CHILE

4th Edition

Where to Stay and Eat
for All Budgets

Must-See Sights
and Local Secrets

Ratings You Can Trust

Fodor's Travel Publications   New York, Toronto, London, Sydney, Auckland
www.fodors.com

FODOR'S CHILE
Editor: Adam Taplin

Editorial Contributors: Josh McIlvain, Christina Knight, Katy Hutter, Tom Azzopardi, Jimmy Langman, Jonathan Yevin, Brian Kleupfel, Jack Trout, Ruth Bradley, Margaret Snook, Nicholas Gill

Editorial Production: Evangelos Vasilakis
Maps & Illustrations: David Lindroth, Craig Cartographic Services, *cartographers*; Bob Blake, Rebecca Baer, *map editors;* William Wu, *information graphics*
Design: Fabrizio LaRocca, *creative director*; Guido Caroti, Siobhan O'Hare, *art directors*; Tina Malaney, Chie Ushio, Ann McBride, Jessica Walsh, *designers*; Melanie Marin, *senior picture editor;* Moon Sun Kim, *cover designer*
Cover Photo: (Horse riders in the Valle de la Muerte in the Cordillera de la Sal in the Atacama desert): Ian Cumming/Axiom
Production/Manufacturing: Angela McLean

4th Edition

ISBN 978-1-4000-1967-0

ISSN 1535-5055

SPECIAL SALES
This book is available at special discounts for bulk purchases for sales promotions or premiums. Special editions, including personalized covers, excerpts of existing books, and corporate imprints, can be created in large quantities for special needs. For more information, write to Special Markets/Premium Sales, 1745 Broadway, MD 6-2, New York, New York 10019, or e-mail specialmarkets@randomhouse.com.

AN IMPORTANT TIP & AN INVITATION
Although all prices, opening times, and other details in this book are based on information supplied to us at press time, changes occur all the time in the travel world, and Fodor's cannot accept responsibility for facts that become outdated or for inadvertent errors or omissions. So **always confirm information when it matters,** especially if you're making a detour to visit a specific place. Your experiences—positive and negative—matter to us. If we have missed or misstated something, **please write to us.** We follow up on all suggestions. Contact the Chile editor at editors@fodors.com or c/o Fodor's at 1745 Broadway, New York, NY 10019.

PRINTED IN THE UNITED STATES OF AMERICA
10 9 8 7 6 5 4 3 2 1

Be a Fodor's Correspondent

Your opinion matters. It matters to us. It matters to your fellow Fodor's travelers, too. And we'd like to hear it. In fact, we need to hear it.

When you share your experiences and opinions, you become an active member of the Fodor's community. That means we'll not only use your feedback to make our books better, but we'll publish your names and comments whenever possible. Throughout our guides, look for "Word of Mouth," excerpts of your unvarnished feedback.

Here's how you can help improve Fodor's for all of us.

Tell us when we're right. We rely on local writers to give you an insider's perspective. But our writers and staff editors—who are the best in the business—depend on you. Your positive feedback is a vote to renew our recommendations for the next edition.

Tell us when we're wrong. We're proud that we update most of our guides every year. But we're not perfect. Things change. Hotels cut services. Museums change hours. Charming cafés lose charm. If our writer didn't quite capture the essence of a place, tell us how you'd do it differently. If any of our descriptions are inaccurate or inadequate, we'll incorporate your changes in the next edition and will correct factual errors at fodors.com immediately.

Tell us what to include. You probably have had fantastic travel experiences that aren't yet in Fodor's. Why not share them with a community of like-minded travelers? Maybe you chanced upon a beach or bistro or B&B that you don't want to keep to yourself. Tell us why we should include it. And share your discoveries and experiences with everyone directly at fodors.com. Your input may lead us to add a new listing or highlight a place we cover with a "Highly Recommended" star or with our highest rating, "Fodor's Choice."

Give us your opinion instantly at our feedback center at www.fodors.com/feedback. You may also e-mail editors@fodors.com with the subject line "Chile Editor." Or send your nominations, comments, and complaints by mail to Chile Editor, Fodor's, 1745 Broadway, New York, NY 10019.

You and travelers like you are the heart of the Fodor's community. Make our community richer by sharing your experiences. Be a Fodor's correspondent.

¡Feliz viaje!

Tim Jarrell, Publisher

CONTENTS

ABOUT THIS BOOK

Our Ratings

Sometimes you find terrific travel experiences and sometimes they just find you. But usually the burden is on you to select the right combination of experiences. That's where our ratings come in.

As travelers we've all discovered a place so wonderful that its worthiness is obvious. And sometimes that place is so unique that superlatives don't do it justice: you just have to be there to know. These sights, properties, and experiences get our highest rating, **Fodor's Choice**, indicated by orange stars throughout this book.

Black stars highlight sights and properties we deem **Highly Recommended**, places that our writers, editors, and readers praise again and again for consistency and excellence.

By default, there's another category: any place we include in this book is by definition worth your time, unless we say otherwise. And we will.

Disagree with any of our choices? Care to nominate a place or suggest that we rate one more highly? Visit our feedback center at www.fodors.com/feedback.

Budget Well

Hotel and restaurant price categories from ¢ to $$$$ are defined in the opening pages of each chapter. For attractions, we always give standard adult admission fees; reductions are usually available for children, students, and senior citizens. Want to pay with plastic? **AE, DC, MC, V** following restaurant and hotel listings indicate whether American Express, Diners Club, MasterCard, and Visa are accepted.

Restaurants

Unless we state otherwise, restaurants are open for lunch and dinner daily. We mention dress only when there's a specific requirement and reservations only when they're essential or not accepted—it's always best to book ahead.

Hotels

Hotels have private bath, phone, TV, and air-conditioning and operate on the European Plan (aka EP, meaning without meals), unless we specify that they use the Continental Plan (CP, with a Continental breakfast), Breakfast Plan (BP, with a full breakfast), or Modified American Plan (MAP, with breakfast and dinner) or are all-inclusive (AI, including all meals and most activities). We always list facilities but not whether you'll be charged an extra fee to use them, so when pricing accommodations, find out what's included.

Many Listings
- ★ Fodor's Choice
- ★ Highly recommended
- ⊠ Physical address
- ✛ Directions
- ⌂ Mailing address
- ☎ Telephone
- 🖷 Fax
- ⊕ On the Web
- ✉ E-mail
- 💳 Admission fee
- ☉ Open/closed times
- Ⓜ Metro stations
- ⊟ Credit cards

Hotels & Restaurants
- ⬚ Hotel
- ⤴ Number of rooms
- ⌂ Facilities
- ¶⊙¶ Meal plans
- ✕ Restaurant
- ⌂ Reservations
- ⌐ Smoking
- ⌱⌱ BYOB
- ✕⬚ Hotel with restaurant that warrants a visit

Outdoors
- ⌐ Golf
- ⛺ Camping

Other
- ☉ Family-friendly
- ⇨ See also
- ⊠ Branch address
- ☞ Take note

Experience Chile

Boy at rodeo, Frutillar

WORD OF MOUTH

"We had an excellent trip to Chile. It was one of the best trips we have had in many years of travel."

—detraveler

WHAT'S NEW
IN CHILE

Chile's Awakening

In the 18 years since its return to democracy, this isolated nation at the end of the world has made great strides on a number of fronts. The World Bank now classifies Chile's national economy as upper-middle income with only moderate debt. Corruption is lower here than anywhere in Latin America, leading to the most competitive economy in the region. A member of the Asia-Pacific Economic Cooperation (APEC) group and an associate member of the regional trade block MERCOSUR, Chile has bilateral trade agreements with the United States, China, Canada, South Korea, and New Zealand, among other countries. On the political front, Chileans have democratically elected four presidents since 1990, including Chile's first female president, Michelle Bachelet. From 2003 to 2006, the number of people living below the poverty line was reduced by 5% (from 18.7% to 13.7%), although income inequality is still a significant concern. For these reasons, Chileans are referred to as the "jaguars" of Latin America. Given their relative anonymity and geographic isolation, they are very proud of this reputation.

Globalization

Due to new economic success and global linkages, Chile is becoming more modern, and, increasingly, globalized. A Subway sandwich shop stands catty-corner to the presidential palace, and there are currently 18 Starbucks in the capital city. South America's tallest building will soon stand in downtown Santiago, at a cost of approximately $400 million. Given its stability and security, Chile is one of the most popular destinations in Latin America for exchange students, and is

also home to the regional headquarters of many multinationals.

Chile's 200th Birthday

Preparations are under way for the 200th anniversary of Chilean independence in 2010. In 2000, former President Lagos created a Bicentenary Commission to oversee the design and implementation of these initiatives, which range from infrastructure development to the preservation of cultural heritage. Some examples of the projects under construction include the Bicentenary Park City, a large-scale, environmentally friendly, urban development project in Santiago; the renovation of the plaza in front of La Moneda, the presidential palace; and a trans-Patagonian railway.

Transguatazo

Transantiago, an ambitious plan to make Santiago's transportation system more efficient and less damaging to the environment, was meant to use the city's subway as its spine while upgraded city buses replaced the much-loved but traffic jam–inducing micros (an older system of independently operated minibuses and vans). However, about a year since its launch and billions later, the system—nicknamed "Transguatazo" (Chilean slang for "flop")—has been deemed a complete failure. Commuters line up for blocks to take the new buses, which run limited routes, while the subway is as crowded as Tokyo's.

The Penguin Revolution

No, we're not talking about the Humboldt or Magellanic varieties found in southern Patagonia, but rather about Chilean secondary-school students who are nicknamed "penguins" after their black-and-white uniforms and tendency to travel in

packs. Their revolution involved a series of strikes in which between 600,000 and 1 million students from around the country demanded reforms relating to the cost and quality of the education system. These student demonstrations were the most significant in the country's history.

The Death of a Dictator

Even after his death in 2006 at the age of 91, former Chilean dictator Augusto Pinochet is still a divisive figure. Pinochet came to power on September 11, 1973, ousting socialist president Salvador Allende, and ruled with an iron fist for the next 17 years. During his government, thousands of people were killed, tortured, or forced into exile. Despite these injustices, approximately one-third of the Chilean population continues to support Pinochet. Many feel that his government is responsible for the strength of the Chilean economy as well as the country's overall stability. His family and other collaborators are involved in an ongoing trial to determine whether they embezzled public funds.

Santiago Gets Hip

Chileans, and particularly Santiaguinos (as the residents of Santiago are called), have lately become much "hipper" and design-savvy. Compared to their fashionista neighbors in Buenos Aires and Rio, Chileans used to have a reputation for being drab and formal. However, with the recent openings of the Museo de la Moda (Fashion Museum) and the design floor of Chile's premier mall Parque Arauco, as well as the gentrification of areas like Bellavista, Santiago offers a richer and more diverse aesthetic experience than it once did. The capital is now a destination in its own right, as opposed to a stop on the way to Chile's other attractions.

"Pelolais," "Pokemona," and Other Chilean Youth

Coming up with new slang is a national pastime in Chile. The latest new words describe duelling urban tribes of Chilean adolescent girls. "Pelolais" (a play on the Spanish for straight hair) refers to young, upper-class girls with long, straight hair, who are always in shape, highly fashionable, and know it. "Pokemona" on the other hand have shorter, unkempt hair and use barrettes, glitter, and stars. They buy second-hand clothes—preferably with Japanese anime themes—and epitomize cool. Keep your eyes open as well for "flaites," "ondulais," and "emos"!

Two New Regions

Chile's two new regions—the XIV Region of Los Rios in the south and the XV Region of Arica-Parinacota in the north—began operating in October 2007. These regions were created to respond to population growth and distribution, as well as to combat the tendency towards centralization of power in Santiago. Other provinces are also exploring the possibility of becoming independent regions.

Telenovelas Are Out; Reality TV Is In!

Telenovelas (the Latin version of soap operas) have long been a Chilean national obsession. However, as elsewhere in the world, reality shows are a new and extremely popular phenomenon. In "Touching the Stars" and "Fame," aspiring stars compete to be the next big thing. In "The Farm," city folk living together on a farm must figure out how to milk cows, raise chickens, and plant fields. Sound familiar? Most of the Chilean "realities," as they are called, are based on North American and European models.

WHAT'S WHERE

1 Santiago. Although it doesn't get the same press as Rio or Buenos Aires, this metropolis of 5 million people is as cosmopolitan as its flashier South American neighbors. Ancient and modern stand side by side in the heart of the city, and the Andes are ever-present to the east.

2 Viña del Mar and Valparaíso. Anchoring the coast west of Santiago, port city Valparaíso has stunning views from the promenades atop its more than 40 hills. Next door, Viña del Mar, home to Chile's beautiful people, has nonstop nightlife and the country's most popular stretch of shoreline.

3 El Norte Chico. A land of dusty brown hills, the "little north" stretches for some 700 km (435 mi) north of Santiago. In the lush Elqui Valley, just about everyone you meet is involved in growing the grapes used to make *pisco,* Chile's national drink. Astronomers flock to the region for the crisp, clear night skies.

4 El Norte Grande. Stark doesn't begin to describe Chile's great north, a region bordering Peru to the north and Bolivia to the east. This is the driest place on Earth, site of the Atacama Desert, where no measurable precipitation has ever been recorded.

5 The Central Valley. Chile's wine country lies south of Santiago, from the Valle Maipo to the Valle Maule. Some of the best wines in the world come from this fertile strip of land trapped between the Pacific and the Andes. A drive through the valley is beautiful any time of year.

6 The Lake District. The austral summer doesn't get more glorious than in this compact 400-km (250-mi) stretch of land between Temuco and Puerto Montt. It has fast become Chile's vacation central, drawing people to resorts such as Pucón, Villarrica, and Puerto Varas. More than 50 snow-covered peaks, many of them still smoldering volcanoes, offer splendid hiking.

7 Chiloé. More than 40 islands sprinkled across the Golfo de Ancud make up the rainy archipelago of Chiloé, home to no-nonsense farmers who have tilled the land for centuries. Dozens of simple wooden churches, constructed by Jesuit missionaries during the colonial era, dot the landscape and are Chiloé's main draw.

8 The Southern Coast. This stretch of coastline between the Lake District and Patagonia is one of the most remote regions on Earth. Anchoring the region's spine is the Carretera Austral, one of the world's amazing, hair-raising, "I survived" road trips. Flying is an easier option, but a cruise south from Puerto Montt in the Lake District through the labyrinth of icy fjords is eminently more stylish.

Magellanic Penguins can be found off of the Southern coast

9 Southern Chilean Patagonia. Look up "end of the world" in the dictionary and you might see a picture of Chile's southernmost region. Impenetrable forests and impassable mountains meant that Chilean Patagonia went largely unexplored until the beginning of the 20th century. It's still sparsely inhabited.

PERU

Arica

Iquique

BOLIVIA

EL NORTE GRANDE
4

Calama

San Pedro de Atacama

Antofagasta

NORTHERN CHILE

PACIFIC OCEAN

EL NORTE CHICO
3

Copiapó

Vallenar

Pan-American Hwy.

La Serena

ARGENTINA

Ovalle

Zapallar
Vina del Mar
Valparaíso
2

SANTIAGO
1

Rancagua

Curicó

Talca

THE CENTRAL VALLEY
5

Chillán

Concepción

0   100 mi

0   100 km

Curicó
Talca

Chillán
Concepción

Pan-American Hwy.

Temuco

Villarrica   Pucón
Valdivia   *THE LAKE DISTRICT*
6
Osorno

Puerto Varas

Puerto Montt

Castro

Isla Grande de Chiloé   **7**   *THE SOUTHERN COAST*

ARGENTINA

PACIFIC OCEAN

Puerto Puyuhuapi

8   Coyhaique   Balmaceda

SOUTHERN CHILE

Cochrane

Parque Nacional
Torres del Paine

Puerto Natales

ARGENTINA

Punta
9   Arenas

Estrecho de Magallanes

Tierra del Fuego

Puerto Williams

CHILE PLANNER

Visitor Info

The national tourist office **Sernatur** (⊕ www.sernatur.cl) has branches in Santiago and major tourist destinations around the country. Sernatur offices, often the best source for general information about a region, are generally open daily from 9 to 6, but break for lunch (usually from 2 to 3).

Safety

The vast majority of visitors to Chile never experience a problem with crime. Violence is a rarity; far more common are pick-pocketing or thefts from purses, backpacks, or rental cars. Women should be particularly careful about walking alone at night in both large cities and small towns. Catcalls are common, but harmless.

Money

Most businesses in major cities accept credit cards and traveler's checks. Note that ATMs in Chile have a special screen—accessed after entering your PIN code—for foreign-account withdrawals. In this case, you need to access your account first via the "foreign client" option.

Eat Well

Chile serves an incredible variety of foods. With such a long coastline, it's no surprise that you can get wonderful seafood. Salmon is caught off the Southern Coast and raised in farms in the Lake District. Other popular catches include sea bass (corvina) and conger eel (congrio). Shellfish such as mussels and scallops are widely available, and locos (abalone) and jaiba (crab) are frequently prepared as chupes (stews) or pasteles (pies). Raw shellfish is best avoided, but cooked with cheese or white wine, lemon, and fresh coriander, it's an excellent introduction to Chilean cuisine. Simply seasoned grilled fish is another Chilean favorite, usually served with steamed potatoes or an ensalada a la chilena (sliced tomatoes and onions).

But fish isn't all that's available. Pastel de choclo is a typical dish that you'll find just about everywhere in Chile. Served in a heavy clay bowl, it's a mixture of minced beef, chicken, olives, hard-boiled egg, and raisins, topped with a layer of creamy mashed corn.

A parrillada is a platter of every cut of meat imaginable—often one order will serve many. Beefsteak a la pobre comes with a fried egg or two on top, plus onions and french fries.

For something lighter try an empanada, which you can order as a starter or a main course. These come most commonly stuffed with meat, olives, egg, and onions (pino), or with cheese (queso); occasionally they'll be stuffed with shellfish (mariscos).

Lunch, which usually begins at 1 or 2, is the most important meal of the day. It can take two hours or more. Some Chileans forgo dinner, making do with an once, a light evening meal similar in style to a high tea. Many restaurants have once meals, which include a sandwich (often ham and cheese), fresh juice, tea, and a dessert. Once is served from 5 to 8; dinner is eaten later than in North America, usually starting anywhere from 8 to 10.

Rest Easy

Hostels. Youth hostels in Chile are not very popular, perhaps due to the prevalence of *residenciales* and other lowcost lodging.

Hotels. Chile's urban areas and resort areas have hotels that come with all of the amenities that are taken for granted in North America and Europe, such as room service, a restaurant, or a swimming pool. Elsewhere you may not have television or a phone in your room, although you will find them somewhere in the hotel. Rooms that have a private bath may have only a shower, and in some cases, there will be a shared bath in the hall. In all but the most upscale hotels, you may be asked to leave your key at the reception desk whenever you leave.

Residenciales. Private homes that rent rooms, *residenciales*, are a unique way to get to know Chile, especially if you're on a budget. Sometimes residenciales are small, very basic accommodations and not necessarily private homes. *Hospedajes* are similar. Many rent rooms for less than $10. Some will be shabby, but others can be substantially better than hotel rooms. They also offer the added benefit of allowing you to interact with locals, though they are unlikely to speak English. Contact the local tourist office for details on residenciales and hospedajes.

Holidays

Shops and services are open on most Chilean holidays except September 18, Christmas Day, and New Year's Day. On these days, shops close and public transportation runs at the bare minimum.

September 18 is Chile's Independence Day, and celebrations last for almost a week. Attending a *fonda* or *ramada* (smaller version of a fonda) is a must. These are parties in which communities gather to eat empanadas, drink *chicha* (a potent drink made from fermented corn), and dance *la cueca*, the national dance. Rodeos are also common this time of year.

Watching the fireworks from Valparaíso or Viña del Mar on New Year's Eve is a remarkable experience. Arrive early to get the best view of the fireworks, which go off at midnight all along the coast. You'll also want to wear clothing that can get wet, since Chileans spray each other with champagne.

When to Go

Chile's seasons are the reverse of the Northern Hemisphere's— that is, June through August are Chile's winter months. If you were to move Chile out of its place on the globe and transfer it to corresponding latitudes in the Northern Hemisphere, you would have a nation stretching from Cancún to Hudson Bay. In other words, expect vast north– south climatic differences.

Tourism peaks during the hot summer months of January and February, except in Santiago, which tends to empty as most Santiaguinos take their summer holiday. Though prices are at their highest, it's worth braving the summer heat if you're interested in lying on the beach or enjoying the many concerts, folklore festivals, and outdoor theater performances offered during this period.

Chile Temperatures

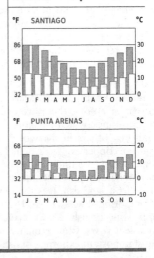

CHILE TODAY

Women and the Family

Over the past 10 years, women in Chile have become increasingly influential in both the government and the private sector. When she began her term in 2006, President Michelle Bachelet launched a campaign to promote gender equality in Chile and named women to a number of influential posts in her cabinet. Despite these advances, salaries for men and women remain unequal in Chile.

Two recent government policies have had a particularly important impact on women and the family. In November 2004, divorce became legal for the first time. Then, in late 2006, state-run hospitals were given clearance to distribute the morning-after pill free of charge. Before the passage of the law legalizing divorce, Chile was one of the few countries in the world to prohibit this practice, which resulted in many Chileans forming new families without legally divorcing. Those who could afford it had their marriages annulled. These new policies have directly challenged the influence of the Roman Catholic Church in Chile (about 70% of Chileans are Catholic), and were vehemently resisted by the powerful conservative sectors of the Chilean population.

Export Industries

Chilean export industries are booming. Foremost among these are the nation's copper mines, which are more productive than any others in the world. In 2006, Chilean copper exports reached a historic high of US$33.3 billion. Chile's principal non-mineral exports include wine, wood, fresh fruit, and fish. It is the fourth-largest exporter of wines to the United States, and while its fish exports have declined in recent years, Chile remains one of the most important exporters of fish and fish-derived products in the world. The main destinations for Chilean exports are the Americas (42% of total exports), Asia (30%), and Europe (24%).

Despite the positive macroeconomic impacts of Chile's vibrant export sector, the success of these businesses has also resulted in a number of domestic conflicts. The mining and salmon industries have been highly criticized for their negative environmental effects. Additionally, the Mapuche, the most significant indigenous group in Chile, have challenged the construction of the Ralco hydroelectric plant, in the Bío Bío region, on environmental, territorial, and cultural grounds. Workers at Codelco, the government-owned copper company, have also repeatedly demanded higher wages and better working conditions. Clearly, large segments of the population have yet to see the benefits of Chile's thriving export industries.

Chilean Identity

Due in part to this economic boom, Chilean identity is in flux. While Chileans are very proud of their nationality and celebrate the *fiestas patrias* (Independence Day holidays) with fervor, they also increasingly value cultural and material imports from abroad. Chileans flock to malls every weekend to buy the latest technological toys, and SUVs are common, despite high gas prices. Many members of the expanding middle class are moving to the suburbs and sending their children to private, bilingual schools; incorporating English words into conversations and having coffee at Starbucks have become status symbols. In recent years, the United States has replaced Europe as the preferred cultural model for many middle- and upper-class Chileans.

Other sectors of the Chilean population, however, resist these influences, including members of the political left and indigenous groups. A number of popular Chilean artists have also commented on Chile's increasingly materialistic and outward-looking culture, including writer Alberto Fuguet and musicians Los Chancho en Piedra and Joe Vasconcelos.

An interesting example of these tensions in Chilean identity is the annual pre-Christmas charity event, the Teletón. Modeled on telethons in the United States, the Teletón is billed as "27 hours of love" and presided over by Chilean TV personality Don Francisco. Despite its growing commercialization—big companies showing off with big donations to strengthen their brand—the event is remarkable not only because it raises large sums of money for handicapped children, but also because almost all Chileans watch it and contribute funds, despite class, ethnic, and geographic differences. The Teletón is truly an expression of modern "Chilenidad" (Chileanism).

Chile on the International Stage

Since its return to democracy, Chile has been active in international politics and trade relations. A strong proponent of free trade, Chile has signed numerous bilateral free trade agreements all over the world, and hopes for the creation of a Free Trade Area of the Americas close to home. It participates actively in the United Nations agencies and has sent Chilean soldiers on UN peacekeeping missions in countries such as Haiti and Iraq. The recent election of Chilean José Miguel Insulza as Secretary General of the Organization of American States makes Chile a high profile force in the hemisphere.

Despite its increasingly important role on the global stage, Chile's relations with its immediate neighbors are somewhat contentious. Chile and Argentina continue to have disputes over natural gas, and Bolivia and Chile have maintained only consular relations since 1978 due to a long-standing conflict over Bolivia's access to the sea. Since 2005, Chile and Peru have been involved in a dispute over the demarcation of the coastline between the two countries. Peru recently elevated its complaint to The Hague. And although President Bachelet is socialist, she has kept fellow socialist presidents Evo Morales (Bolivia) and Hugo Chávez (Venezuela) at arm's length.

Language

It's no coincidence that the book *How to Survive in the Chilean Jungle,* a dictionary of Chilean slang, regularly sells out. Chileans use an astonishing amount of slang—known as "Chilenismos," or "Chileanisms"—on a regular basis. Some common examples are "cachai," "al tiro," and "gringo." "¿Cachai?" is an interrogative that roughly means "get it?" and supposedly comes from the English expression "to catch." "Al tiro" means "right away," but depending on the Chilean and the circumstances, may indicate a time frame of anywhere from 30 seconds to several hours. "Gringo" refers mostly to North Americans, but in some cases may refer to other foreigners. The term is considered relatively neutral and is used freely, but can take on a negative connotation depending on the tone; when used with the diminutive "ito," it can also be affectionate.

TOP CHILE ATTRACTIONS

Valle de la Luna

(A) Part of the Cordillera de Sal, formed where the Andes meet the Atacama Desert, the Valle de la Luna is aptly named: its sand and rock formations create a remarkably moon-like landscape. Come at sunrise or sunset, when a multitude of colors splash across the sky. It's an indescribable experience to watch the full moon rise over the valley.

Torres del Paine

(B) The Torres del Paine, part of the Paine Massif, an Eastern spur of the Andes rising dramatically above the Patagonian steppe, are three granite towers that form the centerpiece of the Torres del Paine National Park in Region XII. In addition to the towers, the park has breathtaking lakes, glaciers, valleys, and forests. Pumas, guanacos, and a wide variety of birds are also found there.

Volcán Villarrica

(C) On a clear day, the perfectly cone-shaped, snow-covered Volcán Villarrica is visible from nearby Pucón, one of the principal destinations in the Chilean Lake District. Adventurous tourists can climb the active volcano, peering into the lava lake within its crater at the summit.

Pablo Neruda's Houses

Isla Negra, La Sebastiana, and La Chascona are the three houses of Chilean Nobel prize–winning poet Pablo Neruda. They are located in Isla Negra (45 minutes south of Valparaíso), Valparaíso, and Santiago, respectively. Given Neruda's eclectic taste and passion for collecting objects, each is distinctive and well worth a visit.

Chiloé's Churches

(D) In addition to its *palafitos* (brightly colored homes built along the water on wooden stilts) and *curanto* (typical dish),

Chiloé is best known for its 150 wooden churches, which were built by Jesuit missionaries during the colonial period. After declaring the churches a World Heritage Site in 2000, UNESCO has been helping to restore many that were damaged or in disrepair. One of the most beautiful and oldest examples is the Iglesia de Santa María de Loreto, located on the small island of Quinchao. The church dates from 1706, and its deep-blue ceiling is adorned with gold stars.

La Moneda and the Plaza de Armas, Santiago

(F) La Moneda is Chile's presidential palace, though the President does not reside there. Time your visit to watch the changing of the guards at 10 AM every other day in the Plaza de la Constitución. Also look for the statue of former president Salvador Allende in the south-east corner of the Plaza. Many believe Allende committed suicide inside La Moneda during the military coup in 1973, although others contend he was assassinated. The Plaza de Armas is the nearby bustling square at Compañía and Estado flanked by impressive buildings such as the Correo Central (central post office), the Municipality of Santiago, and the Cathedral.

Central Coast Beaches

(E) Chile's beaches are a major draw for international and domestic tourism alike. During the summer months of December through March, families from all over Chile come to relax along the wind-swept coast near Viña del Mar and Valparaíso, sharing *asado* and enjoying the bounty of fresh seafood provided by the freezing waters of the Humboldt current. Be sure to include this area on your itinerary if you spend any length of time in Santiago.

TOP EXPERIENCES

See a Rodeo in Rancagua

From September to May, head to Rancagua, a city 87 km (54 mi) south of Santiago, to watch a rodeo. During the event, pairs of *huasos* (Chilean cowboys) round up steers in a *medialuna,* or half-moon-shaped ring. Huasos live in the countryside throughout Chile and wear traditional clothing of flat-topped, wide-brimmed hats, short-vested jackets, sashes, and colorful blankets called *mantas* draped over their shoulders.

Cruise the Fjords in Tierra del Fuego

Beyond Puerto Montt at the far southern end of the Lake District, Chile's coastline fractures into some 1,500 km (932 mi) of jagged inlets, mountains, glaciers, and islands. The terrain has created a longstanding headache for national planning: how to provide access to such an isolated, forbidding region? The answer: by boat. Transport along this sector of the southern coast varies from high-end to utilitarian. At the top of the line are the luxury Cruceros Australis boats, with all the buffet tables and social activities any cruise-ship passenger could desire. At the other end are serviceable, no-frills freighters and ferries, where your fellow passengers will be locals.

Ride the Tren del Vino

A steam engine from the turn of the 20th century will take you through one of Chile's principal wine regions, the Colchagua Valley. Idyllic scenery and vineyards roll by as you taste a selection of Chilean wines and local cheeses. You will also tour the Santa Cruz winery, visit Colchagua Museum, and enjoy a Chilean-style lunch. For those who want to experience Chile's wine country in a less structured way, there are numerous other options including private, group, and self-guided

tours. See "The Pleasures of the Vine," below, for a list of important wineries. *Also see Chapter 3, Central Valley.*

Kayak in Parque Pumalín

Parque Pumalín is the private nature reserve near Puerto Montt created by North American Douglas Tompkins and his wife Kristen. The park contains almost 800,000 acres of temperate rain forests, fjords, waterfalls, and hot springs. The northern section of the park is best visited by kayak. Two kayak tour-guide operators are **Al Sur Expeditions** (⊕ *www. alsurexpeditions.com*) and **Yak Expediciones** (⊕ *www.yakexpediciones.cl*). Al Sur accompanies clients with a small boat, which you can board for meals and to relax.

Soak in the Termas Geométricas

After driving 17 km (10½ mi) from Coñaripe on a rough road, you'll want to spend hours soaking in these simple yet luxurious Japanese-style hot springs. Coñaripe, a small town in the Lake District, has become a hub for tourists and Chilean senior citizens looking to experience the region's numerous hot springs. Our recommendation: skip the others, avoid the crowds, and head straight to the Termas Geométricas. Although a bit more expensive than the other springs (US$24 per person), there are numerous pools to choose from, each with distinctive features and abundant foliage. For a particularly romantic atmosphere, go at night when the pools are illuminated by candlelight.

Eat Curanto in Chiloé

Preparing a traditional curanto is an event in itself, requiring the participation of at least five people. A hole 1½ meters (5 feet) deep is dug in the ground, and its base is then covered with red-hot stones. Ingre-

dients are added on top of that, including shellfish, meat, vegetables, and different potato mixtures called *milcao* and *chapalele*. Leaves from the *pangue* plant, which is common in Chiloé, separate each layer of ingredients, while the entire hole is covered with earth. All of this creates a giant pressure cooker. After about one hour, the curanto can be served. The best place to try curanto is in Chiloé, but the dish is also available in many other parts of Chile.

See Penguins

There are several places to see penguins in Chile. Each year from late September to late March, about 2,000 Magellanic penguin couples head to the Otway Sound near Punta Arenas to mate, lay their eggs, and care for their chicks. The National Humbolt Penguin Reserve is located on Isla Choros and Isla Damas about two hours north of La Serena. The local fishermen-turned-tour-guides will also show you sea lions and dolphins. And off the coast of Puñihuil near Ancud in Chiloé, you can visit one of the few places in the world where these two penguin species—Humbolt and Magellanic—cohabitate.

Ride Valparaíso's Funiculars

Funiculars are an essential means of transportation in the steep port city of Valparaíso, whose historic center was declared a UNESCO World Heritage Site in 2003. There are 42 hills in Valparaíso, and 15 funiculars. The funiculars, which were imported from England and Germany in the early 20th century, may seem a bit rickety, though they are in fact quite safe. Each hill has two cars in motion at any given time—one going up, one going down. Only the brave will risk a look at oncoming cars.

Participate in the La Tirana Festival

La Tirana is the most important folklore festival in Chile. It is held every year on July 16, in the town of La Tirana, in Region I. More than 100,000 people gather for the celebrations, which last a week. Since 1910, the festival has honored the Virgen of Carmen, but its origins are mestizo.

Sandboard in the North

Yes, that's right, you can experience the sister sport of snowboarding on the sand dunes of Chile's Antofagasta region. While going down may be smoother than snowboarding, getting back up is the hard part! With no ski lifts to help you, be prepared to sweat your way to the top of the hill just to start all over again.

Climb Volcán Villarrica

This (active) volcano, located just 20 minutes' drive from Pucón, has become an obligatory climb for the many nature- and adventure-seeking tourists who come to Chile. In winter, many people like to make the ascent and then ski or snowboard down. Don't forget to warm up in one of the thermal baths around the region.

Go Fly Fishing Near Coyhaique

Southern Chile's lakes and streams are a major destination for anglers from the United States and elsewhere. Cast your line in the Río Simpson, where the trout are abundant and rustic European-style fishing lodges await.

QUINTESSENTIAL CHILE

Eat an Asado

Chilean men claim the way to their hearts is through their stomachs. So, clearly, a first step towards understanding the national culture is attending an *asado*. While uninformed tourists might liken the asado to a North American barbecue or an Argentine-style *parillada*, Chileans will be quick to correct them. While Argentine grilled meat is often accompanied with chimichurri, and in the United States by, gasp, ketchup, Chileans accompany their meat with *pebre*, a mixture of tomatoes, cilantro, onions, and *ají* (chilies). Asados are the preferred means of celebrating many occasions in Chile, from birthdays and baptisms to Independence Day. Each event generally has an official or unofficial *asado* ("grill master" might be the U.S. equivalent), although other males may—perhaps a little presumptuously—give suggestions about how the asado could be perfected.

Go to the Beach

During the Chilean summer, many Santiaguinos escape to the beach on weekends. Some own condos or second homes in towns like Cachagua, Zapallar, and Reñaca. Others take day trips to towns like El Quisco and Cartagena. Surfers tend to prefer towns like Pichilemu, farther south, but Maitencillos just north of Valparaíso is also popular with the surfer crowd. Wherever you land, the people-watching is always entertaining. Most Chileans don't actually swim in the water, even in the summer, because of the frigid temperatures produced by the Humbolt current. Instead, be prepared to wade and enjoy the sunbathing. Many towns have fishermen's wharfs where you can buy fresh seafood to cook yourself, or eat at a fish shack by the water.

Jog, Walk, or Bike up Cerro San Cristóbal

If you're looking for a Sunday activity in Santiago, try heading to Cerro San Cristóbal, the city's highest hill. You'll be joined by hundreds of Santiaguinos walking, jogging, or biking up the hill. Walking to the top from the entrance (off Pedro de Valdivia) takes less than an hour. On the way up, stop at some of the park's lovely gardens to cool off. At the top, you can see the gleaming white virgin crowning the summit as well as excellent views of the city. Sunset is a particularly beautiful time to be at the summit, when the sky often turns a kind of blood orange. If you're not feeling inspired to walk back down the hill, take an exhilarating ride in one of the cable cars, which drop you off in the Bellavista neighborhood.

Go to a Soccer Game

Going to any soccer game will give you a sense of how seriously the sport is taken in Chile. However, if you can make a *clásico* between two of Chile's top three teams—la Universidad de Chile, la Universidad Católica, and Colo-Colo—you'll see Chilean fans at their best...and their worst. Watching the game from neutral territory, rather than one of the *hincha* (fan) sections, is the safest option. Don't worry, you'll still see plenty of action!

IF YOU LIKE

Distinctive Cuisine

This thin strip of land at the end of the world has it all: mountains, plains, lakes, rivers, desert, and the sea. Such geographic variety provides breathtaking scenery as well as the ingredients for a distinctive national cuisine. Ocean delicacies such as conger eel, sea bass, king crab, and *locos* (abalone the size of fat clams) are vitally important to Chileans. But the Pacific isn't Chile's only answer to fine dining—European immigrants brought with them a love of robust country cooking. International cuisine has caught on here, too, especially in the cosmopolitan capital, where you can dine in every type of ethnic restaurant from Japanese to Jamaican.

- **Azul Profundo.** For a taste of the capital's best seafood, visit the trendy Bellavista neighborhood, where Azul Profundo serves fresh fish and shellfish *a la plancha* (grilled) or *a la lata* (served on a sizzling plate with tomatoes and onions).

- **Café Turri.** If you couldn't get enough of the seafood in Santiago, visit this elegant 19th-century mansion high above Valparaíso, where simply prepared *jardín de mariscos especial* (a huge platter of the catch of the day) should be enjoyed with a pisco sour on the restaurant's rooftop terrace.

- **Parrilla Los Ganaderos.** Way down south in Punta Arenas, waiters dressed as *gauchos* carve *cordero al ruedo* (roasted lamb) off the spit.

- **Donde Eladio.** The island of Chiloé is famous not only for its churches, but also for a unique dish called *curanto*. Donde Eladio serves this dish, which is a hearty stew of shellfish, chicken, sausages, smoked pork ribs, and potatoes roasted in a buried pit for hours.

Sports & the Outdoors

The Lake District is Chile's outdoor-tourism center, with outfitters and guides ready to fix you up and take you out for any activity your adventurous heart could desire. Fly-fishing, hiking, and rafting top the list, but the entire country has caught the outdoor bug, and activities abound.

- **Sendero de Chile.** Though far from complete, this ambitious project will eventually provide a continuous north–south hiking trail running the entire length of the country. Serious mountaineers from all over the world already flock to Chile to hike different peaks in the Andes.

- **Volcán Ojos del Salado.** El Norte Chico, the world's highest active volcano, it soars to 6,893 meters (22,609 feet). There are dozens of other challenging climbs along the eastern border.

- **Pucón.** Chile's all-around adventure destination is the area around Pucón and Villarrica, where everything from rafting and kayaking to climbing and horseback riding is available.

- **Valle Nevado.** Skiing deserves special mention. Since Chile's seasons are the opposite of the northern hemisphere's, you can ski or snowboard from June to September. Most of Chile's ski resorts are in the Andes close to Santiago. With the top elevations at the majority of ski areas extending to 3,300 meters (10,825 feet), you can expect long runs and deep, dry snow.

- **Chaitén and Futaleufú.** Fly fisherman should explore the trip options in Southern Chile. There are numerous places to fish, most of which are much less crowded and much more remote than any place you may have been before.

Natural Wonders

Norway has fjords. Bavaria has forests. Nepal has mountains. Arizona has deserts. Chile offers all these—so it's understandable if you feel disoriented each time you step off a domestic flight that's whisked you from one region to another.

■ **The Andes.** A defining feature of Santiago is the city's proximity to the Andes. Everywhere else you might go in Chile, the Andes will be there as a defining characteristic, and a reminder of the isolation Chile is now emerging from.

■ **Atacama Desert.** The most arid spot on Earth is in El Norte Grande's Atacama Desert; no measurable precipitation has ever been recorded there. The region's Cerros Pintados form the largest group of geoglyphs in the world.

■ **Volcán Villarrica.** Perpetually smoldering, this volcano in the Lake District is one of the world's most active—although you shouldn't let that fact stop you from hiking to the snow-covered summit. Yet even when Chile's natural wonders can't lay claim to adjectives like "biggest" or "most," they might find themselves at the top of your list of favorites.

■ **Laguna San Rafael.** A looming, fearsome, cobalt-blue mountain of ice, this 4-km (2½-mi) glacier at the southern is a doubly arresting attraction:, it gives off thunderous sounds as chunks of it break off and stir up the water as you pass by (safely on your ship, of course).

■ **Parque Nacional Fray Jorge.** Chile's only cloud forest, and a great retreat from the relentless sun of El Norte Chico.

■ **Torres del Paine.** No photo can ever do justice to the ash-gray, glacier-molded spires of Patagonia's most visited attraction.

The Pleasures of the Vine

Back in the 1980s, when formerly inexpensive California wines started to jump in price, Chilean vintners saw an opening and began to introduce their products to the world. The rest, as they say, is history.

■ **Concha y Toro.** Chile's largest winery has a number of different labels (some made exclusively for the Chilean market) that usually offer good value. It's an easy day trip from Santiago, and the tours are extremely popular.

■ **Matetic.** If you drive between Santiago and the beach towns of Viña del Mar and Valparaíso—or then again, even if you don't—make time to stop at Matetic, a unique property in the San Antonio Valley. There's plenty to see and do, including visit the restaurant, bicycle around the property, and visit the strikingly modern winery.

■ **Tren del Vino.** Making daily trips between the small town of San Alfonso and wine country's hub, Santa Cruz, the Tren del Vino is a chance to taste several of Colchagua's best wineries all in a single place.

■ **Casa Silva.** Since so many of Chile's wineries are in out-of-the-way places, finding one that can turn into an all-day activity makes good sense. Casa Silva is one such place. They have a corral where you can watch traditional Chilean rodeo, a hotel, a restaurant, and a winery. You'll get a taste of what life must have been like in Chilean *haciendas* a century ago.

GREAT ITINERARIES

SANTIAGO & NORTHERN CHILE
10 DAYS

Days 1, 2 & 3: Arrival/Santiago

No matter where you fly from, you'll likely arrive in Chile's capital early in the morning after an all-night flight. Unless you're one of those rare people who can sleep the entire night on a plane and arrive refreshed at your destination, reward yourself with a couple of hours' shut-eye at your hotel before setting out to explore the city.

The neighborhoods, small and large, that make up Santiago warrant at least a day and a half of exploration. A trip up one of the city's hills—like Cerro San Cristóbal in Parque Metropolitano or Cerro Santa Lucía—lets you survey the capital and its grid of streets. Any tour of a city begins with its historic center; the cathedral and commercial office towers on the Plaza de Armas reflect Santiago's old and new architecture, while the nearby Bohemian quarter of Bellavista, with its bustling markets and colorful shops, was built for walking. But Santiago's zippy, efficient metro can also whisk you to most places in the city, and lets you cover ground more quickly. Avoid taking the metro during morning and evening rush hour because of the crowds.

Alas, if you're here in the winter, gloomy smog can hang over the city for days at a time. Your first instinct may be to flee, and one of the nearby wineries in the Valle de Maipo will welcome you heartily.

See Exploring Santiago and Side Trips from Santiago in Chapter 2.

Days 4 & 5: Valparaíso & Viña del Mar

A 90-minute drive west from Santiago takes you to the Central Coast and confronts you with one of Chilean tourism's classic choices: Valparaíso or Viña del Mar! If you fancy yourself one of the glitterati, you'll go for Viña and its chic cafés and restaurants and miles of beach. But "Valpo" offers you the charm and allure of a port city, rolling hills, and cobblestone streets with better views of the sea. Nothing says you can't do both; only 10 km (6 mi) separate the two, and a new metro system connects them. Overnight in either city.

See Valparaíso & Viña del Mar in Chapter 3.

Days 6 & 7: San Pedro de Atacama

You certainly *could* drive the nearly 1,500 km (900 mi) to Chile's vast El Norte Grande, but a flight from Santiago to Calama then a quick overland drive to San Pedro de Atacama will take you no more than 3½ hours. That a town with such a polished tourism infrastructure could lie at the heart of one the world's loneliest regions comes as a great surprise. This is one of the most-visited towns in Chile, and for good reason: it sits right in the middle of the Atacama Desert, with sights all around. You'll need at least two days here to do justice to the alpine lakes, ancient fortresses, Chile's largest salt flat, and the surreal landscape of the Valle de la Luna.

See The Nitrate Pampa in Chapter 5.

del Tamarugal. The largest geoglyph on Earth, the Gigante de Atacama, is nearby.

See Iquique Area in Chapter 5.

Days 9 & 10: Arica/Departure
If you've come this far, head to Chile's northernmost city, with a temperate climate and a couple of creations by French architect Gustave Eiffel. The main attraction, however, is the nearby Museo Arqueológico de San Miguel de Azapa and its famed Chinchorro mummies, which date from 6,000 BC. Their Egyptian cousins are mere youngsters by comparison.

A morning flight on your last day gets you to Santiago in plenty of time to connect with an overnight flight back to North America or Europe.

See Arica Area in Chapter 5.

Transportation
Although it's quite easy, and even preferable, to explore Santiago, Viña del Mar, and Valparaíso using public transportation, a car makes it easier to visit the sights and towns in El Norte Grande. That said, it is possible to get around using buses, which connect most of the cities of El Norte Grande. Once in San Pedro de Atacama or Iquique, you can hook up with various tour agencies to visit sights not accessible by bus. There are frequent flights from Santiago to Calama and from Arica back to Santiago.

Day 8: Iquique
San Pedro to Iquique is a drivable 500-km (300-mi) journey, but a flight up from Calama saves you more hours of precious vacation time. There's not much of interest in Iquique itself, other than some nice white-sand beaches and the nearby ghost town of Humberstone, but the town makes a good base for visiting the hundreds of geoglyphs at the Cerros Pintados—it's the world's largest collection—in the Reserva Nacional Pampa

GREAT ITINERARIES

SANTIAGO & SOUTHERN CHILE
16 DAYS

Days 1 & 2: Santiago
Arrive in Santiago early the morning of your first day. After a brief rest, set out to explore the city's museums, shops, and green spaces using the power of your own two feet and the capital's efficient metro. (⇨ the *"Santiago & Northern Chile"* itinerary above for details.)

See Exploring Santiago in Chapter 2.

Days 3, 4, 5 & 6: The Lake District
Head south 675 km (405 mi) from Santiago on a fast toll highway to Temuco, the gateway to Chile's Lake District, or even better, take one of the frequent hour-long flights. Temuco and environs are one of the best places in the region to observe the indigenous Mapuche culture. About an hour south, and just 15 minutes apart on the shores of Lago Villarica, lie the twin resort towns of flashy, glitzy Pucón and quiet, pleasant Villarrica. Base yourself in the latter if you're in peso-saving mode. Drive south through the region from the graceful old city of Valdivia to Puerto Montt, stopping at the various resort towns. Frutillar, Puerto Octay, and Puerto Varas still bear testament to the Lake District's German-Austrian-Swiss immigrant history. Be sure to make time for one of the region's many hot springs.

See La Araucanía and Los Lagos in Chapter 7.

Days 7, 8, 9, 10 & 11: Parque Nacional Laguna San Rafael
From Puerto Montt, take a five-day round-trip cruise through the maze of fjords down the coast to the unforgetta- ble cobalt-blue glacier in Parque Nacional Laguna San Rafael. If you're lucky, you'll see the huge glacier calving off pieces of ice that cause noisy, violent waves in the brilliant blue water. Transport runs from the utilitarian passenger–auto ferries offered by Navimag and Transmarchilay to the luxury cruises run by Skorpios.

See Parque Nacional Laguna San Rafael in Chapter 9.

Days 12, 13, 14, 15 & 16: Parque Nacional Torres del Paine/Departure
When you return from your cruise back to Puerto Montt, take a spectacular morning flight over the Andes to the Patagonian city of Punta Arenas. On the next day drive north to Puerto Natales, gateway to the Parque Nacional Torres del Paine. You'll need at least two days to wander through the wonders of the park. On your final day, head back to Punta Arenas, stopping en route at one of the penguin sanctuaries, and catch an afternoon flight to Santiago, in time to connect with a night flight home to North America or Europe.

See Parque Nacional Torres del Paine in Chapter 10.

Transportation
A combination of flights, rental cars, and boat works best. From Santiago, drive south to Temuco and then through the various sights and towns of the Lake District. From Puerto Montt, take the boat cruise down to Parque Nacional Laguna San Rafael—book far in advance for January or February—and on your return to Puerto Montt fly into the city of Punta Arenas. From there, drive north to Puerto Natales.

HISTORY YOU CAN SEE

Pre-Colonial Chile

The indigenous groups living in Chile before the arrival of the Spanish can be categorized as the pre-Incan cultures in the north, the Mapuche in the region between the Choapa River and Chiloé, and the Patagonian cultures in the extreme south. Although the Incan Empire extended into Chile, the Mapuche successfully resisted their incursions; there is a debate about how much of Chile the Incans conquered.

What to See: The **geoglyphs** constructed between AD 500 and 1400 in the mountains along ancient northern trade routes are some of the most important in the world. The **Chinchorro mummies,** relics of the Chinchorro people who lived along the northern coast, are the oldest in the world, dating from 6000 BC. They are visible at the Museo Arqueológico de San Miguel de Azapa near Arica. The **Museo Arqueológico Le Paige** in San Pedro de Atacama has an impressive collection of precolonial and colonial objects. In Temuco, the **Museo Regional de la Araucanía** provides a fairly good introduction to Mapuche art, culture, and history. Temuco and its environs also offer a sense of modern Mapuche life. You can buy fair-trade Mapuche textiles and learn about Mapuche weaving at the **Chol-Chol Foundation** 20 minutes outside Temuco. Farther south, the **Museo Salesiano** in Punta Arenas has an interesting collection of artifacts from various Patagonian cultures. Finally, in Santiago, the **Museum of Pre-Columbian Art** has an excellent collection of indigenous artifacts from Mexico to Patagonia.

Colonial Chile

While Ferdinand Magellan and Diego de Almagro both traveled to Chile earlier, it was Pedro de Valdivia who founded Santiago in 1541. Before being killed in battle by a Mapuche chief, Valdivia established a number of other important towns in Chile. The Mapuche successfully resisted Spanish conquest and colonization, ruling south of the Bío Bío river until the 1880s.

What to See: The **Plaza de Armas** is where Pedro de Valdivia founded Santiago in 1541. The **Iglesia San Francisco** is Santiago's oldest structure dating from 1586, although it was partially rebuilt in 1698 and expanded in 1857. The **Casa Colorada** is a well-preserved example of colonial architecture. It was the home of Mateo de Toro y Zambrano, a creole businessman and Spanish soldier, and now houses the Museo de Santiago.

Independence

September 18, 1810—Chilean Independence Day—is when a group of prominent citizens created a junta to replace the Spanish government. However, full independence was achieved several years later in 1818 with the victory of the Battle of Maipú by Bernardo O'Higgins and José de San Martín. Chiloé remained under Spanish control until 1826.

What to See: The **Temple of Maipú** on the outskirts of Santiago was constructed in honor of the Virgin of Carmen, patron saint of Santiago, after the Battle of Maipú. While the original temple was destroyed, its foundations still exist near the new structure built in the 1950s. On Chiloé near Ancud, the **San Antonio Fort** constructed in 1786 is all that remains of Spain's last outpost in Chile. The **Palacio Cousiño** in Santiago, built by one of Chile's most important families in 1871, provides an excellent sense of how the elite lived in an independent, modernizing Chile.

FAQ

How expensive is Chile?

Very, and of course the weak exchange rate doesn't help! According to a recent report by the World Bank, Chile is the second most expensive country in Latin America, after Mexico. Prices of hotels and transportation go up considerably from mid-December through mid-March and again in July and August.

What should I pack for a trip to Chile?

Since many of Chile's attractions are outdoors, packing sturdy, all-weather gear is a good idea. Sunglasses, a hat, and sunscreen are all musts because the ozone layer over Chile is particularly deteriorated. For your electronic gear, keep in mind that you will need a two-pronged plug adaptor and that voltage in Chile is 220 volts, 50 cycles (220V 50Hz).

Do I need to or should I rent a car? Is driving hectic?

You definitely don't need to rent a car in Santiago, since you can take a combination of taxis, buses, and the metro to get around town. For day trips from Santiago to the coast or wine country, renting a car is probably the most convenient option, although buses to these destinations are also frequent and reasonably priced. Be aware of one-way streets and signs indicating right of way. You are not allowed to turn on red at a stop light unless there is a specific sign indicating otherwise. It is recommended, although not essential, to have an international driver's license. A valid U.S. driver's license is accepted at rental-car agencies.

Can I drive between Chile and Argentina?

Yes, you can drive between Chile and Argentina, but there are a few things to keep in mind. First, since it is an international border, be sure to have your passport along with your driver's license. Also, special insurance is required. If you rent a car, the rental company will provide you with a permit to drive into Argentina (for a price, of course), which includes all the necessary paperwork to cross the border (including the insurance). The permit must be requested several days in advance of the day the rental begins. The rental car must be returned in Chile, and the permit is valid for one exit to Argentina and one entrance into Chile. Common border crossings include the route from Santiago to Mendoza and Valdivia to Bariloche.

I have read about a "reciprocity fee." What is it?

All U.S. citizens entering Chile for the first time must pay a reciprocity fee of US$131 before passing customs. U.S. dollars, traveler's checks, and major credit cards are all accepted. The payment is valid until your passport expires.

Do I need to speak Spanish?

It is always helpful to speak the language of the country where you are traveling, but it is less crucial in Chile. Particularly in Santiago, there is generally at least one person who can speak basic English in most restaurants, hotels, and shops. However, if you plan on traveling to less tourist-oriented destinations, many fewer people will speak English, and you may need to resort to non-verbal means of communication or trying out those basic Spanish phrases you learned.

Santiago

Catedral Metropolitana, Plaza de Armas, Santiago

WORD OF MOUTH

"What to do in Santiago? If your tour doesn't take you to El Centro, go there yourself. Walk through the Plaza de Armas, braving the crowds on your way to the Mercado Central, perhaps for lunch at one of the seafood restaurants. Alternatively, spend an afternoon at the Feria de Artesenia by the Los Dominicos Church in Las Condes. You could also take the cable car up Cerro San Cristobel for stunning views, and lunch or dine at the Camino Real with the best wine list in Chile."

—toid

WELCOME TO SANTIAGO

TOP REASONS TO GO

★ **The Andes:** Ever-present jagged mountain peaks ring the capital. Wherever you go, you'll see them and remember that you are at the edge of the world.

★ **Great Crafts Markets:** Fine woolen items, expertly carved figurines, lapis lazuli jewelry, and other handicrafts from across the country are bountiful in Santiago.

★ **Museo Chileno de Arte Precolombino:** Occupying a lovely old building in the center of Santiago that used to be the *Real Aduana* (Royal Customs House), this museum's collection of indigenous pottery, jewelry, and artifacts is a joy for the eye.

★ **World-Class Wineries:** Santiago nestles in the Maipo Valley, the country's oldest wine-growing district. Some of Chile's largest and most traditional wineries—Concha y Toro and Santa Rita—are within an hour's drive of the city and so too is the lovely Casablanca Valley.

2

To LAS CONDES

PROVIDENCIA

1 **Santiago Centro.** Santiago Centro, with the La
Moneda Presidential Palace
and its ministries and law
courts, is the place from
which Chile is governed
and where you'll find most
of the historic monuments
and museums.

2 **La Alameda.** La Alameda, also known as Ave-
nida Libertador Bernardo
O'Higgins, marks the southern boundary of Santiago
Centro and is lined with
sights that include the San
Francisco church and the
Universidad de Chile. Farther
east, past the base of Santa
Lucía, it changes its name
to Avenida Providencia and
then Avenida Las Condes.

KEY

M *Metro stops*
i *Tourist information*
▬ *Cable Car Line*

3 **Parque Forestal.** A
leafy park along the banks
of the Río Mapocho gives
this tranquil district its
name. This is where you'll
find the city's main art
museums as well as, at its
western tip, the bustle of
the Mercado Central fish
market and, on the other
side of the river, the Vega
and Vega Chica markets.

4 **Bellavista & Parque
Metropolitano.** On the
north side of the Río
Mapocho, nestled in the
shadow of the San Cristóbal
Hill, Bellavista is Santiago's
"left bank," a Bohemian district of cafés, small restaurants, crafts shops, aspiring
art galleries, and one of
the homes of Nobel poet
Pablo Neruda.

5 **Parque Quinta Normal
Area.** Slightly off the beaten
track in western Santiago,
the Quinta Normal park is
not only one of the largest
in the city but also home
to four museums. Budget
constraints are apparent in
both the museums and the
park itself but it's still a great
place for a stroll, especially
with children.

6 **Las Condes.** Over the
past couple of decades,
most businesses have
migrated from the crowded
Centro to Las Condes. The
El Golf area, around Plaza
Perú, is the place to find
the city's largest selection
of smart restaurants and
trendy coffee shops.

GETTING ORIENTED

Pedro de Valdivia wasn't
very creative when he
mapped out the streets of
Santiago. He stuck to the
same simple grid pattern
you'll find in almost all of
the colonial towns along
the coast. The city didn't
grow much larger before
the meandering Río
Mapocho impeded these
plans. You may be sur-
prised, however, at how
orderly the city remains.
It's difficult to get lost wandering around downtown.
Much of the city, espe-
cially communities such
as Bellavista, is best
explored on foot. The
subway is probably the
quickest, cleanest, and
most economical way to
shuttle between neighbor-
hoods. To travel to more
distant neighborhoods,
or to get anywhere in the
evening after the subway
closes, you'll probably
want to hail a taxi.

SANTIAGO PLANNER

When to Go

Santiaguinos tend to abandon their city every summer during the school holidays that run from the end of December to early March. February is a particularly popular vacation time, when nearly everybody who's anybody is out of town. If you're not averse to the heat, this can be a good time for walking around the city; otherwise spring and fall are better choices, as the weather is more comfortable. Santiago is at its prettiest in spring when gentle breezes sweep in to clean the city's air of its winter smog and the trees that line the streets burst into blossom and fragrance.

Spring and fall are also good times to drive up through the Cajón del Maipo, when the scenery is at its peak. In fall, too, the vineyards around the city celebrate the *vendimia*—the grape harvest—with colorful festivals that are an opportunity to try traditional Chilean cuisine as well as some of the country's renowned wines. Winters in the city aren't especially cold—temperatures rarely dip below freezing—but days are sometimes gray and gloomy and air pollution is at its worst.

Eat Well & Rest Easy

Dining is one of Santiago's great pleasures. Everything from fine restaurants to informal *picadas,* restaurants that specialize in typical Chilean food, is spread across the city. Menus run the gamut of international cuisines, but don't miss the local bounty—seafood delivered directly from the Pacific Ocean. One of the local favorites is *caldillo de congrio,* the hearty fish stew celebrated by poet Pablo Neruda in his *Oda al Caldillo de Congrio* which is, in fact, the recipe. A *pisco sour*—a cocktail of grape brandy and lemon juice—makes a good start to a meal.

Lunch and dinner are served quite late—beginning at 1 pm for lunch, 7:30 or 8 pm for dinner. People do dress smartly for dinner, but a coat and tie are rarely necessary.

Santiago has more than a dozen five-star hotels, many of them in the burgeoning Las Condes and Vitacura neighborhoods. You won't find better service than at newer hotels such as the lavish Ritz-Carlton. But don't write off the old standbys such as Hotel Plaza San Francisco. Inexpensive small hotels are harder to find but they do exist, especially around the Calle Londres in the city center and in the Providencia district.

WHAT IT COSTS IN CHILEAN PESOS (IN THOUSANDS)

¢	$	$$	$$$	$$$$
RESTAURANTS				
under 3 pesos	3 pesos– 5 pesos	5 pesos– 8 pesos	8 pesos– 11 pesos	over 11 pesos
HOTELS				
under 15 pesos	15 pesos– 45 pesos	45 pesos– 75 pesos	75 pesos– 105 pesos	over 105 pesos

Restaurant prices are based on the median main course price at dinner. Hotel prices are for two people in a standard double room in high season.

Language

Although staff at large hotels mostly speak adequate English and, in some cases, a little French and German, be prepared elsewhere for people to be helpful but to speak little or no English. Taxi drivers, except for the (very expensive) services provided by hotels, won't in general know English, and menus are mostly only in Spanish. Spanish-speaking travelers, even from other Latin American countries, will find that some words, particularly for food, vary.

Safety

Despite what Chileans will tell you, Santiago is no more dangerous than most other large cities and considerably less so than many other Latin American capitals. As a rule of thumb, watch out for your property but, unless you venture into some of the city's outlying neighborhoods, your physical safety is very unlikely to be at risk. Beware of pickpockets particularly in the Centro and on buses.

Other Practicalities

Navigation. In Santiago, it's easy to get your bearings because the Andes Mountains are always there to tell you where the east is. And, to make it even easier, the main districts you'll want to visit—the Centro, Providencia, and Las Condes—form the city's west–east axis, moving gradually up towards the mountains as they become more prosperous. This is the axis served by Line 1 of the subway.

Kids. Chileans love children and are quite likely to stop and admire them. Children are welcome in restaurants, except the most expensive ones at night, where they'll be admitted but raise eyebrows.

Tipping. In restaurants and for tour guides, a 10% tip is usual unless service has been deficient. Taxi drivers don't expect to be tipped but do leave your small change. Visitors need to be wary of parking attendants. During the day, they should only charge what's on their portable meters when you collect the car but, at night, they will ask for money—usually 1,000 pesos—in advance. This is a racket but, for your car's safety, it's better to comply.

Drinking Water. Tap water in Santiago is perfectly safe to drink, but its high mineral content—it's born in the Andes— can disagree with some people. In any case, a wide selection of still and sparkling bottled waters is available.

Getting Here & Around

Air Travel. Santiago's Comodoro Arturo Merino Benítez International Airport, often referred to simply as Pudahuel, is about a 30-minute drive west of the city. Taxis should cost around 16,000 pesos for a trip downtown. Hire one at the desks near customs, rather than using one of the services touted outside. Tickets for bus services cost around 1,500 pesos each at the same desks.

Car Travel. You don't need a car if you're going to stay within the city limits, as most of the downtown sights are within walking distance of each other. A car is the best way to see the surrounding countryside, however. The highways around Santiago are excellent and generally well signposted.

Subway Travel. Santiago's excellent subway system, the Metro, is the best way to get around the main part of the city but isn't very extensive. It is comfortable, inexpensive, and safe. The system operates weekdays 6 am–11 pm, Saturday 6:30 am–10:30 pm, and Sunday 8 am–10:30 pm.

Buses and taxis. Buses are relatively efficient and clean, although very crowded at peak times. Fares on the subway and buses are paid using the same pre-paid smart card (most easily acquired in subway stations). No cash is accepted on buses. Taxis are reasonably priced and plentiful.

Updated by
Ruth Bradley

WHEN IT WAS FOUNDED BY Spanish conquistador Pedro de Valdivia in 1541, Santiago was little more than the triangular patch of land embraced by two arms of the Río Mapocho. Today that area, known as Santiago Centro, is just one of 32 *comunas* that make up the city, each with its own distinct personality. You'd never confuse Patronato, a neighborhood north of downtown filled with Moorish-style mansions built by families who made their fortunes in textiles, with Las Condes, where the modern skyscrapers built by international corporations crowd the avenues. The chic shopping centers of Las Condes have little in common with the outdoor markets in Bellavista.

Perhaps the neighborhoods have retained their individuality because many have histories as old as Santiago itself. Ñuñoa, for example, was a hardworking farm town to the east. Farther away was El Arrayán, a sleepy village in the foothills of the Andes. As the capital grew, these and many other communities were drawn inside the city limits. If you ask Santiaguinos you meet today where they reside, they are just as likely to mention their neighborhood as their city.

Like many of the early Spanish settlements, Santiago suffered some severe setbacks. Six months after the town was founded, a group of the indigenous Picunche people attacked, burning every building to the ground. Undeterred, the Spanish rebuilt in the same spot. The narrow streets that radiated out from the Plaza de Armas in those days are the same ones that can be seen today.

The Spanish lost interest in Santiago after about a decade, moving south in search of gold. But fierce resistance from the Mapuche people in 1599 forced many settlers to retreat to Santiago. The population swelled, solidifying the city's claim as the region's colonial capital. Soon many of the city's landmarks, including the colorful Casa Colorada, were erected.

It wasn't until after Chile finally won its independence from Spain in 1818 that Santiago took the shape it has today. Broad avenues extended in every direction. Buildings befitting a national capital, such as the Congreso Nacional and the Teatro Municipal, won wide acclaim. Parque Quinta Normal and Parque O'Higgins preserved huge swaths of green for the people, and the poplar-lined Parque Forestal gave the increasingly proud populace a place to promenade.

Santiago today is home to more than 6 million people—nearly a third of the country's total population. It continues to spread outward to the so-called *barrios altos* (upper neighborhoods) east of the center. It's also growing upward, as new office towers transform the skyline. Yet in many ways, Santiago still feels like a small town, where residents are always likely to bump into an acquaintance along the city center's crowded streets and bustling plazas.

SAMPLE ITINERARY

Santiago is a compact city, small enough that you can visit all the must-see sights in a few days. Consider the weather when planning your itinerary—on the first clear day your destination should be **Parque Metropolitano**, where you'll be treated to exquisite views from **Cerro San Cristóbal**. After a morning gazing at the Andes, head back down the hill and spend the afternoon wandering the bohemian streets of **Bellavista**, with a visit to Nobel laureate Pablo Neruda's Santiago residence, **La Chascona**. Check out one of the neighborhood's colorful eateries.

The next day, head to **Parque Forestal**, a leafy park that runs along the Río Mapocho. Be sure to visit the lovely old train station, the **Estación Mapocho**. After lunch at the **Mercado Central**, uncover the city's colonial past in Santiago Centro. Requisite sights include the **Plaza de Armas**, around which you'll find the Casa Colorada and the Museo Chileno de Arte Precolombino. Stop for tea in **Plaza Mulato Gil de Castro**. On the third day explore the sights along the **Alameda**, especially the presidential palace of La Moneda and the landmark church, **Iglesia San Francisco**. For a last look at the city, climb **Cerro Santa Lucía**. That night put on your chicest outfit for dinner in the trendy neighborhood of **Las Condes**.

SANTIAGO CENTRO

Shiny new skyscrapers may be sprouting up in neighborhoods to the east, but Santiago Centro is the place to start if you really want to take the pulse of the city. After all, this is the historic heart of Santiago. All the major traffic arteries cross here—creating the usual traffic headaches—and subway lines converge here before whisking riders out to the suburbs. In Santiago Centro you'll find interesting museums, imposing government buildings, and bustling commercial streets. But don't think you'll be lost in a sprawling area—it takes only about 15 minutes to walk from one edge of the neighborhood to the other.

Numbered bullets in the margins correspond to numbered bullets on the Santiago Centro & La Alameda map.

WHAT TO SEE

❶ **Plaza de Armas.** This square has been the symbolic heart of Chile—as
★ well as its political, social, religious, and commercial center—since Pedro de Valdivia established the city on this spot in 1541. The Palacio de los Gobernadores, the Palacio de la Real Audiencia, and the Municipalidad de Santiago front the square's northern edge. The dignified Catedral graces the western side of the square. On any given day, the plaza teems with life—vendors selling religious icons, artists painting the activity around them, street performers juggling fire, and tourists clutching guidebooks. On the eastern side of the plaza you can watch people playing chess. ✉ *Compañía at Estado, Santiago Centro* Ⓜ *Plaza de Armas.*

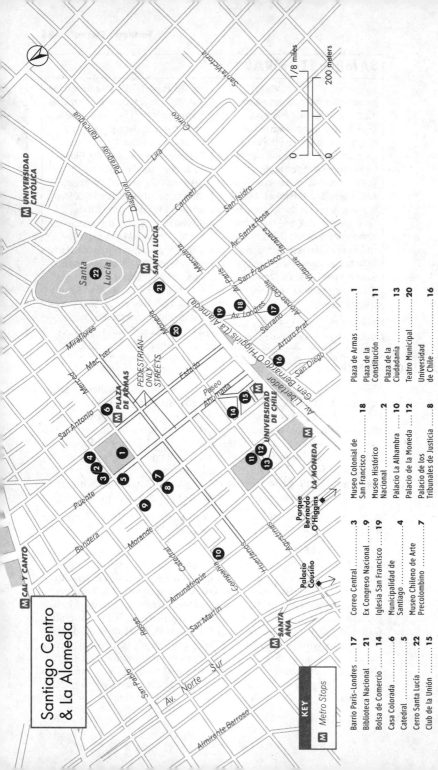

Santiago Centro & La Alameda

KEY

Ⓜ Metro Stops

Barrio París-Londres **17**
Biblioteca Nacional **21**
Bolsa de Comercio **14**
Casa Colorada **6**
Catedral **5**
Cerro Santa Lucía **22**
Club de la Unión **15**

Correo Central **3**
Ex Congreso Nacional **9**
Iglesia San Francisco **19**
Municipalidad de
Santiago **4**
Museo Chileno de Arte
Precolombino **7**

Museo Colonial de
San Francisco **18**
Museo Histórico
Nacional **2**
Palacio La Alhambra **10**
Palacio de la Moneda **12**
Palacio de los
Tribunales de Justicia **8**

Plaza de Armas **1**
Plaza de la
Constitución **11**
Plaza de la
Ciudadanía **13**
Teatro Municipal **20**
Universidad
de Chile **16**

6 **Casa Colorada.** The appropriately named Red House is one of the best-preserved colonial structures in the city. Mateo de Toro y Zambrano, president of Chile's first independent government established in September 1810, once made his home here. It is the house itself that is most interesting but it also contains a modest museum about the history of Santiago. Exhibits are labeled in English. ✉ *Merced 860, Santiago Centro* ☎ *2/633–0723* ✎ *Tues.–Sat. 500 pesos, Sun. free* ☉ *Tues.–Fri. 10–6, Sat. 10–5, Sun. 11–2* Ⓜ *Plaza de Armas.*

5 **Catedral.** Conquistador Pedro de Valdivia declared in 1541 that a house of worship would be constructed at this site bordering the Plaza de Armas. The first adobe building burned to the ground, and the structures that replaced it were destroyed by the earthquakes of 1647 and 1730. The finishing touches of the neoclassical cathedral standing today were added in 1789 by Italian architect Joaquín Toesca. Be sure to see the baroque interior with its line of arches topped by stained-glass windows parading down the long nave and look out for the sparkling silver altar of a side chapel in the south nave. ✉ *Plaza de Armas, Santiago Centro* ☎ *2/696–2777* ☉ *Daily 10–8* Ⓜ *Plaza de Armas.*

3 **Correo Central.** Housed in what was once the ornate Palacio de los Gobernadores, this building dating from 1715 is one of the most beautiful post offices you are likely to see. It was reconstructed by Ricardo Brown in 1882 after being ravaged by fire and is a fine example of neoclassical architecture, with a glass-and-iron roof added in the early 20th century. ✉ *Catedral at Paseo Ahumada, Santiago Centro* ☎ *2/956–5153* ⊕ *www.correos.cl* ☉ *Weekdays 8–7, Sat. 9–2* Ⓜ *Plaza de Armas.*

2 **Museo Histórico Nacional.** The colonial-era Palacio de la Real Audiencia served as the meeting place of Chile's first Congress in July 1811. The building then functioned as a telegraph office before the museum moved here in 1911. It's worth the small admission charge to see the interior of the 200-year-old structure, where exhibits tracing Chile's history from the pre-Conquest period to the 20th century are arranged chronologically in rooms centered around a courtyard. Ask for the free English brochure and audio guide. ✉ *Plaza de Armas, Santiago Centro* ☎ *2/633–1815* ⊕ *www.museohistoriconacional.cl* ✎ *Tues.–Sat. 600 pesos, Sun. free* ☉ *Tues.–Sun. 10–5:30* Ⓜ *Plaza de Armas.*

4 **Municipalidad de Santiago.** Today's city hall for central Santiago can be found on the site of the colonial city hall and jail. The original structure, built in 1552, survived until a devastating earthquake in 1730. Joaquín Toesca, the architect who also designed the presidential palace and completed the cathedral, reconstructed the building in 1785, but it was destroyed by fire a century later. In 1891, Eugenio Joannon, who favored an Italian Renaissance style, erected the structure standing today. On the facade hangs an elaborate coat of arms presented by Spain. The interior is not open to the public. ✉ *Plaza de Armas, Santiago Centro* Ⓜ *Plaza de Armas.*

NEED A BREAK?

Pause for a coffee or a cold beer at one of the two sidewalk cafés on the west side of Plaza de Armas and let the hustle and bustle of the city flow past you. The coffee is better in the more northerly café, the **Faisan D'Or** (⊠ *Plaza de Armas, Santiago Centro* ☎ *2/696–4161*).

⑦ Museo Chileno de Arte Precolombino. If you plan to visit only one museum in Santiago, it should be the Museum of Pre-Columbian Art, a block from the Plaza de Armas. The well-endowed collection of artifacts of the region's indigenous peoples, much of it donated by the collector Sergio Larraín García-Moreno, is displayed in the beautifully restored Royal Customs

FodorśChoice
★

House that dates from 1807. The permanent collection, on the upper floor, showcases textiles and ceramics from Mexico to Patagonia. Unlike many of the city's museums, the displays here are well labeled in Spanish and English. ⊠ *Bandera 361, at Av. Compañía, Santiago Centro* ☎ *2/688–7348* ⊕ *www.museoprecolombino.cl* ☞ *Tues.–Sat. 3,000 pesos, Sun. free* ⊙ *Tues.–Sun. 10–6, public holidays, 10–2* Ⓜ *Plaza de Armas.*

⑧ Palacio de los Tribunales de Justicia. During Augusto Pinochet's rule, countless human-rights demonstrations were held outside the Courts of Justice, which house the country's Supreme Court. The imposing neoclassical interior is worth a look, but men wearing shorts are not admitted. ⊠ *Av. Compañía 1140, Santiago Centro* Ⓜ *Plaza de Armas.*

⑩ Palacio La Alhambra. Santiago's Alhambra palace is tiny and sadly run down but its two patios—the second with its own Fountain of Lions—and richly decorated hall give an idea of its former splendor. It was built in 1860 by Francisco Ignacio Ossa as his family's town house after he made his fortune in silver mining in the north. ⊠ *Compañía 1340,* ☎ *2/698–0875* ⊕ *www.snba.cl* ☞ *Free* ⊙ *Weekdays 11–2 and 5–8* Ⓜ *Plaza de Armas.*

⑨ Ex Congreso Nacional. Once the meeting place for the National Congress (the legislature moved to Valparaíso in 1990), this palatial neoclassical building became the Ministry of Foreign Affairs for a time but was returned to the Senate for meetings after the Ministry moved to the former Hotel Carrera in the Plaza de la Constitución in December 2005. The original structure on the site, the Iglesia de la Compañía de Jesús, was destroyed by a fire in 1863 in which 2,000 people perished. ⊠ *Catedral 1158, Santiago Centro* Ⓜ *Plaza de Armas.*

OFF THE BEATEN PATH

Parque Bernardo O'Higgins. Named for Chile's first president and national hero, whose troops were victorious against the Spanish, this park has plenty of open space for everything from ball games to military parades. Street vendors sell *volantines* (kites) outside the park year-round; high winds make September and early October the prime kite-flying season. Children take advantage of the spring winds to practice this traditional—and highly competitive—pastime and parks start to fill with the *ramadas* at which Chileans gather to drink, eat, dance, and generally celebrate the September 18 Independence Day. ⊠ *Autopista Central between Av. Blanco Encalada and Av. Rondizonni, Santiago Centro* ☎ *2/556-1927* ⊠ *Free* ⊙ *Daily 9-8* Ⓜ *Parque O'Higgins.*

LA ALAMEDA

Avenida Libertador Bernardo O'Higgins, more frequently called La Alameda, is the city's principal thoroughfare. Along with the Avenida Norte Sur and the Río Mapocho, it forms the wedge that defines the city's historic district. Many of Santiago's most important buildings, including landmarks such as the Iglesia San Francisco, stand along the avenue. Others, like Teatro Municipal, are just steps away.

TIMING & PRECAUTIONS

You could spend an hour alone at the Palacio de la Moneda—try to time your visit with the changing of the guard, which takes place every other day at 10 am. Across the Alameda, take at least an hour and a half to explore Iglesia San Francisco, the adjacent museum, and the Barrio París-Londres. You could easily spend a bookish half hour perusing the stacks at the Biblioteca Nacional. Plan for an hour or more at Cerro Santa Lucía with its splendid view of the city.

EXPLORING

㉑ **Biblioteca Nacional.** Near the foot of Cerro Santa Lucía is the block-long classical facade of the National Library. Although it didn't move to its present premises until 1925, this library, founded in 1813, is one of the oldest and most complete in South America. The vast interior includes arcane collections. The second-floor Sala José Toribio Medina (closed Saturday), which holds the most important collection of early Latin American print work, is well worth a look. The three levels of books, reached by curved-wood balconies, are lighted by massive chandeliers. The café on the ground floor is a quiet place to linger over a coffee. ⊠ *La Alameda 651, La Alameda* ☎ *2/360-5200* ⊕ *www.dibam.cl* ⊠ *Free* ⊙ *Apr.-mid-Dec., weekdays 9-7, Sat. 9-2; mid-Dec.-Mar., Sun.-Fri. 9-5:30* Ⓜ *Santa Lucía.*

㉒ **Cerro Santa Lucía.** The mazelike park of Santa Lucía is a hangout for park-bench smoochers and photo-snapping tourists. Walking uphill along the labyrinth of interconnected paths and plazas takes about 30 minutes, or you can take an elevator two blocks north of the park's main entrance (no fee). The crow's nest affords an excellent 360-degree view of the entire city; two stairways lead up from the Plaza Caupolicán esplanade; those on the south side are newer and less slippery. Be careful near dusk as the park, although patrolled, also attracts the occasional

mugger. ⊠*Santa Lucía at La Alameda, La Alameda* ☎*2/664–4206*
⊙*Nov.–Mar., daily 9–8; Apr.–Oct., daily 9–7* Ⓜ*Santa Lucía.*

⑳ **Teatro Municipal.** The opulent Municipal Theater is the city's cultural
center, with performances of opera, ballet, and classical music from
April to November. Designed by French architects, the theater opened
in 1857, with major renovations in 1870 and 1906 following a fire and
an earthquake, and the Renaissance-style building is one of the city's
most refined monuments. The lavish interior deserves a visit. ⊠*Plaza
Alcalde Mekis, Av. Agustinas 794, at Av. San Antonio, La Alameda*
☎*2/463–1000* Ⓜ*Universidad de Chile, Santa Lucía.*

⑭ **Bolsa de Comercio.** Chile's stock exchange is housed in a 1917 French
neoclassical structure with an elegant clock tower surmounted by an
arched slate cupola. Business is now done electronically but you can
visit the old trading floor with its buying and selling circle called *rueda.*
⊠*La Bolsa 64, La Alameda* ☎*2/399–3000* ⊕*www.bolsadesantiago.
com* ▥*Free but you'll be asked to leave identification at the door*
⊙*Weekdays 8–6* Ⓜ*Universidad de Chile.*

⑮ **Club de la Unión.** The facade of this neoclassical building, dating to
1925, is one of the city's finest. The interior of this private club, whose
roster has included numerous Chilean presidents, is open only to members and their guests. ⊠*Alameda at Bandera, La Alameda* Ⓜ*Universidad de Chile.*

⑯ **Universidad de Chile.** From the Club de la Unión, cross through the Universidad de Chile Metro station, with its murals depicting Chilean history painted by Mario Toral, to the main branch of the University of
Chile, the country's largest educational institution. This symmetrical
ochre edifice was completed in 1872, when it was known as the University Palace. It's not officially open to the public, but you are free to
stroll through the grounds. ⊠*La Alameda 1058, La Alameda* Ⓜ*Universidad de Chile.*

⑲ **Iglesia San Francisco.** Santiago's oldest structure, greatest symbol, and
principal landmark, the Church of St. Francis is the last trace of 16th-
century colonial architecture in the city. Construction began in 1586,
and although the church survived successive earthquakes, early trem-
ors took their toll and portions had to be rebuilt several times. Today's
neoclassical tower, which forms the city's most recognizable silhou-
ette, was added in 1857 by architect Fermín Vivaceta. Inside are rough
stone-and-brick walls and an ornate coffered wood ceiling. Visible on
the main altar is the image of the Virgen del Socorro (Virgin of Assistance) that conquistador Pedro de Valdivia carried for protection and
guidance. ⊠*La Alameda 834, La Alameda* ☎*2/638–3238* ⊙*Daily 8
am–8 pm* Ⓜ*Santa Lucía, Universidad de Chile.*

⑱ **Museo Colonial de San Francisco.** This monastery, adjacent to Iglesia San
Francisco, houses the best collection of 17th-century colonial paintings
on the continent. Inside the rooms wrapping around an overgrown
courtyard are 54 large-scale canvases portraying the life of St. Francis
painted in Cuzco, Peru, as well as a plethora of religious iconography.

Most pieces are labeled in Spanish and English. Franciscan friars still occupy the second floor. ⊠ *La Alameda 834, La Alameda* ☎ *2/639–8737* 🖫 *1,000 pesos* ⊙ *Tues.–Sat. 10–1 and 3–6, Sun. 10–2* Ⓜ *Santa Lucía, Universidad de Chile.*

⑰ **Barrio París-Londres.** Many architects contributed to what is frequently referred to as Santiago's Little Europe, among them Cruz Montt, Alamos, and Larraín. The string of small mansion houses lining the cobbled streets of Calles París and Londres sprang up in the mid-1920s on the vegetable patches and gardens that once belonged to the convent adjoining Iglesia San Francisco. The three- and four-story town houses are all unique; some have brick facades while others are done in Palladian style. ⊠ *Londres at París, La Alameda.*

OFF THE BEATEN PATH

Palacio Cousiño. Dating from the early 1870s, this fabulous mansion was built by the wealthy Cousiño-Goyenechea family. All that mining money allowed them to build this palace with amenities such as one of the country's first elevators. The elegant furnishings were—of course—imported from France. ⊠ *Dieciocho 438, La Alameda* ☎ *2/698–5063* 🖫 *2,100 pesos* ⊙ *Tours in English Tues.–Fri. 9:30–1:30 and 2:30–5, weekends 9:30–1:30* Ⓜ *Toesca.*

⑫ **Palacio de la Moneda.** Originally the royal mint, this sober neoclassical edifice designed by Joaquín Toesca in the 1780s and completed in 1805 became the presidential palace in 1846 and served that purpose for more than a century. It was bombarded by the military in the 1973 coup, when Salvador Allende defended his presidency against the assault of General Augusto Pinochet before committing suicide there. The two central courtyards are open to the public, and tours of the interior can be arranged by e-mail with at least two days' notice. ⊠ *Plaza de la Constitución, Moneda between Teatinos and Morandé, La Alameda* ☎ *2/690-4000* ✉ *visitas@presidencia.cl* ⊙ *Daily 10:30–6* Ⓜ *La Moneda.*

⑪ **Plaza de la Constitución.** Palacio de la Moneda and other government
★ buildings line Constitution Square, the country's most formal plaza. The changing of the guard takes place every other day at 10 am within the triangle defined by 12 Chilean flags. Adorning the plaza are four monuments, each dedicated to a notable national figure: Diego Portales, founder of the Chilean republic; Jorge Alessandri, the country's leader from 1958 to 1964; Eduardo Frei Montalva, president from 1964 to 1970; and Salvador Allende (1970–73). ⊠ *Moneda at Morandé, La Alameda* Ⓜ *La Moneda.*

⑬ **Plaza de la Ciudadanía.** On the south side of the Palacio de la Moneda, this plaza was inaugurated in December 2006 as part of a program of public works in preparation for the celebration of the bicentenary of Chile's Independence in 2010. Beneath the plaza is the Centro Cultural del Palacio La Moneda, a new arts center that sometimes has interesting exhibitions but too often echoes with emptiness. The crafts shop there has top-quality work. ⊠ *Plaza de la Ciudadanía 26, La Alameda* ☎ *2/355–6500* ⊕ *www.ccplm.cl* ⊙ *Daily 10–7:30* Ⓜ *La Moneda.*

PARQUE FORESTAL

After building a canal in 1891 to tame the unpredictable Río Mapocho, Santiago found itself with a thin strip of land that it didn't quite know what to do with. The area quickly filled with the city's refuse. A decade later, under the watchful eye of Enrique Cousiño, it was transformed into the leafy Forest Park. It was and still is enormously popular with Santiaguinos. Parque Forestal is the perfect antidote to the spirited Plaza de Armas. The eastern tip, near Plaza Baquedano—also known as Plaza Italia—is distinguished by the Wagnerian-scale Fuente Alemana (German Fountain), donated by the German community of Santiago. The bronze-and-stone monolith commemorates the centennial of Chilean Independence.

Numbered bullets in the margins correspond to numbered bullets on the Parque Forestal map.

TIMING & PRECAUTIONS

You can have a pleasant, relaxing day strolling through the city's most popular park, losing yourself in the art museums, and exploring the Mercado Central. In Plaza Mulato Gil de Castro, allot at least 30 minutes for the Museo de Artes Visuales and adjoining Museo Arqueológico. You can easily spend an hour or two in the Museo Nacional de Bellas Artes and the Museo de Arte Contemporáneo. Vega Chica and Vega Central are usually crowded, so keep an eye on your personal belongings. When the markets are closing around sunset, it's best to return to safer neighborhoods south of the river.

WHAT TO SEE

㉓ ★ Estación Mapocho. This mighty edifice, with its trio of two-story arches framed by intricate terra-cotta detailing, is as elegant as any train station in the world. The station was inaugurated in 1913 as a terminus for trains arriving from Valparaíso and points north, but steam engines no longer pull in here. A major conversion transformed the structure into one of the city's principal arts and conference centers. The Centro Cultural Estación Mapocho houses two restaurants, a fine bookstore and café, and a large exhibition hall and arts space. The cavernous space that once sheltered steam engines now hosts musical performances and other events. ⊠ *Plaza de la Cultura, Independencia at Balmaceda, Parque Forestal* ☎ *2/361–1761* ⊕ *www.estacionmapocho.cl* ☉ *Daily 9–7* Ⓜ *Puente Cal y Canto.*

㉔ Mercado Central. At the Central Market you'll find a matchless selection of creatures from the sea. Depending on the season, you might see the delicate beaks of *picorocos,* the world's only edible barnacles; *erizos,* the prickly shelled sea urchins; or heaps of giant mussels. If the fish don't capture your interest, the architecture may: the lofty wrought-iron ceiling of the structure, reminiscent of a Victorian train station, was prefabricated in England and erected in Santiago between 1868 and 1872. Diners are regaled by musicians in the middle of the market, where two restaurants compete for customers. You can also find a cheap, filling meal at a stand along the market's southern edge.

2

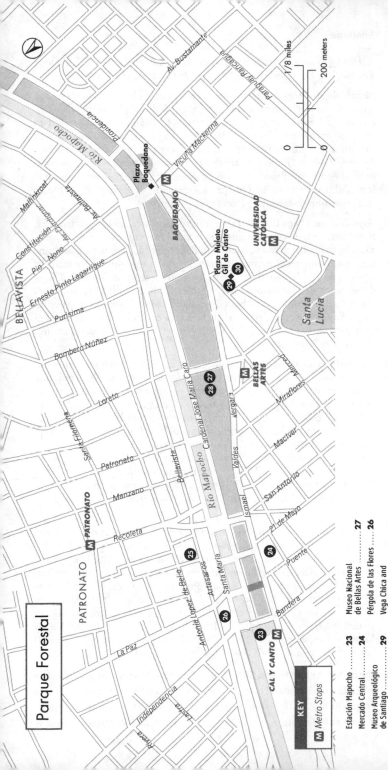

Parque Forestal

✉ *Ismael Valdés Vergara 900, Parque Forestal* ☎*2/696–8327* ⊘ *Sun.–Thurs. 6–5, Fri. 6 am–8 pm, Sat. 6–6* Ⓜ *Puente Cal y Canto.*

㉖ **Pérgola de las Flores.** Santiaguinos come to the Trellis of Flowers to buy wreaths and flower arrangements to bring to the city's two nearby cemeteries. *La Pérgola de las Flores,* a famous Chilean musical, is based on the conflict that arose in the 1930s when the mayor of Santiago wanted to shut down the market, then located near the Iglesia San Francisco on the Alameda. Find a chatty florist at one of the two open-air markets—Pégola San Francisco and Pérgola Santa María—and you may learn all about it. ✉ *Av. La Paz at Artesanos, Recoleta* ☎*No phone* ⊘ *Daily sunrise–sunset* Ⓜ *Puente Cal y Canto.*

㉕ **Vega Chica and Vega Central.** From fruit to furniture, meat to machinery, these lively markets stock just about anything you can name. Alongside the ordinary items you can find delicacies like *piñones,* giant pine nuts found on monkey puzzle trees. If you're undaunted by crowds, try a typical Chilean meal in a closet-size eatery or *picada.* Chow down with the locals on *pastel de choclo,* a pie filled with ground beef, chicken, olives, and boiled eggs and topped with mashed corn. As in any other crowded market, be extra careful with your belongings. ✉ *Antonia López de Bello between Av. Salas and Nueva Rengifo, Recoleta* Ⓜ *Patronato.*

㉗ **Museo Nacional de Bellas Artes.** Unfortunately, Chile's main art museum now has only a small part of its excellent collection of Chilean painting on display, confining it to just six small rooms on the second floor and organizing it confusingly around arcane themes rather than chronologically. The rest of the museum is given over to temporary exhibitions of varying interest. The elegant, neoclassical building, which was originally intended to house the city's school of fine arts, has an impressive glass-domed ceiling that illuminates the main hall. Guided tours in English are available in January and February. ✉ *Bounded by José M. de la Barra and Ismael Valdés Vergara, Parque Forestal* ☎*2/633–0655* ⊕ *www.dibam.cl* ✆ *Tues.–Sat. 600 pesos, Sun. free* ⊘ *Tues.–Sun. 10–7* Ⓜ *Bellas Artes.*

㉘ **Museo de Arte Contemporáneo.** After an ambitious restoration effort, the elegant Museum of Contemporary Art no longer has its rather dilapidated interior. Located in the western end of the building housing the Museo de Bellas Artes, the museum showcases a collection of modern Latin American paintings, photography, and sculpture. The museum is run by the art school of Universidad de Chile, so it isn't afraid to take risks. Look for Fernando Botero's pudgy *Caballo* sculpture gracing the square out front. ✉ *Bounded by José M. de la Barra and Ismael Valdés Vergara, Parque Forestal* ☎*2/977–1741* ⊕ *www.mac.uchile.cl* ✆ *600 pesos* ⊘ *Tues.–Sat. 11–7, Sun. 11–6* Ⓜ *Bellas Artes.*

NEED A BREAK? The pleasant Plaza Mulato Gil de Castro, a cobblestone square off the colorful Calle José Victorino Lastarria, is an unexpected treat. In the midst of it is **Pérgola de la Plaza** (✉ *Parque Forestal* ☎*2/639–3604*), which serves snacks as well as full meals. Just a block east from Calle José Victorino Lastarria is

Emporio La Rosa (⊠ *Merced 191 Parque Forestal* 🕾 *2/638–9257*), which is famous for its homemade ice creams in a rainbow of flavors.

㉚ **Museo de Artes Visuales.** This dazzling museum of contemporary art dis-
★ plays the combined private holdings of Chilean industrial moguls Manuel Santa Cruz and Hugo Yaconi and has one of the finest collections of
contemporary Chilean art. The building itself is a masterpiece: six gallery levels float into each other in surprising ways. The wood floors and
Plexiglas-sided stairways create an open and airy space where, depending on what's on display when you visit, you'll see paintings and sculptures by Roberto Matta, Arturo Duclos, Gonzalo Cienfuegos, Roser
Bru, José Balmes, and Eugenio Dittborn, among others. ⊠ *José Victorino Lastarria 307, at Plaza Mulato Gil de Castro, Parque Forestal*
🕾 *2/638–3502* ⊕ *www.mavi.cl* 🕙 *Tues.–Sat. 1,000 pesos (includes
Museo Arqueológico de Santiago), Sun. free* ☉ *Tues.–Sun. 10:30–6:30*
Ⓜ *Universidad Católica.*

㉙ **Museo Arqueológico de Santiago.** This archaeological museum, devoted
specifically to the indigenous peoples of Chile, more than makes up
for its small size with the quality of the exhibits, labeled in English
and Spanish. Artifacts include an outstanding collection of the Andean
headwear used to distinguish different ethnic groups, pottery, jewelry,
and a collection of the woven bags used by Andean peoples to carry
the coca leaves that sustained them during their long treks at high altitudes. It is located inside the Museo de Artes Visuales. ⊠ *José Victorino
Lastarria 307, 2nd fl., Parque Forestal* 🕾 *2/664–9337* ⊕ *www.mavi.
cl* 🕙 *Tues.–Sat. 1,000 pesos (includes Museo de Artes Visuales), Sun.
free* ☉ *Tues.–Sun. 10:30–6:30* Ⓜ *Universidad Católica.*

**OFF THE
BEATEN
PATH**

Parque de las Esculturas. Providencia is mainly a commercial district, but
it has one of the city's most captivating—and least publicized—public
parks. Here, the gardens are filled with sculptures by Chile's top artists. Because of its pastoral atmosphere, the park is popular with joggers and cuddling couples. In the center is a wood pavilion that hosts
art exhibitions. To get here from the Los Leones Metro stop, walk a
block north to the Río Mapocho and cross the bridge to Avenida Santa
María. The park is on your left.

BELLAVISTA & PARQUE METROPOLITANO

If you happen to be in Santiago on one of those lovely winter days when
the sun comes out after rain has cleared the air, head straight for Parque
Metropolitano. In the center is Cerro San Cristóbal, a hill reached via
a cable car, known as the teleférico, or by an older funicular railway. A
journey to the top of the hill rewards you with spectacular views of the
city nestling below the snow-covered Andes Mountains. In the shadow
of Cerro San Cristóbal is Bellavista. The neighborhood has but one
sight—the poet Pablo Neruda's hillside home of La Chascona—but it's
perhaps the city's best place to wander. You're sure to discover interesting antiques shops, bustling outdoor markets, and adventurous and
colorful eateries.

Numbered bullets in the margins correspond to numbered bullets on the Bellavista & Parque Metropolitano map.

TIMING & PRECAUTIONS

Plan on devoting an entire day to seeing Parque Metropolitano's major attractions. During the week the park is almost empty, and you can enjoy the views in relative solitude. Avoid walking down if you decide to watch the sunset from the lofty perch—the area is not well patrolled. Give yourself at least an hour to wander through Bellavista, and another hour for a tour of La Chascona.

WHAT TO SEE

32 **Cerro San Cristóbal.** St. Christopher's Hill, within Parque Metropolitano, is one of the most popular tourist attractions in Santiago. From the western entrance at Plaza Caupolicán you can walk—it's a steep but enjoyable one-hour climb—or take the funicular. Either route leads you to the summit, which is crowned by a gleaming white statue of the Virgen de la Inmaculada Concepción. If you are coming from the eastern entrance, you can ascend in the cable car or *teleférico* that leaves seven blocks north of the Pedro de Valdivia Metro stop. The ride, with four passengers per colored-glass bubble, can be terrifying for acrophobics. Tree branches whack at your lift as you glide over the park. There is limited parking for 2,000 pesos at the Pío Nono entrance and free parking at the Pedro de Valdivia entrance. ⊠ *Cerro San Cristóbal, Bellavista* ☎ *2/730–1300* ⊕ *www.parquemet.cl* ☜ *Round-trip funicular 1,400 pesos; round-trip cable car 1,600 pesos* ◷ *Park: daily 8:30 am–9 pm. Funicular: Mon. 1–8:30, Tues.–Fri. 10–8:30, weekends 10–9. Cable car: Mon. 12:30–8:00, Tues.–Fri. 10:30–8:00, weekends 10:30–8:30* Ⓜ *Baquedano, Pedro de Valdivia.*

35 **Jardín Botánico Mapulemu.** Gravel paths lead you to restful nooks in the Mapulemu Botanical Garden dedicated to native-Chilean species. Every path and stairway seems to bring you to better views of Santiago and the Andes. Sunday mornings there are tai chi, yoga, and aerobics free of charge. ⊠ *Cerro San Cristóbal, Bellavista* ☎ *2/730–1300* ☜ *Free* ◷ *Daily 10–6* Ⓜ *Pedro de Valdivia, Baquedano.*

36 **Jardín Japonés.** The tranquil Japanese Garden affords a sumptuous view over the skyscrapers of Las Condes and Bellavista. Paths edged with bamboo lead past lily ponds and a gazebo beside a trickling fountain. ⊠ *Cerro San Cristóbal, Bellavista* ☎ *2/730–1300* ☜ *Free* ◷ *Daily 10–6* Ⓜ *Pedro de Valdivia, Baquedano.*

33 **Jardín Zoológico.** The Zoological Garden is a good place to see examples of Chilean animals, some nearly extinct, that you might not otherwise encounter. As is often the case with many older zoos, the creatures aren't given a lot of room. ⊠ *Cerro San Cristóbal, Bellavista* ☎ *2/730–1334* ⊕ *www.zoologico.cl* ☜ *2,000 pesos* ◷ *Tues.–Sun. 10–6 (in winter, closes at 5)* Ⓜ *Baquedano.*

34 **Plaza Tupahue.** The middle stop on the teleférico deposits you in the center of Parque Metropolitano. The main attraction here in summer is the delightful **Piscina Tupahue,** an 82-meter (269-foot) pool with a rocky

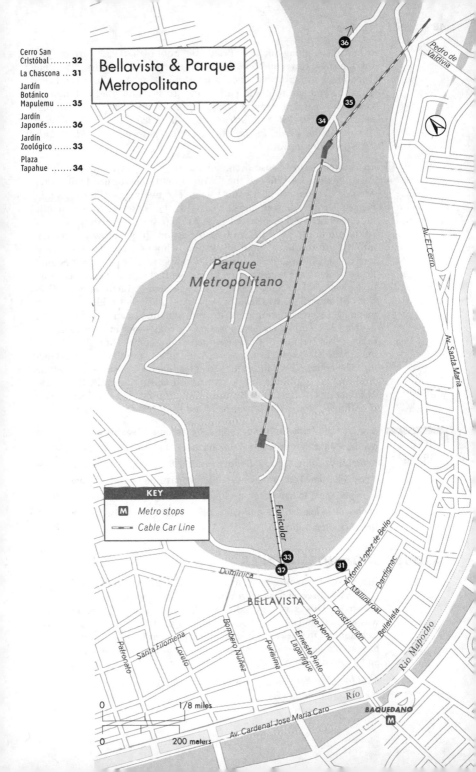

Bellavista & Parque Metropolitano

Parque
Metropolitano

KEY

Ⓜ *Metro stops*

▭▭▭ *Cable Car Line*

Funicular

Dominica

BELLAVISTA

Antonio López de Bello

Dardignac

Mallinkroat

Bellavista

Constitución

Pío Nono

Ernesto Pinto Lagarrigue

Purísima

Bombero Núñez

Loreto

Santa Filomena

Patronato

Río Mapocho

Av. Santa María

Av. El Cerro

Pedro de Valdivia

Río

0   1/8 miles

0   200 meters

Av. Cardenal José María Caro

BAQUEDANO
Ⓜ

crag running along one side. Beside the pool is the 1925 **Torreón Victoria,** a stone tower surrounded by a trellis of bougainvillea. If Piscina Tupahue is too crowded, try the nearby **Piscina Antilén.** From Plaza Tupahue you can follow a path below to **Plaza de Juegos Infantiles Gabriela Mistral,** a popular playground. ⊠ *Cerro San Cristóbal, Bellavista* ☏ *2/730–1300* ⊠ *Entry to park in vehicle 2,000 pesos, Piscina Tupahue 5,000 pesos, Piscina Antilén 6,000 pesos* ⊘ *Nov.–Mar., daily 10–6* Ⓜ *Pedro de Valdivia.*

㉛ ★ **La Chascona.** This house designed by the Nobel prize–winning poet Pablo Neruda was dubbed the "Woman with the Tousled Hair" after Matilde Urrutia, the poet's third wife. The two met while strolling in nearby Parque Forestal, and for years the house served as a romantic hideaway before they married. The pair's passionate relationship was recounted in the 1995 Italian film *Il Postino.* Tours allow you to step into the extraordinary mind of the poet whose eclectic designs earned him the label "organic architect." Winding garden paths, stairs, and bridges lead to the house and its library stuffed with books, a bedroom in a tower, and a secret passageway. Scattered throughout are collections of butterflies, seashells, wineglasses, and other odd objects that inspired Neruda's tumultuous life and romantic poetry. Neruda, who died in 1973, had two other houses on the coast—one in Valparaíso, the other in Isla Negra. All three are open as museums. Though it's not as magical as Isla Negra, La Chascona can still set your imagination dancing. The house is on a little side street leading off Constitución. On the weekends it's advisable to book your visit ahead of time. ⊠ *Fernando Márquez de la Plata 0192, Bellavista* ☏ *2/777–8741* ⊕ *www.neruda. cl* ⊠ *English tour: 3,500 pesos* ⊘ *Tues.–Sun. 10–6* Ⓜ *Baquedano.*

NEED A BREAK?

A short walk from La Chascona is Calle Antonia López de Bello, a street overflowing with bars and restaurants. Here, the café **Off the Record** (⊠ *Antonia López de Bello 0155, Bellavista* ☏ *2/ 823–2803* ⊘ *Weekdays 9 am– 3 am, Sat. 6 pm–3 am*) has a decidedly bohemian air. The wooden booths, for example, seem to have been designed with witty conversation and artistic bonhomie in mind. Black-and-white photographs recall visitors from Pablo Neruda to Uma Thurman.

PARQUE QUINTA NORMAL AREA

Just west of downtown is shady Parque Quinta Normal, a 75-acre park with three museums within its borders and another just across the street. This is an especially good place to take the kids. The park was created in 1841 as a place to experiment with new agricultural techniques. On weekdays it is great for quiet strolls; on weekends you'll have to maneuver around noisy families. Pack a picnic or a soccer ball and you'll fit right in.

Numbered bullets in the margins correspond to numbered bullets on the Parque Quinta Normal map.

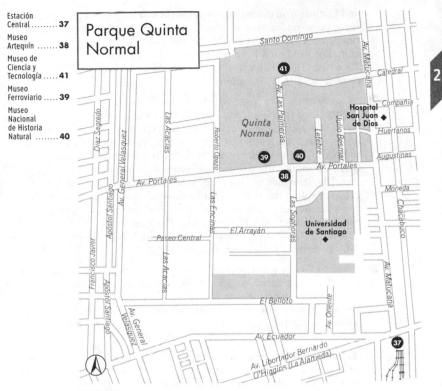

TIMING

You can visit the museums in and around the park, stroll along a wooded path, and even row a boat on a (rather dirty) lake, all within a few hours. The planetarium is open to the public only on weekends.

WHAT TO SEE

Museo Nacional de Historia Natural. The National Museum of Natural History is the centerpiece of Parque Quinta Normal. Paul Lathoud, a French architect, designed the building for Chile's first International Exposition, in 1875. After suffering damage from successive earthquakes, the neoclassical structure was rebuilt and enlarged. Though the exhibits are slightly outdated, the large dioramas of stuffed animals against painted backdrops are still intriguing and the skeleton of an enormous blue whale hangs in the central hall, delighting children of all ages. Exhibits are not labeled in English but guided tours in English are available by prior arrangement. ⊠*Parque Quinta Normal s/n* ☎*2/680–4615* ⊕*www.dibam.cl* ✉*Tues.–Sat. 600 pesos, Sun. free* ☉*Tues.–Sat. 10–5:30, Sun. 11–6* Ⓜ*Quinta Normal.*

Museo Ferroviario. Chile's once-mighty railroads have been relegated to history, but this acre of Parque Quinta Normal keeps a bit of the romance alive. More than a dozen steam locomotives and three passenger coaches are set within quiet gardens with placards in Spanish and English. You can board several of the trains. Among the collection is the cross-Andes express, which operated between Chile and Argentina from 1910 until 1971. ☒ *Av. Las Palmas, Parque Quinta Normal* ☏2/681–4627 ⊕*www.corpdicyt.cl* ☒*500 pesos* ☉*Apr.–Nov., Tues.–Fri. 10–6, weekends 11–6; Dec.–Mar., Tues.–Fri. 11–5, weekends noon–5* Ⓜ*Quinta Normal.*

㊳ **Museo Artequín.** The resplendent Pabellón París houses this interactive
Ⓒ museum that teaches the fundamentals of art to children, but the pavilion itself—with its glass domes, Pompeian-red walls, and blue-steel columns—is the real jewel. It was designed by French architect Henri Picq to house Chile's exhibition in the 1889 Paris International Exposition (where Gustave Eiffel's skyline-defining tower was unveiled). After the show the structure was shipped back to Santiago. Weekdays, school groups explore the two floors of reproductions of famous artworks and didactic areas. On weekends there are more guides available to explain the pavilion's history. ☒ *Av. Portales 3530, Parque Quinta Normal* ☏2/682–5367 ⊕*www.artequin.cl* ☒*800 pesos* ☉*Tues.–Fri. 9–6, weekends 11–6* Ⓜ*Quinta Normal.*

㊶ **Museo de Ciencia y Tecnología.** Children will spend a happy half hour
Ⓒ with this small science-and-technology museum's interactive exhibits while adults can peruse its collection of old phonographs, calculators, and computers. ☒*Parque Quinta Normal* ☏2/681–8808 ⊕*www. corpdicyt.cl* ☒*800 pesos* ☉*Tues.–Fri. 10–5:15, weekends 11–5:15* Ⓜ*Quinta Normal.*

Planetario. The Universidad de Santiago's planetarium dome mimics a universe of stars with a weekend show open to the general public. During the week it buzzes with schoolchildren only. ☒*La Alameda 3349, Estación Central* ☏2/718–2900 ⊕*www.planetariochile.cl* ☒*2,250 pesos* ☉*Weekend shows: usually at 11:30, 3:30, and 4:30 (although subject to some variation)* Ⓜ*Estación Central.*

**OFF THE
BEATEN
PATH**

Cementerio General. It may be an unusual tourist attraction, but this cemetery in the northern part of the city reveals a lot about traditional Chilean society. After passing through the lofty stone arches of the main entrance you'll find well-tended paths lined with marble mausoleums, squat mansions belonging to Chile's wealthy families. The 8- or 10-story "niches" farther along—concrete shelves housing thousands of coffins—resemble middle-class apartment buildings. Their inhabitants lie here until the rent runs out and they're evicted. Look for former President Salvador Allende's final resting spot. A map at the main entrance to the cemetery can help you find it. Two-hour guided tours in Spanish, costing 2,100 pesos, start at 9:30, 11:30, and 3:30 weekdays, and there's also a 9 pm tour on Wednesday, Friday, and Saturday. Reservation required for night tours. ☒ *Av. Prof. Alberto Zañartu 951, Recoleta* ☏2/737–9469 ⊕*www.cementeriogeneral.cl* ☉*Daily 8:30–6* Ⓜ*Cementerios.*

㊲ **Estación Central.** Inaugurated in 1897, Central Station is the city's last remaining train station, serving the south as far as Chillán. The greenish iron canopy that once shielded the engines from the weather is flanked by two lovely beaux arts edifices. A lively market keeps this terminal buzzing with activity. ✉ *La Alameda 3170, Estación Central* ☎ *2/376–8500* 🎫 *Free* 🕐 *Daily 6 am–midnight* Ⓜ *Estación Central.*

OFF THE BEATEN PATH

Barrio Concha y Toro. Don't be put off by the shops selling car spares at the entrance to this intimate little neighborhood on the north side of La Alameda between avenues Brasil and Ricardo Cumming. Developed in the 1920s on land belonging to a mining branch of the Concha y Toro family—another branch founded the vineyard of the same name—its short winding streets spanning out from a central plaza have an eclectic mixture of neoclassical, art deco, and baroque houses, many of them designed by the same architects who worked on the Barrio París-Londres. ✉ *Concha y Torós, La Alameda* Ⓜ *República.*

2

VITACURA

TIMING
Vitacura is not only Santiago's top shopping spot; it is also—with its tree-shaded streets, gardens, and wide sidewalks—a great place for a stroll, especially on a Saturday morning when you'll see residents out jogging, walking their dogs, or simply picking up a newspaper and some fragrant fresh bread. Allow an hour to see the Museo de la Moda.

WHAT TO SEE
☺ **Museo de la Moda.** This Fashion Museum, opened in 2007 by a son
★ of Jorge Yarur Banna, one of Chile's most successful textile barons, hosts small but choice exhibitions around different themes using a collection of clothes—mostly women's dresses—that dates back to the 1600s. Housed in the Yarur family's former home, which was designed by Chilean architects in the style of Frank Lloyd Wright in the early 1960s and decorated by a brother of Roberto Matta, one of Chile's most famous painters, the museum also offers a fascinating insight into the lifestyle of the Chilean oligarchy in the run-up to the upheaval of Salvador Allende's socialist government and the ensuing military coup. The main rooms are on show with their original furnishings, and the pink 1958 Ford Thunderbird driven by Mr. Yarur's wife is parked in a courtyard. The museum café serves excellent light meals and snacks at very reasonable prices and, on weekends, has a special brunch menu. ✉ *Av. Vitacura 4562 Vitacura* ☎ *2/218–7271* ⊕ *www.mmyt.cl* 🎫 *3,000 pesos* 🕐 *Tues.–Sun. 10–7* Ⓜ *No metro.*

WHERE TO EAT

Santiago can be overwhelming when it comes to dining, as hundreds of restaurants are strewn about the city. No matter what strikes your fancy, there are likely to be half a dozen eateries within easy walking distance. Tempted to taste hearty Chilean fare? Pull up a stool at one of the counters at Vega Central and enjoy a traditional pastel de choclo. Craving seafood? Head to the Mercado Central, where you can choose from the fresh fish brought in that morning. Want a memorable meal? Trendy new restaurants are opening every day in neighborhoods like Bellavista, where hip Santiaguinos come to check out the latest hot spots.

In the neighborhood of Vitacura, a 20- to 30-minute taxi ride from the city center, a complex of restaurants called Borde Río attracts an upscale crowd. El Golf, an area including Avenida El Bosque Norte and Avenida Isidora Goyenechea in Las Condes, has numerous restaurants and cafés. The emphasis is on creative cuisine, so you'll often be treated to familiar favorites with a Chilean twist. This is one of the few neighborhoods where you can stroll from restaurant to restaurant until you find exactly what you want.

Remember that Santiaguinos dine a little later than the rest of us. Most fancier restaurants don't open for lunch until 1. (You may startle the cleaning staff if you rattle the doors at noon.) Dinner begins at 7:30 or 8, although most places don't get crowded until after 9. Many eateries close for a few hours before dinner. Many restaurants are closed on Sunday night.

BELLAVISTA

$$$
SEAFOOD
Fodor'sChoice
★
✕ **Azul Profundo.** When it opened, this was the only restaurant you'd find on this street near Parque Metropolitano. Today it's one of dozens of restaurants in trendy Bellavista, but its two-level dining room—with walls painted bright shades of blue and yellow, and racks of wine stretching to the ceiling—ensure that it stands out in the crowd. Choose your fish from the extensive menu—swordfish, sea bass, shark, flounder, salmon, trout, and haddock are among the choices—and enjoy it *a la plancha* (grilled) or *a la lata* (served on a sizzling plate with tomatoes and onions). ⊠ *Constitución 111, Bellavista* ☏ *2/738–0288* ✎ *Reservations essential* ☐ *AE, DC, MC, V* Ⓜ *Baquedano.*

$$
SPANISH
✕ **La Bodeguilla.** This authentic Spanish restaurant is a great place to stop for a glass of sangria after tackling Cerro San Cristóbal. After all, it's right at the foot of the funicular. The dozen or so tables are set among wine barrels and between hanging strings of garlic bulbs. Nibble on tasty tapas like *chorizo riojano* (a piquant sausage), *pulpo a la gallega* (octopus with peppers and potatoes), and *queso manchego* (a mild white cheese) while perusing the long wine list. Then consider ordering the house specialty—*cabrito al horno* (oven-roasted goat). ⊠ *Av. Dominica 5, Bellavista* ☏ *2/732–5215* ☐ *AE, DC, MC, V* ⊗ *Closed Sun.* Ⓜ *Baquedano.*

$$$
CHILEAN
Fodor'sChoice
★
✕ **Como Agua Para Chocolate.** Inspired by Laura Esquivel's romantic 1989 novel *Like Water for Chocolate,* this Bellavista standout is part restaurant, part theme park. It focuses on the aphrodisiacal qualities of food, so it shouldn't be surprising that one long table is actually an iron bed, with place settings arranged on a crisp white sheet. The food compares to the decor like the film version compares to the book: it's good, but not nearly as imaginative. *Ave de la pasión,* for instance, means Bird of Passion. It may be just chicken with mushrooms, but it's

served on a copper plate. ⊠*Constitución 88, Bellavista* ☏*2/777–8740* ☐*AE, DC, MC, V* Ⓜ*Baquedano.*

$ ✗**Galindo.** Join artists and the young crowd of Bellavista for traditional
CHILEAN Chilean food in an old adobe house. This restaurant goes back 60 years when it started life as a canteen for local workmen and, although it gets crowded, it's a great place to try *pastel de choclo* or a hearty *cazuela*, a typical meat and vegetable soup that is a meal in itself. It also has the advantage of being open on Sunday. ⊠*Dardignac 098, Bellavista* ☏*2/777–0116* ☐*AE, DC, MC, V* Ⓜ*Baquedano.*

$$ ✗**Muñeca Brava.** Decorated with movie memorabilia, this restaurant
CHILEAN also names some of its dishes in the same style. Calling a starter of mushrooms stuffed with smoked salmon and cheese *Sexo con Amor*, or Sex with Love, also the name of a popular Chilean movie, may be stretching it but the food, especially the meat, is good. Or simply enjoy the relaxed atmosphere with a drink at the large bar which dominates the restaurant. ⊠*Mallinkrodt 170, Bellavista* ☏*2/732–1388* ☐*AE, DC, MC, V* ☉*Sunday* Ⓜ*Baquedano.*

$$–$$$ ✗**Patio Bellavista.** While not a restaurant *per se*, this lively complex of
ECLECTIC bars and eateries, with its art galleries and crafts shops, stretches from Pío Nono to Constitución between Calle Bellavista and Dardignac. Open daily from 10 am to the early hours of the morning, it offers alternatives that range from an Irish pub to a sushi bar and from Peruvian to Arab food. ⊠*Pío Nono 73, Bellavista* ☏*2/777–4582* ⊕*www. patiobellavista.cl* Ⓜ*Baquedano.*

CENTRO

$$ ✗**Les Assassins.** Although this appears at first glance to be a rather
FRENCH somber bistro, nothing could be further from the truth. The service is friendly, and the Provence-influenced food is first-rate. The steak au poivre and beef bourguignonne would make a Frenchman's mouth water. If you want to practice your Spanish, you're in luck: there's always a line of talkative locals in the cozy ground-floor bar, but English—and, of course, French—is also spoken. ⊠*Merced 297, Parque Forestal* ☏*2/638–4280* ☐*AE, DC, MC, V* ☉*Closed Sun. No lunch Sat.* Ⓜ*Universidad Católica.*

$$ ✗**Atelier del Parque.** Alluding to its artistic leanings, this restaurant's
CHILEAN menus come on palettes with their own paintbrushes. On offer are creations named for artists, such as the Da Vinci (inky black fettuccine tossed with squid, scallops, and prawns). Although it gets crowded, you can usually find an isolated table in the many little dining rooms, including one reached by a wrought-iron spiral staircase. A connected gallery showcases temporary exhibits of art and sculpture. ⊠*Santo Domingo 528, Parque Forestal* ☏*2/639–5843* ☐*AE, DC, MC, V* ☉*Closed Sun. No lunch Sat.* Ⓜ*Bellas Artes.*

$$ ✗**Blue Jar.** This restaurant, although only a block from the Palacio de
CHILEAN la Moneda, is an oasis of quiet on a small pedestrian street, and its
Fodor'sChoice food—simple but creative dishes using the best and freshest Chilean
★ ingredients—appeals to locals and visitors alike, whether it's a sandwich, a salad and a bowl of soup, a full lunch, or a hearty breakfast.

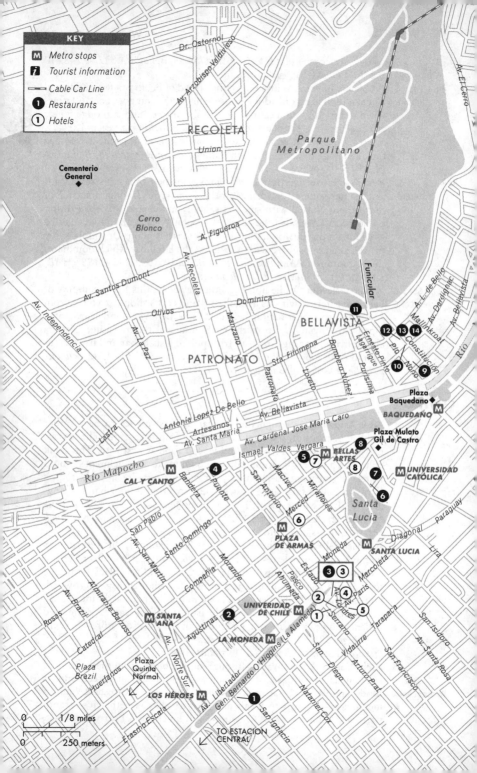

KEY

Ⓜ *Metro stops*

ⓘ *Tourist information*

▭▭▭ *Cable Car Line*

❶ *Restaurants*

① *Hotels*

Dr. Ostornol

Av. Arzobispo Valdivieso

RECOLETA

Union

Cementerio General ◆

Cerro Blanco

A. Figueroa

Parque Metropolitano

Funicular

Av. El Cerro

Av. Recoleta

Av. Santos Dumont

Dominica

Olivos

Manzana

Av. La Paz

PATRONATO

Sta. Filomena

BELLAVISTA

Ernesto Pinto Lagarrigue

Purisima

Pio Nono

A. L. de Bello

Av. Dardignac

Av. Bellavista

Río

❶❶

❶❷ ❶❸ ❶❹

❶⓪

⑨

Bombero Núñez

Loreto

Patronato

Av. Independencia

Av. 1a. Paz

Lastra

Antonia Lopez De Bello

Artesanos

Av. Santa María

Av. Bellavista

Av. Cardenal Jose Maria Caro

Plaza Baquedano ◆

BAQUEDANO Ⓜ

Río Mapocho

CAL Y CANTO Ⓜ

Bandera

Puente

❹

Ismael Valdes Vergara

❺ ❼

Maciver

Merced

BELLAS ARTES

Plaza Mulato Gil de Castro ◆

❽

❽ ❼

Ⓜ UNIVERSIDAD CATÓLICA

San Pablo

Santo Domingo

Av. San Martín

Morande

Compañía

San Antonio

Miraflores

❻

Ⓜ PLAZA DE ARMAS

Santa Lucia

❻

SANTA LUCIA Ⓜ

Diagonal

Paraguay

Lira

Almirante Barroso

Av. Brazil

Rosas

Catedral

Plaza Brazil

Huerfanos

Plaza Quinta Normal

Plaza Norte Sur

Ⓜ SANTA ANA

Agustinas

❷

UNIVERIDAD DE CHILE

Ⓜ

Ahumada

Paseo

Estado

Moneda

❸ ❸

② ④ Av. Paris

Av. Londres

① ❺

San Diego

Serrano

Marcoleta

Nataniel Cox

Vidaurre

Arturo Prat

Tarapaca

San Francisco

San Isidro

San Santa Rosa

LA MONEDA Ⓜ

LOS HÉROES Ⓜ

Av. Gen. Bernardo O'Higgins (La Alameda)

San Ignacio

❶

Erasmo Escala

0 1/8 miles

0 250 meters

↙ TO ESTACIÓN CENTRAL

Restaurants ▼

Hotels ▼

2

Where to Stay & Eat
in Santiago Centro
& Bellavista

The menu changes monthly but not its hallmark hamburgers made from three different cuts of beef—one for flavor, one for texture, the other for color—with a little bacon fat added to keep them moist, and its wine list offers some of Chile's most interesting labels at very reasonable prices. Reservations are advisable for lunch, particularly for an outside table. It closes at 8:30, so arrive early for evening drinks, sandwiches, and snacks. ⊠*Almirante L. Gotuzzo 102, at Moneda, Santiago Centro* ☎*2/696–1890* ⊟*AE, DC, MC, V* ⊘*Closed weekends* Ⓜ*Moneda.*

$$$
CHILEAN

✕**Bristol.** Guillermo Rodríguez, who supervised the kitchen here for 16 years and won just about all the country's culinary competitions, left recently. Now under his right-hand man Axel Manríquez, the restaurant retains his style with dishes like marinated scallops over octopus carpaccio and cold tomato and pepper sauce. The only disappointment is the restaurant's lack of windows with a view. ⊠*Hotel Plaza San Francisco, La Alameda 816, Santiago Centro* ☎*2/639–3832* ⊟*AE, DC, MC, V* Ⓜ*Universidad de Chile.*

$$
CHILEAN
★

✕**Confitería Torres.** José Domingo Torres, a chef greatly in demand amongst the Chilean aristocracy of his day, decided in 1879 to set up shop in this storefront on the Alameda. It remains one of the city's most traditional dining rooms, with red-leather banquettes, mint-green tile floors, and huge chandeliers with tulip-shaped globes. The food, such as *lomo al ajo arriego* (sirloin sautéed with peppers and garlic), now comes from recipes by the mother of owner Claudio Soto Barría. This restaurant also has a branch for snacks and light meals in the Centro Cultural Palacio La Moneda. ⊠*Alameda 1570, Santiago Centro* ☎*2/688–0751* ⊟*AE, DC, MC, V* ⊘*Closed Sun.* Ⓜ*Universidad de Chile.*

$
SEAFOOD
Fodor'sChoice
★

✕**Donde Augusto.** What was once a simple seafood stand has taken over almost all the interior of Mercado Central. If you don't mind the unhurried service and the odd tear in the tablecloth, you may have the time of your life dining on everything from sea urchins to baby eel. Placido Domingo eats here on every visit to Chile, attended to by the white-bearded Segovian Augusto Vásquez, who has run Donde Augusto for more than four decades. Go for simple dishes like the *corvina a la plancha* (grilled sea bass), which is mouthwateringly good. Get here early, as it closes at 5 pm Sunday–Thursday and 6 on Saturday; it's open until 8 on Friday. ⊠*Mercado Central, Santiago Centro* ☎*2/672–2829* ⊟*AE, DC, MC, V* ⊘*No dinner* Ⓜ*Puente Cal y Canto.*

$$
FRENCH

✕**Gatopardo.** It's a bit of a stretch to call this a French restaurant, but you can order delicious fare like the perfectly grilled entrecôte. Some of the dishes, especially the fish, also have a strong Peruvian influence. The glass-roofed dining room is especially inviting on sunny afternoons. The bright-orange building sits among a cluster of eateries south of Plaza Mulato Gil de Castro. ⊠*José Victorino Lastarria 192, Parque Forestal* ☎*2/633–6420* ⊟*AE, DC, MC, V* ⊘*Closed Sun. No lunch Sat.* Ⓜ*Universidad Católica.*

$$
LATIN-
AMERICAN

✕**Victorino.** Cozy in winter and refreshingly cool in summer, this little restaurant offers an attractive mixture of Chilean and Peruvian dishes. Try the Patagonian lamb cooked in Carménère wine with garlic paste.

Many dishes also incorporate indigenous ingredients such as quinoa and *merquén,* a traditional seasoning used by Chile's Mapuche people. In summer, sit on the little patio with a fountain that looks out onto the street. ⊠ *José Victorino Lastarria 128, Parque Forestal* ☎*2/639–5263* ▤*AE, DC, MC, V* Ⓜ *Universidad Católica.*

LAS CONDES

$$$ ✕**Akarana.** Although this restaurant doesn't serve just fish, seafood
SEAFOOD   does feature prominently on a refreshingly creative menu of what New Zealand owner Dell Taylor—also of Café Melba—describes as "Pacific Rim cuisine." Fresh tuna from Easter Island is the restaurant's most popular dish and there are also plenty of Asian flavors, any of which can be neatly rounded out with a wicked Chocolate Temptation dessert. Reservations are a good idea. ⊠ *Reyes Lavalle 3310, Las Condes* ☎*2/231–9667* ▤*AE, DC, MC, V* Ⓜ *El Golf.*

$$$$ ✕**Anakena.** Designed to resemble an outdoor market, this elegant eat-
THAI   ery emphasizes fresh ingredients. You can order Thai favorites like pad thai (rice noodles, peanuts, egg, sprouts, and shrimp), but the best items on the menu are those that combine the cooking style of Asia with those of Europe and South America. To start, there's a wide selection of spring rolls with interesting combinations of seafood and vegetables. If it's on the menu, don't pass up the grilled swordfish in a basil beurre blanc. There's a separate entrance for the restaurant, so you don't have to enter through the lobby of the Grand Hyatt. ⊠ *Grand Hyatt Santiago, Av. Kennedy 4601, Las Condes* ☎*2/950–3179* ▤*AE, DC, MC, V* Ⓜ *No metro.*

$$$ ✕**Bice.** This restaurant's small, two-tiered dining room has soaring ceil-
ITALIAN   ings that lend it a dramatic flair, while gleaming floors of alternating stripes of dark and light wood add a touch of contemporary glamour. The service is a breed apart—white-jacketed waiters zip around, attending to your every need. The menu leans toward imaginatively prepared pastas, such as linguine with scallops, razor clams, shrimp, and mussels. Be sure to leave room for desserts such as the *cioccolatíssimo,* a hot, chocolate soufflé with melted chocolate inside, served with an exquisite *dulce de leche* ice cream. ⊠ *Hotel Inter-Continental, Av. Luz 2920, Las Condes* ☎*2/381–5500* ⌂ *Reservations essential* ▤*AE, DC, MC, V* Ⓜ *Tobalaba.*

$$ ✕**Boulevard Parque Arauco.** In Santiago's largest shopping mall, this
ECLECTIC   open-air food court has 33 cafés and restaurants and, with the advantage of being open on Sundays, is a great alternative for a drink or meal after a movie at the Showcase Parque Arauco cinema multiplex. It is also conveniently close to the Hyatt, Marriott, and Kennedy hotels. Children like the ice creams at Munchi's or Emporio La Rosa and the pizzas at Santa Pizza, but there are more sophisticated alternatives such as El Otro Sitio, a Peruvian restaurant that serves large and powerful pisco sours, and the popular Vendetta restaurant. Skip the disappointing Asian Bistro though. ⊠ *Av. Kennedy 5413, Las Condes* ☎*2/299–0500* ⊕ *www.parquearauco.cl* Ⓜ *No metro.*

$ ✕**Café Melba.** Almost unheard of in Santiago, this storefront restau-
CAFÉS   rant serves breakfast all day. If you're particularly hungry, order "The
Works"—baked beans, mushrooms, sausage, and bacon. Drink it
down with a caffe latte, served in a large white bowl. The interior is
open and airy, with wooden tables scattered about the wood-floored
dining room. In warm weather, grab a seat on the covered patio in
front. Get here early, as it closes around 7:30 pm on weekdays and 4 on
weekends. ⊠*Don Carlos 2898, off Av. El Bosque Norte, Las Condes*
☎*2/232–4546* ▤*AE, DC, MC, V* ⊘*No dinner* Ⓜ*Tobalaba.*

$$$$ ✕ **Coco Loco.** What's "loco" here is the price people plunk down for the
SEAFOOD   king crab. They come from the far south of Chile and one is enough for
two people, but does that justify a price tag of over $100? The other
items on the menu, such as the *risotto marinero* with a variety of shellfish, are better value. The dining room, with impressionistic murals of
waves (they might remind you of Vincent van Gogh's *Starry Night*), is
full of whimsy. ⊠*Av. El Bosque Norte 0215, Las Condes* ☎*2/233–
8930* ⌁*Reservations essential* ▤*AE, DC, MC, V* Ⓜ*Tobalaba.*

$$$ ✕ **Le Due Torri.** For excellent homemade pastas, head to this longtime
ITALIAN   favorite. If you think the *agnolotti,* stuffed with ricotta cheese and spin-
ach, resembles a feathered hat, you're right. The affable owner, who
was in Italy during World War II, intentionally shaped it like a nurse's
cap. The rear of the dining room, with its small cypress trees and a cor-
ner pergola, is traditional; seating in the front is more contemporary.
The name of the restaurant, by the way, refers to the two towers erected
by the dueling Garisenda and Asinelli families in the owner's native
Bologna. ⊠*Av. Isidora Goyenechea 2908, Las Condes* ☎*2/231–3427*
⌁*Reservations essential* ▤*AE, DC, MC, V* Ⓜ*Tobalaba.*

$$ ✕ **Gernika.** The Basque owners of this wood-and-stone restaurant have
SPANISH   created a little slice of their homeland with graceful stone arches, tap-
estries bearing ancient coats of arms, and even jai alai equipment. Head
upstairs to the more intimate upper level, which has three well-deco-
rated private dining salons. Chilean seafood is cooked with Spanish
flair, as in the *congrio donostiarra* (conger eel coated in chili sauce and
fried in olive oil). Delicious *centolla* (king crab) is brought in from the
chilly waters of Tierra del Fuego. Several hearty selections from Spain's
Rioja region appear on the wine list. ⊠*Av. El Bosque Norte 0227, Las
Condes* ☎*2/232–9954* ⌁*Reservations essential* ▤*AE, DC, MC, V*
⊘*No lunch Sat.* Ⓜ*Tobalaba.*

$$$ ✕ **Matsuri.** With a sleek design that calls to mind Los Angeles as much
JAPANESE   as Tokyo, this restaurant in the Grand Hyatt is one of Santiago's most
stylish eateries. After passing through a foyer painted vivid red, you
enter the calm dining area with a view of a waterfall. Downstairs are a
sushi bar and two tatami rooms (no shoes allowed, but slippers are pro-
vided) with sliding screens for privacy, and upstairs are two grill tables.
⊠*Grand Hyatt Santiago, Av. Kennedy 4601, Las Condes* ☎*2/950–
3051* ▤*AE, DC, MC, V* Ⓜ*No metro.*

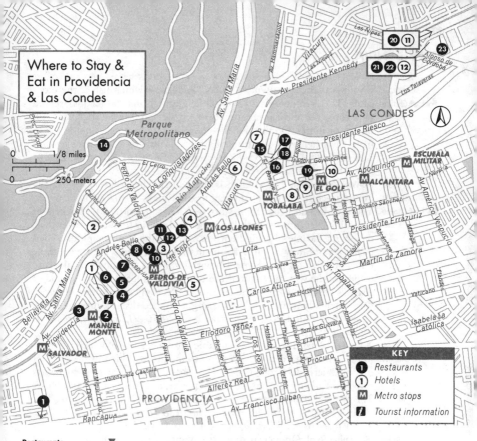

Where to Stay & Eat in Providencia & Las Condes

0   1/8 miles
0   250 meters

Restaurants ▼

Akarana	....	19
Anakena	....	21
Aquí Está Coco	....	7
Astrid y Gaston	....	6
Bice	....	20
Boulevard Parque Arauco	....	23
Café del Patio	....	5
Café Melba	....	16
Camino Real	....	14
Coco Loco	....	18
De Cangrejo a Conejo	......	1

Eladio	....	13
El Cid	....	4
El Huerto	....	12
El Parrón	....	3
Gernika	....	17
Le Due Torri	....	15
Le Flaubert	....	11
Liguria	....	2, 9
Lomit's	....	10
Mare Nostrum	....	8
Matsuri	....	22

Hotels ▼

Chilhotel	....	1
Director El Golf	....	9
Four Points By Sheraton	....	4
Grand Hyatt Santiago	.....	12
Hotel Orly	....	3
Neruda Express	....	8
Radisson Plaza Santiago	....	6
Ritz-Carlton	....	10

Santiago Marriott Hotel	....	11
Santiago InterContinental	....	7
Santiago Park Plaza	....	5
Sheraton Santiago and San Cristóbal Tower	....	2

PROVIDENCIA

$$
SEAFOOD
Fodor'sChoice
★

✗**Aquí Está Coco.** The best seafood in Santiago is served here; ask your waiter—or friendly owner "Coco" Pacheco—which fish is the day's catch. This is a good place to try Chile's famous *machas* (clams), served with tomatoes and Parmesan cheese, or *corvina* (sea bass) grilled with plenty of butter. Don't miss the cellar, where you can sample wines from the extensive collection of Chilean vintages. ⊠*La Concepción 236, Providencia* ☎*2/235–8649* ⚖*Reservations essential* ⊟*AE, DC, MC, V* ⊘*Closed Sun.* Ⓜ*Pedro de Valdivia.*

$$$$
CHILEAN
Fodor'sChoice
★

✗**Astrid y Gaston.** The kitchen is the real star here—every seat in the pumpkin-color dining room has a great view of the chefs at work. You couldn't do better than start with the agnolotti, little pockets of squid-ink pasta stuffed with king crab and cherry tomatoes. After that, try one of the one-of-a-kind entrées, such as the lamb shank drenched in *pisco* (a brandy distilled from small grapes) and served with three kinds of yucca, or the parrot fish with tamarind and ginger. Make sure to peruse the wine list, one of the best in town. Save room for one of Astrid's desserts, such as the creamy confection called *suspiro limeña,* "sigh of a lady from Lima": a meringue-topped dish of dulce de leche. ⊠*Antonio Bellet 201, Providencia* ☎*2/650–9125* ⚖*Reservations essential* ⊟*AE, DC, MC, V* Ⓜ*Pedro de Valdivia.*

$
VEGETARIAN

✗**Café del Patio.** The chef uses organic produce, some of which is grown in the owner's garden, at this vegetarian eatery hidden in the back of quaint Galería del Patio. The chef's salad—with lettuce, tomato, hearts of palm, and Gruyère cheese—is exquisite, as is the vegetarian ravioli. The menu also includes pizzas. At night, Café del Patio turns into a bar. ⊠*Av. Providencia 1670, Providencia* ☎*2/236–1251* ⊟*AE, DC, MC, V* ⊘*Closed Sun. No lunch Sat.* Ⓜ*Pedro de Valdivia.*

$$$$
CHILEAN

✗**Camino Real.** On a clear day, treat yourself to the stunning views of the city through the floor-to-ceiling windows at this restaurant atop Cerro San Cristóbal. The menu lists such dishes as pork tenderloin in mustard sauce with caramelized onions, and warm scallop salad with quail eggs and asparagus. Oenophiles appreciate the many Chilean vintages in the wine cellar. Neophytes can head across a central courtyard to Bar Dalí, where the servers can organize an impromptu *degustación* of a half dozen varietals. ⊠*Parque Metropolitano, Bellavista* ☎*2/232–3381* ⚖*Reservations essential* ⊟*AE, DC, MC, V* Ⓜ*Pedro de Valdivia, Baquedano.*

$$$

✗**De Cangrejo a Conejo.** Heavy wooden double doors bring you into the large, high-ceilinged interior of this hip eatery. Tables and chairs of pale wood and steel have been thoughtfully arranged around a long curving bar, and flourishing greenery extends out into the patio garden. The menu reflects its name, serving everything from *cangrejo* (crab) to *conejo* (rabbit). ⊠*Av. Italia 805, Providencia* ☎*2/634–4041* ⊟*AE, DC, MC, V* ⊘*No lunch Sat. Closed Sun.* Ⓜ*Bustamante.*

$$$$
CHILEAN
Fodor'sChoice
★

✗**El Cid.** Considered by critics to be one of the city's top restaurants, El Cid is the culinary centerpiece of the classic Sheraton Santiago. The dining room, which overlooks the pool, has crisp linens and simple place settings. All the excitement here is provided by the food, which is served with a flourish. Don't miss the famous grilled seafood—king

2

crab, prawns, squid, and scallops with a sweet, spicy sauce. If you're
new to Chilean cuisine, you can't go wrong with the excellent lunch
buffet, which includes unlimited wine. ⊠ *Av. Santa María 1742, Providencia* ☎ *2/233–5000* ⊟ *AE, DC, MC, V* Ⓜ *Pedro de Valdivia.*

$ ✕**Eladio.** You can eat a succulent *bife de chorizo* (sirloin) or mouthwa-
CHILEAN tering *costillas de cerdo* (pork ribs) or just about any other meat cooked
as you like and enjoy it with a good bottle of Chilean wine—and your
pockets wouldn't be much lighter. Finish with a slice of *amapola*
(poppy-seed) sponge cake. This restaurant also has a branch in Bellavista at Pío Nono 251. ⊠ *Providencia 2250, Providencia* ☎ *2/231–4224*
⊟ *AE, DC, MC, V* ☉ *Closed Sun.* Ⓜ *Los Leones.*

$$$ ✕**Le Flaubert.** With table lamps casting a warm glow, racks full of
FRENCH magazines, and walls covered with black-and-white photographs, this
little eatery could be in any small town in France. The menu of the
day, written on a blackboard, might tempt you with such dishes as a
traditional coq au vin—cooked to perfection. Homesick Brits come
here to reminisce over freshly baked scones and refreshing cups of
tea. There's a large, shady patio garden where the staff doesn't mind
if you linger over a cup of coffee. ⊠ *Orrego Luco 0125, Providen-
cia* ☎ *2/231–9424* ⊟ *AE, DC, MC, V* ☉ No *dinner Sun. and Mon.*
Ⓜ *Pedro de Valdivia.*

$ ✕**El Huerto.** Long Santiago's star vegetarian restaurant, this wood-pan-
VEGETARIAN eled eatery in the heart of Providencia has lost some of its creativity and
flair but its hearty soups and freshly squeezed juices still make it worth
a visit. La Huerta, a sister café next door, has faster service and slightly
more economical prices. ⊠ *Orrego Luco 054, Providencia* ☎ *2/233–
2690* ⊟ *AE, DC, MC, V* ☉ No *lunch Sun.* Ⓜ *Pedro de Valdivia.*

$$ ✕**Liguria.** This extremely popular picada is always packed, so you might
CHILEAN have to wait to be seated in the chandelier-lighted dining room or at
one of the tables that spill out onto the sidewalk. A large selection of
Chilean wine accompanies such favorites as *cazuela* (a stew of beef or
chicken and potatoes) and sandwiches of *mechada* (tender and thinly-
sliced beef). There are three branches in the neighborhood, but each has
its own personality. ⊠ *Av. Providencia 1373, Providencia* ☎ *2/235–
7914* ⊟ *AE, DC, MC, V* ☉ *Closed Sun.* Ⓜ *Manuel Montt* ⊠ *Pedro de
Valdivia 047, Providencia* ☎ *2/334–4346* ⊟ *AE, DC, MC, V* ☉ *Closed
Sun.* Ⓜ *Pedro de Valdivia* ⊠ *Luis Thayer Ojeda 019, Providencia*
☎ *2/231–1393* ⊟ *AE, DC, MC, V* ☉ *Closed Sun.* Ⓜ *Tobalaba.*

$ ✕**Lomit's.** There's nothing particularly smart about Lomit's, a tradi-
CHILEAN tional and rather old-fashioned Chilean restaurant, but it unfailingly
serves up some of the city's best *barros lucos,* steak sandwiches overflowing with melted cheese. You can eat at the long wooden bar and
watch the sandwich maker at work, or find a small table to the side
(prices are a bit lower at the *mesón* than at the *mesas*). ⊠ *Av. Providencia 1980, Providencia* ☎ *2/233–1897* ⊟ *AE, DC, MC, V* Ⓜ *Pedro
de Valdivia.*

$$$ ✕**Mare Nostrum.** Mare Nostrum doesn't look like a seafood restaurant.
SEAFOOD In fact, the only clue that it specializes in fish is the subtle ship's-wheel
pattern in the deep-blue carpeting. All the focus here is on the food,

which leans toward Peruvian specialties like ceviche (raw fish marinated in lemon juice) and *tiradito* (similar but without onion). A standout is the *ambrosia de pulpo*, a spicy grilled octopus. The friendly staff is happy to help you negotiate the menu or pick just the right wine. ✉ *La Concepción 281, Providencia* ☎ *2/251–5691* ⚑ *Reservations essential* ☰ *AE, DC, MC, V* ⊘ *No dinner Sun.* Ⓜ *Pedro de Valdivia.*

$$ ✕ **El Parrón.** One of the city's oldest restaurants, dating from 1936, it
CHILEAN   specializes in grilled meats. You can watch the action in the kitchen through enormous windows. The dining areas are large and slightly impersonal, but the extensive wine list and menu make up for them. The congenial, wood-paneled bar is the perfect place to sample the refreshing national aperitif—the pisco sour. For dessert try a popular Chilean street-trolley offering, *mote con huesillos* (peeled wheat kernels and dried peaches). ✉ *Av. Providencia 1184, Providencia* ☎ *2/251–8911* ☰ *AE, DC, MC, V* ⊘ *No dinner Sun.* Ⓜ *Manuel Montt.*

VITACURA

$$$ ✕ **Agua.** Talk about minimalist—this gleaming glass box of a dining
CHILEAN   room is almost devoid of ornamentation. But that's because the food here gets all the attention. This is the upmarket member of a group of restaurants that also includes Mestizo (see below), Vendetta in the Boulevard del Parque Arauco, and Miguel Torres Vinos & Tapas on Vitacura's Avenida Isidora Goyenechea. At Agua, start with scallops and roasted peppers with lettuce and a mango vinaigrette, then move on to lamb chops marinated in coffee and finish with a crepe of cherries cooked in ginger and lemon verbena. If you get here before your reservations, stroll around the tony shops on the nearby streets. ✉ *Av. Nueva Costanera 3467, Vitacura* ☎ *2/374–1540* ⚑ *Reservations essential* ☰ *AE, DC, MC, V* Ⓜ *No metro.*

$$$$ ✕ **Europeo.** You're in for a fine meal at this trendy yet relaxed eatery
SEAFOOD   on Santiago's most prestigious shopping avenue. The menu changes
Fodor'sChoice   regularly but leans toward fish—try the succulent *mero*—but this is
★   also one of the few places in town that serves wild game, such as venison ragout. ✉ *Av. Alonso de Córdova 2417, Vitacura* ☎ *2/208–3603* ⚑ *Reservations essential* ☰ *AE, DC, MC, V* Ⓜ *No metro.*

$$ ✕ **Le Fournil.** Rumor has it that the French owners import even their
FRENCH   flour from France at this authentic boulangerie. The *plato del dia* (dish of the day) is always a tasty concoction, but equally good bets are the mixed green salad with grilled goat's cheese and the succulent carpaccio of salmon. But the tarte tatin steals the show—large, thick chunks of perfectly baked apple atop a thin layer of pastry, served with a scoop of creamy vanilla ice cream. The shady terrace is lovely, but the upstairs dining room is the place for a romantic meal. If you like the baguettes, a little shop lets you take them home. ✉ *Av. Vitacura 3841, Vitacura* ☎ *2/228–0219* ☰ *AE, DC, MC, V* Ⓜ *No metro.*

$$$ ✕ **Ibis de Puerto Varas.** Nattily nautical sails stretch taut across the ceiling,
SEAFOOD   pierced here and there by mastlike wood columns, and the walls are a splashy blue at this seafood restaurant. Choose from appetizers such as squid in bell pepper vinaigrette with baby onions or smoked salmon on a bed of watercress. *Panqueque Ibis* is a pancake stuffed with shrimp,

2

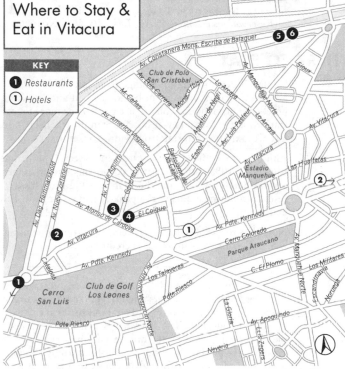

Where to Stay &
Eat in Vitacura

calamari, and scallops; the whole thing is sautéed in butter, flambéed in cognac, and served with a spinach-and-cream sauce. ⊠*Borde Río, Av. Monseñor Escrivá de Balaguer 6400, Vitacura* ☎*2/218–0111* ⚘*Reservations essential* ☰*AE, DC, MC, V* Ⓜ*No metro.*

$$ ✕**Mestizo.** This restaurant, with its view over the Parque Bicentenario,
LATIN- is a bit out of the way but is well worth the trip for a leisurely lunch or,
AMERICAN on a summer evening, to sip a perfect and generous-sized pisco sour as
Fodor's Choice the sun sets betweens the hills. The restaurant's design, with a roof sup-
★ ported on large boulders, makes the best of its setting and the eclectic menu brings together some of the best of Chilean and Peruvian cuisine. With an emphasis on fish, it also offers some great meat dishes such as *plateada,* a slow-cooked cut of beef, on a bed of mashed potatoes and basil. Reservations are not essential except for the terrace tables, which are the best in good weather. ⊠*Av. Bicentenario 4050, Vitacura* ☎*9/7477–6093* ☰*AE, DC, MC, V* ☉*No dinner Sun.* Ⓜ*No metro.*

$$$ ✕**Zanzíbar.** Although you can order hummus or lamb stew, this osten-
MIDDLE sibly Middle Eastern restaurant is more about conjuring up an exotic
EASTERN atmosphere than re-creating the cuisine of the region. (The first clue would be that Zanzibar isn't in the Middle East.) The food is tasty, but the real reason to come is to glide across the multicolor mosaic floors and settle into a chair placed beneath dozens of silver lanterns. Tables are just as fanciful, with designs made from pistachio nuts, red

peppers, and beans. It's all a bit over-the-top, but fun nonetheless. ⊠*Borde Río, Av. Monseñor Escrivá de Balaguer 6400, Vitacura* ☏*2/218–0118* ⚭*Reservations essential* ☰*AE, DC, MC, V* Ⓜ*No metro.*

WHERE TO STAY

Santiago's accommodations range from luxurious *hoteles* to comfortable *residenciales,* which can be homey bed-and-breakfasts or simple hotel-style accommodations. The city also has more than a dozen five-star properties. Most newer hotels are in Providencia and Las Condes, a short taxi or Metro ride from Santiago Centro.

Although the official room rates are pricey, you'll find discounts, usually of 10%–20%, in off-peak seasons or for longer stays. Call several hotels and ask for the best possible rate. It's a good idea to reserve in advance during the peak seasons (January, February, July, and August).

Note that the 19% sales tax is removed from your bill if you pay in U.S. dollars or with an overseas credit card.

CENTRO

$ ▣ **Andes Hostel.** Backpackers and budget-conscious families can ask to ✆   block off one of the four- or six-bed dormitories at this excellent hostel, opened in mid-2006. The basement has a well-equipped kitchen and pleasant dining room with three large tables and a television. Older kids love the pool table in the ground-floor lobby/common room. The location—opposite a subway station in the heart of the Parque Forestal, surrounded by museums, cool cafés, and restaurants—is hard to beat. **Pros:** This old house has been beautifully converted, is spotlessly clean, and has a great rooftop terrace. **Cons:** Some of the private rooms, with or without bathroom, are very small. ⊠*Monjitas 506, Santiago Centro* ☏*2/632–9990* ⊕*www.andeshostel.com* ⇆*6 rooms, 3 with bath; 9 dormitories* ⚭*In-hotel: bar, public Wi-Fi, public Internet, no-smoking rooms* ☰*AE, DC, MC, V* ⃝*CP* Ⓜ*Bellas Artes.*

$ ▣ **Foresta.** Staying in this seven-story hotel across the street from Cerro Santa Lucía is like visiting an elegant old home that has seen better days. It's still a good deal but the decoration is dated and tired. The best rooms are those on the upper floors overlooking the hill, although those at the back are quieter. A rooftop restaurant-bar is a great place to enjoy the view. **Pros:** Great location with the quaint cafés and shops of Plaza Mulato Gil de Castro just around the corner. **Cons:** Rooms are small, although for a few thousand extra pesos, the *matrimonial* rooms—with a double bed instead of the twin beds of double rooms—have a sitting area. ⊠*Victoria Subercaseaux 353, Santiago Centro* ☏*2/639–6261* ⇆*35 rooms* ⚭*In-room: refrigerator, no a/c. In-hotel: restaurant, room service, bar, public Wi-Fi, public Internet, laundry service, parking (no fee)* ☰*AE, DC, MC, V* ⃝*CP* Ⓜ*Bellas Artes.*

2

$$$ 📺 **Hotel Fundador.** On the edge of the quaint Barrio París-Londres, the Hotel Fundador has recently been renovated and rooms, although small, are bright and airily attractive. Make sure to take a stroll on the iron bridge across Calle Londres that links the hotel's two halves. Amenities include a small indoor pool. This hotel also has business on its mind, so there are plenty of meeting rooms with high-tech equipment. The same Chilean company also owns the award-winning Hotel Remota in Puerto Natales in the far south of Chile and, following Fundador's renovation, plans to offer joint deals for the two hotels. **Pros:** Tucked away from downtown traffic noise; on the doorstep of a subway station. **Cons:** Not an area for a stroll at night; few restaurants or bars in the immediate vicinity. ✉ *Paseo Serrano 34, Santiago Centro* ☎ *2/387–1200* 🖷 *2/387– 1300* ⊕ *www.hotelfundador.cl* 🖵 *119 rooms, 28 suites* ⚘ *In-room: safe, dial-up, refrigerator. In-hotel: restaurant, room service, bar, Wi-Fi, pool, gym, laundry service, parking (no fee), no-smoking rooms* ▭ *AE, DC, MC, V* 🏵 *BP* Ⓜ *Universidad de Chile.*

¢–$ 📺 **Hotel París.** In the heart of Barrio París-Londres stands this mansion-turned-hotel. Pass through the large lobby and you'll find a quaint courtyard garden. Rooms are old-fashioned and have just the basic furnishings but are very clean. Those in the more comfortable half, which you reach via a marble staircase, are more spacious and are just a few thousand pesos extra. **Pros:** Excellent value for a very modest price; friendly service. **Cons:** Breakfast room far too small for hotel size but it's extra and there are alternatives nearby. ✉ *París 813, La Alameda* ☎ *2/664–0921* 🖷 *2/639–4037* 🖵 *52 rooms* ⚘ *In-room: no a/c, no TV (some). In-hotel: bar, public Internet, no-smoking rooms, no elevator* ▭ *AE, DC, MC, V* 🏵 *EP* Ⓜ *Universidad de Chile, Santa Lucía.*

$$$ 📺 **Hotel Plaza San Francisco.** Across from Iglesia San Francisco, this busi-
Fodor's Choice   ness hotel has everything traveling executives need. Between meetings
★   there's plenty to do: take a dip in the sparkling indoor pool, work out in the fitness club, or stroll through the art gallery. Recent redecoration has given the hotel's wood paneling and the rich reds, oranges, and greens of its decor a lighter, more modern touch. Its spacious rooms have large beds, and double-paned windows keep out the downtown noise. **Pros:** Helpful English-speaking staff; the Bristol (see restaurants) offers interesting cuisine. **Cons:** Other good restaurants and bars are a Metro or taxi-ride away. ✉ *La Alameda 816, Santiago Centro* ☎ *2/639–3832, 800/223–5652 toll-free in U.S.* 🖷 *2/639–7826* ⊕ *www.plazasanfran-cisco.cl* 🖵 *136 rooms, 9 suites* ⚘ *In-room: safe, refrigerator, ethernet. In-hotel: restaurant, room service, bar, pool, gym, public Wi-Fi, laundry service, no-smoking rooms, parking (no fee)* ▭ *AE, DC, MC, V* 🏵 *BP* Ⓜ *Universidad de Chile.*

$ 📺 **Hotel Santa Lucía.** The rooms at this centrally located hotel are on the small side and are a little tired looking—after all, it's been around for 50 years. But they're spotlessly clean and avoid most traffic noise because of their position above an office building. The large terrace restaurant, unusually quiet given its location, serves nothing but typical Chilean fare. For the quietest rooms, ask to overlook Huérfanos, which is pedestrian, rather than San Antonio with its heavy bus traffic. **Pros:** Comfortably furnished rooms with good beds; excellent maintenance.

Cons: Not an attractive area at night. ⊠*San Antonio 327, Paseo Huér-*
fanos 779, Santiago Centro ☎*2/639–8201* 🖷*2/633–1844* ⊕*www.*
hotelsantalucia.cl ⟿*70 rooms* ⚷*In-room: no a/c, safe, refrigerator.*
In-hotel: restaurant, laundry service, public Internet, parking (fee), no-
smoking rooms ⊟*AE, DC, MC, V* ❢⎉*CP* Ⓜ*Plaza de Armas.*

$ 📶**Hotel Vegas.** This colonial-style building, adorned with a bullet-
shaped turret on the corner, sits in the heart of the charming Barrio
París-Londres. Rooms here are spacious and filled with comfortable
modern furnishings. All have plenty of windows—ask for one of the
two double rooms with a sitting room inside the turret so you'll have a
view of gently curving Calle Londres. **Pros:** A good location for downtown sightseeing. **Cons:** Some rooms smell musty; cramped lobby, bar
and café. ⊠*Londres 49, Santiago Centro* ☎*2/632–2498 or 2/632–*
2514 🖷*2/632–5084* ⊕*www.hotelvegas.net* ⟿*20 rooms* ⚷*In-room:*
refrigerator. In-hotel: room service, bar, public Wi-Fi, laundry service,
no elevator ⊟*AE, DC, MC, V* ❢⎉*BP* Ⓜ*Universidad de Chile.*

¢–$ 📶**Residencial Londres.** This 1920s-era hotel in the picturesque Barrio
París-Londres is just a stone's throw from most of the city's major
sights. Rooms are spacious, with high ceilings ringed by detailed mold-
ings and expansive wood floors. The best rooms have stone balconies
overlooking this charmingly atypical neighborhood. **Pros:** The staff is
friendly and helpful. **Cons:** Except for the beautiful lobby, very poor
maintenance, with badly peeling paint in some bathrooms; dirty mattresses long past their throw-out date. ⊠*Londres 54, Santiago Cen-*
tro🖷🖷*2/638–2215* ⊕*www.londres.cl* ⟿*25 rooms* ⚷*In-room: no*
a/c, no phone, no TV. In-hotel: no elevator ⊟*No credit cards* ❢⎉*EP*
Ⓜ*Universidad de Chile.*

LAS CONDES

$$ 📶**Director El Golf.** The decoration at this hotel is dated and the smell
of air freshener in the corridors is off-putting but, aside from its loca-
tion near the center of the El Golf business and restaurant area, it has
an important plus in that rooms—all spacious suites—have a kitch-
enette and small dining area. The service is friendly and very efficient.
This hotel also has another less conveniently located branch at Ave-
nida Vitacura 3600. **Pros:** A good choice for longer-stay visitors who
don't want to eat out every night. **Cons:** No-smoking rooms not avail-
able. ⊠*Carmencita 45, Las Condes* ☎*2/498–3000* 🖷*2/498–3010*
⊕*www.director.cl* ⟿*49 suites* ⚷*In-room: kitchen, safe, refrigerator,*
Wi-Fi, ethernet. In-hotel: restaurant, room service, bar, gym, public
Internet, laundry service, parking (no fee) ⊟*AE, DC, MC, V* ❢⎉*CP*
Ⓜ*El Golf, Tobalaba.*

$$$$ 📶**Grand Hyatt Santiago.** The soaring spire of the Grand Hyatt resembles
Fodor's Choice a rocket (and you might feel like an astronaut when you're shooting up
★ a glass elevator through a 24-story atrium). The rooms wrap around
the cylindrical lobby, providing a panoramic view of the Andes. As
you might guess from the pair of golden lions flanking the entrance,
the theme is vaguely Asian, which is why two of the three award-win-
ning restaurants are Thai and Japanese. (Senso, which is Tuscan, is

also well worth a visit.) Duke's, the spitting image of an English pub, fills to standing capacity each day after work hours. **Pros:** The garden is particularly lovely and the Atrium Lounge serves famed afternoon teas. **Cons:** Rather out of the way and, although one of city's main shopping malls is close, there isn't much else except the junction of two major highways. ⊠ *Av. Kennedy 4601, Las Condes* ☎*2/950–1234* 📠*2/950–3155* ⊕*www.santiago.hyatt.com* 🛏*287 rooms, 23 suites* ♿ *In-room: safe, refrigerator, ethernet. In-hotel: 3 restaurants, room service, bar, public Wi-Fi, tennis courts, pool, gym, concierge, laundry service, parking (no fee), no-smoking rooms* ☰*AE, DC, MC, V* ❏*BP* Ⓜ*No metro.*

$$ 🏨**Neruda Express.** This "express" branch of the larger Hotel Neruda (on Avenida Pedro de Valdivia) has recently been redecorated and the rooms are tastefully modern, spacious, and luminous. Ask for one of the two suites on the 2nd floor or one of the "superior" rooms on the 9th to 11th floors; they cost the same as a standard room. Although all windows have double glass, rooms on Avenida Apoquindo still get traffic noise; those at the back are quieter. **Pros:** Location on the edge of fashionable Las Condes. **Cons:** Fawlty-Towers service has its charm but can also be very irritating. ⊠ *Vecinal 40, at Av. Apoquindo, Las Condes* ☎*2/233–2747* 📠*2/232–1662* ⊕*www.hotelneruda.cl* 🛏*50 rooms, 2 suites* ♿ *In-room: safe, refrigerator, Wi-Fi. In-hotel: public Internet, laundry service, parking (no fee), no-smoking rooms* ☰*AE, DC, MC, V* ❏*CP* Ⓜ*El Golf, Tobalaba.*

$$$ 🏨**Radisson Plaza Santiago.** Santiago's World Trade Center is also home to the Radisson, a combination that will make sense to many corporate travelers. The windows here are huge, with three wide glass panels for triptych perspectives of the city and the Andes beyond. The upholstered leather chairs and wood paneling in meeting rooms make it clear the hotel is serious in its attitude toward luxury. Even standard rooms have nice touches like wooden writing desks and small sitting areas with plush sofas. **Pros:** All the comfort and facilities of a top hotel at a more modest price; easy walking distance to the Metro. **Cons:** Major construction projects in the immediate area. ⊠ *Av. Vitacura 2610, Las Condes* ☎*2/203–6000, 888/20–1718 toll-free in U.S.* 📠*2/203–6001* ⊕*www.radisson.com/santiagocl* 🛏*134 rooms, 25 suites* ♿ *In-room: safe, refrigerator. In-hotel: restaurant, room service, bar, public Wi-Fi, pool, gym, concierge, laundry service, parking (no fee), no-smoking rooms* ☰*AE, DC, MC, V* ❏*BP* Ⓜ*Tobalaba.*

$$$$ 🏨**Ritz-Carlton.** The rather bland brick exterior of this 15-story hotel, the first Ritz-Carlton in South America, belies the luxurious appointments within. Mahogany-paneled walls, cream marble floors, and enormous windows characterize the splendid two-story lobby, which faces a small leafy plaza just off busy Avenida Apoquindo. Elegant furnishings upholstered in brocade, and silk floral fabrics dominate the large guest rooms. Under a magnificent glass dome on the top floor you can swim or work out while pondering the panorama, smog permitting, of the Andes and the Santiago skyline. **Pros:** Prime location close to the main El Golf business and restaurant area. **Cons:** Almost the same comfort is available in other five-star hotels at much lower prices.

✉*El Alcalde 15, Las Condes* ☎*2/470–8500* 🖷*2/470–8501* ⊕*www.*
ritzcarlton.com ↻*187 rooms, 18 suites* ♿*In-room: safe, refrigerator,*
ethernet. In-hotel: 2 restaurants, bar, room service, public Wi-Fi, pool,
gym, concierge, laundry service, parking (no fee), no-smoking rooms
🞖*AE, DC, MC, V* 🍽*BP* Ⓜ*El Golf.*

$$$$ 🎭**Santiago InterContinental.** Attendants wearing top hats usher you into
the two-story marble lobby of one of the city's top hotels. Beyond the
reception desk there is a string of comfortable lounge areas, including
one next to an indoor waterfall. In the rear is Bice, one of the city's
most memorable restaurants. The rooms are sumptuous, with doors
made from handsome panels of the native blond wood called *mañío.*
Five executive floors have express check-in, a sleek private dining area
with open bar, and an elegant meeting room on the 11th floor. **Pros:**
Easy walking distance from the El Golf business and restaurant area.
Cons: Lengthy walk to the Metro; bad traffic congestion around the
hotel. ✉*Av. Vitacura 2885, Las Condes* ☎*2/394–2000* 🖷*2/394–*
2075 ⊕*www.interconti.com/santiago* ↻*281 rooms, 14 suites* ♿*In-*
room: safe, refrigerator, ethernet. In-hotel: 2 restaurants, bars, room
service, public Wi-Fi, pool, gym, concierge, executive floors, laun-
dry service, parking (no fee), no-smoking rooms 🞖*AE, DC, MC, V*
🍽*BP* Ⓜ*Tobalaba.*

$$$$ 🎭**Santiago Marriott Hotel.** The first 25 floors of this gleaming copper
tower house the Marriott. An impressive two-story, cream marble lobby
has full-grown palm trees in and around comfortable seating areas. Visitors who opt for an executive room can breakfast in a private lounge
while scanning the newspaper and marveling at the snowcapped Andes.
There's no need to venture out for entertainment, either: there are wine-
tastings in the Latin Grill restaurant and theme evenings, with live
music, in the Café Med. **Pros:** Excellent, friendly service in a spacious
setting. **Cons:** Located in a suburban neighborhood, it's a bit removed
from the action. ✉*Av. Kennedy 5741, Las Condes* ☎*2/426–2000,*
800/468–4000 toll-free in U.S. and Canada 🖷*2/426–2001* ⊕*www.*
santiagomarriott.com ↻*280 rooms, 60 suites* ♿*In-room: safe, refrig-*
erator, ethernet. In-hotel: 2 restaurants, bar, room service, public Wi-Fi,
pool, gym, concierge, laundry service, parking (no fee), no-smoking
rooms 🞖*AE, DC, MC, V* 🍽*BP* Ⓜ*No metro.*

PROVIDENCIA

$ 🎭**Chilhotel.** Good mid-range hotels are few and far between in Santiago
and this small hotel is one of the few, and great value for money. For
about what you'd pay for a dinner for two, you get a room that's clean
and comfortable. Those overlooking the palm-shaded courtyard in back
are especially lovely. It's in a funky old house, so no two rooms are
alike. See a few before you decide. And talk about location—you're on
a quiet side street, yet dozens of restaurants and bars are steps away.
Pros: Excellent service closely supervised by owners; just a 10-min-
ute Metro ride away from downtown sightseeing. **Cons:** Small size of
rooms. ✉*Cirujano Guzmán 103, Providencia* ☎*2/264–0643* 🖷*2/264–*
1323 ⊕*www.chilhotel.cl* ↻*17 rooms* ♿*In-room: safe, refrigerator.*

In-hotel: restaurant, laundry service, public Wi-Fi, no elevator ▭AE, DC, MC, V |○|BP Ⓜ*Manuel Montt.*

$$ 🏨**Four Points By Sheraton.** The heart of Providencia's shopping district is just steps away from this eight-year-old hotel, a favorite with savvy business visitors to the city. Rooms are a generous size and, like the rest of the hotel, have most of the comforts and facilities of a much more expensive establishment. The cool rooftop terrace, with a small pool, is a real pleasure in summer, when you can relax with a pisco sour and take in the city views. **Pros:** Excellent value for money. **Cons:** The pubs on nearby Calle Suecia were once great for partying but have slid into drug-dealing and prostitution, although the immediate area of the hotel is perfectly safe at night. ✉*Av. Santa Magdalena 111, Providencia* ☎*2/750–0300* 📠*2/750–0350* ⊕*www.fourpoints. com* 🛏*112 rooms, 16 suites* ♿*In-room: safe, refrigerator, ethernet. In-hotel: restaurant, room service, bar, public Wi-Fi, pool, spa, gym, laundry service, parking (no fee), no-smoking rooms* ▭AE, DC, MC, V |○|BP Ⓜ*Los Leones.*

$$ 🏨**Hotel Orly.** Finding a treasure like this in the middle of Providencia is

Fodor'sChoice nothing short of a miracle. The shiny wood floors, country-manor fur-

★ nishings, and glass-domed breakfast room make this hotel as sweet as it is economical. Rooms come in all shapes and sizes, so ask to see a few before you decide. Cafetto, the downstairs café, owned by the hotel but also open to the public, serves some of the finest coffee drinks in town. **Pros:** Attractively decorated; excellent maintenance. **Cons:** Difficult to get a room on short notice. ✉*Av. Pedro de Valdivia 027, Providencia* ☎*2/231–8947* 📠*2/334–4403* ⊕*www.orlyhotel.com* 🛏*25 rooms, 3 suites* ♿*In-room: safe, refrigerator. In-hotel: restaurant, room service, laundry service, parking (no fee), public Wi-Fi, no-smoking rooms* ▭AE, DC, MC, V |○|BP Ⓜ*Pedro de Valdivia.*

$$$$ 🏨**Santiago Park Plaza.** It bills itself as a "classic European-style" hotel, and the receptionists that greet you from behind individual mahogany desks certainly call to mind the Continent. The color scheme, in rich burgundy and dark green with cream accents, extends to the adjoining Park Lane restaurant, whose chef masterfully combines international and Chilean cuisine. Although the glass-covered pool on the top floor is tiny, it has a great view. **Pros:** In the heart of Providencia with a Metro station on the doorstep. **Cons:** Some people find the predominant "English" reds and greens of the decor make the hotel gloomy. ✉*Av. Ricardo Lyon 207, Providencia* ☎*2/372–4000* 📠*2/233–6668* ⊕*www.parkplaza.cl* 🛏*104 rooms, 6 suites* ♿*In-room: safe, refrigerator, ethernet. In-hotel: restaurant, bar, public Wi-Fi, pool, gym, laundry service, parking (no fee), no-smoking rooms* ▭AE, DC, MC, V |○|BP Ⓜ*Los Leones.*

$$$$ 🏨**Sheraton Santiago and San Cristóbal Tower.** Two distinct hotels stand side by side at this lovely resort. The Sheraton Santiago is certainly a luxury hotel, but the adjoining San Cristóbal Tower is in a class by itself, popular with business executives and foreign dignitaries who value its efficiency, elegance, and impeccable service. A lavish, labyrinthine marble lobby links the two hotels, its fine restaurants, and a large hotel convention center. Pampering is not all that goes on at the

San Cristóbal Tower—attentive staff members at the business center can provide you with everything from secretarial services to Internet access. The modern rooms have elegant linens and are decorated with rich fabrics. **Pros:** The service in both hotels is really top-notch. **Cons:** On the north side of the Mapocho river, this hotel is a taxi ride away from the nearest Metro station and from business, restaurant, and shopping areas. ⊠ *Av. Santa María 1742, Providencia* ☎ *2/233–5000* 🖷 *2/234–1729* ⊕ *www.sheraton.cl* ⬎ *Sheraton Santiago: 369 rooms, 14 suites. San Cristóbal Tower: 130 rooms, 9 suites* ⚒ *In-room: safe, refrigerator, ethernet. In-hotel: 3 restaurants, bars, public Wi-Fi, tennis court, pools, gym, concierge, laundry service, no-smoking rooms* ▤ *AE, DC, MC, V* ⎮◎⎮*BP* Ⓜ *No metro.*

VITACURA

$ 🖾 **Acacias de Vitacura.** The extraordinary location of this hotel—in the midst of towering eucalyptus and acacia trees thought to be more than a century old—is unforgettable. It's a pleasure to drink your morning coffee in the lush garden under one of the oversize umbrellas. The rooms here are simple but bright, decorated with pale creams and tans. The owner's collection of old carriages gives the hotel a quirky personality. **Pros:** A lovely, peaceful setting. **Cons:** A 20-minute taxi ride, and much longer at peak times, from the city's business areas and sights. ⊠ *El Manantial 1781, Vitacura* ☎ *2/211–8601* 🖷 *2/212–7858* ⊕ *www.hotelacacias.cl* ⬎ *31 rooms, 2 suites* ⚒ *In-room: safe, refrigerator, ethernet. In-hotel: restaurant, public Wi-Fi, pool, gym, parking (no fee)* ▤ *AE, DC, MC, V* ⎮◎⎮*BP* Ⓜ *No metro.*

$$$ 🖾 **Hotel Kennedy.** This glass tower may seem impersonal but small details show the staff cares about keeping guests happy. Bilingual secretarial services and an elegant boardroom are among the pluses for visiting executives. The Aquarium restaurant serves international cuisine and has a cellar full of excellent Chilean wines. **Pros:** This hotel prides itself on the quality of its restaurant. **Cons:** Out of the way with no Metro station nearby. ⊠ *Av. Kennedy 4570, Vitacura* ☎ *2/290–8100* 🖷 *2/219–3272* ⊕ *www.hotelkennedy.cl* ⬎ *113 rooms, 10 suites* ⚒ *In-room: safe, refrigerator, ethernet. In-hotel: restaurant, room service, bar, public Wi-Fi, pool, gym, laundry service, parking (no fee), no-smoking rooms* ▤ *AE, DC, MC, V* ⎮◎⎮*BP* Ⓜ *No metro.*

NIGHTLIFE & THE ARTS

Although it can't rival Buenos Aires or Rio de Janeiro, Santiago buzzes with increasingly sophisticated bars and clubs. Santiaguinos often meet for drinks during the week, usually after work when most bars have happy hour. Then they call it a night, as most people don't really cut loose until Friday and Saturday. Weekends commence with dinner beginning at 9 or 10 and then a drink at a pub. (This doesn't refer to an English beer hall; a pub here is a bar with loud music and a lot of seating.) No one thinks of heading to the dance clubs until 1 am, and they stay until 4 or 5 am.

THE ARTS

With dozens of museums scattered around the city, it's clear Santiaguinos also have a strong love of culture. Music, theater, and other artistic endeavors supplement weekends spent dancing the night away.

DANCE

The venerable **Ballet Nacional Chileno** (⊠ *Av. Providencia 043, Providencia* ☎ *2/634–4746*), founded in 1945, performs from its repertoire of more than 150 pieces at the Teatro Universidad de Chile near Plaza Baquedano.

FILM

Santiago's many cinemas screen movies in English with Spanish subtitles. Movie listings are posted in *El Mercurio* and other dailies. Admission is generally between 3,000 and 4,000 pesos, with reduced prices on Monday to Wednesday and for matinees. The newest multiplexes—with mammoth screens, plush seating, and fresh popcorn—are in the city's malls. Most of the city's art cinemas tend to screen international favorites. The old standby is **El Biógrafo** (⊠ *José Victorino Lastarria 181, Santiago Centro* ☎ *2/633–4435*), which shows foreign films on its single screen. It's on a colorful street lined with cafés.

Affiliated with one of the city's universities, the **Centro de Extensión Universidad Católica** (⊠ *La Alameda 390, Santiago Centro* ☎ *2/354–6507*) has interesting festivals as well as art exhibitions. **Cine Arte Normandie** (⊠ *Av. Tarapacá 1181, Santiago Centro* ☎ *2/697–2979*) is a popular, cheap theater south of Iglesia San Francisco. **CineHoyts Huérfanos** (⊠ *Paseo Huérfanos 735, Santiago Centro* ☎ *600/500–0400*) has four screens while the nearby **CineHoyts San Augustín** (⊠ *San Antonio 144, Santiago Centro* ☎ *600/500–0400*) has eight.

Among the best theaters in town is the **Cinemark 12** (⊠ *Av. Kennedy 9001, Las Condes* ☎ *600/586–0058*), in the Alto Las Condes mall. Its dozen screens show the latest releases. In the Parque Arauco mall, **Showcase Cinemas Parque Arauco** (⊠ *Av. Kennedy 5413, Las Condes* ☎ *2/565–7025*) has the city's most modern facility. **Tobalaba** (⊠ *Av. Providencia 2563, Las Condes* ☎ *2/231–6630*) shows arty and foreign films.

MUSIC

Parque de las Esculturas (⊠ *Av. Santa María between Av. Pedro de Valdivia Norte and Padre Letelier, Providencia* ☎ *No phone*) hosts numerous open-air concerts in the early evenings in summer. The **Teatro Municipal** (⊠ *Plaza Alcalde Mekis, Av. Agustinas at Av. San Antonio, Santiago Centro* ☎ *800/471–000* ⊕ *www.municipal.cl*), Santiago's 19th-century theater, presents excellent classical concerts, opera, and ballet by internationally recognized artists from March to December. **Teatro Oriente** (⊠ *Av. Pedro de Valdivia, between Costanera and Av. Providencia, Providencia* ☎ *2/251–5321* ⊕ *www.teatroriente.cl*) has a classical music season and hosts some more popular concerts. The Coro Sinfónico and the Orquesta Sinfónica, the city's highly regarded chorus and orchestra, perform near Plaza Baquedano at the

Teatro Universidad de Chile (✉*Av. Providencia 043, Providencia* ☎*2/634–5295* ⊕*teatro.uchile.cl*).

THEATER

Provided that you understand at least a little Spanish, you may want to take in a bit of Chilean theater. Performances take place all year, mainly from Thursday to Sunday around 8 pm. In January, the year's best plays are performed at the Estación Mapocho and other venues in a program called the **Festival Internacional Teatro A Mil** (☎*2/735–6167* ⊕*www.stgoamil.cl*). The name refers to the admission price of 1,000 pesos (just over $2).

The city's best-equipped theater and some of the most interesting plays are to be found in the **Matucana 100** arts center (✉*Matucana 100, Quinta Normal* ☎*2/682–4502* ⊕*www.m100.cl*). The following theaters produce a mix of Latin American comedies and dramas: **Teatro Bellavista** (✉*Dardignac 0110, Bellavista* ☎*2/735–2395*); **Teatro Aparte** (✉*Ernesto Pinto Lagarrigue 179, Bellavista* ☎*2/738–0861*); and **Teatro Mori** (✉*Constitución 183, Bellavista* ☎*2/777–6246*), which also has another theater in the Parque Arauco shopping mall, usually showing comedy.

The well-respected ICTUS theater company performs in the **Teatro la Comedia** (✉*Merced 349, Santiago Centro* ☎*2/639–1523*).

NIGHTLIFE

Bars and clubs are scattered all over Santiago, but a handful of streets have such a concentration of establishments that they resemble block parties on Friday and Saturday nights. Try pub-crawling along Avenida Pío Nono and neighboring streets in Bellavista. The crowd here is young, as the drinking age is 18. To the east in Providencia, the area around the Manuel Montt Metro station attracts a slightly older and better-heeled crowd.

What you should wear depends on your destination. Bellavista has a mix of styles ranging from blue jeans to basic black and, in general, the dress gets smarter the farther east you move, but remains casual.

Note that establishments referred to as "nightclubs" are almost always female strip shows. The cheesy signs in the windows usually make it quite clear what goes on inside.

BARS & CLUBS

BELLAVISTA

El Toro (✉*Loreto 33, Bellavista* ☎*2/737–5937*) is packed every night of the week including Sunday. The tables are spaced close enough that you can eavesdrop on the conversations of the models and other celebrities who frequent the place. **La Casa en el Aire** in the Patio Bellavista (✉*Constitución 40, Bellavista* ☎*2/762–1161*) is a great place to listen to live bands. For jazz, go to **Perseguidor** (✉*Antonia Lopéz de Bello 0126, Bellavista* ☎*2/777–6763*). The **Libro Café** (✉*Purísima 165, Bellavista* ☎*2/735–3901*) is a late-night haunt for starving artists and those who wish they were. If you're hungry, head here for a tortilla and a carafe of the house red..

CENTRO

At the base of Cerro Santa Lucía, **Catedral** (⊠ *José Miguel de la Barra 407, Parque Forestal* ☎ *2/638–4734*) is a smart new bar, popular with the thirties crowd. It serves food but the same building also houses Opera, its upmarket restaurant partner. Identifiable by the leering devil on the sign, **El Diablito** (⊠ *Merced 336, Parque Forestal* ☎ *2/664–3048*) is a charming hole-in-the-wall. The dimly lighted space is popular with the after-work crowd. A secret meeting place during the Pinochet regime, **El Rincón de las Canallas** (⊠ *San Diego 379, Santiago Centro* ☎ *2/699–1309*) still requires a password to get in (*Chile libre*, meaning "free Chile"). The walls are painted with political statements such as *Somos todos inocentes* ("We are all innocent").

LAS CONDES

Flannery's (⊠ *Encomenderos 83, Las Condes* ☎ *2/233–6675*), close to the main drag of Avenida El Bosque Norte, is an honest-to-goodness pub serving Irish food, beer, and occasionally Guinness on tap. **Pub Licity** (⊠ *Av. El Bosque Norte 0155, Las Condes* ☎ *2/293–5984*) is a large, popular, glass-fronted building permanently teeming with people in their twenties and early thirties.

PROVIDENCIA

From the doorway, **Casa de Cena** (⊠ *Almirante Simpson 20, Providencia* ☎ *2/222–8900*) looks like your average hole-in-the-wall, but it's actually a gem. Most nights a guitar player wanders through the maze of wood-paneled rooms singing folk songs while the bartender listens to endless stories from inebriated regulars.

Bar Yellow (⊠ *General Flores 47, Providencia* ☎ *2/946–5063*) is a newer and more alternative place that has great food as well as drinks. Try the chips and, if it's on the menu, the Thai soup with shrimp. And the staff really do speak English. Closed Sundays.

GAY & LESBIAN CLUBS

Once mostly underground, Santiago's gay scene is bursting at the seams. Although some bars are so discreet they don't have a sign, others are known by just about everyone. Clubs like Bunker, for example, are so popular that they attract a fair number of nongays. There's a cluster of gay restaurants and bars on the streets parallel to Avenida Pío Nono in Bellavista. There's not as much for lesbians in Santiago, however, although some women can be found at most establishments catering to men.

On Bellavista's main drag, **Bokhara** (⊠ *Pío Nono 430, Bellavista* ☎ *2/732–1050*) is one of the city's largest and most popular gay discos. It has two dance floors playing house and techno. **Bunker** (⊠ *Bombero Nuñez 159, Bellavista* ☎ *2/737–1716*), a mainstay of the gay scene, is in a cavernous space with numerous platforms overlooking the dance floor. Don't get here too early—people don't arrive until well after midnight. Note that it's open only Friday and Saturday. The venerable

Fausto (⊠ *Av. Santa María 0832, Providencia* ☎2/777–1041), in business for more than 20 years, has polished wood paneling that calls to mind a gentlemen's club. The disco pumps until the wee hours.**Máscara** (⊠*Purísima 129, Bellavista* ☎2/737–4123) is a lesbian disco.

If you're looking for a place to kick back with a beer, try **Friends** (⊠*Bombero Nuñez 365, Bellavista* ☎2/777–3979). Live music performances and shows take place on Thursday, Friday, and Saturday.

Vox Populi (⊠*Ernesto Pinto Lagarrigue 364, Bellavista* ☎2/738–0562) is a longtime favorite in Bellavista.

SALSA CLUBS

Havana Salsa (⊠*Dominíca 142, Bellavista* ☎2/737–1737) thumps to the beat of salsa and merengue from Thursday to Saturday night. At **Ilé Habana** (⊠*Bucarest 95, Providencia* ☎2/231–5711) you can boogie to the beat of a live band. There are salsa lessons Tuesday–Saturday from 8:30–9:30 pm at 2,000 pesos.

SPORTS & THE OUTDOORS

ATHLETIC CLUBS & SPAS

All of Santiago's larger hotels have health clubs on the premises, usually with personal trainers on hand to assist you with your workout. Even if you aren't staying at a particular hotel, you can usually pay to use the facilities for the day. **Balthus** (⊠*Av. Monseñor Escrivá de Balaguer 5970, Vitacura* ☎2/410–1414 ⊕*www.balthus.cl*) is the city's top health club. This high-tech marvel has all the latest equipment. You feel healthier just by walking into the complex, a sleek series of riverside structures in concrete and glass. There are eight tennis courts, spas, pools, and numerous fitness programs.

The modern **Spa Mund** (⊠*Cardenal Belarmino 1075, Vitacura* ☎2/678–0200 ⊕*www.spamund.cl*) is a sprawling aquatic spa where you can relax in saunas and hot tubs. Better yet, pamper yourself with a facial.**Rolf Nathan** (⊠*Reina Astrid 879, Las Condes* ☎2/21–8263 ⊕*www.corplascondes.cl*), owned by the Las Condes municipality, also has a good swimming pool open to the public.

BICYCLING

Santiago has no shortage of public parks, and they provide good opportunities to see the city. If you're ambitious you can even pedal up Cerro San Cristóbal, the city's largest hill. You can rent mountain bikes for 8,700 pesos from **Lys** (⊠*Av. Miraflores 537, Santiago Centro* ☎2/633–7600).

HORSE RACING

Betting on horses is popular in Santiago, which is the reason you'll see so many Teletrak betting offices. The city has two large race-tracks. Races take place Friday and alternating Mondays at **Club Hípico** (⊠ *Blanco Encalada 2540, Santiago Centro* ☎ *2/693–9600* ⊕ *www. clubhipico.cl*), south of downtown. El Ensayo, an annual race that's a century-old tradition, is held here in early November. **Hipódromo Chile** (⊠ *Hipódromo Chile 1715, Independencia* ☎ *2/270–9237* ⊕ *www. hipodromo.cl*) is the home of the prestigious Gran Premio Internacional, which draws competitors from around South America. Regular races are held Saturday and alternating Thursdays.

SKIING

If you're planning on hitting the slopes, **KL Ski Rental** (⊠ *Augusto Mira Fernández 14248, Las Condes* ☎ *32/2817–366* ⊕ *www.kladventure. com*) not only rents skis and snowboards, but also arranges transportation to and from the nearby ski areas.

SOCCER

Chile's most popular spectator sport is soccer, but a close second is watching the endless bickering among owners, trainers, and players whenever a match isn't going well. First-division *fútbol* matches, featuring the city's handful of local teams, are held in the **Estadio Nacional** (⊠ *Av. Grecia 2001, Nuñoa* ☎ *2/238–8102*), southeast of the city center. Soccer is played year-round, with most matches taking place on weekends. It was here in the Estadio that Pinochet's henchmen held thousands of political opponents in 1973, including Chilean folk singer Victor Jara. To assure that he would never again provoke Chileans to action with his music, Jara's hands were mutilated before he was put to death.

SHOPPING

Vitacura is, without a doubt, the destination for upscale shopping. Lined with designer boutiques where you'll find SUVs double parked out front, Avenida Alonso de Córdova is Santiago's equivalent of 5th Avenue in New York or Rodeo Drive in Los Angeles. "Drive" is the important word here, as nobody strolls from place to place. Although buzzing with activity, the streets are strangely empty. Here you'll see names like Emporio Armani, Louis Vuitton, and Hermès. Other shops are found on nearby Avenida Vitacura and Avenida Nueva Costanera.

Providencia, another of the city's most popular shopping districts, has rows of smaller, less luxurious boutiques. Avenida Providencia slices through the neighborhood, branching off for several blocks into the parallel Avenida 11 de Septiembre. The shops continue east to Avenida El Bosque Norte, after which Avenida Providencia changes its name to

Avenida Apoquindo and the neighborhood becomes Las Condes. In Providencia, some of the best shops are in **Drugstore** (✉ *Av. Providencia 2124, Providencia* ☎ *2/490–1241* ⊕ *www.drugstoreprovidencia.cl*), a small three-story shopping center.

Bohemian Bellavista attracts those in search of the perfect woolen sweater or the right piece of lapis lazuli jewelry. Santiago Centro is much more down-to-earth. The Mercado Central is where anything fishy is sold, and nearby markets like Vega Chica and Vega Central sell just about every item imaginable. Stores downtown usually face the street, which makes window-shopping more entertaining. Pedestrian streets around the Plaza de Armas are crowded with children licking ice-cream cones, older women strolling arm in arm, and business executives sitting under wide umbrellas having their shoes shined.

Shops in Santiago are generally open weekdays 10–7 and Saturday 10–2. Malls are usually open daily 10–10.

> ## WHAT TO LOOK FOR
>
> All manner of fine woolen items, carvings, lapis lazuli, and other handicrafts can be acquired at street markets, in the Pueblito Los Dominicos—a craft "village" in one of the city's parks—or at shops like those run by Artesanías de Chile, a foundation that selects top-quality work and ensures artisans receive a fair price. An hour's drive from Santiago, the quaint village of Pomaire is famous for its brown *greda*, the earthenware pottery that is a common feature of Chilean tables.

MARKETS

Aldea de Vitacura (✉ *Av. Vitacura 6840, Vitacura* ☎ *2/219–3161*) is a pleasant outdoor market where you can browse among the various stands selling local and national craftwork. It's open daily 11–9.

Centro Artesanal Santa Lucía, an art fair just across La Alameda from the base of Cerro Santa Lucía, is an excellent place to find Aymara and Mapuche crafts. It's open daily 10–7.

Bellavista's colorful **Feria Artesanal Pío Nono,** held in the park at the start of Avenida Pío Nono, comes alive every night of the week. It's even busier on weekends, when more vendors gather in Parque Domingo Gómez to display their handicrafts.

Pueblito Los Dominicos (✉ *Av. Apoquindo 9085, Las Condes* ☎ *2/201–9749* ⊕ *www.pueblitolosdominicos.com*) is a "village" of more than 200 shops where you can find everything from fine leather to semiprecious stones and antiques. There's also a wonderful display of cockatoos and other live birds. It's a nice place to visit, especially on weekends when traveling musicians entertain the crowds. It's open daily 10:30–8 in summer and 10–7 in winter. Next door is an attractive whitewashed church dating from the late 18th century. It's rather far from the main drag, so take a taxi, but an extension of the metro, due to be completed in December 2009, will link it to Providencia and the Centro.

SHOPPING MALLS

In Santiago, the shopping malls are so enormous that they have become attractions in their own right. Some even provide free transportation from the major hotels.

Alto Las Condes (⊠*Av. Kennedy 9001, Las Condes* ☎*2/299–6965*) has over 200 shops, three department stores, a multiplex, and a seemingly endless food court. Also here is a supermarket, appropriately named Jumbo, where the staff members wear roller skates while restocking the shelves. It carries excellent Chilean wines.

Parque Arauco (⊠*Av. Kennedy 5413, Las Condes* ☎*2/299–0500*) is a North American–style shopping center with an eclectic mix of designer boutiques, including clothing outlets like Benetton, Ralph Lauren, and Laura Ashley. Chile's three largest department stores—Falabella, Ripley, and Almacenes París—sell everything from perfume to plates. The tonier shops are mostly in the outdoor Boulevard which also has a wide selection of restaurants.

The **Mall del Centro** (⊠*Puente 689, Santiago Centro* ☎*2/361–0011*) is a smaller version of Parque Arauco, with fewer international brands but a more central location.

SPECIALTY SHOPS

ANTIQUES

West of Estación Mapocho is **Antiguedades Balmaceda** (⊠*Av. Brasil at Balmaceda, Santiago Centro* ☎*No phone* ⊘*Daily 10:30–7*), a warehouse filled with antiques dealers. On display is everything from furniture to books to jewelry.

More upmarket antiques shops are to be found in a small shopping center on Avenida Providencia at Bucarest, and in the basement of the Lo Castillo shopping center on Avenida Vitacura, one block up from the corner of Avenida Alonso de Córdova.

BOOKS

A cluster of bookstores can be found along Avenida Providencia in what is known as the Galería El Patio. The most interesting is **Libreria Australis** (⊠*Av. Providencia 1670, Providencia* ☎*2/236–8054*), which stocks nothing but travel-related items. You can find travel guides in English as well as Spanish, language dictionaries, and beautiful photography books highlighting the region's natural wonders. Also in Galería El Patio, **Librería Books** (⊠*Av. Providencia 1652, Providencia* ☎*2/235–1205*) stocks secondhand English books, including novels and non-fiction.

CLOTHING

If you've ever wondered where the men of Santiago buy their proper toppers, head to **Donde Golpea El Monito** (⊠*21 de Mayo 707, Santiago Centro* ☎*2/638–4907*). At this downtown shop, in business for nearly a century, the friendly staff will teach you the difference between a *texano* (cowboy hat) and a *paño* (a more formal hat).

In Vitacura, you can wrap yourself in style on and near Avenida Alonso de Córdova. Make sure to ring the bell at these shops, as they usually keep their doors locked. (They don't let just anybody in.) Looking a bit like a fortress, **Hermès** (⊠ *Av. Alonso de Córdova 2526, Vitacura* 🕾 *2/374–1576*) occupies some prime real estate on the main drag. Chilean women spend hours selecting just the right scarf. Yards and yards of cashmere fill the window of **Matilde Medina** (⊠ *Av. Vitacura 3660, Vitacura* 🕾 *2/206–6153*). She imports her beautiful scarves and sweaters from England.

Ralph Lauren (⊠ *Av. Vitacura 3634, Vitacura* 🕾 *2/228–3011*) has a relaxed atmosphere and a friendly staff. At **Wool** (⊠ *Av. Alonso de Córdova 4098, Vitacura* 🕾 *2/208–8767*) you can find a wide variety of items fashioned from the eponymous fiber.

GALLERIES

Galleries are scattered around the city, and admission is usually free. The newspaper *El Mercurio* lists current exhibitions in its Saturday supplement *Vivienda y Decoración*. True to its name, **Casa Naranja** (⊠ *Santo Domingo 528, Parque Forestal* 🕾 *2/639–5843*) is a house painted a particularly vivid shade of orange. Inside, past the restaurant, is a gallery filled with pieces by local artists.

Bellavista, which is full of small galleries and where restaurants often put on exhibitions, is the place to scout the work of young artists—but it is Vitacura that is the heart of the more consolidated gallery scene. See works by local artists at **Galería Animal** (⊠ *Av. Alonso de Córdova 3105, Vitacura* 🕾 *2/371–9090*). The large-scale pieces include sculpture and other types of installations. There's an outdoor café if all this art makes you peckish. **Galería Isabel Aninat** (⊠ *Espoz 3100, Vitacura* 🕾 *2/481–9870*) hosts exhibitions of international artists and also has a smaller showroom on the Boulevard of the Parque Arauco shopping mall. A space that was an important gallery in the 1970s is now called **Trece** (⊠ *Av. Nueva Costanera 3980, Vitacura* 🕾 *2/378–1981*). The warehouse-like space is perfect for massive works.

HANDICRAFTS

FodorsChoice **Artesanías de Chile** (⊠ *Av. Bellavista 0357, Bellavista* 🕾 *2/777–8643*
★ ⊕ *www.artesaniasdechile.cl*), a foundation created by the wife of President Ricardo Lagos, is one of the best places to buy local crafts. The work is top quality and you know that the artisans are getting a fair price. The foundation also has shops in the Pueblito Los Dominicos and in the Centro Cultural Palacio La Moneda. The staff at **Pura** (⊠ *Av. Isidora Goyenechea 3226, Las Condes* 🕾 *2/333–3144*) has picked out the finest handicrafts from around the region. Here you can find expertly woven blankets and throws, colorful pottery, and fine leather goods, but it's expensive. For everything from masks to mosaics, head to **Manos de Alma** (⊠ *General Salvo 114, Providencia* 🕾 *2/235–3518*).

JEWELRY

Chile is one of the few places in the world where lapis lazuli, a brilliant blue mineral, is found in abundance. In Bellavista, a cluster of shops deals solely in lapis lazuli, selling a range of products made from this

semiprecious stone: paperweights, jewelry, and chess sets. Several larger shops selling lapis lazuli are dotted around the rest of the city.

Blue Stone (✉*Av. Nueva Costanera 3863, Vitacura* ☏*2/207–4180*) has lovely original designs. Near Plaza Mulato Gil de Castro is **Rocco** (✉*José Victorino Lastarria 53, Santiago Centro* ☏*2/633–4036*), one of the best destinations in Santiago Centro.

WINE

Chileans have discovered just how good their vintages are, and wine-shops have popped up everywhere. **El Mundo del Vino** (✉*Av. Isidora Goyenechea 2931, Las Condes* ☏*2/584–1172*) is a world-class store with an international selection, in-store tastings, wine classes, and books for oenophiles. It also has shops in the Alto Las Condes and Parque Arauco shopping malls and in Patio Bellavista. **La Vinoteca** (✉*Av. Isidora Goyenechea 2966, Las Condes* ☏*2/334–1987*) proudly proclaims that it was Santiago's first fine wineshop. It also has a shop at the airport for last-minute purchases.

SIDE TRIPS FROM SANTIAGO

For more than a few travelers, Santiago's main attraction is its proximity to the continent's best skiing. Three world-class ski resorts lie just outside the city, and another is only a little farther away. Others are curious to see the region where their favorite wines are produced. The wineries around Santiago provide the majority of the country's excellent exports. The Cajón del Maipo, deep in the Andes, is irresistible for those who want to soak in a natural hot spring, stroll through picturesque mountain villages where low adobe houses line the roads, or just take in the stark but majestic landscape.

It's also possible to take day trips to Pomaire, a crafts village some 70 km (43 mi) west of Santiago, or to go farther afield to Valparaíso, Viña del Mar, or Isla Negra *(⇨Chapter 3).*

WINERIES CLOSE TO SANTIAGO

CENTRAL MAIPO

Don Francisco Undurraga Vicuña founded **Viña Undurraga** in 1885 in the town of Talagante, 34 km (21 mi) southwest of Santiago. The opulent mansion he built here has hosted various visiting dignitaries, from the queen of Denmark to the king of Norway. Today you can tour the house and the gardens—designed by Pierre Dubois, who planned Santiago's Parque Forestal—or take a look at the facilities, and enjoy a tasting. Reserve ahead for a spot on a tour in English or Spanish. Viña Undurraga is along the way to Pomaire, so you might visit both in the same day. ✉*Camino a Melipilla, Km 34, Talagante* ☏*2/372–2850* ⊕*www.undurraga.cl* 🎫*7,000 pesos* ☉*Tours: weekdays 10, 11:30, 2, and 3:30; weekends and holidays 10, 11:30, and 1:00.*

Viña De Martino. The De Martino family has been making fine wine in Isla de Maipo since the 1930s and were the first to bottle carmenère, Chile's signature grape. The winery is a strong proponent of organic viticulture. Its winemaking team has done ground-breaking work in seeking out the country's finest terroirs. ⊠*Manuel Rodríguez 229, Isla de Maipo* ☎*2/819–2062* ✆*vinoteca@demartino.cl* ⊕*www.demartino.cl* ☉*Daily* ⚷*Reservations essential.*

ALTO MAIPO

Some of Chile's finest red wines hail from the eastern sector of the valley, known as "Alto Maipo." There are a number of wineries—old and new, big and small—snugged up into the foothills of the Andes Mountains.

Viña Concha y Toro. Chile's largest producer is consistently good in every price range, from the most inexpensive table wines to some of Chile's finest—and priciest—labels. Melchor de Concha y Toro, who once served as Chile's minister of finance, built the *casona,* or manor house, in 1875. He was among the first to import French vines, making this a cutting-edge winery since its foundation in 1883. The hour-long tour includes a stroll through the century-old gardens and vineyards, a look at the modern facilities, and a visit to the *Casillero del Diablo,* the famed cellar where Don Melchor kept his finest stock, with tastings of three wines along the way. Want more? Finish up at the new wine bar to taste special labels with specially paired tapas, or combine this with lunch at nearby Viña Santa Rita. Reserve your tour a few days ahead for a weekday tour, or a week ahead for the popular weekend tours. ⊠*Av. Virginia Subercaseaux 210, Pirque* ☎*2/476–5269 or 2/476–5680* ⊕*www.conchaytoro.com* ☎*Standard tour: 6,000 pesos. Private tour: 12,000 pesos* ☉*Daily (except holidays) 10–7. Spanish tours: 10:30, 11, 12, 4. English tours: 10, 11:30, 3* ⚷*Reservations Essential.*

The property that is now home to **Viña Santa Rita,** Chile's third-largest winery, played an important historical role in Chile's battle for independence. Legend has it that in 1814, then-owner Doña Paula Jaraquemada saved the lives of revolutionary hero Bernardo O'Higgins and his 120 soldiers by hiding them in the winery's cellars and refusing to let the Spanish enter. (Santa Rita's 120 label commemorates the event.) The existing winery was founded in 1880 with vines, equipment, and winemakers imported from France. The Pompeian-style manor house built in 1880 is now the pricey 16-room Casa Real Hotel, owned by, but operated separately from, the winery. The house, its neo-gothic chapel, and the beautiful park that surrounds them are strictly off limits to all but the hotel's VIP guests. Winery visitors are quite welcome, however, to enjoy the well-prepared Chilean fare offered at its Casa de Doña Paula restaurant, a delightful place for lunch before or after the tour. The new Andean Museum on-site is open to the public free of charge and is highly recommended. Tours take you down into the winery's musty cellars, which are worthy of Edgar Allan Poe. Built by French engineers in 1875 using a limestone- and egg-white stone masonry technique called *cal y canto,* the fan-vault cellars have been named a national monument. The wine was once made and stored in the 120-year-old casks made of *raulí* wood that are now on display. Note that you must reserve a week ahead for these tours. ⊠ *Camino Padre Hurtado 0695, Alto Jahuel-Buín* ☎ *2/362–2520* ⊕ *www.santarita.com* ✉ *Standard tours: 8,000 pesos. Lunch tours: free with minimum restaurant consumption of 16,500 pesos* ⊙ *Bilingual Spanish and English tours: Tues.–Fri. at 10, 11:30, and 4. Lunch tours: Tues.–Sun. 2 tours per day.*

Viña Antiyal. Chilean winemaker Alvaro Espinoza and his wife Marina Ashton harvested their first organically grown grapes from biodynamically managed vines in their own front yard back in 1998 and thus was born Chile's first ultra-premium "garage wine." They've grown a bit since then, and have another parcel higher in the mountains, but they still only produce just 20,000 bottles (each numbered by hand) of their red-blend, Antiyal. Tours are personalized, with emphasis on their environmentally friendly winegrowing. Llamas, alpacas, geese, and the family dog wander the vineyards. Visits should be arranged well in advance (e-mail contact is best) for a personalized tour with tasting. ⊠ *Padre Hurtado 68, Buín* ☎ *2/821–4224* ✉ *marina@antiyal. cl* ⚠ *Reservations essential.*

WHERE TO EAT

$$$ ✕ **La Casa de Doña Paula.** A century-old colonial building with thick adobe walls houses Viña Santa Rita's restaurant. Beneath the exposed beams of the peaked wooden ceiling, the restaurant is decorated with old religious sculptures and portraits, including one of Paula Jaraquemada, who owned the land at the time of the revolution. If you plan to lunch here, arrive in time to join the winery's 12:15 tour. Locally raised meats are the draw here; try the delicious *costillar de cerdo* (pork ribs). For dessert, the house specialty is *ponderación*, a crisp swirl of fried dough atop vanilla ice cream and caramel syrup. ⊠ *Viña Santa Rita, Camino Padre Hurtado 0695, Alto Jahuel-Buín* ☎ *2/362–2594* ⊕ *www.santarita.com* ⚠ *Reservations essential* ☰ *AE, DC, MC, V* ⊙ *Closed Mon. No dinner.*

POMAIRE

You can easily spend a morning or afternoon wandering around the quaint village of Pomaire, a former settlement of indigenous people comprising nothing more than a few streets of single-story adobe dwellings. On weekends Pomaire teems with people who come to wander around, shop, and lunch in one of the picadas specializing in empanadas and other typical Chilean foods.

Pomaire is famous for its brown *greda*, or earthenware pottery, which you'll likely come across in one form or another throughout Chile. Order pastel de choclo and it will nearly always be served in a round, simple clay dish—they're heavy and retain the heat, so the food is brought to the table piping hot.

The village bulges with bowls, pots, and plates of every shape and size, not to mention other objects such as piggy banks, plant pots, vases, and figurines. You can purchase these items at shops and open-air markets around town. An average bowl will set you back no more than 300 to

2

400 pesos; an oven dish might cost between 2,000 and 3,000 pesos. The quality varies, so it's worth taking a look around before you buy.

The workmanship at **Nativa** (⊠ *Roberto Bravo 53, 78, and 366* ☎ *2/832–5693*) is among the best you'll find. Vases and other items are extremely delicate.

Pomaire, which lies 70 km (43 mi) west of Santiago, is easy to find. It's clearly signposted to your right off the Autopista del Sol. You can also take any of the buses that depart frequently from Terminal San Borja in downtown Santiago.

WHERE TO EAT

$$ ✕ **La Greda.** Named for the earthenware pottery that made this village famous, La Greda is a great place for grilled meats. Try the *filete la greda,* a steak covered with a sauce of tomatoes, onions, and mushrooms, and topped with cheese. The expansive outdoor dining room has vines winding around the thick wood rafters. If the weather is cool, the staff will light a fire in the woodstove to keep things toasty. ⊠ *Manuel Rodríguez 251, at Roberto Bravo* ☎ *2/831–1166* ⊟ *AE, DC, MC, V.*

$$ ✕ **Los Naranjos.** An eclectic collection of gramophones could be reason enough to come and lunch here, but more than anything diners come back time and again for the excellent Chilean food. If you're hungry try the *pernil de chancho* (leg of pork)—it's succulent and fit for an army. This is also a good place to try one of the national staples such as pastel de choclo—a delicious concoction of minced beef, chicken, olives, and boiled egg, topped with a creamy layer of mashed corn. Sunday there's often a traditional Chilean dance show to entertain you while you eat. ⊠ *Roberto Bravo 44* ☎ *2/831–1791* ⊟ *AE, DC, MC, V.*

SKI RESORTS

No wonder skiing aficionados from around the world head to Chile: the snowcapped mountains to the east of Santiago have the largest number of runs not just in Chile or South America, but in the entire Southern Hemisphere. The other attraction is that the season here lasts from June to September, so savvy skiers can take to the slopes when everyone else is hitting the beach.

There are three distinct ski areas within easy reach of Santiago—El Colorado, La Parva, and Valle Nevado—with a total of 46 lifts that can carry you to the top of 1,260 acres of groomed runs. To reach these areas, follow Avenida Las Condes eastward until you leave Santiago. Here, you begin an arduous journey up the Andes, making 40 consecutive hairpin turns. The road forks when you reach the top, with one road taking the relatively easy 16-km (10-mi) route east to Valle Nevado, and the other following a more difficult road north to Farellones and La Parva.

About 160 km (100 mi) north of Santiago and close to the Argentine border is Portillo, the oldest ski area in South America. It's a three-hour drive from the city, so a day trip would be exhausting. The only accommodation is Hotel Portillo with its two nearby lodges, which requires a minimum one-week stay. To reach Portillo from Santiago, take the Américo Vespucio beltway north and exit onto the Los Libertadores Highway to Los Andes. From Los Andes, take the International Highway (Ruta 60) east until you reach the resort.

EL COLORADO

The closest ski area to Santiago is Cerro Colorado. At its base is the village of Farellones, with a couple of ski runs for beginners, and farther up is El Colorado, which has 568 acres of groomed runs—the most in Chile. There are 20 runs here: 15 beginner, 3 intermediate, and 2 expert. You'll find a few restaurants and pubs in the village but most are down in Farellones. Ski season here runs mid-June to end-September. ☎ 2/889–9200 ⊕ www.elcolorado.cl ⊠ 20,000–28,000 pesos ⊗ Mid-June–end-Sept.

LA PARVA

About 3 km (2 mi) up the road from Farellones, La Parva is a colorful conglomeration of private homes set along a handful of mountain roads. At the resort itself there are 14 ski runs, most for intermediate skiers. La Parva is positioned perfectly to give you a stunning view of Santiago, especially at night. ⊠ *Office in Santiago: Av. El Bosque Norte 0177, 2nd floor, Las Condes* ☎ 2/339–8482 ⊕ www.laparva.cl ⊠ 25,000 pesos ⊗ June–Sept.

WHERE TO STAY

$$$$ 🏨 **Condominio Nuevo Parva.** The best place to stay in La Parva is this complex of spacious, modern apartments that sleep between six and eight people. Linens are provided, but maid service is extra. You can rent only by the week, so plan for a lot of skiing. Valle Nevado and the other ski areas are a short drive away. ⊠ *Nueva La Parva 77* ☎ 2/339–8490 ⊕ www.laparva.cl 🛏 38 apartments ⚙ In-room: kitchen. In-hotel: pool, no elevator ☱ AE, DC, MC, V ⊗ Closed Oct.–May.

VALLE NEVADO

Valle Nevado, just 13 km (8 mi) beyond La Parva, is Chile's largest ski region—a luxury resort area with 12 ski lifts that take you up to 40 runs. There are a few slopes for beginners, but Valle Nevado is intended for skiers who like a challenge. Two of the extremely difficult runs from the top of Cerro Tres Puntas are labeled "Shake" and "Twist." If that doesn't intimidate you then you might be ready for some heliskiing. The helicopter whisks you to otherwise inaccessible peaks where you can ride a vertical drop of up to 2,500 meters (8,200 feet).

A ski school at Valle Nevado gives pointers to everyone from beginners to experts. As most of the visitors here are European, the majority of the instructors are from Europe. Equipment rental runs about 25,000 pesos a day. ☎ 2/477–7000 ⊕ www.vallenevado.com ⊠ 22,500 pesos ⊗ Mid-June–Sept.

WHERE TO STAY

Three hotels dominate Valle Nevado; staying at one gives you access to the facilities at the other two. The larger two—Puerta del Sol and

Valle Nevado—are part of the same complex. The three hotels share restaurants, which serve almost every type of cuisine. Rates include lift tickets, ski equipment, breakfast, and dinner. Peak season is July and August; prices drop sharply in June or September when there are plenty of cheap offers.

$$$$ ☷ **Puerta del Sol.** The largest of the Valle Nevado hotels, Puerta del Sol can be identified by its signature sloped roof. Rooms here are larger than those at Tres Puntas, but still rather small. One good option are the "altillo rooms," which have a loft bed that gives you more space. North-facing rooms cost more but have unobstructed views of the slopes. Since all three hotels share facilities, Puerta del Sol is your best value. ✉ *Valle Nevado* ☎ *2/477–7000, 800/669–0554 toll-free in U.S.* 📠 *2/477–7734* ⊕ *www.vallenevado.com* ⇨ *124 rooms* ⚿ *In-room: safe, refrigerator. In-hotel: 2 restaurants, room service, public Wi-Fi, laundry service* ☰ *AE, DC, MC, V* ⊙ *Closed Oct.–May* ⊺○*|MAP.*

$$$$ ☷ **Tres Puntas.** It bills itself as a hotel for young people, and Tres Puntas may indeed remind you of a college dormitory. The closet-size rooms come with either bunk beds or two single beds and maybe a night table. And the tiny wooden balconies are just big enough for two people. In short, these rooms are for people who intend to be on the slopes all day. Inside is a pub and a lively restaurant with karaoke. ✉ *Valle Nevado* ☎ *2/477–7000, 800/669–0554 toll-free in U.S.* 📠 *2/477–7734* ⊕ *www.vallenevado.com* ⇨ *89 rooms* ⚿ *In-room: safe, refrigerator. In-hotel: restaurant, bar, laundry service* ☰ *AE, DC, MC, V* ⊙ *Closed Oct.–May* ⊺○*|MAP.*

$$$$ ☷ **Valle Nevado.** Valle Nevado's most extravagantly priced lodge provides ski-in ski-out convenience. Rooms here are larger than at the other two hotels, and all have balconies. Off season, it's possible to trek by horse or on foot from here to the foot of El Plomo, which is more than 5,000 meters (16,400 feet) high. ✉ *Valle Nevado* ☎ *2/477–7000, 800/669–0554 toll-free in U.S.* 📠 *2/477–7734* ⊕ *www.vallenevado. com* ⇨ *53 rooms* ⚿ *In-room: safe, refrigerator, Wi-Fi. In-hotel: restaurant, room service, bar, pool, gym, laundry service* ☰ *AE, DC, MC, V* ⊺○*|MAP.*

PORTILLO

This ski area north of Santiago is renowned for its slopes, where numerous world speed records have been recorded. It also has the best views of any of the area's ski resorts. The slopes here were discovered by engineers building the now-defunct railroad that linked Chile to Argentina. After the railroad was inaugurated in 1910, skiing aficionados headed here despite the fact that there were no facilities available. Hotel Portillo, the only accommodation in the area, opened its doors in 1949, making Portillo the country's first ski resort, and went on to host the World Ski Championships in 1966.

The facilities at the hotel are reserved for hotel guests, but you can dine in the *auto-servicio* (cafeteria-style) restaurant if you're here for the day. ☎ *2/263–0606* ⊕ *www.skiportillo.com* ⇦ *24,500 pesos* ⊙ *Mid-June–mid-Oct.*

WHERE TO STAY

$$$$ ☷**Hotel Portillo.** Staying here feels a bit like going off to camp: every Saturday a new group settles in for a week's worth of outdoor activities. Besides skiing there's skating on the Laguna del Inca and even swimming in the heated outdoor pool. Big windows in the guest rooms showcase mountain views or the more prized view of the lake. Family-style apartments come with bunk beds for children. The hotel also has two lodges nearby offering cheaper accommodation. ✉ *Los Andes* ☎*2/361–7000 hotel, 2/263–0606 office in Santiago, 800/829–5325 toll-free in U.S.* 🖷*2/361–7080* ⊕*www.skiportillo.com* ⬦*120 rooms, 5 suites, 15 apartments* ⎙*In-room: safe, refrigerator, Wi-Fi. In-hotel: 4 restaurants, bar, pool, gym, laundry service* ▤*AE, DC, MC, V* ⭘*AI.*

SANTIAGO ESSENTIALS

TRANSPORTATION

BY AIR

Santiago's Comodoro Arturo Merino Benítez International Airport, often referred to simply as Pudahuel, is about a 30-minute drive west of the city.

Among the U.S. carriers, American serves Santiago from Dallas and Miami, and Delta connects from Atlanta. LAN flies nonstop to Santiago from both Miami and Los Angeles and with a layover in Lima from New York. Air Canada has direct flights from Toronto while Air France-KLM flies nonstop from Paris and Iberia has nonstop flights from Madrid.

Most of the major Central and South American airlines also fly to Santiago, including Aerolíneas Argentinas, Aeroméxico, Avianca, Copa, Gol, Taca, Tam, and Varig.

LAN has daily flights from Santiago to most cities throughout Chile. Aircomet Chile and Sky also fly to most large cities within Chile.

Airport Comodoro Arturo Merino Benítez International Airport (☎*2/690–1900* ⊕*www.aeropuertosantiago.cl*).

Carriers Aerolíneas Argentinas (☎*2/210–9300*). **Aircomet Chile** (☎*600/625–0000*). **American Airlines** (☎*2/679–0000*). **Avianca** (☎*2/270–6613*). **Copa** (☎*2/200–2100*). **Delta Airlines** (☎*800/202–020*). **LAN** (☎*600/565–2000*). **Sky** (☎*600/600–2828*). **Taca** (☎*800/461–133*).

AIRPORT TRANSFERS

Taxis from Santiago to the airport run on the meter plus a small extra charge for tolls and should come out at around 15,000 pesos. To take a taxi from the airport to the city, use Taxiofficial, the official service, or one of the handful of regulated companies that have desks just outside the exit from customs. They all charge the same price of around 16,000 pesos for a trip downtown.

CentroPuerto, which runs buses every 10 minutes between the airport and Terminal Los Héroes, charges about 1,300 pesos. Tur-Bus has service between the airport and its own terminal near Los Héroes Metro station; it departs every half hour and costs 1,500 pesos. The buses stop en route at the Pajaritos Metro station. Many locals prefer to get off there and take the subway to avoid the downtown traffic.

Transvip and Tur Transfer operate minibus service between the airport and various locations in the city. The cost is about 3,800 pesos.

Note that there is no Metro service to the airport.

Contacts CentroPuerto (☎ 2/601–9883). **Taxiofficial** (☎ 2/690–1381). **Transvip** (☎ 2/677–3000). **Tur-Bus** (☎ 2/601–9573). **Tur Transfer** (☎ 2/677–3600).

BY BUS
TO & FROM SANTIAGO

All the country's major highways pass through Santiago, which means you won't have a problem catching a bus to almost any destination. Finding that bus, however, can be a problem. The city has four main terminals, each with buses heading in different directions. Terminal Los Héroes is on the edge of Santiago Centro near Los Héroes Metro station. Several companies have buses to points north and south from this station. The other three stations are clustered around the Universidad de Santiago Metro station. The modern Terminal San Borja (also known as Terminal Norte) has buses headed north and west. Terminal Santiago is the busiest, with dozens of small companies going west to the coast and to the south. Terminal Alameda, which handles only Tur-Bus and Pullman Bus, is for coastal and southern traffic. Terminal Los Héroes and Terminal Santiago also handle a few international routes, heading to far-flung destinations such as Buenos Aires, Rio de Janeiro, and Lima.

Several bus companies run regularly scheduled service to the Andes in winter. Skitotal buses depart from the office on Avenida Apoquindo and head to all of the ski resorts. Buses depart at 8:45 am; a round-trip ticket costs 10,000 pesos. Also available for hire here are taxis—(65,000 pesos) and 12-person minibuses (90,000 pesos). Manzur Expediciones runs minibuses to Portillo on Saturday and Sunday for 15,000. Buses leave at 7:15 am from the Plaza Baquedano in front of the Teatro Universidad de Chile. Prior booking is essential.

Manzur also offers a round-trip ticket to Lo Valdés Mountain Center in Cajón del Maipo and the Baños de Colina hot springs. Buses, which run daily in summer, but only Saturday and Sunday the rest of the year, leave at 7:30 am from the Plaza Baquedano in front of the Teatro Universidad de Chile. The round trip to Lo Valdés costs 8,000 pesos; prior booking is essential. Sit on the right side of the bus for a good view of the river.

Bus Companies Manzur Expediciones (⊠ *Sótero del Río 475, Santiago Centro* ☎ 2/777–4284). **Pullman Bus** (⊠ *Terminal Alameda, Estación Central* ☎ 2/779–2106). **Skitotal** (⊠ *Av. Apoquindo 4900, Las Condes* ☎ 2/246–6881). **Tur-Bus** (⊠ *Terminal Alameda, Estación Central* ☎ 2/270–7500).

Bus Depots Terminal Alameda (✉ *La Alameda 3750, Estación Central* ☎ *2/270–7500*). **Terminal Los Héroes** (✉ *Tucapel Jiménez 21, Estación Central* ☎ *2/420–0099*). **Terminal San Borja** (✉ *San Borja 184, Estación Central* ☎ *2/776–0645*). **Terminal Santiago** (✉ *La Alameda 3848, La Alameda* ☎ *2/376–1755*).

WITHIN SANTIAGO

Don't mention the word *Transantiago* to Santiaguinos unless you have plenty of time to listen to a litany of complaints. The new bus system—a mixture of trunk routes on main arteries served by long articulated buses and shorter "feeder" routes connecting individual neighborhoods to these arteries and the Metro subway—was billed to bring modernity and efficiency to the old, anarchic system. Instead, its introduction in February 2007 plunged the city into a chaos from which it has only gradually and partially recovered, and Santiaguinos still resent the change inflicted upon them.

The best advice is to avoid the city's buses (called *micros*), if possible, during the morning and evening rush hours. The queues will tell you all you need to know. During the rest of the day, it is actually quite a sensible form of transport. The bus map, available at Metro stations, is difficult to understand and not altogether accurate, but bus stops and the buses themselves are fairly clearly labeled.

To use the buses, you must have a pre-paid smart card (known as *Bip!*) since no cash is accepted. This can be acquired at Metro stations. The standard fare is 380 pesos and allows you to combine different buses to reach your destination during a two-hour period.

BY CAR

You don't need a car if you're not going to venture outside the city limits, as most of the downtown sights are within walking distance of each other. To get to other neighborhoods, taxis are inexpensive and the subway system is safe and efficient. After you dodge a line of cars speeding through a red light or see the traffic snarls during rush hour, you may be glad you don't have to drive in the city.

A car is the best way to see the surrounding countryside, however, and the highways around Santiago are excellent. Between May and August, rain can cause roads in low-lying areas to flood. If you're headed north or south, you'll probably use the Pan-American Highway, also called Ruta 5. To reach Valparaíso, Viña del Mar, or the northernmost beach resorts on the Central Coast, take Highway 68; for the southern beaches, take Ruta 78.

It can take up to two hours to reach the region's three major ski resorts, which lie 48–56 km (30–35 mi) from Santiago. The road is narrow, winding, and full of Chileans racing to get to the top. If you decide to drive, make sure you have either a four-wheel-drive vehicle or snow chains, which you can rent along the way. The chains are installed for about 8,000 pesos. Don't think you need them? There's a police checkpoint just before the road starts to climb into the Andes, and if the weather is rough they'll make you turn back. To reach Valle Nevado, Farellones, and La Parva, take Avenida Kennedy or Avenida

Las Condes east. Signs direct you once you get into the mountains. Portillo is three hours north of Santiago. Call the hotel there ahead of time to find out about road conditions.

To reach Cajón del Maipo, head south on Avenida José Alessandri until you reach the Rotonda Departamental, a large traffic circle. There you take Camino Las Vizcachas, following it south into the valley.

CAR RENTALS

Renting a car is convenient in Santiago, as most companies have offices at the airport and downtown. The international agencies generally rent compact cars with unlimited mileage and insurance coverage for about 40,000 pesos a day. They can provide ski-equipped vehicles for climbs to the Andes. Reputable local agencies include Bengolea, Chilean, and Rosselot, whose rates can be as low as 20,000 pesos a day.

Agencies Alamo (⊠ *Airport* ☎ *2/690–1370* ⊠ *Av. Francisco Bilbao 2846, Providencia* ☎ *2/225–4117*). **Avis** (☎ *2/690–1382* ⊠ *Airport* ☎ *2/795–3990* ⊠ *Hotel Radisson, Av. Vitacura 2610, Las Condes* ☎ *2/596–8760*). **Bengolea** (⊠ *Av. Francisco Bilbao 1047, Providencia* ☎ *2/204–9021*). **Budget** (⊠ *Airport* ☎ *2/690–1386* ⊠ *Av. Francisco Bilbao 1439, Providencia* ☎ *2/362–3205*). **Chilean** (⊠ *Bellavista 0183, Bellavista* ☎ *2/737–9650*). **Hertz** (⊠ *Airport* ☎ *2/601–0477* ⊠ *Av. Andrés Bello 1469, Providencia* ☎ *2/496–1000*). **Rosselot** (⊠ *Airport* ☎ *2/690–1317* ⊠ *Av. Francisco Bilbao 2045, Providencia* ☎ *2/381–2200*).

BY SUBWAY

Santiago's subway system is the best way to get around town. The Metro is inexpensive and safe, although it gets very crowded at peak hours. The system operates Monday–Saturday 6 am–11 pm, Saturday 6:30 am–10:30 pm, and Sunday 8 am–10:30 pm. Línea 1 runs east–west along the axis of the Río Mapocho. This is the most popular line, and perhaps the most useful, because it runs past most of the heavily touristed areas. Línea 5 runs north–south except at its northern tip, where it bends to the west to connect with the Bellas Artes, Plaza de Armas, and Quinta Normal stations. Línea 2 also runs north–south; it's rarely used by nonresidents because it heads to residential areas. This is also the case of Línea 4, which runs from Tobalaba south and west to Puente Alto and La Cisterna.

Every station has an easy-to-read map of all the stations and the adjoining streets. Buy tickets in any station at the glass booths or at the nearby machines. You'll see locals using a prepaid smart card, known as *Bip!*—because of the noise the sensor makes—but for a short stay buy individual tickets which cost 380 to 420 pesos, depending on the time of day. Deposit your ticket in the turnstile and pass through; tickets are not returned.

When you wave a *Bip!* card in front of a sensor of the turnstiles, it automatically deducts the fare. You can put any amount over 500 pesos on a card.

Subway Information Metro de Santiago (☎ *600/422-3330* ⊕ *www.metrosantiago.cl*).

BY TAXI

It's easy to flag a taxi down in Santiago except during the morning rush hour or when it's raining. The average ride costs around 2,000 to 3,000 pesos. The driver will turn the taxi meter on when you start your journey; it should read 250 pesos, the minimum charge. Taxi drivers don't always know where they are going and frequently ask directions; it's a good idea to carry a map. Radio-dispatched cabs are slightly more expensive but will pick you up at your door.

Taxi Companies Alborada (☎ *2/246–4900*). **Alto Oriente** (☎ *2/226–2116*). **Andes Pacífico** (☎ *2/225–3064 or 2/204–0104*). **Apoquindo** (☎ *2/211–6073*).

BY TRAIN

Chileans once boasted about the country's excellent rail service, but there's little left today aside from the limited service from Santiago to points south. Santiago's Estación Central, at the Metro station of the same name, is where you catch trains headed to the Central Valley. Note that you can also purchase tickets for the trains at the Estación Metro Universidad de Chile.

Trains run from Santiago through the larger cities of Rancagua, Curicó, Talca, and Chillán.

Contacts Estación Central (✉ *La Alameda 3170, Santiago Centro* ☎ *600/585– 5000* ⊕ *www.efe.cl*). **Estación Metro Universidad de Chile** (✉ *Local 10, La Alameda* ☎ *600/585–5000*).

CONTACTS & RESOURCES

BANKS & EXCHANGE SERVICES

Unlike other South American countries, Chile rarely accepts U.S. dollars. (The exception is larger hotels, where prices are often quoted only in dollars.) Credit cards are accepted everywhere in Santiago's most touristy areas.

You can exchange money in many places in the city. Banks in Santiago are open weekdays 9–2, and *casas de cambio* (currency-exchange offices) are open weekdays 9–7 and Saturday 9–3. They normally cluster together; in Providencia, for example, along Pedro de Valdivia, just before La Costanera, there are three or four and there are also plenty in the center of the city.

Automatic teller machines dispense only Chilean pesos. They are ubiquitous but, although most have instructions in English, not all are linked to the Plus and Cirrus systems. Look at the stickers on the machine to find the one you need. To use an ATM issued by a foreign bank, select the *"extranjeros/foreign clients"* option from the menu.

Banks American Express (✉ *Av. Isidora Goyenechea 3621, Las Condes* ☎ *2/350– 6700*). **Santander Santiago** (✉ *Bandera 140, Santiago Centro* ☎ *600/320–3000* ✉ *Av. Providencia 2667, Providencia* ☎ *600/320–3000* ✉ *Av. Apoquindo 3575, Las Condes* ☎ *600/320–3000*).

2

EMERGENCIES

Santiago has three main pharmacy chains, Ahumada, Cruz Verde, and Salcobrand, which all have branches in every part of the city. Few are open 24 hours, but many are open until midnight. There's a good one downtown near the Plaza de Armas at Paseo Ahumada and Huérfanos.

Emergency Numbers Ambulance (☎*131*). **Fire** (☎*132*). **Police** (☎*133*).

Hospitals Clínica Alemana (⊠*Av. Vitacura 5951, Las Condes* ☎*2/210–1334*). **Clínica Las Condes** (⊠*Lo Fontecilla 441, Las Condes* ☎*2/210–4000*). **Clínica Santa María** (⊠*Av. Santa María 0500, Providencia* ☎*2/461–2000*).

Late-Night Pharmacy Farmacias Ahumada (⊠*Ahumada 301, at Huérfanos, Santiago Centro* ☎*2/631–3003*).

ENGLISH-LANGUAGE MEDIA

The Instituto Chileno-Norteamericano de Cultura has a selection of books in English, as well as English-language periodicals. Librería Inglesa sells new books, but the prices are high. For popular newspapers and magazines in English, check the kiosks on the pedestrian mall of Paseo Ahumada in Santiago Centro or the kiosk on the top floor of the Parque Arauco Mall (Avenida Kennedy 5413) in Las Condes.

Bookstores Instituto Chileno-Norteamericano de Cultura (⊠*Moneda 1467, Santiago Centro* ☎*800/200–863*). **Librería Inglesa** (⊠*Av. Pedro de Valdivia 47, Providencia* ☎*2/231–6270* ⊠*Av. Vitacura 5950, Vitacura* ☎*2/219–3080*⊠*Huérfanos 669, Local 11, Santiago Centro* ☎*2/638–7118*).

INTERNET, MAIL & SHIPPING

In Santiago there are plenty of Internet cafés; you're likely to find several around your hotel. Most larger hotels provide business services, but these can be expensive. Santiago also has plenty of free Wi-Fi hotspots. Look, for example, for the signposted areas in some of the main Metro stations.

Correo Central—Santiago's main post office—is housed in the ornate Palacio de los Gobernadores, in Santiago Centro on the north side of the Plaza de Armas. It is open weekdays 8–7, Saturday 9–2. There is a second downtown branch near the Palacio de la Moneda, as well as one in Providencia near the Manuel Montt Metro stop and one in Las Condes at El Golf stop.

For overnight delivery, DHL and Federal Express have offices in different parts of the city.

Internet Cafés Comunicaciones S.A.F. (⊠*Apoquindo 4572, Las Condes* ☎*2/206–6378*). **Cyber & Market** (⊠*Almirante Pastene 62, Providencia* ☎*2/236–8743*). **Isinet** (⊠*Calle Londrés 30, La Alameda* ☎*2/632–9155*). **Uribe-Larry** (⊠*Merced 618, Parque Forestal* ☎*2/663–1990*).

Post Office Correo Central (⊠*Catedral at Paseo Ahumada, Santiago Centro* ☎*2/956–5153* ⊕*www.correos.cl*).

Shipping Services DHL (⊠*San Francisco 301, Santiago Centro* ☎*2/280–2000* ⊠*Bandera 204, Santiago Centro* ☎*2/697–1081*⊠*Av. 11 de Septiembre*

2070, Providencia ☎ *2/234–1516).***Federal Express** (✉ *Fray Camilo Henríquez 190, Santiago Centro* ☎ *800/363–030* ✉ *Av. Providencia 1951, Providencia* ☎ *800/363–030).*

TOURS

Sernatur *(⇨ Visitor Information)*, the national tourism agency, maintains a listing of experienced individual tour guides who will take you on a half-day tour of Santiago and the surrounding area for about 25,000 pesos. These tours are a great way to get your bearings when you have just arrived in the city. They can also greatly enrich your visit. In museums, for example, they often provide information not generally available to the public and are especially helpful in museums with little or no signage in English.

Altué Active Travel arranges adventure trips such as white-water rafting on nearby rivers and hiking to the mouths of volcanoes. Chilean Travel Services and Sportstour handle tours of both Santiago and other parts of Chile. Chip Travel has several interest tours available, including a "human rights legacy" tour of sites that are reminders of dictator Augusto Pinochet's 17-year regime.

With more than a dozen locations, Turismo Cocha, founded in 1951, is one of the city's biggest private tour operators. It arranges tours of the wineries of the Cajón del Maipo and the beach resorts of Valparaíso and Viña del Mar, in addition to the usual city tours. It also has offices in the domestic and international terminals of the airport as well as in some of the larger hotels.

Tour Operators Altué Active Travel (✉ *General Salvo 159, Providencia* ☎ *2/235–1519* 📠 *2/235-3085* ⊕ *www.altue.com).* **Chilean Travel Services** (✉ *Antonio Bellet 77, Office 202, Providencia* ☎ *2/251-0400* 📠 *2/251-0423* ⊕ *www.cts turismo.cl).* **Chip Travel** (✉ *Av. Santa Maria 227, Office 12, Bellavista* ☎ *2/735-9044* 📠 *2/735-2267* ⊕ *www.chipsites.com).* **Sportstour** (✉ *Av. El Bosque Norte 500, 15th fl., Las Condes* ☎ *2/549-5260* 📠 *2/549-5290* ⊕ *www.sportstour.cl).* **Turismo Cocha** (✉ *Av. El Bosque Norte 0430, Las Condes* ☎ *2/464-1000* 📠 *2/464-1025* ✉ *Pedro de Valdivia 0169, Providencia* ☎ *2/464-1600* 📠 *2/464-1699* ✉ *Agustinas 1039, Santiago Centro* ☎ *2/464-1970* 📠 *464-1960* ⊕ *www.cocha.com).*

VISITOR INFORMATION

Sernatur, the national tourist service, stocks maps and brochures. The Providencia office, in a building with saffron-color columns, is near the Manuel Montt Metro stop. It is open weekdays 8:45–6 and Saturday 9–2. It also has an information desk in the arrivals hall of Santiago's Comodoro Arturo Merino Benítez International Airport, open daily 9–8.

Sernatur Providencia (✉ *Av. Providencia 1550, Providencia* ☎ *2/731-8310* ⊕ *www.sernatur.cl).*

The Central Coast

The Pontificia Universidad Catolica de Valparaiso

WORD OF MOUTH

"I agree that the Santiago/Valparaiso combo is a good one for your one week trip. As for staying in Vina or Valpo, yes they are right next to each other, but Vina would probably be the better choice as it is more of a beach town, where Valpo is more of an industrial city. Both are worth visiting, but Vina should make a better base."

—msteacher

WELCOME TO
THE CENTRAL COAST

TOP REASONS
TO GO

★ **Riding the Ascensores:** Valparaíso's steep hills are smoothed out a bit by the *ascensores*, or funiculars, that shuttle locals between their jobs near the port and their homes in the hills.

★ **Beautiful Beaches:** Thousands of Santiaguinos flock to the Central Coast's beaches every summer, where dozens and dozens of seafood shacks serve the masses.

★ **Superb Shopping:** The streets of Cerro Alegro and Cerro Concepción in Valparaíso are lined with shops selling everything from finely wrought jewelry to hand-tooled leather, while Viña has everything from large department stores and outlet malls to trendy shops and boutiques.

★ **Seafood straight from the net:** Almost every town on the Central Coast has its own wharf where fishermen land with last night's catch. Bustling with shoppers, the caleta offers an excellent biology lesson on the diversity of sealife in addition to, of course, many a gastronomic treat.

1 Valparaíso & Viña del Mar. The twin cities of Chile's Central Coast could not be more different. The winding streets of Valparaíso, a once great port that considers San Francisco a distant cousin, are filled with historic monuments to 19th-century glory. Thanks to a tourism boom and UNESCO's recent naming of the city as a World Heritage Site, a cultural renaissance is underway here. Meanwhile, neighboring Viña del Mar has the country's largest casino, some of Chile's most elegant hotels, and a sharp nightlife scene that make it an excellent place to blow off some steam.

2 The Southern Beaches. Isla Negra, the oceanside retreat of Pablo Neruda, South America's most famous poet, is the main attraction south of Valparaíso. Along the way, don't miss the relaxed charms of Algarrobo or Quintay, a forgotten former whaling station.

3 The Northern Beaches. The beaches north of Viña have something for every type of traveler, from the beautiful young crowd at Reñaca and the summer bustle of Concón to easygoing Maintencillo and stunning Zapallar, the exclusive seaside resort for Santiago's rich and powerful.

GETTING ORIENTED

3

The Central Coast lies two hours west of Santiago, across the Coastal mountains. Dominated by the overlapping cities of Valparaíso and Viña del Mar, this is where stressed *santiaguinos* come to sunbathe, party, and gorge on seafood every moment they can. In the summer, even the smallest resort can heave with visitors but outside of January and February, they can be very quiet.

Museo Francisco Fonck, Viña Del Mar

THE CENTRAL COAST PLANNER

When to Go

It seems that all of Chile heads to the coast in the summer months of January and February. This can be a great time to visit, with the weather at its warmest, and the nightlife hopping. But it's also a tough time to find a room, especially on weekends. Make reservations as far in advance as possible. Spring (September, October, and November) and fall (March, April and May) can be great times to visit, when the days are warm and breezy, and the nights cool. Consider visiting during the shoulder months of December and March, which have good weather, but also provide relative solitude in which to explore.

Festivals & Seasonal Events

The annual Festival Internacional de la Canción (International Song Festival) takes place during a week in mid-February in Viña del Mar. The concerts are broadcast live on television. Most towns have colorful processions on the Día de San Pedro on June 29. A statue of St. Peter, patron saint of fisherfolk, is typically hoisted onto a fishing boat and led along a coastal procession.

Eat Well & Rest Easy

Dining is one of the great pleasures of visiting the Central Coast. It's not rare to see fishermen bringing the day's catch straight to the restaurants that inevitably line the shore. Your server will be happy to share with you which fish were caught fresh that day. Try *corvina a la margarita* (sea-bass in shellfish sauce) or *ostiones a la parmesana* (clams served with melted Parmesan cheese). The more daring can also try a batch of raw shellfish bought direct from the fishermen and served with a dash of lemon. With the exception of major holidays, reservations are almost never required for restaurants here. Most restaurants close between lunch and dinner: from 3 or 4 to 7 or 8.

Because the central beach resorts were developed by and for the Santiago families who summer here, they are dominated by vacation homes and apartments, although new, often upmarket, hotels have been built especially around Valparaíso, Viña del Mar, Reñaca, and Concón. Cabañas, somewhat rustic cabins with a kitchenette and one or more bedrooms, are designed to accommodate families on tighter budgets. An even more affordable option is a *residencial* (guesthouse), often just a few rooms for rent in a private home.

WHAT IT COSTS IN CHILEAN PESOS (IN THOUSANDS)				
¢	$	$$	$$$	$$$$
RESTAURANTS				
under 3 pesos	3 pesos– 5 pesos	5 pesos– 8 pesos	8 pesos– 11 pesos	over 11 pesos
HOTELS				
under 15 pesos	15 pesos– 45 pesos	45 pesos– 75 pesos	75 pesos– 105 pesos	over 105 pesos

Restaurant prices are based on the median main course price at dinner. Hotel prices are for a standard double room in high season, excluding tax.

Beaches

To the vast majority of Chileans, summer holiday means one thing: heading to the beach. Whether on the banks of a southern lake, one of the north's deserted coves, or one of the pleasant towns of the central coast, from late December to early March, the beaches are packed. Even where the water is safe enough to enter, the icy Humboldt Current, rushing up from Antarctica, means only the young and the brave can bear more than a few seconds up to their chests.

There is little reason to move. Wandering salesmen constantly wander by, plying ice creams, drinks, and other goodies. And watch out for the promotoras, scantily clad young women promoting everything from batteries to beer.

Where permitted, Chileans will set up a *parrilla* for one of their famous *asados*, grilling meat and sausages over a charcoal fire. The athletic may rouse themselves for a game of *paleta*, batting a tennis ball back and forth with a small wooden racket. If you want to escape the crowds, try walk along to the next beach, which may be surprisingly empty though just a few hundred meters away. The southern end of Maitencillo or the north of Papudo are particularly suitable for exploration.

Strong sun protection in Chile is essential, due to the nearby hole in the ozone layer. Even if the day begins in a fog, the mist quickly burns off, leaving you vulnerable to the sun's rays. Be sure to pack a hat, strong sunblock, and something to cover you up. You might even consider a beach umbrella, often available to rent right on the beach. Once the sun goes down, temperatures can fall quickly as sea breezes pick up, so bring a light jacket or sweater as well.

Sample Itinerary

Plan to spend at least two days in **Valparaíso,** where you can ride a few funiculars and explore the cobbled streets. While you're here, a good day trip is an excursion to Pablo Neruda's waterfront home nearby in **Isla Negra.** You'll want to take a day or so to stroll around the bustling beach town of **Viña del Mar.** After that you can drive north along the coastal highway, stopping for lunch in either **Concón** or **Maitencillo.** From there you can return to Viña del Mar or continue on to spend a night in **Zapallar.**

Getting Here & Around

Air Travel. The Central Coast is served by Lan Airlines via Santiago's Aeropuerto Comodoro Arturo Merino Benítez, an hour and a half flight from either Viña del Mar or Valparaíso.

Bus Travel. There is hourly bus service (3,700 pesos, two hours on the road) between Santiago and both Valparaíso and Viña del Mar. Tur-Bus and other companies leave from Santiago's Terminal Alameda. Smaller companies serving the other beach resorts depart from Santiago's Terminal Santiago.

Car Travel. Since it's so easy to get around in Valparaíso and Viña del Mar, there's no need to rent a car unless you want to travel to other towns on the coast.

Train Travel. The bright, spacious Merval commuter train links Valparaíso with Viña del Mar. It runs every 12 minutes from 6:30 AM to 10.30 PM.

Money Matters

All but the smallest Central Coast towns have at least one ATM, and both Valparaíso and Viña del Mar have dozens of them. ATMs at well-distributed Banco de Chile branches also give cash advances on international credit cards. Most restaurants and hotels accept major credit cards.

Updated
by Tom
Azzopardi

MOST PEOPLE HEAD TO THE CENTRAL COAST for a single reason: the beaches. Yes, some may be drawn by the rough grandeur of the wind-swept coastline, with its rocky islets inhabited by sea lions and penguins, but those in search of nature generally head south to Chiloé and Patagonia or north to the Atacama Desert. Yet this stretch of coastline west of Santiago has much more than sun and surf.

The biggest surprise is the charm of Valparaíso, Chile's second-largest city—known locally as Valpo. Valparaíso shares a bay with Viña del Mar but the similarities end there. Valparaíso is a bustling port town with a jumble of colorful cottages nestled in the folds of its many hills. Viña del Mar has lush parks surrounding neoclassical mansions and a long beach lined with luxury high-rises. Together they form an interesting contrast of working class and wealth at play.

The *balnearios* (small beach towns) to the north of the twin cities have their own character, often defined by coastal topography. Proximity to Santiago has resulted in the development—in some cases overdevelopment—of most of them as summer resorts. At the beginning of the 20th century, Santiago's elite started building vacation homes. Soon after, when trains connected the capital to beaches, middle-class families started spending their summers at the shore. Improved highway access in recent decades has allowed Chileans of all economic levels to enjoy the occasional beach vacation. Late December–mid-March, when schools let out for summer vacation and Santiago becomes torrid, the beaches are packed. Vacationers frolic in the chilly sea by day, and pack the restaurants and bars at night. The rest of the year, the coast is relatively deserted and, though often cool and cloudy, a pleasantly tranquil place to explore. Local *caletas*—literally meaning "coves," where fishing boats gather to unload their catch, usually the site of local fishing cooperatives—are always colorful and lively.

VALPARAÍSO & VIÑA DEL MAR

Viña del Mar and Valparaíso (Vineyard of the Sea and Paradise Valley, respectively) each maintain an aura that warrants their dreamy appellations. Only minutes apart, these two urban centers are nevertheless as different as twin cities can be. Valparaíso won the heart of poet Pablo Neruda, who praised its "cluster of crazy houses," and it continues to be a disorderly, bohemian, charming town. Valparaíso's lack of beaches keeps its mind on matters more urban, if not urbane.

Viña del Mar, Valparaíso's glamorous sibling, is a clean, orderly city with miles of beige beach, a glitzy casino, manicured parks, and shopping galore. Viña, together with nearby Reñaca, is synonymous with the best of life for vacationing Chileans. Its beaches gleam, its casino rolls, and its discos sizzle.

VALPARAÍSO

10 km (6 mi) south of Viña del Mar via Avenida España, 120 km (75 mi) west of Santiago via Ruta 68.

Valparaíso's dramatic topography—45 *cerros,* or hills, overlooking the ocean—requires the use of winding pathways and wooden *ascensores* (funiculars) to get up many of the grades. The slopes are covered by candy-color houses—there are almost no apartments in the city—most of which have exteriors of corrugated metal peeled from shipping containers decades ago. Valparaíso has served as Santiago's port for centuries. Before the Panama Canal opened, Valparaíso was the busiest port in South America. Harsh realities—changing trade routes, industrial decline—have diminished its importance, but it remains Chile's principal port.

Most shops, banks, restaurants, bars, and other businesses cluster along the handful of streets called *El Plan* (the flat area) that are closest to the shoreline. *Porteños* (which means "the residents of the port") live in the surrounding hills in an undulating array of colorful abodes. At the top of any of the dozens of stairways, the *paseos* (promenades) have spectacular views; many are named after prominent Yugoslavian, Basque, and German immigrants. Neighborhoods are named for the hills they cover.

With the jumble of power lines overhead and the hundreds of buses that slow down—but never completely stop—to pick up agile riders, it's hard to forget you're in a city. Still, walking is the best way to experience Valparaíso. Be a careful where you step, though—locals aren't very conscientious about curbing their dogs.

GETTING HERE & AROUND

By car from Santiago, take Ruta 68 west through the coastal mountains and the Casablanca valley, as far as you can go, until the road descends into Valparaíso's Avenida Argentina, on the city's eastern edge. If you don't have a car, Tur-Bus, Pullman and Condor buses leave several times an hour for Valparaíso and Viña del Mar from Santiago. Tur-Bus and Pullman both leave from Terminal Alameda (Metro *Universidad de Santiago*) while Condor and Sol del Pacifico use Terminal Santaigo (Metro *Estación Central*) or alternatively you can save yourself a crawl through Santiago by catching a bus from Metro Pajaritos on the city's western edge. If you're using Valparaíso as your hub, you can use Pullman Bus to get to most coastal towns south of the city. Tur-Bus heads north to Cachagua, Zapallar, Papudo, and other towns. Sol del Pacifico also runs buses to the northern beaches. Valparaíso has two information booths: one at Muelle Prat that is supposedly open daily 10–2 and 3–6 (although in real life the hours vary wildly).

TIMING & PRECAUTIONS

Your need a good pair of shoes to fully appreciate Valparaíso. Walking past all the sights, exploring the museums, and enjoying a meal and drinks makes for a long, full day. You might visit La Sebastiana the next morning to give yourself more time to linger. Definitely bring sunblock

Valparaíso

Bahía de Valparaíso

Antonio Varas

**Ascensor
Artillería**

Plaza
Advana

Artillería

Av. Carampangue

Márquez

Victoria

San Martín

Clave

Cobo

Av. Errázuriz

Serrano

**Ascensor
El Peral**

Av. Tomás Ramos

Castillo

Estación
Puerto

Blanco
Cochrane

Prat

**Ascensor
Concepción**

Esmeralda

Papudo

Concepción

Urriola

Templeman

Av. Pedro Montt

Monte Alegre

Morrison

Munich
Hospital

**Estación
Bellavista**

Magarena

Bellavista

Puerto

O'Higgins

Av. Brasil

Salvador

Condell

Cumming

*Cementerio
Católico*

*Cementerio
de Disidentes*

Cumming

Av. Ecuador

*Plaza
Bismarck*

KEY

i *Tourist Information*

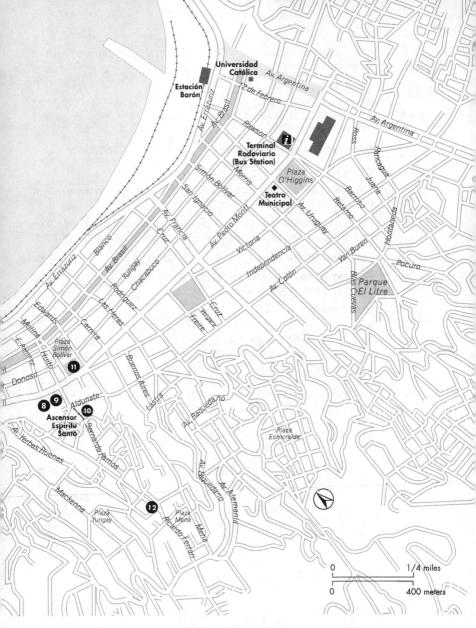

Estación
Barón

Universidad
Católica

Av. Argentina

12 de Febrero

Av. Errázuriz

Brasil

Rawson

Terminal
Rodoviario
(Bus Station)

Morris

Simón Bolívar

San Ignacio

Plaza
O'Higgins

Teatro
Municipal

Av. Uruguay

Av. Argentina

Ross

Rancagua

Juana

Av. Pedro Montt

Victoria

Independencia

Av. Colón

Retamo

Barroso

Van Buren

Hontaneda

Pocuro

Parque
El Litre

Blas Cuevas

Av. Francia

Cruz

Av. Errázuriz

Blanco

Av. Brasil

Yungay

Chacabuco

Rodríguez

Las Heras

Carrera

Edwards

Molina

E. Ramírez

Hurto

Plaza
Simón
Bolívar

11

Donoso

8 **9**

Aldunate

10

Ascensor
Espíritu
Santo

Av. Yerbas Buenas

Bernardo Ramos

Buenos Aires

Lastra

Cruz
Vergara

Freire

Av. Baquedano

Plaza
Esmeralda

Mackenna

Plaza
Yungay

12

Plaza
Mena

Plaza
Ricardo Ferrari

Av. Baquedano

Av. Alemania

Mena

0   1/4 miles

0   400 meters

or a hat. Even if it's cloudy when you start, the sun often comes out by afternoon.

ESSENTIALS

Bus Contacts Pullman Bus (☎ *32/221-6663*). **Sol del Pacífico** (☎ *32/221-3776*). **Tur-Bus** (☎ *32/221-2028*). **Valparaíso Bus Depot** (✉ *Av. Pedro Montt 2800* ☎ *32/223-7209*).

Currency Exchange Banco de Chile (✉ *Cochrane 785* ☎ *32/356-500*).

Internet World Next Door (✉ *Blanco 692* ☎ *32/222-7148*).

Mail & Shipping DHL (✉ *Plaza Sotomayor 95* ☎ *32/221-3654*). **Valparaíso Post Office** (✉ *Southeast corner of Plaza Sotomayor*).

Medical Assistance Farmacias Ahumada (✉ *Pedro Montt No 1881-1895* ☎ *32/221-5524*). **Hospital Carlos Van Buren** San Ignacio 725 (☎ *32/220-4000*).

Rental Cars Rosselot (✉ *Victoria 2675* ☎ *32/352-365*)

Visitor & Tour Info Tourism Office (✉ Condell 1490 ☎ 32/293-9262). **Valparaíso Muelle Prat office** (✉ *Muelle Prat*

EXPLORING

MAIN ATTRACTIONS

❼ Cerro Concepción. Ride the Ascensor Concepción to this hilltop neighborhood covered with houses and cobblestone streets. The greatest attraction is the view, which is best appreciated from Paseo Gervasoni, a wide promenade to the right when you exit the ascensor, and Paseo Atkinson, one block to the east. Over the balustrades that line those paseos lie amazing vistas of the city and bay. Nearly as fascinating are the narrow streets above them, some of which are quite steep. Continue uphill to Cerro Alegre, which has a bit of a bohemian flair. ✉ *Ascensor Concepción, Prat.*

❻ Muelle Prat. Though its name translates as Prat Dock, the muelle is actually a wharf with steps leading to the water. Sailors from the ships in the harbor arrive in *lanchas* (small boats), or board them for the trip back to their vessels. It's a great place to watch the activity at the nearby port, and the ships anchored in the harbor. To get a closer look, you can board one of the lanchas—it costs 1,000 pesos for the trip out to a ship and back, or 20,000 pesos for a 60-minute tour of the bay. Here you'll find the tourist information office and a row of souvenir shops. One of the city's best seafood restaurants, Bote Salvavidas, is a few steps away. ✉ *Av. Errázuriz at Plaza Sotomayor.*

❶❷ La Sebastiana. People come to La Sebastiana to marvel at the same ocean
★ that inspired so much of Pablo Neruda's poetry. The house is named for Sebastián Collado, a Spanish architect who began it as a home for himself but died before it was finished. The incomplete building stood abandoned for 10 years before Neruda finished it, revising the design (Neruda had no need for the third-floor aviary or the helicopter landing pad) and adding curvaceous walls, narrow stairways, a tower, and a polymorphous character.

A maze of twisting stairwells leads to an upper room where a video shows Neruda enunciating the five syllables of the city's name over and again as he rides the city's ascensores. His upper berth contains his desk, books, and some original manuscripts. What makes the visit to La Sebastiana memorable, however, is Neruda's nearly obsessive delight in physical objects. The house is a shrine to his many cherished things, such as the beautiful orange-pink bird he brought back embalmed from Venezuela. His lighter spirit is here also, in the carousel horse and the pink-and-yellow barroom stuffed with kitsch. ⊠*Ferrari 692* ☎*32/225–6606* ⊕*www.neruda.cl* ⊠*2,500 pesos* ☉*Oct.–Feb., Tues.–Sun. 10:30–7; Mar.–Sept., Tues.–Sun. 10:10–6.*

🔟 **Museo a Cielo Abierto.** The Open Sky Museum is a winding walk past 20 official murals (and a handful of unofficial ones) by some of Chile's best painters. There's even one by the country's most famous artist, Roberto Matta. The path is not marked—there's no real fixed route—as the point is to get lost in the city's history and culture. ⊠*Ascensor Espíritu Santo up to Cerro Buenavista.*

② **Museo Naval y Marítimo de Valparaíso.** Atop Cerro Artillería is the large neoclassical mansion that once housed the country's naval academy. It now contains a maritime museum, with displays that document the history of the port and the ships that once defended it. Cannons positioned on the front lawn frame the excellent view of the ocean. ⊠*Ascensor Artillería up to Paseo 21 de Mayo 46* ☎*32/243–7651* ⊠*500 pesos* ☉*Tues.–Sun. 10–5.30.*

① **Paseo 21 de Mayo.** Ascensor Artillería pulls you uphill to Paseo 21 de Mayo, a wide promenade surrounded by well-tended gardens and stately trees from which you can survey the port and a goodly portion of the city through coin-operated binoculars. A gazebo—a good place to escape the sun—seems to be hanging in midair. Paseo 21 de Mayo is in the middle of Cerro Playa Ancha, one of the city's more colorful neighborhoods. ⊠*Ascensor Artillería at Plaza Advana.*

⑤ **Plaza Sotomayor.** Valparaíso's most impressive square, Plaza Sotomayor, serves as a gateway to the bustling port. **Comandancia en Jefe de la Armada,** headquarters of the Chilean navy, is a grand, gray building that rises to a turreted pinnacle over a mansard roof. At the north end of the plaza stands the **Monumento de los Héroes de Iquique,** which honors Arturo Prat and other heroes of the War of the Pacific. In the middle of the square (beware of traffic—cars and buses come suddenly from all directions) is the **Museo del Sitio.** Artifacts from the city's mid-19th-century port, including parts of a dock that once stood on this spot, are displayed in the open under glass. ⊠*Av. Errázuriz at Cochrane.*

IF YOU HAVE TIME

⑨ **Galería Municipal de Arte.** This crypt in the basement of the Palacio Lyon is the finest art space in the city. Temporary exhibits by top-caliber Chilean artists are displayed on stone walls under a series of brick arches. It's easy to miss the entrance, which is on Calle Condell just beyond the Museo de Historia Natural de Valparaíso. ⊠ *Condell 1550* 📞 *32/2939–568* 🎫 *Free* ⊙ *Mon.–Sat. 10–6.30.*

❸ Mercado Central. Before *supermercados* became popular, locals did all their grocery shopping in markets such as this one topped by an enormous octagonal glass roof. On the ground floor you'll find produce piled high on tables and tumbling out of baskets, and upstairs is whatever types of fish the boats brought in that morning. A dozen different eateries serve up the catch of the day. Watch your wallet, as this place can get crowded. ⊠ *Cochrane between Valdivia and San Martín* 📞 *No phone.*

NEED A BREAK?

While exploring Cerro Bellavista, be sure to stop for a coffee at **Gato Tuerto** (⊠ *Hector Calvo Jofré 20* 📞 *32/220–867*), the One-Eye Cat. This meticulously restored 1910 Victorian house, painted eye-popping shades of yellow and blue, affords lovely views. It's also a popular nightspot.

---

❽ Museo de Historia Natural de Valparaíso. Within the Palacio Lyon, one of the few buildings to survive the devastating 1906 earthquake is this rather outdated natural history museum. Among the more unusual exhibits are a pre-Columbian mummy, newborn conjoined twins in formaldehyde, and stuffed penguins. ⊠ *Condell 1546* 📞 *32/254–4840* 🎫 *600 pesos* ⊙ *Tues.–Sat. 10–1 and 2–6, Sun. 10–2.*

❹ Museo del Mar Lord Cochrane. There's a small collection of naval paraphernalia, but the real reason for a visit is to the see the house itself, constructed for Lord Thomas Cochrane. The colonial-style house, with its red tile roof and stately wood columns, is one of the most beautiful in Valparaíso. As you might expect for an admiral's abode, it has wonderful views of the port. The museum was due to close for renovation work but should reopen by the end of 2008. ⊠ *Merlet 195* 📞 *32/293–9558* 🎫 *600 pesos* ⊙ *Tues.–Sun. 10–6.*

NEED A BREAK?

If you can't get enough of the views from Paseo 21 de Mayo, stroll down the stairs that run parallel to the ascensor to the small restaurant, **Poseidon** (⊠ *Subida Artillería 99* 📞 *32/346–713*). With a terrace superbly perched on a high corner overlooking the city, this makes a great spot for a cool drink.

⓫ Plaza Victoria. The heart of the lower part of the city is this green plaza
ↂ with a lovely fountain bordered by four female statues representing the seasons. Two black lions at the edge of the park look across the street to the neo-Gothic cathedral and its unusual freestanding bell tower. Directly to the north is **Plaza Simon Bolívar,** which delights children with swings, slides, and simple carnival rides. ⊠ *Condell at Molina.*

WHERE TO EAT

$$–$$$ ✕ **Bote Salvavidas.** This restaurant on Muelle Prat has great views of the harbor from its glass-walled dining room. As you might guess, it specializes in seafood. Dishes such as *congrio margarita* (conger eel with shellfish sauce), *caldillo de marisco* (shellfish chowder), and *pastel de jaiba* (crab pie) are among the popular specialties. ⊠ *Muelle Prat* 📞 *32/2251–477* 🖃 *AE, DC, MC, V* ⊙ *No dinner Sun.*

¢–$ ✗**Brighton.** Nestled below the eponymous bed-and-breakfast on the edge of Cerro Concepción, this popular restaurant has an amazing view from its black-and-white-tiled balcony. Vintage advertisements hang on the walls of the intimate dining room. A limited menu includes such standards as *machas a la parmesana* (razor clams Parmesan) and seviche, as well as several kinds of crepes and hearty Chilean sandwiches. An extensive wine list and cocktail selection make it a popular nightspot, especially on weekends, when there's live music. ✉*Paseo Atkinson 151* ☎*32/2223–513* ▤*AE, DC, MC, V.*

$$–$$$ ✗**Café Turri.** Near the top of Ascensor Concepción, this 19th-century
Fodor'sChoice mansion commands one of the best views of Valparaíso. It also has
★ some of the finest seafood. House specialties such as sea bass or shrimp in almond sauce are alone worth the effort of driving to the coast from Santiago. If you're a seafood lover, splurge on the *jardín de mariscos especial,* which is a huge platter of the catch of the day. Outside there's a terrace and inside are two floors of dining rooms. The old-fashioned service, overseen by the affable owner, is excellent. ✉*Templeman 147, at Paseo Gervasoni* ☎*32/2252–091, 32/236–5307* ▤*AE, DC, MC, V.*

¢ ✗**Casino Social J. Cruz M.** This eccentric restaurant is a Valparaíso institution, thanks to its legendary status for inventing the *chorillana* (minced beef with onions, cheese, and an egg atop french fries), which is now served by most local restaurants. There is no menu—choose either a plate of chorillana for two or three, or *carne mechada* (stewed beef), with a side of french fries, rice, or tomato salad. Glass cases choked with dusty trinkets surround tables covered with plastic cloths in the cramped dining room. You may have to share a table. The restaurant is at the end of a bleak corridor off Calle Condell. ✉*Condell 1466* ☎*32/211–225* ▤*No credit cards.*

$–$$$ ✗**Coco Loco.** It takes a little more than an hour to turn 360 degrees in this impressive *giratorio* (revolving restaurant), meaning you can savor all the smashing views of the city. The vast menu ranges from *congrío frito con un compot de anis y papaya* (fried sea-bass with papaya and aniseed compote) to ostrich steak with seasalt and ginger. ✉*Blanco 1781* ☎*32/227–614* ⌕*Reservations essential* ▤*AE, DC, MC, V* ☾*No dinner Sun.*

$$–$$$ ✗**La Colombina.** This restaurant is in an old home on Cerro Alegre, one of the city's most beautiful hilltop neighborhoods. Dining rooms on two floors are notable for their elegant furnishings, stained-glass windows, and impressive views of the city and sea. Seafood dominates the menu, with such inventive dishes as sea-bass in olive and parsley sauce, or Magallanic lamb roasted with plums, mushrooms, bacon, and orange. Choose from a list of 80 national wines. **Pros:** Good value in the heart of Valparaíso's World Heritage Site. **Cons:** Lacks the modern conveniences which are basic elsewhere. ✉*Paseo Apolo 91, off Paseo Yugoslavo, Cerro Alegre* ☎*32/223–6254* ▤*AE, DC, MC, V* ☾*Mar.– Aug. No dinner, Sep.t–Feb. Lunch and dinner.*

¢–$ ✗**Donde Carlitos.** A stone's throw from the port are dozens of eateries specializing in whatever was caught that morning. You won't find any fresher fish than at this tiny storefront restaurant near Mercado Central. Through a window on the street you can watch the chefs

Chilean Coastal Cuisine

"In the turbulent sea of Chile lives the golden conger eel," wrote Chilean poet Pablo Neruda in a simple verse that leaves the real poetry for the dinner table. To many, dining is the principal pleasure of a trip to the Central Coast. Along with that succulent conger eel, *congrio*, menus here typically have *corvina* (sea bass), a whitefish called *reineta*, and the mild *lenguado* (sole). The appetizer selection, which is invariably extensive, usually includes *ostiones* (scallops), *machas* (razor clams), *camarones* (shrimp), and *jaiba* (crab). Because lobster is extremely rare in Chilean waters, it's more expensive here than just about anywhere in the world.

Fish and meat dishes are often served alone, which means that if you want french fries, mashed potatoes, a salad, or *palta* (avocado), you have to order it as an *agregado* (side dish). Bread, a bowl of lemons, and a sauce called *pebre* (a mix of tomato, onion, coriander, parsley, and often chili) are always brought to the table. Valparaíso is known for a hearty, cheap meal called *chorillana*—a mountain of minced steak, onions, cheese, and eggs on a bed of french fries.

–Mark Sullivan

prying open oysters and rolling razor clams into empanadas. The simple dining room has a half dozen tables under chandeliers shaped like—you guessed it—ships' wheels. ⊠*Blanco 166* ▭*No credit cards* ⊗*No dinner.*

$$ ✕ **Pasta y Vino.** Everything isn't black and white at this extremely popu-
Fodor'sChoice lar restaurant on Cerro Concepción. The innovative food, served in
★ the monochromatic dining room, comes in eye-popping colors. Even the fanciful breads, which seem to swirl out of the basket, are lovely shades of brown. Start with clams on the half shell flavored with ginger and lime, then move on to strawberry gnocchi in a champagne sauce or ravioli filled with duck in a rich port wine reduction. The wine list, focusing on local vintages, is impressive. The hip young staff in floor-length black aprons couldn't be more accommodating. ⊠*Templeman 352* ☎*32/249–6187* ⋐*Reservations essential* ▭*AE, DC, MC, V.*

WHERE TO STAY

$ ▤ **Brighton B&B.** This bright-yellow Victorian house enjoys an enviable
Fodor'sChoice location at the edge of tranquil Cerro Concepción. The house is fur-
★ nished with brass beds and other antiques chosen by owner Nelson Morgado, who taught architecture for two decades at the University of Barcelona. The terrace of its restaurant and three of its six rooms have vertiginous views of the bay. One room has a private balcony that is perfect for a romantic breakfast. Room size varies considerably—only the so-called suite (just a larger room) is spacious—but all are charming. ⊠*Paseo Atkinson 151* ☎*32/222–3513* ▤*32/259–8802* ⊕*www.brighton.cl* ⊷*9 rooms* ⌂*In-room: no a/c, no phone. In-hotel: restaurant, bar, laundry service, no elevator* ▭*AE, DC, MC, V* ⦿*CP.*

$$-$$$ ⊞**Casa Thomas Somerscales.** Perched high atop Cerro Alegre, this palm-
Fodor'sChoice shaded mansion has an unobstructed view of the sea. As befits an ele-
★ gant home from the 19th century, its rambling hallways and wooden
staircases lead to rooms of various shapes and sizes. Ask for Number
8, which has lovely French doors and a private terrace where you can
enjoy your breakfast. All rooms at this boutique hotel are impecca-
bly furnished with antique armoires and bureaus and beds piled high
with imported linens. Dozens of trendy shops and restaurants are
steps away. **Pros:** A chance to imagine life in Valparaíso's Victorian
apogee. **Cons:** It's a steep climb back to your room at night. ⊠*San
Enrique 446, Cerro Alegre* ☎*32/233–1379* ⊕*www.hotelsomerscales.cl*
🛏*8 rooms* ♨*In-room: safe, DVD, cable TV, Internet, Wi-Fi, minibar,
no elevator* ⊟*AE, DC, MC, V* ⊙*CP.*

$$-$$$ ⊞**Gran Hotel Gervasoni.** Set in a sprawling Victorian mansion that
Fodor'sChoice spreads across five floors, the Gervasoni is a chance to step back in
★ time into Valparaíso's past. Finding your room will involve navigating
dark corridors and descending steep stairways, but the atmosphere is
addictive. Ask to see the wine cellar below the restaurant, a dark place
once used to hold slaves. The city's mind-boggling topography means
that the hotel has three entrances on different floors. **Pros:** A chance
to imagine life in Valparaíso's Victorian apogee. **Cons:** The steep stairs
may not suit all legs and the views are rather spoiled by a concrete
office block. ⊠*Paseo Gervasoni 1, Cerro Concepción* ☎*32/223–
9236* ⊕*www.hotelgervasoni.com* 🛏*14 rooms* ♨*In-room: cable TV,
Wi-Fi, room service, no A/C, no elevator, laudnry service, restaurant,
bar* ⊟*AE, DC, MC, V* ⊙*CP.*

$ ⊞**Hostal La Colombina.** The location here is excellent: on a quiet street
just up the hill from the Ascensor Concepción, near Paseo 21 de Mayo
in the heart of Cerro Concepción. Dozens of shops and restaurants are
on the nearby streets. Rooms in this old house may be sparsely furnished, but they are ample, with high ceilings and wooden floors. Most
have big windows, though none of them have much of a view. **Pros:**
Good location. **Cons:** A bit austere. ⊠*Concepción 280* ☎*32/223–
4980* ⊕*www.lacolombina.cl* 🛏*8 rooms without bath* ♨*In-room: no
a/c, no phone, no TV. In-hotel: bar* ⊟*AE, DC, MC, V* ⊙*CP.*

$ ⊞**Manoir Hotel Atkinson.** One of new boutique hotels which are filling
up fashionable Cerro Concepcion and Cerro Alegre, this cozy house
lies at the end of Paseo Atkinson and near many local attractions. The
French-Chilean owners have carefully preserved many of this 19th-
century building's original features, including beautiful stained-glass
windows and tastefully elegant furnishings, plenty of artwork, and a
piano in the lobby. **Pros:** Many of Valparaíso's best restaurants are
just a block or two away. **Cons:** Despite location, many of the rooms
lack seaviews. ⊠*Paseo Atkinson 165* ☎*32/235–1313* 📠*32/745–642*
⊕*www.hotelatkinson.cl* 🛏*6 rooms, 1 suite* ♨*In-room: no a/c, Wi-Fi,
cable TV, safe, minibar. In-hotel: dining room, room service, laundry
service* ⊟*AE, DC, MC, V* ⊙*CP.*

$ ⊞**Puerta de Alcalá.** The rooms surround a five-story atrium flooded with
light at this centrally-located hotel. They have little personality, but are
clean and well equipped, with a few little extras. Those facing the street

are bright, but can be noisy on weekends. If you're a light sleeper, take a room in the back. Try to get a room on the fourth floor—the lower floors get less sunlight because they are blocked by the building next door. There's a decent restaurant and bar on the ground level. **Pros:** One of few hotels in Valparaíso in downtown area. **Cons:** Those facing the street are bright, but can be noisy on weekends. ⊠ *Pirámide 524, at Condell* ☎ *32/227–478* 🖨 *32/745–642* ⊕ *www.hotelpuertadealcala. cl* 🖙 *21 rooms* ⚏ *In-room: no a/c, Wi-Fi. In-hotel: restaurant, room service, bar, laundry service, minibar* ▭ *AE, DC, MC, V* ⏰| *CP.*

$–$$$ 🖳 **Ultramar.** No, you're not seeing spots. Those huge polka dots in the bathroom are part of the whimsical design at Ultramar, the city's first real boutique hotel. The candy-color stripes and bold geometric patterns are like nothing this country has ever seen. They come as a complete surprise, as the hotel is housed in a staid-looking brick building dating from 1907. **Pros:** The café on the first floor hosts occasional art exhibits while terrace boasts eye-popping views of the bay. **Cons:** Just about the only caveat is the location, which is a bit far from the action. ⊠ *Tomás Peréz 173, Cerro Cárcel* ☎ *32/2210–000* ⊕ *www.hotelultra-mar.cl* 🖙 *16 rooms* ⚏ ▭ *AE, DC, MC, V.*

NIGHTLIFE & THE ARTS

Valparaíso has an inordinate number of nocturnal establishments, which run the gamut from pubs to tango bars and salsa dance clubs. Thursday through Saturday nights most places get crowded between 11 PM and midnight. Young people stay out until daybreak. The main concentrations of bars and clubs are on Subida Ecuador, near Plaza Anibal Pinto, and a block of Avenida Errázuriz nearby. Cerro Concepción, Alegre, and Bellavista have quieter options, many with terraces perfect for admiring the city lights.

BARS   It's not surprising that there are a handful of bars surrounding the dock. The rougher ones west of Plaza Sotomayer are primarily patronized by sailors, whereas those to the east welcome just about anybody. A short walk east of Plaza Sotomayor, **Bar Inglés** (⊠ *Cochrane 851* ☎ *32/221–4625*) has dark-wood paneling and the longest bar in town. You can also order decent food. The huge antique mirrors of **Bar La Playa** (⊠ *Serrano 567* ☎ *32/221–8011*), just west of Plaza Sotomayor, give it a historic feel. It becomes packed with party animals after midnight on weekends in January and February. **Valparaíso Eterno** (⊠ *Almirante Señoret 150* ☎ *32/222–8374*), one block from Plaza Sotomayor, is filled with paintings of Valparaíso and floor-to-ceiling graffiti lovingly supplied by patrons. It opens only on weekends.

DANCE CLUBS   Some of the city's hottest dance clubs are found on the streets east of Plaza Sotomayer. Among the top dance clubs is **Aché Havana** (⊠ *Av. Errázuriz 1042* ☎ *9/521–9872*), which plays mostly salsa and other Latin rhythms. Nearby are several other large dance clubs: **Bulevar** (⊠ *Av. Errázuriz 1154* ☎ *No phone*) has eclectic music on weekend nights. The basement **Eterno** (⊠ *Blanco 698* ☎ *32/221–9024*) plays only Latin dance music, and opens weekends only.

There is also a cluster of bars along the streets that lead uphill from Plaza Anibal Pinto. The four-story **Mr. Egg** (⊠*Ecuador 50* ☎*No phone*) has a bar on the ground floor and a dance club above it.

LIVE MUSIC Tango dancing is so popular in Valparaíso that you might think you were in Buenos Aires. On Cerro Concepción, **Brighton** (⊠*Paseo Atkinson s/n* ☎*32/222–3513*) has live bolero music on Friday and tango on Saturday, starting at 11 PM. Its black-and-white tile terrace overlooks the city's glittering lights.Dance to live tango music weekends at **Cinzano** (⊠*Anibal Pinto 1182* ☎*32/221–3043*), an old-fashioned watering hole facing Plaza Anibal Pinto. The walls above the bar are decorated with scenes of old Valparaíso, including some notable shipwrecks.

If you want to see the lights of the city, several of the most popular establishments are perched on the nearby hills. On Cerro Alegre, **La Colombina** (⊠*Papudo 526* ☎*32/221–9891*) has live Latin music weekend nights. Tiny **Color Café** (⊠*Papudo 612* ☎*32/225–1183*), on Cerro Concepción, serves up live Latin music on weekends. Cerro Bellavista's **Gato Tuerto** (⊠*Hector Calvo Jofré 205* ☎*32/222–0867*) hosts live Latin music on weekends in a lovely Victorian mansion with a city view.

Weekends, **Entre Socios** (⊠*Ecuador 75*), on the upper end of the Subita Ecuador, plays alternative music.Concert fans should check out **La Piedra Feliz** (⊠*Av. Errázuriz 1054* ☎*32/225–6788*), which hosts performances by Chile's best bands Tuesday–Saturday. The music starts at 9 PM weeknights and 11 PM weekends. Wednesday is jazz night.There's live Latin music weekends at **El Triunfo** (⊠*Ecuador 27* ☎*32/257–428*).

FILM **Cine Hoyts** (⊠*Av. Pedro Montt 2111* ☎*600/5000–400*), across from Parque Italia, is a state-of-the-art theater showing American releases on five screens. The restaurant **Valparaíso Mi Amor** (⊠*Papudo 612* ☎*32/219–891*) screens 16-millimeter films about Valparaíso made by owner Nelson Cabrera, as well as European features.

THEATER **Ex-Cárcel de Valparaíso** (⊠*El Castro s/n* ☎*32/225–0891*), a crumbling former prison on Cerro Cárcel, is a haunting space often used for plays and concerts. Off Plaza O'Higgins, the lovely old **Teatro Municipal de Valparaíso** (⊠*Uruguay 410* ☎*32/225–7480*) hosts symphonies, ballet, and opera May–November.

SPORTS & THE OUTDOORS

BEACHES If it's beaches you're after, head to Viña del Mar or one of the other resort towns along the coast. Valparaíso has only one notable beach, **Playa Las Torpederas,** a sheltered crescent of sand east of the port. Though less attractive than the beaches up the coast, it does have very calm water. A short bus ride south of the city is **Laguna Verde,** a completely undiscovered stretch of shore that is absolutely gorgeous. There are no eateries, so make sure to pack a picnic.

BOATING Informal boat operators at **Muelle Prat** take groups on a 60-minute circuit of the bay for 2,000 pesos per person. If you have several people, consider hiring your own boat for 20,000 pesos.

SOCCER Valparaíso's first-division soccer team is the **Santiago Wanderers** (⊠*Independencia 2061* ☎*32/221–7210*). Matches are usually held Monday at the Estadio Municipal in Playa Ancha.

SHOPPING

Outside of Santiago, there are more shops in Valparaíso than anywhere else in Chile. The country's major department store chain, **Ripley** (⊠*Condell 1646* ☎*32/265–2531*), is across from Plaza Victoria. The fifth floor has a food court.

If it's handicrafts you're looking for, head to the bohemian neighborhoods of Cerro Concepción and Cerro Alegre. There are dozens of workshops where you can watch artisans ply their crafts. On Cerro Concepción, **Paraíso del Arte** (⊠*Abtao 529* ☎*32/239–357*) has a wonderful collection of paintings and mosaics. Most days you'll find artists hard at work. In the same building as Paraíso del Arte, **Trio** (⊠*Abtao 529-B* ☎*32/239–357*) carries beaded handbags and funky jewelry. **Taller Arte en Plata** (⊠*Pasaje Templeman 8* ☎*9/315–0438*) displays necklaces, bracelets, and rings, almost all made from silver.

On Cerro Alegre, **Taller Antiquina Artesania en Cero** (⊠*San Enrique 510* ☎*9/378–1006*) has handmade leather items ranging from belts to satchels. **Paulina Acuña** (⊠*Almirante Montt 64* ☎*9/871–8388*), a small boutique downhill from Cerro Alegre, sells an unusual collection of handicrafts, including painted glass, candles, jewelry, and clothing.

Cooperativa Artesanal de Valparaíso (⊠*Av. Pedro Montt at Las Heras* ☎*No phone*) is a daily market where you can buy local crafts. The weekend flea market, **Feria de Antigüedades** (⊠*Av. Argentina at Plaza O'Higgins* ☎*No phone*), has an excellent selection of antiques.

VIÑA DEL MAR

130 km (85 mi) northwest of Santiago.

Viña del Mar has high-rise apartment buildings that tower above its excellent shoreline. Here are wide boulevards lined with palms, lush parks, and mansions. Miles of beige sand are washed by heavy surf. The town has been known for years as Chile's tourist capital (a title being challenged by several other hot spots), and is currently in the midst of some minor refurbishment.

Viña, as it's popularly known, has the country's oldest casino, excellent hotels, and an extensive selection of restaurants. To some, all this means that Viña del Mar is modern and exciting; to others, it means the city is lacking in character. But there's no denying that Viña del Mar has a little of everything—trendy boutiques, beautiful homes, interesting museums, a casino, varied nightlife, and, of course, one of the best beaches in the country.

GETTING HERE & AROUND

From Santiago, take Ruta 68 west through the coastal mountains, turning off to Viña del Mar as the vineyards of the Casablanca valley give way to eucalyptus forests. The spectacular twisting access road (Agua

CASABLANCA WINE TASTING

Don't miss the chance to stop at this convenient mid-point for the drive between Santiago and the coast. As you come out of the Zapata tunnel (at kilometer 60 on Ruta 68), the importance of wine production to the local economy will be obvious. Vineyards carpet the floor of the Casablanca Valley for as far as the eye can see. Just 30 years ago most winemakers consider this area inhospitable for wine grapes, yet today it is at the forefront of the country's wine industry. Experts have come to recognize the valley's proximity to the sea as its main asset, because cooler temperatures give the grapes more time to develop flavor as they ripen.

Almost all wineries are open to visitors. Choices for activities might include a tour, a tasting, lunch at an on-premises restaurant, or even an overnight stay (all for a price, of course). Although most offer tours on a daily basis, call ahead to ensure someone is available to show you around.

If you want to visit more than one winery, the **Casablanca Valley Wine Producers Association** (⊕ *www.casablancavalley.cl* ☎ *32/274–3755* or *32/274–3933*) runs one-day and two-day visits.

Casas del Bosque, nestled in among rolling vine-covered hills just outside the town of Casablanca, offers a vineyard tour in an old wagon, a tour of the winemaking facilities and a tasting. During March and April, the main harvest months, you can learn even more about the production process with the chance to pick your grapes and take them for selection and pressing. Like many wineries in the valley, Casas del Bosque has its own restaurant, Tanino. ⊠ *Hijuela No 2, Casablanca* ☎ *2/480–6900* or *32/377–9431* ⊕ *www.casasdelbosque.cl.*

Viña Matetic, which straddles the border between the Casablanca valley and the adjacent San Anontio valley, may take prize for the region's most stunning bodega. Set into a ridge overlooking vines on both sides, it resembles a futuristic bunker worthy of a James Bond villain, with sloping passageways revealing glimpses into the barrels stored below. A couple of kilometers away, the winery's octagonal restaurant looks out over beautifully manicured gardens, in the middle of which is a recently restored guest house with three elegantly-decorated rooms available to rent. ⊠ *Fundo Rosario, Lagunillas Casablanca* ☎ *2/583–8660* ⊕ *www.mateticvineyards.com.*

Chile's vineyard and orchard lands, which are well-protected from many diseases and pests by the Andes mountains, the Pacific Ocean, and the Atacama desert, generally require the use of much fewer pesticides than those in other countries. **Emiliana Orgánico** is a celebration of this fact. Visitors can learn about some innovative organic practices, the most interesting of which is the use of ladybugs and llamas for pest control and fertilization, respectively. Tours can be arranged to include lunch or dinner. ⊠ *Ruta 68, kilometer 70 Casablanca* ☎ *9/225—5679* ⊕ *www.emiliana.cl.*

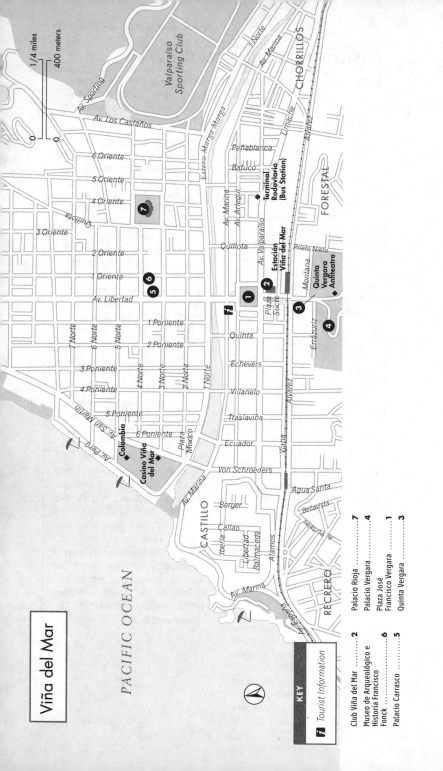

Viña del Mar

PACIFIC OCEAN

1/4 miles

400 meters

0

0

Valparaíso
Sporting Club

CHORRILLOS

Av. Sporting

Av. Los Castaños

6 Oriente

5 Oriente

4 Oriente

3 Oriente

2 Oriente

1 Oriente

Quillota

Estero Marga Marga

Peñablanca

Batuco

Terminal
Rodoviario
(Bus Station)

FORESTAL

Av. Marina

Av. Arlegui

Quillota

Estación
Viña del Mar

Prieto Nieto

Montana

Quinta
Vergara
Anfiteatro

Av. Valparaíso

Plaza
Sucre

Errázuriz

Av. Libertad

1 Poniente

2 Poniente

Quinta

Echevers

Villanelo

Traslaviña

Ecuador

Von Schroeders

3 Poniente

4 Poniente

5 Poniente

6 Poniente

7 Norte

6 Norte

5 Norte

4 Norte

3 Norte

2 Norte

1 Norte

Viana

Álvarez

Agua Santa

Bellavista

Av. Portales

Av. San Martín

Av. Perú

Colombia

Casino Viña
del Mar

Plaza
México

Av. Marina

Berger

Callao

Iberia

Libertad

Balmaceda

Álamos

CASTILLO

Av. Marina

RECREO

Av. España

RECREO

KEY

i Tourist Information

Club Viña del Mar **2**

Museo de Arqueológico e
Historia Francisco
Fonck **6**

Palacio Carrasco **5**

Palacio Rioja **7**

Palacio Vergara **4**

Plaza José
Francisco Vergara **1**

Quinta Vergara **3**

Santa), through hills dotted with Chilean palm trees, drops you on Avenida Alvarez, just a couple of blocks from downtown Viña del Mar. Tur-Bus, Condor, Pullman, and Sol del Pacífico all run buses to Viña del Mar. Tur-Bus leaves from its Alameda terminal. Viña del Mar has the best tourist office on the coast, offering fistfuls of helpful maps and brochures. It's north of Plaza Vergara at the corner of Avenida Libertad and Avenida Marina. It's open weekdays 9–2 and 3–7, weekends 10–2 and 3–7. There's also a friendly kiosk on Avenida Valparaíso that's open Monday–Saturday 10–2 and 3–7.

ESSENTIALS

Currency Exchange Banco de Chile (⊠ *Av. Valparaíso 667* ☎ *32/648–760*).

Internet OKA Comunicaciones (⊠ *Av. Valparaíso 242* ☎ *32/713–712*). **286 Rue Valparaíso** (⊠ *Av. Valparaíso 286* ☎ *32/710–140*).

Medical Assistance Farmacias Ahumada (⊠ *Avenida Valparaíso no 505* ☎ *32/269–1343*). **Hospital Dr Gustavo Fricke** (⊠ *Avenida Alvarez 1532* ☎ *32/265–2200*).

Visitor & Tour Information Viña del Mar main office (⊠ *Av. Libertad at Av. Marina* ☎ *32/269–330*).

Viña del Mar branch office (⊠ *Av. Valparaíso at Villanelo* ☎ *32/683–355*).

EXPLORING

② **Club Viña del Mar.** It would be a shame to pass up a chance to see this private club's magnificent interior. The neoclassical building, constructed in 1901 of materials imported from England, is where wealthy locals come to play snooker. Nonmembers are usually allowed to enter only the grand central hall, but there are often tours of the building during the week. The club hosts occasional concerts during which you may be able to circumambulate the second-floor interior balcony. ⊠ *Plaza Sucre at Av. Valparaíso* ☎ *32/268–0016*.

NEED A BREAK? Even die-hard shoppers may be overwhelmed by the myriad shops along Avenida Valparaíso. Take a load off at 286 Rue Valparaíso (⊠ *Av. Valparaíso 286* ☎ *32/710–140*), a café with tables on the sidewalk. Enjoy a cappuccino, a milk shake, or perhaps a crepe.

⑥ **Museo de Arqueológico e Historia Francisco Fonck.** A 500-year-old stone *moai* (a carved stone head) brought from Easter Island guards the entrance to this archaeological museum. The most interesting exhibits are the finds from Easter Island, which indigenous people call Rapa Nui, such as wood tablets displaying ancient hieroglyphics. The museum, named for groundbreaking archaeologist Francisco Fonck—a native of Viña del Mar—also has an extensive library of documents relating to the island. ⊠ *4 Norte 784* ☎ *32/268–6753* *1,500 pesos* ⊙ *Tues.–Fri. 10–6, Sat.–Sun. 10–2*.

⑤ **Palacio Carrasco.** Set in a shady park, this Italian-style mansion is now the home of the city's archives, library, and cultural center. The grand facade is its best feature, but the interior is also worth a look. A few rooms are set aside for temporary exhibits, usually of works by local artists. ✉ *Av. Libertad 250* 🕾 *32/269–708* 💺 *Free* ⊙ *Mon.–Sat. 9.30–7, Sun. 10–1.30.*

❼ Palacio Rioja. This grand palace was built by Spanish banker Francisco Rioja immediately after the earthquake that leveled much of the city in 1906. It contains a decorative-arts museum showcasing a large portion of Rioja's belongings and a conservatory, so there's often music in the air. Performances are held in the main ballroom. The beautifully landscaped grounds are great for shady lounging or a picnic. ✉ *Quillota 214* 🕾 *32/689–665* 💺 *300 pesos* ⊙ *Tues.–Sun. 10–1:30 and 3–5:30.*

❹ Palacio Vergara. The neo-Gothic Palacio Vergara, erected after the 1906
★ earthquake as the residence of the wealthy Vergara family, houses the **Museo de Bellas Artes.** Inside is a collection of classical paintings dating from the 15th to the 19th century, including works by Rubens and Tintoretto. A highlight is the intricate parquet floor—you'll be given booties to wear over your shoes so as not to scuff it up. ✉ *Av. Errázuriz 593* 🕾 *32/273–8438, 32/226–9425* 💺 *600 pesos* ⊙ *Tues.–Sun. 10–1.30 and 3–5.30.*

❶ Plaza José Francisco Vergara. Viña del Mar's central square, Plaza Vergara is lined with majestic palms. Presiding over the east end of the plaza is the patriarch of coastal accommodations, the venerable Hotel O'Higgins, which has seen better days. Opposite the hotel is the neo-classical Teatro Municipal de Viña del Mar, where you can watch a ballet, theater, or music performance. To the west on Avenida Valparaíso is the city's main shopping strip, a one-lane, seven-block stretch with extra-wide sidewalks and numerous stores and sidewalk cafés. You can hire a horse-drawn carriage to take you from the square past some of the city's stately mansions.

NEED A BREAK? In search of a great place to watch the sunset? Head to **Enjoy Del Mar** (✉ *Av. Perú 100* 🕾 *32/500–703*), an ultramodern restaurant right on the beach. Locals eschew the food and come instead for coffee and a view of the sky turning various shades of pink, purple, and green.

❸ Quinta Vergara. Lose yourself on the paths that wind amid soaring eucalyptus trees on the grounds that contain one of Chile's best botanical gardens. An amphitheater here holds an international music festival, *Festival Internacional de la Canción de Viña del Mar,* in February. ✉ *Av. Errázuriz 563* 🕾 *32/477–310* 💺 *Free* ⊙ *Daily 7–6.*

WHERE TO EAT

$–$$$ ✗ **Armandita.** Meat-eaters need not despair in this city of seafood saturation. A rustic restaurant half a block west of Avenida San Martín serves almost nothing but grilled meat, including various organs. The menu includes popular dishes such as *lomo a lo pobre* (flank steak served on a bed of french fries and topped with a fried egg). The *parrillada especial,* a mixed grill of steak, chicken, ribs, pork, and sausage, serves two or three people. ✉ *6 Norte 119* 🕾 *32/268–1607* ▭ *AE, DC, MC, V.*

$$ ✕**Delicias del Mar.** Former television chef Raúl Madinagoitía, who once
Fodor'sChoice had his own program, presides over the kitchen here. The menu lists
★ such seafood delicacies as Peruvian-style seviche, stuffed sea bass, and
machas *curadas* (steamed clams with dill and melted cheese). Oeno-
philes are impressed by the extensive, almost exclusively Chilean wine
list. Save room for one of the excellent desserts, maybe crème brûlée,
chocolate mousse, or cheesecake with a raspberry sauce. ⊠*Av. San
Martín 459* ☎*32/290–1837* ▭*AE, DC, MC, V.*

$–$$$ ✕**San Marcos.** More than five decades after Edoardo Melotti emigrated
here from northern Italy, the restaurant maintains a reputation for
first-class food and service. A modern dining room with abundant foliage and large windows overlooks busy Avenida San Martín. Farther
inside, the two dining rooms in the house the restaurant originally
occupied are elegant and more refined. The menu includes the traditional gnocchi and cannelloni, as well as *lasagna di granchio* (crab
lasagna) and *pato arrosto* (roast duck). Complement your meal with a
bottle from the extensive wine list. ⊠*Av. San Martín 597* ☎*32/297–
5304* ▭*AE, DC, MC, V.*

$–$$ ✕**Shitake.** With so much fresh fish available, it's a wonder that it's taken
so long for sushi and sashimi to catch on with locals. Now that it has,
it's hard to find a block downtown that lacks a Japanese restaurant. A
favorite with locals is Sushi Taro, which occupies a few gold and beige
rooms on Avenida San Martín. The tempura is flavorful, especially
when it incorporates juicy Ecuadorean shrimp. Sushi here is a group
activity—you can order platters of anywhere from 17 to 103 pieces.
⊠*Av. San Martín 419* ☎*32/290–1458* ▭*AE, MC, V.*

WHERE TO STAY

$$ ✕▥**Cap Ducal.** This ship-shaped building on the waterfront was
inspired by transatlantic ocean liners, but it takes a bit of imagination
to see what the architect had in mind. Like the building, rooms are
oddly shaped, but they are nicely decorated with plush carpets and
pastel wallpaper. Those on the third floor have narrow balconies. Be
sure to ask for a view of Reñaca, or you may see, and hear, the high-
way. The three-level restaurant serves seafood that tops the view. Try
the congrio *a la griega* (conger eel with a mushroom, ham, and cream
sauce) or *pollo a la Catalana* (chicken with an olive, mushroom, and
tomato sauce). **Pros:** Unique architecture. **Cons:** Noise of traffic can
spoil the great views. ⊠*Av. Marina 51* ☎*32/262–6655* 🖷*32/266–
5478* ⊕*www.capducal.cl* ⇝*23 rooms, 3 suites* ⚿*In-room: no a/c,
safe. In-hotel: restaurant, bar, laundry service, minibar* ▭*AE, DC,
MC, V* ¶◯*BP.*

$$$$ ▥**Hotel Del Mar.** A rounded facade, echoing the shape of the adjacent
Fodor'sChoice Casino Viña del Mar, means that almost every room at this ocean-
★ front hotel has unmatched views. The exterior is true to the casino's
neoclassical design, but spacious guest rooms are pure 21st century,
with sleek furnishings, original modern art, and sliding glass doors
that open onto balconies. Marble floors, fountains, abundant gardens,
and impeccable service make Hotel Del Mar one of Chile's most luxu-
rious. An eighth-floor spa and infinity pool share the view. A stay here
includes free access to the upscale casino, which evokes Monaco rather

than Las Vegas. **Pros:** The Savinya restaurant was recently named as Chile's best outside Santiago. **Cons:** The constant chiming of gaming machines may grate but there are ways to escape. ✉*Av. San Martín 199* ☎*32/250-0800* 🖷*32/250-0801* ⊕*www.enjoy.cl* ↵*50 rooms, 10 suites* ♿*In-room: safe, data port. In-hotel: 3 restaurants, bar, pool, spa, concierge, laundry service, minibar* ⊟*AE, DC, MC, V* ⦿*BP.*

$$ 🛏**Hotel Gala.** Modern rooms in this upscale 14-story hotel have panoramic views of the city. The rooms are spacious, and large windows let in lots of light. The bathrooms are crisp and clean and outfitted in white tile. There's a small heated pool next to the bar. One block from the Avenida Valparaíso shopping strip, Gala is near most of the city's attractions. **Pros:** Great views in the heart of downtown Viña. **Cons:** One down point is the staff, which seems stretched a bit thin. ✉*Arlegui 273* ☎*32/232-1500* 🖷*32/689-568* ⊕*www.gala.cl* ↵*64 rooms, 12 suites* ♿*In-room: dial-up, Wi-Fi In-hotel: restaurant, bar, pool, laundry service, minibar* ⊟*AE, DC, MC, V* ⦿*BP.*

$$–$$$ ✗🛏**Hotel Oceanic.** Built on the rocky coast between Viña and Reñaca,
★   this boutique hotel has luxurious rooms with gorgeous ocean views. Rooms are cheerful, decorated in bright shades of pink and orange. The pool area, perched on the rocks below, is occasionally drenched by big swells. Although there's no beach access, the sands of Salinas are a short walk away. The restaurant is one of the area's best, serving French-inspired dishes such as shrimp crepes, *filete café de Paris* (tenderloin with herb butter), and congrio *oceanic* (conger eel in an artichoke mushroom sauce). **Pros:** Watch the waves on the rock from your hotel terrace. **Cons:** Though the setting is great, it's a long way out of Viña. ✉*Av. Borgoño 12925, north of town* ☎*32/283-0006* 🖷*32/283-0390* ⊕*www.hoteloceanic.cl* ↵*30 rooms, 1 suite* ♿*In-room: no a/c, safe, dial-up. In-hotel: restaurant, room service, bar, pool, minibar, no elevator* ⊟*AE, DC, MC, V* ⦿*BP.*

★   ✗🛏**Sheraton Miramar.** This sophisticated city hotel certainly earns it name, as you can do almost everything here while gazing at the sea. The striking white architecture has quickly made it a landmark in the city, attracting many of the big name stars who perform at the summer music festival. Another highlight is the downstairs Baltus spa, where guests can alternate between a heated pool and one of two outdoor pools, one of which is carved into the rocks and filled by the tide. Fishes and the occasional crab may drift by as you enjoy the view. **Pros:** Difficult to bear comfort with spectacular views. **Cons:** The area around the hotel is blighted by one of Viña's main access roads. ✉*Av. Marina 15* ☎*32/238-8600* 🖷*32/283-0390* ⊕*www.sheraton.cl* ↵*142 rooms, 4 suites* ♿*In-room: cable TV, safe, ethernet. In-hotel: 2 restaurants, Wi-Fi, room service, bar, 3 pools, minibar* ⊟*AE, DC, MC, V* ⦿*BP.*

$ 🛏**Tres Poniente.** Come for the personalized service and for many of the same amenities as larger hotels at a fraction of their rates. Rooms are carpeted, nicely furnished, and impeccably clean. Two "apartments," larger rooms in back, are ideal for small families. Complimentary breakfast and light meals are served at the bright café in front, behind which is a small lounge with armchairs and a sofa. The small hotel is half a block from busy 1 Norte, but is remarkably quiet. **Pros:** Good value on a quiet backstreet. **Cons:** It's a long walk from the beach or Vina's main attractions. ⊠ *3 Poniente 70, between 1 and 2 Norte* ☏ *32/297–7822* 🖷 *32/247–8576* ⊕ *www.hotel3poniente.com* ↝ *12 rooms* ⬩ *In-room: no a/c, safe. In-hotel: bar, laundry service, no-smoking rooms, Wi-Fi, Internet, minibar, no elevator* ⊟ *AE, DC, MC, V* ⏍ *BP.*

NIGHTLIFE & THE ARTS

Viña's nightlife varies considerably according to the season, with the most glittering events concentrated in January and February. There are nightly shows and concerts at the casino and frequent performances at Quinta Vergara. During the rest of the year, things get going only on weekends. Aside from the casino, late-night fun is concentrated in the area around the intersection of Avenida San Martín and 4 Norte, the shopping strip on Avenida Valparaíso, and the eastern end of the alley called Paseo Cousiño. Viña residents tend to go to Valparaíso to party to live music, since it has a much better selection.

BARS Though it's surrounded by the dance clubs and loud bars of Paseo Cousiño, **Kappi Kua** (⊠ *Paseo Cousiño 11-A* ☏ *32/977–331*) is a good place for a quiet drink. **Margarita** (⊠ *Av. San Martín 348* ☏ *32/972–110*) is a popular watering hole late at night. The namesake cocktail is a killer. **Rituskuan** (⊠ *Av. Valparaíso at Von Schroeders* ☏ *9/305–0340*) is colorful and has excellent beer and electronic music.

CASINO With a neoclassical style that wouldn't be out of place in a classic James Bond movie, **Casino Viña del Mar** (⊠ *Av. San Martín 199* ☏ *32/250–0600*) has a restaurant, bar, and cabaret, as well as roulette, blackjack, and 1,500 slot machines. It's open nightly until the wee hours of the morning most of the year. There's a 3,000-peso cover charge. People dress up to play here, especially in the evening.

DANCE CLUBS The popular **El Burro** (⊠ *Paseo Cousiño 12-D* ☏ *No phone*) opens only Friday and Saturday. **El Mezón con Zeta** (⊠ *Paseo Cousiño 9* ☏ *No phone*) has a small dance floor. Viña's most sought-out dance club is **Scratch** (⊠ *Bohn 970* ☏ *32/978–219*), a long block east of Plaza Sucre.

The impossible-to-spell **Zeuz's** (⊠ *Arlegui 829* ☏ *No phone*) is the hottest gay disco on the coast. Don't get here before 1:30 or 2, when the extravagant drag shows on the balcony stop all the action on the dance floor.

FILM **Cine Arte** (⊠ *Plaza Vergara 142* ☏ *32/882–998*) is an art-house theater on the west side of Plaza Vergara. **Cinemark Marina Arauco** (⊠ *Av. Libertad 1348* ☏ *32/688–188*) has four screens showing American flicks. You can catch newly released American films on eight screens at the **Cinemark Shopping Viña** (⊠ *Av. 15 Norte 961* ☏ *32/993–388*), but it's a little far from the center of town.

THEATER **Teatro Municipal de Viña del Mar** (⊠ *Plaza José Francisco Vergara s/n* ☏ *32/681–739*), a lovely neoclassical auditorium in the center of the city, hosts frequent theatrical productions, as well as music and dance performances.

SPORTS & THE OUTDOORS

BEACHES Just north of the rock wall along Avenida Peru is a stretch of sand that draws throngs of people December–March. Viña del Mar really has just one **main beach**, bisected near its southern end by an old pier, though its parts have been given separate names: Playa El Sol and Playa Blanca. South of town, on the far side of Cerro Castillo, the small **Playa Caleta Abarca** receives fewer sun worshippers than the main beach. A short drive north of town is the tiny **Las Salinas**, a crescent of sand that has the calmest water in the area.

GOLF You can play 18 holes Tuesday–Sunday at the **Granadilla Country Club** (⊠ *Camino Granadilla s/n* ☎ *32/689–249*). It's an established course in Santa Inés—a 10-minute drive from downtown. The green fees are 56,000 pesos, and they rent clubs for 15,000 pesos, but you need to make a reservation.

HORSE
RACING
Valparaíso Sporting Club (⊠ *Av. Los Castaños 404* ☎ *32/689–393*) hosts horse racing every Wednesday. The Clásico del Derby, Chile's version of the Kentucky Derby, takes place the first Sunday in February. Rugby, polo, cricket, and other sports are also played here.

SOCCER Everton is Viña del Mar's soccer team. Matches are held at the 19,000-seat **Estadio Sausalito** (⊠ *Laguna Sausalito* ☎ *32/978–250*), which hosted World Cup matches in 1962.

SHOPPING

Viña's main shopping strip is **Avenida Valparaíso** between Cerro Castillo and Plaza Vergara, where wide sidewalks accommodate throngs of shoppers. Stores here sell everything from shoes to cameras, and there are also sidewalk cafés, bars, and restaurants. South of Plaza Vergara is the city's largest department store, **Ripley** (⊠ *Sucre 290* ☎ *32/384–480*). **Falabella** (⊠ *Sucre 250* ☎ *32/264–740*) is a popular small department store south of Plaza Vergara. For one-stop shopping, locals head to the mall. **Viña Shopping** (⊠ *Av. 15 Norte at 2 Norte* ☎ No phone), on the north end of town, is a longtime favorite. Next door to Viña Shopping is **Mall Marina Arauco** (⊠ *Av. 14 Norte at 2 Oriente* ☎ No phone), which is even bigger.

Local crafts are sold at the **Cooperativa de Artesanía de Viña del Mar** (⊠ *Quinta 220, between Viana and Av. Valparaíso* ☎ No phone).On the beach, near the pier at Muelle Vergara, the **Feria Artesanal Muelle Vergara** is a crafts fair open daily in summer and on weekends the rest of the year.There are also collections of **handicraft stands** on the road to Reñaca.

THE SOUTHERN BEACHES

Once a dominion of solitude and sea, the stretch of coastline south of Valparaíso has seen much development, not all of it well planned, over the past few decades. A succession of towns here caters to the beach-bound hordes January and February. Though none of the towns is terribly attractive, a few of the beaches are quite nice. The main reason

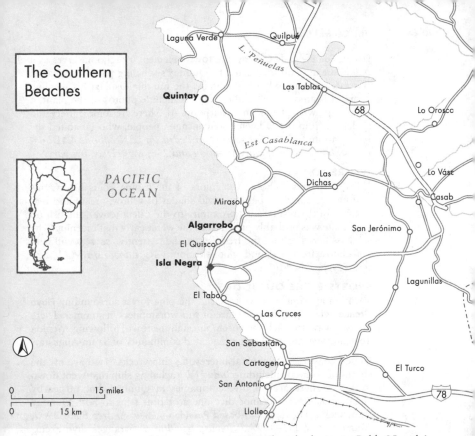

The Southern Beaches

PACIFIC OCEAN

0   15 miles
0   15 km

to visit—and it's a great one—is to take a look at poet Pablo Neruda's hideaway at Isla Negra. Here you can see the various treasures he collected during his lifetime.

Because large waves create dangerous undertows at some southern beaches, pay attention to warning flags: red means swimming is prohibited, whereas green, usually accompanied by a sign reading PLAYA APTA PARA NADAR (beach suitable for swimming), is a go-ahead signal.

QUINTAY

★ *30 km (19 mi) south of Valparaíso.*

Not too long ago, migrating sperm whales could still be seen from the beaches at Quintay. The creatures were all but exterminated by the whaling industry that sprang up in Quintay in 1942. Whaling was banned in 1967, and Quintay returned to being a quiet fishing village. If you wonder what the coast used to be like before condos began springing up, head to this charming spot. Just past the handful of brightly colored fishing boats on the little beach is the nearly abandoned **whaling factory.** Walk around its skeletal remains—parts are now used as an open-air shellfish hatchery.

Escuela San Pedro de Quintay, the town's elementary school, serves as a makeshift museum dedicated to Quintay's whaling past. Jose Daniel Barrios, a former whaler, maintains the humble display; his whaling contract is among the exhibits. Others include photos of the plant, a whale gun, whale teeth, and a harpoon. Also here are some pottery and skeletons from the indigenous Aconcagua people, who inhabited the region around 1300. ⊠ *Escuela San Pedro s/n* ☎ *No phone* 🖃 *Donation* ⊙ *Jan. and Feb., daily 10–noon and 2–6; Mar.–Dec., hrs vary.*

WHERE TO EAT

$–$$ ✕ **Los Pescadores.** Echoing the colors of the fishing boats below, this seafood restaurant is painted vivid shades of yellow, green, and red. Because of the restaurant's proximity to the caleta (cove), the fish on your plate was probably pulled from the water early that morning. The sea bass here is about the freshest around. Attentive servers will help you choose from the good wine selection. ⊠ *Costanera s/n* ☎ *32/362–068* ▤ *AE, DC, MC, V.*

SPORTS & THE OUTDOORS

BEACHES   Vacation apartments have replaced the pine forest surrounding **Playa Grande,** which gets its fair share of sun worshippers in summer. There are two ways to reach the beach: through the town, following Avenida Teniente Merino, or through the gated community of Santa Augusta.

DIVING   Chile's coastline has several interesting shipwrecks. Two are off the shores of Quintay, including *Indus IV*, a whaling ship that went down in 1947. There are no dive companies in Quintay, but in nearby Algarrobo, Cinco Oceanos dive operator runs trips to both Quintay shipwrecks. The Santiago-based **Poseidon** (⊠ *Av. Andrés Bello 2909, Santiago* ☎ *2/231–3597* ⊕ *www.posseidon.cl*) arranges dive excursions to the wrecks of Quintay.

ALGARROBO

35 km (22 mi) south of Quintay.

The largest town south of Valparaíso, Algarrobo is the first in a string of balnearios spread along the coast to the south. Though Algarrobo isn't the prettiest, it has a winding coastline with several yellow-sand beaches, and consequently attracts throngs of sun worshippers.

GETTING HERE & AROUND

From Valparaíso, follow Ruta 68 back to Santiago and turn off onto Ruta F90 just before Casablanca. From there it is approximately 35 km (22 mi) to Algarrobo. Pullman and Turbus travel regularly to Algarrobo from the Alameda Terminal (Metro Universidad de Santiago) in Santiago. Most of Algarrobo's main beaches lie within easy walking distance of the town. Regular buses run from here along the coast to El Quisco and Isla Negra further south.

ESSENTIALS

Currency Exchange Banco de Chile (⊠ *Carlos Alessandri 1666, Algarrobo* ☎ *35/482–857*).

Medical Assistance Hospital Claudio Vicuña (⌧ *Carmen Guerrero 945, San Antonio* ☎ *35/201–301*). **Cruz Verde** (⌧ *Avenida Carlos Alessandri 1915-1923* ☎ *35/489–065*).

Visitor & Tour Info Municipal Tourist Office (⌧ *Avenida Peñablanca 250* ☎ *35/483–615*).

EXPLORING

Next to Playa San Pedro is the private yacht club, **Club de Yates Algarrobo.** In February, boats from all over the country participate in one of Chile's most important nautical events here: the Regata Mil Millas Náuticas.

The **Cofradía Náutica,** a private marina at the end of a point south of town, harbors some of the country's top yachts.

Just offshore from the Cofradía Náutica is a tiny island called **Isla de los Pájaros Niños,** a penguin sanctuary that shelters more than 300 Humboldt and Magellan penguins. The upper crags of the island are dotted with hundreds of little caves dug by the penguins using their legs and beaks. Though only members are allowed in the marina, a path leads to the top of a nearby hill from which you can watch the flightless birds through binoculars.

WHERE TO STAY & EAT

$-$$ ✕**Algarrobo.** The only waterfront restaurant in Algarrobo has an expansive terrace overlooking the beach. The extensive menu is almost exclusively seafood, including half a dozen types of fish served with an equal number of sauces. Ostiones *pil pil* (spicy scallop scampi) and *loco apanado* (fried abalone) are popular starters. Finish with sole or sea bass steamed, grilled, or served *a lo pobre* (topped with a fried egg). ⌧ *Av. Carlos Alessandri 1505* ☎☐ *35/481–078* ☰ *AE, DC, MC, V.*

$$ ▦**Hotel Pacífico.** This older hotel in the heart of town, a block from Playa Las Cadenas, has bland but comfortable rooms. The main building dates from the 1940s, with polished wooden floors and a nice lounge with a fireplace. Spacious rooms on the second floor have seen better days, but a few in front overlook the sea. A newer—1960s—annex is stacked against the hillside. **Pros:** Spacious rooms with views over ocean. **Cons:** Hotel is looking its age with some rooms rather worn. ⌧ *Av. Carlos Alessandri 1930* ☎ *35/482–865* ☐ *35/481–040* ⊕ *www. hotel-pacifico.cl* ⌁ *79 rooms* ⌂ *In-room: no a/c. In-hotel: restaurant, bar, pool, laundry service, no elevator* ☰ *AE, DC, MC, V* ⦿ *BP.*

$ ▦**Pao Pao.** Llamas trim the grass around the cabanas spread here
★ across a forested ridge north of town. The octagonal pine cabanas range from cozy studios that sleep two to two-bedroom apartments complete with wooden decks and hot tubs. Only some have views of the water at Playa Grande. All of the cabanas have giant windows and well-stocked kitchenettes; most have small fireplaces. **Pros:** The rural setting makes it ideal for families. **Cons:** The adjacent restaurant opens only on weekends outside of January and February. ⌧ *Camino Mirasol 170* ☎☐ *35/482–145 or 35/481–264* ⊕ *www.turismopaopao.cl* ⌁ *22 cabins* ⌂ *In-room: no a/c, kitchen, cable TV. In-hotel: restaurant, pool, laundry service, minibar, no elevator* ☰ *No credit cards.*

$ ⚏**San Alfonso del Mar.** This set of imposing apartment buildings on
★ Algarrobo's northern edge is a record-breaker. The eight hectare, one
thousand meter, turquoise blue seawater pool that stretches the length
of the complex is officially (it's in the *Guiness Book of Records*) the
world's largest. That attracts swimmers, kayakers and even yachters.
The spacious suites, all with terraces overlooking the ocean, sleep up
to 10 and guests also have access to their own spa, supermarket, ice
cream parlor and even an aquarium, so there is plenty to keep a young
and old occupied with having to stray. **Pros:** Avoid the chilly Humboldt Current in style. **Cons:** If you do feel the need to stray, it's a
long walk to town. ✉*Camino Algarrobo–Mirasol*⚏*35/481–398
or 2/202–0231* ⊕*www.sanalfonso.cl* ↩*Most apartments privately
owned, only small number available to rent* ⚘*In-room: kitchen, cable
TV. In-hotel: aquarium, spa, restaurants, bar, pool, laundry service*
⊟*No credit cards.*

SPORTS & THE OUTDOORS

BEACHES Algarrobo's nicest beach is **Playa El Canelo,** in a secluded cove south of
town. It's an idyllic spot of fine yellow sand, calm blue-green water,
and a backdrop of pines. Though quiet most of the year, it can get
crowded in January and February. Follow Avenida Santa Teresita south
to Avenida El Canelo and the pine forest of Parque Canelo. Guarded
parking there costs 2,000 pesos. If you want seclusion, follow the trail
that leads southwest from Playa El Canelo, past the guano-splotched
outcropping called Peñablanca, to the smaller **Playa Canelillo.** South of
Algarobbo, **El Quisco** is a gesture of summer, nothing but a long beach
of pale sand guarded on either end by stone jetties. In the middle of the
beach is a boulder with a 15-foot-high, six-pronged cactus sculpture
perched atop it. South of the beach is the blue-and-yellow caleta, where
boats anchored offshore create a picturesque composition. In summer,
the beach is packed on sunny days, as visitors outnumber *Quisqueños*
(locals) about 10 to 1.

The second-nicest beach in Algarrobo is **Playa Grande.** The beige sand
stretches northward from town for several miles. There's usually rough
surf, which can make it dangerous for swimming. Massive condomin-
ium complexes on either end of this beach spill thousands of vacationers onto it every summer. The most popular beach in town is tiny **Playa
San Pedro**; a statue of Saint Peter in the sand next to the wharf marks
the spot. It's small, but the waters are surrounded by a rocky barrier
that keeps them calm and good for swimming. **Playa Las Cadenas,** on
the north end of town, has a waterfront promenade. The name, Chain
Beach, refers to the thick metal links lining the sidewalk, which were
recovered from a shipwreck off Algarrobo Bay.

DIVING **Pablo Zavala** runs boat dives to half a dozen spots from the Club de
Yates (✉*Av. Carlos Alessandri 2447* ⚏*9/9435–4835*).

ISLA NEGRA

6 km (4 mi) south of El Quisco.

"I needed a place to work," Chilean poet and Nobel laureate Pablo Neruda wrote in his memoirs. "I found a stone house facing the ocean, a place nobody knew about, Isla Negra." Neruda, who bought the house in 1939, found much inspiration here. "Isla Negra's wild coastal strip, with its turbulent ocean, was the place to give myself passionately to the writing of my new song," he wrote.

Fodor'sChoice A must-see for Pablo Neruda's ardent admirers, **Casa-Museo Isla Negra** ★ is a shrine to his life, work, and many passions. The house, perched on a bluff overlooking the ocean, displays the treasures—from masks and maps to seashells—he collected over the course of his remarkable life. Although he spent much time living and traveling abroad, Neruda made Isla Negra his primary residence later in life. He wrote his memoirs from the upstairs bedroom; the last pages were dictated to his wife here before he departed for the Santiago hospital where he died of cancer. Neruda and his wife are buried in the prow-shaped tomb area behind the house.

Just before Neruda's death in 1973, a military coup put Augusto Pinochet in command of Chile. He closed off Neruda's home and denied all access. Neruda devotees chiseled their tributes into the wooden gates surrounding the property. In 1989 the Neruda Foundation, started by his widow, restored the house and opened it as a museum. Here his collections are displayed as they were while he lived. The living room contains—among numerous other oddities—a number of bowsprits from ships hanging from the ceiling and walls. Neruda called them his "girlfriends."

You can enter the museum only with a guide, but there are excellent English-language tours every half hour. The tour will help you understand Neruda's many obsessions, from the positioning of guests at the dinner table to the east–west alignment of his bed. Objects had a spiritual and symbolic life for the poet, which the tours make evident. ⊠ *Camino Vecinal s/n* 🕾🕾 *35/461–284* ⊕ *www.neruda.cl* ✉ *3,000 pesos* ⊙ *Tues.–Sun. 10–2, 3–6.*

WHERE TO STAY & EAT

$–$$ ✕ **El Rincón del Poeta.** Inside the entrance to the Neruda museum, this small restaurant has a wonderful ocean view, with seating both indoors and on a protected terrace. The name translates as Poet's Corner, a theme continued in the small but original menu. Corvina *Neruda* is a sea bass fillet in a mushroom, artichoke, and shrimp cream sauce, and congrio *Garcia Lorca* is conger eel topped with tomato, sausage, and melted cheese. The house specialty is *pastel de centolla* (king crab pie), and they have lighter dishes such as chicken crepes, salmon seviche, and a spicy squid scampi. ⊠ *Casa-Museo Isla Negra, Camino Vecinal s/n* 🕾 *35/461–774* ▭ *No credit cards* ⊙ *Closed Mon.*

$–$$ ✕ ⛺ **La Candela.** Wander along the same rocky shore that Neruda once explored while staying at La Candela. The owner, Chilean folk singer

CLOSE UP

Neruda's Inspiration

First of all, let's clear up one thing: Isla Negra may mean "Black Island," but this little stretch of rugged coastline is not black, and it is not an island. This irony must have appealed to Nobel Prize–winning poet Pablo Neruda, who made his home here for more than three decades.

Of his three houses, Pablo Neruda was clearly most attached to Isla Negra. "Ancient night and the unruly salt beat at the walls of my house," he wrote in one of his many poems about his home in Isla Negra. It's easy to see how this house, perched high above the waves crashing on the purplish rocks, could inspire such reverie.

Neruda bought this house in 1939. Like La Sebastiana, his house in Valparaíso, it had been started by someone else and then abandoned.

Starting with the cylindrical stone tower, which is topped by a whimsical weather vane shaped like a fish, he added touches that could only be described as poetic. There are odd angles, narrow hallways, and various nooks and crannies, all for their own sake.

What is most amazing about Isla Negra, however, is what he chose to place inside. There's a tusk from a narwhal in one room, and figureheads from the fronts of sailing ships hanging overhead in another. There are huge collections ranging from seashells to bottles to butterflies. And yet it is also just a house, with a simple room designed so he could gaze down at the sea when he needed inspiration.

–Mark Sullivan

Rosario "Charo" Cofré, was a good friend of the Nerudas—note the photos in the lobby. If there's a crowd, she'll often sing a few songs. Many of the large guest rooms have fireplaces, and about half overlook the sea through the pines. The restaurant serves a vast selection of clams, sea bass, shrimp, and other seafood in numerous sauces. Country-style rooms have pale-wood furnishings and beds piled high with comforters. **Pros:** Seaside cosiness a short walk from Neruda's house. **Cons:** Not somewhere to stay in touch with the rest of the world. ✉ *De la Hostería 67* ☎ *35/461–254* 🖷 *35/462–531* ⊕ *www.candela.cl* 🛏 *20 rooms* ᨞ *In-room: no a/c, no phone, no TV, Wi-Fi. In-hotel: restaurant, bar, laundry service, no elevator* 🖃 *AE, DC, MC, V* ⊗ *CP.*

THE NORTHERN BEACHES

To the north of Viña del Mar, the Pacific collides with the rocky offshore islands and a rugged coastline broken here and there by sandy bays. The coastal highway runs from Viña del Mar to Papudo, passing marvelous scenery along the way. Between Viña and Concón, it winds along steep rock faces, turning inland north of Concón, where massive sand dunes give way to expanses of undeveloped coastline. The farther north you drive, the greater the distance between towns, each of which is on a significantly different beach. Whether as a day trip from Viña, or on a series of overnights, this stretch of coast is well worth exploring.

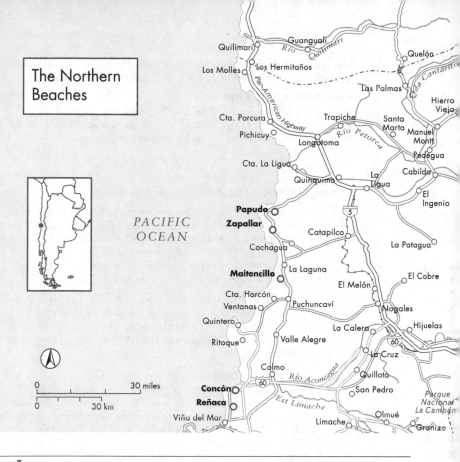

The Northern Beaches

Guanguali
Río Quilimarí
Quilimarí
Los Molles   Los Hermitaños
Quelón
La Cantarito
Las Palmas
Hierro
Viejo
Cta. Porcura
Trapiche   Santa
Marta   Manuel
Pichicuy
Río Petorca   Montt
Longotoma
Pedegua
Cta. La Ligua
Cabildo
Quinquimo   La
Ligua   El
Ingenio
Papudo
5
Zapallar
Catapilco
Cachagua   La Patagua
Maitencillo   La Laguna
El Cobre
El Melón
Cta. Horcón
Ventanas   Puchuncaví   Nogales
Quintero   Hijuelas
La Calera
Ritoque   Valle Alegre   60
La Cruz
Colmo   Quillota
Río Aconcagua   San Pedro
60
Parque
Concón   Nacional
Reñaca   Est Limache   La Campana
Viña del Mar   Olmué
Limache   Granizo

PACIFIC
OCEAN

0 _____ 30 miles
0 _____ 30 km

REÑACA

6 km (4 mi) north of Viña del Mar (follow Avenida Jorge Montt).

Thousands of Chileans flock to Reñaca every summer for one, and only one, reason—the crashing waves. You need merely contemplate this wide stretch of golden sand pounded by aquamarine waves, glistening beneath an azure sky, to understand why it's so popular. Contemplate it on a January or February afternoon, though, and you're likely to have trouble discerning the golden sand for the numerous bodies stretched across it. Vacation apartments are stacked up the steep hillside behind the beach, and on summer nights the bars and restaurants are packed. If you're seeking solitude, continue up the coast.

WHERE TO EAT

$–$$ ✕**Delicias del Mar.** At this seafood standout, you can watch through the
Fodor's Choice wide windows as the waves crash against the rocks across the street.
★ The second- and third-floor dining rooms are set back a bit so that everyone can enjoy the sun and surf. It's what comes out of the kitchen, however, that keeps people coming back. Start with seviche or *gratín de jaiba* (crab casserole), then feast on *salmón de rosita* (salmon on a bed

of spinach), or corvina *rellena* (sea bass stuffed with crab, spinach, and mushrooms). ⊠*Av. Borgoño 16000* ☎*32/289–0491* ▤*AE, MC, V.*

NIGHTLIFE & THE ARTS
The dance club **Kamikaze** (⊠*Av. Vicuña Mackenna 1106* ☎*32/834–667*), west of town, draws a young crowd. **Margarita** (⊠*Av. Central 150* ☎*32/836–398*) hosts live music on weekend nights.

CONCÓN

11 km (7 mi) north of Reñaca, along Avenida Borgoño.

How to explain the lovely name Concón? In the language of the Changos, *co* meant "water," and the duplication of the sound alludes to the confluence of the Río Aconcagua and the Pacific. When the Spanish arrived in 1543, Pedro de Valdivia created an improvised shipyard here that was destroyed by natives, leading to one of the first clashes between indigenous and Spanish cultures in central Chile.

Today, the town that holds the name is packed with high-rise apartment buildings, though it does have decent ocean views. The attraction lies to the north and south: the rugged coastal scenery along the road that connects it to Reñaca, and the sand dunes that rise up behind the beaches north of town.

GETTING HERE & AROUND
Concón, occupying a long stretch of coast on the south bank of the mouth of the Aconcagua river, lies 11 km (7 mi) north of Reñaca along the spectacular Avenida Borgoño (check out the houses built into the cliffs). If coming direct from Santiago, take Ruta 5 north until Km 109 and take the turning to Quillota all the way to the coast. Buses from Viña del Mar leave regularly from Plaza Francisco Vergara.

ESSENTIALS
Currency Exchange Banco de Chile (⊠*Avenida Concón Reñaca 710* ☎*32/246–8592*).

Medical Assistance Farmacias Ahumada (⊠*Av. Manantiales No 1121* ☎*32/281–3571*).

EXPLORING
North of town across from a large wooden restaurant is **Isla de Lobos,** a small rocky island that shelters a permanent population of sea lions, which can be viewed from shore. ⊠*Costanera, 9 km (5½ mi) north of Concón.*

Roca Oceánico is a massive promontory covered with scrubby vegetation. Footpaths that wind over it afford excellent views of Viña del Mar and Valparaíso—and of the sea churning against black volcanic rock below. ⊠*Costanera, 1 km (½ mi) north of Isla de Lobos.*

3

WHERE TO STAY & EAT

$-$$ ✕**Aquí Jaime.** Owner Jaime Vegas is usually on hand, seating customers
Fodor's Choice and scrutinizing the preparation of such house specialties as *lenguado*
★ *jaime* (sole in a mushroom and shrimp sauce), *arroz a la valenciana*
(paella packed with seafood), and *albacora portuguesa* (grilled sword-
fish topped with shrimp-tomato flambé). Perhaps this is why the small
restaurant perched on a rocky promontory next to Caleta Higuerillas
has one of the best reputations in the region. Large windows let you
watch the waves crashing just below, passing boats and pelicans, and
the coast that stretches northward. ⊠*Av. Borgoño 21303* ☎*32/281–
2042* ▤*AE, DC, MC, V* ◷*No dinner Sun. and Mon.*

$ ▥**Bahía Bonita.** Perched on a hilltop overlooking Concón, this all-suites
Fodor's Choice hotel is painted pale shades of yellows and oranges. All the rooms have
★ flower-filled terraces—some more than one—overlooking the crashing
waves. Living rooms and full-size kitchens packed with elegant plates
and glassware make this a great place for a family or several friends.
Some of the larger rooms can easily sleep five or six. An indoor heated
pool makes it a year-round possibility. **Pros:** The apartments have plenty
of space to spread out. **Cons:** A steep climb from the beach. ⊠*Av. Borgoño 22040, Subida San Fabián, Con-Con* ☎*32/281-8757* ⊕*www.
aparthotelbahiabonita.cl* ⇖*12 suites* ⊘*In-room: safe, kitchen. In-
hotel: pool, laundry service, Wi-Fi* ▤*AE, DC, MC, V* ⦿*CP.*

Fodor's Choice ▥**Radisson Concón.** Rising out of a craggy headland with spectacular
★ views up and down the coast, this hotel blends almost seamlessly into
it surroundings. The rough rock walls, huge bright windows, and red
leather upholstery also make this one of Chile's most stylish hotels.
Do not miss the beautiful roof terrace or the indoor pool of heated
seawater. **Pros:** Escape the summer crowds of larger towns, while still
just a walk from the beach. **Cons:** Hard floors and a cool atmosphere
make this less than ideal for children. ⊠*Av. Borgoño 23333, Concón*
☎*32/254-6400* ⊕*www.radisson.cl* ⇖*50 rooms* ⊘*In-room: safe,
mini-bar, Wi-Fi. In-hotel: pools, spa, sauna, laundry service* ▤*AE,
DC, MC, V* ⦿*CP.*

BEACHES The southernmost beach in Concón, **Playa Los Lilenes** is a tiny yellow-
sand cove with calm waters. After the wharf is **Playa Las Bahamas,** the
beach favored by surfers and windsurfers. At the north end of town is
the gray-sand **Playa La Boca.** It was named Mouth Beach because the Río
Aconcagua flows into the Pacific here, which makes the water murky.
Concón's nicest beach is **Playa Ritoque,** a long, wide, golden strand that
starts several miles north of town and stretches northward for several
miles. Access is good at Punta de Piedra, 5 km (3 mi) north of town,
where guarded parking costs 2,000 pesos per day. You can reenact
scenes from *The English Patient* 1 km (½ mi) north of here, where
the vast sand dunes that resemble those in the movie rise up behind
the beach.

HORSEBACK **Sol y Mar** (⊠*Camino a Quintero, Km 5* ☎*32/813–675*) has horseback
RIDING excursions on the beach or to the sand dunes that can be combined
with kayaking or boat trips on a nearby lake.

MAITENCILLO

20 km (12 mi) north of Quintero.

This town is a mass of cabanas and eateries spread out along the 4-km (2½-mi) Avenida del Mar. Two long beaches are separated by an extended rocky coastline that holds the local caleta. To complement the abundant sand and surf, there is a decent selection of restaurants, bars, and accommodations. The coast south of the town is almost completely undeveloped and a magnet for seabirds.

GETTING HERE & AROUND

From Concón, follow Ruta F30 E north turning inland from the coast past Quintero until signs show the turnoff for Maitencillo and La Laguna. If coming from Santiago, take Ruta 5 Norte and turn off at the turning for Catapilco (just after the El Melón tunnel) and follow the road to the coast.

ESSENTIALS

Medical Assistance Posta Rural Maitencillo (⊠ *Padre E. del Río s/n* ☎ *32/277–1715*).

Visitor & Tour Info Municipal Tourism Office (⊠ *Avenida Bernardo O'Higgins 70, Puchancavi* ☎ *32/279–1085*).

EXPLORING

Off the coast from Cachagua, several miles north of Maitencillo, is the **Monumento Nacional Isla Cachagua,** a protected island inhabited by Magellan and Humboldt penguins. No one is allowed on the island, but you can ride around in a small boat that can be hired at the Caleta de La Laguna or Caleta de Zapallar. You can also view the island from the beach below Cachagua, though you need binoculars to watch the penguins wobble around.

WHERE TO EAT

$ ✕ **La Canasta.** Serpentine bamboo tunnels connect rooms, and slabs of wood suspended by chains serve as tables: the scene could be straight from *The Hobbit*. A small menu changes regularly, but includes dishes such as *cordero a la ciruela* (lamb with a cherry sauce) and corvina *queso de cabra* (sea bass with goat cheese). Although it's across from the beach, there's no view. ⊠ *Av. del Mar 593* ☎ *32/277–1026* ⊟ *AE, DC, MC, V.*

$-$$ ✕ **La Tasca de Altamar.** Old nautical equipment decorates the interior of this spacious restaurant across the street from the ocean. The ample, almost exclusively marine menu ranges from such Chilean standards as *ostiones a la parmesana* (scallops in melted cheese) and *perol de machas* (steamed razor clams with onions and parsley) to delicious, but exorbitantly priced, half lobsters. A pair of fireplaces warm things up when wintry winds blow. ⊠ *Av. del Mar 3600* ☎ *32/772–132* ⊟ *AE, DC, MC, V* ⊙ *Closed Wed. Mar.–Dec.*

$$-$$$ ✕🏨 **Marbella.** Golf fairways, pine trees, and ocean vistas surround a four-story white-stucco resort building. Spacious, colorful rooms are decorated with original art and have large terraces with views of Mait-

encillo Bay. The circular Mirador restaurant has great views and interesting menu selections, such as sea-bass with clams sautéed in pesto, and *filete del bosque Marbella* (steak stuffed with wild mushrooms and vegetable confit). The only drawback is the distance from the beach—you need a car if you also want to explore the coast. ✉ *Carretera Concón–Zapallar, Km 38* ☎ *32/2772–020 or 800/211–108* 🖷 *32/2772–030, 2/206–0554 in Santiago* ⊕ *www.marbella.cl* ⇆ *78 rooms* ♨ *In-room: safe, dial-up. In-hotel: 2 restaurants, room service, bar, tennis courts, pools, spa, bicycles, laundry service, minibar* ⊟ *AE, DC, MC, V* ¶ *BP, FAP, MAP.*

WHERE TO STAY

$$ ⊡ **Altamar Aparthotel.** All the rooms in this brick-red building with
★ a vaguely New England feel have ocean views, though those on the third floor have the best ones. They are spotless, bright, and nicely decorated, with sliding glass doors that open onto either a terrace or balcony, most of which are surrounded by flowers. All of them have well-stocked kitchenettes, but they range in size from studios to one-bedroom apartments with sofa beds and large furnished terraces complete with grills. **Pros:** Enjoy breakfast on your terrace over looking the ocean. **Cons:** Less centralized contact with other guests. ✉ *Av. del Mar 3600* 🖷 *32/772–150* ⊕ *www.altamaraparthotel.cl* ⇆ *18 apartments* ♨ *In-room: no a/c, kitchen. In-hotel: restaurant, pool, laundry service, no elevator* ⊟ *AE, DC, MC, V.*

$ ⊡ **Cabañas Hermansen.** Set in an overgrown garden, these cabanas feel far away from everything. (In reality, they're just across from the beach.) A jumble of walkways leads uphill to the rooms. Stone fireplaces and wood walls add to the rustic feel. Ask for one of the newer rooms at the top of the hill, as they have a few nice touches like river-rock showers. **Pros:** The best place to escape the crowds without leaving Maitencillo. **Cons:** Like almost everywhere in Maitencillo, you have to cross a busy road to reach the beach. ✉ *Av. del Mar 592* ☎ *32/771–028* ⊕ *www. hermansen.cl* ⇆ *15 rooms* ♨ *In-room: kitchen (some). In-hotel: restaurant, bar, no elevator* ⊟ *No credit cards.*

SPORTS & THE OUTDOORS

BEACHES On the north side is the largest beach in town, the extra-wide **Playa Larga.** It's often pounded by big surf. The light-gray sand of **Playa Aguas Blancas** lies to the south of a rock outcropping, protected from the swells, and consequently is good for swimming.

Nearby, in the town of Quintero, there are beaches and hidden coves that can be hard to find, or may require a bit of a hike to reach. **Playa Los Enamorados** is a short walk from the Parque Municipal. Surfing is popular at **Playa El Libro,** which is reached from Hermanos Carrera or Balmaceda via concrete stairs. Swimming is prohibited here, but kids play in the little pools that form behind the rocks. If you follow Avenida 21 de Mayo to its end, you come to **Playa Durazno,** a small, unattractive gray-sand beach that does have calm water. **Playa El Caleuche,** beyond the rocks at the end of Playa Durazno, is safe for swimming.

GOLF The **Marbella Country Club** (✉ *Carretera Concón–Zapallar, Km 35* ☎ *32/277–2403*) has 27 holes of golf—without a doubt some of the best on the coast—in an exclusive environment. The tennis and paddle-tennis courts are available only to members and to guests of the Marbella resort. Green fees for hotel guests are 22,000 pesos, whereas nonguests pay 42,000 pesos during the week and 52,000 pesos on weekends.

HANG GLIDING *Parapente,* a seated version of hang gliding, is popular here. **Parapente Aventura** (✉ *Lomas del Rincón s/n, Puchuncaví* ☎ *9/7919–9292 or 9/332–2426*) has classes and two-person trips for beginners.

HORSEBACK RIDING In Cachagua, **Club Ecuestre Cachagua** (✉ *Costanera s/n, Cachagua* ☎ *33/771–596*) runs horseback tours to scenic overlooks.

ZAPALLAR

★ *48 km (30 mi) north of Concón along the Camino Concón-Zapallar.*

An aristocratic enclave for the past century, Zapallar doesn't promote itself as a vacation destination. In fact, it has traditionally been reluctant to receive outsiders. The resort is the brainchild of Olegario O'Valle, who owned property here. In 1893, following an extended stay in Europe, O'Valle decided to re-create the Riviera on the Chilean coast. He allotted plots of land to friends and family with the provision that they build European-style villas. Today the hills above the beach are dotted with these extravagant summer homes. Above them are the small, tightly packed adobes of a working-class village that has developed to service the mansions.

GETTING HERE & AROUND
From Maitencillo, follow Ruta F30 E north over the clifftops until signs indicate the turning for Zapallar. If coming from Santiago, take Ruta 5 Norte and turn off at the turning for Catapilco and follow the road to the coast.

ESSENTIALS
Currency Exchange Banco de Chile (✉ *Ramón Calderón O.* ☎ *33/291–516*).

Medical Assistance Cruz Verde (✉ *Avenida Cachagua No 34* ☎ *33/772–056*).

EXPLORING
Zapallar's raison d'être is **Playa Zapallar,** a crescent of golden sand kissed by blue-green waters, with a giant boulder plopped in the middle. Cropped at each end by rocky points and backed by large pines and rambling flower gardens, it may well be the loveliest beach on the Central Coast.

At the south end of Playa Zapallar is a rocky point that holds **Caleta de Zapallar,** where local fisherfolk unload their boats, sell their catch, and settle in for dominoes. The view of the beach from the caleta and adjacent restaurant, El Chiringuito, is simply gorgeous. On the other side of the point, a trail leads over the rocks to rugged but equally impressive views.

↻ Up the hill from Caleta de Zapallar is the **Plaza del Mar Bravo**. Rough Sea Square has a park with yet another ocean view and a large playground. In January and February, there are usually mule rides for kids.

Note: There are no signs pointing the way down to the beach, and few signs even telling you on what road you happen to be traveling. Locals are happy to point the way.

WHERE TO STAY & EAT

$–$$ ✕ **El Chiringuito.** Pelicans, gulls, and cormorants linger among the fishing boats anchored near this remarkable seafood restaurant. Since it's next door to the fishermen's cooperative, the seafood is always the freshest. For starters choose from *machas* (razor clams), *camarones* (shrimp), or *ostiones* (scallops) cooked *al pil pil* (with chili sauce and garlic), *a la parmesana* (with cheese), or *a la crema* (with a cream sauce). Then sink your teeth into any of half a dozen types of fish, served with different sauces. The dining room—with a floor of crushed shells and hand-carved chairs resembling sea creatures—is a delight. ⊠*Caleta de Zapallar s/n* ☎*33/741–024* ⊟*No credit cards* ☉*No dinner weekdays Mar.–Dec.*

Fodor'sChoice

★

$–$$ ✕ **Restaurante Cesar.** There's no better way to escape the afternoon sun than to snag one of the bright red tables at this terrace restaurant. The thatched parasols above you sway gently in the breeze. In winter, cozy up to a large fireplace in the dining room. The menu has an ample seafood selection, including many different dishes using swordfish and sole, as well as beef and chicken dishes, and is complemented by an extensive wine list. ⊠*Playa Zapallar* ☎*9/9280–3420* ⊟*No credit cards.*

$$–$$$ ▦ **Isla Seca.** Bougainvillea and cypress trees surround two identical moss-green buildings with well-appointed, spacious rooms. If you choose those with *terraza y vista al mar,* you get picture windows and narrow balconies with wonderful views of the rocky coast and blue Pacific. The suites on the corners have views on two sides, but lack terraces. The airy restaurant, with its black-and-white tile floor and original art, has style to rival anything in Miami Beach. It leads directly out to a terrace wrapping around a sparkling pool. A staircase leads down to the beach. **Pros:** Quiet, feels secluded. **Cons:** Not all rooms have ocean view. ⊠*Camino Costero Ruta F-30-E No 31* ☎*33/741–224* ⊟*33/741–228* ⊕*www.hotelislaseca.cl* ⬎*36 rooms, 6 suites* ♿*In-room: no a/c, safe. minibar, Wi-Fi. In-hotel: restaurant, bar, pool, bicycles, no elevator* ⊟*AE, DC, MC, V.*

Fodor'sChoice

★

TENNIS

Zapallar's **Club de Tenis** (⊠*Costanera s/n* ☎*33/741–551*) has 14 clay courts scattered around a forested hillside above town. Nonmembers pay 5,000 pesos per game.

PAPUDO

11 km (7 mi) north of Zapallar.

In a letter dated October 8, 1545, Spanish conquistador Pedro Valdivia wrote: "Of all the lands of the New World, the port of Papudo has a goodness above any other land. It's like God's Paradise: it has a gentle temperate climate; large, resounding mountains; and fertile lands."

Today a jumble of apartment buildings and vacation homes detracts from the view Valdivia once admired, but the beaches and coast north of town remain quite pleasant. For years Papudo was connected to Santiago by a train that no longer runs. You can still find bits of that history in the quiet resort town.

A block from the beach is the **Palacio Recart,** built in 1910. The yellow building, which now holds municipal offices, hosts occasional art and history exhibitions. ⊠ *Costanera s/n* ☎ *No phone.*

Near the south end of town is the lovely **Iglesia Parroquial de Papudo,** a 19th-century church. It was once part of a convent that has been replaced by vacation apartments. ⊠ *Costanera s/n* ☎ *No phone* ⊙ *Jan. and Feb., weekends.*

WHERE TO STAY & EAT

$–$$ ✕ **El Barco Rojo.** In 1913, a French ship called the *Ville de Dijon* sank off the coast of Papudo. The beams, doors, portholes, and other sundry parts were salvaged to build The Red Ship. Poet Pablo Neruda once frequented the spot. The ceiling is papered with love letters to the restaurant written by patrons. Tables and chairs are a delightful hodgepodge of styles and colors, and the tiny bar is eclectically furnished with bric-a-brac. The menu is dominated by seafood, but includes such treats as fried empanadas filled with cheese and basil. ⊠ *Av. Irarrazaval 300* ☎ *33/791–488* ☐ *AE, DC, MC, V* ⊙ *Closed Mon.–Thurs. Mar.–Dec.*

$ ☷ **Hotel Carande.** The only respectable hotel in town, Carande has carpeted rooms devoid of charm but just a short walk from the beach. It's worth paying the extra money for a room on the third floor to have a sea view over the rooftops. There's a restaurant on the second floor, and the lobby has a fireplace that usually has a fire burning in winter. **Pros:** Great views down to the beach. **Cons:** Lacks personality. ⊠ *Chorillos 89* ☎ *33/791–105* ☐ *33/791–118* ⊕ *www.hotelcarande.cl* ⮥ *29 rooms* ☖ *In-room: no a/c, refrigerator. In-hotel: restaurant, bar, no elevator* ☐ *AE, DC, MC V.*

BEACHES

Chileans migrate to Papudo from Santiago every summer to play on its beaches. **Playa Chica,** the small beach on the south end of town, is well protected and safe for swimming. Papudo's most popular beach is **Playa Grande,** a wide strand that stretches northward from the Barco Rojo for more than a mile. You have to do a bit of walking to reach **Playa Durazno.** It's an attractive beach north of Playa Grande—past the condominiums—that is lined with pine trees and protected by a rocky barrier offshore.

El Norte Chico

Elqui Valley

WORD OF MOUTH

"My favorite part of Chile was the Elqui Valley, it's just magical at night, but it might be a bit far for you considering your other plans."
—Notorious MEG

WELCOME TO EL NORTE CHICO

TOP REASONS TO GO

★ **Sugar-Sand Beaches:** The sugary sand, turquoise water, and warm breezes make El Norte Chico's beaches among the best in the country. During the summer months of January and February, you may have to fight for a place in the sun.

★ **Southern Skies:** Chile's northern desert has some of the clearest skies in the world, making it a top destination for international star gazers and scientists. There are six astronomical observatories in El Norte Chico and while Vicuña's Mamalluca is the most accessible, you can also visit the others if you make arrangements ahead of time.

★ **Crafts & Jewelry:** Unusual crafts are plentiful in El Norte Chico. The Elqui Valley is known for the beautiful ceramics of the Diaguita people, which often come in zoomorphic shapes with intricate geometric patterns. In La Serena, jewelry and items crafted from the locally mined combarbalita are particularly lovely.

Town of Vicuña

1 The Elqui Valley. Hot sun, cool pisco sours, and a heaven full of stars every night. Only an hour's drive from La Serena but a world apart from the bustling regional capital, the Elqui Valley is an inspirational place. It's easy to see where Chilean Nobel prize–winning poet Gabriela Mistral, raised in the Valley, got her inspiration.

2 The Huasco Valley. The desert here not only has a variety of flowers, but some are unique to this valley. On the coast, Parque Nacional Llanos de Challe is the best spot to view *el desierto florido*, a spectacular flowering that happens every four or five years.

Elqui Valley

3 The Copiapó Valley. Copiapó itself is a hot, inland town where the mining industry's newly minted wealthy are building new hotels and homes. But just 15 minutes outside of Copiapó is the realm of the desert, where quail and lizards scamper beneath the shadows of cacti and rocks bear mysterious carvings.

Tres Erres Pisco winery, Elqui

ANT⭘FAGASTA

Parque Nacional Pan de Azúcar

Diego de Almagro

El Salvador

Salar de Pedernales

Chañaral

PACIFIC OCEAN

Potrerillos

La Ola

Inca del Oro

Cerro Ermitanno

Caldera

Salar de Maricunga

31

Bahía Inglesa

5

Copiapó

3

Parque Nacional Nevado Tres Cruces

Cta. del Medio

Tierra Amarilla

Los Azules

ATACAMA

Los Loros

La Guardia

Parque Nacional Llanos de Challe

Algarrobal

Las Juntas

2

Huasco

Vallenar

Freirina

5

Alto del Carmen

Cta. Sarco

Domeyko

Gonay

Cerro del Toro

Cta. Chañaral

Las Breas

La Higuera Los Hornos

El Romeral

La Serena

1

Cerro Las Tortolas

Coquimbo

41

Monte Grande

Andacollo

Vicuña

Tongoy

Pisco Elqui

Quebrada Seca

Ovalle

Monte Patria

Parque Nacional Fray Jorge

5

Punitaque

Central Los Molles

San Marcos

Tulahuén

Cta Morritos

Combarbalá

Puerto Oscuro

COQUIMBO

ARGENTINA

Illapel

Salamanca

Río Choapa

0   50 miles

Quilimari

0   75 km

VALPARAÍSO

GETTING ORIENTED

El Norte Chico is a vast region spreading some 700 km (435 mi) between Río Aconcagua and Río Copiapó. You'll need more than one base to explore the entire area. In the south, La Serena is a good place to start if you're going to the Elqui Valley. Vallenar, on the Río Huasco, is where you'll want to be if your destination is the flowering desert. Copiapó, near the region's northern border, is a convenient stop if you're headed to Parque Nacional Nevado Tres Cruces.

EL NORTE CHICO PLANNER

When to Go

During the summer months of January and February, droves of Chileans and Argentines flee their stifling hot cities for the relative cool of El Norte Chico's beaches. Although it is an exciting time to visit, prices go up and rooms are hard to find. Make your reservations at least a month in advance. For a little tranquility, visit when the high season tapers off in March. Moving inland you'll find the weather is mild all year. The almost perpetually clear skies explain why the region has the largest concentration of observatories in the world. The temperatures drop quite a bit when you head to the mountains.

Health & Safety

Naturally, in the desert, drinking plenty of non-alcoholic fluids is crucial, as is protecting your face and body from the sun's powerful rays. Get a good pair of sunglasses for driving, as the glare can be intense. Keep in mind that pisco sours, though they may go down as smooth as lemonade, are a powerful drink, so a moderate intake is recommended.

Eat Well & Rest Easy

El Norte Chico is not known for its gastronomy, but the food here is simple, unpretentious, and often quite good. Along the coast you'll find abundant seafood. Don't pass up the *merluza con salsa margarita* (hake with butter sauce featuring almost every kind of shellfish imaginable) or *choritos al vapor* (mussels steamed in white wine). Inland you come across country-style *cabrito* (goat), *conejo* (rabbit), and *pinchones escabechadas* (baby pigeons). Don't forget to order a pisco sour, the frothy concoction made with the brandy distilled in the Elqui Valley.

People in El Norte Chico generally eat a heavy lunch around 2 PM that can last two hours, followed by a light dinner around 10 PM. Reservations are seldom needed, except in the fanciest restaurants. Leave a 10% tip if you enjoyed the service.

The good news is that lodging in El Norte Chico is relatively inexpensive. Your best bet is often the beach resorts, which have everything from nice cabanas to high-rise hotels. The bad news is that away from the areas that regularly cater to tourists you may have to make do with extremely basic rooms with shared baths.

WHAT IT COSTS IN CHILEAN PESOS (IN THOUSANDS)				
¢	$	$$	$$$	$$$$
RESTAURANTS				
under 3 pesos	3 pesos– 5 pesos	5 pesos– 8 pesos	8 pesos– 11 pesos	over 11 pesos
HOTELS				
under 15 pesos	15 pesos– 45 pesos	45 pesos– 75 pesos	75 pesos– 105 pesos	over 105 pesos

Restaurant prices are based on the median main course price at dinner. Hotel prices are for a double room in high season, excluding tax.

Norte Chico—there are even cloth napkins. **Pros:** Excellent swimming pool and comfy rooms. **Cons:** Some bathroom fixtures could use updating. ⊠*Sargento Aldea 101* ☎*51/411–301* 🖨*51/411–144* ⊕*www. hosteriavicuna.cl* ⤶*14 rooms* ⌂*In-room: no a/c. In-hotel: restaurant, bar, tennis court, pool, laundry service, parking (no fee)* ⊟*AE, DC, MC, V* ⦿*CP.*

$ ★ 🏨**Hotel Halley.** In a pretty colonial house with wood trim and white walls, this inn has carefully decorated rooms filled with authentic circa-1950s radios and more doilies than you could possibly imagine. There's a small, rather shallow swimming pool in the back. **Pros:** Quaint with central location. **Cons:** Small pool, old-fashioned. ⊠*Gabriela Mistral 542* ☎*51/412–070* 🖨*51/412–070* ⤶*11 rooms, 1 suite* ⌂*In-room: no a/c, refrigerator. In-hotel: pool, public Internet, parking (no fee), no-smoking rooms* ⊟*AE, DC, MC, V* ⦿*CP.*

4

NIGHTLIFE & THE ARTS

Pub Kharma (⊠*Gabriela Mistral 417* ☎*51/419–738*) occasionally hosts live music. Otherwise, the bar plays Bob Marley almost exclusively and pays further homage to the reggae legend with posters.

SHOPPING

You can buy local handicrafts, especially ceramics and jewelry, at the **Poblado Artesenal,** a collection of artisan stands on the Plaza de Armas. It's open daily 10–5.

PISCO ELQUI

10 km (6 mi) south of Monte Grande, 43 km (27 mi) east of Vicuña via Ruta D-485.

Once known as La Unión, this pisco-producing village, perched on a sun-drenched hillside, received its current moniker in 1939. Gabriel González Videla, at that time the president of Chile, renamed the village in a shrewd maneuver to ensure that Peru would not gain exclusive rights over the term "pisco." The Peruvian town of Pisco also produces the heady brandy.

GETTING HERE & AROUND

Take Ruta 41 to the turn for Paihuana (Ruta D-485). Follow this serpentine, narrow road about 12 km (7½ mi) into Pisco Elqui. Buses and colectivos run with frequency between La Serena, Vicuña, and Pisco Elqui. A bus or colectivo between Vicuña and Pisco Elqui costs about 1,500 pesos.

ESSENTIALS

Bus Contacts Solar de Elqui (☎*51/215–946*). **Valle de Elqui colectivo** (☎*51/411–695 or 51/224–517*). **Via Elqui** (☎*51/312–422*).

EXPLORING

This idyllic village of fewer than 600 residents has two pisco plants.

★ The **Disteleria Mistral** (☎*51/451–358* ⊕*www.piscomistral.cl*), on the main road, is Chile's oldest distillery. It produces the famous Tres Erres brand, perhaps Chile's finest. In the older section of the plant, maintained strictly for show, you can see the antiquated copper cauldrons and wooden barrels. The distillery arranges daily tours for 4,000 pesos, from 11 AM until 6 PM, followed by tastings where you can sample a pisco sour.

About 4 km (2½ mi) past Pisco Elqui you come upon the **Los Nichos** distillery (☎ 51/411–085), which hosts free daily tours and tastings.

Tiny **Monte Grande,** 6 mi north of Pisco Elqui, recalls a time of simpler pleasures. This picturesque village in the midst of rolling hills is home to both pisco and poetry. On the neighboring hillsides and in the valley below, farmers cultivate the grapes used to make pisco.

Gabriela Mistral, born in nearby Vicuña, grew up in Monte Grande. Her family lived in the schoolhouse where her elder sister taught. The **Casa Escuela** has been turned into a museum and displays some relics from the poet's life. Her tomb is on a nearby hillside. ⊠ *Central plaza* ☎ *51/451–015* 🎟 *600 pesos* ⊙ *Tues.–Sun. 10–1 and 3–6.*

WHERE TO STAY & EAT

¢–$ 🖭 **Complejo Turístico Gabriela Mistral.** The cabanas at this hotel are comfortable, although some are a bit dark. The pool is shallow, but can be a great place to wallow after a day of exploring the sun-drenched valley. **Pros:** Economical. **Cons:** A bit dated and cramped. ⊠ *Arturo Prat 59* ☎ *51/451–086* ⊕ *www.valledeelqui.cl* 🛏 *12 rooms, 12 cabanas* ⚒ *In-room: no a/c, no phone, no TV. In-hotel: restaurant, pool, laundry service* ⊟ *No credit cards.*

$$ 🖭 **Refugio Misterios de Elqui.** These six grass-roof cabanas surround a pleasant pool, where you can relax with a pisco sour and enjoy the delightful sunshine. The views of the mountains from the open-air restaurant are outstanding. **Pros:** Lovely, rustic, and clean. First class all the way. **Cons:** Footpaths a bit steep. ⊠ *Arturo Prat s/n* 🖭 *51/451-126* ⊕ *www.misteriosdeelqui.cl* 🛏 *6 cabanas* ⚒ *In-room: no a/c, no phone, no TV. In-hotel: restaurant, bar, pool* ⊟ *DC, MC, V* ⍟ *.BP.*

¢–$ ✕🖭 **El Tesoro de Elqui.** Beautiful gardens with flowers of e˙ .y imagin-
★ able shape and size surround this hotel's nicely decor˙ .ı cabanas. At the lovely pool you can laze around in the world-˙ .ous Elqui Valley sunshine and take in the panoramic view of ˙ Andes. The restaurant, which serves as a meeting place for tra˙ .rs, has an international menu. The tasty spaghetti Bolognese m˙ .s a welcome change from Chilean country cuisine. Ask for one ˙ .ıe rooms with a skylight. **Pros:** Rooms with views of the stars. ˙ .ı. **Cons:** Hard to navigate paths at night to reach rooms. ⊠ *A ˙ ıo Prat s/n* ☎ *51/451–069* ⊕ *www. tesoro-elqui.cl* 🛏 *5 rooms ˙ ın-room: no a/c, no phone, no TV. In-hotel: restaurant, pool ⊨ .ı, MC, V* ⍟ *BP.*

NIGHTLIFE & TH˙ .ıTS

There isn't much to do at night in Pisco Elqui but lie on your back and enjoy the brilliant stars. **Los Jugos** (🖭 *No phone*), on the corner of the plaza, serves incredible fresh-fruit drinks. Try the *jugo de frambuesa* (raspberry juice). At night time, **La Escuela** on Arturo Prat, between all the hotels, is a comfy joint, piping in jazz and American pop tunes.

CLOSE UP

Chile's National Drink

Distilled from muscat grapes grown in the sunbaked river valleys of El Norte Chico, pisco is indisputably Chile's national drink. This fruity, aromatic brandy is enjoyed here in large quantities—most commonly in a delightful elixir known as a pisco sour, which consists of pisco, lemon juice, and sugar. A few drops of bitters on top is optional. Some bars step it up a notch by adding whipped egg white to give the drink a frothy head. Another concoction made with the brandy is piscola—the choice of many late-night revelers—which is simply pisco mixed with soda. Tea with a shot of pisco is the Chilean answer to the common cold, and it may just do the trick to relieve a headache and stuffy nose. Whichever way you choose to take your pisco, you can expect a pleasant, smooth drink.

Chileans have enjoyed pisco, which takes its name from *pisku*, the Quechuan word for "flying bird," for more than 400 years. The drink likely originated in Peru—a source of enmity between the two nations. In 1939, Chilean President Gabriel González Videla went so far as to change the name of the town of La Unión to Pisco Elqui in an attempt to gain exclusive rights over the name pisco. But Peru already had its own town south of Lima named Pisco. The situation is currently at a standoff, with both countries claiming they have the better product.

The primary spots for pisco distillation are the Huasco and Elqui valleys; the latter is particularly renowned for the quality of its grapes. The 300 days of sunshine per year here make these lush valleys perfect for cultivating muscat grapes. The distillation process has changed very little in the past four centuries. The fermented wine is boiled in copper stills, and the vapors are then condensed and aged in oak barrels for three to six months—pisco makers call the aging process "resting." The result is a fruity but potent brandy with between 30% and 50% alcohol.

–Gregory Benchwick and Brian Kleupfel

SHOPPING

Fresh fruit marmalade and preserves are sold in the town's main plaza. You can also head to the pisco distilleries to pick up a bottle of freshly brewed pisco.

ANDACOLLO

54 km (34 mi) southeast of La Serena.

The compact town of Andacollo, an important gold and silver mining center since the 16th century, makes a pleasant stopover between Ovalle and La Serena. Here you'll find one of Chile's most famous religious icons. The wooden image of the Virgen de Andacollo, deemed miraculous by the Vatican in 1901 for its putative power to cure disease, draws some 150,000 pilgrims to the town each year from December 23 to 26 for the Fiesta Grande de la Virgen. During the festival, the statue is decorated and paraded through the streets.

★ The Virgen de Andacollo sits on a silver altar in the small **Templo Antiguo,** on Plaza Videla, the town's main square. This church, built in the 17th century, has a museum of the offerings given to the virgin in hopes of her miraculous assistance.

The **Basilica,** which was inaugurated in 1893 after nearly 20 years of construction, is by far the largest structure in the town. With a 40-meter-high (130-foot-high) dome and two giant steeples, it towers over everything else.

OVALLE

88 km (55 mi) south of La Serena via Ruta 43.

Ovalle will always suffer in comparison to its fair sister to the north, La Serena, for it has no beaches or breezes. However, Ovalle can be a starting point for a morning tour or a stopping-off point for lunch, and it does serve as a good base for trips to the Monumento Natural Pichasca or the Valle del Encanto. Moving toward modernity, in 2008 Ovalle looks forward to a new pedestrian mall, and on the outskirts of town, a four-star hotel. But if you have a choice for an overnight stay, La Serena is it.

GETTING HERE & AROUND

Ovalle is about an hour from La Serena directly via Ruta 43; a 15-minute drive on Ruta 45 out of Ovalle will take you to the Valle del Encanto; just beyond that to the west is the intersection with the Pan-American Highway (Ruta 5). There is daily bus service from Santiago (five hours) and La Serena (one hour). On the way into town you'll pass plenty of signs for *queso de cabra* (goat cheese) and field after field of muscatel grapes (used for pisco) and acre upon acre of avocado—a nice break after the bleak desert stretches of the Pan-American.

ESSENTIALS

Bank/Currency Exchange Banco de Chile (✉ *Victoria 261* ☎ *53/660–600*).

Bus Contacts Ovalle bus station (✉ *Maestranza 443* ☎ *53/626–707*).

Hospital Hospital Dr. Antonio Tirado Lanas De Ovalle (✉ *Ariztia 7* ☎ *53/660–100*).

Post Office Correos de Chile (✉ *Plaza de Armas*).

Tour Info Ovalle Tour (✉ *Libertad 456,* ☎ *53/626–696*).

EXPLORING

The town's shady **Plaza de Armas** is a pleasant place to pass an afternoon.

On the Plaza de Armas, the **Iglesia San Vicente Ferrer** is worth a visit. Constructed in 1849, the church was damaged by an earthquake in 1997 and remains open, albeit in a semi-dilapidated state.

★ Unlike geoglyphs, which are large-scale figures chiseled into the landscape, petroglyphs are small pictures carved onto the rock surface. One of Chile's densest collections of petroglyphs can be found in **Valle del Encanto.** The 30 images in the Valley of Enchantment were most likely etched by the Molle culture between AD 100 and 600. The figures wear ceremonial headdresses hanging low over large, expressive eyes. On occasion a guide waits near the petroglyphs and will show you the best of the carvings for a small fee. To reach the site, take Ruta 45 west from Ovalle. About 19 km (12 mi) from the town head south for 5 km (3 mi) on a rough, dry road. ✉*24 km (15 mi) west of Ovalle* ☎*No phone* ✇*Free* ⊘*Daily 8–7:30.*

A tourist complex cut from the rough land, **Termas de Socos** is a very pleasant hot springs. The waters, which spout from the earth at 28°C (82°F), are said to have incredible healing powers. Curative or not, the waters here are extremely relaxing. ✉*24 km (15 mi) west of Ovalle on Ruta 45* ☎*53/198–2505 or 2/236–3336* ⊕*www.termasocos.cl* ✇*1,000 pesos* ⊘*Daily 8–8.*

Heading toward the Andes you come across **Monumento Natural Pichasca,** a forest of petrified tree trunks. These play host to dozens of fossils, such as imprints of leaves and outlines of small animals. Nearby is a cave beneath a stone overhang that housed indigenous peoples thousands of years ago. Inside you'll find some cave paintings by the Molle people. ✉*50 km (31 mi) northeast of Ovalle on Camino Ovalle–Río Hurtado* ☎*No phone* ✇*1,000 pesos* ⊘*Daily 8:30–4:30.*

WHERE TO EAT

$ ✗**Bavaria.** Because of the country's large number of German immigrants, most Chilean cities have at least one Bavarian-theme restaurant. This one, part of a national chain, evokes the old country with wood beams and checkered yellow tablecloths. Entrées like *pollo a la plancha* (grilled chicken) are a bit bland, but wholesome and filling. ✉*Vicuña Mackenna 161-B* ☎*53/630–578* ▭*AE, MC, V.*

$ ✗**Neus.** Local engineering entrepreneur Nelson La Torre ("Neus") runs this joint and whips up a mean bowl of fetuccine with salsa a la Oscar, or if you're lucky, some freshly arrived fish from the coast. He may also turn on the "magic sing" Karaoke machine later in the evening—fasten your safety belts. ✉*Coquimbo 347* ☎*53/623–393* ▭*AE, MC, V.*

WHERE TO STAY

$ ▥**Hotel El Turismo.** A pleasant hotel in the center of town, Hotel El Turismo has spacious and well-kept rooms. Ask for a room facing the Plaza de Armas. **Pros:** Newly renovated, in center of town. **Cons:** Next to disco. ✉*Victoria 295* ☎*53/623–258* 📠*53/433 243* ⇆*30 rooms* ⌂*In-room: no a/c, refrigerators. In-hotel: restaurant, laundry service* ▭*MC, V* ⦿*CP.*

$ ▥**Hotel Termas de Socos.** This rustic hotel, about 33 km (20 mi) west of Ovalle, allows you unlimited access to the hot springs at Termas de Socos. The rooms have large, comfortable beds, and many have expansive picture windows looking out over the surrounding desert. Also available are relaxing massages and private hot tubs. The service, unfortunately, is a little inattentive. **Pros:** Big beds, access to hot springs. **Cons:** Remote, and inattentive service. ✉*Termas de Socos*

WILDLIFE

Situated between the mountains and the sea, the Central Valley has a host of wildlife, despite its barren appearance. Look for the Andean Fox (zorro andino) in Parque Fray Jorge, or the California Quail (cordoniz) hopping along the desert floor of the Valle del Encanto. Just an hour's cruise from La Serena is the national reserve of the Chaplinesque Humboldt Penguin, and you'll also see a host of sea lions (lobos marinos) and other sea creatures out there, such as the Brown Pelican. If you're very lucky, and you keep still long enough, you may even spot a puma at night in the Elqui Valley. CONAF—the Corporación Nacional Forestal de Chile (⊕ www. conaf.cl)—maintains Chile's national parks and forests, and can provide information on El Norte Chico's more remote regions. In La Serena check for tours to national parks and the interior. In Copiapó you can arrange trips to the altiplano. The Web page ⊕ www.jacobita.cl has a large listing and photo gallery of plants, rodents, insects, birds, and mammals that subsist in the Norte Chico.

☎ 53/681–021 ⊕ www.termasocos.cl ☜ 28 rooms ☆ In-room: no a/c. In-hotel: restaurant, room service, bar, pool, laundry service ☰ AE, MC, V ⊙ BP.

PARQUE NACIONAL FRAY JORGE

Fodor'sChoice *110 km (68 mi) south of La Serena.*
★

The thought of a patch of land that is rich with vegetation and animal life in the heart of El Norte Chico's dry, desolate landscape seems to defy logic. But Parque Nacional Fray Jorge, a UNESCO world biosphere reserve since 1977, has a small cloud forest similar to those found in Chile's damp southern regions. The forest, perched 600 meters (1,968 feet) above sea level, receives its life-giving nourishment from the *camanchaca* (fog) that constantly envelops it. Within this forest you'll come across ferns and trees found nowhere else in the region. A slightly slippery boardwalk leads you on a 20-minute tour. Budget time for the park as part of a longer day—the idea of "national park" in Chile is different from the concept in North America, and the "park" part of Fray Jorge is rather small. Although interesting, Fray Jorge will not take a lot of time to see, but there is a picnic table where you can lunch and watch the fog drift over the Pacific Ocean below. ⊠ *At Km 387 of Pan-American Hwy., take dirt road 27 km (11 mi) west* ☎ *No phone* ☜ *1,600 pesos* ⊙ *Daily 9–4:30.*

THE HUASCO VALLEY

At least twice a decade the desert bursts into life in a phenomenon called "el desierto florido." If you are lucky enough to visit the area during these times, you'll see the desert covered with colorful flowers, some of which exist only in this region. You can see the desierto florido in most of El Norte Chico, and the Parque Nacional Llanos de Challe

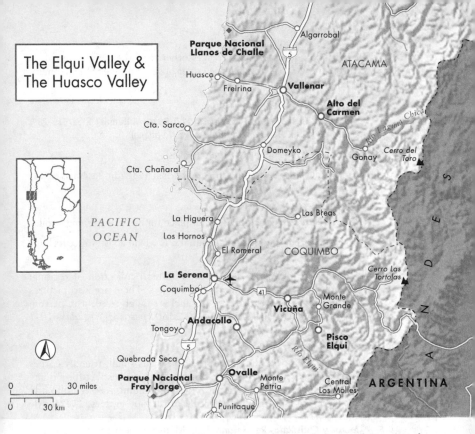

The Elqui Valley & The Huasco Valley

Parque Nacional Llanos de Challe

Algarrobal

ATACAMA

Huasco

Freirina

Vallenar

Alto del Carmen

Río Laguna Chica

Cta. Sarco

Domeyko

Gonay

Cerro del Toro

Cta. Chañaral

PACIFIC OCEAN

La Higuera

Las Breas

COQUIMBO

Los Hornos

El Romeral

Cerro Las Tortolas

La Serena

Coquimbo

Vicuña

Monte Grande

Andacollo

Tongoy

Pisco Elqui

Quebrada Seca

Río Elqui

Parque Nacional Fray Jorge

Ovalle

Monte Patria

Central Los Molles

ARGENTINA

Punitaque

0   30 miles

0   30 km

A N D E S

on the coast is an excellent place to view the flowering desert, but the Huasco Valley in particular has a lovely and large variety of flora.

The Huasco Valley sees far fewer visitors than the Elqui Valley, giving you the feeling that you've beaten the crowds. Climbing into the Andes from Vallenar, the valley's largest city, you reach the Upper Huasco Valley. The Valle del Carmen, a subregion of the Huasco Valley, has several quaint villages, such as Alto del Carmen and San Felix.

VALLENAR

188 km (116 mi) north of La Serena.

There isn't a reason to visit Vallenar, the transportation hub of the Huasco Valley, other than to use it as a base for visiting Parque Nacional Llanos de Challe or Alto del Carmen. Vallenar was founded in 1789 by Ambrosio O'Higgins, who named the town after his home in Ballinagh, Ireland.

GETTING HERE & AROUND

Vallenar lies midway between La Serena and Copiapó, on Ruta 5. Several bus companies such as Buses Palauta and Buses Vallemar travel through the Huasco Valley (also going inland to Alto del Carmen, for example), departing from places other than the main terminal on Arturo Prat, which is home to the larger buses that take the Pan-American Highway.

ESSENTIALS

Bus Contacts Buses Palauta (☏ 51/612–117). Buses Vallemar (☏ 51/619–289). **Bus Station** (✉ Av. Matta and Arturo Prat ☏ No phone).

Post Office Correos Chile (✉ Plaza O'Higgins).

Visitor & Tour Info Sernatur, Chilean Tourism (✉ Plaza de Armas ☏ 51/619–215).

EXPLORING

The large **Plaza O'Higgins** is a pleasant place for an early evening stroll.

The **Iglesia Porroquial,** on the main square, is worth a visit to see its huge copper dome.

On display at the **Museo de Huasco** is a small collection of regional indigenous artifacts like pottery and textiles. There are also pictures of the flowering desert for those not lucky enough to see it in person. ✉ Sargento Aldea 742 ☏ 51/611–320 ☐ 600 pesos ☉ Weekdays 10–1 and 3–6, Sat. 10–12:30.

WHERE TO EAT

$ ✕ **Il Boccato.** Opposite the Plaza de Armas, this small, friendly corner pizza place with a brightly lighted interior is your best bet for a quick bite. Choose from myriad menu options, including a zesty pollo a la plancha. There's also a wide selection of seafood entrées. ✉ Plaza de Armas ☏ 51/614–609 ☐ AE, DC, MC, V.

$ ✕ **Moros y Christianos Restaurant.** This Mediterranean-style restaurant, named for the Spanish festivals commemorating the wars between the Moors and the Christians, serves flavorful fish and meat dishes. ✉ Pan-American Hwy. at entrance to Vallenar ☏ 51/614–600 ⚓ Reservations essential ☐ AE, DC, MC, V ☉ Closed Mon.

WHERE TO STAY

$ ⊡ **Hostería de Vallenar.** The best lodging in Vallenar, this comfortable hostelry has basic rooms with wood furniture. The staff is friendly and helpful. The restaurant features some Brazilian specialties like *feijoada*, a hearty stew of black beans and sausage. **Pros:** Good location in town. **Cons:** Basic rooms. ✉ Alonso de Ercilla 848 ☏ 51/614–195 ☐ 51/614–538 ⊕ www.hotelesatacama.cl ☞ 30 rooms ☖ In-room: no a/c, refrigerator. In-hotel: restaurant, bar, pool, laundry service, public Wi-Fi ☐ AE, DC, MC, V ☉| CP.

$ ⊡ **Hotel Cecil.** A pleasant garden with a pool makes Hotel Cecil a good budget lodging choice. The rooms are spotless, but the baths are a bit small. **Pros:** Cheap. **Cons:** No frills. ✉ Arturo Prat 1059 ☏ 51/614–071 ⊕ www.hotelcecil.cl ☞ 18 rooms ☖ In-room: no a/c. In-hotel: room service, pool, laundry service, ethernet ☐ No credit cards ☉| CP.

NIGHTLIFE & THE ARTS

La Casona (⊠*Serrano 1475* ☏*51/611–600*) caters to an older crowd and heats up with dancing on the weekends. You can dance to salsa and other Latin rhythms on the town's largest dance floor at **Cubaire** (⊠*Serrano 1398* ☏*No phone*).

ALTO DEL CARMEN

40 km (25 mi) southeast of Vallenar.

Not far from where El Transito and El Carmen rivers join to form the Huasco you'll find Alto del Carmen, a quaint town whose inhabitants dedicate themselves to cultivating the muscat grapes used to make pisco. In addition to pisco, the town is famous for making *pajarete*, a sweet wine.

GETTING HERE & AROUND

From the Pan-American Highway (Ruta 5) at Vallenar, take Route C-485 about 45 km (28 mi) directly to Alto del Carmen. If you're flying from Santiago, fly to Copiapó, drive about 150 km (93 mi) south to Vallenar on Ruta 5, and then on to Alto del Carmen via C-485. The bus trip to Vallenar from Santiago is about 9 hours; tack on another 90 minutes for service to Alto de Carmen on any of the city's colectivos or smaller bus lines, which run from various points.

The **Planta Pisquera Alto del Carmen,** just outside town, hosts free tours and tastings daily from 8 AM to 8 PM.

About 26 km (16 mi) east of Alto del Carmen in the Valle del Carmen you'll find the precious town of **San Felix,** whose central plaza, white-washed church, and pleasant markets shouldn't be missed. There's also a pisco distillery here.

PARQUE NACIONAL LLANOS DE CHALLE

78 km (48 mi) northwest of Vallenar, 99 km (61 mi) north of Huasco.

There is no better place in El Norte Chico to view the desierto florido than this desolate coastal park. Every four or five years it is transformed into a carpet of reds, greens, and blues when there's sufficient rainfall to awaken the dormant bulbs below the dry, cracked earth. The park, spanning 450 square km (174 square mi), was formed to protect the *Garra de León,* a rare plant with an intoxicating red bloom that grows in only a few parts of the Huasco region. There are also a number of unusual species of cactus in the park—pacul, napina, and quisco flourish here. ⊠*About 17 km (11 mi) north of Vallenar, turn west off Pan-American Hwy. Take this road 82 km (51 mi) to the coast* ☏*No phone* 💲*Free.*

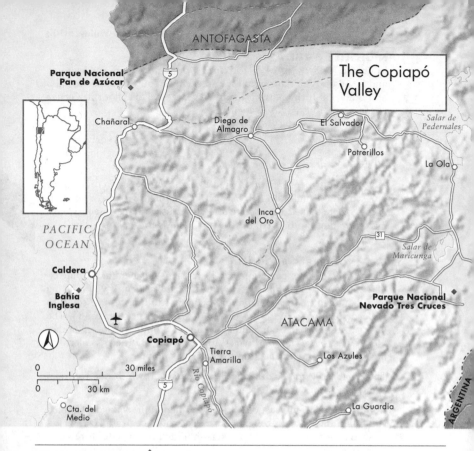

THE COPIAPÓ VALLEY

The region once known as Copayapu, meaning "cup of gold" in the Andean Quechua language, was first inhabited by the Diaguitas around AD 1000. The Incas arrived several hundred years later in search of gold. Conquistador Diego de Almagro, who passed this way in 1535, was the first European to see the lush valley.

During the 19th century the Copiapó Valley proved to be a true cup of gold when prospectors started large-scale mining operations in the region. But today, the residents of the valley make their living primarily from copper.

The northernmost city in the region, Copiapó, lies at the end of the world. Here the semiarid El Norte Chico gives way to the Atacama Desert. Continuing north from Copiapó there is little but barren earth for hundreds of miles.

COPIAPÓ

145 km (90 mi) north of Vallenar.

Copiapó was officially founded in 1744 by Don Francisco Cortés, who called it Villa San Francisco de La Selva. Originally a *tambo*, or resting place, Copiapó was where Diego de Almagro recuperated after his grueling journey south from Peru in 1535. The 19th-century silver strikes solidified Copiapó's status as an important city in the region.

GETTING HERE & AROUND

Copiapó's Desierto de Atacama airport (DAT) is a bit more than one hour's flying time from Santiago and connects to other points in El Norte Chico and El Norte Grande via Sky and LAN airlines. The DAT is about an hour from Copiapó but more like 30 minutes from Caldera—think of it as a big triangle. Hertz and Econorent both have locations at DAT airport. Copiapó is a straight shot north from Vallenar on Ruta 5, and its terminal is serviced by all major bus lines. To the north, about 45 minutes to one hour via Route 5, lie the beaches of Caldera and Bahía Inglesa.

ESSENTIALS

Air Travel Avant (⊠ *Colipí 510* ☎ *52/217–285* ⊕ *www.avant.cl*). **LAN** (⊠ *Colipí 101* ☎ *52/213–512* ⊕ *www.lan.com*). **Sky** (⊠ *Colipí 526* ☎ *52/214–640* ⊕ *www. skyairline.cl*).

Bank Banco del Estado (⊠ *Los Carrera 2242* ☎ *52/355–489*).

Bus Contacts Copiapó station (⊠ *Chañarcillo 680* ☎ *52/213–793*).

Hospital Hospital de Copiapó San José (⊠ *Los Carrera 1320* ☎ *52/473–100* ⊕ *www.hospitalcopiapo.cl*).

Post Office Correos de Chile (⊠ *Los Carrera 691* ☎ *52/355–489*).

Rental Cars Avis (⊠ *Rómulo Peña 102* ☎ *52/210–413* ⊕ *www.avis.com*). **Budget** (⊠ *Ramón Freire 50* ☎ *52/216–272* ⊕ *www.budget.cl*). **Hertz** (⊠ *Copayapu 173* ☎ *52/213–522* ⊕ *www.hertz.cl*).

Visitor & Tour Info Cobre Tour (⊠ *Av. Bernardo O'Higgins 640* ☎ *52/211–072*). **Sernatur, Chilean Tourism** (⊠ *Los Carrera 691* ☎ *52/212–838 or 52/231–510*). **Turismo Atacama** (⊠ *Los Carrera 716* ☎ *52/214–767*).

EXPLORING

In the center of Copiapó lies **Plaza Prat,** a lovely park lined with 100-year-old pepper trees.

English architect William Rogers built the neoclassical **Iglesia Catedral Nuestra Señora del Rosario,** facing the central square, in the middle of the 19th century.

The 1872 **Iglesia San Francisco** is a red-and-white candy cane of a church. The adjacent Plaza Godoy has a statue of goatherd Juan Godoy, who accidentally discovered huge silver deposits in nearby Chañarcillo.

The **Museo Mineralógico** offers a geological history of the region and what is perhaps the country's largest collection of rocks and minerals.

There are more than 2,000 samples, including some found only in the Atacama Desert. The museum even displays a few meteorites that fell in the area. ⊠*Colipí at Rodriguez* ☎*52/206–606* ⊕*www.unap. cl/museomin/index2.htm* ☒*500 pesos* ⊙*Mon., Wed., and Fri. 10:30–noon and 4–5:30; Tues. and Thurs. 10:30–noon and 6:30–8.*

A historic home that once belonged to the wealthy Matta family now houses the **Museo Histórico Regional,** dedicated to the natural history of the area. Regional archives suggest that the house was originally built by mining engineer Felipe Santiago Matta between 1840 and 1850. ⊠*Atacama 98* ☎*52/212–313* ☒*600 pesos* ⊙*Mon. 2:30–6, Tues.–Thurs. 9–6, weekends 10–12:45.*

WHERE TO STAY

$
★ 🏨**Hotel La Casona.** Beautiful gardens surround this quaint country inn with a red facade. Entering through wooden doors you reach the sunny lobby. To one side is a dining area with oak furniture and blue-and-white-checked tablecloths—an excellent place to enjoy your complimentary pisco sour. The rooms, decorated in blue, can get hot in summer. **Pros:** Quaint, friendly service. **Cons:** Far from center, rooms very hot in summer. ⊠*Av. Bernardo O'Higgins 150* ☎☎*52/217–277* ⊕*www.lacasonahotel.cl* ⤳*10 rooms* ⚐*In-room: no a/c. In-hotel: restaurant, bar, laundry service* ⊟*AE, DC, MC, V* ⦿❘*BP.*

$$ 🏨**Hotel Chagall.** Although it appears a little run-down on the outside, this business hotel has clean, modern rooms. Ask to see a few before you decide, as some are very dark. The bar, decorated with lots of kelly green, is reminiscent of an Irish pub. You won't find Guinness on tap here, however, so you'll have to settle for a well-made pisco sour. **Pros:** Recently renovated, modern. **Cons:** Some rooms are dark, as is the lobby. ⊠*Av. Bernardo O'Higgins 760* ☎*52/352–900* ☎*52/352–935* ⊕*www.chagall.cl* ⤳*88 rooms* ⚐*In-room: no a/c (some), refrigerator. In-hotel: restaurant, bar, laundry service* ⊟*AE, DC, MC, V* ⦿❘*BP.*

$$ 🏨**Hotel Miramonti.** This central hotel has clean, modern rooms decorated in the same shade of mauve you'll find in the lobby and hallways. The staff is friendly and helpful. Arched-back wooden chairs and blue tablecloths fill the country-style restaurant. The international menu here is heavy on seafood, and includes great merluza and *ostiones* (oysters). **Pros:** Modern and state-of-the-art. **Cons:** Near bus station, ugly location. ⊠*Ramón Freire 731* ☎☎*52/210–440* ⊕*www.miramonti.cl* ⤳*47 rooms* ⚐*In-room: no a/c, safe, refrigerator. In-hotel: restaurant, bar, laundry service, public Wi-Fi* ⊟*AE, DC, MC, V.*

NIGHTLIFE & THE ARTS

Because there are lots of students in town from the Universidad de Atacama (UDA), nightlife in Copiapó can be lively, with bars hosting bands, and a few dance clubs that rage all night to salsa beats. **Discoteque Splash** (⊠*Juan Martinéz 46* ☎*52/215–948*) is your best bet for late-night dancing. Outside town, the **Drive-In Esso Pub** (⊠*Near exit ramp from Pan-American Hwy.* ☎*52/211–535*) is perhaps the most innovative bar in northern Chile—it's in a converted gas station. **La Tabla** (⊠*Los Carreras 895* ☎*52/233–029*), near Plaza Prat, has live music, very expensive drinks, and good food.

SHOPPING

The **Casa de la Cultura** (⊠*Av. Bernardo O'Higgins 610, on Plaza Prat* ☎*52/210–824*) has crafts workshops and a gallery displaying works by local artists. On Friday there is a frenzied **fruit market** when locals pack the normally tranquil Plaza Godoy.

BAHÍA INGLESA

68 km (42 mi) northwest of Copiapó.

Some of the most beautiful beaches in El Norte Chico can be found at Bahía Inglesa, which was originally known as Puerto del Inglés because of the number of English buccaneers using the port as a hideaway. It's not just the beautiful white sand that sets these beaches apart, however: it's also the turquoise waters, the fresh air, and the fabulous weather. Combine all this with the fact that the town has yet to attract large-scale development and you can see why so many people flock here in summer. If you are fortunate enough to visit during the low season, you'll likely experience a tranquility rarely felt in Chile's other coastal towns.

GETTING HERE & AROUND

Follow the Pan-American Highway about one hour north until the small towns of Caldera and Bahía Inglesa come into view: you may smell the salty Pacific before you see the buildings. Buses big and small, as well as taxi colectivos, service Caldera, and from Caldera itself it's a 10-minute cab ride to Bahía Inglesa. To the north lies Antofagasta, about 6 hours by car or bus on the Pan-American Highway.

WHERE TO STAY & EAT

$ ✕**El Pateao.** With ocean views and the region's best food, this bohemian
★ bistro is a must for anyone staying in the area. The innovative contemporary menu lists such culinary non sequiturs as curry dishes and *tallarines con mariscos* (a pan-Asian noodle concoction served with shellfish and topped with cilantro). On the sand-covered porch you can sit in a comfy chair and watch the sunset. ⊠*Av. El Morro 756* ☎*No phone* ▭*No credit cards.*

$$ ▦**Apart Hotel Playa Blanca.** If you are tired of indistinguishable chain hotels, a cabana at Playa Blanca may just do the trick. These cabins are more like condos, complete with comfortable living rooms and full kitchens. Relax on a chaise longue by the pool, an asymmetrical beauty. This is a great place for kids, as there is a play area with a slide and jungle gym. **Pros:** Right on the water, hear the waves crash from your bed. **Cons:** A dark walk at night from wherever you're coming from. ⊠*Camino de Martín 1300* ☎*52/316–044* 🖶*52/316–468* ✍*olivo. norte@ia.cl* ⟲*10 cabanas* ⚿*In-room: no a/c, kitchen. In-hotel: pool, public Wi-Fi* ▭*No credit cards.*

$$ ▦**Hotel Rocas de Bahía.** This sprawling modern hotel, straight from *The*
Fodor'sChoice *Great Gatsby,* has rooms with huge windows facing the sea. You'll also
★ find large beds and Southwestern-style furniture in the rooms. Take a dip in the glistening waters of the bay, or head up to the rooftop pool. **Pros:** Can't beat the views. **Cons:** On same road as main disco

in town, which is open until dawn on weekends. ⊠*Av. El Morro 888* ☎*52/316–005* 🖷*52/316–032* ⊕*www.rocasdebahia.cl* ⇝*36 rooms* ⚒*In-room: no a/c, safe. In-hotel: restaurant, room service, pool, bicycles, public Wi-Fi, laundry service* ☰*AE, DC, MC, V* ⧖*BP.*

NIGHTLIFE & THE ARTS

There are few true bars in Bahía Inglesa except in the hotels, but outside the city, on the way north to Caldera, you'll find several discos that are always packed during high season. You can dance at **Discoteque Loreto** (⊠*Camino Bahía Inglesa* 🖀*No phone*), which lies midway between Bahía Inglesa and Caldera. Head to the funky **El Plateao** (⊠*Av. El Morro 756* 🖀*No phone*) to listen to reggae and Cuban tunes. **Takeo** (⊠*Camino Bahía Inglesa s/n* 🖀*No phone*)attracts a mature, salsa-dancing crowd.

SPORTS & THE OUTDOORS

BEACHES There are several easily accessible beaches around Bahía Inglesa. **Playa La Piscina** is the town's main beach. The rocky outcroppings and sugary sand are reminiscent of the Mediterranean. **Playa Las Machas,** the town's southernmost beach, is especially relaxing because few tourists have discovered it.

WATER SPORTS There are all types of water sports in the area. **Morro Ballena Expediciones** (⊠*El Morro s/n, on south end of beach* 🖀*No phone*) arranges fishing, kayaking, and scuba-diving trips.The Chilean surfing craze has caught on a bit here, and **Atacama Surf** (🖀*9/484–6769* ⊕*www.atacamasurf. com*), run by an enterprising Basque transplant, offers bodyboard, kite-surfing, and longboard lessons.

CALDERA

74 km (46 mi) northwest of Copiapó.

An important port during the silver era, Caldera today is a slightly run-down town with decent beaches and friendly people. The memories of piracy still haunt the port—a former pirate hideout—which is used today to export grapes and copper.

GETTING HERE & AROUND

This is a straight one-hour shot up the coastal highway from Copiapó, whether you're taking the bus, a colectivo, or your own vehicle. It's also about a one-hour drive from the Desierto de Atacama airport, should you choose to arrive from the capital in style.

EXPLORING

Near the beach is the **Estacion Ferrocarril,** once the terminus of Chile's first railroad. There's a tourist-information kiosk here.

The large, Gothic-towered **Iglesia de San Vincente de Paul,** on the town's main square, was built in 1862.

WHERE TO STAY & EAT

$ ✕**Nuevo Miramar.** Huge windows overlook the pier at this excellent seafood restaurant. One of the most elegant eateries in Caldera, the Nuevo Miramar has tables with fine linens and cloth napkins. Bow-tied waiters, all extremely attentive, will tell you the catch of the day. ✉*Gana 90* ☎*52/315–381* ⌕*Reservations essential* ▤*No credit cards.*

$ ⛺**Hostería Puerta del Sol.** These A-frame cabanas have small kitchens and dining areas and a view of the bay. The showers pour out wonderfully hot water, a nice touch after a long day of exploring. There is also a pool, which could be quite pleasant if it were filled to the top. **Pros:** Great bay views, peaceful atmosphere. **Cons:** You have to be careful walking up and down the steep hill. ✉*Wheelwright 750* ☎*52/315–205* 🖷*52/315–507* ⌂*7 cabanas* ⌕*In-room: no a/c, kitchen. In-hotel: bar, pool, laundry service, public Wi-Fi* ▤*AE, DC, MC, V.*

$ ⛺**Motel Portal del Inca.** This string of red cabanas has a tennis court and an inviting pool surrounded by lounge chairs. There's also a playground, making this an excellent choice if you are traveling with children. The rooms are simple, with furnishings that may have been popular back in the 1970s. **Pros:** Family friendly. **Cons:** Very old fashioned with dated decor. ✉*Carvallo 945* ☎🖷*52/315–252* ⊕*www.portaldelinca.cl* ⌂*25 cabanas* ⌕*In-room: no a/c, kitchen. In-hotel: bar, tennis court, pool, laundry service, public Internet* ▤*No credit cards.*

NIGHTLIFE & THE ARTS

Many of Caldera's bars are open only in summer, when the town is packed with vacationing South Americans. The funky **Bartolomeo** (✉*Wheelwright 747* ☎*No phone*) plays eclectic music; if you're hungry, chow down on the various tapas. **Pub Entre Jotes** (✉*Wheelwright 485* ☎*No phone*), with a terrace overlooking the port, is a good place to enjoy the sunset, but it's only open for the high season of January and February. The pub hosts live music on weekends, although it's often just a man playing a keyboard.

BEACHES

The town's main beach is **Playa Copiapina.** North of the pier, **Playa Brava** stretches as far as you can see. About 4 km (2½ mi) to the south of town you come upon the pleasant sandy beach of **Playa Loreto.**

PARQUE NACIONAL PAN DE AZÚCAR

🕑 *100 km (62 mi) north of Caldera.*

★ Some of Chile's most spectacular coastal scenery is in Parque Nacional Pan de Azúcar, a national park that stretches for 40 km (25 mi) along the coast north of the town of Chañaral. Steep cliffs fall into the crashing sea, their ominous presence broken occasionally by white-sand beaches. These isolated stretches of sand make for excellent picnicking. Be careful if you decide to swim, as there are often dangerous currents.

Within the park you'll find an incredible variety of flora and fauna. Pelicans can be spotted off the coast, as can sea lions and sea otters, cormorants, and plovers (similar to sandpipers but with shorter beaks). There are some 20 species of cacti in the park, including the rare copiapoa, which resembles a little blue pincushion. The park also shelters rare predators, including the desert fox. In the pueblo of Caleta Pan de Azúcar, a tiny fishing village, you can get information from the CONAF-run kiosk (CONAF is the national forestry service, Corporación Nacional Forestal).

Offshore from Caleta Pan de Azúcar is a tiny island that a large colony of Humboldt penguins calls home. You can hire local fisherfolk to bring you here. Negotiate the price, which should be around 7,000 pesos. About 10 km (6 mi) north of the village, Mirador Pan de Azúcar affords spectacular views of the coastline. Another 30 km (19 mi) to the north is Las Lomitas. This 700-meter (2,296-foot) cliff is almost always covered with the *camanchaca* (fog), which rolls in from the sea. A huge net here is used to catch the fog and condense it into water. ⊠*An unpaved road north of the cemetery in Chañaral leads to Caleta Pan de Azúcar* ☎*No phone* ⊕*www.conaf.cl* ✉*1,000 pesos* ☉*Park daily, ranger kiosk daily 8:30–12:30 and 2–6.*

GETTING HERE & AROUND
You can take Route C-120 from Chañaral for 29 km (18 mi) directly into the park, or Route C-110 from Pan-American Highway Km marker 1,410.

WHERE TO STAY
$ 🏠 **Hostería Chañaral.** Leaps and bounds above the other places in Chañaral, where you will mostly likely stay the night when visiting the park, the Hostería Chañaral has well-maintained rooms and clean baths with plenty of hot water. A restaurant on the premises serves good seafood. **Pros:** Clean, plenty of hot water. **Cons:** Smallish rooms ⊠*Muller 268* ☎*52/480–050* 🖷*52/480–554* ↯*34 rooms* ♿*In-room: no a/c. In-hotel: restaurant, bar, laundry service* ☰*AE, MC, V* � 🍴*CP.*

El Norte Grande

Ichu (Bunchgrass), Puna de Atacama (Atacama Plateau)

WORD OF MOUTH

"My husband and I do not speak Spanish but managed to tour Atacama area by ourselves. We flew from Santiago to Calama. We rented a car at Calama airport and drove to San Pedro de Atacama where we stayed as a base. Road signs are clearly posted, so you can easily visit Moon valley, Flamenco Natural Reserve, Chug Chug Geoglyphs, and lakes such as Laguna Verde."

—mochi

WELCOME TO EL NORTE GRANDE

TOP REASONS TO GO

★ **Valle de la Luna:** Within the Reserva Nacional los Flamencos lies the Valle de la Luna, a place most visitors to northern Chile will not want to miss. This magical moon-like landscape, filled with dusty gray desert sand dunes and deep valleys, is one of the top places in Chile to watch the sunset.

★ **Flora & Fauna:** Yes, the Atacama Desert is one of the driest places on earth. But head to the Chilean Altiplano, just a few hours east of Arica, and you'll find an abundance of fauna and, depending on the season, flora. Pink flamingos dot the edges of volcanic lakes like Lago Chungará on the Bolivian border, and slender brown vicuñas—treasured for their fur, the finest of the American camelids—run in small herds through the sparse grasslands.

★ **Pristine Beaches:** Pristine sands line the shore near Arica and Iquique. They are packed during summer months, but outside of these you just might have the beach to yourself.

1 The Nitrate Pampa. Snowcapped volcanoes dominate the landscape to the east, making mornings in this region especially memorable. The vast lunar landscapes around San Pedro de Atacama make for days' worth of fascinating trekking. Just watching the sun—or moon—rise over the dunes is worth the trip itself. And bird-lovers will find the Reserva Nacional de Flamencos well worth the high-altitude adjustment for a chance to see hundreds of pink flamingos against the backdrop of shimmering blue and green lakes.

2 San Pedro & The Atacama Desert. If you get beyond the hype and the hippies, San Pedro is a great place, albeit expensive. But the range of outdoor activities, from sandboarding to hiking to biking, and the breathtaking sights, including moon-like landscapes, volcanoes, flamingos, and Incan graveyards, make it a must-see stop in the North. Spend your mornings hiking, biking, and boarding, afternoons swimming, and nights beside a blazing outdoor fire in the patio of one of San Pedro's down-home but delicious eateries, gazing up at the star-filled heavens.

3 Iquique Area. The port of Iquique is the world's largest exporter of fish meal, but its heyday was as a nitrate center in the 19th century. Fading mansions remain and this regional capital is still a popular destination. From here you can do a day trip to the hot springs of Mamiña, also glimpsing the ghost town of Humberstone, while getting to the petroglyph Gigante de Atacama—Chile's largest—in time for the sunset.

4 Arica Area. Arica, at the intersection of Chile, Bolivia, and Peru, is part of the "land of eternal spring" and its pedestrian-mall eateries can ease even the most impatient traveler into a chair for a day. Sights to see include mummies dating to 6000 BC, Aymara markets, and national parks with alpine lakes and herds of vicuña.

Traditional designs, Atacama Desert

Church, San Pedro de Atacama

GETTING ORIENTED

Only if you enjoy the solitude and desolation of the desert should you venture into El Norte Grande. The Atacama Desert is barren until it explodes in a riot of color every four or five years when unusual amounts of rain awaken dormant flower bulbs. But you won't have every place to yourself, exactly. San Pedro de Atacama is one of the continent's hotspots, a mecca for outdoor-sports enthusiasts, New Age crystal gazers, birdwatchers, and sandboarders. If you miss the human touch, board a 4 AM van full of fellow travelers heading out to the steaming geysers. Resting between two giant branches of the Andean mountains is the *altiplano*, or high plains, where you'll see natural marvels such as crystalline salt flats, geysers, and volcanoes. You'll also spot flocks of flamingos and herds of vicuña, a cousin to the llama. The best bases for exploration are San Pedro de Atacama, Iquique, and Arica.

5

EL NORTE GRANDE PLANNER

When to Go

In the height of the Chilean summer, January and February, droves of Chileans and Argentines mob El Norte Grande's beaches. Although this is a fun time to visit, prices go up and finding a hotel can be difficult. Book your room a month or more in advance. The high season tapers off in March, an excellent time to visit if you're looking for a bit more tranquillity. If you plan to visit the altiplano, bring the right clothing. Winter can be very cold, and summer sees a fair amount of rain.

Health & Safety

The main concern you should have in the North is the sun: a hat and sunblock are always a good idea. Use common sense: don't be flashy with cash or expensive cameras. The North is relatively tranquil, but when venturing out from the center of any town into other neighborhoods, it's always safer to take a cab than to walk (and to ask the place where you are to call one for you).

Eat Well & Rest Easy

The food of El Norte Grande is simple but quite good. Along the coast you can enjoy fresh seafood and shellfish, including *merluza* (hake), *corvina* (sea bass), *ostiones* (oysters), and *machas* (similar to razor clams but unique to Chile), to name just a few. Seviche (a traditional Peruvian dish made with raw, marinated fish) is also available in much of El Norte Grande, but make sure you sample it in a place where you are confident that the fish is fresh. Fish may be ordered *a la plancha* (grilled in butter and lemon) or accompanied by a sauce such as *salsa margarita* (a butter-based sauce comprising almost every shellfish imaginable). As you enter the interior region you'll come across heartier meals such as *cazuela de vacuno* (beef stew served with corn on the cob and vegetables) and *chuleta con arroz* (beef with rice).

People in the north generally eat a heavy lunch around 2 PM that can last two hours, followed by a light dinner around 10 PM. Reservations are seldom needed, except in the poshest of places. Leave a 10% tip if you enjoyed the service.

Lodging in El Norte Grande is relatively inexpensive. However, some accommodations that bill themselves as "luxury" hotels haven't been remodeled or painted in years. Ask to look at a room before deciding. Few small towns have hotels, so you will have to make do with guesthouses with extremely basic rooms and shared bathrooms.

WHAT IT COSTS IN CHILEAN PESOS (IN THOUSANDS)

	¢	$	$$	$$$	$$$$
RESTAURANTS					
	under 3 pesos	3 pesos–5 pesos	5 pesos–8 pesos	8 pesos–11 pesos	over 11 pesos
HOTELS					
	under 15 pesos	15 pesos–45 pesos	45 pesos–75 pesos	75 pesos–105 pesos	over 105 pesos

Restaurant prices are based on the median main course price at dinner. Hotel prices are for a double room in high season, excluding tax.

Folklore & Festivals

Every town in the region celebrates the day honoring its patron saint. Most are small gatherings attended largely by locals. One fiesta not to be missed takes place in La Tirana from July 12 to 18. During this time some 80,000 pilgrims converge on the town to honor the Virgen del Carmen with dancing in the streets.

Geoglyphs

In addition to the Gigante de Atacama, the world's largest geoglyph at 86 meters (282 feet) high, there are geoglyphs throughout El Norte Grande. The rock art at Cerros Pintados comprises the largest collection of geoglyphs in South America. More than 400 images adorn this hill in Reserva Nacional Pampa del Tamarugal. Figures representing birds, animals, people, and geometric patterns appear to dance along the hill. Farther north, the Tiliviche geoglyphs decorate a hill sitting not far from the modern-day marvel of the Pan-American Highway. These geoglyphs, most likely constructed between AD 1000 and 1400, during the Inca reign, depict a large caravan of llamas. All of these llamas are headed in the same direction—toward the sea—a testament, perhaps, to the geoglyphs' navigational use during the age when llama trains brought silver down to the coast in exchange for fish.

Sample Itinerary

You'll have to hustle to see much of El Norte Grande in less than a week. You can spend at least two days in **San Pedro de Atacama,** visiting the incredible sights such as the bizarre moonscape of the Valle de la Luna and the desolate salt flats of the Salar de Atacama. For half a day soak in the hot springs in the tiny town of **Pica,** then head to the nitrate ghost town of Humberstone. On the way to Iquique, take a side trip to the **Gigante de Atacama,** the world's largest geoglyph. After a morning exploring Iquique, head up to **Arica,** the coastal town that bills itself as the "land of eternal spring." Be sure to visit the Museo Arqueológico de San Miguel de Azapa to see the Chinchorro mummies. Stop in **Putre** to catch your breath before taking in the flamingos at **Parque Nacional Lauca** or the vicuñas, llamas, and alpacas of **Reserva Nacional Las Vicuñas.**

Getting Here & Around

Air Travel. There are no international airports in El Norte Grande, but from Santiago you can transfer to a flight headed to Antofagasta, Calama, Iquique, or Arica. Round-trip flights can run up to 300,000 pesos or more. The cities within El Norte Grande are far apart, so flying between them can save you time and provide more comfort. Aerolineas del Sur (AirComet), Sky Airline, and LAN offer services with prices ranging from 28,000 to 105,000 pesos. Sky's daily service will often stop in all three regional airports to and from Santiago.

Bus Travel. Travel between the larger towns and cities in El Norte Grande is easy, but there may be no bus service to some smaller villages or the more remote national parks. No bus company has a monopoly, so shop around for the best price and note there are often several bus stations in each city.

Car Travel. A car is definitely the best way to see El Norte Grande. Driving in the cities can be a little hectic, but highway travel is usually smooth sailing and the roads are generally well maintained. Ruta 5, more familiarly known as the Pan-American Highway, bisects all of northern Chile. Ruta 1, Chile's answer to California's Highway 101, is a beautiful coastal highway running between Antofagasta and Iquique.

5

Updated by
Brian Kluepfel

A LAND OF ROCK AND earth, terrifying in its austerity and vastness, El Norte Grande is one of the world's most desolate regions. Spanning some 1,930 km (1,200 mi), Chile's Great North stretches from the Río Copiapó to the borders of Peru and Bolivia. Here you will find the Atacama Desert, the driest place on Earth—so dry that in many parts no rain has ever been recorded.

Yet people have inhabited this desolate land since time immemorial, and indeed the heart of El Norte Grande lies not in its geography but in its people. The indigenous Chinchorro people eked out a meager living from the sea more than 8,000 years ago, leaving behind the magnificent Chinchorro mummies, the oldest in the world. High in the Andes, the Atacameño tribes traded livestock with the Tijuanacota and the Inca. Many of these people still cling to their way of life, though much of their culture was lost during the colonial period.

Although the Spanish first invaded the region in the 16th century, El Norte Grande was largely ignored by Europeans until the 1800s, when huge deposits of nitrates were found in the Atacama region. The "white gold" brought boom times to towns like Pisagua, Iquique, and Antofagasta. Because most of the mineral-rich region lay beyond its northern border, Chile declared war on neighboring Peru and Bolivia in 1878. Chile won the five-year battle and annexed the land north of Antofagasta, a continuing source of national pride for many Chileans. With the invention of synthetic nitrates, the market for these fertilizers dried up and the nitrate barons abandoned their opulent mansions and returned to Santiago. El Norte Grande was once again left on its own.

What you'll see today is a land of both growth and decay. The glory days of the nitrate era are gone, but copper has stepped in to help fill that gap (the world's largest open-pit copper mine is here). El Norte Grande is still a land of opportunity for fortune-seekers, as well as for tourists looking for a less-traveled corner of the world. It is a place of beauty and dynamic isolation, a place where the past touches the present in a troubled yet majestic embrace.

THE NITRATE PAMPA

The vast *pampa salitrera* is an atmospheric introduction to Chile's Great North. Between 1890 and 1925 this region was the site of more than 100 *oficinas de salitre,* or nitrate plants. For a glorious period Chile was the king of production of the fertilizer saltpeter (sodium nitrate), led by the "Father of Nitrate," Englishman James Humberstone. The Dover-born chemist applied James Shanks' method of producing sodium nitrate, and soon it was used throughout Chile. The War of the Pacific fought by Chile, Peru, and Bolivia was caused at least in part by the desire for these rich deposits beneath the Atacama Desert. The invention of synthetic nitrates spelled the end for all but a few plants. Crumbling nitrate works lay stagnant in the dry desert air, some disintegrating into dust, others remaining a fascinating testament to the white gold that for a time made this one of Chile's richest regions.

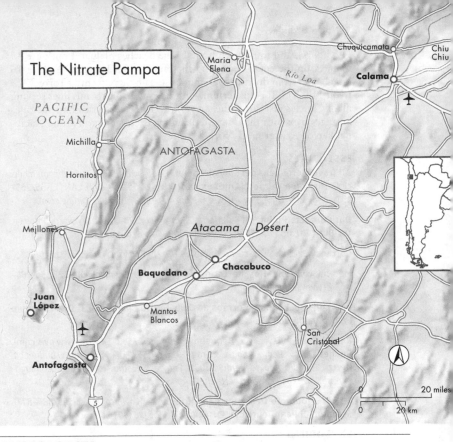

The Nitrate Pampa

PACIFIC
OCEAN

Chuquicamata
Chiu
Chiu

Maria
Elena
Río Loa
Calama

Michilla

ANTOFAGASTA

Hornitos

Mejillones
Atacama Desert

Baquedano Chacabuco

Juan
López

Mantos
Blancos

San
Cristóbal

Antofagasta

0   20 miles
0   20 km

ANTOFAGASTA

565 km (350 mi) north of Copiapó.

Antofagasta is the most important—and the richest—city in El Norte Grande. It was part of Bolivia until 1879, when it was annexed by Chile in the War of the Pacific. The port town became an economic powerhouse during the nitrate boom. With the rapid decline of nitrate production, copper mining stepped in to keep the city's coffers filled.

Many travelers end up spending a night in Antofagasta on their way to the more interesting destinations like San Pedro de Atacama, Iquique, and Arica, but a few sights here are worth a look. Around two in the afternoon the city shuts down most of the streets in the center of town, making for pleasant afternoon shopping and strolling.

GETTING HERE & AROUND

Antofagasta's airport, 30 minutes from downtown, is a regular stop on Sky Airline's northern run, about a two-hour flight from Santiago. From Caldera in the south, it's a six- to seven-hour ride up the Pan-American Highway by bus or car, but at least on this stretch you'll see some of the ocean. The bus terminal on LaTorre is just a short walk from downtown. Regular buses leave to Calama (3 hours), San Pedro

(4½ hours), and Iquique (6 hours). The beaches of Juan Lopez are 45 minutes up the coast road, and the famous "La Portada" a mere 16 km (10 mi) from downtown—minibuses run there from LaTorre 2723 frequently. The Tur-Bus terminal, for one of the bigger bus lines serving all of Chile, is just down the street on LaTorre. Desertica Expediciones arranges trips into the interior, including excursions to Parque Nacional Pan de Azucar in El Norte Chico.

ESSENTIALS

Air Travel Aerolineas del Sur/AirComet (☎ *55/452–050* ⊕ *www.aircometchile. cl*). **Cerro Moreno Airport (Antofagasta) (CNF)** (☎ *55/269–077*). **LAN** (☎ *55/265– 151* ⊕ *www.lan.com*). **Sky Airline** (☎ *55/459–090* ⊕ *www.skyairline.com*).

Bus Contacts Pullman (✉ *LaTorre 2805* ☎ *600/320–3200* ⊕ *www.pullman.cl*). **Tur-Bus** (✉ *LaTorre 2751* ☎ *600/660–6600* ⊕ *www.turbus.cl*).

Currency Exchange Casa de Cambios (✉ *1818 Sotomayor* ☎ *55/312–063*).

Medical Assistance Hospital Leonardo Guzman (✉ *Av. Argentina 1962* ☎ *55/204– 571* ⊕ *www.hospantof.cl*).

Post Office & Shipping Correos de Chile (✉ *Washington 2623*). **DHL** (✉ *Arturo Prat 260* ☎ *55/260–209*).

Rental Cars Avis (✉ *Av. Baquedano 364* ☎ *55/563–140* ⊕ *www.avis.com*). **Budget** (✉ *Av. Pedro Aguirre Cerda 13358* ☎ *55/214–445* ⊕ *www.budget.cl*). **Hertz** (✉ *Pedro Aguirre Cerda 15030, Parque Industrial La Portada, Antofagasta* ☎ *55/428–042* ⊕ *www.hertz.cl*).

Visitor & Tour Info Desertica Expediciones (✉ *La Torre 2732* ☎ *55/386–877*). **Sernatur, Chilean Tourism** (✉ *Maipu 240* ☎ *55/264–016*).

EXPLORING

High above Plaza Colón is the **Torre Reloj**, the clock tower whose face is a replica of London's Big Ben. It was erected by British residents in 1910.

The historic customs house, the town's oldest building, dates from 1866. Housed inside is the **Museo Regional de Antofagasta**, which displays clothing and other bric-a-brac from the nitrate era. ✉ *Bolívar 188* ☎ *55/227–016* ⊕ *www.dibam.cl/sdm_m_antofagasta/* ☒ *600 pesos* ⊙ *Tues.–Fri. 9–5, weekends 11–2.*

WHERE TO EAT

¢ ✕ **Café del Centro.** A people-watcher's paradise on the city's main walking route, Plaza Prat, this is a nice place for a *café cortado* (an espresso "cut" with a bit of milk), a slice of lemon pie, or a sandwich, while watching "Anto" stroll by. ✉ *Paseo Prat 490, corner of LaTorre* ☎ *No phone* ▭ *DC, MC, V.*

$$$$ ✕ **Club de Yates.** This seafood restaurant with nice views of the port caters to yachting types, which may explain why the prices are a bit higher than at other restaurants in the area. The food is quite good, especially the *ostiones a la parmesana* (oysters with Parmesan cheese). The maritime theme is taken to the extreme—the plates, curtains, tablecloths, and every decoration imaginable come in the mandatory navy

blue. The service is excellent. ⊠ *Av. Balmaceda 2705* ☎ *55/284–116* ♨ *Reservations essential* ⊟ *AE, DC, MC, V.*

¢ ✗ **Don Pollo.** This rotisserie restaurant prepares some of the best roasted chicken in Chile—a good thing, because it's the only item on the menu. The thatched-roof terrace is a great place to kick back after a long day of sightseeing. ⊠ *Ossa 2594* ☎ *No phone* ⊟ *No credit cards.*

$$ ✗ **Restaurant Arriero.** Serving up traditional dishes from Spain's Basque
★ country, Arriero is the place to go for delicious barbecued meats. A healthy selection of national wines supplements the menu. The restaurant is in a pleasant Pyrenees-style inn decorated with traditional cured hams hanging from the walls. The owners play jazz on the piano almost every evening. ⊠ *Condell 2644* ☎ *55/264–371* ⊟ *AE, DC, MC, V.*

WHERE TO STAY

$$ ⊡ **Hotel Antofagasta.** Part of the deluxe Panamericana Hoteles chain,
★ this high-rise on the ocean comes with all the first-class luxuries, from an elegant bar with a grand piano to a lovely kidney-shape pool. The rooms, which have ample bathrooms and plenty of closet space, are comfortably furnished, and some have ocean views. Suites are considerably more expensive ($$$$). A semiprivate beach is just steps from the hotel's back door. **Pros:** Nice beachfront location, top-rate rooms and service. **Cons:** Expensive, a bit sterile. ⊠ *Av. Balmaceda 2575* ☎ *55/228–811* 🖷 *55/268–415* ⊕ *www.hotelantofagasta.cl* ⇱ *145 rooms, 18 suites* ♨ *In-room: safe, refrigerator, Wi-Fi. In-hotel: restaurant, room service, bar, pool, gym, laundry service* ⊟ *AE, DC, MC, V* �‖*BP.*

$ ⊡ **Marsal Hotel.** This modern and clean hotel faces busy Calle Arturo Prat, so be sure to ask for one of the pleasant rooms in the back. All the rooms have nice touches like desks. The service here is quite friendly—the staff goes out of its way to recommend restaurants and arrange excursions. **Pros:** A quick walk from downtown's pedestrian mall, economical. **Cons:** A bit outdated in terms of style and furnishings. ⊠ *Arturo Prat 867* ☎ *55/268–063* 🖷 *55/221–733* ⊕ *www.marsalhotel.cl* ⇱ *18 rooms* ♨ *In-room: no a/c. In-hotel: laundry service, minibar* ⊟ *AE, DC, MC, V* ❋‖*CP.*

NIGHTLIFE & THE ARTS

Nightlife in El Norte Grande often means heading to the *schoperias,* beer halls where the almost entirely male clientele downs *schops* (draft beers) served by scantily clad waitresses. The drinking generally continues until everyone is reeling drunk, maybe dancing to the jukebox tunes. If this is your idea of fun, check out the myriad schoperias in the center of town around the Plaza Colón.

If you're not quite ready for the schoperia experience (and for many these are not the most pleasant places to spend an evening), don't worry: there are also a few bars where you can have a quiet drink. With its swinging saloon-style doors and a great waitstaff donning cowboy hats and blue jeans, the **Country Pub** (⊠ *Salvador Reyes 1025* ☎ *55/371–751*) is lots of fun. The music doesn't go country, however, staying instead on the modern side of pop (think Beyonce). Antofagasta's elite head to **Wally's Pub** (⊠ *Antonino Toro 982* ☎ *55/223–697*), an American-style grill with American-style prices.

SHOPPING

You don't want to miss out on the people-watching or the shopping on the *plaza peotonal* (pedestrian mall) that runs for four blocks along Calle Arturo Prat. There are electronics shops, a Fallabella (Macy's-type national chain), sporting-goods stores for the outdoors enthusiast or collector of Chilean soccer jerseys, cafés, and jewelry shops.

On the corner of Manuel A. Matta and Maipú you'll find the **Mercado Central,** a fruit and vegetable market with blue-and-yellow walls. Behind the market is the **Plaza del Mercado,** where artisans sell handmade jewelry and healing crystals, and where the occasional outdoor performance takes place.

JUAN LÓPEZ

38 km (24 mi) north of Antofagasta.

Those turned off by the hustle and bustle of Antofagasta will likely be charmed by Juan López, a hodgepodge of pastel-color fishing shacks and a picturesque *caleta* (cove). In high season, January and February, the beaches are crowded and dirty. The rest of the year you may have the white, silken sand to yourself for a nice stroll or swim.

GETTING HERE & AROUND

Juan López is just a hop up the coastal road from Antofagasta, and in the busy season there are plenty of minibuses and colectivos making the trip. It's about 30–40 minutes' drive time.

EXPLORING

On the coast about 13 km (8 mi) south of Juan López lies **La Portada,** an offshore volcanic rock that the sea has carved into an arch. It's one of the most photographed natural sights in the country. Many local travel agencies include La Portada as part of area tours.

WHERE TO STAY & EAT

$ ✕ **Restaurant Vitoco.** This restaurant, decorated with native textiles, serves a fixed meal of chicken or grilled fish. The food is good and the kitchen is spotless. ⊠ *Manzana 8* ☎ *55/383-071* ▤ *No credit cards.*

¢ ⛺ **Hosteria Sandokan.** An airy garden complete with chirping caged birds surrounds the nicest place to stay in Juan López. Hosteria Sandokan has basic but clean rooms with shared baths. The hotel's terrace restaurant, which serves excellent seafood, affords great views of the pelicans going about their business. **Pros:** Beautiful garden, good views. **Cons:** Shared bathroom. ⊠ *Fernando Bull s/n* ☎ *55/223-302* ⛨ *6 rooms without bath* ♿ *In-room: no a/c, no phone, no TV. In-hotel: restaurant* ▤ *No credit cards.*

BEACHES

People come to Juan López for the beaches, and there are plenty from which to choose, both around town and within a short drive. The most popular beach is **Balneario Juan López,** a small strip of white sand near the center of town. It can get uncomfortably crowded in summer. If you want a bit more elbow room, head to the beaches outside town. Picturesque **Playa Acapulco** is in a small cove north of Balneario Juan López. **Playa Rinconada,** about 5 km (3 mi) south of Juan López, is lauded by locals for its warm water.

CHACABUCO

★ *70 km (43 mi) northeast of Antofagasta.*

Many nitrate plants of the *pampa salitrera* (literally "saltpeter plains"), as well as the company towns that housed their workers, still survive. A mysterious dot on the desert landscape, the ghost town of Chacabuco is a decidedly eerie place. More than 7,000 employees and their families lived here when the Oficina Chacabuco (a company mining town that was made a National Monument in 1971) was in operation between 1922 and 1944. Today you'll find tiny houses, their tin roofs flapping in the wind and their walls collapsing. You can wander through many of the abandoned and restored buildings and take a look inside the theater, which has been restored to the way it looked when this was a boomtown.

During the first years of Augusto Pinochet's military regime, Chacabuco was used as a prison camp for political dissidents. The artwork of prisoners still adorns many of the walls. Do not walk around the town's exterior, as land mines from this era are still buried here. ✉ *70 km (43 mi) northeast of Antofagasta on Pan-American Hwy.* ☎ *No phone* 🎫 *1,000 pesos* 🕐 *Daily 7 AM–8 PM.*

EN ROUTE

Founded by a British company in 1926, **María Elena** is a dusty place that warrants a visit if you want to see a functioning nitrate town. It's home to the employees of the region's last two nitrate plants. The 8,000 people who live in María Elena are proud of their history—nearly every house has a picture of the town hanging inside. A tiny but informative museum on the town's main square houses many artifacts from the nitrate boom as well as a few from the pre-Columbian era. The town is about 148 km (92 mi) north of Chacabuco.

CALAMA

215 km (133 mi) northeast of Antofagasta.

The discovery of vast deposits of copper in the area turned Calama into the quintessential mining town, and therein lies its interest. People from the length of Chile flock to this dusty spot on the map in hopes of striking it rich in "the land of sun and copper"—most likely working for Codelco, Chile's biggest company, which has three mines in the surrounding area. A modern-day version of the boomtowns of the 19th-century American West, Calama is rough around the edges, but it does possess a certain energy.

Founded as a *tambo,* or resting place, at the crossing of two Inca trails, Calama still serves as a stopover for people headed elsewhere. Some people traveling to San Pedro de Atacama end up spending the night here, and the town does have a few attractions of its own.

GETTING HERE & AROUND

Daily flights from Santiago via Sky, AirComet, and LAN arrive 20 minutes from downtown at Calama's El Loa airport (CJC). Bus service to neighboring San Pedro is frequent and fast—it's only about an hour between the two towns. To points north, you can fly to Iquique and Arica in an hour (if you can avoid the puddle-jumper service which adds a few stops), but a bus or car will take you 7 and 9 hours, respectively. Be very careful when passing the mining company trucks that may slow your journey.

ESSENTIALS

Air Travel Aerolineas del Sur/AirComet (☎ *600/625-0000* ⊕ *www.air cometchile.cl*). **El Loa Airport (CJC)** (☎ *55/312-348*). **LAN** (☎ *55/313-927* ⊕ *www. lan.com*). **Sky Airline** (☎ *55/310-090* ⊕ *www.skyairline.com*).

Currency Exchange Banco de Estado (⊠ *Sotomayor 1848* ☎ *55/535-500*).

Medical Services Hospital Cisternas (⊠ *Av. Dr. Carlos Cisternas 2253* ☎ *55/342-347*).

Post Office & Shipping Correo de Chile (⊠ *Mackenna at Granaderos*). **DHL** (⊠ *Sotomayor 1952* ☎ *55/340-570*).

Rental Cars Avis (⊠ *Latorre 1498* ☎ *55/319-797* ⊕ *www.avis.com*). **Budget** (⊠ *Parque Industrial Apia Sitio 1-C* ☎ *55/361-072* ⊕ *www.budget.cl*). **Hertz** (⊠ *Granaderos 1416* ☎ *55/341-380* ⊕ *www.hertz.cl*).

Visitor & Tour Info Sernatur, Chilean Tourism (☎ *55/364-176*).

EXPLORING

The gleaming copper roof of **Catedral San Juan Bautista** (⊠ *Ramírez at Av. Granaderos*), on Plaza 23 de Marzo, the city's main square, testifies to the importance of mining in this region.

The **Museo Arqueológico y Etnológico,** a natural history museum in the well-manicured Parque El Loa, depends heavily on dioramas to explain the region's pre-Columbian past. Nearby is a replica of the quaint church in neighboring Chiu Chiu. ⊠ *Parque El Loa, south of town on Av. Bernardo O'Higgins* ☎ *55/340-112* ⊠ *200 pesos* ☉ *Tues.–Fri. 10–1 and 3–5:30, weekends 3–6.*

WHERE TO EAT

$ ✕ **Cactus Restaurant & Bar.** An after-work crowd haunts this Mexican-theme restaurant, where a mandatory cow skull adorns one of the walls. South-of-the-border favorites like flautas, taquitos, and chimichangas dominate the menu. Many regulars crowd around the tables for the two-for-one mojitos and Cuba libres. ⊠ *Sotomayor 1901* ☎ *55/312-367* ⊟ *AE, DC, MC, V.*

$$ ✕ **Café Caruso.** This little slice of the Mediterranean coast in the Chilean desert is tastefully appointed with rich wood furniture and walls painted in muted copper-red tones. Caruso hits the high notes with a delicious set lunch (the roast pork is delectable). If you prefer, you can just hang out with a cup of coffee or glass of wine and check out the old photos of Calama's proud past. ⊠ *Avaroa 1702* ☎ *55/364-872* ⊟ *No credit cards.*

CHUQUICAMATA

The trucks never stop rolling, and the machinery never stops grinding, at Chuquicamata, the world's biggest open-pit mine, located just outside of Calama. Nine-hundred workers split three eight-hour shifts, digging, transporting, and processing the metal on which Chile runs.

Chuquicamata is part of CODELCO's operation, the state-owned coopera-tive that is a legacy of President Salvador Allende's nationalization of copper in 1970 (with four mines and one metallurgic division, it's the country's largest company). Chuqui-camata alone produces 640,000 tons of copper per year.

One is dwarfed by the sheer scale of "Chuqui," as locals call it: it's 5 km long, 2 km wide, and 1 km deep. It takes any of the 96 trucks, some of which have beds 12 meters wide, a half hour to navigate the winding road to the bottom of the pit. The monstrous German-made trucks cost a pretty penny, about $4 million, and are refueled by pressure-hoses in the same way Formula One cars are gassed up. After all, a 4,000-liter (1,000-gallon) tank could take a while to fill the conventional way. Even the tires cost about $20,000 apiece. Because they run night and day, the trucks require constant maintenance and generally only about 80 are in operation at any one time. The most modern cranes can shovel out up to 50 tons of rock at a time and require one operator, while in years gone by 20-ton cranes required a crew of 12.

Copper goes through a three-stage separation process, beginning with the rocks being crushed, milled, and "floated" through water. This results in about 33% pure copper, and an intense smelting process refines that to 99%. Anodes, operating like giant magnets, remove other metals like gold and silver, resulting in a final product that is 99.9% pure copper. A byproduct of the process, Molyb-denum, is even more precious than copper because of its high melting point, and is set aside for later sale as well.

Stare into the vast pit of Chuquica-mata and you'll be convinced that Chile uncovered untold riches below the barren Atacama Desert. In 2006, CODELCO profits totaled more than $9 billion, and with market demand increasing in Asia, where 45% of its product is shipped, that number seems certain to rise in the short term. While Chileans may brag about their wine and pisco, there's little doubt that their economy runs on copper.

There is a small museum at the mine's entrance where you can get a close-up view of the machinery used to make such big holes. Tours are in Spanish and English. Reserve in advance by phone or by e-mail. It's about a 20-minute taxi ride (5,000 pesos) from downtown Calama. ✉ *16 km (10 mi) north of Calama* ☎ *55/322–122* ⊕ *www.codelco.cl* ✉ *reservas@codelco.cl.* ✉ *By dona-tion* ⊙ *Tours weekdays at 2* PM.

–Brian Kluepfel

WHERE TO STAY

$ ★ ⊡ **Hotel El Mirador.** This friendly bed-and-breakfast around the corner from Plaza 23 de Marzo is set in a colonial-style house built in the 19th century. Inside it's a charmer, with cheerful yellow rooms that are both clean and comfortable. A tasteful, antiques-filled salon leads to an enclosed courtyard where a Continental breakfast is served. **Pros:** Homey feel, short walk to shopping and restaurants. **Cons:** Some street noise. ⊠*Sotomayor 2064* ☎☎*55/340–329* ⊕*www.hotelmirador.cl* ⮑*14 rooms* ♿*In-room: no a/c, no phone, Wi-Fi. In-hotel: laundry service, public Wi-Fi* ⊟*AE, DC, MC, V* ⦿*CP.*

$ ⊡ **Park Hotel Calama.** It's easy to see why international mining consultants frequent this top-notch hotel. The rooms have giant beds made up with luxurious linens, and the steaming showers feel great after a day of exploring the surrounding desert. A pool, a lovely garden, and an excellent restaurant serving international cuisine round out the hotel's attractions. **Pros:** Nice swimming pool, relaxing lounge. **Cons:** Nothing within walking distance. ⊠*Camino Aeropuerto 1392* ☎*55/319–900* ☎*55/319–901* ⊕*www.parkplaza.cl* ⮑*102 rooms, 6 suites* ♿*In-room: safe, ethernet. In-hotel: restaurant, room service, bar, tennis court, pool, gym, laundry service, public Wi-Fi, airport shuttle* ⊟*AE, DC, MC, V* ⦿*BP.*

NIGHTLIFE & THE ARTS

Calama is the land of the schoperia—locals say there are more schoperias than people. Come payday at the mine, these drinking halls fill up with beer-swilling workers. The schoperias near Plaza 23 de Marzo are less raucous than the ones farther from downtown. The **Afogata Bar** (⊠*MacKenna 1977* ☎*No phone*), from the Spanish word for bonfire, lives up to its name with a blazing fireplace. A twentysomething crowd packs into this cavelike setting, highlighted by mock petroglyphs on the walls. On weekends head to **Pub Anaconda** (⊠*Granaderos 2663* ☎*55/345–834*), an upscale, two-level bar that attracts foreigners and locals alike. Pop and cumbia are played here at top volume, so bring your earplugs.

Cine Teatro Municipal (⊠*Ramírez 2034* ☎*55/342–864*) screens recent Hollywood movies. It also stages the occasional play or concert.

SHOPPING

Locals sell clothing and jewelry at the covered markets off the pedestrian mall of Calle Ramírez. There are also markets on Calle Vargas between Latorre and Vivar. On Balmaceda, the road to the airport, the Calama Mall includes a movie theater screening the latest Hollywood releases. A new casino is set to open in 2008 as well.

SAN PEDRO & THE ATACAMA DESERT

The most popular tourist destination in El Norte Grande (and perhaps all of Chile), San Pedro de Atacama sits in the heart of the Atacama Desert and in the midst of some of the most breathtaking scenery in the country. A string of towering volcanoes, some of which are still

CHIU CHIU

In contrast to the sprawling industrial center of Calama, Chiu Chiu, 32 km (20 mi) away in a lush valley near the Río Loa, is a vision of the region's agrarian past. Inhabitants still make their living growing carrots and other vegetables in this pastoral town.

Across from Chiu Chiu's main square is the **Iglesia de San Francisco**. Built in 1674, it's one of the oldest churches in the altiplano. A cactus-shingle roof tops the squat building's whitewashed adobe walls. No nails were used in its construction—rafters and beams are lashed together with leather straps. On October 4, things get lively when the 500 inhabitants congregate in the nearby central plaza to celebrate the town's patron saint, St. Francis of Assisi. Chiu Chiu is just a turn off the road between Calama and San Pedro, and makes for a nice stopping-off point.

5

active, stands watch to the east. To the west is La Cordillera de Sal, a mountain range composed almost entirely of salt. Here you'll find such marvels as the Valle de la Luna (Valley of the Moon) and the Valle de la Muerte (Valley of Death), part of the Reserva Nacional los Flamencos. The desolate Salar de Atacama, Chile's largest salt flat, lies to the south. The number of attractions in the Atacama area does not end there: alpine lakes, steaming geysers, colonial villages, and ancient fortresses all lie within easy reach.

The area's history goes back to pre-Columbian times, when the Atacameño people scraped a meager living from the fertile delta of the San Pedro River. By 1450 the region had been conquered by the Incas, but their reign was cut short by the arrival of the Europeans. Spanish conquistador Pedro De Valdivia, who eventually seized control of the entire country, camped here in 1540 while waiting for reinforcements. By the 19th century San Pedro had become an important trading center and was a stop for llama trains on their way from the altiplano to the Pacific coast. During the nitrate era, San Pedro was the main resting place for cattle drives from Argentina.

SAN PEDRO DE ATACAMA

★ *100 km (62 mi) southeast of Calama.*

With its narrow streets lined with whitewashed and mud-color adobe houses, San Pedro centers around a small Plaza de Armas teeming with artisans, tour operators, and others who make their living catering to tourists.

GETTING HERE & AROUND

There is direct van shuttle service to San Pedro from the Calama airport, which should be arranged in advance. It's a one-hour-plus drive or bus ride (1,500 pesos) from Calama on Ruta 23. Take good care if driving at sundown as there are many accidents at this time due to vis-

San Pedro & the
Atacama Desert

ibility issues. Tur-Bus and a few other companies serve San Pedro, and
the bus terminal is just a few blocks from downtown at the intersection of Lincacabur and Domingo Atienz. If planning other trips around
Chile, there's a Tur-Bus ticket window here. There are myriad tour
agencies in San Pedro de Atacama. Cosmo Andino Expediciones offers
excellent tours with well-informed guides to the Salar de Uyuni and
other destinations.

SAFETY & PRECAUTIONS
Take good care driving on the road between Calama and San Pedro as
many accidents happen around sundown, when the blinding altiplano
sun hits the horizon, hindering visibility.

ESSENTIALS
There is an emergency clinic in San Pedro on the main plaza, but the
nearest proper hospital is in Calama. There are no banks, but on the
main plaza there is a Banco de Chile ATM machine across from the
regional museum.

Visitor & Tour Info **Cosmo Andino Expediciones** (⊠ *Caracoles s/n* ☎ *55/851–069*).
Sernatur, Chilean Tourism (⊠ *Toconao at Gustavo LePaige* ☎ *55/851–420*).

EXPLORING

The 1744 **Iglesia San Pedro,** to the west of the square, is one of the altiplano's largest churches. It was miraculously constructed without the use of a single nail—the builders used cactus sinews to tie the roof beams and door hinges. ⊠ *Gustavo Le Paige s/n* ☏ *No phone* ⊙ *Daily 9–2 and 3–8.*

Fodor's Choice
★

The **Museo Arqueológico Gustavo Le Paige** exhibits an awe-inspiring collection of artifacts from the region, including fine examples of textiles and ceramics. The museum traces the history of the area from pre-Columbian times through the Spanish colonization. The most impressive exhibit is the well-preserved, fetal-positioned Atacameño mummy with her swatch of twisted black hair. Most of the items on display were gathered by the founder, Jesuit missionary Gustavo Le Paige. ⊠ *Padre Le Paige 380, at Paseo Artesenal* ☏ *55/851–002* ⊕ *www.ucn.cl* ⊡ *2,000 pesos* ⊙ *Weekdays 9–12 and 2–6, weekends 10–noon and 2–6.*

■
**NEED A
BREAK?**

The altiplano sun burns bright and hot in San Pedro, so stop In at Babalu Heladeria (⊠ *Caracoles 160* ☏ *No phone*) to sample one of 52 flavors of ice cream. Stop at Café Cuna (⊠ *Tocopilla 359* ☏ *55/851–999*) for sweet, fresh juices and excellent specials for lunch or dinner. The dining area is in a huge courtyard with chañar trees.

Just 3 km (2 mi) north of San Pedro lies the ancient fortress of **Pukara de Quitor.** This group of stone structures at the entrance to the Valle de Catarpe was built in the 12th century to protect the Atacameños from invading Incas. It wasn't the Incas but the Spanish who were the real threat, however. Spanish conquistador Pedro de Valdivia took the fortress by force in 1540. The crumbling buildings were carefully reconstructed in 1981 by the University of Antofagasta. ⊠ *On road to Valle Catarpe* ☏ *No phone* ⊡ *1,200 pesos* ⊙ *Daily 8–8.*

The archaeological site of **Tulor,** 9 km (5½ mi) southwest of San Pedro, marks the remains of the oldest known civilization in the region. Built around 800 BC, the village of Tulor was home to the Linka Arti people, who lived in small mud huts resembling igloos. The site was uncovered only in the middle of the 20th century, when Jesuit missionary Gustavo Le Paige excavated it from a sand dune. Archaeologists hypothesize that the inhabitants left because of climatic changes and a possible sand storm. Little more about the village's history is known, and only one of the huts has been completely excavated. As one of the well-informed guides will tell you, even this hut is sinking back into the obscurity of the Atacama sand. ⊠ *9 km (5½ mi) southwest of San Pedro, then 3 km (2 mi) down the road leading to the Valle de la Luna* ☏ *No phone* ⊡ *1,500 pesos* ⊙ *Daily 8–8.*

WHERE TO EAT

$$
★
✕ Café Adobe. With a lattice-covered dining area surrounding a blazing fire and a terrace that is open to the stars, Café Adobe is San Pedro's finest eatery. The regional and international cuisine is excellent, and the animated (at times downright frenetic) waitstaff makes for a unique

dining experience. At night, a white-capped chef grills meat in the center courtyard. Try the perfectly seasoned steaks, the cheesy quesadillas, or any of the pasta dishes. There's an Internet café in the rear. ⊠*Carcoles 211* ☎*55/851–132* ⊟*AE, DC, MC, V.*

$ ✕ **Casa Piedra.** This rustic stone structure (*piedra* means "stone") affords views of the cloudless desert skies from its central courtyard. As at most San Pedro eateries, a blazing fire keeps you company. The *congrio* (eel) and salmon are among the best choices on the menu, which includes international and local dishes. Specialty sauces spice up any dinner. ⊠*Caracoles 225* ☎*55/851–271* ⊟*AE, DC, MC, V.*

WHERE TO STAY

$$$ ⊡ **Hotel Altiplánico.** This boutique hotel just outside the center of San Pedro has the look and feel of an altiplano pueblo. A river-stone walkway leads you from room to room, each with its own private terrace. Muted whites predominate in the guest chambers, which also have thatched roofs, thick warm comforters, and cool stone-tiled bathrooms featuring nice hot showers. **Pros:** Refreshing pool, friendly service, nice showers. **Cons:** Tricky walk from downtown in the dark—bring a flashlight. ⊠*Domingo Atienza 282* ☎*55/851–212* 📠*55/851–238* ⊕*www.altiplanico.cl* ⟿*29 rooms, 3 apartments* ⟳*In-room: no a/c, no phone, no TV. In-hotel: restaurant, pool, laundry service, public Wi-Fi, public Internet* ⊟*AE, DC, MC, V* ❘❙❘*BP.*

$$$$ ⊡ **Hotel Explora.** Is it a modern monstrosity or an expressionist show-
★ piece? Hotel Explora, built by the same company that constructed the much-lauded Hotel Explora in Parque Nacional Torres del Paine, attracted much criticism for not fitting in with the local architecture. On the other hand, it has also won architectural prizes for its skewed lines and sleek courtyard. The hotel, which has three-, four-, and seven-day all-inclusive stays—with tours, meals, and drinks included—delivers the best service and amenities of any lodging in northern Chile. The wood-and-tile floors and wall-to-wall windows make the views from each room more enjoyable. **Pros:** Top-notch, all-inclusive service. **Cons:** Expensive. ⊠*Domingo Atienza s/n* ☎*55/851–110* 📠*55/851–115* ⊕*www.explora.com* ⟿*52 rooms* ⟳*In-room: no a/c, safe, Wi-Fi, no TV. In-hotel: restaurant, bar, pools, bicycles, laundry service, public Wi-Fi, airport shuttle, parking (no fee), no-smoking rooms* ⊟*AE, DC, MC, V* ❘❙❘*AI.*

$$$ ⊡ **Hotel Kimal.** This adobe-walled dwelling has comfortable rooms and a cheery central courtyard dotted with islands of desert shrubbery. The rooms are pleasantly airy, with skylights and reed ceilings. The excellent restaurant serves Chilean fare. The pool is ideal for cooling off after your desert exploration. **Pros:** Close to center of town. **Cons:** Pool is on small side. ⊠*Domingo Atienza 452* ☎*55/851–030* 📠*55/851–152* ⊕*www.kimal.cl* ⟿*19 rooms* ⟳*In-room: no a/c, no TV, safe. In-hotel: restaurant, pool, laundry service, public Internet* ⊟*AE, DC, MC, V* ❘❙❘*BP.*

$ ⊡ **Hotel Tambillo.** A good budget alternative, Hotel Tambillo has simple, rather drab rooms along a long, outdoor walkway. The garden, with a thatched-roof sitting area, is a nice place to relax. There's also a good restaurant. **Pros:** Economical rates. **Cons:** A bit run-down. ⊠*Gustavo Le*

Paige 159 🏢📠*55/851–078* ⊕*www.hoteltambillo.cl* 🛏*15 rooms* ⚬*In-room: no a/c, no phone, no TV. In-hotel: restaurant* ▭*No credit cards.*

$$$

Fodor'sChoice

★

🏨 **Lodge Andino Terrantai.** An architectural beauty with river-stone walls, Lodge Andino Terrantai has high-ceilinged rooms highlighted by beautiful tile floors and big beds piled with down comforters. Hand-carved furnishings add a rustic feel. Throw open the huge windows to let in the morning breeze. The candlelit restaurant, perfect for a romantic dinner, serves international fare. There's also a tiny, natural-rock plunge pool. The hotel is just a block away from the Plaza de Armas. **Pros:** Beautiful hotel, and great location for walking to the plaza. **Cons:** No room TV. ✉*Tocopilla 411* 📞*55/851–145* 📠*55/851–037* ⊕*www.terrantai. cl* 🛏*21 rooms* ⚬*In-room: no TV. In-hotel: restaurant, room service, pool, laundry service, public Wi-Fi* ▭*AE, DC, MC, V* ◐*BP.*

NIGHTLIFE & THE ARTS

The bohemian side of San Pedro gets going after dinner and generally ends around 1 AM. Most of the bars and small cafés are on Caracoles. It's all pretty mellow and your choices pretty much limited to whether you want to sit outside by a fire or inside, where it's a bit warmer. **Café Export** (✉*Caracoles at Toconao* 📞*55/851–547*) is smaller and more intimate than the other bars in town. There's a pleasant terrace out back. **La Estaka** (✉*Caracoles 259B* 📞*55/851–201*) is a hippie bar with funky decor, including a sculpted dragon hanging on one of the walls. Reggae music rules, and the international food isn't half bad either.

SPORTS & THE OUTDOORS

San Pedro is an outdoors-lover's dream. There are great places for biking, hiking, and horseback riding in every direction. Extreme-sports enthusiasts can try their hand at sandboarding on the dunes of the Valle de la Muerte. Climbers can take on the nearby volcanoes. The only trouble is the crowds. At the Valle de la Luna, for example, you'll sometimes encounter a caravan of 20 or 30 tourists scurrying toward the top of the large sand dune to watch the sunset. The number of tour agencies and outfitters in San Pedro can be a bit overwhelming: shop around, pick a company you feel comfortable with, ask questions, and make sure the company is willing to cater to your needs.

Whatever your sport, keep in mind that San Pedro lies at 2,400 meters (7,900 feet). If you're not acclimated to the high altitude, you'll feel tired much sooner than you might expect. Also remember to slather on the sunscreen and drink plenty of water.

BIKING

An afternoon ride to the Valle de la Luna is unforgettable, as is a quick trip to the ruins of Tulor. You can also head to the Salar de Atacama. Bike rentals can be arranged at most hotels and tour agencies. A bike can be rented for a half day for 3,000 pesos and for an entire day for 5,000 pesos.

HIKING

There are hikes in all directions from San Pedro. Good hikes include trips through the Valle de la Muerte, as well as to the ruins of Pukara de Quitor. **Cosmo Andino Expediciones** (✉*Caracoles s/n* 📞*55/851–069*) runs excellent treks with well-informed guides.

5

HORSEBACK RIDING
San Pedro has the feeling of a Wild West town, so why not hitch up your horse and head out on an adventure? Although the sun is quite intense during the middle of the day, sunset is a perfect time to visit Pukara de Quitor or Tulor. An overnight journey to the Salar de Atacama or the Valle de La Luna is a great way to see the region at a relaxed pace. **Herradura** (⊠ *Tocopilla s/n* ☎ *55/851–087* ✐ *laherraduraatacama@hotmail. com*) provides horses and guides.

SANDBOARDING
It's like snowboarding, only hotter. Many agencies offer a three-hour sandboarding excursion into the Valle de la Muerte from 8 AM to 11 AM—the intelligent way to beat the desert heat. These tours run about 12,000 pesos (US$24) and include an instructor. If you're brave and have your own transportation, you can rent just the board for 4,000 pesos (US$8). There is also a combination sandboarding-and-sunset tour for 15,000 pesos which closes the day with a desert sunset over the Valle de la Luna. Contact **Altiplano Aventura** (⊠ *Toconao 441-E* ☎ *55/851–039*) or **Expediciones Corvatch** (⊠ *Tocopilla 406* ☎ *55/851–087*) for information.

STARGAZING
Chile is known worldwide for the visibility of its nighttime skies, due to the exceptionally dry climate. **SPACE** (⊠ *166 Caracoles* ☎ *55/851–935* ⊕ *www.spaceobs.com*) is a small observatory just outside of town with five telescopes and nightly tours operated by a French immigrant to the area.

SHOPPING

Just about the entire village of San Pedro is an open-air market. Shopping here is fun, but prices are probably about 20% to 30% higher than in neighboring areas and you'll find many of the same products: the traditional altiplano ponchos (aka serapes), jewelry, and even musical instruments. The **Feria Artesenal**, just off the Plaza de Armas, is bursting at the seams with artisan goods. Here, you can buy high-quality knits from the altiplano, such as sweaters and other woolen items. **Galeria Cultural de Pueblos Andinos** (⊠ *Caracoles s/n, east of town* ☎ *No phone*) is an open-air market selling woolens and crafts. **Mallku** (⊠ *Caracoles s/ n* ☎ *No phone*) is a pleasant store carrying traditional altiplano textiles, some up to 20 years old. **Rayo de La Luna** (⊠ *Caracoles 378* ☎ *09/473–9018*) sells jewelry made by local artisans.

GEYSERS DEL TATIO

95 km (59 mi) north of San Pedro.

The world's highest geothermal field, the Geysers del Tatio are a breathtaking natural phenomenon. The sight of dozens of *fumaroles,* or geysers, throwing columns of steam into the air is unforgettable. A trip to El Tatio usually begins at 4 AM, on a guided tour, when San Pedro is still cold and dark (any of the tour agencies in San Pedro can arrange this trip). After a three-hour bus trip on a relentlessly bumpy road you reach the high plateau about daybreak. (The entrance fee is covered if you are on a tour.) The jets of steam are already shooting into the air as the sun slowly peeks over the adjacent cordillera. The rays of light illuminate the steam in a kaleidoscope of chartreuses, violets, reds, oranges, and blues. The vapor then silently falls onto the sulfur-stained crust of the geyser field. As the sun heats the cold, barren land, the force of the geysers gradually diminishes, allowing you to explore the mud pots and craters formed by the escaping steam. Be careful, though—the crust is thin in places and people have been badly burned falling into the boiling-hot water. On your way back to San Pedro, you may want to stop at the **Termas de Puritama** (✉5,000 pesos) hot springs. A hot soak may be just the thing to shake off that early morning chill. *3,500 pesos.*

RESERVA NACIONAL LOS FLAMENCOS

10 km (6 mi) south and east of San Pedro.

Many of the most astounding sights in El Norte Grande lie within the boundaries of the protected Reserva Nacional los Flamencos. This sprawling national reserve to the south and east of San Pedro encompasses a wide variety of geographical features, including alpine lakes, salt flats, and volcanoes.

GETTING HERE & AROUND
Any of the San Pedro tour companies will take you to the Reserva, but if you're in your own vehicle, take the road toward Toconao for 33 km (20½ mi) to the park entrance.

EXPLORING
You can get information about the Reserva Nacional los Flamencos at the station run by CONAF, the Chilean forestry service. ✉*CONAF station near Laguna Chaxa* ☎*No phone* ⊕*www.conaf.cl* ✉*2,000 pesos* ⊙*Daily 8:30–1 and 2:30–6:30.*

★ About 10 km (6 mi) south of San Pedro you arrive at the edge of the **Salar de Atacama,** Chile's largest salt flat. The rugged crust measuring 3,000 square km (1,158 square mi) formed when salty water flowing down from the Andes evaporated in the stifling heat of the desert. Unlike other salt flats, which are smooth surfaces of crystalline salt, the Salar de Atacama is a jumble of jagged rocks. **Laguna Chaxa,** in the middle of Salar de Atacama, is a very salty lagoon that is home to three of the New World's four species of flamingos. The elegant pink-and-white birds are mirrored by the lake's glassy surface. Near Laguna Chaxa, beautiful plates of salt float on the calm surface of **Laguna Salada.**

It's possible to take a three- to five-day, four-wheel-drive organized tour from San Pedro into Bolivia's massive and mysterious **Salar de Uyuni,** the world's largest salt flat. Beware: the accommodations—usually clapboard lodgings in small oasis towns—are rustic to say the least, but speeding along the Salar de Uyuni, which is chalkboard flat, is a treat. Nearby are geysers, small Andean lagoons, and islands of cactus that stand in sharp contrast to the sea-like salt flat.

★ One of the most impressive sights in Reserva Nacional los Flamencos is the 4,350-meter-high (14,270-foot-high) **Laguna Miscanti**, an awe-inspiring blue lake that merits a few hours of relaxed contemplation.

Laguna Miñeques, a smaller lake adjacent to Laguna Miscanti, is spectacular. Here you will find vicuña and huge flocks of flamingos attracted by the warm waters.

★ Very few places in the world can compare to the **Valle de la Luna** (⊠*14 km [9 mi] west of San Pedro*). This surreal landscape of barren ridges, soaring cliffs, and pale valleys could be from a canvas by Salvador Dalí. Originally a small corner of a vast inland sea, the valley rose up with the Andes. The water slowly drained away, leaving deposits of salt and gypsum that were folded by the shifting of the Earth's crust and then worn away by wind and rain. It's best to visit Valle de la Luna in the late afternoon to take advantage of the incredible sunsets from atop the immense sand dune.

Not far from the Valle de la Luna, just on the other side of Ruta 98 which leads to Calama, are the reddish rocks of the **Valle de la Muerte.** Jesuit missionary Gustavo Le Paige, who in the 1950s was the first archaeologist to explore this desolate area, discovered many human skeletons. These bones are from the indigenous Atacameño people, who lived here before the arrival of the Spanish. He hypothesized that the sick and the elderly may have come to this place to die.

IQUIQUE AREA

The waterside town of Iquique itself is rather dreary, but the area holds many sights that merit a visit. Wander down to the port and *muelles* (fishing piers) and watch the fishing boats come in; while you're there, imagine the key battle of the War of the Pacific being waged offshore in 1879, or Sir Francis Drake and his gang of brigands arriving to sack the town in 1577. You can find out more about this history at the Museo Naval.

A stone's throw from Iquique, nitrate ghost towns like Humberstone sit in eternal silence. Farther inland you encounter the charming hot-spring oases of Pica and Mamiña and the enigmatic Gigante de Atacama, the world's largest geoglyph.

IQUIQUE

390 km (242 mi) northwest of Calama.

Iquique is the capital of Chile's northernmost region, but it wasn't always so important. For hundreds of years it was a tiny fishing community. After the arrival of the Spanish the village grew slowly into a port. The population, however, never totaled more than 100. It was not until the great nitrate boom of the 19th century that Iquique became a major port. Many of those who grew rich on nitrate moved to the city and built opulent mansions, almost all of which still stand today.

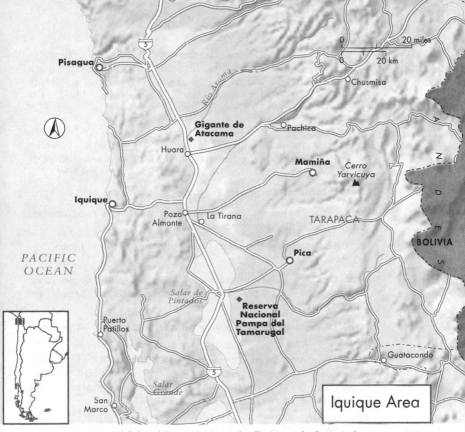

Iquique Area

Many of the old mansions are badly in need of repair, however, giving the city a rather worn-down look. The boom went bust, and those who remained turned again to the sea to make a living. Today Iquique is the world's largest exporter of fish meal.

At the base of a coastal mountain range, Iquique is blessed with year-round good weather. This may explain why it's popular with vacationing Chilean families, who come for the long stretches of white beaches as well as the *zona franca,* or duty-free zone.

GETTING HERE & AROUND

Iquique's Diego Aracena airport (IQQ) is about 45 minutes from downtown proper (35 km [22 mi]; 12,000 pesos in taxi fare) and is served by the three major airlines: Sky, Air Comet, and LAN. Iquique is about seven hours via bus or car from Calama (400 km [249 mi]); once you've turned off the Pan-American Highway it's a narrow, serpentine road down to the town, so don't try passing any of the big trucks or other vehicles that may be slowing you down. The tourist sights of Mamiña, Pica, and the Gigante de Atacama can all be done in one day's driving, and if you don't want to drive yourself, two tour companies in town offer all-inclusive tours. There are two official taxi stands, one on Plaza Prat and one on the pedestrian street of Baquedano. Both will quote you rates to and from the airport, as well as day tours to nearby sites like the Gigante de Atacama, Humberstone, and Mamiña. To get to Pica, La Tirana, and the surrounding sights from Iquique, head south on Ruta 5 (Pan-American Highway) to Km 1,800 (Cruce Sara). Head east on Ruta 685. As for rental cars, the best deals are in Iquique but cars rented here can't be taken out of the area.

ESSENTIALS

Air Travel Aerolineas del Sur/AirComet (☎ *600/625-0000* ⊕ *www.air cometchile.cl*). **Diego Aracena Airport (IQQ)** (☎ *57/407-000*). **LAN** (☎ *57/427-600* ⊕ *www.lan.com*). **Sky Airline** (☎ *57/415-031* ⊕ *www.skyairline.com*).

Currency Exchange Agreement Exchange (✉ *Galeria Lynch 3 y 4*).

Medical Asístanse Hospital Dr. E. Torres Galdames (✉ *Héroes de la Concepción #502* ☎ *57/395-555* ⊕ *www.hospitaliquique.cl*)

Post Office & Shipping Correos de Chile (✉ *Bolívar 485*). **DHL** (✉ *Aníbal Pinto 695, Iquique* ☎ *57/472-820*).

Rental Cars Avis (✉ *Manuel Rodriguez 730* ☎ *57/574-330* ⊕ *www.avis.com*). **Budget** (✉ *Bulnes 542* ☎ *57/416-322* ⊕ *www.budget.cl*). **Hertz** (✉ *Aníbal Pinto 1303* ☎ *57/510-432*).

Taxis Taxi Aeropuerto (✉ *Baquedano corner of Wilson* ☎ *57/419-004* or *57/415-916*).

Visitor & Tour Info Avitours (✉ *Baquedano 997* ☎ *57/429-368* ⊕ *www.avitours. cl*). **Geotour** (✉ *Baquedano 982* ☎ *57/428-984* ⊕ *www.geotour.cl*). **Sernatur, Chilean Tourism** (✉ *Aníbal Pinto 436* ☎ *57/419-241* ⊕ *www.sernatur.cl*). **Unita Turismo** (✉ *Baquedano corner of Plaza Prat* ☎ *57/342-300*).

EXPLORING

Life in the city revolves around the **Plaza Prat,** where children ride bicycles along the sidewalks and adults chat on nearly every park bench. The 1877 **Torre Reloj,** with its gleaming white clock tower and Moorish arches, stands in the center of the plaza.

Leading out from Plaza Prat is **Calle Baquedano,** a pedestrian mall with wooden sidewalks. This is a great place for an afternoon stroll past some of Iquique's salitrera-era mansions, or for a leisurely cappuccino in one of the many sidewalk cafés. An antique trolley runs the length of the mall.

Unlike most cities, Iquique does not have a cathedral on the main plaza. Here instead you'll find the sumptuous **Teatro Municipal,** built in 1890 as an opera house. The lovely statues on the Corinthian-columned facade represent the four seasons. If you're lucky you can catch one of the infrequent plays or musical performances here. ✉ *Plaza Prat* ☎ *57/411-292* 🎫 *Tickets 1,500–5,000 pesos* ⊙ *Daily 8–7.*

★ For a tantalizing view into the opulence of the nitrate era, visit the Georgian-style **Palacio Astoreca.** This palace, built in 1903, includes such highlights as the likeness of Dionysus, the Greek god of revelry; a giant billiard table; and a beautiful skylight over the central hall. An art- and natural-history museum on the upper level houses modern works by Chilean artists and such artifacts as pottery and textiles.

⊠*Av. Bernardo O'Higgins 350* ☎*57/425–600* ⊕*www.iqq.cl/palacio astoreca* ⊠*Free* ☉*Tues.–Fri. 10–1 and 4–7, weekends 11–2.*

Along the historic Calle Baquedano is the **Museo Regional,** a natural-history museum of the region. It showcases pre-Columbian artifacts such as deformed skulls and arrowheads, as well as an eclectic collection from the region's nitrate heyday. ⊠*Baquedano 951* ☎*57/411–214* ⊠*Free* ☉*Weekdays 9–5:30, weekends 10–5.*

The **Museo Naval,** in the old customs house, has displays about the Battle of Iquique in 1879, when the Chileans claimed Iquique from their neighbors to the north. Here you can get a glimpse at what the soldiers wore during the war and at the antiquated English arms used by Chilean army. A well-hidden corridor displays photos and descriptions of two-dozen bird species of the Chilean seashore. ⊠*Sotomayor and Anibal Pinto* ☎*57/402–121* ⊠*200 pesos* ☉*Weekdays 10–1 and 4–7, weekends 10–1.*

WHERE TO EAT

$ ✕**Boulevard.** Excellent seafood is served in a variety of ways at this intimate, candlelit restaurant. The cuisine is an interesting mélange of French and international recipes—try the "Normand," mixed fish in a creamy sauce, topped with a baked-cheese crust. There's live music on weekends. ⊠*Baquedano 790* ☎*57/413–695* ⚑*Reservations essential* ▭*MC, V.*

¢ ✕**Cafe Cioccolatá.** The phrase, "a clean, well-lighted place" fits perfectly here. Chock-full of espresso drinks, cakes, and speciality concoctions like Café Verdi, Café Rossini, the "Rolling Stone," and the "Monkie," this is a good people-watching spot with decent snacks as well. ⊠*A. Pinto 487* ☎*57/413–010* ▭*AE, MC, DC, V.*

$$ ✕**Casino Español.** This venerable gentleman's club on Plaza Prat has
Fodor'sChoice been transformed into a palatial Spanish restaurant, with beautiful
★ Moorish architecture that calls to mind the Alhambra in Granada. The service is good, though rather fussy, and the food is extravagant in the traditional Andalucian style. The paella *Valenciana* is quite good, as is the variety of sauces that accompany the freshly caught fish. Don't miss the *salsa Carolina,* a rich combination of garlic and fresh herbs. Try a side of *pure catalan* (mashed potatoes with bacon, onion, and grilled peppers). ⊠*Plaza Prat 584* ☎*57/423–284* ⚑*Reservations essential* ▭*AE, DC, MC, V.*

$$ ✕**Club Nautico Cavancha.** Located away from the center of the city, this seafood restaurant treats you to views of Playa Cavancha. It's very stylish, right down to the cloth napkins (a rarity in El Norte Grande). Try the sole stuffed with shrimp in a lemon-cognac sauce, the shrimp in a pepper-whisky sauce, or the paella for two, served by friendly bow-tied waiters. ⊠*Los Rieles 110* ☎*57/432–896* ⚑*Reservations essential* ▭*DC, MC, V.*

$ ✕**Neptuna.** When the doors open at lunch time, locals fill this seafood-lovers' paradise for the four "menu" items, including seviche, cabrilla (a type of sea bass), and a *caldillo de pescado,* a three-fish stew. A large selection of Chilean wines complements the food. The nautical paraphernalia on display includes large sea-turtle shells affixed to the wall. ⊠*Riquelme 234* ☏*No phone* ▭*AE, DC, MC, V.*

$ ✗**Restaurant Protectora.** A soaring molded ceiling and a huge chandelier overlook this elegant contemporary restaurant next to the Teatro Municipal. The international menu includes such succulent items as lamb cooked in mint sauce and *merluza con salsa margarita* (hake in a creamy seafood sauce). The service, though a bit doting, is top-notch. ⊠*Thompson 207* ☏*57/421–923* ▭*AE, DC, MC, V.*

$ ✗**Split Café.** This café, on the lower floor of the Croatian Community Center on Plaza Prat, pays tribute to the thousands of immigrant workers from the Dalmatian coast who came to Chile in the late 19th and early 20th centuries. Teas, coffees, and seven-flavor cake—a Croatian specialty—highlight the menu. There are also tasty sandwiches. Replicas of the coats of arms from Croatia, Slovenia, and Dalmatia sit proudly above the counter. The new pub opens at 5 PM. ⊠*Plaza Prat 310* ☏*57/316–541* ▭*AE, DC, MC, V.*

$$ ✗**Taberna Barracuda.** An immensely popular bar and grill, Taberna Bar-
★ racuda serves everything from tapas to rib-eye steak. The wine list is good, making this an ideal place to sample some of Chile's labels. A general sense of joviality and merriment here harkens back to the decadent days of the nitrate boom. Antiques ranging from brass instruments to time-stained photos decorate the labyrinthine, salitrera-era house. ⊠*Gorostiaga 601* ☏*57/427–969* ⚓*Reservations essential* ▭*AE, DC, MC, V* ⊙*Closed Sun. mid-June–early Sept.*

WHERE TO STAY

$–$$ ☷**Hotel Arturo Prat.** The only thing this luxury hotel in the heart of Iquique's historic district lacks is access to the ocean. To make up for this, it has a very pleasant rooftop pool area decorated with white umbrellas and navy-blue sails. The rooms are all comfortable and modern, though some look out onto the parking lot. Ask for one of the newer rooms, which are several notches above the rooms in the older section of the hotel. The Arturo faces the central square, and the restaurant, which serves good but somewhat uninspired fare, sits right on Plaza Prat. **Pros:** Central location, friendly staff. **Cons:** A bit cavernous, some rooms nicer than others. ⊠*Anibal Pinto 695* ☏*57/520–000* 🖷*57/520–050* ⊕*www.hotelarturoprat.cl* 📞*81 rooms, 9 suites* ⚏*In-room: no a/c (some), safe (some). In-hotel: restaurant, room service, bar, pool, laundry service* ▭*AE, DC, MC, V* ⏍BP.

$ ☷**Hotel Atenas.** Housed in a venerable nitrate-era mansion on the
★ beach, Hotel Atenas is truly a taste of the city's history. Antiques and wood furnishings fill most of the rooms. There are more modern rooms in the back, but these are not nearly as charming. The honeymoon suite has a giant tub where you can imagine the nitrate barons bathing in champagne. There's also a pleasant pool in the garden. **Pros:** Near beaches, quaint. **Cons:** Borders on old-fashioned. ⊠*Los Rieles 738* ☏*57/431–100* 🖷*57/421–534* 📞*40 rooms, 3 suites* ⚏*In-room: no a/c, safe. In-hotel: restaurant, room service, pool, laundry service, public Wi-Fi, public Internet* ▭*AE, DC, MC, V* ⏍CP.

$$ ☷**Sunfish.** On Playa Cavancha, Sunfish has very large, very modern rooms, many with views of the beach. Though the hotel lacks char-

acter, the royal-blue exterior will certainly catch your eye. There's a small rooftop pool surrounded by a tacky artificial-grass terrace. **Pros:** Close to the beach. **Cons:** A bit 1970s in style. ⊠*Amunategui 1990* ☎*57/419–000* 🖷*57/419–001* ⊕*www.sunfish.cl* ⟳*45 rooms* ♨*In-room: safe, refrigerator. In-hotel: restaurant, bar, pool, laundry service, public Wi-Fi* ▤*AE, DC, MC, V* ⦿|*BP.*

$$$–$$$$ 🏨**Terrado Suites.** A skyscraper at the southern end of Playa Cavancha, the Terrado is Iquique's most upscale hotel. A marble entryway leads you down to the comfortable lounge and restaurant area. Overstuffed sofas, Andean prints, and hardwood accents decorate the large suites, which have private balconies. The pool and underground sauna are a delight after a day in the desert. **Pros:** Everything you'd need in one place, done with elegance. **Cons:** A bit much; you might forget you're in Chile. ⊠*Los Rieles 126* ☎*57/437–878* 🖷*57/437–755* ⊕*www.terrado.cl* ⟳*91 suites* ♨*In-room: no a/c (some), safe, refrigerator, Wi-Fi. In-hotel: 2 restaurants, room service, bar, pools, gym, laundry service, airport shuttle* ▤*AE, DC, MC, V* ⦿|*BP.*

NIGHTLIFE & THE ARTS

Iquique really gets going after dark. Young vacationers stay out all night and then spend the next day lazing around on the beach.

BARS   Bars, most of which feature folk and jazz performances, get crowded around midnight. **Bar Sovia** (⊠*Tarapaca 173* ☎*57/517–015*), perhaps the North's only microbrewery, is a relaxed place for a frothy brew. For sunset drinks and excellent empanadas head to **Choza Bambu** (⊠*Arturo Prat s/n, Playa Cavancha* ☎*57/519–002*). **Runas** (⊠*Arturo Prat 2996* ☎*57/518–738*) caters to the 30-plus crowd with live bands playing the likes of the Eagles and Kiss. One of the city's most popular bars is **Van Gogh** (⊠*Ramirez 805* ☎*57/319–847*), with impressive murals of the Dutch master's work filling the walls and live music on weekends.

DANCE CLUBS   At about 2 AM the beachfront discos start filling with a young, energetic crowd. Check out the dance clubs along Playa Brava and just south of town. **Kamikaze** (⊠*Bajo Molle, Km 7* ☎*No phone*), part of a popular chain of discos, is jam-packed on weekends with young people dancing to salsa music. **Timber House** (⊠*Bolívar 553* ☎*57/422–538*) has a disco upstairs and an Old West–style saloon downstairs.

BEACHES

⟲ Just south of the city center on Avenida Balmaceda is **Playa Cavancha,** a long stretch of white, sandy beach that's great for families and often crowded. You can stroll along the boardwalk and touch the llamas and alpacas at the petting zoo. There's also a walk-through aquarium housing a group of *yacares*, small crocodiles that inhabit the rivers of Bolivia, Argentina, and Uruguay. For bars and eateries you'll have to head back to town or the peninsula. If you crave solitude, follow the coast south of Playa Cavancha for about 3 km (2 mi) on Avenida Balmaceda to reach **Playa Brava,** a pretty beach that's often deserted. The currents here are quite strong, so swimming is not recommended. **Playa Blanca,** 13 km (8 mi) south of the city center on Avenida Balmaceda, is a sandy spot that you can often have all to yourself.

SHOPPING

Many Chileans come to Iquique with one thing on their minds—shopping. About 3 km (2 mi) north of the city center is the **Zona Franca**—known to locals as the Zofri—the only duty-free zone in the country's northern tip. This big, unattractive mall is stocked with cheap cigarettes, alcohol, and electronic goods. Remember that large purchases, such as personal computers, are taxable upon leaving the country. ✉ *Av. Salitrera Victoria* ☎ *57/515–100* ⊕ *www.iquique.cl* ⊙ *Mon. 4–9, Tues.–Fri. 10–9, Sat. 10–2 and 5–9.*

EN ROUTE   One of the last nitrate plants in the region, **Humberstone** closed in 1960 after operating for nearly 200 years. Now it's a ghost town where ancient machines creak and groan in the wind. You can wander through the central square and along the streets of the company town, where almost all of the original buildings survive. The theater, with its rows of empty seats, is particularly eerie. ✉ *45 km (28 mi) east of Iquique on the Pan-American Hwy.* ☎ *57/324–642* 🎫 *1,000 pesos* ⊙ *Daily 9–5.*

MAMIÑA

125 km (78 mi) east of Iquique.

An oasis cut from the brown desert, the tiny village of Mamiña has hundreds of hot springs. Renowned throughout Chile for their curative powers, these springs draw people from around the region. Every hotel in town has the thermal water pumped into its rooms, so you can enjoy a soak in the privacy of your own *tina*, or bathtub. The valley also has several public pools fed by thermal springs. The town itself is perched on a rocky cliff above the terraced green valley where locals grow alfalfa.

GETTING HERE & AROUND

Mamiña is 125 km (78 mi) from Iquique proper: go back to Ruta 5, and head south briefly before taking Ruta A-65 directly east into Mamiña. If you'd also like to see Tambillo (a resting spot on the Inca trail), take the turnoff for Ruta A-651. For the adventurous and hard-of-bottom, there are minivans which head to Mamiña from Iquique.

EXPLORING

Most directions in town are given in relation to the Mamiña bottling plant, which produces the popular mineral drinking water sold in many Chilean shops.

If you'd like to wallow in the mud, try a soothing mud bath in a secluded setting at **Barros El Chino** (✉ *Near the Mamiña bottler* ☎ *No phone* 🎫 *1,000 pesos*). After your bath you can bake in the sun on a drying rack and then leap into one of the plunge pools to wash the stinky brown stuff off your skin.

Baños Ipla (✉ *Near the Mamiña bottler* ☎ *No phone* 🎫 *1,000 pesos*) lets you soak in large public tinas.

A fountain near the Baños Ipla called the **Vertiente del Radium,** with slightly radioactive spring water, is said to cure every type of eye malady.

The simple, charming **Iglesia Nuestra Señora del Rosario** in the central plaza dates to 1632. The church's twin bell towers are unique in Andean Chile. A garish electric sign mars the front of the building.

A two-hour hike from Mamiña will bring you to **Pukara del Cerro Inca,** a great place to watch the sunset. Here you'll find interesting petroglyphs left by the Incas and an excellent view of the valley. To find it, head west on the trail a block west of the bottler.

WHERE TO STAY & EAT

$$ ★ ✕🖼 **Hotel los Cardenales.** Two highlights of this hotel are its lovely garden and its pool, which is covered by an awning to protect you from the fierce rays of the sun. All rooms have private tubs that fill with spring water—most tubs are on the small side, but the one in the honeymoon suite is big enough for two. At the pleasant restaurant terrace you can enjoy views of the valley. A fixed menu includes a soup or cazuela, and grilled meat. Pro: Nice views. Con: A bit dated in every sense. ✉ *Camino Barros El Chino s/n* ☎ *57/517–000 or 09/553–0934* 🛏 *10 rooms, 1 suite* 🛁 *In-room: no a/c, no phone, no TV (some). In-hotel: restaurant, pool* ═ *No credit cards* ⎮🍽AI.

$ ✕🖼 **Hotel Refugio del Salitre.** You reach the Hotel Refugio del Salitre, on the hill in the northern part of the valley, by a series of flower-lined walkways. Although the rooms here have seen better days (the carpets are a bit threadbare), the tubs are big and the king-size towels are luxurious. The views of the alfalfa-laden valley from your bath are also quite nice. Your stay includes all meals, with dinners of grilled fish or meat that are served in the wood-floor restaurant. Pros: Location, nice country feel. Con: A bit threadbare. ✉ *Av. El Tambo 1* ☎ *57/751–203* 🖨 *57/751–203* 🛏 *40 rooms* 🛁 *In-room: no a/c, no phone. In-hotel: restaurant, bar, pool* ═ *No credit cards* ⎮🍽AI.

PICA

114 km (71 mi) southeast of Iquique.

From a distance, Pica appears to be a mirage. This oasis cut from the gray and brown sand of the Atacama Desert is known for its fruit—the limes used to make pisco sours are grown here. A hint of citrus hangs in the air, because the town's chief pleasure is sitting in the Plaza de Armas and sipping a *jugo natural,* fresh-squeezed juice of almost any fruit imaginable, including mangoes, oranges, pears, and grapes. You can buy a bag of any of those from a vendor for the bus trip back to Iquique.

Most people come to Pica not for the town itself but for the incredible hot springs at **Cocha Resbaladero.** Tropical green foliage surrounds this lagoonlike pool cut out of the rock, and nearby caves beckon to be explored. It is quite a walk, about 2 km (1 mi) north of town, but well worth the effort. You can also drive here. ✉ *Gen. Ibañez* ☎ *No phone* 🎫 *1,000 pesos* 🕐 *Daily 8–8.*

WHERE TO STAY & EAT

$ ✕**Los Naranjos.** This is a popular place among the locals because of the inexpensive lunch specials, usually featuring a meat or fish dish. It's nothing fancy, little more than long tables in a low-slung dining room. ⊠*Barboza 200, at Esmeralda* ☎*57/741–318* ⊟*No credit cards.*

¢ ✕**San Andres.** Locals speak highly of this family-style restaurant at the Hotel San Andres serving a fixed lunch. The northern Chilean fare, which usually includes a cazuela and chicken or beef entrée, is delicious. ⊠*Av. Balmaceda 197* ☎*57/741– 319* ⊟*No credit cards.*

$ ✕**Hotel los Emelios.** Birds chirp-
★ ing in the garden and a refreshing plunge pool make this comfortable, homey, family-owned B&B your best bet in Pica. The small rooms have nice linens on the somewhat lumpy beds. Breakfast is served on the terrace in the back, where you'll enjoy bread with marmalade and tea or coffee. **Pros:** Friendly staff. **Cons:** Feels more like a hostel than a hotel. ⊠*L. Cochrane 213* ☎*57/741–126* 🖷*57/741–126* 📞*7 rooms* ⚅*In-room: no a/c, no phone. In-hotel: restaurant, pool, laundry service* ⊟*No credit cards* ⦿*CP.*

> ### LA TIRANA FESTIVAL
>
> With only 250 residents, La Tirana is usually a quiet place. The sleepy town awakens each year from July 12 to 18, when 80,000 people in colorful masks and costumes converge here, filling the square with riotous dancing (don't plan on staying as there are no hotels). The object of this merriment is one of Chile's most important religious icons, the Virgen del Carmen (also known as the Virgen de la Tirana).
>
> The statue is found inside the **Santuario de la Tirana**, on the main plaza. The **Museo del Salitre**, on Tirana's main plaza houses artifacts from the nitrate era. ⊠*Opposite Santuario de la Tirana on the main plaza* ☎*No phone* ⊕*www.museodelsalitre.cl* 📧*Free* ⊙*Mon.–Sat. 8:30–1 and 3–8.*

RESERVA NACIONAL PAMPA DEL TAMARUGAL

96 km (60 mi) southeast of Iquique.

The tamarugo tree is an anomaly in the almost lifeless desert. These bushlike plants survive where most would wither because they are especially adapted to the saline soil of the Atacama. Over time they developed extensive root systems that search for water deep beneath the almost impregnable surface. Reserva Nacional Pampa del Tamarugal has dense groves of tamarugos, which were almost wiped out during the nitrate era when they were felled for firewood. At the entrance to this reserve is a CONAF station. ⊠*24 km (15 mi) south of Pozo Almonte on Pan-American Hwy.* ☎*57/751–055* 📧*Free.*

Fodor'sChoice The amazing **Cerros Pintados** *(Painted Hills)*, within the Reserva Nacio-
★ nal Pampa del Tamarugal, are well worth a detour. Here you'll find the largest group of geoglyphs in the world. These figures, which scientists believe ancient peoples used to help them navigate the desert, date from AD 500 to 1400. They are also enormous—some of the figures are decipherable only from the air. Drawings of men wearing pon-

chos were probably intended to point out the route to the coast to the llama caravans coming from the Andes. More than 400 figures of birds, animals, and geometric patterns adorn this 4-km (2½-mi) stretch of desert. There is a CONAF kiosk on a dirt road 2 km (1 mi) west of the Pan-American Highway. ⊠*45 km (28 mi) south of Pozo Almonte* ☎*57/751–055* 🔖*1,000 pesos* ⊙*Daily 9:30–6.*

GIGANTE DE ATACAMA

84 km (52 mi) northeast of Iquique.

The world's largest geoglyph, the Gigante de Atacama, measures an incredible 86 meters (282 feet). The Atacama Giant, thought to represent a chief of an indigenous people or perhaps created in honor of Pachamama (Mother Earth), looks a bit like a space alien. It is adorned with a walking staff, a cat mask, and a feathered headdress that resembles rays of light bursting from his head. The exact age of the figure is not known, but it certainly hails from before the arrival of the Spanish, perhaps around AD 900. The geoglyph, which is on a hill, is best viewed just before dusk, when the long shadows make the outline clearer. To get here from Iquique, head north on Ruta 5, take Ruta A-483 toward Chusmiza (east), then turn west at Huara and travel for 14 km (8 mi). ⊠*Cerro Unita, 14 km (8 mi) west of the turnoff to Chusmiza* ☎*No phone* 🔖*Free.*

PISAGUA

168 km (104 mi) north of Iquique.

Pisagua, one of the region's most prominent ports during the nitrate era, at one time sustained a population of more than 8,000 people. Many of the mansions built at that time are still standing, although others have fallen into disrepair. During Pinochet's regime Pisagua was the site of a prison, which was later used as hotel and has since closed. Today, there are only around 100 inhabitants in Pisagua—fisherfolk and guano harvesters primarily. The echoes of the Pinochet massacres and the bygone era of decadence still haunt the oceanfront village.

The town's most famous sight, the **Torre Reloj**, built in 1887 from Oregon pine, stands on a hill overlooking the city, its blue and white paint peeling in the hot coastal sun. This clock tower, which was constructed by Alexandre Gustave Eiffel, is an excellent place to catch views of the town and its port.

The **Teatro Municipal** testifies to the wealth the town once possessed. Built in 1892 at the height of the nitrate boom, the once-lavish theater has grand touches, such as the painted cherubs dancing across the ceiling. The theater sits right on the edge of the sea, and waves crash against its walls, throwing eerie echoes through the empty, forgotten auditorium. You can get the key, and a very informative free tour, from a woman in the tourist kiosk opposite the theater.

WHERE TO EAT

¢ ✕**Restaurant La Picada de Don Gato.** This terrace restaurant, recommended by locals, serves simple but exquisite seafood. The shellfish dishes, especially the ostiones a la parmesana, are particularly delicious. Don't let the plastic chairs, which look like they belong in a bus station, distract you from the great food. ⊠*Arturo Prat 127* ☎*57/731–511* 🖃*No credit cards.*

ARICA AREA

At the very tip of Chile, Arica is the country's northernmost city. This pleasant community on the rocky coast once belonged to Peru. In 1880, during the War of the Pacific, Chilean soldiers stormed El Morro, a fortress set high atop a cliff in Arica. Three years later, much of the land north of Antofagasta that was once part of Peru and Bolivia belonged to Chile. Though the Arica of today is fervently Chilean, you can still see the Peruvian influence in the streets and market stalls of the city. Indigenous women still sell their goods and produce in the town's colorful markets.

Inland from Arica, the Valle Azapa cuts its way up into the mountains, a strip of green in a land of brown. Here, the excellent Museo Arqueológico de San Miguel de Azapa contains the world's oldest mummies. They were left behind by the Chinchorro people who inhabited Chile's northern coast during pre-Hispanic times. Ascending farther up the mountains toward the Bolivian border you pass through the pleasant indigenous communities of Socoroma and Putre. These towns, though far from picturesque, are good resting points if you're planning to make the journey to the 4,000-meter-high (13,120-foot-high) Parque Nacional Lauca and the neighboring Reserva Nacional Las Vicuñas. The beautiful Lago Chungará, part of Parque Nacional Lauca, lies near Bolivia, creating what is probably the country's most impressive border crossing.

ARICA

301 km (187 mi) north of Iquique.

Arica boasts that it is "the land of the eternal spring," but its temperate climate and beaches are not the only reason to visit this small city. Relax for an hour or two on the Plaza 21 de Mayo. Walk to the pier and watch the pelicans and sea lions trail the fishing boats as the afternoon's catch comes in, or walk to the top of the Morro and imagine battles of days gone by, or wonder at the magnitude of modern shipping as Chilean goods leave the port below by container.

Arica is gaining notice for its great surfing conditions, and in 2007 hosted the Rip Curl Pro Search as part of an international competition sponsored by beer giant Foster's. A shop on the main pedestrian mall, **Huntington Surf Shop** (⊠*21 de Mayo 493*) caters to those brought into town by the waves. Arica also has a surfing school, **Escuela de Surf** (☎*58/310–524 or 9/282–5175*).

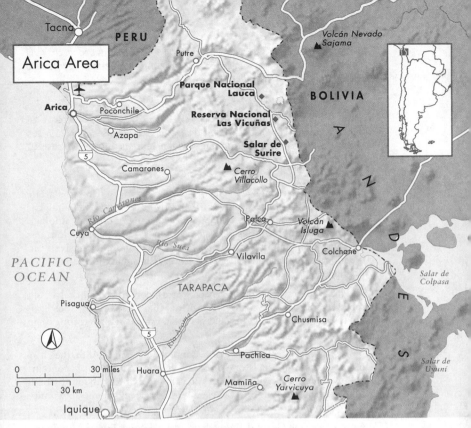

GETTING HERE & AROUND

Arica is a true international crossroads: planes arrive daily from Santiago (Sky, LAN, Air Comet), buses pull in from La Paz, and colectivos laden with four passengers head in both directions for Tacna and the Peruvian border. The airport is about 15 minutes north of town (a taxi fare is about 5,000 pesos). The bus terminal is a quick five-minute taxi ride to downtown. Vans leave in the morning from Patricio Lynch if you want a local's experience of getting to Putre; you can also take colectivos there for a bargain rate (about US$1) to the museum out on Azapa Valley (15- to 20-minute ride). Arica is about four or five hours north of Iquique by auto or bus (300 km [187 mi]).

ESSENTIALS

Air Travel Arica Chacalluta Airport (ARI) (☎ 58/211–116). **LAN** (☎ 58/251–641 ⊕ www.lan.com). **Sky Airline** (☎ 58/251–816 ⊕ www.skyairline.com).

Currency Exchange Banco Santander (✉ 21 de Mayo 359 ☎ 600/320–3000).

Hospital Centro Clinico Militar Arica (✉ S. Velasquez 1700 ☎ 58/232–478).

Post Office & Shipping Correos de Chile (✉ Arturo Prat 305). **DHL** (✉ Colón 351 ☎ 58/256–753).

Rental Cars Budget (⊠ *Colón 996* ☎ *58/258–911* ⊕ *www.budget.cl*). **Avis** (⊠ *Gillermo Sanchez 660* ☎ *58/584–821* ⊕ *www.avis.com*). **Hertz** (⊠ *Baquedano 999* ☎ *58/231–487* ⊕ *www.hertz.cl*).

Taxis Taxi Tarapaca (☎ *58/221–000 or 58/424–000*).

Visitor & Tour Info Geotour (⊠ *Bolognesi 421* ☎ *58/253–927* ⊕ *www.geotour.cl*). **Raices Andinas** (⊠ *Paseo Thompson, Feria 3 Esquinas* ☎ *58/233–305* ⊕ *www.raicesandinas.com*). **Sernatur, Chilean Tourism** (⊠ *San Marcos 101* ☎ *58/252–054*).

EXPLORING

The well-respected agency called Geotour arranges trips to Parque Nacional Lauca, the Salar de Surire, and the Reserva Nacional Las Vicuñas. Most Arica-based companies can arrange a one-day altiplano tour for about 15,000 pesos. Raices Andinas, near Plaza Colón, has two- and three-day options, which allow for a more expansive visit. The tour includes a stop at a Hare Krishna ashram in the Azapa Valley for a delicious vegetarian lunch.

On Plaza Colón is the **Iglesia de San Marcos,** constructed entirely from iron. Alexandre Gustave Eiffel, designer of that famed eponymous Parisian tower, had the individual pieces cast in France before erecting them in Arica in 1876.

Across from Parque General Baquedano, the **Aduana de Arica,** the city's former customs house, is one of Eiffel's creations. It currently contains the town's cultural center, where you can find exhibits about northern Chile, old photographs of Arica, and works by local painters and sculptors. ☎*No phone* ⊠*Free* ⊙*Daily 10–6.*

North of Parque General Baquedano is the defunct **Estación Ferrocarril,** the train station for the Arica–La Paz railroad. Though trains no longer run across the mountains to the Bolivian capital, there are round-trip journeys four times a week to the altiplano. The 1913 building houses a small museum with a locomotive and other remnants of the railroad. ☎*No phone* ⊠*Free* ⊙*Daily 10–6.*

Hanging over the town, the fortress of **El Morro de Arica** is impossible to ignore. This former Peruvian stronghold was the site of one of the key battles in the War of the Pacific. The fortress now houses the **Museo de las Armas,** which commemorates that battle. As you listen to the proud drumroll of military marches you can wander among the uniforms and weapons of past wars. ⊠*Reached by footpath from Calle Colón* ☎*58/254–091* ⊠*600 pesos* ⊙*Daily 8–8.*

Fodor's Choice ★ A newcomer to the museum scene is Arica's **Museo del Mar,** a well-maintained and colorful collection of more than 1,000 seashells and oceanic oddities from around the world. The owner has traveled the globe for more than 30 years to bolster his collection, which includes specimens from Africa, Asia, and you guessed it—Arica. ⊠*Sangra 315* ⊕*www.museodelmardearica.cl* ⊠*1,000 pesos* ⊙*Mon.–Sat. 10–2 and 4–8.*

Fodor's Choice ★ A must for any visitor to El Norte Grande is the **Museo Arqueológico de San Miguel de Azapa.** In an 18th-century olive-oil refinery, this museum

CLOSE UP

Eiffel's Other Tower

An extremely ambitious man, Alexandre Gustave Eiffel designed buildings and bridges all over the world, so when Peruvian president José Balta invited him to construct a new church, Eiffel leaped at the chance. (Before the War of the Pacific, much of what is northern Chile was part of Peru or Bolivia.) The structure was originally intended for the coastal town of Ancón, but when a great earthquake felled Arica's cathedral in 1868, the parts that had already been fabricated in Eiffel's Parisian workshop were rerouted.

Eiffel took advantage of new building materials—for example, iron—in constructing the Iglesia de San Marcos, a job that took five years. The plates and girders were cast in an iron foundry in Paris and transported to Arica, where they were carefully

assembled. The only part of this marvel of Gothic-style architecture that is wood is the massive front door. Eiffel's structure withstood a harrowing test just two years after completion, when an earthquake and storm surge pummeled the town. In 2001, it stood tall again when parts of Arica succumbed to yet another temblor.

In addition to the church and customs house in Arica, Eiffel also designed a clock tower in the Chilean town of Pisagua. In neighboring Peru you can see the cathedral—made of more traditional stone—that Eiffel designed for the town of Tacna in 1870 and the bridge he designed for Arequipa in 1882. All this happened before his famed Parisian tower was built in 1889.

–Brian Kluepfel

houses an impressive collection of artifacts from the cultures of the Chinchorros (a coastal people) and Tijuanacotas (a group that lived in the antiplano). Of particular interest are the Chinchorro mummies, the oldest in the world, dating to 6000 BC. The incredibly well–preserved mummies are arranged in the fetal position, which was traditional in this area. To look into their wrinkled, expressive faces is to get a glimpse at a history that spans more than 8,000 years. The tour ends at an olive press that functioned until 1956, a reminder of the still-thriving industry in the surrounding valley. The museum is a short drive from Arica. You can also make the 20-minute journey by colectivo from Patricio Lynch for about 600 pesos. ⊠ *12 km (7 mi) south of town on the route to Putre* ☎ *58/205–551* ⊕ *www.uta.cl/masma* ✉ *1,000 pesos* ☉ *Jan. and Feb., daily 10–6; Mar.–Dec., daily 9–8.*

WHERE TO EAT

$ ✕ **Casino La Bomba.** In the old fire station, Casino La Bomba is more of a cultural curiosity than a culinary one. That said, the traditional food isn't bad, and the service is friendly. You'll have to maneuver around the parked fire trucks to get inside, where you are greeted by wagonwheel furnishings and a menu heavy on grilled fish and roasted chicken. ⊠ *Colon 357* ☎ *58/231–312* ⊟ *No credit cards.*

$ ✕ **Club de Deportes Náuticos.** This old yacht club with views of the port serves succulent seafood dishes in a relaxed terrace setting. One of the friendliest restaurants in town, this former men's club is a great place to meet the old salts of the area. Bring your fish stories. ⊠*Thompson 1* ☎*58/254–738* ⊟*MC, V.*

$ ✕**El Rey de Mariscos.** Locals call this the best seafood restaurant in town, for good reason. The *corvina con salsa margarita* (sea bass in a seafood-based sauce) is a winner, as is the *paila marina,* a hearty soup stocked with all manner of fish. The dreary fluorescent lights and faux-wood paneling give this restaurant on the second story of a concrete-block building an undeserved down-at-the-heels air. ⊠*Colon 565* ☎*58/229–232* ⊟*AE, DC, MC, V.*

$$ ✕**Maracuyá.** Wicker furniture enhances the cool South Pacific atmosphere of this pleasant, open-air restaurant that literally sits above the water on stilts. The international menu focuses on fish. The seafood, lauded by locals, is always fresh; ask the waiter what the fishing boats brought in that day. House specialties include octopus grilled in lemon and olive oil, salmon in an orange sauce, and sea bass in the pineapple-flavored *salsa amazonia.* ⊠*Av. Comandante San Martin 0321* ☎*58/227–600* ⊟*AE, DC, MC, V.*

WHERE TO STAY

$$–$$$ ✕▥**Hotel Arica.** The finest hotel in Arica, this first-class establishment
★   sits on the ocean between Playa El Laucho and Playa Las Liseras. The rooms, which are elegant if a bit dated, have views of the ocean and great showers with plenty of hot water. The courteous and attentive staff can help set up sightseeing tours or book a table at a local eatery. The hotel's tony restaurant ($), which takes advantage of the ocean views, serves fresh seafood cooked to order, including crab, octopus, and tuna. Don't pass up the conger eel chowder. **Pros:** Beautiful setting, nice restaurant. **Cons:** Somewhat dated, far from downtown. ⊠*Av. Comandante San Martin 599* ☎*58/254–540* ⊟*58/231–133* ⊕*www. panamericanahoteles.cl* ↩*108 rooms, 13 suites, 20 cabanas* ⌂*In-room: safe. In-hotel: restaurant, room service, tennis court, pool, gym, children's programs (ages 2–10, summer only), laundry service, refrigerator* ⊟*AE, DC, MC, V* ⦿|*BP.*

$–$$ ▥**Hotel El Paso.** This modern lodging in the center of Arica surrounds a landscaped courtyard and a pool with a swim-up bar. Though not on the ocean, it's a short walk from any of the city's beaches. The superior rooms, with newer furnishings and larger televisions, are a far better value than the standard ones. **Pros:** Modern, close to beach. **Cons:** Somewhat sterile. ⊠*Av. General Velasquez* ☎*58/230–808* ⊟*58/231–965* ⊕*www.hotelelpaso.cl* ↩*71 rooms, 10 suites* ⌂*In-room: no a/c, safe. In-hotel: restaurant, bar, tennis court, pool, laundry service, parking (no fee), public Internet, refrigerator* ⊟*AE, DC, MC, V* ⦿|*BP.*

$ ▥**Hotel Plaza Colon.** This small hotel is a good option if you don't mind being so far from the beach. You are close to the downtown attractions, including the historic Iglesia de San Marcos. The pink-wall rooms are small but clean. **Pros:** Friendly staff, walking distance to shopping and restaurants. **Cons:** A bit dated, small rooms. ⊠*San Marcos 261* ☎*58/254–424* ⊟*58/231–244* ⊕*www.hotelplazacolon. cl* ↩*39 rooms* ⌂*In-room: no a/c. In-hotel: restaurant, room service, laundry service, parking (no fee), refrigerator, public Internet* ⊟*AE, DC, MC, V* ⦿|*CP.*

$ **Hotel Saint Gregory.** Although it's quite a hike from Arica's city center, this pleasant oceanfront hotel is great for weary travelers who simply want to relax on the beach. Some of the rooms and common areas have dated decor, but the hotel is still a good value. Many rooms have their own hot tubs. **Pros:** Romantic setting. **Cons:** Far from anything. ✉ *Av. Comandante San Martin 1020* ☎ *58/233–320* 🌐 *www.hotelsaintgregory.cl* *28 rooms, 8 suites* *In-room: kitchen (some). In-hotel: restaurant, bar, pool, airport shuttle, parking (no fee), public Internet* *AE, DC, MC, V* *CP.*

NIGHTLIFE & THE ARTS

You can join the locals for a beer at one of the cafés lining the pedestrian mall of 21 de Mayo. These low-key establishments, many with outdoor seating, are a great place to spend an afternoon watching the passing crowds. An oddity in Arica is the attire of the servers in various tranquil cafés and tea salons (usually called "café con piernas" or "cafés with legs"): women serve coffee and tea dressed in lingerie.

5

In the evening you won't have trouble finding the city's many watering holes. For a more refined setting, try the lively, funky **Barrabas** (✉ *18 de Septiembre 520* ☎ *58/230–928*), a bar and adjoining disco that attracts Arica's younger set. **Discoteca SoHo** (✉ *Buenos Aires 209* ☎ *58/215–892*), near Playa Chinchorro, livens things up weekends with the sounds of pop and cumbia. The beachfront **Puesta del Sol** (✉ *Raul Pey 2492* ☎ *58/216–150*) plays '80s tunes and appeals to a slightly older crowd. Weekends you can enjoy live music on the pleasant terrace.

BEACHES

Part of the reason people flock to Arica is the beaches. The surf can be quite rough in some spots, so look for—and heed—signs that say NO APTA PARA BAÑARSE ("no swimming"). South of El Morro, **Playa El Laucho** is the closest to the city, and thus the most crowded. It's also a bit rocky at the bottom. South of Playa El Laucho you'll find **Playa Brava,** with a pontoon that keeps the kids occupied. At the somewhat secluded white-sand **Playa Chinchorro,** 2 km (1 mi) north of the city, you can rent Jet Skis in high season.

SHOPPING

Calle 21 de Mayo is a good place for window-shopping. **Calle Bolognesi,** just off Calle 21 de Mayo, is crowded with artisan stalls selling handmade goods. The length of **Calle Chacabuco,** four blocks north of Calle 21 de Mayo, is closed to traffic on Sunday for a market featuring everything from soccer jerseys to bootleg CDs.

The **Feria Internacional** on Calle Máximo Lira sells everything from bowler hats (worn by Aymara women) to blankets to batteries. The Terminal Pesquero next door offers an interesting view of fishing, El Norte Grande's predominant industry. Located outside the city in the Azapa Valley, the **Poblado Artesenal** (✉ *Hualles* ☎ *58/222–683*) is an artisan cooperative designed to resemble an altiplano community. This is a good place to pick up traditionally styled ceramics and leather.

PARQUE NACIONAL LAUCA

★ *47 km (29 mi) southeast of Putre.*

On a plateau more than 4,000 meters (13,120 feet) above sea level, the magnificent Parque Nacional Lauca shelters flora and fauna found in few other places in the world. Cacti, grasses, and a brilliant emerald-green moss called *llareta* dot the landscape. Playful vizcacha—rabbitlike rodents with long tails—laze in the sun, and llamas, graceful vicuñas, and alpacas make their home here as well. About 10 km (6 mi) into the park is a CONAF station with informative brochures. ⊠ *Off Ruta 11* ☎ *58/250–570 in Arica* ⊕ *www.conaf.cl* ☐ *Free.*

Within the park, off Ruta 11, is the altiplano village of **Parinacota**, one of the most beautiful in all of Chile. In the center of the village sits the whitewashed **Iglesia Parinacota,** dating from 1789. Inside are murals depicting sinners and saints and a mysterious "walking table," which parishioners have chained to the wall for fear that it will steal away in the night. An interesting Aymara cultural commentary can be found in the Stations of the Cross, which depict Christ's tormenters not as Roman soldiers, but as Spanish conquistadors. Opposite the church you'll find crafts stalls run by Aymara women in the colorful shawls and bowler hats worn by many altiplano women. Only 18 people live in the village, but many more make a pilgrimage here for annual festivals such as the Fiesta de las Cruces, held on May 3, and the Fiesta de la Virgen de la Canderlaria, a three-day romp that begins on February 2.

About 8 km (5 mi) east of Parinacota are the beautiful **Lagunas Cotacotani,** which means "land of many lakes" in the Quechua language. This string of ponds—surrounded by a desolate moonscape formed by volcanic eruptions—attracts many species of bird, including Andean geese.

Lago Chungará sits on the Bolivian border at an amazing altitude of 4,600 meters (15,100 feet) above sea level. Volcán Parinacota, at 6,330 meters (20,889 feet), casts its shadow onto the lake's glassy surface. Hundreds of flamingos make their home here. There is a CONAF-run office at Lago Chungará on the highway just before the lake. ⊠ *From Ruta 11, turn north on Ruta A-123* ☎ *No phone* ⊕ *www.conaf.cl* ☐ *Free* ☉ *CONAF office daily 8–8.*

RESERVA NACIONAL LAS VICUÑAS

★ *121 km (75 mi) southeast of Putre.*

Although it attracts far fewer visitors than neighboring Parque Nacional Lauca, Reserva Nacional Las Vicuñas contains some incredible sights—salt flats, high plains, and alpine lakes. And you can enjoy the vistas without running into buses full of tourists. The reserve, which stretches some 100 km (62 mi), has a huge herd of graceful vicuñas. Although quite similar to their larger cousins, llamas and alpacas, vicuñas have not been domesticated. Their incredibly soft wool, among the most prized in the world, led to so much hunting that these creatures were threatened with extinction. Today it is illegal to kill a vicuña. Getting to this reserve, unfortunately, is quite a challenge. There is no public transportation, and the roads are passable only in four-wheel-drive vehicles. Many people choose to take a tour out of Arica. ✉*From Ruta 11, take Ruta A-21 south to park headquarters* ☎*58/250–570 in Arica* ⊕*www.conaf.cl.*

SALAR DE SURIRE

126 km (78 mi) southeast of Putre.

After passing through the high plains, where you'll spot vicuña, alpaca, and the occasional desert fox, you'll catch your first glimpse of the sparkling Salar de Surire. Seen from a distance, the salt flat appears to be a giant white lake. Unlike its southern neighbor, the Salar de Atacama, it's completely flat. Three of the four New World flamingos (Andean, Chilean, and James') live in the nearby lakes. ✉*South from Reserva Nacional Las Vicuñas on Ruta A-235* ☎*58/250–570* ⊕*www. conaf.cl* 🎫*Free.*

5

The Central Valley

Chilean cowboys at rodeo, San Fernando, Central Valley

WORD OF MOUTH

"I did enjoy my tour of [the wineries]. We had a private guide that, apparently, the folks at winery knew, so he took us to areas inside that the bigger tours didn't see. That was fun! I would go with a guide for that reason alone."

—guimbymoy

WELCOME TO THE CENTRAL VALLEY

TOP REASONS TO GO

★ **Wine Tasting:** The Central Valley is the heart of Chile's wine country. Vineyards for both table and wine grapes abound and are pretty hard to miss—in fact, the Pan-American Highway runs through some of the longest continuous vineyards in the world.

★ **Rowdy Rodeos:** The Central Valley is also home to the *huaso,* a cousin of the Argentine *gaucho. Huasos,* in their typical flat-topped, wide-brimmed hats, are a common sight around Rancagua, where they flock to the national *Medialuna* (rodeo arena) for their favorite sport.

★ **Scenic Train Rides:** Chile's train service has dwindled over the years—like everywhere else, it seems—but a special treat for train lovers remains in the Central Valley. The Wine Train is a restored steam engine that dates to 1907 accompanied by wood-paneled passenger cars from the 1920s. It runs between San Fernando and Santa Cruz.

1 Maipo Valley. Take a breather from the fast pace of the capital and ease into the calm and charm of rural life. Only a short drive south of Santiago, the Andes highlands and many vineyards make a great day trip—or use Maipo as the starting point for a longer multi-valley sidetrip.

2 Rapel Valley. Chile's agricultural heartland is the rodeo country home of the *huaso,* with his wide-brimmed hat and jaunty smile. There's some mighty fine wine, too. The valley is divided into two wine appellations, Cachapoal to the north around Rancagua and Colchagua to the south around Santa Cruz.

3 Curicó Valley. Dormant volcanoes make a gorgeous backdrop for the valley's extensive vineyards, and Curicó's charming plaza fills with excitement and grape stomping each April for one of the country's most traditional wine fests. If wine's not your thing, try the upscale Vichuquén Lake resort near the coast or camping at Siete Tazas National Park.

4 Maule Valley. Scratch any surface and you'll find plenty of rural tradition and natural beauty. The O'Higginiano Museum and the Villa Huilquilemu in Talca beautifully portray the area's cultural heritage, and Chile's only local train still makes daily runs to the coast. Vineyards old and new pepper the stunning countryside.

PACIFIC OCEAN

Constitución

Chanco

Cobquecura

Quirihue

Coelemu

Tomé

Talcahuano

Concepción

Isla Santa María

San Pedro

Lota

Arauco

La Laja

Curanilahué

Lebú

Nacimiento

Parque Nacional Nahuelbuta

Angol

Cañete

Contulmo

Collipulli

Puren

Valparaíso
VALPARAÍSO
5
San Antonio
SANTIAGO
Talagante
REGIÓN
Melipilla
Paine
METROPOLITANA
Graneros
Sewell
Rancagua
1
Coya
LIBERTADOR GENERAL
BERNARDO O'HIGGINS
Peumo
2
Termas de
Pichilemu
San
Cauquenes
Bucamlemu
Fernando
Reserva
Nacional
Llico
Santa
Río los
Cruz
Cipreses
Vichuquén
Chimbarongo
Iloca
Hualañé
Curicó
Molina
Peteroa
MAULE
Reserva
Nacional
Gualleco
4
Radal
5
Siete Tazas
Descabezado
Río Maule
Grande
Talca
San Clemente
San Javier
Reserva
Nacional
Villa Allegre
Colbún
Altos del Lircay
Cauquenes
Linares
Longaví
Parral
Nevado
Longaví
A
San Carlos
N
Chillán
Pinto
D
Bulnes
Termas de
ARGENTINA
Recinto
Chillán
E
Pemuco
Cabrero
Chillán
S
Yungay
Parque Nacional
Laguna del Laja
Antuco
5
Los
Quilleco
0   50 miles
Ángeles
BIO-BIO
0   75 km
Munchen
Copahue
Copahue
Termas de
Pemehue

GETTING ORIENTED

Geographically speaking, the Central Valley isn't really a valley at all, but rather an "Intermediate Depression" between two mountain ranges, the younger, higher Andes to the east and the much older and lower Coastal Range to the west. The two intermingle in northern Chile and separate just north of Santiago, leaving a fertile flatland between them that runs south to the Bío Bío, where the Coastal Mountains gradually descend into the Pacific Ocean. Chile's wine appellation (called the *Denominación de Orígen,* or DO) system follows municipal subdivisions, and therefore the large Central Valley DO is divided into the four sub-regions of the Maipo Valley (Santiago sits in its center), the Rapel Valley (usually divided into Cachapoal and Colchagua), the Curicó Valley (around the city of Curicó), and the Maule Valley (which runs south from Talca).

6

THE CENTRAL VALLEY PLANNER

When to Go

Timing your visit to the Central Valley really depends on what you want to do there. January and February are peak summer vacation months in Chile, so the parks are open and the beaches are full. The weather will be clear and sunny—cool in the mountains and on the coast, and quite hot in between, making this the best time for many outdoor activities. If winter sports are your thing, your safest bet is to come from June to August, although the snow may last into September.

If it's the wineries that draw you to the Central Valley, however, consider that grapes are picked from late February through early May, depending on the varietal and area. This is certainly the best time to visit a vineyard, since you can see everything from crushing to bottling, and if you visit on a weekend, you'll also stand a good chance finding one of the many harvest festivals that take place throughout the region at this time of year. But don't overlook a visit at any other time of year; the wineries offer tastings and fun activities year-round.

Eat Well & Rest Easy

No matter where or when you eat in the Central Valley, a good bottle of local wine is likely to be on the table, so knowing a handful of wine-related words will doubtless come in handy. *Vino* is the Spanish word for wine; red is *tinto* (never *rojo*) and white is *blanco*. You'll want to drink them by the *copa*, or wine glass, and *desgustación* and *cata* both refer to a formal wine tasting.

Central Valley cuisine tends to be hearty fare based on locally raised beef and pork, served with local vegetables and followed by fruit-based desserts. These will always be accompanied by regional—usually red—wine. Most Chileans eat a big lunch around 1 PM and have a light dinner late in the evening. If you want to try real, home-style Chilean cooking, your best bet is to follow suit and look for lunch at the same time, even though you may need to adopt the local siesta habit as well. In the summer look for popular favorites such as *porotos granados* (fresh cranberry beans with corn, squash, and basil), *humitas* (Chilean tamales) with fresh-sliced tomatoes, or *pastel de choclo* (a savory ground-beef base served in a clay bowl, sometimes with a piece of chicken, and always generously slathered with a rich grated corn topping). Desserts are often simply fresh fruits served in their own juice. Do watch for the refreshing *mote con huesillo* served cold as a drink or dessert. Begin by eating the *mote*, a type of wheat hominy; then slurp up the juice from the *huesillo*, a large dried peach, and leave the peach for the final act of this three-course treat.

WHAT IT COSTS IN CHILEAN PESOS (IN THOUSANDS)

¢	$	$$	$$$	$$$$
RESTAURANTS				
under 3 pesos	3 pesos–5 pesos	5 pesos–8 pesos	8 pesos–11 pesos	over 11 pesos
HOTELS				
under 15 pesos	15 pesos–45 pesos	45 pesos–75 pesos	75 pesos–105 pesos	over 105 pesos

Restaurant prices are based on the median main course at dinner. Hotel prices are for a double room in high season, excluding tax.

Folklore & Festivals

The harvest season, or *crush* as it is often called, is the most important time of the year in wine country. Most of Chile's wine-producing regions mark the moment with a Fiesta de la Vendimia, or harvest festival. They take place throughout the region in March and April, but the biggest and most spectacular are held in Colchagua and Curicó, where they include grape-stomping competitions and harvest queen contests. Maule, the other notable festival, kicks off the year with its Carmenère Festival in January, in honor of the very Chilean red wine grape.

Not every fiesta is wine related, of course. Catholic roots run deep here, and many ancient religious festivals remain, such as those in honor of San Pedro and San Pablo, the patron saints of fishermen, on June 29 in fishing villages all along the coast. San Sebastian, the much persecuted, arrow-pierced saint, draws thousands of devotees to Yumbel (108 km [68 mi] from Concepción) on January 20. And during the fiesta de San Francisco, held October 4 in the small colonial-era village of Huerta de Maule, 38 km (24 mi) southwest of Talca, more than 200 huasos gather from all over Chile for a day of horseback events, including races around the central square.

Sample Itinerary

If you can afford it, spend at least one night at Hacienda Los Lingues. The restored ranch near **Rancagua** gives you a sense of what life was like for the aristocrats who lived here centuries ago. Or head directly to **Santa Cruz,** where you can relax in modern comfort at the Santa Cruz Plaza Hotel and explore another perfectly preserved hacienda outside town at the Museo San José del Carmen de El Huique. Santa Cruz is the king of Chilean wine tourism, so be sure to visit at least one. Surfing enthusiasts should continue west to **Pichilemu** for world-class surfing. Head back to the Pan-American Highway and continue south through **Curicó,** stopping at the Viña Miguel Torres Restaurant, right off the highway, for lunch, then on to the lovely city of **Talca.** This is a good home base for visiting a number of Maule Valley wineries, the rodeo at San Clemente, or exploring into the nearby mountains. Drive east to **Termas de Chillán,** which has hot springs, skiing in winter, hiking in summer, and amazing mountain scenery year-round. Head to Concepción, the region's largest city, to grab your flight to Santiago.

Getting Here & Around

Bus Travel. The two big bus companies in the region, Pullman Bus and Tur-Bus, offer regular departures that leave precisely on time from Santiago's Alameda Terminal bound for Rancagua, Talca, Curicó, Chillán, and Concepción. One-way fare from Santiago to Chillán runs about 10,000 pesos.

Car Travel. Traveling by car is often the most convenient way to see the region. The Central Valley is sliced in half by Chile's major highway, the Pan-American Highway, also called Ruta 5, which passes through all of the major towns in the region. Be sure to have cash on hand for the frequent tolls, which are rather high and increase on weekends and holidays. Keep your receipt; some smaller exits have toll booths, and you can avoid the fare by showing your paid ticket.

Train Travel. The train remains an excellent way to travel through the Central Valley. Express trains from Estación Central in Santiago to the cities of Rancagua, Curicó, Talca, Chillán, and Concepción are comfortable and faster than taking the bus or driving. Oenophiles should consider the wine train from San Fernando to Santa Cruz.

Updated by
Margaret
Snook

THE CENTRAL VALLEY IS CHILE'S heartland. The combination of rich soils, long, warm, and dry summers offset by cold and rainy winters, and abundant supplies of Andean meltwater for irrigation, makes this ideal farm land. It is also the perfect place to grow wine grapes, and as such, wine has been a very big deal in much of the Central Valley for four centuries.

The Central Valley is a straight shot down the Pan-American Highway between the volcanic cones of the Andes on the west and the lower Coastal Mountains to the east. As you head south, the relatively dry foliage of the short, scrubby indigenous bushes gives way to more verdant pastures and eventually to thick pine and eucalyptus forests.

It's about a five-hour drive straight south from Santiago to Chillán and nearly another hour east to Concepción, but do plan to stop and explore along the way. The valley holds something for everyone. Head west into the mountains to visit mining towns, relax at a hot-springs spa, climb rock walls, ski, or hike through a nature reserve. Veer off to the coast for lovely beaches and swimming (if you can stand the cold Pacific waters), excellent surfing, and outstanding seafood. And of course, no matter which way you turn, you can't help but see thousands of acres of vineyards and the wineries that produce some of Chile's finest wines. Most of the valleys have Wine Route (Ruta del Vino) associations that are happy to help visitors plan tours of the wineries.

VALLE RAPEL: COLCHAGUA & CHACHAPOAL

RANCAGUA

87 km (54 mi) south of Santiago along the Pan-American Hwy.

In 1814, the hills around Rancagua were the site of a battle in the War of Independence known as the *Desastre de Rancagua* (Disaster of Rancagua). Chilean independence fighters, including Bernardo O'Higgins, held off the powerful Spanish army for two days before being captured. In the resulting blaze, much of the town was destroyed.

Despite its historical significance and current importance as a regional commercial center, it has relatively little to offer in terms of tourism. If you find yourself in town, do, by all means, visit the historic area around the central Plaza or take in a rodeo in the national *Medialuna* or rodeo arena, but otherwise, skip the city and head straight for one of the more interesting attractions outside of town, such as a copper mine, a hot springs, a nature reserve, or a winery.

GETTING HERE & AROUND

Rancagua is just a short one-hour hop due south from Santiago by car or bus. It's a bit faster by train, and much too close to justify flying. Wheeled transport will take the Pan-American Highway, while rail options follow along beside it. Traffic heading out of Santiago is often sluggish, and delays due to roadwork are frequent, but the highway is

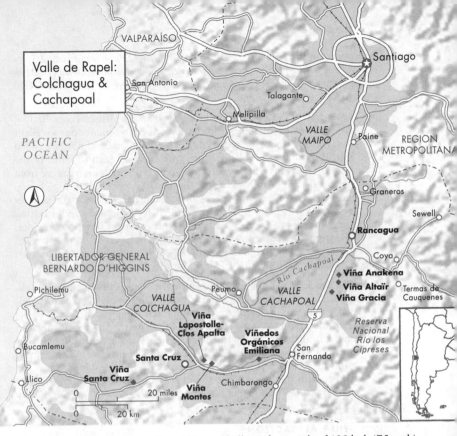

Valle de Rapel:
Colchagua &
Cachapoal

VALPARAÍSO

Santiago

San Antonio

Talagante

Melipilla

VALLE
MAIPO

Paine

PACIFIC
OCEAN

REGION
METROPOLITANA

Graneros

Sewell

Rancagua

Coya

LIBERTADOR GENERAL
BERNARDO O'HIGGINS

Pichilemu

Peumo

Río Cachapoal

VALLE
CACHAPOAL

Viña Anakena

Viña Altaïr
Viña Gracia

Termas de
Cauquenes

VALLE
COLCHAGUA

Viña
Lapostolle-
Clos Apalta

Viñedos
Orgánicos
Emiliana

5

Reserva
Nacional
Río los
Cipreses

Bucamlemu

Santa Cruz

San
Fernando

Viña
Santa Cruz

Illico

20 miles

0   20 km

Viña
Montes

Chimbarongo

generally in good condition and allows for speeds of 120 kph (75 mph)
for most of the route.

ESSENTIALS

Bus Contacts Rancagua Terminal de Buses (✉ *Dr. Salinas 1165* ☎ *72/225–425*).
Rancagua Terminal al Sur (✉ *Ocarrol 1039* ☎ *72/230–340*). **Tur Bus** (✉ *Ocarrol
1175* ☎ *72/241–117*).

Currency Exchange Forex Cambios y Servicios Ltda (✉ *Astorga 367, Rancagua*).
Ifex Cambios (✉ *Campos 363, Of. 4*).

Post Office Correos Chile Rancagua (✉ *Campos at Cuevas* ☎ *72/230–413*).

Visitor & Tour Info Sernatur Rancagua (✉ *German Riesco 277, Offices 11–12*
☎ *72/230–413* ⊕ *www.sernatur.cl*).

EXPLORING

WINERIES

Viña Anakena. Based in the Andean sector of the Cachapoal Valley known
as "Alto Cachapoal," this winery has properties in a number of Chilean
wine regions to ensure the finest results for each variety. Their labels
include symbols inspired by the motifs found in Chile's various indigenous cultures. Visits include a tour of the vineyards and cellars, the
varietal garden, the view from the scenic overlook, along with tastings of

reserva or premium lines. ✉*Camino Pimpenela s/n, Requinoa* ☎*2/552–535* ✑*saladeventas@anakenawines.cl* ⊕*www.anakenawines.cl* ✉*Basic tour: 4,000 pesos. Premium tour: 9,000 pesos* ⊙*Daily 10:30–4:30* ✑*Reservations essential.*

Viña Altaïr. Inspired by the brightest star in the Aquila constellation, this French-Chilean joint venture was formed to produce one excellent wine: Altaïr. Today the winery offers a second celestial bottling called Sideral. Both are red blends from grapes grown high foothills of the Andes. The winery offers three different types of tours ranging from a basic visit to horseback riding through the vineyards and high into the hills. There's even a spectacular nocturnal version that includes a moonlight ride on horseback through the vineyards and a tasting under the stars. All tours include tastings of one or both house wines. The stunning view comes free of charge. ✉*Fundo Totihue, Camino Pimpinela s/n, Requinoa* ☎*2/477–5598* ⊕*www.altairwines.com* ✉*14,000–72,000 pesos* ⊙*Mon.–Sat.* ✑*Reservations essential.*

Viña Gracia. The Córpora Company has a number of wineries throughout Chile and actually has two in Cachapoal. Viña Gracia, near Requinoa, offers a number of tour options that range from a brief cellar visit and tasting of two wines for 4,000 pesos per person up to a deluxe four-hour visit with lunch in the Gracia open kitchen that overlooks the vineyards (22,000 pesos). The menus, which change with the season and availability of produce, are designed especially to pair with the house's finest wines. ✉*Camino Totihue s/n, Requinoa* ☎*2/240–7678* ⊕*www.gracia.cl* ✉*4000–22,000 pesos* ⊙*Daily* ✑*Reservations essential.*

OTHER ATTRACTIONS

Today's Rancagüinos enjoy relaxing in the city's central square, the **Plaza de los Héroes.** A statue of the valiant war hero and future first president Bernardo O'Higgins on horseback stands proudly in the center of the plaza, and although each side of the statue's base quotes one of his famous sayings, curiously enough, there is nothing that indicates to outsiders and newcomers who the statue represents.

A block north of the plaza along Calle Estado is the **Iglesia de la Merced,** an 18th-century church that was declared a national monument not only for its beauty, but because of its place in the city's fateful history. It was in this bell tower that O'Higgins waited in vain for reinforcements during the battle for independence. The twin spires, in a somber neoclassical style, are a fitting memorial.

The three-room **Museo Regional de Rancagua** re-creates a typical 18th-century home, complete with period furniture and religious artifacts. A small collection of 19th-century weaponry is the type that would have been used in the momentous Battle of Rancagua. Dioramas re-create this dramatic moment in the country's quest for independence. The whitewashed colonial building is a few blocks south of Plaza de los Héroes. ✉*Estado 685, at Ibieta* ☎*72/230–976* ⊕*www.museorancagua.cl* ✉*600 pesos, includes Casa de Pilar de Esquina* ⊙*Tues.–Fri. 10–6, weekends 9–1.*

Casa del Pilar de la Esquina, across the street from the Museo Regional de Rancagua, once belonged to Fernando Errázuriz Aldunate, who helped draft the country's constitution. In addition to displays on the area's history, including the daily lives of its indigenous cultures, there are often modern-art exhibits on the first floor. ⊠ *Estado 682, at Ibieta* ☎ *72/221–524* 🖃 *500 pesos* 🕙 *Tues.–Sun. 10–5.*

Numerous trails lead through thick forests of cypress trees at **Reserva Nacional Río los Cipreses,** a 92,000-acre national reserve 50 km (31 mi) east of Rancagua. Occasionally you'll reach a clearing where you'll be treated to spectacular views of the mountains above. CONAF, the national parks service, has an office here with informative displays and maps. Hiking, swimming, and horseback riding are all available. Just south of the park is the spot where a plane carrying Uruguayan university students crashed in 1972. The story of the group, part of which survived three months in a harsh winter by resorting to cannibalism, was told in the book and film *Alive.* ⊠ *Carretera del Cobre s/n* ☎ *72/297–505* 🌐 *www.conaf.cl* 🖃 *2,000 pesos* 🕙 *Daily 8:30–6.*

On the southern banks of the Río Cachapoal about 20 km (12½ mi) east of Rancagua, the **Termas de Cauquenes** spout mineral-rich water that has been revered for its medicinal properties since colonial days. The Spanish discovered the 48°C (118°F) springs in the late 1500s, and basic visitor facilities have existed since the 1700s. José de San Martín, who masterminded the defeat of Spanish forces in Chile, is said to have relaxed here before beginning his campaign. Naturalist Charles Darwin, who visited in 1834, wrote that the springs were situated in "a quiet, solitary spot, with a good deal of wild beauty." The beautiful gothic-style bathhouse with its high, vaulted ceilings, stained-glass windows, and classic colonial-style ceramic floor patterns was built in 1867 and remains in excellent condition. It holds about two dozen rooms with the original marble tubs that are filled with spring water for 20-minute baths, or you can choose a modern whirlpool version for one or two people. Massages and medical pedicures (no nail polish) are also available. Overnight guests at the spa also have exclusive access to a naturally heated swimming pool. Whether you stay at the spa or are just passing through for the day, don't leave without having at least one meal at the extraordinary restaurant. To reach the springs, take Ruta 32 from Rancagua to Coya and then head south for 5 km (3 mi). ⊠ *Termas de Cauquenes s/n, Machalí* ☎ *72/899–010* 🌐 *www. termasdecauquenes.cl* 🕙 *Daily 8–6:30* 🖃 *Individual bath: 5,000 pesos. Individual whirlpool: 6,500 pesos. Double whirlpool: 12,000 pesos.*

Mina El Teniente and Sewell. High in the mountains north of Termas de Cauquenes, 60 km (37 mi) northeast of Rancagua, the El Teniente Mine is the world's largest subterranean copper mine, in operation since colonial times. In 1905 the city of Sewell, known as the "city of stairs," was constructed at 2,130 meters (6,988 feet) above sea level to house miners, and was later abandoned in the early 1970s. Sewell was declared a UNESCO World Heritage site in 2006. Guided tours of both the mine and the city can be arranged by the Rancagua tour operator **VTS** (☎ *72/210–290* 🌐 *www.vts.cl*).

WHERE TO STAY & EAT

$$$ ✕ **Juan y Medio.** On the north-bound side of the Pan-American Highway, between the towns of Requinoa and Rosario, this well-loved Chilean diner is a must for hearty appetites. It began as a humble truck stop in 1946 and established a tremendous reputation for its trucker-sized portions of Chilean favorites, such as whopping steaks and ribs grilled over a wood fire, or slow-cooked *cazuelas* and stews that will leave you wanting nothing more than a hammock and a long nap. The original eatery burned to the ground in 2006, and Chilean travelers mourned the loss until it reopened, much bigger and a bit splashier, a year later. It seats up to 500 people and fills fast on busy weekends. Stop at noon—or at 6—to beat the local crowd, which tends to eat much later. One of the dining rooms overlooks a simple play area for children that also has a very large bird cage with many attractive species. ✉ *Ruta 5, Km 108, Rosario* ☎ *72/521–726* ▭ *AE, DC, MC, V.*

$$$$ Fodor's Choice ★ ✕ **Hacienda Los Lingues.** One of Chile's best-preserved colonial haciendas, this estate southeast of Rancagua has remained in the same family for four centuries. Staying here is a bit like traveling back in time: 17th- and 18th-century adobe buildings hold spacious rooms furnished with brass beds and heated by woodstoves. The hacienda is part of a 20,000-acre working ranch with extraordinary horses and miles of trails through the foothills. Manicured gardens, timeless porticos, and plush living rooms provide idyllic spots for relaxation. Deluxe four-course Continental dinners, served in the garden or sumptuous dining room, make use of fine china, crystal, and silverware and are complemented by the definitive Chilean wine list. Use this as home base for visits to local wineries or olive oil mills, the Sewell mining city high in the Andes, or spend a relaxing day at the estate riding horses or bicycles. **Pros:** Plenty to do. **Cons:** Somewhat isolated. ✉ *Ruta 5 S, Km 124 s/n, San Fernando* ☎ *2/431–0510* 🖷 *2/431–0501* 🌐 *www.loslingues.com* *16 rooms, 2 suites* *In-room: no a/c, safe, no TV. In-hotel: restaurant, room service, bar, tennis court, pool, bicycles, laundry service, no elevator* ▭ *AE, DC, MC, V.*

$$–$$$ ✕ **Hotel Termas de Cauquenes.** The main attractions of this hotel are the mineral baths, the thermal swimming pool, and one of the region's best restaurants, with spectacular meals served up by Swiss father-daughter team René and Sabine Acklin. Despite its great location overlooking the Río Cachapoal, the hotel doesn't have much of a view. Only the restaurant and a few rooms in the *pabellón del río* (river building) afford glimpses of the boulder-strewn river. Dating from the 1960s, the pabellón's rooms are smallish and somewhat spartan. Rooms in the older *patio central* building are spacious but lack views. Everything is a bit timeworn, and the decor is uninspired. **Pros:** Spa facilities, location. **Cons:** A bit plain. ✉ *Termas de Cauquenes s/n, Machalí* ☎ *72/899–010* 🖷 *72/899–009* 🌐 *www.termasdecauquenes.cl* *38 rooms, 12 suites* *In-room: refrigerator, no a/c. In-hotel: restaurant, room service, pool, laundry service, no elevator* ▭ *AE, DC, MC, V* *BP, FAP, MAP.*

HORSEBACK RIDING

A working horse ranch, **Hacienda Los Lingues** (☎ *02/431–0510*) offers mountain rides on world-class steeds. The rides, which cost $25 per hour, take you past flora like the *lingue* (a tree from which the ranch's name was derived) and the *quillay*, a plant whose dried leaves are used for making medicinal teas. Farther from the ranch you might spot owls high in the trees.

RODEO

One of the great highlights of life in Rancagua includes excursions to the **National Rodeo Arena**: the *Medialuna Monumental,* especially in late March, when it is host to the national championship. This is a great opportunity to glimpse *huaso* tradition in its full glory: horsemanship, riding and cow-herding skills, traditional foods, crafts, music, and dance. ⊠*Av. Germán Ibarra s/n, at Av. España, Rancagua* ☎*72/221–286* ✉*medialuna_rancagua@ entelchile.net* ⊕*www.rodeochileno.cl.*

HUASOS
The Chilean rodeo, which is quite unlike the American version, consists of a competition between pairs of riders who must demonstrate their skills in horsemanship and teamwork in pinning a young bull against a padded section of the corral. The National Championship takes pace in Rancagua the first weekend of April, while preliminaries and other competitions take place throughout the region from August through May.

SANTA CRUZ

180 km (112 mi) southwest of Santiago; 104 km (65 mi) southwest of Rancagua via the Pan-American Hwy. to San Fernando, then southwest on I-50.

This once sleepy village has become the height of rural chic in recent years, due, in large part, to the booming Colchagua Valley wine industry, which produces many of Chile's award-winning red wines. It has an attractive central plaza surrounded by a mix of modern and traditional architecture, including an imposing 19th-century church, the town hall, the Colchagua Museum, the Wine Route office, and the grand Hotel Santa Cruz Plaza.

This is farm country par excellence, and *huasos* in their wide-brimmed flat-topped *chupalla* hats are as common behind the wheel of a pickup truck as they are on horseback. They take pride in their traditional dress, and often seek out formal occasions to don their short-cropped black or white jacket, pin-striped black pants, colorful woven sash-belt, and short black boots, to which they strap jangling silver spurs and knee-high black spats. You'll probably see the *cueca*, Chile's national dance, performed at some point during your visit to Colchagua.

Santa Cruz is the perfect home base for visiting the Colchagua wineries that extend out to the east and west, mostly along Route I-50. Be sure to visit the Colchagua Museum on the Plaza—it's one of the country's finest.

GETTING HERE & AROUND

Getting to Santa Cruz is easiest by car; just hop back on the Pan-American Highway (Route 5), and head south 55 km (34 mi) to San Fernando. Pass the first exit north of the city and continue another 2 km

HISTORY OF CHILEAN WINE

Fans of Chilean wines owe a debt to missionaries who arrived here in the 16th century. Spanish priests, who needed wine to celebrate the Catholic Mass, planted the country's first vineyards from Copiapó in the north to Concepción in the south. Of course not all wine was intended for such religious purposes, and vines were quickly sent north and planted in the Maipo Valley around Santiago to fill the "spiritual" void experienced by the early Spanish settlers—many of whom were soldiers and sailors.

Fast-forward a few centuries to the rise of cross-Atlantic travel and trade that began in the 19th century. Wealthy Chileans, many with new fortunes made in the mining industry, returned from European visits with newfound appreciation for French food, dress, architecture, and lifestyles. Many began building their own Chilean-style chateaux, particularly on the outskirts of Santiago. French varietals such as cabernet sauvignon, malbec, and carmenère thrived in the Central Valley's rich soils and the near-perfect climate, and thus Chile's second "wine boom" was launched.

Chilean wineries did not keep pace with the rest of the world, however, and rather stagnated throughout much of the 20th century. But with the introduction of modern equipment such as stainless steel tanks in the late 1980s, the country soon caught global attention. Fresh national and international investment in the industry made Chilean wine a tasty and affordable option. Continued advances in growing techniques and wine-making methods throughout the 1990s and into the early 21st century have resulted in the production of exceedingly excellent wines of premium and ultra-premium quality with increasingly hefty price tags. Wine exports increase annually, and in 2007 Chile sold more than $1.25 billion in wine to more than 90 countries.

—Margaret Snook

(1 mi) to the next exit marked "Santa Cruz, Carretera del Vino, Pichilemu." This is I-50, the "Wine Highway," which takes you west through wine country and on to the coast to Pichilemu, surf capital of Chile. It is very easy to visit most of the valley's wineries by car; in fact, you will see a number of them along the way on this aptly named route.

If using public transportation, take a bus or train to San Fernando and then take the local bus or *colectivo* (a shared taxi with a fixed route) to Santa Cruz. On most Saturdays you can also take the Wine Train from San Fernando to the Santa Cruz station.

ESSENTIALS
Bus Contacts San Fernando Terminal (✉ *Manso de Velasco s/n* ☎ *72/713–912*). **Santa Cruz Terminal** (✉ *Casanova 478* ☎ *72/822–191*).

Currency Exchange BCI (✉ *Plaza de Armas 286-A, Santa Cruz* ☎ *72/825–059*).

Medical Asístanse Hospital de Santa Cruz (✉ *Av. Errázuriz 920* ☎ *72/822–032*).

EXPLORING

WINERIES

The Colchagua Valley wineries had the good sense to band together back in the 1990s, when Chile's latest wine boom was just getting started. The move to form the **Ruta del Vino de Colchagua** has paid off handsomely, not only for marketing purposes, but for organizing world-class wine tourism options. It's no joke; Colchagua was named "World's Best Wine Region" by *Wine Enthusiast* in 2005—which locals are very happy to mention. The Wine Route's office, next to the Santa Cruz Plaza Hotel on the main square, provides basic information about its 18 member wineries and arranges guided tours in English to most of them. Though most wineries do have their own guides, few of them speak English, and some accept only visits arranged by Ruta del Vino. The office arranges tours to two or three vineyards, with or without lunch, starting at about 20,000 pesos per person and up depending on the complexity of the tour. The harvest season—March and April—kicks off with the *Fiesta de la Vendimia* (grape harvest festival) and is always a great time to visit. ⊠*Plaza de Armas 298* ☎*72/823-199* ⊕*www.colchaguavalley.cl* ☉ *Weekdays 9–7:30, weekends 10–6:30.*

Viñedos Orgánicos Emiliana (VOE). This biodynamic farm is one of Chile's most interesting wine projects. It's just nature and the human hand at work here—no agrochemicals at all—and the results are stunning. Roaming animals manage to keep the bugs and weeds under control, while close attention to cosmic cycles indicates when to plant and when to reap. It's a beautiful winery with a fascinating story and great wines to back it up. ⊠*Camino Lo Moscoso s/n, Placilla, Nancagua* ☎*9/327-4019* ✍*wineshop@emiliana.cl* ⊕*www.voe.cl* ✍*Reservations essential.*

Fodor'sChoice
★
Viña Montes. Founded in 1987 in the Curicó Valley as Discover Wine, this highly successful premium wine producer has since moved its center of operations to the renowned Apalta sector of Colchagua and has changed its name to Montes, after its star winemaker and owner. Known for its deep, rich, concentrated, oaky red wines and crisp whites (most also oaked), every bottle has a stylized angel on the label. The new gravity-flow winery—launched in 2004—was designed according to Feng Shui principles. Tour options vary from simple to quite elaborate, and may include a ride up the steep hills for lunch overlooking the valley, hiking the botanical trails, or horseback riding through the vineyards. ⊠*Parcela 15, Millahue de Apalta, Santa Cruz* ☎*72/825-417* ✍*lafinca@ monteswines.com* ⊕*www.monteswines.com* ✍*Reservations essential.*

Viña Lapostolle-Clos Apalta. Owned by the Marnier family of France—yes, the GRAND Marnier family—Chile's Viña Lapostolle has its main facility right on the main road; you'll pass it along the way. It's attractive enough, but hold out for the new winery in Apalta. The barrel-stave-shaped beams rising impressively above the vineyards are a tip-off that this has got to be one of the most impressive wineries in the world. Built into a hillside to facilitate the gravity flow process, the grapes are taken to the top floor, where they are separated by hand, then dropped into tanks on the floor below, then racked to barrels on the floor below, and so forth, six floors down into the hillside, where

6

PHYLLOXERA

When it comes to wine, Europe got the short end of the stick in the 19th-century global diffusion of wine. Native vines from the United States arrived in the Old World infested with phylloxera, a deadly insect that devastated European vineyards and nearly destroyed the Old World industry entirely. Eventually most of the world's wine regions were affected by this dreaded louse, but to this day Chile has avoided it altogether and is the only wine-producing country in the world to remain phylloxera-free. No one can say for sure why, but weather, geographic isolation, and a healthy dose of old-fashioned good luck all seem to play an essential part. The same conditions make organic and even biodynamic farming relatively easy, and sustainable agriculture increasingly common. Even those who have not jumped on the ecological bandwagon have little reason to use pesticides and other agrochemicals.

they are finally trucked out and shipped around the world. Join one of the three daily tours with tastings (US$40), or stay for lunch at the fabulous guest house (US$120). If you're in the mood for luxury, for US$650 you can book a night in one of the exclusive cabins up on the hill. ⊠ *Camino San Fernando a Pichilemu, Km 36, Cunaquito s/n, Santa Cruz* ☎ *72/321–803* ⊕ *www.closapalta.com* ✉ *US$40–$120* ⚘ *Reservations essential.*

Viña Santa Cruz. Chilean businessman Carlos Cardoen not only owns the Santa Cruz Plaza Hotel, but the winery of the same name as well. This relatively new project is dedicated to producing premium red wines in the Lolol sector of the Colchagua Valley. If you've seen the hotel, you already know that Cardoen does not do things half way, and a visit to the winery will only confirm that observation. In addition to the things you would normally find at any winery (vineyards, stainless steel tanks, oak barrels), this one also includes a cable car to make sure visitors get a bird's-eye view of the valley. On top of the hill is a replica "indigenous village" that represents three separate Chilean native cultures: Aymará, Mapuche, and Rapa Nui. There are also an astronomical center, a gastronomical center, and a wine and gift shop. ⊠ *Carretera I-72, Km 25, Lolol* ☎ *2/221–9090* ⊕ *www.vinasantacruz.cl* ⚘ *Reservations essential.*

OTHER ATTRACTIONS

One great way to explore the wine region around Santa Cruz is by taking the 1913 steam engine known as the **Tren del Vino.** The train leaves from the nearby town of San Fernando every Saturday morning (transfers are also available from Santiago), and chugs through the scenic Colchagua Valley, home to more than a dozen wineries. As well as making vineyard visits and tasting wine on board, you can also opt to stop for lunch at the Santa Cruz Plaza Hotel, or visit the Colchagua Museum. The trains leave the San Fernando Station at 10:30 AM; the tours are approximately 8 hours long (12 if you're transferring from Santiago). You must pre-book by phone or online. ☎ *2/470–7403*

⊕*www.trendelvinochile.cl* ✉*42,000 pesos; 50,000 pesos with transfer from Santiago.*

In the center of the palm-lined **Plaza de Armas** is a colonial-style bell tower with a carillon that chimes every 15 minutes; inside the tower you'll find the town's tourist office.

Facing the central square is the fortresslike **Iglesia Parroquial,** an imposing white stucco structure built in 1817.

★ The attractive **Museo de Colchagua,** built in colonial style at the end of the 20th century, focuses on the history of the region. It's the largest private natural history collection in the country, and second only in size to Santiago's Museo Nacional de Historia Natural. Exhibits include pre-Columbian mummies; extinct insects set in amber that must be viewed through special lenses; the world's largest collection of silver work by the indigenous Mapuche; and the only known original copy of Chile's proclamation of independence. A few early vehicles and wine-making implements surround the building. The museum is the creation of Santa Cruz native and international businessman Carlos Cardoen. The placards are only in Spanish, but a video provides some information in English about the museum's collection. ✉*Av. Errázuriz 145* ☎*72/821–050* ⊕*www. museocolchagua.cl* ✉*3,000 pesos* ☉*Tues.–Sun. 10–6.*

★ **Museo San José del Carmen de El Huique,** lends an invaluable look into the lifestyle of Chile's 19th-century rich and famous. Construction was begun on the current house in 1829 and finally completed with the inauguration of the chapel in 1852. The Errázuriz family, who can trace the 2,600-acre estate back through family lines to 1756, donated it to the Chilean Army in 1975. It was reopened as a museum in the 1990s and is now the only remaining estate of its kind in Chile that has been preserved intact and open to the public.

Visitors not only see the sumptuous suites full of collections of opal glass, lead crystal, bone china, antique furniture, and family portraits evoking Chile's aristocratic past, but even more interesting, also get to see how the other half lived. The tour includes the servants' quarters, kitchens, and the estate's 16 working patios, each dedicated to a specific household chore, such as laundry, butchering, or cheese making.

The local guides are very knowledgeable and have many tales to tell, as many grew up hearing family stories about working at the estate. The tour ends with a visit to the chapel, which has Venetian blown-glass balustrades around the altar and the choir loft. Sunday-morning mass is held in the chapel at 11:30. Visits are by prior reservation only, and English-speaking guides are available with sufficient notice. ✉*26 km (16 mi) north of Santa Cruz to Palmilla, turn left to the Estación Colchagua, then turn right and follow the signs to museum* ☎*72/933–083* ✉*2,000 pesos* ☉*Tues.–Sun. 10–5.*

★ **Espíritus de Colchagua.** Take a short walk from the main plaza to the door of this classic adobe Colchagua house for a unique tour, but be sure to call first. This is a family operation dedicated to making delicious liqueurs and brandies from 21 different types of fruits, nuts, herbs,

6

and spices. For the basic tour (9,000 pesos), they'll show you how it's done, complete with a tasting. A more elaborate option includes drinks made from the house spirits served with tasty bites made with their home-grown organic produce (15,000 pesos). And of course you can buy a bottle or two of your favorite(s) at discounted prices. ⊠ *Nicolás Palacio 221* ☎*72/822–754* ☉ *Tours: Thurs.–Sun. 11, 3, 7.*

WHERE TO STAY & EAT

$$ ✕ **Los Varietales.** The restaurant at the Hotel Santa Cruz Plaza is by far
★ the best in town. The menu features typical Chilean dishes prepared with flair and made to pair well with the extensive list of Colchagua Valley wines available by glass or bottle. The 11,900-peso executive lunch special includes appetizer, main course, dessert, and wine (of course). In warmer months, the trellised terrace in back is a great spot for lunch. ⊠ *Plaza de Armas 286* ☎*72/821–010* ⊟*AE, DC, MC, V.*

$$ ✕ **Pan Pan Vino Vino & Mistela.** This two-in-one restaurant duo about
★ 6 km (4 mi) outside Santa Cruz in Cunaco has something for everyone at affordable prices. The original restaurant, **Pan Pan Vino Vino,** is set in the old bakery that once supplied the daily bread for the Cunaco Hacienda. The enormous old brick oven is now part of the restaurant's attractive interior. The kitchen focuses on turning local products into sophisticated fare, such as curried lamb stew, eggplant casserole with polenta, and braised quail. The newer **Mistela** next door shares the same management, but offers typical Chilean dishes on the terrace in a more rustic setting. The menus are interchangeable, however, so don't worry if you want fancy and your dining partner wants home cooking—here, all you have to do is decide where to sit. ⊠ *Camino San Fernando a Santa Cruz, Km 31 s/n, Cunaco* ☎*72/858–059* ⊟*AE, DC, MC,* ☉*No dinner Sun.* ⊕*www.panpanvinovino.cl.*

$$$ ⊡ **Hotel Santa Cruz Plaza.** This beautiful, colonial-style hotel on the
★ Plaza de Armas may look historic, but it's less than a decade old. Behind the yellow facade adorned with wooden columns are Spanish-style arches, hand-painted tiles, antique reproductions, and stained glass. Guest rooms are small but charming, with orange stucco walls and French doors that open onto balconies. Those in back are quieter and overlook a creek crossed by wooden footbridges, and a curvaceous pool surrounded by lush foliage. The complex includes the AlmaCruz Shop, which sells exquisite crafts goods, and a wine shop that offers Colchagua Valley wines and Espíritu de Colchagua liqueurs. By mid-2008 they'll offer wine massages in the new spa facility, and a casino is slated to open its doors by year-end. **Pros:** Great restaurant, good location. **Cons:** Rooms can be on the small side. ⊠ *Plaza de Armas 286* ☎*72/209–600, 2/470–7474 in Santiago* 🖷*72/823–445, 2/470–7447 in Santiago* ⊕*www.hotelsantacruzplaza.cl* ⥱*113 rooms, 9 suites* ⌂*In-room: safe, Wi-Fi. In-hotel: 2 restaurants, room service, bars, pool, laundry service* ⊟*AE, DC, MC, V* ⦾*BP.*

HORSEBACK RIDING

Punta del Viento Cabalgatas (⊠ *Fundo El Arrayán* ☎*09/728–4784*) runs horseback tours to the top of a peak that affords a panoramic view of the vineyards that make up much of the Valle de Colchagua.

SHOPPING

The **Asociación de Artesanos** (⊠*Av. Rafael Casanova* ☎*No phone*), near the Viña La Posada, sells high-quality leather goods, embroidered tapestries, and clay figurines. If you're a fan of all things horses, be sure to check out **Machovero** on Almendroza, just a few blocks from the plaza, for a broad selection of saddles and other riding gear fit for your favorite *huaso*.

About 5 km (3 mi) west of the plaza on the road to San Fernando is a colorful adobe house that holds the **Doña Selina** boutique (⊠*Ruta I-50* ☎*072/931–166*), where you can buy local jams, straw hats, ceramics, wood carvings, and other unique handicrafts. If you want a souvenir you can't find elsewhere, head to **La Lajuela**, a hamlet 8 km (5 mi) southeast of Santa Cruz. Residents here weave *chupallas,* straw hats made from a fiber called *teatina* that is cut, dyed, dried, and braided by hand.

VALLE CURICÓ

CURICÓ

6

113 km (71 mi) south of Rancagua along the Pan-American Hwy.

Curicó, which means "black water" in Mapudungún, the native Mapuche language, was founded in 1743. Today this agro-industrial center is the provincial capital and the gateway to the Curicó wine valley. The Plaza de Armas is one of the most attractive in the Central Valley; it is a center of activity year-round, but fills to capacity for the Fiesta de la Vendimia (wine harvest festival) each March. Most of the wineries are south of the city and easily reached from the Pan-American Highway. Other points of interest are found toward the Andes or on the coast.

GETTING HERE & AROUND

Return to the Pan-American Highway and head south for just a short 50 km (31 mi) to Curicó. You can also take an inter-urban bus to Curicó, or head back to San Fernando and hop the train for the very quick trip south. Once you're in Curicó, you can get around by local bus, taxi, or *colectivo*. And if you're visiting wineries, be sure to contact the Ruta del Vino de Curicó; they'll help you make the arrangements for visits and transport, and can also include visits to other sites of interest, such as Radal Siete Tazas or Vichuquén.

ESSENTIALS

Bus Contacts Curicó Terminal (⊠*Arturo Prat 780* ☎*75/328–575*). **Pullman del Sur** (⊠*Camilo Henríquez 253* ☎*75/310–387*).

Currency Exchange Banco de Chile (⊠*Estado 390*).

Medical Asístanse Clínica Curicó (⊠*Chacabuco 121*). **Hospital Curicó** (⊠*Carmen 321, at Villota* ☎*75/206–200, 75/206–206 emergencies*).

Post Office Correos Chile (⊠*Carmen s/n* ☎*75/310–000*).

Visitor & Tour Info Curicó Tourism Office (⊠*Manso de Velasco 744*). **Ruta del Vino** (⊠*Arturo Prat 301-A* ☎🖨*75/328–972* ⊕*www.rutadelvinocurico.cl*).

SURFING IN PICHILEMU

Chile has a burgeoning surfing scene that, surprisingly, is only an hour's drive from the wineries of Colchagua. The little coastal town of Pichilemu dates to the early 19th century, and today is a popular beach town, especially with the younger crowd, most of whom come to catch the waves…and the nightlife. This is Chile's prime surf spot, and people come from around the world to test their skills. There are three main sectors for surfing. Beginners should start at La Puntilla, known for its long, even waves of 1 to 4 meters (3 to 13 feet) during the winter months (March through November). Those with a bit more experience can check out El Infiernillo—about a ¼ mi south—where the rocky conditions will make it clear why it's called the "Little Hell." But the area's big draw is clearly Punta de Lobos, where the conditions leave novices on the beach and the experts with the challenge of maneuvering the 6-meter (20-foot) waves. This is widely considered the best surfing in South America year-round. And if you're up to it, you might even compete in the International Surfing Championship held here each year in late November.

Pichilemu is easy to reach by car or bus from Santa Cruz. If you're driving, head north out of town to Palmilla, turn left, and continue on I-50 all the way to the coast. The paved road is in good condition and leads through wine country and over the coastal mountains and then down again through pine-lined curves to the coast. Buses are also readily available from San Fernando and Santa Cruz directly to Pichilemu.

EXPLORING

WINERIES

Just south of Curicó and immediately off the Pan-American Highway is **Viña Miguel Torres,** one of Chile's most visitor-savvy vineyards. The tour begins with an orientation video that provides a glossy overview of the winery, with its roots in the family winery in Catalonia, Spain, and Miguel Torres's choice to set up shop in Chile while his sister opted for California. Torres was a leader in Chile's wine revolution and is credited as the first in Chile to use a stainless steel tank—now *de rigueur*—in the late 1970s. He also brought another tradition from his native Iberia: the annual wine harvest festival that takes place in Curicó's main plaza. Be sure to visit the restaurant, definitely one of the finest in the area. ⊠ *Ruta 5 S, Km 195* ☎ *75/564–121* ⊕ *www.migueltorres.cl* 🖾 *5,000 pesos* ⊙ *Daily 10–6.*

The vineyard that surrounds **Viña San Pedro** in the Molina sector of the valley is one of the largest and oldest in Latin America. The first vines were planted here in 1701. The winery is also among the most modern, with 28 half-million-liter stainless-steel tanks producing more wine than any other competitor except Concha y Toro. San Pedro's top of the line is the premium Cabo de Hornos (which is Spanish for Cape Horn), followed by 1865 (the year the winery was founded), and Castillo de Molina. The bottling plant has a sleek glass dome and a second-floor viewing platform. There's also a great little wine shop

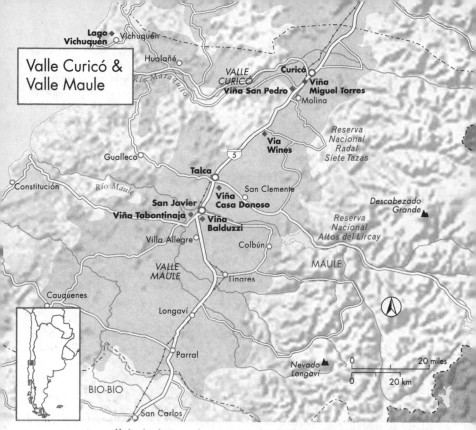

Valle Curicó & Valle Maule

just off the highway where you can pick up some real bargains. Tours can be arranged through the Ruta del Vino office in Curicó. ⊠ *Ruta 5 S, Km 205* ☎ *75/492–770, 2/477–5300 in Santiago* ⊕ *www.sanpedro. cl* ⊙ *Weekdays 9:30–5:30.*

OTHER ATTRACTIONS

The lovely **Plaza de Armas** has a pretty fountain ringed by statues of dancing nymphs. Nearby is an elaborate bandstand that was constructed in New Orleans in 1904.

The **Iglesia San Francisco,** five blocks east of the central plaza, houses a statue of the Virgen de la Velilla that was brought from Spain in 1734. It has been named a national monument.

The local **Ruta del Vino** (⊠ *Arturo Prat 301-A* ☎📠 *75/328–972* ⊕ *www. rutadelvinocurico.cl*) office provides basic information and offers a wide variety of tours that range from basic half-day visits to a single winery to combination packages that include hiking, biking, and rafting options. English-speaking guides are available.

A 13,000-acre national reserve 70 km (43 mi) southeast of Curicó, **Reserva Nacional Radal Siete Tazas** is famous for the unusual "Seven Tea-cups," a series of pools created by waterfalls along the Río Claro. From the park entrance, where you'll find a CONAF station, the falls are a short hike away. Farther along the trail are two other impressive cascades: the Salto Velo de la Novia (Bridal Veil Falls) and Salto de la Leona (Lioness Falls). The park is home to a wide range of flora and fauna. Black woodpeckers, hawks, and eagles are common throughout the park, and condors nest in the highest areas. If you're lucky, you might catch a glimpse of the scarce *loro tricahue*, an endangered species that is Chile's largest and most colorful parrot. Camping is permitted in the park, which is snowed over in winter. October–March is the best time to visit. ⊠ *Camino Molina–Parque Inglés* ☎ *71/228–029* ⊕ *www. conaf.cl* ☜ *3,000 pesos* ⊙ *Daily 8:30–6.*

LAGO VICHUQUÉN

112 km (69 mi) west of Curicó.

An hour's drive from Curicó, the lake is a popular place for water sports such as sailing and water-skiing. The town itself, about 8 km (5 mi) away, is worth a visit for its museum, but has little to offer in terms of dining or lodging. Black-necked swans are a common sight on meandering Lago Vichuquén and nearby Laguna Torca, which is a protected area.

The **Museo Colonial de Vichuquén** displays ceramics, stone tools, and other artifacts collected from pre-Hispanic peoples. ⊠ *Av. Manuel Rodríguez s/n* ☎ *75/400–045* ☜ *700 pesos* ⊙ *Daily 10–1 and 4–6.*

WHERE TO STAY & EAT

$ ✕⌂ **La Hostería.** This two-story structure constructed entirely of native woods affords unparalleled views of Lago Vichuquén, with many rooms overlooking the lake from private decks. The hotel has excellent water-sports facilities. The discotheque is a popular nightspot, and the restaurant is the best on the lake—many people from nearby accommodations arrive by motorboat. **Pros:** Beautiful location. **Cons:** Somewhat remote. ⊠ *Sector Aquelarre, Lago Vichuquén* ☎ *75/400–018* 🖶 *75/400–030* ⊕ *www.lagovichuquen.cl* ⤵ *12 rooms* & *In-room: no a/c, no TV. In-hotel: restaurant, bar, bicycles, laundry service, beachfront, no elevator* ⊟ *AE, DC, MC, V* ⧉ *BP.*

$$ ⌂ **Marina Vichuquén.** The comfortable Marina Vichuquén has an enviable location right on the shore and makes use of it with its own marina. Many rooms have nice views of the lake and the surrounding pine forests. There are plenty of opportunities for water sports, including a sailing school for children. If you want to explore the nearby countryside, you can rent horses or mountain bikes. **Pros:** Plenty to do. **Cons:** Somewhat remote. ⊠ *Sector Aquelarre, Lago Vichuquén* ☎ *75/400–271* 🖶 *75/400–274* ⊕ *www.marinavichuquen.cl* ⤵ *18 rooms* & *In-room: no a/c, no TV. In-hotel: restaurant, bar, tennis court, pool, bicycles, laundry service, public Internet, no elevator* ⊟ *AE, DC, MC, V* ⧉ *BP.*

VALLE MAULE

Talca is the capital of Maule, Chile's largest wine valley. Dozens of wineries are scattered throughout the region, which begins north of Talca in San Rafael and extends south to the regional border at the Perquilauquén River, just south of Parral. Most are roughly grouped into two areas: east of the highway around San Clemente, or slightly west of the highway around San Javier and Villa Alegre. Maule is an up-and-coming region; it was long ignored as backward, but insightful winemakers have discovered its value for producing excellent red wines.

TALCA

56 km (35 mi) south of Curicó on the Pan-American Hwy. .

Straddling the banks of the Río Claro, Talca is not only Maule's most important industrial center; it is also one of the most appealing towns in the Central Valley. It was founded in 1692 and intelligently designed on a regimented grid pattern divided into quadrants—*poniente* means west and *oriente* east; *sur* means south and *norte* north—centered around the pretty Plaza de Armas. Be sure to take some time to check out its native and exotic trees.

6

GETTING HERE & AROUND

No surprises here; once again it's back to the Ruta 5 (Pan-American Highway) for an easy ride to Talca, about 40 mi (65 km) south of Curicó. If you're a train enthusiast, find an excuse to hop aboard Chile's only remaining local train and head to Constitución on the coast. It runs twice a day and takes you through some gorgeous scenery you won't be able to see any other way.

ESSENTIALS

Bus Contacts Talca Terminal (⊠*2 Sur 1920* ☎*71/243–270*).

Currency Exchange Banco del Estado (⊠*1 Sur 971* ☎*71/223–285*).

Medical Asístanse Hospital de Talca (⊠*1 Norte 13 Oriente s/n* ☎*71/209–100*).

Post Office Talca (⊠*1 Oriente 1150* ☎*71/227–271*).

Rental Cars Rosselot (⊠*Av. San Miguel 2710* ☎*71/247-979*).

Visitor & Tour Info Talca (⊠*1 Poniente 1281* ☎*71/226–940*).

EXPLORING

WINERIES

The **Valle del Maule Ruta del Vino** office, east of Talca, arranges visits to about a dozen wineries. It can provide transportation and an English-speaking guide, which simplifies and enriches a visit. The office is in the **Villa Cultural Huilquilemu,** a hacienda built in 1850 that also holds a small museum of religious art and local culture. ⊠*Camino a San Clemente, Km 7* ☎*71/246–460* ⊕*www.chilewineroute.com* ✉*500 pesos* ☻*Tues.–Fri. 9–1 and 3–6:30, weekends noon–6.*

Continued on page 230

Wines of Chile & Argentina

The wine regions of both Chile and Argentina are set against the backdrop of the Andes. And while these mountains do play an important role in the making of wine in both countries, Chile and Argentina have very different traditions and strengths.

— by Margaret Shook —

Although wine-loving Spaniards settled both countries in the 16th century, only Chile's wine industry developed quickly, largely because the land around Santiago was particularly good for growing grapes. Buenos Aires, on the warm and humid Atlantic coast, however, was hardly an ideal place for viticulture. Mendoza, Argentina's present-day wine wonderland, was impossibly far away to be a reliable supplier of wine to the capital until the railroad united it with the coast in the mid-19th century.

Chile also experienced a boom in the 19th century as new, French-inspired wineries sprang up. Both countries continued without significant change for more than 100 years, until the 1990s international wine boom sparked new interest in South American wines. Big investments from France, Spain, Italy, the United States, and elsewhere—plus some extraordinary winemakers—have made this an exciting place for oenophiles to visit.

(left) Bottle of Maradona red wine; (background) Errazuriz Winery, Chile.

NEIGHBORS ACROSS THE ANDES

CHILE

In the early days, the emphasis was on growing cheap wine to consume domestically. Then, in the middle of the 20th century, Chile's political turmoil caused the business to stagnate. It wasn't until the 1980s that wine exports became a major business, and today Chile exports more than it imports.

Chile's appellation system names its valleys from north to south, but today's winegrowers stress that the climatic and geological differences between east and west are more significant. The easternmost valleys closest to the Andes tend to have less fog, more hours of sunlight, and greater daily temperature variations, which help red grapes develop deep color and rich tannins while maintaining bright acidity and fresh fruit characteristics. On the other hand, if you're after crisp whites and bright Pinots, head to the coast, where cool fog creeps inland from the sea each morning and Pacific breezes keep the vines cool all day.

Interior areas in the Central Valley are less prone to extremes and favor varieties that require more balanced conditions, such as Merlot, and Chile's own rich and spicy Carmenère. Syrah, a relatively new grape in Chile, is doing well in both cold and warm climates.

BE SURE TO TASTE:

Sauvignon Blanc: Cool-climate vineyards from Elqui to Bío Bío are producing very exciting Sauvignon with fresh green fruit, crisp acidity, and often an enticing mineral edge.

Carmenère: Chile's signature grape arrived in Chile during the mid-19th century from France, where it was usually a blending grape in Bordeaux. Over time Chileans forgot about it, mistaking it for Merlot, but during the Chilean boom times of the 1990s they realized that they had a very unique grape hidden amongst the other vines in their vineyards.

Cabernet Sauvignon: The king of reds grows well nearly wherever it's planted, but rarely with the elegance, balance, and structure it develops in the Alto Maipo.

Syrah: Chile produces two distinct styles of this grape. Be sure to try both: luscious and juicy from Colchagua or enticingly spicy from coastal areas, such as Elqui or San Antonio.

Malbec: True, this is Argentina's grape, but Chile produces some award-winning bottling that has appealing elegance and balance.

Vina Cousino Macul; Santiago, Chile.

Miguel Torres, Chile.

Winery tour, Chile.

Bodega Tres Erres, Chile.

ARGENTINA

Unlike Chile, Argentina exports far less wine than it consumes, and much of its wine is produced in accordance with local tastes and wallets. The 1990s wine boom sparked a greater emphasis on export, and following new investments, the country is now widely recognized for the quality of its red wines, particularly its signature Malbec.

Autumnal Las Compuertas vineyard, with the Andes beyond.

Broad-shouldered Argentina looks west to the Andes, for a life-giving force. Its wine regions receive no cooling maritime influence, as Chile's do, and its vineyards rely on the mountain altitudes not only to irrigate its lands, but also to attenuate the effects of the blazing sun. The climate here is capricious, so producers must be ever-prepared for untimely downpours, devastating hailstorms, and scorching, dehydrating Zonda winds.

BE SURE TO TASTE:

Malbec: Just one sip of Argentina's most widely known wine evokes gauchos and tangos. Deep, dark, and handsomely concentrated, this is a must-try on its home turf.

Malbec and Merlot, Bodega Norton, Luján de Cuyo.

Cabernet Sauvignon: Argentine Cabs are big, bold, and brawny, as is typical of warmer climates. They're perfect with one of those legendary Argentine grilled steaks.

Red Blends: The red blends here may be mixtures of classic Bordeaux varietals with decidedly Argentine results, or audacious combinations that are only possible in the New World.

Torrentés: Argentina's favorite white has floral overtones, grown most often in Cafayate, in the northwestern province of Salta.

Estancia Colome; Salta province, Argentina.

TASTING TIPS ON BOTH SIDES OF THE BORDER

1. The number one wine travel rule in Chile and Argentina? Make reservations! Unlike wineries in the U.S., most wineries are not equipped to receive drop-in visitors.

2. Don't expect wineries to be open on Sunday. Winery workers need a day off too.

3. The distances between wineries can be much longer than they look on the map.

Be sure to allot plenty of travel time, and plan on no more than three or four wineries per day.

4. Do contact the wine route offices in the region you're visiting. They can be extremely helpful in coordinating visits to wineries and other local attractions.

5. Hire a driver, or choose a designated driver. That's sage advice in any wine region.

Botellas.

GREAT WINE ITINERARIES

ALTO MAIPO ITINERARY

Plenty of wineries are within reach of a day trip from Santiago. You can save some money by hiring a taxi to take you out (it should cost around $70 for a half day), but brush up on your Spanish first. Alternatively, for around US$160 your hotel can put you in touch with a trusted guide for a full day trip. They may have better access to the wineries than you would on your own.

Concha y Toro. Start the day at one of Chile's oldest and best known wineries, located just outside of the capital in the town of Pirque. The village is charming, the estate's park is lovely, the cellars are beautiful, and the tour efficient.

Haras de Pirque. Horses are the owners' first love, which is plain to see. You'll pass the breeding farm and the race track on the way to this horseshoe-shaped winery tucked up into the Andean hills. Reservations are strictly required.

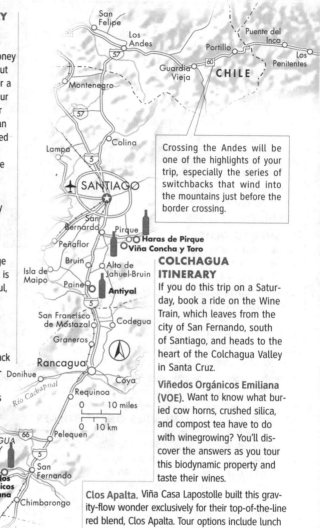

Crossing the Andes will be one of the highlights of your trip, especially the series of switchbacks that wind into the mountains just before the border crossing.

COLCHAGUA ITINERARY

If you do this trip on a Saturday, book a ride on the Wine Train, which leaves from the city of San Fernando, south of Santiago, and heads to the heart of the Colchagua Valley in Santa Cruz.

Viñedos Orgánicos Emiliana (VOE). Want to know what buried cow horns, crushed silica, and compost tea have to do with winegrowing? You'll discover the answers as you tour this biodynamic property and taste their wines.

Antiyal. One of Chile's first boutique-garage wineries, Antiyal only makes two red blends, both of which are organic and biodynamic.

Now head to the Pan American Highway for the fast route back to Santiago.

Clos Apalta. Viña Casa Lapostolle built this gravity-flow wonder exclusively for their top-of-the-line red blend, Clos Apalta. Tour options include lunch on the patio overlooking the valley.

Viña Santa Cruz. More than just a winery, this is an entire wine complex. Take the a cable car to the "indigenous village" at the top of the hill, where the view can't be beat.

Head into Santa Cruz for lunch at **Los Varietales,** in the Santa Cruz Plaza Hotel and a visit to the must-see **Colchagua Museum.** Take a break, if you're tempted, and spend the night in the hotel, otherwise turn back toward Santiago.

Catena Zapata winery.

ARGENTINA ITINERARY

The charming city of Mendoza is the logical home base for exploring Argentine wine country, and the country's finest wineries surround the city.

Ruca Malén. This smallish winery is less than 10 years old and offers a friendly, personalized tour with tastings of its Malbec, Cabernet, and Chardonnay wines. The restaurant is a good place to stop for lunch.

Finca & Bodega Carlos Pulenta. Owned by one of Argentina's most renowned winemakers, Carlos Pulenta, this elegantly modern winery has glass walls that expose the vineyard's soil profiles.

Bodega Catena Zapata. Rising like a Mayan temple from the fertile soil, this winery produces some of Argentina's most memorable blended wines.

WINERY-ARCHITECTURE ITINERARY

Fans of spectacular architecture will enjoy visiting Argentina's wineries. Big, modern, sometimes whimsical, and often surprising, many of these enormous high-tech facilities have restaurants and even lodgings to make the long distances between them bearable. Plan for a long day in the beautiful Valle de Uco visiting some striking examples.

Bodegas Salentein. A perfect example of the "winery-plus" experience in South American wine tourism, this property is a work of art set against a natural backdrop of the Andes, complete with cultural center, restaurant, chapel, and award-winning wines.

Andeluna. The Rutini family has long made wine in Argentina, and its newest endeavor is at the relatively high altitude of 1,300 meters (4,265 feet). Check out the house wines at the wine bar or one of the other tasting centers, or chat in the kitchen as the chef prepares your meal.

Bodegas y Viñedos O. Fournier S.A. End your day at this highly unusual building that looks, from a distance, like a city of Oz for the new millennium. An enormous, flat roof seems to hover over the building, and the large U-shaped ramp accommodates gravity-flow winemaking.

6

IN FOCUS WINES OF CHILE & ARGENTINA

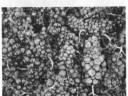

Colchagua Valley Chile.

CROSSING THE ANDES

Mendoza, Argentina; Andean foothills, wine harvest.

■ If you're coming all the way to South America to taste wine, be sure to visit both sides of the Andes. There are frequent hour-long jet flights between Santiago and Mendoza for US$200-$300 that provide a spectacular condor's-eye view of the craggily snow-covered peaks below.

■ If you are visiting in the summer months and have time for the day-long, 250 km (155 mi) overland route, by all means take it. Know that you will most likely have to get a roundtrip car rental. Most companies will not allow one-way international crossings. Better to rent a car in Santiago or Buenos Aires to see the wineries in each country, then fly or catch a bus to cross the border. On the Argentina side, a flight from Buenos Aires to Mendoza can save time.

■ Roads are well-maintained and reasonably marked. Take Ruta 57 north from Santiago to the small city of Los Andes, then head east on Ruta 60 toward the mountains and the Argentine border, where the highway's name changes to Ruta 7, to Mendoza.

■ Crossing the Andes will be one of the highlights of your trip, especially the series of switchbacks that wind into the mountains as you approach the Portillo Ski Resort (a nice place for lunch) just before the border crossing some 8,200 feet above sea level. Be aware that the Libertadores Pass is often closed for days at a time during the winter months, so don't risk it unless you're willing to spend several days sleeping in your car while you wait for things to clear up. Be sure to bring a jacket any time of year, as it can be very chilly at that altitude.

■ Plan a couple of stops along the way; make the Portillo Ski Resort your last stop on the Chilean side, where you can visit the Laguna del Inca at nearly 10,000 feet. On the Argentine side, stop for gas and a bite to eat in Upsallata, about 100 km (65 miles) before reaching Mendoza.

WINE TASTING 101

TAKE A GOOD LOOK.
Hold your glass by the stem, raise it to the light, and take a close look at the wine. Check for clarity and color. (This is easiest to do if you can move the glass in front of a white background.) Any tinge of brown means that the wine is over the hill or has gone bad.

BREATHE DEEP.
1. Sniff the wine once or twice to see if you can identify any smells.

2. Swirl the wine gently in the glass. Aerating the wine this way releases more of its aromas. (It's called "volatilizing the esters," if you're trying to impress someone.)

3. Take another long sniff. You might notice that experienced wine tasters spend more time sniffing the wine than drinking it. This is because this step is where the magic happens. The number of scents you might detect is almost endless, from berries, apricots, honey, and wildflowers to leather, cedar, or even tar. Does the wine smell good to you? Do you detect any "off" flavors, like wet dog or sulfur?

AT LAST! TAKE A SIP.
1. Swirl the wine around your mouth so that it makes contact with all your taste buds and releases more of its aromas. Think about the way the wine feels in your mouth. Is it watery or rich? Is it crisp or silky? Does it have a bold flavor, or is it subtle? The weight and intensity of a wine are called its body.

2. Hold the wine in your mouth for a few seconds and see if you can identify any developing flavors. More complex wines will reveal many different flavors as you drink them.

SPIT OR SWALLOW.
The pros typically spit, since they want to preserve their palate (and sobriety!) for the wines to come, but you'll find that swallowers far outnumber the spitters in the winery tasting rooms. Whether you spit or swallow, notice the flavor that remains after the wine is gone (the finish).

Swirl

Sniff

Sip

Via Wines. Via Wines, the northernmost winery in the Maule Valley, in San Rafael, is a company with a sense of humor. Its most recognizable brand, "Oveja Negra," means black sheep. A visit will take you through the modern winery and olive oil operations, and, if you are so inclined, you can ride in a carriage or on a horse through the gorgeous vineyards with the Andes Mountains serving as a backdrop. The guesthouse offers very comfortable accommodations, complete with home-cooked meals including breads and meats prepared in the traditional adobe oven. In the evening, relax with a game of pool or a good book in the reading room. ⊠ *Fundo Las Chilcas, San Rafael* ☎ *71/651–000* ⊕ *www.viawines.com* ⚑ *Reservations essential.*

Ten minutes east of Talca along a dirt road are the massive iron gates that mark the entrance to **Viña Casa Donoso,** a red hacienda with a barrel-tile roof. The vineyards themselves climb up into the Andean foothills. The estate was once called Domain Oriental, because it is east of the city, but today it bears the name of the family who owned it for many generations before it was purchased by four Frenchmen in 1989. The oenological work is performed by a skilled Chilean staff, and the results are auspicious. The colonial-period manor house also has three rooms available to guests. ⊠ *Fundo La Oriental, Camino a Palmira, Km 3.5* ☎ *71/242–506* ⊕ *www.casadonoso.cl* ⚑ *6,000 pesos* ☽ *Weekdays 9–4, weekends 10:30–5:30* ⚑ *Reservations essential.*

In San Javier itself is **Viña Balduzzi.** Albano Balduzzi, descended from 200 years of Italian winemakers, built the 40-acre estate here in 1900. Today his great-grandson, Jorge López-Balduzzi, is in charge and pumps out a million liters of wine each year. The premium label features varietals such as cabernet sauvignon, sauvignon blanc, carmenère, merlot, and a sweet late-harvest chardonnay. Tours include a peek at the cellars that stretch underneath the property, and the collection of antique machinery, as well as a tasting. Within the estate is a beautiful expanse of oak and cedar trees that's perfect for a picnic. ⊠ *Av. Balmaceda 1189* ☎ *73/322–138* ⊕ *www.balduzzi.cl* ⚑ *5,000 pesos* ☽ *Mon.–Sat. 9–5:30.*

☺ ★ **Viña Tabontinaja / Gillmore.** The Gillmores, who own this winery, are a creative bunch. In addition to making truly fine red wines (sold as Viña Gillmore), they have created a fun place to stop and spend a couple of hours or stay on for a night or two. There's an impressive zoo on-site that includes a puma, a rare Chilean deer called a *huemul,* and a raucous group of peacocks, as well as other animals. An adobe chapel has been turned into a museum, and there's a village project going on next door that sells wine and local crafts today, but that has plans to expand to include a variety of cultural items and events.

This is a great place to stay while on the way south. Its odd-looking guest houses made from ancient recycled fermentation tanks provide all the comforts of home, as well as a wood-burning hot tub and great food. Take the Pan-American Highway to the "Camino a Constitución" south of San Javier. Head east over the Loncomilla River and through the rolling hills of the Coastal Mountains for 20 km (12½ mi); Tabontinaje is on the right. ⊠ *Camino a Constitución, Km 20,*

San Javier 📠*73/197–5539* ⊕*www.tabontinaja.com* ✉*5000 pesos* &*Reservations essential.*

OTHER ATTRACTIONS

You can make out the city's orderly colonial design from **Cerro de la Virgen,** a hill that affords a panoramic view of Talca and the vineyards in the distance.

One of the most pleasant stretches of green is **Avenida Bernardo O'Higgins,** a cedar-lined boulevard popular with joggers, skaters, and strolling couples. At its western tip is the Balneario Río Claro, where you can hire a boat to paddle down the river.

The **Museo O'Higginiano,** one block east of the Plaza de Armas, is a pink colonial mansion that belonged to Albano Pereira, a tutor of national hero Bernardo O'Higgins. As Chile's first president, O'Higgins signed the country's proclamation of independence in this house in February 1818. Declared a national monument in 1971, it now houses the city's fine-arts museum, which has a collection of more than 500 paintings by local artists. There's also an impressive armory of 19th-century *carabinas* (carbines) from Europe and America. The Chilean name for the police force, *carabineros,* is derived from this word. ⊠*1 Norte 875, at 2 Oriente* 📠*71/210–428* ⊕*www.dibam.cl* ✉*Free* ⊙*Tues.–Fri. 10–7, weekends 10–2.*

There may be no better way to get to know the Central Valley than by taking a ride on Chile's only remaining *ramal* (branch-line railroad), which runs from Talca to the coastal city of Constitución. The 100-km (62-mi) **Ramal Talca–Constitución** makes a slow trip to the coast—it's 2½ hours each way—stopping for about 15 minutes at each of the small towns en route. In Constitución you'll be able to admire the coastal cliffs and rock formations. The train departs Talca's Estación de Tren daily at 7:30 AM, returning at 4 PM. In high season (December–April) a train also leaves at 11 and returns at 9. A good option is to arrange a tour on which you take the train to Constitución, then board a van to visit nearby sand dunes and other natural attractions. Contact **EFE, the national train service** (📠*71/674–824* ⊕*www.efe.cl*) for more information on the train tour.

The town of **San Clemente,** 16 km (10 mi) southeast of Talca, hosts the best rodeo in the region September–April, with riding, roping, dances, and beauty-queen competitions. The events take place weekends 11–6. The national championship selections are held here toward the end of the season.

WHERE TO STAY & EAT

$ ✕**Rubén Tapia.** This top-tier Central Valley restaurant, named for its
Fodor'sChoice chef-owner Rubén Tapia, is renowned for its refined service and out-
★ standing cuisine. The elegant dining rooms make you feel like a guest in someone's home. The spacious bar, which displays mostly local wines, is a nice spot for a cocktail. Signature dishes include a *caldillo de congrio dorado* (conger eel stew) that is reputed to be Pablo Neruda's recipe, curried salmon, *lomo estilo corralero* (tenderloin in a shellfish sauce), and *chupe de locos* (abalone casserole topped with shredded cheese).

Even more unusual is the jambalaya, made with shrimp, chicken, and ham and served in a leaf of red lettuce. ✉*2 Oriente 1339* ☏*71/215–991* ⊕*www.rubentapia.cl* ⊟*AE, DC, MC, V* ⊗*Closed Sun.*

$ ✕**Vivace.** Hardwood, tiles, and brick decorate the warm dining room, and window tables overlook the lovely tree-lined boulevard at Vivace, one of Talca's most popular restaurants. The Italian menu includes the familiar, such as lasagna Bolognese, but also original entrées, such as *conejo mediterraneo* (rabbit with vegetables in a sherry sauce), fettuccine *con ragú de ciervo* (with a venison sauce), and fettuccine *con ragú de cordero* (with a curried lamb–and–pistachio sauce). The restaurant occupies a refurbished home half a block northwest of the Plaza de Armas, on the diagonal road. ✉*Isodoro del Solar 50* ☏*71/238–337* ⊟*AE, DC, MC, V* ⊗*Closed Sun.*

$ 🏨**Hostal del Puente.** This quiet, family-run hotel, at the end of a dusty street two blocks west of the Plaza de Armas, is quite a bargain. Simple carpeted rooms have small desks and windows that open onto a portico or overlook the parking area in back. Ask for one of the older rooms in the front, where a narrow garden holds níspero and cherry trees. The owners provide inexpensive breakfasts and free travel advice. **Pros:** Great budget option. **Cons:** No frills. ✉*1 Sur 407*☏☏*71/220–930* ⊕*www.hostaldelpuente.cl* ⟲*14 rooms* ⚇*In-room: no a/c, no phone. In-hotel: no-smoking rooms* ⊟*No credit cards.*

$ 🏨**Hotel Terrabella.** Half a block west of the Plaza de Armas, this hotel has rooms that although neither especially bright nor spacious, are tasteful and spotless. The ground floor holds a small lounge and a restaurant enclosed in glass walls with a view of the backyard and swimming pool. The shady lawn is hemmed by gardens, and the friendly staff make this a pleasant, if not luxurious, place to stay. **Pros:** Location. **Cons:** No frills. ✉*1 Sur 641* ☏☏*71/226–555* ⊕*www.hotelterrabella.cl* ⟲*29 rooms, 2 suites* ⚇*In-room: no a/c, safe, dial-up. In-hotel: restaurant, room service, pool, laundry service* ⊟*AE, DC, MC, V* ⏐◯⏐*BP.*

NIGHTLIFE

Pura Candela (✉*Isidoro del Solar 38* ☏*41/236–505*), in a colorful house just northwest of the Plaza de Armas, draws a young professional crowd Wednesday to Saturday. There's live Latin music on Friday and Saturday evenings, as well as a cover charge.

HORSEBACK RIDING

Horseback-riding tours are an excellent way to explore the amazing mountain scenery east of Talca. **Achibueno Expediciones** (✉*Ruta L-45, Km 8, Linares*☏☏*73/375–098*) runs 2- to 10-day horseback trips through the Andes that pass waterfalls, hot springs, and mountain lakes. **Expediciones Quizapu** (✉*Casilla 421* ☏*71/621–592*) arranges three- to seven-day horseback expeditions that combine camping and overnight stays in rustic farmhouses.

SHOPPING

The **Centro Artesanal Antumapu** (✉*1 Sur 1330, Galería Bavaria* ☏*No phone*) sells work by 17 local artisans, including ceramics, jewelry, leather, and woolen goods. The **Mercado Central** (✉*1 Sur, between 4 and 5 Oriente* ☏*No phone*) has stands filled with ceramics, copperware, baskets, and other handicrafts.

The Lake District

Lake Llanquihue with Mount Osorno Volcano in background, Puerto Varas, Lake District

7

WORD OF MOUTH

"Last year my wife and I crossed the lakes from Puerto Varas (Chile) to Bariloche (Argentina) on a boat and bus excursion, and enjoyed it very much. Most of the crossing was by boat, very scenic. Don't think crossing by car or by bus would be as nice."

–caldnj

WELCOME TO
THE LAKE DISTRICT

TOP REASONS TO GO

★ **Volcanoes:** Volcán Villarrica and Volcán Osorno are the conical, iconic symbols of the northern and southern Lake District, respectively, but some 50 other volcanoes loom and fume in this region. Not to worry; eruptions are rare.

★ **Stunning Summer Nights:** Southern Chile's austral summer doesn't get more glorious than January and February, when sunsets don't fade until well after 10 PM, and everyone is out dining, shopping, and enjoying the outdoors.

★ **Lakes and Rivers:** The region may sport a long Pacific coastline, but everyone flocks to the inland lakes to swim, sun bathe, kayak, sail, and more. The region also hosts numerous wild rivers that are, among other things, excellent for fly fishing.

★ **Soothing Hot Springs:** Chile counts some 280 thermal springs, and a good many of the well-operated ones are in the Lake District, the perfect place to pamper yourself after a day of outdoor adventure and sightseeing.

1 La Araucanía. It may not be called Los Lagos, but La Araucanía contains some of Chile's most spectacular lake scenery. Several volcanoes, among them Villarrica and Llaima, two of South America's most active, loom over the region. Burgeoning Pucón, on the shore of Lago Villarrica, has become the tourism hub of southern Chile. Other quieter alternatives exist, however. Lago Calafquén, farther south, begins the seven-lake Siete Lagos chain that stretches across the border to Argentina.

2 Los Lagos. Los Lagos, the southern half of the Lake District, is a land of snowcapped volcanoes, rolling farmland, and, of course, the shimmering lakes that give the region its name. This landscape is literally a work in progress, as it's part of the so-called Ring of Fire encircling the Pacific Rim. Most of Chile's 55 active volcanoes are here.

Volcan Villaricca

Lake Caburgua

GETTING ORIENTED

The Lake District's altitude descends sharply from the towering peaks of the Andes on the Argentine border, to forests and plains, and finally to sea level, all in the space of about 200 km (120 mi). Throughout the region, big volcanoes burst into view alongside the many large lakes and winding rivers. Architecture and gastronomy here are unlike anywhere else in Chile, much of it heavily influenced by the large-scale German colonization of the 1850s and '60s. The Pan-American Highway (Ruta 5) runs straight down the middle, making travel to most places in the region relatively easy. It connects the major cities of Temuco, Osorno, and Puerto Montt, but bypasses Valdivia by 50 km (30 mi). A drive from Temuco to Puerto Montt should take less than four hours. Flying between the hubs is a reasonable option. The region also now has a passenger train connecting Temuco and Puerto Montt, as well as many towns in between.

7

THE LAKE DISTRICT PLANNER

When to Go

Most Chileans not on holiday on the Central Coast head here during southern Chile's glorious summer, between December and March. For fishermen, the official fishing season commences the second Friday of November and runs through the first Sunday of May. Visiting during the off-season is no hardship, though, and lodging prices drop dramatically. An increasing number of smog-weary Santiaguinos flee the capital in winter to enjoy the Lake District's brisk, clear air or to ski and snowboard down volcanoes and Andean hills. Just be prepared for wind and rain.

Festivals & Seasonal Events

Summer, with its better weather and ample presence of vacationers, also means festival season in the Lake District. In late January and early February, Semanas Musicales de Frutillar brings together the best in classical music. Villarrica hosts a Muestra Cultural Mapuche in January and February that shows off Mapuche art and music. During the first week of October, Valdivia hosts a first-class, nationally acclaimed international film festival.

Eat Well & Rest Easy

Meat and potatoes characterize the cuisine of this part of southern Chile. The omnipresent *cazuela* (a plate of rice and potatoes with beef or chicken) and *pastel de choclo* (a corn, meat, and vegetable casserole) are solid, hearty meals. Arguably the greatest gifts from the waves of German immigrants were their tasty *küchen,* rich fruit-filled pastries. (Raspberry is a special favorite here.) Sample them during the late-afternoon *onces,* the coffee breaks locals take to tide them over until dinner. The Germans also brought their beer-making prowess to the New World; Valdivia, in particular, is home base to the popular Kunstmann brand.

If you've traveled in Europe, you may feel at home in the Lake District, where most of the lodgings resemble old-world hotels. Many hostelries, even the newly built ones, are constructed in Bavarian-chalet style echoing the region's Germanic heritage. A handful of lodgings—Temuco's Hotel Continental, Pucón's Hotel Antumalal, and Puerto Octay's Hotel Centinela—are also historic landmarks that shouldn't be missed.

Rates usually include a Continental breakfast of coffee, cheese, bread, and jam. Although most of the places listed here stay open all year, call ahead to make sure the owners haven't decided to take a well-deserved vacation during the March–November off-season.

WHAT IT COSTS IN CHILEAN PESOS (IN THOUSANDS)				
¢	$	$$	$$$	$$$$
RESTAURANTS				
under 3 pesos	3 pesos– 5 pesos	5 pesos– 8 pesos	8 pesos– 11 pesos	over 11 pesos
HOTELS				
under 15 pesos	15 pesos– 45 pesos	45 pesos– 75 pesos	75 pesos– 105 pesos	over 105 pesos

Restaurant prices are based on the median main course price at dinner. Hotel prices are for a double room in high season, excluding tax.

Adventure Travel

Awash in rivers, mountains, forests, gorges, and its name-sake lakes, this part of the country is Chile's outdoors capi-tal. Outfitters traditionally are concentrated in the northern resort town of Pucón and the southern Puerto Varas, but firms up and down this 400-km-long (240-mi-long) slice of Chile can rent you equipment or guide your excursions.

The increasing popularity of such excursions means that everybody and their brother and sister seem to want a slice of the adventure küchen. Quality varies widely, especially in everybody's-an-outfitter destinations such as Pucón. Ask questions about safety and guide-to-client ratios. (A few unscrupulous businesses might take 20 climbers up the Vil-larrica volcano with a single guide.) Also, be brutally frank with yourself about your own capabilities: Are you really in shape for rappelling? Or is bird-watching more your style? This is nature at its best and sometimes at its most powerful.

Sample Itinerary

On your arrival into **Temuco,** spend the afternoon shopping for Mapuche handicrafts at the city's Mercado Municipal. Rise early the next morning and drive to **Villarrica** or **Pucón,** where you can spend the day exploring a beauti-ful area, maybe taking a dip in one of the nearby thermal springs. The next day take a hike up Volcán Villarrica. Day four means a drive south to **Valdivia,** where you can spend the afternoon visiting the modern-art and history mu-seums on Isla Teja. Catch an evening cruise along the Río Valdivia. Rise early the next day and drive to the Bavarian-style village of **Frutillar** on Lago Llanquihue. Visit the Museo Colonial Alemán and wind up the afternoon partaking of the Chilean onces ritual with a cup of coffee and küchen. Head for **Puerto Varas** the next day for a thrilling rafting excursion on the nearby Río Petrohué. Save **Puerto Montt** for your final day, and spend the afternoon shopping for handicrafts in the Angelmó market stalls. Finish with a sea-food dinner at one of the market's lively restaurants.

Getting Here & Around

Air Travel. None of the Lake District's airports—Osorno, Puerto Montt, Temuco, and Valdivia—receives international flights; flying here from another country means connecting in Santiago. Of the four cities, Puerto Montt has the greatest frequency of domestic flights.

Bus Travel. There's no short-age of bus companies travel-ing the Pan-American Highway (Ruta 5) from Santiago south to the Lake District. The buses, which are very comfortable, have assigned seating and aren't too crowded. Tickets may be purchased in advance.

Car Travel. It's easier to see more of the Lake District if you have your own vehicle. The Pan-American Highway through the region is a well-maintained four-lane toll highway. Bring plenty of small bills for the frequent toll booths you'll encounter.

Train Travel. Chile's State Rail-way Company, the Empresa de los Ferrocarriles del Estado, has daily service southward from Santiago's Alameda station as far as Temuco on its Terra Sur trains. Trains run daily all year; the overnight trip takes about nine hours. From Temuco, you can board another train south to Puerto Montt and several towns in between. Shuttle-bus service to and from Pucón and Villarrica runs in conjunction with the trains.

7

Updated
by Jimmy
Langman

AS YOU TRAVEL THE WINDING road of the Lake District, the snow-capped shoulders of volcanoes emerge, mysteriously disappear, then materialize again, peeping through trees or towering above broad valleys. The sometimes difficult journey through breathtaking mountain passes is inevitably rewarded by views of a glistening lake, vibrant and blue. You might be tempted to belt out "The hills are alive...," but this is southern Chile, not Austria. With densely forested national parks, a dozen large lakes, easy access to transportation and facilities, and predominantly small, family-run lodgings, this area has come pretty close to perfecting tourism.

The Lake District is the historic homeland of Chile's indigenous Mapuche people, who revolted against the early Spanish colonists in 1598, driving them out of the region. They kept foreigners out of the area for nearly three centuries. Though small pockets of the Lake District were controlled by Chile after it won its independence in 1818, most viewed the forbidding region south of the Río Bío Bío as a separate country. After a treaty ended the last Mapuche war in 1881, Santiago began to recruit waves of German, Austrian, and Swiss immigrants to settle the so-called "empty territory" and offset indigenous domination. The Lake District took on the Bavarian-Tyrolean sheen still evident today.

LA ARAUCANÍA

La Araucanía is the historic home of the Araucano, or Mapuche, culture. The Spanish both feared and respected the Mapuche. This nomadic society, always in search of new terrain, was a moving target that the Spaniards found impossible to defeat. Beginning with the 1598 battle against European settlers, the Mapuche kept firm control of the region for almost 300 years. After numerous peace agreements failed, a treaty signed near Temuco ended hostilities in 1881 and paved the way for the German, Swiss, and Austrian immigration that would transform the face of the Lake District.

TEMUCO

675 km (405 mi) south of Santiago on the Pan-American Hwy., Ruta 5.

This northern gateway to the Lake District acquired a bit of pop-culture cachet as the setting for a segment in 2004's *The Motorcycle Diaries,* a film depicting Che Guevara's prerevolutionary travels through South America in the early 1950s. But with its office towers and shopping malls, today's Temuco would hardly be recognizable to Guevara. The city has a more Latin flavor than the communities farther south. (It could be the warmer weather and the palm trees swaying in the pleasant central park.) It's also an odd juxtaposition of modern architecture and indigenous markets, of traditionally clad Mapuche women darting across the street and business executives talking on cell phones, but, oddly enough, it all works. This is big-city life Chilean style, and it warrants a day if you have the time.

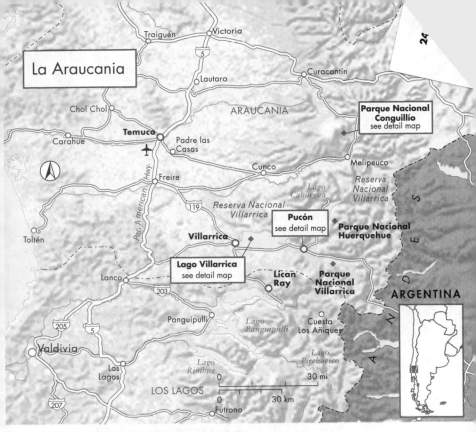

GETTING HERE & AROUND

At least a dozen bus lines serve Temuco; it's an obligatory stop on the long haul between Santiago and Puerto Montt. The city also hosts Manquehue airport, 6 km (4 mi) southwest of town, which has daily connections to Santiago and other Chilean cities. At the airport, in addition to taxis, there are several transfer services that can take you into town. If you're going to Villarrica or Pucón, you'll probably come through here as well. The Pan-American Highway, Ruta 5, runs through the city, and is paved, but several of the outlying roads connecting Temuco to smaller, rural towns are two-lanes and unpaved. Be careful on such roads, as the Chilean auto accident rate due to passing cars is not very good.

ESSENTIALS

Bus Contacts Buses JAC (⊠ *Corner of Balmaceda and Aldunate* ☎ *45/465–500*). **Cruz del Sur** (⊠ *Terminal de Buses, Av. Vicente Pérez Rosales 1609* ☎ *45/730– 310*). **Temuco** (⊠ *Av. Rudecindo Ortega* ☎ *45/257–904*). **Tur-Bus** (⊠ *Lagos 538* ☎ *45/278–161*).

Currency Exchange Germaniatour (⊠ *Manuel Montt 942, Local 5* ☎ *45/ 958–080*).

Internet Net & Cofee (⊠ *Portales 873* ☎ *45/940–001*).

Medical Asístanse Farmacias Ahumada (⊠ *Av. Alemania 505* ☎ *45/246–992*).
Hospital de Temuco (⊠ *Manuel Montt 115* ☎ *45/212–525*).

Post Office Correos de Chile (⊠ *Av. Diego Portales 801*).

Rental Cars Avis (⊠ *Vicuña Mackenna 448* ☎ *45/237–575*). **Budget** (⊠ *Vicuña Mackenna 399* ☎ *45/232–715*). **Hertz** (⊠ *Las Heras 999* ☎ *45/318–585*).

Visitor & Tour Info Sernatur (⊠ *Claro Solar and Bulnes* ☎ *45/312–857*). **Temuco Tourist Office** (⊠ *Mercado Municipal* ☎ *45/203–345*).

EXPLORING

Bustling **Plaza Aníbal Pinto,** Temuco's central square, is ringed with imported palm trees—a rarity in this part of the country. A monument to the 300-year struggle between the Mapuche and the Spaniards sits in the center.

The small subterranean **Galería de Arte** displays rotating exhibits by Chilean artists. ⊠ *Plaza Aníbal Pinto* ☎ *45/236–785* ≌ *Free* ☾ *Mon.– Sat. 10–8, Sun. 1–8.*

The city's modern **Catedral de Temuco** sits on the northwest corner of the central square, flanked by an office tower emblazoned with a cross.

Lined with lime and oak trees, a shady secondary square called **Plaza Teodoro Schmidt** lies six blocks north of the Plaza Aníbal Pinto. It's ruled over by the 1906 Iglesia Santa Trinidad, an Anglican church that is one of the city's oldest surviving structures.

Housed in a 1924 mansion, the **Museo Regional de la Araucanía** covers the history of the area. It has an eclectic collection of artifacts and relics, including musical instruments, utensils, and the country's best collection of indigenous jewelry. Upstairs, exhibits document the Mapuche people's three-century struggle to keep control of their land. The presentation could be more evenhanded: the rhetoric glorifies the Central European colonization of this area as the *pacificación de la Araucanía* (taming of the Araucanía territories). But the museum gives you a reasonably good Spanish-language introduction to Mapuche history, art, and culture. ⊠ *Av. Alemania 84* ☎ *45/730–062* ≌ *600 pesos* ☾ *Weekdays 9–5:45.*

★ Author Pablo Neruda was Chile's most famous train buff. (Neruda spent his childhood in Temuco and his father was a rail worker.) Accordingly, the city has transformed its old rail yard into the **Museo Nacional Ferroviario Pablo Neruda,** a well-laid-out museum documenting Chile's rail history and dedicated to the author's memory. Thirteen locomotives (one diesel and 12 steam) and nine train carriages are housed in the round engine building. Scattered among the exhibits are snippets from Neruda's writings: "Trains were dreaming in the station, defenseless, sleeping, without locomotives," reads one wistful reflection. Exhibits are labeled in Spanish, but an English-speaking guide is on hand if you need translation. The museum lies a bit off the beaten path, but if trains fascinate you, as they did Neruda, it's worth the short taxi ride from downtown. Twice-monthly tourist rail excursions to Valdivia, using the museum's restored 1940 steam locomotive, are worth an afternoon of your time. ✉*Av. Barros Arana 565* ☎*45/973–940* 🗫*1,000 pesos* ◷*Tues.–Sun. 9–6.*

The imposing **Monumento Natural Cerro Ñielol** is the hillside site where the 1881 treaty between the Mapuche and the Chilean army was signed, allowing for the city of Temuco to be established. Trails bloom with bright red *copihues* (a bell-like flower with lush green foliage), Chile's national flower, in autumn (March–May). The monument, not far from downtown, is part of Chile's national park system. ✉*Av. Arturo Prat, 5 blocks north of Plaza Teodoro Schmidt* 🗫*1,000 pesos* ◷*Jan.–Mar., daily 8 AM–11 PM; Apr.–Nov., daily 8:30–12:30 and 2:30–6.*

The small **Museo de Chol Chol** in Temuco exhibits a collection of animal-shaped ceramics and textiles with bold rhomboid and zigzag designs—both are distinctively Mapuche specialties—as well as old black-and-white photographs. A *fogón*, the traditional cooking pit, graces the center of the museum. ✉*Balmaceda s/n* ☎*45/613–350* 🗫*300 pesos* ◷*Tues.–Sun. 9–6.*

WHERE TO EAT

$$ ✕**Centro Español.** The basement dining room of Centro Español, an association that promotes Spanish culture in Temuco, is open to all for lunch and dinner. You have your choice of four or five rotating prix-fixe menus. There will always be something Spanish, something seafood, and something meaty to choose from. *Jamón de Serrano,* a salty type of ham, is a specialty. ✉*Av. Bulnes 483* ☎*45/210–343* 🖃*AE, DC, MC, V.*

$ ✕**Confitería Central.** Coffee and homemade pastries are the specialties of this café, but sandwiches and other simple dishes are also available. Steaming-hot empanadas are served on Sunday and holidays, and during the week you'll swear all of Temuco stops by for a quick bite for lunch among the clattering of dishes and the army of waitresses maneuvering their way around the tables. ✉*Av. Bulnes 442* ☎*45/210–083* 🖃*DC, MC, V.*

$$ ✕**El Fogón.** Decorated with primary colors—yellow walls, red tablecloths, and blue dishes—this place certainly stands out in pastel-hue Temuco. The Chilean-style *parrillada,* or grilled beef, is the specialty of the house. Barbecue here has subtler spices than its better-known Argentine counterpart. The friendly owners will gladly take the time to explain the menu to the uninitiated. Even though it's close to downtown, you should splurge on a cab if you're coming to this dark street at night. ✉*Aldunate 288* ☎*45/737–061* 🖃*No credit cards.*

$ ✕**Mercado Municipal.** In the central market around the produce stalls are small stands offering such typical Chilean meals as cazuela and pastel de choclo. Many have actually taken on the trappings of sit-down restaurants, and a few even have air-conditioning. The complex closes at 8 in summer and 6 the rest of the year, so late-night dining is not an option. ✉*Manuel Rodríguez 960* ☎*No phone* 🖃*No credit cards.*

$$$ ✕**La Pampa.** Wealthy local professionals frequent this upscale modern steak house for its huge, delicious cuts of beef and the best *papas fritas* (french fries) in Temuco. Although most Chilean restaurants douse any kind of meat with a creamy sauce, this is one of the few exceptions: the entrées are served without anything but the simplest of seasonings.

The People of the Land

The Mapuche profoundly affected the history of southern Chile. For almost 300 years this indigenous group fought to keep colonial, then Chilean powers out of their land. The Spanish referred to these people as the Araucanos, from a word in the Quechua language meaning "brave and valiant warriors." In their own Mapudungun language, today spoken by some 400,000 people, the word *Mapuche* means "people of the land." In colonial times only the Spanish missionaries seemed to grasp what this meant. "There are no people in the world," one of them wrote, "who so love and value the land where they were born."

Chilean schoolchildren learning about the Mapuche are likely to read about Lautaro, a feared and respected young chief whose military tactics were instrumental in driving out the Spanish. He cunningly adopted a know-thy-enemy strategy that proved tremendously successful in fending off the colonists. Students are less likely to hear about the tightly knit family structure or nomadic lifestyle of the Mapuche. Even the region's two museums dedicated to Mapuche culture, in Temuco and Valdivia, traditionally focused on the three-century war with the Spaniards. They toss around terms like *pacificación* (meaning "to pacify" or "to tame") to describe the waves of European immigrants who settled in the Lake District at the end of the 1800s, the beginning of the end of Mapuche dominance in the region.

Life has been difficult for the Mapuche since the signing of a peace treaty in 1881. Their land was slowly taken by the Chilean government. Some 200,000 Mapuche today are living on 3,000 *reducciones* (literally meaning "reductions"), operated much like the system of reservations in the United States. Other Mapuche have migrated to the cities, in particular fast-growing Temuco, in search of employment.

A resurgence in Mapuche pride these days takes several forms, some peaceful, some militant. Mapuche demonstrations in Temuco are now commonplace, many calling attention to deplorable conditions on the reducciones. Some are seeking the return of their land, while others are fighting against the encroachment of power companies damming the rivers and logging interests cutting down the forests. News reports occasionally recount attacks and counterattacks between indigenous groups and farmers in remote rural areas far off the beaten tourist path.

Awareness of Mapuche history is increasing. (Latest census figures show that about 1 million of Chile's population of 15 million can claim some Mapuche ancestry.) Both major museums have devoted more of their space to the art, language, and culture of this people. Both institutions spend ample time these days discussing the group's distinctive textiles, with their bold rhomboid, triangular, and zigzagging lines. Both museums also devote considerable space to traditional animal-shaped pottery.

There is also a newfound interest in the Mapuche language and its seven dialects. Mapudungun poetry movingly describes the sadness and dilemma of integration into modern life and of becoming lost in the anonymity of urban life. Never before really understood by others who shared their land, the Mapuche may finally make their cause known.

–Jeffrey Van Fleet

✉ *Caupolicán 0155* ☎ *45/329–999* ♨ *Reservations essential* 🖃 *AE, DC, MC, V* ⊗ *No dinner Sun.*

WHERE TO STAY

$–$$ 🖼 **Don Eduardo Hotel.** Orange inside and out, this pleasant nine-story hotel is made up entirely of cozy furnished apartments, with comfortable chairs and dining areas. All have two or three bedrooms and kitchenettes. The many business travelers who frequent the place appreciate the work areas, with desks and shelves. An eager-to-please staff tends to your needs. **Pros:** Work areas in rooms, spacious. **Cons:** No gym, no safe in room. ✉ *Bello 755* ☎ *45/214–133* 🖷 *45/215–554* ⊕ *www. hoteldoneduardo.cl* ⇄ *46 rooms, 14 suites* ♿ *In-room: no a/c, refrigerator (some), Wi-Fi. In-hotel: restaurant, room service, public Internet, laundry service, public Wi-Fi, parking, no-smoking rooms* 🖃 *AE, DC, MC, V* ⦿*BP.*

$$ 🖼 **Holiday Inn Express.** This hotel is one of five of the chain's outlets in Chile. If you're looking for something uniquely Chilean about the place, you won't find it, but you will find all the U.S.-style amenities, including the do-it-yourself breakfast for which the chain is known— its selling point for guests who stay here. You're quite a way from downtown, but it's a good option if you have a vehicle. **Pros:** Modern, comfortable. **Cons:** Location is relatively far from the center of Temuco. ✉ *Av. Rudecindo Ortega 1800* ☎ *45/223–300* 🖷 *45/224– 100* ⊕ *www.hiexpress.com* ⇄ *62 rooms* ♿ *In-room: no a/c, safe, Wi-Fi. In-hotel: pool, gym, laundry service, parking, no-smoking rooms* 🖃 *AE, MC, V* ⦿*BP.*

$ 🖼 **Hotel Aitué.** The exterior of this hotel is unimposing; in fact, its covered drive-up entry, set back from the road, might cause you to drive right past it. Once you're inside, though, you'll find that this small, pleasant business-class hotel has bright, airy rooms with a tan-and-lavender color scheme. They're on the smallish side, but cozy and comfortable, and come complete with refrigerators and music systems. **Pros:** Well-equipped rooms, comfortable. **Cons:** Hard to find the hotel. ✉ *Antonio Varas 1048* ☎ *45/211–917* 🖷 *45/212–608* ⊕ *www.hotel aitue.cl* ⇄ *35 rooms* ♿ *In-room: no a/c, safe, refrigerator, ethernet, Wi-Fi. In-hotel: no elevator, laundry service, public Internet, parking, no-smoking rooms* 🖃 *AE, DC, MC, V* ⦿*CP.*

$ ✕🖼 **Hotel Continental.** If you appreciate faded elegance and don't mind
★   an uneven floorboard or two, some peeling paint, and few conveniences, the 1890 Continental is for you. Checkered in black-and-white tiles, the lobby has leather furniture, antique bronze lamps, and handsome *alerce* and *raulí* (native wood) trims. Rooms, painted in ash-blue and cream tones, have hardwood floors and lofty ceilings. The hotel has hosted Nobel laureates Pablo Neruda and Gabriela Mistral, and former president Salvador Allende. The restaurant ($$) serves delicious French cuisine. Good choices include the steak au poivre and the salade niçoise. **Pros:** A hotel with character; good location, great food. **Cons:** Rooms feel cold and damp, old furniture. ✉ *Antonio Varas 708* ☎ *45/238–973* 🖷 *45/233–830* ⊕ *www.turismochile.cl/continental/* ⇄ *40 rooms, 20 with bath* ♿ *In-room: no a/c, no TV (some). In-hotel: restaurant, bar, no elevator, parking* 🖃 *AE, DC, MC, V* ⦿*CP.*

7

$$ ✕▦**Hotel Frontera.** This lovely old hotel is really two in one, with *nuevo* (new) and *clásico* (classic) wings facing each other across Avenida Bulnes. Tastefully decorated rooms have double-pane windows to keep out the street noise. Opt for the less expensive rooms in the newer wing—they're nicer anyway. La Taberna, the downstairs restaurant on the clásico side ($$), has excellent steak and seafood dining. An orchestra plays and people dance on weekends. **Pros:** Centrally located, good restaurant, nice rooms: **Cons:** No Wi-Fi in rooms. ⊠*Av. Bulnes 733–726* ☎*45/200–400* 🖷*45/200–401* ⊕*www.hotelfrontera.cl* ⬍*90 rooms, 10 suites* ♿*In-room: no a/c, ethernet (some), refrigerator, safe (some). In-hotel: restaurant, room service, bar, laundry service, refrigerator, executive floor, public Wi-Fi, parking* ▭*AE, DC, MC, V* ⏴◍⏵*BP.*

$$–$$$ ▦**Hotel Terraverde.** Temuco's most luxurious lodging combines all the comforts of a modern hotel with the style of a hunting lodge. The dramatic, glass-enclosed spiral staircase leads off the stone-wall lobby with its huge fireplace and has a view of Cerro Ñielol. Cheerful rooms have lovely wood furnishings. Rates include a huge breakfast buffet, a nice change from the roll and coffee served at many other lodgings in the region. It's part of Chile's Panamericana Hoteles chain. **Pros:** Breakfast buffet, luxurious feeling. **Cons:** Lacks intimacy of smaller hotels. ⊠*Av. Arturo Prat 220* ☎*45/239–999, 2/234–9610 in Santiago* 🖷*45/239–455, 2/234–9608 in Santiago* ⊕*www.panamericanahoteles. cl* ⬍*64 rooms, 6 suites* ♿*In-room: no a/c, safe, refrigerator, ethernet, Wi-Fi. In-hotel: restaurant, room service, bar, pool, laundry service, public Internet, airport shuttle, no-smoking rooms, parking* ▭*AE, DC, MC, V* ⏴◍⏵*BP.*

$ ▦**Hotel Turismo.** Originally established as a budget accommodation, this three-story hotel retains its bland facade. The interior has been upgraded, however, with a comfortable lobby and rooms with their own music systems, cushy beds, and tables and chairs. A lime-green color scheme dominates throughout. **Pros:** Comfortable, nice beds. **Cons:** Lime-green color scheme. ⊠*Av. Lynch 563* ☎☎*45/951–090* ⊕*www.hotelturismotemuco.cl* ⬍*30 rooms* ♿*In-room: no a/c, safe, refrigerator. In-hotel: restaurant, bar, laundry service, parking, public-Wi-Fi* ▭*AE, DC, MC, V.*

NIGHTLIFE

Temuco is a city with several universities, and as such has a thriving nightlife. **Geronimo** (⊠*Antonio Varas 983* ☎*45/230–041*) is in the center of the city, and has live music mostly oriented toward young adults. **Taberna del Bucanero** (⊠*Bulnes 315* ☎*45/214–468*), a pub and disco with a pirate theme, features especially good mixed drinks.**Jalisco Tex-Mex** (⊠*Hochstetter 435* ☎*45/243–254*) is a pub-restaurant with Mexican food and lively margaritas.

SPORTS & THE OUTDOORS

CONAF (⊠*Bilbao 931* ☎*45/298–100*) administers Chile's national parks and provides maps and other information about them. In summer it also organizes hikes in Parque Nacional Conguillío. The agency is strict about permits to ascend the nearby volcanoes, so expect to show evidence of your climbing ability and experience.

SHOPPING

Temuco is ground central for the Mapuche Nation. Here you will find the gamut of Mapuche Indian handicrafts, from carpets to sweaters to sculpture. The **Mercado Municipal** (✉*Manuel Rodríguez 960* ☎*No phone*) is one of the best places in the country to find Mapuche woolen ponchos, pullovers, and blankets. The interior of the 1930 structure has been extensively remodeled, and is quite open and airy. The low-key artisan vendors share the complex with butchers, fishmongers, and fruit sellers. There is no bargaining, but the prices are fair. It opens daily at 8, but closes around 3 on Sunday.

A little more rough-and-tumble than the Mercado Municipal is the **Feria Libre** (✉*Barros Arana at Miraflores*). You can bargain hard with the Mapuche vendors who sell their crafts and produce in the blocks surrounding the railroad station and bus terminal. Leave the camera behind, as the vendors aren't happy about being photographed. It's open from about 7 to 2 Monday–Saturday.

Casa de la Mujer Mapuche (✉*Portales 1190* ☎*45/233–886*), an indigenous women's center, lets you shop for textiles, ponchos, and jewelry in its display room, with a minimum of fuss. (The organization even handles catalog sales.) Proceeds support social development programs. It's open weekdays, 9–1.

Across the Río Cautín from Temuco is the suburb of **Padre Las Casas** (✉*2 km [1 mi] southeast of Temuco*), a Mapuche community whose center is populated by artisan vendors selling locally crafted woodwork, textiles, and pottery under the auspices of the town's rural development program. You can purchase crafts here weekdays 9–5. **Farmacia Herbolaria Mapuche Makewelawen** (✉*Aldunate 245* ☎*45/951–620*) offers ancestral Mapuche remedies for everything from a simple head cold to cancers to improving sexual performance.

PARQUE NACIONAL CONGUILLÍO

126 km (78 mi) northeast of Temuco.

Volcán Llaima, which erupted as recently as 1994 and has shown constant, but not dangerous, low levels of activity since 2002, is the brooding centerpiece of Parque Nacional Conguillío. The 3,125-meter (10,200-foot) monster, one of the continent's most active volcanoes, has altered the landscape—much of the park's southern portion is a moonscape of hardened lava flow. But in the 610-square-km (235-square-mi) park's northern sector there are thousands of umbrella-like araucaria pines, also known as monkey puzzle trees.

The Sierra Nevada trail is the most popular for short hikes. The three-hour trek begins at park headquarters on Laguna Conguillío, continuing northeast to Laguna Captrén. One of the inaugural sections of the Sendero de Chile, a hiking and biking trail, passes through the park. Modeled on the Appalachian Trail in the United States, the project will eventually span the length of the country. Completion is expected around 2010.

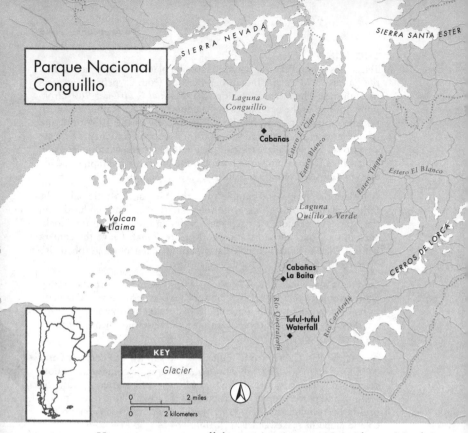

Parque Nacional
Conguillio

SIERRA NEVADA

SIERRA SANTA ESTER

*Laguna
Conguillío*

◆ **Cabañas**

Estero El Claro

Estero Blanco

Estero Tiuque

Estero El Blanco

**Volcan
Llaima** ▲

*Laguna
Quililo o Verde*

CERROS DE LORCA

**Cabañas
La Baita** ◆

Río Carrileufú

Río Quetralquín

**Tuful-tuful
Waterfall** ◆

KEY
⌇⌇⌇ *Glacier*

0   2 miles
0   2 kilometers

Heavy snow can cut off the area in winter, so November to March is
the best time to visit the park's eastern sector. Conguillío's western sector, Los Paraguas, comes into its own in winter because of a small ski
center. ⊠*Entrances at Melipeuco and Curacautín* ☎*45/736–200 in
Temuco* ⊠*2,500 pesos* ☉*Dec.–Mar., daily 8 AM–10 PM; Apr.–Nov.,
daily 8–5.*

GETTING HERE & AROUND
About 126 km (78 mi) northeast of Temuco, the roads are paved until
the town of Curacautin; from there it's 40 km (25 mi) on gravel and
dirt roads to the Conguillío Park. The roads are marked with signs
leading to the park.

WHERE TO STAY
$–$$ 🏨 **Cabañas Conguillío.** Close to the park, this property rents basic four-
person cabins built around the trunks of araucaria trees. All come
with kitchen utensils, stoves, and cooking fuel. Also here are an on-site
restaurant and a small store where you can stock up on provisions.
Pros: Close to park. **Cons:** Closed most of year. ⊠*Laguna Conguillío*
☎*45/581–253* 🛏*6 cabins* ♿*In-room: no a/c, no phone, no TV. In-
hotel: restaurant, parking.* ▭*No credit cards* ☉*Closed Apr.–Nov.*

VILLARRICA

87 km (52 mi) southeast of Temuco via the Pan-American Hwy. and a paved road southeast from Freire.

Villarrica was founded in 1552, but the Mapuche wars prevented extensive settlement of the area until the early 20th century. Founded by the Spanish conqueror Pedro de Valdivia, it was a Spanish fortress built primarily to serve as a base for gold mining in the area. The fortress's mission succeeded up until 1599, when the Mapuche staged an uprising here and destroyed the original town. On December 31, 1882, a historic meeting between more than 300 Mapuche chiefs and the Chilean government was held in Putue, a few kilometers outside of the town. The next day, the town was re-founded. Today this pleasant town of about 40,000 people, situated on the lake of the same name, is in one of the loveliest, least-spoiled areas of the southern Andes, and has stunning views of the Villarrica and Llaima volcanoes. To Villarrica's eternal chagrin, it lives in the shadow of Pucón, a flashier neighbor several miles down the road. Many travelers drive through without giving Villarrica a glance, but they're missing out. Villarrica has some wonderful hotels that won't give you a case of high-season sticker shock. Well-maintained roads and convenient public transportation make the town a good base for exploring the area.

GETTING HERE & AROUND

Located southeast of Temuco, Villarrica can be reached by a paved, two-lane road, from the town of Freire, or farther to the south, from Loncoche. Several bus lines serve the town. For about 2,000 pesos, buses leave every hour from the Temuco bus terminal and arrive in Villarrica about one hour later.

ESSENTIALS

Bus Contacts Buses JAC (✉ *Bilbao 610* ☎ *45/467–777*).

Currency Exchange Christopher Exchange (✉ *Pedro Valdivia 1033*). **Turcamb** (✉ *Camilo Henriquez 576*).

Internet Central de Llamadas (✉ *Camilo Henriquez 567* ☎ *45/413–640*).

Medical Asístanse Hospital (✉ *San Martin 460* ☎ *45/411–169*).

Rental Cars Hertz (✉ *Picarte 640* ☎ *45/218–316*). **Renta Car Castillo** (✉ *Anfion Munoz 415* ☎ *45/411–618*).

Visitor & Tour Info Villarrica Tourist Office (✉ *Pedro de Valdivia 1070* ☎ *45/206–618*).

EXPLORING

Feria Mapuche is a fine market featuring some of the best local artisans that make Mapuche handicrafts. You'll find all kinds of items, from sweaters and ponchos to wooden figurines. ✉ *Corner of Pedro de Valdivia with Julio Zebers.* ⊙ *Jan. and Feb., daily 9–noon.*

The municipal museum, **Museo Histórico y Arqueológico de Villarrica**, displays an impressive collection of Mapuche ceramics, masks, leather,

OUTDOOR ADVENTURES AT A GLANCE

Pucón. Located near a variety of lakes, rivers, forests, and parks, and just 20 minutes from the 2,847-meter-high (9,341-foot-high) Villarrica Volcano, Pucón is without doubt one of Chile's top spots for adventure sports. The (active) volcano itself has become an obligatory climb for the many nature- and adventure-seeking tourists who come to Chile. In winter, the volcano is a favorite spot for skiing and snowboarding. Nearby Trancura River is a rafting, kayaking, and fishing paradise. Villarrica Lake and Calburga Lake are two outstanding lakes for fishing, swimming, kayaking, and water-skiing. There are several worthy nature hikes close to Pucón, featuring some of the most beautiful forest in Chile, including the Cani Sanctuary, Huerquehue National Park, and Conguillo National Park.

Puerto Varas. This small, tranquil town on the edge of Lake Llanquihue in the southern Lake District is one of Chile's most popular destinations for adventure-sports enthusiasts. The lake itself frequently boasts strong winds suitable for first-class windsurfing and sailing. At Canopy Lodge of Cascadas, the largest canopy area in Chile, not far from Puerto Varas, you can zip-line through canyons and forest 70 meters (230 feet) high. The Petrohué River offers the opportunity for rafting, and along with numerous other rivers in the area, great fishing. Biking alongside the lake is a popular trip, too. Vicente Pérez Rosales Park and Alerce Andino Park have good trails for hiking and camping. And there is the Osorno Volcano for treks, skiing, and snowboarding. Some two hours from Puerto Varas is Cochamó Valley, a fantastic spot that

has drawn comparisons to Yosemite Park in California for its high granite mountain cliffs, waterfalls, and overall landscape. This is a rock-climbing paradise and a hiker's dream, with exceptional horseback-riding trails, too. Just south from Cochamó is Puelo, a river valley in the shadow of the Andes mountains. It's the launching point for some of Chile's best fly fishing, in addition to great hiking and other outdoors action.

Valdivia. A complex network of 14 rivers cuts through the landscape in and around this southern Chilean city, forming dozens of small islands. About 160 km (99 mi) of the river system are navigable in waters ranging from 5 to 20 meters (16½ to 66 feet) deep. That makes ideal territory for kayaking, canoeing, and sailing, among other water sports. Valdivia is also near the Pacific coast. Curinanco beach, 25 km (15½ mi) from Valdivia, is considered a prime spot for fishing. Then there are the intact coastal temperate rainforests on the outskirts of town, secluded areas with beautiful scenery for long hikes and camping trips. At the private nature park Oncol, just 22 km (14 mi) from Valdivia, are hiking trails and an 870-meter (2,854-foot) treetop canopy course.

Osorno. Osorno itself is no outdoor wonder, but within an hour's drive you can reach Puyehue National Park, one of Chile's best hiking areas, and several lakes for fishing and boating, such as Rupanco. To the west, there is horseback riding, fishing, and hiking along the Pacific coast and at the indigenous network of parks Mapu Lahual, which is managed by Huilluiche Indian communities.

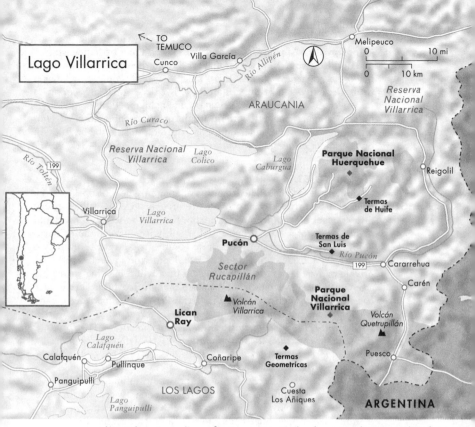

Lago Villarrica

TO TEMUCO

Cunco Villa García Río Allipén Melipeuco

0 _____ 10 mi
0 _____ 10 km

ARAUCANIA

Río Curaco

Reserva Nacional Villarrica Lago Colico Lago Caburgua

Reserva Nacional Villarrica

Parque Nacional Huerquehue

Reigolil

Río Toltén 199

Termas de Huife

Villarrica Lago Villarrica

Pucón

Termas de San Luis

Río Pucón 199 Cararrehue

Sector Rucapillán

Carén

Volcán Villarrica

Parque Nacional Villarrica

Lican Ray

Volcán Quetrupillán

Lago Calafquén

Coñaripe

Termas Geométricas

Puesco

Calafquén Pullinque

Panguipulli

LOS LAGOS

Cuesta Los Añiques

ARGENTINA

Lago Panguipulli

and jewelry. A replica of a *ruca* graces the front yard. It's made of thatch so tightly entwined that it's impermeable to rain. ✉ *Pedro de Valdivia 1050* ☎ *45/415–706* 💲*200 pesos* ◷ *Jan. and Feb., Mon.–Sat. 9–1 and 6–10; Mar.–Dec., Mon.–Sat. 9–1 and 3–7:30.*

WHERE TO EAT

$$ ✗ **Café 2001.** For a filling sandwich, a homemade küchen, and an espresso or cappuccino brewed from freshly ground beans, this is the place to stop in Villarrica. Pull up around a table in front or slip into one of the quieter booths by the fireplace in the back. The *lomito completo* sandwich—with a slice of pork, avocado, sauerkraut, tomato, and mayonnaise—is one of the best in the south. ✉ *Camillo Henríquez 379* ☎ *45/411–470* ▭ *AE, DC, MC, V.*

$$ ✗ **La Cava de Roble.** This is a great, elegant grill with exotic and traditional types of meat and an extensive wine list. One standout dish: deer in cranberry sauce, with quinoa, toasted almonds, cabbage, and spinach. ✉ *Valentin Letelier 658* ☎ *45/416–446* ▭ *AE, DC, MC, V.*

$ ✗ **El Rey de Marisco.** You'll find friendly service and assorted seafood dishes here, such as trout and clams with Parmesan cheese. If you can, call ahead of time to reserve a table with a view of the lake. ✉ *Valentin Letelier 1030* ☎ *45/412–093* ▭ *AE, DC, MC, V.*

$ ✕**The Travellers.** Martin Golian and Juan Pereira met by happenstance, and decided to open a place serving food from their homelands—and a few other countries. The result is a place that serves one or two dishes from Germany, Thailand, China, Italy, Mexico, and many countries in between. While you chow down on an enchilada, your companions might be having spaghetti with meatballs or sweet-and-sour pork. Dining on the front lawn under umbrella-covered tables is the best option on a summer evening. ⊠ *Valentín Letelier 753* ☎*45/413–617* ⊟*AE, DC, MC, V.*

WHERE TO STAY

$$ 🏨**Hostería de la Colina.** The friendly American owners of this hostería,
Fodor's Choice Glen and Beverly Aldrich, provide attentive service as well as special
★ little touches like homemade ice cream. Rooms in the half-century-old main house are a mix of large and small, with carpets and/or hardwood floors, all tastefully decorated with wood furnishings. Two bright, airy hillside cottages are carpeted and wood paneled and have private patios. There's a hot tub heated by a wood-burning stove, and a serene *vivero* (greenhouse) and garden that attracts birds. The terrace has stupendous views of Lago Villarrica. **Pros:** Homemade ice cream, friendly service, ambience. **Cons:** No TV. ⊠ *Las Colinas 115, Casilla 382* 🏠🏠*45/411–503* ⊕*www.hosteriadelacolina.com* ⏎*10 rooms, 2 cabins* 🛏*In-room: no a/c, no phone, no TV. In-hotel: bar, restaurant, room service, water sports, bicycles, laundry service, public Wi-Fi, parking* ⊟*AE, DC, MC, V* �’❍|*BP.*

$$ 🏨**Hotel El Ciervo.** Villarrica's oldest hotel is an unimposing house on a quiet street, but inside are elegant details such as wrought-iron fixtures and wood-burning fireplaces. Spacious rooms, some with their own fireplaces, have huge beds and sparkling bathrooms. Just outside is a lovely pool and a secluded patio. Rates include an enormous German breakfast with loads of fruit, muesli, and fresh milk. El Ciervo also has all-inclusive seven-day tour packages. **Pros:** Spacious rooms. **Cons:** A bit plain. ⊠ *General Körner 241* ☎*45/411–215* 🏠*45/413–884* ⊕*www.hotelelciervo.cl* ⏎*13 rooms* 🛏*In-room: no a/c, Wi-Fi. In-hotel: restaurant, bar, room service, pool, laundry service, public Internet, public Wi-Fi, no elevator, parking, no-smoking rooms* ⊟*AE, DC, MC, V* �’❍|*BP.*

$$ 🏨**El Parque.** You can take in the commanding views of Lago Villarrica from just about anywhere at this 70-year-old, rustic and quaint retreat—the comfy lobby, the sitting area, the restaurant, or the warmly colored guest rooms. Eleven modern cabins amble down the hill to a private beach and dock. Each cabin, which accommodates two to eight people, comes with a kitchen, fireplace, and terrace. You are on your own here, but lots of personalized attention is yours for the asking. **Pros:** Views of lake, comfortable. **Cons:** Outside of main towns of Pucón and Villarrica. ⊠ *Camino Villarrica–Pucón, Km 2.5* ☎*45/411–120* 🏠*45/411–090* ⊕*www.hotelelparque.cl* ⏎*8 rooms, 10 cabins* 🛏*In-room: no a/c, Wi-Fi. In-hotel: restaurant, bar, room service, tennis court, pool, beachfront, laundry service, no elevator, public Wi-Fi, parking, no-smoking rooms* ⊟*AE, DC, MC, V* ❍|*BP.*

$$$$ 🏨 **Villarrica Park Lake Hotel.** This sumptuous old European spa with modern touches is the perfect mix of old-world plush and clean, uncluttered design. There's ample use of hardwood in the bright, spacious common area and the rooms—each with its own balcony and lake view—that descend down a hill toward Lago Villarrica. **Pros:** Lake view, upscale. **Cons:** Expensive, half way between Pucón and Villarrica. ✉*13 km (8 mi) east of Villarrica on the road to Pucón* 🕾*45/450–000, 2/207–7070 in Santiago* 🖷*45/450–202, 2/207–7020 in Santiago* ⊕*www.vplh.cl/* ⇌*70 rooms, 11 suites* ♿*In-room: safe, refrigerator, ethernet. In-hotel: restaurant, room service, bars, pools, gym, spa, beachfront, laundry service, public Internet, public Wi-Fi, airport shuttle, parking, no-smoking rooms* ▭*AE, DC, MC, V* ❢|*BP.*"

SPORTS & THE OUTDOORS

The friendly, knowledgeable folks at **Flor del Lago** (✉*Camino a Pedregoso, Km 9* 🕾*45/415–455* ⊕*www.flordellago.cl*) will take you on half- or full-day horseback-riding excursions in the forests surrounding Lago Villarrica.

PUCÓN

25 km (15 mi) east of Villarrica.

The resort town of Pucón, on the southern shore of Lago Villarrica, attracts all manner of Chileans young and old. By day, there are loads of outdoor activities in the area. The beach on Lago Villarrica feels like one of Chile's popular coastal beach havens near Viña del Mar. By night, the young people flock to the major nightspots and party 'til dawn. The older crowd has a large array of fine restaurants and trendy shops to visit. Pucón has many fans, though some lament the town's meteoric rise to fame. Still, this is the place to have fun all 24 hours of the day in southern Chile. Be warned, however, that accommodations are hard to come by in February, which is easily the busiest month. And outside of summer, December to March, most stores, restaurants, and pubs here close down.

With Volcán Villarrica looming south of town, a color-coded alert system on the Municipalidad (city hall) on Avenida Bernardo O'Higgins signals volcanic activity, and signs around town explain the colors' meanings: green—that's where the light almost always remains—signifies "normal activity," indicating steam being let off from the summit with sulfuric odors and constant, low-level rumblings; yellow and red indicate more dangerous levels of activity. Remember: the volcano sits 15 km (9 mi) away, and you'll be scarcely aware of any activity. Indeed, ascending the volcano is the area's most popular excursion.

GETTING HERE & AROUND

Pucón has only a small air strip 2 km (1 mi) outside of town for private planes, but the national airlines such as LAN and Sky fly regularly to Temuco. From Temuco, Buses JAC has frequent service to Pucón. Roads that connect Pucón to Ruta 5, the Pan-American Highway, are paved from both Loncoche and Freire. In Pucón, there are several taxis that can move you about but the town itself is small and in most cases you will just need your two feet.

ESSENTIALS

Bus Contacts JAC (✉ *corner of Palguin and Uruguay* ☎ *45/443–693*). **Tur-Bus** (✉ *Palguin 383* ☎ *45/481–870*).

Currency Exchange Banco BCI (✉ *Fresia 174*). **Banco Santander** (✉ *Av. Bernardo O'Higgins 308*).

Internet Unid@d G (✉ *Av. Bernardo O'Higgins 415* ☎ *45/444–918*).

Medical Asístanse Hospital San Francisco (✉ *Uruguay 325* ☎ *45/441–177*).

Post Office Correos de Chile (✉ *Fresia 183*).

Rental Cars Christopher Car (✉ *Bernardo O'Higgins 335* ☎ *45/449–013*). **Hertz** (✉ *Miguel Ansorena 123* ☎ *45/441–664*). **Pucon Rent A Car** (✉ *Av. Colo Colo 340* ☎ *45/443–052*).

Visitor & Tour Info Pucón Tourist Office (✉ *Av. Bernardo O'Higgins 483* ☎ *45/293–002*).

EXPLORING

Mapuche Museo. A small, private museum, it houses an array of Mapuche artifacts, including musical instruments, masks, rock sculptures, pipes, and other items representative of Mapuche culture and history. ✉ *Capoulican 243* ☎ *45/441–963* ⊕ *www.puconline.cl/museo* 🎫 *1,000 pesos* ⊗ *Jan. and Feb., daily 11–1 and 6–10; Mar.–Dec., daily 11–1 and 3–7.*

Termas Geometricas. Chile is volcano country, and around Pucón are numerous natural hot springs. This is one of the best. Seventeen natural hot-spring pools, many of them secluded, dot the dense native forest. Each thermal bath has its own private bathrooms, lockers, and deck. ✉ *3 km (2 mi south of Villarrica National Park* ☎ *9/7477–1708* ⊕ *www.termasgeometricas.cl* 🎫 *14,000 pesos* ⊗ *Jan. and Feb, daily 10–10; Mar.–Dec., daily 11–8.*

Parque Cuevas Volcanicas. After a short hike uphill, you'll find this cave half-way up Volcán Villarrica, right next to a very basic visitor center. The place first opened up in 1968 as a cave for spelunkers to explore, but eventually tourism proved more lucrative. A short tour takes you deep into the electrically illuminated cave via wooden walkways that bring you close to the crystallized basalt formations. Your tour guide may make occasional hokey references to witches and pumas hiding in the rocks, but it's definitely worth a visit—especially if uncooperative weather prevents you from partaking of the region's other attractions and activities. ✉ *Volcán Villarrica National Park* ⊕ *www.cuevas volcanicas.cl* 🎫 *12,000 pesos* ⊗ *Daily 10–7.*

WHERE TO EAT

$ ✕ **Arabian Restaurant.** The Apara family knows how to whip up tasty falafel or *shawarma* (a pita-bread sandwich filled with spicy beef or lamb). Most everyone opts for the outdoor tables over the tiny indoor dining area. ✉ *Fresia 354* ☎ *45/443–469* ▭ *No credit cards.*

Pucón

Lago
Villarrica

La Peninsula

Playa Grande

Clemente Holzapfel

Carlos Ansorena

Pasaja Luck

Pedro de Valdivia

Alderete

Mapuche
Museum

General Urrutia

O'Higgins

Caupolican

Lincoyan

Fresia

Miguel Ansorena

Palguin

Arauco

Colo Colo

Brasil

Chile

Uruguay

Paraguay

Peru

Ecuador

Peru

Sebastian Engler

Pacfic Nappe

Camino Internacional

TO ARGENTINA

TO VILLARRICA

Hotels ▼		Restaurants ▼	
Apart Hotel Del Volcán ... **14**	Hotel Huincahue **6**	Arabian Restaurant **10**	La Grilla **9**
¡école! **8**	Hotel Los Maitenes **13**	Cassis **5**	La Maga **4**
Gran Hotel Pucón **1**	Hotel Malalhue **18**	Empanadas y	Nau Kana **12**
Gudenschwager Hotel **3**	Kila Leufu **16**	Hamburguesas	¡Viva Perú! **11**
Hotel Antumalal **15**	La Casona de Pucon **2**	Lleu-Lleu **7**	
Hotel Huincahue **6**	Termas de San Luis **17**		

$ ✕**Cassis.** Formerly called the Patagonia Express, this is a wonderful café and restaurant. Fruit-filled pastries are baked fresh all day long and the coffee is good. The restaurant has a varied menu of sandwiches, pizza, and more with an extensive wine list. In summer, this is an especially great ice-cream stop—head for one of the tables outside on the sidewalk. This place also stays quite lively on summer nights until about 3 AM. ⊠*Pedro de Valdivia 333* ☎*45/444–715* ▭*AE, DC, MC, V.*

¢   ✕**Empanadas y Hamburguesas Lleu-Lleu.** This is the place in Pucón to eat Chile's famous empanadas, a sort of hot pastry filled with diverse ingredients. Try the vegetarian empanada. They also have good sandwiches. They are open every day from 10 AM to 7 AM, which makes it a popular destination for the late-night bar crowd. They can also deliver to your hotel. ⊠*520 General Urrutia* ▭*No credit cards.*

$$$ ✕**La Grilla.** The best seafood in Pucón is served here, so don't be frightened off by the nondescript dining room: basic wooden tables and the ubiquitous nautical theme. You'll receive a free welcoming pisco sour when you arrive. ⊠*Fresia at Urrutia* ☎*45/442–294* ▭*AE, DC, MC, V.*

$$$ ✕**La Maga.** Argentina claims to prepare the perfect parrillada, or grilled beef, but here's evidence that Uruguayans just might do it best. Watch the beef cuts or salmon turn slowly over the wood fire at the entrance. Wood, rather than charcoal, is the key, says the owner, Emiliano Villanil, a transplant from Punta del Este. The product is a wonderfully smoked, natural taste, accented with a hint of spice in the mild *chimichurri* (a tangy steak sauce). ⊠*Fresia 125* ☎*45/444–277* ▭*AE, DC, MC, V* ⊘*Closed Mon. Apr.–Dec.*

$$ ✕**Nau Kana.** Tired of the same ole Chilean food offerings? Come here to sample excellent dishes from Thailand, Japan, Vietnam, Indonesia, and Arabia. Try the Gary Ga, for example, a Vietnamese dish of curried chicken breast with basil, tomato, mushroom, and coconut milk over Arab rice. It's also a good place for cocktails. Open only at night, after 7:30 PM. ⊠*Fresia 236* ☎*45/444–677* ▭*AE, DC, MC, V.*

$$$ ✕**¡Viva Perú!** As befits the name, Peruvian cuisine reigns supreme at this restaurant with rustic wooden tables. Try the *ají de gallina* (hen stew with cheese, milk, and peppers) or the seviche, thoroughly cooked but served cold. You can dine on the porch, a nice option for a pleasant summer night—and take advantage of the two-for-one pisco sours nightly until 9 PM. You can also order to carry out. ⊠*Lincoyan 372* ☎*45/444–025* ▭*AE, DC, MC, V.*

WHERE TO STAY

$$–$$$$ 🏨 **Apart Hotel Del Volcán.** In keeping with the region's immigrant heritage, the furnishings of this chalet-style hotel look like they come straight from Germany. Checked fabrics cover carefully fluffed duvets in the guest apartments. Many of the generously proportioned apartments also have balconies. Each unit in this centrally located hotel sleeps up to six people. **Pros:** Kitchen, central location, large apartments. **Cons:** No restaurant. ⊠*Fresia 420* ☎*45/442–055* 🖷*45/442–053* ⊕*www.aparthoteldelvolcan.cl* ⬐*18 apartments* ⚷*In-room: no a/c, safe, kitchen, refrigerator, Wi-Fi. In-hotel: gym, concierge, parking (no fee), no-smoking rooms* ▭*AE, DC, MC, V* ⧡*BP.*

$$ ▣ **La Casona de Púcon.** In a beautiful, recently restored 1930s southern Chile-style mansion made entirely of native woods, this bed-and-breakfast opened in late 2007 and is set to become one of Pucón's best lodging options. The rooms are immaculate, tastefully decorated, and the common areas make you feel at home. Located on the town plaza, just a block from the beach, it's also a prestigious address. **Pros:** Homey feeling, tasteful decoration, on the plaza. **Cons:** No restaurant. ⊠ *Lincoyan 48* ☎ *45/443–179* ⊕ *www.lacasonadepucon.cl* ⤻ *11 rooms, 1 suite* ♿ *In-room: no a/c, safe, ethernet, Wi-Fi. In-hotel: no elevator, laundry service, public Wi-Fi, airport shuttle, parking, no-smoking rooms* ⊟ *AE, DC, MC, V* ⥲ *BP.*

$ ✕▣ **¡école!** It's part hostel and part beach house—and takes its name **Fodor'sChoice** from a Chilean expression meaning "Right on!" Cozy two-, three-, and ★ four-person rooms can be shared or private. The vegetarian restaurant ($), a rarity in the Lake District, merits a trip in itself. You can choose among truly international options, such as lasagna, burritos, and moussaka, and eat in the sunny courtyard or small dining room. The environmentally conscious staff can organize hiking and horseback-riding trips and expeditions to volcanoes and hot springs, as well as arrange for Spanish lessons and massages. **Pros:** Great food in restaurant, easy to meet other travelers, eco-conscious. **Cons:** Some rooms are noisy, toilets don't always work. ⊠ *General Urrutia 592* ☎☎ *45/441–675* ⊕ *www.ecole.cl* ⤻ *21 rooms, 9 with bath* ♿ *In-room: no a/c, no phone, no TV, Wi-Fi. In-hotel: restaurant, bar, public Wi-Fi, no-smoking rooms, no elevator* ⊟ *AE, DC, MC, V.*

$$$$ ▣ **Gran Hotel Pucón.** The outside of Pucón's largest hotel is quite *gran* and imposing in true alpine-lodge style. Its location right on the shore provides direct access to the beach. The rooms are scattered among three buildings, and although perfectly acceptable, they're disappointingly contemporary; the exterior gets your hopes up for something more old-world. Depending on which side of the buildings you are on, though, you do get stupendous views of either the lake or Volcán Villarrica. The hotel is enormously popular among Chileans who come here for the summer holiday, so you won't find much peace and quiet, especially in summer. **Pros:** Loaded with activities, good location. **Cons:** Noise, rooms aren't especially worth the price. ⊠ *Clemente Holzapfel 190* ☎ *45/913–300, 2/429–6100 in Santiago* ⊕ *www.gran hotelpucon.cl* ⤻ *274 rooms, 141 apartments, 14 suites* ♿ *In-room: no a/c, safe, kitchen (some), refrigerator (some). In-hotel: 2 restaurants, bar, room service, pools, gym, spa, beachfront, water sports, bicycles, children's programs, laundry service, concierge, public Internet, public Wi-Fi, airport shuttle, parking, no-smoking rooms* ⊟ *AE, DC, MC, V* ⥲ *BP, MAP.*

$$ ▣ **Gudenschwager Hotel.** The Chilean-born, Los Angeles–raised owner of this property, Pablo Guerra, has taken one of Pucón's oldest lodgings and given it a complete (and much appreciated) overhaul, stripping the paint and reexposing the original wood walls and the old radiators. They've placed queen beds in every room and installed little touches, such as safety rails in the bathtubs, which you rarely see in large hotels in Chile, let alone small inns of this size. They bill a few of the more

simply furnished rooms on the top floor as "backpacker" rooms, and they are a definite cut above Pucón's typical budget lodgings. Location is everything here: sitting on the peninsula that juts out into Lago Villarrica, the deck affords both lake and volcano views. **Pros:** Great location, rooms are good. **Cons:** No phone or TV. ⊠ *Pedro de Valdivia 12* 🕾 *45/442–025* 🖷 *45/442–326* ⊕ *www.hogu.cl* 🖅 *20 rooms* ⮜ *Inroom: no a/c, no phone, no TV. In-hotel: restaurant, bar, public Wi-Fi, no-smoking rooms* ▭ *AE, DC, MC, V* ⫟⊙⫟*BP.*

$$$$ 🏨 **Hotel Antumalal.** A young Queen Elizabeth stayed here in the 1950s,
★ as did actor Jimmy Stewart—and the Antumalal hasn't changed very much since. The decor, styles, and colors from that decade have all been maintained at this family-run hotel, which has the feel of a country inn. It's perched atop a cliff just outside town above Lago Villarrica, and its cozy rooms have fireplaces and huge windows overlooking the spectacularly landscaped grounds. If you tire of relaxing with a refreshing pisco sour on the wisteria-shaded deck, just ask owner Rony Pollak to arrange an adventure for you. Favorites include fly-fishing, whitewater rafting, and volcano climbing. **Pros:** Secluded location, fireplace in room, architecture of hotel. **Cons:** The hotel looks its age at times. ⊠ *Casilla 84* 🕾 *45/441–011* 🖷 *45/441–013* ⊕ *www.antumalal.com* 🖅 *15 rooms, 3 suites* ⮜ *In-room: no a/c, safe. In-hotel: restaurant, bar, room service, tennis courts, pool, gym, spa, beachfront, water sports, laundry service, public Internet, public Wi-Fi, airport shuttle, parking, no-smoking rooms, no elevator* ▭ *AE, DC, MC, V* ⫟⊙⫟*BP.*

$$$ 🏨 **Hotel Huincahue.** In a town whose motto could be "Bigger is better" when it comes to lodging, the elegant Huincahue is a refreshing find. The German-style hotel sits close to the center of town on the main plaza. Lots of windows brighten the lobby and library, which is warmed by a roaring fire. Bright, airy rooms come furnished with wrought-iron and blond-wood furniture. Rooms on the second floor have small balconies. Rates include a hearty American breakfast. **Pros:** Location next to plaza, breakfasts. **Cons:** Steep price for what you get. ⊠ *Pedro de Valdivia 375* 🕾 *45/443–540* 🖷 *45/442–728* 🖅 *20 rooms* ⮜ *In-room: no a/c, safe. In-hotel: bar, pool, public Wi-Fi, laundry service, parking, no-smoking rooms* ▭ *AE, DC, MC, V* ⫟⊙⫟*BP.*

$$ 🏨 **Hotel Los Maitenes.** Situated in the center of Pucón, on the most important street for shopping and eating, this is a good quality option. Rooms are clean and comfortable, with pleasantly decorated fresh pine-wood walls, bright colored bed covers, and colorful paintings. Some rooms have good views. Room 11 is slightly bigger, and the best of the lot. **Pros:** Central location. **Cons:** Some rooms on the small side. ⊠ *Fresia 354* 🕾 *45/441–820* ⊕ *www.hotelmaitenes.cl* 🖅 *11 rooms* ⮜ *In-room: no a/c, no phone, safe, Wi-Fi. In-hotel: room service, no elevator, public Wi-Fi, parking, no-smoking rooms* ▭ *V, MC, AE, DC.*

$$ 🏨 **Hotel Malalhue.** Dark wood and volcanic rock were used in building
Fodor's Choice this hotel at the edge of Pucón on the road to Calburga. It's about a 15-
★ minute walk from the hubbub of downtown, but Malalhue's many fans see that as a selling point. The cozy sitting room just off the lobby with fireplace and couches is so inviting you may want to linger there for hours. But the guest rooms, with their plush comforters and pillows,

beckon, too. The top-floor "superior" rooms under the gables are more spacious and contain vaulted ceilings; they're a few thousand pesos more than the "standard" rooms, which are perfectly acceptable in their own right and in the same style as the "superiors," though smaller. **Pros:** Rooms are comfortable, sitting room. **Cons:** 15-minute walk to town. ✉ *Camino Internacional 1615* ☎ *45/443–130* 🖷 *45/443–132* ⊕ *www.malalhue.cl* ⬙ *24 rooms* ⚿ *In-room: no a/c, safe. In-hotel: bar, restaurant, room service, laundry service, public Internet, public Wi-Fi, no-smoking rooms, parking, no elevator* ▭ *AE, DC, MC, V* ⏃ *BP.*

$ ☷ **Kila Leufu and Ruka Rayen.** As part of a growing agro-tourism trend in Chile, a Mapuche family has opened up two guest houses in the countryside, 15 minutes from Pucón. Kila Leufu provides an authentic glimpse at Mapuche farming life, complete with authentic Mapuche cooking. Here, you can bake bread and milk the cows if you like, or just relax and read. Ruka Rayen, a second guest house next to Palguin River, which is a hot kayaking spot, is run by a Mapuche woman and her Austrian husband. They speak English and a number of other languages and provide not just comfortable lodging but an array of outdoor adventure activities, from horseback rides to hot-springs visits to treks in local nature areas. **Pros:** Mapuche influence, countryside location. **Cons:** No TV, outside of Pucón. ✉ *Camino a Curarrehe, Puente Cabedane* ☎ *09/711–8064* ⊕ *www.kilaleufu.cl* ⬙ *11 rooms, 5 with bath* ⚿ *In-room: no a/c, no phone, no TV. In hotel: bicycles, water sports, parking, laundry service* ▭ *No credit cards* ⏃ *FAP.*

$$$ ☷ **Termas de San Luis.** The famous San Luis hot springs are the main attraction of this hideaway east of Pucón. Here you can rent a rustic cabin that sleeps up to six people. Rates include the option of all or some meals—cabins are not kitchen equipped—and free use of the baths. If you're not staying, 5,500 pesos gets you a day of soaking in the thermal springs and mud baths. **Pros:** Access to hot springs. **Cons:** Distance from Pucón. ✉ *Carretera Internacional, Km 27, Catripulli* ☎🖷 *45/412–880* ⊕ *www.termasdesanluis.cl* ⬙ *6 cabins* ⚿ *In-room: no a/c. In-hotel: 2 restaurants, bar, pools, children's programs, no elevator* ▭ *No credit cards* ⏃ *BP, FAP, MAP.*

NIGHTLIFE

Pucón has a fantastic nightlife in summer. There are several bars south of Avenida Bernardo O'Higgins. But a local favorite is the friendly **Mamas & Tapas** (✉ *Av. Bernardo O'Higgins 597* ☎ *45/449–002*). It's de rigueur among the expat crowd. Light Mexican dining morphs into DJ-generated or live music lasting into the wee hours. Across the street from Mamas & Tapas is the equally welcoming **Bar Esquina** (✉ *Av. Bernardo O'Higgins 630* ☎ *45/441–070*), a popular bar for drinks, food, and dancing. A few kilometers outside of town is the large, fun discotheque **Fire** (✉ *Camino a la Balsa s/n* ☎ *9/275–5362*).

SPORTS & THE OUTDOORS

At first glance Pucón's myriad outfitters look the same and sell the same slate of activities and rentals; quality varies, however. The firms listed below get high marks for safety, professionalism, and friendly service. Although a given outfitter might have a specialty, it usually offers other activities as well. Pucón is the center for rafting expeditions in the northern Lake District, with Río Trancura just 15 minutes away, making for easy half-day excursions on Class III–V rapids.

Friendly, French-owned **Aguaventura** (✉ *Palguín 336* ☎ *45/444–246* ⊕ *www.aguaventura.com*) outfits for rafting, as well as canoeing, kayaking, snowshoeing, and snowboarding. They specialize in trekking up the volcano for a ski descent, although you should be an expert skier if you want to join them. Alex Goly, an accomplished guide to all of Chile, works with Aguaventura and can take you on informative natural history and geography climbs in the area.

Anden Sport (✉ *Av. Bernardo O'Higgins 535* ☎ *45/441–574*) is a good bet for bikes, snowboards, snowshoes, and skis.

Huepil Malal (✉ *Km 27, Carretera a Huife* ☎ *09/643–2673 or 09/643–3204* ⊕ *www.huepil-malal.cl*) arranges horseback riding in the nearby Cañi mountains, with everything from half-day to six-day excursions.

Politur (✉ *Av. Bernardo O'Higgins 635* ☎ *445/441–373* ⊕ *www.politur.com*) can take you rafting on the Río Trancura, trekking in nearby Parque Nacional Huerquehue, on ascents of the Volcán Villarrica, and skydiving.

★ **Sol Y Nieve** (✉ *Av. Bernardo O'Higgins and Lincoyan* ☎☎ *45/463–860*) runs rafting trips and hiking and skiing expeditions. It takes groups up Villarrica Volcano.

PARQUE NACIONAL HUERQUEHUE

35 km (21 mi) northeast of Pucón.

Unless you have a four-wheel-drive vehicle, this 124-square-km (48-square-mi) park is accessible only in summer. (And even then, a jeep isn't a bad idea.) It's worth a visit for the two-hour hike on the Lago Verde trail beginning at the ranger station near the park entrance. You head up into the Andes through groves of araucaria pines, eventually reaching three startlingly blue lagoons with panoramic views of the whole area, including distant Volcán Villarrica. ☎ *45/298–221 in Temuco* 💰 *2,200 pesos* 🕙 *Dec.–Mar., daily 8* AM*–10* PM*; Apr.–Nov., daily 8–6.*

WHERE TO STAY

$$$$ 🍴 **Termas de Huife.** Just outside Parque Nacional Huerquehue, this resort lets you relax in three steaming pools set beside an icy mountain stream. At the spa you can enjoy an individual bath, a massage, or both. The complex includes a handful of luxurious cabins, all of which have enormous tubs you can fill with water from the hot springs. Those just visiting for the day—hours are 9 AM–10 PM—pay 9,500 pesos for entry. If you lack your own wheels, the office in Pucón offers twice-daily shuttle service for 14,000 pesos round-trip. There's also a country house past the spa where you can soak in privacy. **Pros:** Access to hot springs and park. **Cons:** Price is steep. ✉ *33 km (20 mi) from Pucón on the road to Caburga* ☎☎ *45/197–5666* ⊕ *www.termashuife.cl* 🛏 *11*

cabins ☼*In-room: no a/c, safe, refrigerator. In-hotel: restaurant, bar, pool, spa, parking, no elevator* ☰*AE, DC, MC, V* ⊧◯⫿*BP.*

PARQUE NACIONAL VILLARRICA

Fodor'sChoice
★

15 km (9 mi) south of Pucón.

One of Chile's most popular national parks, Parque Nacional Villarrica has skiing, hiking, and many other outdoor activities. The main draw, however, is the volcano that gives the 610-square-km (235-square-mi) national park its name. You don't need to have any climbing experience to reach Volcán Villarrica's 3,116-meter (9,350-foot) summit, but a guide is a good idea. The volcano sits in the park's Sector Rucapillán, a Mapuche word meaning "house of the devil." That name is apt, as the perpetually smoldering volcano is one of South America's most active. CONAF closes off access to the trails at the slightest hint of volcanic activity they deem to be out of the ordinary. It's a steep uphill walk to the snow line, but doable any time of year. All equipment will be supplied by any of the Pucón outfitters that organize daylong excursions for about 30,000 pesos per person. Your reward for the six-hour climb is the rare sight of an active crater, which continues to release clouds of sulfur gases and explosions of lava. You're also treated to superb views of the nearby volcanoes, the less-visited Quetrupillán and Lanín. ⊠*15 km (9 mi) south of Pucón* ☎*45/298–221 in Temuco* ⊡*1,100 pesos* ◷*Daily 8–6.*

7

WHERE TO STAY

$ ⌂**Volcán Villarrica.** This camping area run by CONAF is in the midst of a forest of *coigüe,* Chile's massive red oaks. The site charges 8,800 pesos per person and provides very basic toilets. ⊠*Sector Rucapillán* ☎*45/298–221 in Temuco* ☰*No credit cards.*

SKIING

The popular **Ski Pucón** (⊠*Parque Nacional Villarrica* ☎*45/441–901* ⊕*www.skipucon.cl*), in the lap of Volcán Villarrica, is one of the best-equipped ski areas in southern Chile, with 20 runs for varying levels of experience, nine rope tows, three double-chair tows, and equipment rental. The facility offers snowboarding, too. The ski season usually begins early July and can sometimes run through mid-October. High-season rates run 18,000 pesos per day; 15,000 pesos per half day. There are also a restaurant, coffee shop, boutique shop for various skiing accessories, and skiing and snowboard classes. Information about the facility can also be obtained from the Gran Hotel Pucón.

LICAN RAY

30 km (18 mi) south of Villarrica.

In the Mapuche language, Lican Ray means "flower among the stones." This pleasant, unhurried little resort town of just 1,688 inhabitants is on Lago Calafquén, the first of a chain of seven lakes that spills over into Argentina. You can rent rowboats and sailboats along the shore, which is also a fine spot to soak up sun. It must be admitted that Lican Ray is not as perfectly manicured as Pucón. With but one paved street, a lot of dust gets kicked up on a dry summer day.

GETTING HERE & AROUND

You can reach Lican Ray via the paved Ruta 199 from Temuco and Villarrica. From Valdivia and points south, take Ruta 203 to Panguipulli, then travel on dirt and gravel roads north to Lican Ray. There is daily and frequent bus service to the town from nearby locales such as Villarrica.

ESSENTIALS

Visitor & Tour Info Lican Ray Tourist Office (⊠ *General Urrutia 310* ☎ *45/431–201*).

WHERE TO EAT

$$$ ✕ **Cábala Restaurant.** Impeccable service is the hallmark of this Italian restaurant on Lican Ray's main street. The brick-and-log building has plenty of windows so you can watch the summer crowds stroll by as you enjoy pizza and pasta. ⊠ *General Urrutia 201* ☎ *45/431–176* ▤ *AE, DC, MC, V* ⊘ *Closed Apr.–Nov.*

$$ ✕ **The Ñaños.** Hearty meats and stews are the offerings at Lican Ray's most popular eatery. Most people partake of cazuela or pastel de choclo on the plain covered terrace on the main street, but the wood-trimmed dining room is a lot cozier, especially if the place is doing one of its trout fries on a summer evening. ⊠ *General Urrutia 105* ☎ *45/431–021* ▤ *DC, MC, V.*

WHERE TO STAY

$ 🛏 **Hostal Hoffman.** Owner Maria Hoffman keeps attentive watch over this little house just outside town. You can get lost in the plush chairs as you read a book in the sitting room. Equally plush and comfy are the bright, airy rooms with lots of pillows and thick, colorful quilts on the beds. Rates include a huge breakfast with lots of homemade breads and pastries. **Pros:** Comfy rooms, breakfast. **Con:** Small. ⊠ *Camino a Coñaripe 100* ☎ *45/431–109* ⌖ *5 rooms* ⌂ *In-room: no a/c, no phone, dial-up. In-hotel: café, laundry service, public Internet, parking* ▤ *No credit cards* ⊘*BP.*

$ 🛏 **Hotel Inaltulafquen.** This rambling old house sits in a garden on a quiet street fronting Playa Grande. The rooms are simple, but bright and airy and filled with plants. The cozy restaurant serves Chilean dishes. There's soft music playing in the background, but someone is bound to sit down at the piano and encourage the crowd to sing along. **Pro:** Restaurant. **Con:** A bit quiet. ⊠ *Punulef 510* ☎ *45/431–115* ⌖ *6 rooms, 2 with bath* ⌂ *In-room: no a/c, no phone, no TV (some). In-hotel: restaurant, bar, laundry service, no elevator* ▤ *DC, MC, V* ⊘*BP.*

BEACHES

The peninsula on which Lican Ray sits has two gray-sand beaches. **Playa Chica,** the smaller of the beaches near Lican Ray, is south of town. It's popular for swimming. **Playa Grande** stretches along a few blocks on the west side of Lican Ray and has choppy water. Swimming is best avoided here.

LOS LAGOS

Some of Chile's oldest cities are in Los Lagos, yet you may be disappointed if you come looking for colonial grandeur. For a region so conscious of its heritage, history is not much in evidence. Wars with indigenous peoples kept the Spaniards, then Chileans, from building here for 300 years. An earthquake of magnitude 9.5, the largest recorded in history, was centered near Valdivia and rocked the region on May 22, 1960. It destroyed many older buildings in the region and produced a tsunami felt as far away as Japan.

Eager to fill its *tierras baldías* (uncultivated lands) in the 19th century, Chile worked tirelessly to promote the country's virtues to German, Austrian, and Swiss immigrants looking to start a new life. The newcomers quickly set up shop, constructing breweries, foundries, shipyards, and lumberyards. By the early part of the 20th century, Valdivia had become the country's foremost industrial center, aided in large part by the construction of a railroad from Santiago. To this day the region retains a distinctly Germanic flair, and you might swear you've taken a wrong turn to Bavaria when you pull into towns such as Frutillar or Puerto Octay.

VALDIVIA

120 km (72 mi) southwest of Villarrica.

If you have time for just one of the Lake District's four hub cities, make it Valdivia. The city gracefully combines Chilean wood-shingle construction with the architectural style of the well-to-do German settlers who colonized the area in the late 1800s. But the historic appearance is a bit of an illusion, as the 1960 earthquake destroyed all but a few old riverfront structures. The city painstakingly rebuilt its downtown area, seamlessly mixing old and new buildings. Today you can enjoy evening strolls through its quaint streets and along its two rivers, the Valdivia and the Calle Calle.

Various tour boats leave from the docks at Muelle Schuster along the Río Valdivia for a one-hour tour around nearby Isla Teja. Expect to pay about 3,000 pesos. If you have more time, a five-hour excursion takes you to Niebla near the coast for a visit to the colonial-era forts. A four-hour tour north transports you to Puncapa, the site of a 16th-century Jesuit church and a nature sanctuary at San Luis de Alba de Cruces. Most companies charge 10,000–12,000 pesos for either of the longer tours. Each tour company offers all three excursions daily during the December–March high season, and you can always sign on to one at the last minute. Most will not operate tours for fewer than 15 passengers, however, which makes things a bit iffy during the rest of the year.

GETTING HERE & AROUND

Like most other major cities in the Lakes District, Valdivia is served by Ruta 5, the Pan-American Highway. The city also has an airport with

frequent flights by national airlines such as LAN, and the nation's bus lines regularly stop here as well. Valdivia's bus terminal is located by the river at the cross section of Munoz and Prat. Some outlying towns and sites around Valdivia you may want to visit, however, are only connected by dirt roads.

ESSENTIALS

Bus Contacts Buses JAC (✉ *Anfión Muñoz 360* ☎ *63/333–343*). **Cruz del Sur** (✉ *Anfión Muñoz 360* ☎ *63/213–840*). **Valdivia Bus Depot** (✉ *Anfión Muñoz 360* ☎ *63/212–212*).

Currency Exchange Arauco (✉ *Galeria Arauco, Local 24*). **Banco Santander** (✉ *Pérez Rosales 505*). **Corp Banca** (✉ *Picarte 370*).

Internet Café Phonet (✉ *Libertad 127* ☎ *63/341–054*). **Centro Internet Libertad** (✉ *Libertad 7*).

Medical Asístanse Farmacias Ahumada (✉ *Av. Ramón Picarte 310* ☎ *63/257–889*). **Hospital Regional Valdivia** (✉ *Simpson 850* ☎ *63/297–000*).

Post Office Correos de Chile (✉ *Av. Bernardo O'Higgins 575*).

Rental Cars Assef y Mendez (✉ *General Lagos 1335* ☎ *63/213–205*). **Autovald** (✉ *Vicente Pérez Rosales 660* ☎ *63/212–786*). **Avis** (✉ *Beauchef 619* ☎ *63/278–455*). **Budget** (✉ *Picarte 1348* ☎ *63/340–060*).

Visitor & Tour Info Sernatur (✉ *Av. Arturo Prat 555* ☎ *63/213–596*).**Valdivia Tourist Office** (✉ *Terminal de Buses, Anfión Muñoz 360* ☎ *63/212–212*).

EXPLORING

❶ Valdivia's imposing modern **Catedral de Nuestra Señora del Rosario** faces the west side of the central plaza. A small museum inside documents the evangelization of the region's indigenous peoples from the 16th through 19th centuries. ✉ *Independencia 514* ☎ *63/232–040* 💲 *Free* ⊙ *Masses: weekdays 7 AM and noon, Sat. 8 AM and 7 PM, Sun. 10:30 AM, noon, and 7 PM; museum: Dec.–Mar., Tues.–Sun. 10–1 and 3–7; Apr.–Nov., Tues.–Fri. 10–1 and 3–7.*

❸ The awning-covered **Mercado Fluvial,** in the southern shadow of the bridge leading to Isla Teja, is a perfect place to soak up the atmosphere of a real fish market. Vendors set up early in the morning; you hear the thwack of fresh trout and the clatter of oyster shells as they're piled on the side of the market's boardwalk fronting the river. If the sights, sounds, and smells are too much for you, fruit and vegetable vendors line the other side of the walkway opposite the river. ✉ *Av. Arturo Prat at Libertad* ☎ *No phone* ⊙ *Mon.–Sat. 8–3.*

❷ The city's 1918 **Mercado Municipal** barely survived the 1960 earthquake intact, but it thrives again after extensive remodeling and reinforcement as a shopping-dining complex. A few restaurants, mostly hole-in-the-wall seafood joints, but some quite nice, share the three-story building with artisan and souvenir vendors. ✉ *Block bordered by Av. Arturo Prat, Chacabuco, Yungay, and Libertad* ☎ *No phone* ⊙ *Dec.–Mar., daily 8 AM–10 PM; Apr.–Nov., daily 8 AM–8:30 PM.*

❻ For a historic overview of the region, visit the **Museo Histórico y Antropológico Maurice van de Maele,** on neighboring Isla Teja. The collection focuses on the city's colonial period, during which it was settled by the Spanish, burned by the Mapuche, and invaded by Dutch corsairs. Downstairs, rooms re-create the interior of the late-19th-century Anwandter mansion that belonged to one of Valdivia's first immigrant families; the upper floor delves into Mapuche art and culture. ✉ *Los Laureles, Isla Teja* ☎ *63/212–872* 💲 *1,500 pesos* ⊙ *Daily 10–8.*

❺ 👶 The **Museo Philippi,** under construction at this writing, sits behind the history and anthropology museum. It bears the name of 19th-century Chilean explorer and scientist Bernardo Philippi and will be designed to foster an interest in science among young people. ✉ *Los Laureles, Isla Teja* ☎ *63/212–872* 💲 *1,200 pesos* ⊙ *Dec.–Feb., Tues.–Sun. 10–1 and 2–6; Mar.–Nov., Tues.–Sun. 10–1 and 2–8.*

❹ Fondly known around town as the "MAC," the **Museo de Arte Contemporáneo** is one of Chile's foremost modern-art museums. This Isla Teja complex was built on the site of the old Anwandter brewery destroyed in the 1960 earthquake. The minimalist interior, formerly the brewery's warehouses, contrasts sharply with ongoing construction of a modern glass wall fronting the Río Valdivia, a project slated for completion by 2010, Chile's bicentennial. The museum has no permanent collection; it's a rotating series of temporary exhibits by contemporary Chilean

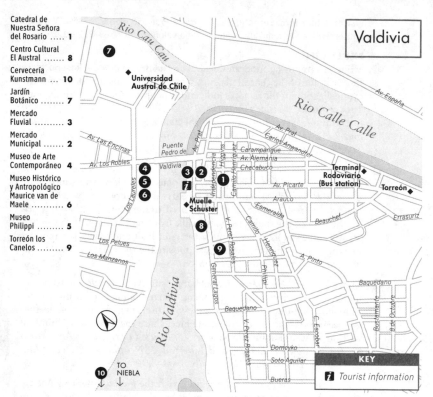

artists. ⊠*Los Laureles, Isla Teja* ☎*63/221–968* ⊕*www.macvaldivia.*
uach.cl 🎟*1,200 pesos* ⊗*Daily 10–2 and 4–8.*

⑧ A walk south of downtown on Yungay and General Lagos takes you
through a neighborhood of late-19th- and early-20th-century houses
that were spared the ravages of the 1960 earthquake. One of these
houses dates from 1870 and accommodates the **Centro Cultural El Austral.** It's worth the stop if you have an interest in period furnishings.
⊠*Yungay 733* ☎*63/213–6588* ⊕*www.macvaldivia.uach.cl* 🎟*Free*
⊗*Tues.–Sun. 10–1 and 4–7.*

⑨ Just south of the Centro Cultural El Austral lies the **Torreón Los Canelos,**
one of two fortress towers constructed in 1774 to defend Valdivia from
constant indigenous attacks. Both towers—the other sits on Avenida
Picarte between the bus terminal and the bridge entering the city over
the Río Calle Calle—were built in the style of those that guarded the
coasts of Andalusia, in southern Spain. A wall and moat connected the
two Valdivia towers in the colonial era, effectively turning the city into
an island. ⊠*General Lagos at Yerbas Buenas.*

⑦ The **Jardín Botánico,** north and west of the Universidad Austral campus,
is awash with 1,000 species of flowers and plants native to Chile. It's
a lovely place to wander among the alerce, cypress, and laurel trees

whatever the season—and if you can't make it to Conguillío National Park to see the monkey puzzle trees, this is the place to see them—but it's particularly enjoyable in spring and summer. ⊠ *Isla Teja* 🕾 *63/221–313* 🎫 *Free* ⊙ *Dec.–Feb., daily 8–8; Mar.–Nov., daily 8–4.*

❿ Valdivia means beer to many Chileans, and **Cervecería Kunstmann** brews the country's beloved lager. The Anwandter family immigrated from Germany a century-and-a-half ago, bringing along their beer-making know-how. The *cervecería* (brewery), on the road to Niebla, hosts interesting guided tours by prior arrangement. There's also a small museum and a souvenir shop where you can buy the requisite caps, mugs, and T-shirts; plus a pricey restaurant serving German fare. ⊠ *Ruta 350 No. 950* 🕾 *63/222–570* 🎫 *Free* ⊙ *Restaurant and museum, daily noon–midnight.*

To protect the all-important city of Valdivia, the Spanish constructed a series of strategic fortresses at Niebla, where the Valdivia and Tornagaleones rivers meet. Portions of the 1671 **Fuerte de Niebla** and its 18 cannons have been restored. The ground on which the cannons sit is unstable; you can view them from the ramparts above. The old commander's house serves as a small museum documenting the era's military history. ⊠ *1 km (½ mi) west of entrance to Niebla* 🕾 *No phone* 🎫 *1,000 pesos, Wed. free* ⊙ *Jan. and Feb., daily 10–7; Mar.–Dec., daily 11–6.*

Across the estuary from the Fuerte de Niebla, the 1645 **Castillo San Sebastián de la Cruz** is large and well preserved. In the January–February summer season, historic reenactments of Spanish military maneuvers take place daily at 4 and 6. To get there, you will need to rent a small boat, which only costs about 700 pesos at the marina near Fuerte de Niebla. ⊠ *1 km (½ mi) north of Corral* 🎫 *1,000 pesos* ⊙ *Jan. and Feb., Tues.–Sun. 10–7; Mar.–Dec., Tues.–Sun. 11–6 Closed on Mondays.*

WHERE TO EAT

¢ ✕ **Café Haussmann.** The excellent *crudos* (steak tartare), German-style sandwiches, and delicious küchen here are testament to the fact that Valdivia was once a mecca for German immigrants. The place is small—a mere four tables and a bar—but it's that rarest of breeds in Chile: a completely nonsmoking restaurant. ⊠ *Av. Bernardo O'Higgins 394* 🕾 *63/213–878* 🖃 *AE, DC, MC, V* ⊙ *Closed Sun.*

$$ ✕ **La Calesa.** Head to this centrally located, well-known restaurant for a good introduction to Peruvian cuisine. Try the *ají* (chicken stew with cheese, milk, and peppers), but be careful not to burn your mouth. Peruvian dishes, particularly the stews, are spicier than their Chilean counterparts. ⊠ *Yungay 735* 🕾 *63/225–467* 🖃 *AE, DC, MC, V* ⊙ *Closed Sun. No lunch Sat.*

$$ ✕ **Camino de Luna.** The Way of the Moon floats on a barge on the Río Valdivia, just north of the Pedro de Valdivia bridge. As the city is only a few miles from the ocean, it's no surprise that seafood is a specialty here. The *congrío calle calle* (conger eel in a cheese-and-tomato sauce) is particularly good. Tables by the windows offer views of Isla Teja. ⊠ *Av. Arturo Prat Costanera s/n* 🕾 *63/213–788* 🖃 *AE, DC, MC, V.*

$$$ ✕**Salón de Té Entrelagos.** This swanky café caters to Valdivian business executives, who come here to make deals over sandwiches (try the Isla Teja—with grilled chicken, tomato, artichoke hearts, asparagus, olives, and red peppers), decadent crepes, and desserts. In the evenings, the atmosphere feels less formal—the menu is exactly the same—as the Entrelagos becomes a place to meet friends and converse well into the night. ⊠*Vicente Pérez Rosales 640* ☎*63/218–333* ⊟*AE, DC, MC, V.*

WHERE TO STAY

$ 🏨**Aires Buenos Hostal.** Well situated near Valdivia's downtown, this renovated, old and strikingly handsome house is a great find. The price is cheap, but the place is clean, friendly, and warm. It's mostly a backpackers' haven, but there are some private rooms that will make the older crowd feel at home. **Pros:** Price, location. **Cons:** Not many amenities, noise in ground-floor rooms. ⊠*Garcia Reyes 550* ☎*63/206–304* ⊕*www.airesbuenos.cl* ⇆*10 rooms, 5 with bath* ♿*In-room: no a/c, no phone, no TV, Wi-Fi. In-hotel: public Internet, public Wi-Fi, parking, no-smoking rooms* ⊟*AE, DC, MC V* ⦿*BP.*

¢ ⛰**Complejo Turístico Isla Teja.** The campsites at this facility sit in the middle of an apple orchard with an attractive view of the Río Valdivia. There's electricity and hot showers. ⊠*Los Cipreses 1125, Isla Teja* ☎*63/213–584* 🖷*63/225–855.*

$ 🏨**Hotel El Castillo.** A grand 1920s German-style house sits at Niebla's main intersection on the riverfront and has been converted into this lovely bed-and-breakfast with lots of knickknacks, antiques, and cuckoo clocks in the common areas. Rooms have more modern amenities, but retain the old wood finishing, and overlook either the river or the pool and back gardens. A new wing has been added, but it blends so seamlessly with the original house that you can't tell where one ends and the other begins. **Pros:** Nice ambience, rooms good. **Cons:** No restaurant. ⊠*Antonio Ducce* ☎*63/282–061* 🖷*63/219–133* ✉*hotelelcastillo@hotmail.com* ⇆*11 rooms, 2 cabins* ♿*In-room: no a/c. In-hotel: pools, no elevator, parking, no-smoking rooms* ⊟*AE, DC, MC, V* ⦿*BP.*

$$ 🏨**Hotel Isla Teja.** This affordable hotel doubles as student housing for the nearby Universidad Austral, though a section is always open for non-university guests. The rooms are quiet and comfortable, with modern amenities. **Pros:** Rooms are comfortable. **Cons:** Not close to town. ⊠*Las Encinas 220, Isla Teja* ☎*63/215–014* 🖷*63/214–911* ⊕*www. hotelislateja.cl* ⇆*90 rooms* ♿*In-room: no a/c, Wi-Fi (some). In-hotel: restaurant, bar, room service, no elevator, laundry service, concierge, executive floor, public Internet, public Wi-Fi, airport shuttle, parking* ⊟*AE, DC, MC, V* ⦿*CP.*

$$–$$$ 🏨**Hotel Naguilán.** You can relax at this charming hotel's poolside gar-
★ den while watching the boats pass by on the Río Valdivia. Rooms in the property's newer building are bigger, with balconies and more modern furnishings; the older rooms, in a building that dates from 1890, are smaller and a bit dated, with lime-green carpeting, but they have more character, and are cheaper. Service-wise, you're in good hands here: as soon as you check in, a waiter will appear to offer you a welcome pisco

sour. **Pros:** Good service, river location. **Cons:** No Wi-Fi in rooms. ⊠*General Lagos 1927* ☎*63/212–851* 📠*63/219–130* ⊕*www.hotel naguilan.com* 🛏*33 rooms, 3 suites* ♿*In-room: no a/c, refrigerator (some), dial-up. In-hotel: restaurant, bar, room service, pool, laundry service, no elevator, public Wi-Fi, parking, no-smoking rooms* ▭*AE, DC, MC, V* ⦿|*BP.*

$$$ 🏨**Hotel Puerta del Sur.** Expect lavish pampering with top-notch service at this highly regarded lodging. Spacious rooms, all with views of the river, are decorated in soft lavender tones. Play a few games of tennis, then hit the pool or relax in the hot tub. You're near the edge of town here, so this is a good place to stay if you have your own car. **Pros:** Good service, lots of activity options. **Cons:** At edge of town. ⊠*Los Lingues 950, Isla Teja* ☎*63/224–500* 📠*63/211–046* ⊕*www. hotelpuertadelsur.com* 🛏*45 rooms, 3 suites* ♿*In-room: safe, refrigerator, DVD, Wi-Fi. In-hotel: restaurant, bars, room service, tennis court, pool, gym, spa, bicycles, laundry service, concierge, executive floor, public Internet, public Wi-Fi, parking* ▭*AE, DC, MC, V* ⦿|*BP.*

$ 🏨**Los Renovales.** In a renovated home on the banks of the Calle Calle River, just a seven-minute drive from the center of Valdivia, this relatively new hotel offers hospitality and tranquility in a setting you may not want to leave. The rooms are ample, with lots of natural light, and many have a nice view of the river. The quality of the service and facilities in relation to price is excellent. **Pros:** Value for money, river setting, homey environment. **Cons:** No pool or other luxuries. ⊠*Pedro Aguirre Cerda 1415* ☎*63/278–562* ⊕*www.losrenovales.cl* 🛏*9 rooms, 2 suites* ♿*In-room: safe, ethernet, Wi-Fi. In-hotel: restaurant, room service, bar, no elevator, laundry service, public Internet, public Wi-Fi, parking* ▭*AE, DC, MC, V* ⦿|*BP.*

SPORTS & THE OUTDOORS

Numerous rivers, lush coastal temperate rainforests, and the Pacific coastline are some of the attractions for sports lovers in and around Valdivia. This is a great place for anything related to the river. Bird watching is a joy, particularly when you can witness the rare black-necked swans, one of the world's smallest swans, which have made the Valdivia area their main habitat despite pollution problems from a nearby pulp mill.

Valdivia-based tour operator **Pueblito Expediciones** (⊠*San Carlos 188* ☎*63/245–055* ⊕*www.pueblitoexpediciones.cl*) organizes marvelous rafting, kayaking, and nature appreciation trips on nearby rivers.An astonishing variety of wetland birds inhabits this part of the country. **Hualamo** (☎*09/642–3143* ⊕*www.hualamo.com*) lets you get a close look if you join its bird-watching and natural-history tours based out of a lodge 20 km (12 mi) upriver from Valdivia.

NIGHTLIFE

Here in the hometown of Austral University of Valdivia, a major Chilean university, the nightlife is lively and fun, particularly in and around the downtown area known as Calle Esmeralda. Bars, discos, and pubs are not just student-oriented, though; there are also many establishments in Esmeralda and elsewhere in the city that cater to older folks.

New York Discotheque (⊠ *Km 6 Camino a Niebla* ☎ 63/299–999) is an upbeat discotheque for mostly the younger crowd. **El Legado Bar** (⊠ *Esmeralda 657* ☎ 63/207–546) is a very cool jazz bar in the heart of the Esmeralda bar scene. **Papadaki's** (⊠ *Esmeralda 677* ☎ 63/246–700), a combination bar-disco, is a popular hangout that also sometimes has live music.

SHOPPING

Affiliated with the restaurant of the same name next door, **Entrelagos** (⊠ *Vicente Pérez Rosales 622* ☎ 63/212–047) has been whipping up sinfully rich chocolates for more than three decades, and arranges them with great care in the storefront display windows. Most of what is sold here is actually made at Entrelagos's factory outside town, but a small army of chocolate makers is on-site to let you see, on a smaller scale, how it's done, and to carefully package your purchases for your plane ride home.

EN ROUTE

Isla Huapi. Some 20% of Chile's 1 million Mapuche live on *reducciones*, or reservations. One of the most welcoming communities is on Isla Huapi, a leafy island in the middle of deep-blue Lago Ranco. It's out of the way—about 80 km (48 mi) southeast of Valdivia—but worth the trip for those interested in Mapuche culture. A boat departs from Futorno, on the northern shore of the lake, at 7 AM Monday, Wednesday, and Friday, returning at 5 PM. The pastoral quiet of Isla Huapi is broken once a year in January or February with the convening of the island council, in conjunction with the Lepún harvest festival. You are welcome during the festival, but be courteous and unobtrusive with your camera.

OSORNO

107 km (65 mi) southeast of Valdivia, via Ruta 5, Pan-American Hwy.

Workaday Osorno is the least visited of the Lake District's four major cities. It's one of the oldest in Chile, but the Mapuche prevented foreigners from settling here until the late 19th century. Like other communities in the region, it bears the imprint of the German settlers who came here in the 1880s. Osorno, situated in a bend of the Río Rahue, makes a convenient base for exploring the nearby national parks.

GETTING HERE & AROUND

Osorno is about a 1½-hour flight from Santiago. By car, Osorno is reached by the paved Ruta 5, or Pan-American Highway. There is also passenger train service via Temuco. All the main bus lines serve Osorno on a frequent basis.

ESSENTIALS

Bus Contacts Buses Vía Octay (⊠ *Errázuriz 1400* ☎ 64/237–043). **Osorno Bus Depot** (⊠ *Errázuriz 1400* ☎ 64/234–149).

Currency Exchange Banco BCI (⊠ *MacKenna 801*). **Cambiotur** (⊠ *MacKenna 1010*).

Hier ist alles so Deutsch

You'll meet people in the Lake District with names like María Schmidt or Pablo Gudenschwager. At first, such juxtapositions sound odd, but, remember, this melting pot of a country was liberated by a man, good Irishman that he was, named Bernardo O'Higgins.

The Lake District's Germanic origins can be traced to one Vicente Pérez Rosales. (Every town and city in the region names a street for him, and one of Puerto Montt's more fabulous lodgings carries his name.) Armed with photos of the region, Don Vicente, as everyone knew him in his day, made several trips on behalf of the Chilean government to Germany, Switzerland, and Austria in the mid-19th century. His mission? To recruit

waves of European immigrants to settle the Lake District and end 300 years of Mapuche domination in the region once and for all.

Thousands signed on the dotted line and made the long journey to start a new life in southern Chile. It was a giant leap of faith for the original settlers, but it didn't hurt that the region looked just like the parts of Central Europe that they'd come from. The result was *küchen,* sausage, and a good old-fashioned work ethic mixed with a Latin-spirited, oom-pah-pah gemütlichkeit. But don't bother to dust off that high-school German for your trip here; few people speak it these days.

—Jeffrey Van Fleet

Internet Chat-Mail-MP3 (⊠ *Patricio Lynch 1334*). **Internet Skype** (⊠ *MacKenna 939* ☎ *64/319–707*).

Medical Asístanse Farmacias Ahumada (⊠ *Eleuterio Ramírez 981* ☎ *64/421–561*). **Hospital Base Osorno** (⊠ *Dr. Guillermo Bühler 1765* ☎ *64/235–571*).

Post Office Correos de Chile (⊠ *Av. Bernardo O'Higgins 645*).

Visitor & Tour Info Osorno Tourist Office (⊠ *Plaza de Armas* ☎ *64/218–714*). **Sernatur** (⊠ *Bernardo O'Higgins 667* ☎ *64/237–575*).

EXPLORING

Mapu Lahual. One of Osorno's main attractions is this network of indigenous parks spread over nine Huilluiche Indian communities on the Pacific coast, amid 50,000 hectares of temperate rainforest. The communities offer four tour programs, from one to seven days in duration. However you choose to see these parks, you will find some of the most spectacular nature areas in Chile. In addition, you will get a first-hand look at indigenous culture and have the opportunity to buy native handicrafts. ⊠ *Ramirez 116, oficina 7, Osorno* ☎ *08/186–3083* ⊕ *www.mapulahual.cl.*

Osorno's friendly **tourist office** arranges free daily tours in summer. Each day has a different focus: walks around the city, fruit orchards, or nearby farms are a few of the offerings. ⊠ *North side of Plaza de Armas* ☎ *64/264–250* 🎫 *Free* ⊙ *Office: Dec.–Feb., daily 8–8; Mar.–Nov., weekdays 9–1 and 2:30–6. Tours: daily 10:30.*

The 1960 earthquake left Osorno with little historic architecture, but a row of **19th-century houses** miraculously survived on Calle Juan Mackenna between Lord Cochrane and Freire. Their distinctively sloped roofs, which allow adequate drainage of rain and snow, are replicated in many of Osorno's newer houses.

The modern **Catedral de San Mateo Apostol** fronts the Plaza de Armas and is topped with a tower resembling a bishop's mitre. "Turn off your cell phone," the sign at the door admonishes those who enter. "You don't need it to communicate with God." ⊠*Plaza de Armas* ☎*No phone* ◷*Mass: Mon.–Sat. 7:15 PM; Sun. 10:30, noon, and 8:15.*

The **Museo Municipal Osorno** contains a decent collection of Mapuche artifacts, Chilean and Spanish firearms, and exhibits devoted to the German settlement of Osorno. Housed in a pink neoclassical building dating from 1929, this is one of the few older structures in the city center. ⊠*Manuel Antonio Matta 809* ☎*64/238–615* ⊠*Free* ◷*Mon.–Thurs. 9:30–5:30, Fri. 9:30–4:30, Sat. 2–6.*

WHERE TO EAT

$ ✕**Café Central.** You can dig into a hearty American-style breakfast in the morning, and burgers and sandwiches the rest of the day, at this diner on the Plaza de Armas. The friendly, bustling staff speaks no English, but if it's clear you're North American, an English menu will be presented to you with great fanfare. ⊠*Av. Bernardo O'Higgins 610* ☎*64/257–711* ▭*DC, MC, V.*

$$ ✕**Club Alemán.** This was the first in a network of German associations in southern Chile. Established in 1862, it predated the first big waves of European immigration. Despite the exclusive-sounding name, anyone can dine here. Options are limited, however. There's usually a choice of four or five rotating prix-fixe menus for lunch and dinner, often including a seafood stew or a hearty cazuela, and lots of tasty küchen and other pastries for dessert. ⊠*Av. Bernardo O'Higgins 563* ☎*64/232–784* ▭*AE, DC, MC, V.*

WHERE TO STAY

$ ⊡**Gran Hotel Osorno.** Osorno's grande dame, built in the era when art deco was all the rage, has stood the test of time. The five-story hotel has an unbeatable location on the Plaza de Armas. The rooms, although a tad dark, are clean and comfortable. Mercifully, the hotel's Power Disco has closed, though the neon sign still blinks out front. **Pros:** Great location. **Cons:** A bit tired interior. ⊠*Av. Bernardo O'Higgins 615* ☎*64/232–171* ⊞*64/239–311* ✐*granhotelosorno@entelchile.net* ⤳*70 rooms* ⌂*In-room: no a/c, safe, refrigerator. In-hotel: restaurant, bar, laundry service, public Wi-Fi* ▭*AE, DC, MC, V.*

$$$ ⊡**Hotel García Hurtado de Mendoza.** This stately hotel two blocks from the Plaza de Armas is one of Osorno's nicest lodgings. Classical lines grace the traditional furnishings and complement the subdued fabrics of the bright and airy guest rooms. **Pros:** Good location, rooms are pleasant. **Cons:** Dated-looking common spaces. ⊠*Juan Mackenna 1040* ☎*64/237–111* ⊞*64/237–115* ⊕*www.hotelgarciahurtado.cl* ⤳*31 rooms* ⌂*In-room: no a/c, ethernet, Wi-Fi. In-hotel: restaurant,*

bar, room service, laundry service, public Internet, public Wi-Fi, parking, no-smoking rooms ▤AE, DC, MC, V ⦿|BP.

$ 🏨**Hotel Innsbruck.** Osorno's most Germanic hotel, the Innsbruck has half-timbered walls and cheery flower boxes in the windows. Rooms are small and simply furnished with little more than beds, nightstands, and televisions, but the vaulted ceilings make them seem spacious. **Pros:** Classic Patagonia. **Cons:** ✉*Manuel Rodríguez 941* 🕾*64/242–000* ⌖*hinnsbruck@telsur.cl* ⟿*16 rooms* ♿*In-room: no a/c. In-hotel: bar, no elevator, laundry service, parking* ▤*AE, DC, MC, V* ⦿|*CP.*

$$ 🏨**Hotel Lagos del Sur.** Business travelers frequent Osorno more than leisure travelers do, and this place near the Plaza de Armas provides attentive service and a quiet place to work. Warm golds and greens make a splash in sparkling white guest rooms. The color scheme echoes the building's dark-green exterior. Doubles include a small sitting room off to one side. **Pros:** Good for business travel. **Cons:** A bit tattered. ✉*Av. Bernardo O'Higgins 564* 🕾*64/243–244* 🖷*64/243–696* ⊕*www.hotelagosdelsur.cl* ⟿*20 rooms* ♿*In-room: no a/c, Wi-Fi. In-hotel: bar, laundry service, no elevator, parking, public Internet, public Wi-Fi* ▤*AE, DC, MC, V* ⦿|*CP.*

SHOPPING

Osorno's city government operates the **Centro de Artesanía Local** (✉*Juan MacKenna at Ramón Freire*), a complex of 46 artisan vendors' stands built with steeply sloped roofs in the style of the Calle MacKenna houses. Woodwork, leather, and woolens abound. Prices are fixed but fair. It's open January and February, daily 9 AM–10 PM, and March–December, daily 10–8.

EN ROUTE An Osorno business executive's love for tail fins and V-8 engines led him to establish the **Auto Museum Moncopulli.** His particular passion is the little-respected Studebaker, which accounts for 50 of the 80 vehicles on display. Elvis and Buddy Holly bop in the background to put you in the mood. ✉*Ruta 215, 25 km (16 mi) east of Osorno, Puyehue* 🕾*64/210–744* ⊕*www.moncopulli.cl* 🎫*2,000 pesos* ⊙*Dec.–Mar., daily 10–8; Apr.–Nov., daily 10–6.*

PARQUE NACIONAL PUYEHUE

81 km (49 mi) east of Osorno, via Ruta 215.

Chile's most popular national park, Parque Nacional Puyehue draws crowds who come to bask in its famed hot springs. Most never venture beyond them, and that's a shame. A dozen miles east of the Aguas Calientes sector lies a network of short trails leading to evergreen forests with dramatic waterfalls.

Truly adventurous types attempt the five-hour hike to the summit of 2,240-meter (7,350-foot) Volcán Puyehue. As with most climbs in this region, CONAF rangers insist on ample documentation of experience before allowing you to set out. Access to the 1,070-square-km (413-square-mi) park is easy: head due east from Osorno on the highway leading to Argentina. ✉*Ruta 215* 🕾*64/197–4572* 🎫*800 pesos* ⊙*Dec.–Feb., daily 8 AM–9 PM; Apr.–Oct., daily 8–8.*

WHERE TO STAY

$$ ☐**Termas Aguas Calientes.** Just a few kilometers up the road from Termas Puyehue, this is a more affordable, somewhat more independent way to enjoy hot springs and see Puyehue Park. The triangular-shaped cabins are comfortable and well-equipped, and there are two campgrounds costing 6,000 or 10,000 pesos per day. The use of thermal pools costs 6,000 pesos. Their spa offers massages (including a chocolate massage) and facial treatments. ⊠ *Camino Antillanca, Km 4, Puyehue National Park* ☎ *64/331–710* ⊕ *www.termasaguascalientes.com* ⤶ *26 cabins* ⚷ *In-room: no a/c, no phone, kitchen, refrigerator. In-hotel: restaurant, pools, spa, parking* ☰ *AE, DC, MC, V.*

$$$–$$$$ ☐**Termas Puyehue Wellness and Spa Resort.** Probably Chile's most
★ famous hot-springs resort, this grandiose stone-and-wood lodge sits on the edge of Parque Nacional Puyehue. Make no mistake: the place is enormous, with a slate of activities to match, offering everything from darts to skiing. Yet, despite its huge popularity, and the fact that something is always going on, it can be a surprisingly nice place to relax. Most people come for a soak in the thermal pools. The rooms and common areas here mix starkly modern and 19th-century Germanic features: chrome, hardwoods, and even some modern art happily share the same space. The hotel recently changed to an "all-inclusive" concept in which meals, drinks, excursions, and use of the pools and thermal baths are included in the price of the room. If you're not staying as a guest, an all-day pass for the use of the springs and pools, with meals included, is 30,000 pesos weekdays, 35,000 pesos on weekends and holidays. ⊠ *Ruta 215, Km 76, Puyehue* ☎ *64/232–881, 2/293–6000 in Santiago* 🖨 *64/236–988, 2/283–1010 in Santiago* ⊕ *www.puyehue.cl* ⤶ *137 rooms* ⚷ *In-room: no a/c, safe, refrigerator, Wi-Fi. In-hotel: 3 restaurants, room service, bar, tennis courts, pools, gym, spa, bicycles, water sports, children's programs, laundry service, concierge, public Internet, public Wi-Fi, airport shuttle, parking* ☰ *AE, DC, MC, V* ⦿*BP.*

PUERTO OCTAY

50 km (30 mi) southeast of Osorno, via Ruta 5, the Pan-American Hwy.

The story goes that a German merchant named Ochs set up shop in this tidy community on the northern tip of Lago Llanquihue. A phrase uttered by customers looking for a particular item, "¿Ochs, hay...?" ("Ochs, do you have...?"), gradually became "Octay." With spectacular views of the Osorno and Calbuco volcanoes, the town was the birthplace of Lake District tourism: a wealthy Santiago businessman constructed a mansion outside town in 1912, using it as a vacation home to host his friends. (That structure is now the area's famed Hotel Centinela.) Puerto Octay doesn't have the frenetic energy of neighboring Frutillar and Puerto Varas, but its many fans enjoy its less-frenzied, more-authentic nature.

GETTING HERE & AROUND

Puerto Octay is easily accessible on paved roads from Ruta 5, the Pan-American Highway. It's less than an hour north of Puerto Montt.

WHERE TO STAY & EAT

$$ ✕ **Restaurant Baviera.** Because it's on the Plaza de Armas, this is a popular lunch stop for tour groups. Baviera serves solid German fare—schnitzel, sauerkraut, sausage, and küchen are among the favorites. Beer steins and other Bavarian paraphernalia lining the walls evoke the old country. ⊠ *German Wulf 582* ☎ *64/391–460* ▭ *No credit cards.*

$$$ ▦ **Hotel Centinela.** Simple and elegant, the venerable 1912 Hotel Centi-
★ nela remains one of Chile's best-known accommodations. This imposing wood-shingled lodge with a dramatic turret sits amid 20 forested acres at the tip of Península Centinela jutting into Lago Llanquihue. Britain's Edward VII, then Prince of Wales, was the most famous guest (but there's some mystery as to whether his future wife, American divor-cée Wallis Simpson, accompanied him). Imposing beds and armoires fill the huge rooms in the main building. The cabins, whose rates include three meals a day delivered to the door, are more modern than the rooms in the lodge. ⊠ *Península de Centinela, 5 km (3 mi) south of Puerto Octay* ☎☎ *64/391–326* ⊕ *www.hotelcentinela.cl* ⤵ *11 rooms, 1 suite, 18 cabins* ♨ *In-room: no a/c, no TV (some). In-hotel: restaurant, bar, beachfront, no elevator* ▭ *AE, DC, MC, V* ❦ *BP, FAP.*

$ ▦ **Zapato Amarillo.** Backpackers make up the majority of the clientele
★ here, but this is no scruffy youth hostel. This modern alerce-shingled house with wood-paneled rooms affords a drop-dead gorgeous view of Volcán Osorno outside town. Armin Dubendorfer and Nadi Muñoz, the eager-to-please Chilean-Swiss couple that owns it, will arrange guided horseback-riding, hiking, and cycling tours, as well as cheese-fondue evening gatherings. Rates include an excellent buffet breakfast that uses local fruits and dairy products. You also have access to the kitchen. ⊠ *2 km (1 mi) north of Puerto Octay on road to Osorno* ☎☎ *64/210–787* ⊕ *www.zapatoamarillo.cl* ⤵ *7 rooms, 2 with bath* ♨ *In-room: no a/c, no phone, no TV. In-hotel: bicycles, laundry facilities, public Internet, no elevator* ▭ *No credit cards* ❦ *BP.*

FRUTILLAR

30 km (18 mi) southwest of Puerto Octay.

Halfway down the western edge of Lago Llanquihue lies the small town of Frutillar, a destination for European immigrants in the late 19th century and, today, arguably the most picturesque Lake District community. The town—actually two adjacent hamlets, Frutillar Alto and Frutillar Bajo—is known for its perfectly preserved German architecture. Don't be disappointed if your first sight of the town is the nondescript neighborhood (the Alto) on the top of the hill; head down to the charming streets of Frutillar Bajo that face the lake, with their picture-perfect view of Volcán Osorno.

GETTING HERE & AROUND
About 45 minutes north of Puerto Montt, on Ruta 5, Pan-American Highway. Several bus lines make stops here on Santiago–Puerto Montt routes.

ESSENTIALS
Currency Exchange **Banco Santander** (⊠*Av. Philippi 555* ☎*65/421–228*).

Medical Assistance **Farmacia Frutillar** (⊠*Av. Carlos Richter 170*). **Hospital Frutillar** (⊠*Las Piedras* ☎*65/421–386*).

Visitor and Tour Information **Informacion Turistica** (⊠*Costanera Philippi in front of boat dock* ☎*65/421–080*). **Secretaria Muncipal de Turismo** (⊠*Av. Philippi 753* ☎*65/421–685*).

EXPLORING
Each year, in late January and early February, the town hosts **Semanas Musicales de Frutillar,** an excellent series of mostly classical concerts (and a little jazz) in the lakeside Centro de Conciertos y Eventos, a semi-outdoor venue inaugurated for the 2006 festival. Ticket prices are a reasonable 3,000–10,000 pesos. ⊠*Av. Phillipi 1000* ☎*65/421–290* ⊕*www.semanasmusicales.cl.*

Culture in Frutillar is not only about Semanas Musicales these days. In the Centro de Conciertos y Eventos is also housed the **Teatro del Lago,** with a year-round schedule of concerts, art shows, and film. Events take place every week. ⊠*Av. Phillipi 1000* ☎*65/422–954* ⊕*www. teatrodellago.cl.*

★ You step into the past when you step into one of southern Chile's best museums, the **Museo Colonial Alemán.** Besides displays of the 19th-century agricultural and household implements, this open air museum has full-scale reconstructions of buildings—a smithy and barn, among others—used by the original German settlers. Exhibits at this complex administered by Chile's Universidad Austral are labeled in Spanish and, *natürlich,* German, but there are also a few signs in English. A short walk from the lake up Avenida Arturo Prat, the museum also has beautifully landscaped grounds and great views of Volcán Osorno. ⊠*Av. Vicente Pérez Rosales at Av. Arturo Prat* ☎*65/421–142* ☜*1,800 pesos* ⊙*Dec.–Feb., daily 10–7; Mar.–Nov., daily 10–2 and 3–5.*

WHERE TO EAT
¢ ✕**Café Capuccini.** Sink into one of the plush couches here and write some postcards while you nurse a gourmet coffee drink on a chilly evening. If the couches are taken—they are in demand—grab one of the small tables adorned with a musical-score lampshade. All have superb lake and volcano views out the curving, sweeping picture window. This café in the new Centro de Conciertos y Eventos complex caters mostly to a pre- and post-theater crowd, but it serves up light fare (sandwiches, küchen, and desserts) on brown stoneware to anyone, any day. ⊠*Av. Phillipi 1000* ☎*65/422–900* ▭*No credit cards.*

$$ ✕**Club Alemán.** One of the German clubs that dot the Lake District, this restaurant in the center of town has a selection of four or five rotating prix-fixe menus that cost 3,500 pesos. There will always be a meat and

seafood option—often steak and salmon—with soup, salad, and dessert. Don't forget the küchen. ✉*Philippi 747* ☎*65/421–249* ⊟*AE, DC, MC, V.*

$$ ✗**Guten Apetit.** Right on the waterfront, with tables both outdoors and inside, this is a warm and friendly place with good food. It's the standard southern Chilean menu, from clam stews and Barros Lucos (a classic Chilean sandwich of beef and melted cheese) to large beef and chicken dishes. But they also have a few German imports such as Chuletas Kasler, a German pork chop. In summer, a pianist busts out a variety of tunes from 12:30 to 4 PM every day. ✉*Balmaceda 98* ☎*65/421–145* ⊟*AE, DC, MC.*

WHERE TO STAY

$$ ▦**Hotel Ayacara.** A beautiful, yellow and green house on the lakefront, this bed-and-breakfast is one of Frutillar's best. The service is friendly, the rooms are a delight. **Pros:** Fun and friendly. **Cons:** Not much privacy. ✉*Av. Philippi corner of Pedro Aguirre* ☎*65/421–550, 2/430–7000 in Santiago* ⊕*www.hotelayacara.cl* ⤳*8 rooms* ⚴*In-room: no a/c, Wi-Fi. In-hotel: restaurant, room service, bar, beachfront, no elevator, laundry service, public Wi-Fi, parking, no-smoking rooms* ⊟*AE, DC, MC, V* ◎|*BP.*

$$ ▦**Hotel Elun.** From just about every vantage point at this hillside lodging just south of town—the lobby, the library, and, of course, the guest rooms—you have a spectacular view of Lago Llanquihue. Each room has huge bay windows framing Volcán Osorno. The blue of the facade is repeated in the rooms, which have polished wood furniture. Add the exceptionally attentive owners to the mix, and you have a real find. **Pros:** Great views. **Cons:** A bit homely. ✉*Costanera Sur* ☎*65/420–055* ▤*65/420–170* ⊕*www.hotelelun.cl* ⤳*14 rooms, 3 suites* ⚴*In-room: no a/c, safe, refrigerator. In-hotel: restaurant, bar, room service, bicycles, laundry service, no elevator, public Internet, public W-Fi, parking, no-smoking rooms* ⊟*AE, DC, MC, V* ◎|*BP.*

$$ ▦**Hotel Kaffee Bauernhaus.** Gingerbread cutouts and swirls adorn this pretty 1911 home-turned-inn. You couldn't ask for a much better location—the property is right on the lake, although only one guest room has a lake view. All, however, are wood paneled and tastefully decorated with flowered bedspreads and curtains. The German breakfast is substantial. **Pros:** Great location. **Cons:** Not all rooms have a view. ✉*Av. Philippi 663* ☎*65/420–003* ⊕*www.interpatagonia.com/bauernhaus* ⤳*8 rooms* ⚴*In-room: no a/c, no TV (some). In-hotel: restaurant, no elevator, public Wi-Fi, parking* ⊟*AE, DC, MC, V* ◎|*BP.*

$$ ▦**Hotel Serenade.** The names of the guest rooms here reflect musical compositions—like *Fantasia* and *Wedding March*—and each door is painted with the first few sheet-music bars of the work it's named for. Inside are plush quilts and comforters, hardwood floors, and throw rugs. The cozy sitting room, overlooking a quiet side street, is another lovely place to relax. The musical theme makes this an especially appropriate place to stay during the Semanas Musicales de Frutillar in late January. ✉*Pedro Aguirre Cerda 50* ☎*65/420–332* ⤳*6 rooms* ⚴*In-room: no a/c, no TV. In-hotel: no elevator, laundry service, parking* ⊟*No credit cards* ◎|*CP.*

$–$$ 🏨**Hotel Villa San Francisco.** The location of this highly recommended
★ hotel could not be better, situated on a small hill overlooking the lake.
At the tranquil end of the Costanera, or lakeside road, it has a spectacular view of the town and volcanoes while just a minute's walk from
all the sights and sounds of Frutillar. All the rooms have that lake view,
along with their own private terrace. The hotel also has a pleasant pool
and a cozy bar and restaurant. This is a place to relax. Francisco Fayula
de la Corte, its Spanish owner, took over the hotel in 1999 and has
transformed it into Frutillar's top lodging choice. **Pros:** Lakeside view,
good value for price, tranquil but close to town. **Cons:** Some rooms are
small. ⊠*Avda. Phillipi 1503* ☎*65/421–531* ⊕*www.villasanfrancisco.
cl* ⟳*15 rooms* ♿*In-room: no a/c, Wi-Fi. In-hotel: restaurant, room
service, bar, pool, gym, beachfront, no elevator, laundry service, public
Wi-Fi, parking* ⊟*AE, DC, MC, V* ⊺⊙⊺*BP.*

$$ ✕🏨**Salzburg Hotel & Spa.** Rooms at this Tyrolean-style lodge com-
mand excellent views of the lake. Cozy cabins and slightly larger bun-
galows, all made of native woods, are fully equipped with kitchens
and private terraces. The staff will gladly organize fishing trips. The
restaurant ($$) serves some of the best smoked salmon in the area.
Pros: Great view, lots of privacy. **Cons:** Need a car to get around.
⊠*Costanera Norte* ☎*65/421–589* 🖨*65/421–599* ⊕*www.salzburg.
cl* ⟳*31 rooms, 9 cabins, 5 bungalows* ♿*In-room: no a/c, no TV. In-
hotel: restaurant, bar, pool, spa, laundry service, parking, no elevator*
⊟*AE, DC, MC, V* ⊺⊙⊺*BP.*

7

BEACHES

Packed with summer crowds, the gray-sand **Playa Frutillar** stretches for
15 blocks along Avenida Philippi. From this point along Lago Llanquihue you have a spectacular view due east of the conical Volcán Osorno,
as well as the lopsided Volcán Puntiagudo.

PUERTO VARAS

27 km (16 mi) south of Frutillar via Ruta 5, Pan-American Hwy.

A small but fast-growing resort town on the edge of Lago Llanquihue,
Puerto Varas is renowned for its view of the Osorno and Calbuco volcanoes. Stunning rose arbors and Germanic-style architecture grace the
many centuries-old houses and churches that dot this tranquil town.
Every year new hotels here crop up as tourism continues to rise significantly. Tons of cafés, trendy restaurants, an excellent casino, and
a budding bar scene all point towards Puerto Varas's ascendancy as a
serious challenge to Pucón, the region's top vacation spot.

GETTING HERE & AROUND

Puerto Varas is only about a 20-minute drive from the center of nearby
Puerto Montt, making it a virtual suburb of that large city. You can
get to the Puerto Montt airport via a 40-minute drive south on Ruta 5.
Most of the bus lines that serve Puerto Montt make obligatory stops
in Puerto Varas on their way north or south. Around town, there are
numerous taxis and several minivan buses, which have various stops,
the most prominent one on Avenida Salvador near the corner of Calle

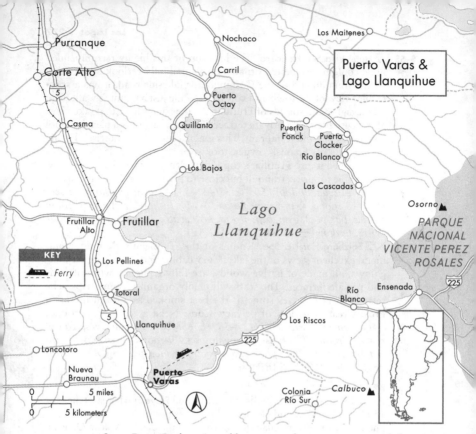

Santa Rosa. Both taxis and buses can take you to countryside locations such as Ensenada as well as Puerto Montt for a minimal cost. You can cross to Argentina via bus or boat.

ESSENTIALS

Bus Contacts Buses JAC (✉ *Walker Martinez 227* ☎ *65/236–000*).**Cruz del Sur** (✉ *Walker Martinez 239-B* ☎ *65/231–925*). **Tur-Bus** (✉ *Salvador 1093* ☎ *65/233–787*).

Currency Exchange Banco Santander (✉ *Del Salvador 399* ☎ *65/237–255*). **Travelsur** (✉ *San Pedro 451* ☎ *65/236–000*).

Medical Assistance Clinica Alemana (✉ *Otto Bader 810* ☎ *65/239–100*). **Farmacia Cruz Verde** (✉ *San Francisco 400* ☎ *65/234–293*).**Farmacia Salco** (✉ *Del Salvador 400* ☎ *65/234–544*).

Post Office Correos de Chile (✉ *San José 242*).

Rental Cars Hunter Rent-a-Car (✉ *San José 130* ☎ *65/237–950 or 65/522–454*).

Visitor & Tour Info Casa del Turista (✉ *Piedra Plen, in front of Plaza de Armas* ☎ *65/237–956*). **Oficina de Turismo** (✉ *San Francisco 441* ☎ *65/233–477*).

WHERE TO EAT

$ ✗**Café Danes.** A friendly café-restaurant next to Santa Isabel Supermarket on Puerto Varas's main drag, Calle Del Salvador, the restaurant offers a set lunch menu as well as a range of plates, from sandwiches to beef and chicken dishes served up the Chilean way. The large beef and vegetarian empanadas and the illustrious küchen are not to be missed. ✉*Del Salvador 441* ☎*65/232–371* ⊟*No credit cards.*

$ ✗**Donde El Gordito.** You'll find great seafood here. Some of the fish is personally caught by the avid fisherman owner, El Gordito, who is usually on hand with his wife to wait tables and ring up checks. This little eatery, housed inside a downtown fishmarket, also has entertaining decor, some of it chosen by its owner and some of it given to him by the many tourists that luckily find their way to his food. ✉*San Bernardo 560* ☎*65/233–425* ⚓*reservations recommended* ⊟*AE, DC, MC, V.*

$$ ✗**Mediterraneo.** This gourmet restaurant and bar has a privileged view of the lake and volcanoes, while offering up a constantly changing menu of sophisticated beef, chicken, and seafood plates that combine the best of the local culinary scene with Mediterranean-style cooking. Reserve a table by the window. ✉*Santa Rosa 68* ☎*65/237–268* ⊟*AE, DC, MC, V.*

$$ ✗**La Olla.** This lakeside restaurant does not look like much, but it
★ serves the best fish and seafood dishes in Chile, according to its legion of fans. The specialties of the house are seafood empanadas and other, more simply elegant preparations. The place is almost always full during peak hours, so reserve a table ahead of time. ✉*Av. Vicente Pérez Rosales 1071* ☎*65/234–605* ⚓*Reservations essential* ⊟*AE, DC, MC, V.*

WHERE TO STAY

$$ ⊞**Los Alerces Hotel & Cabanas.** Across the street from the town's most popular beach for swimming and tanning, this is a clean, comfortable option. Wood-paneled walls and paintings of flowers predominate. The cabins on-site are a perfect place for a family stay. For business travelers, the extensive meeting facilities are a bonus. The hotel pool is inviting, too. **Pros:** Close to beach, large cabins. **Cons:** It's a hike to walk to town. ✉*Av. Vicente Pérez Rosales 1281* ☎*65/235–985* ⊕*www. hotellosalerces.cl* ⇥*44 rooms, 10 cabins* ⚐*In-room: no a/c, refrigerator, Wi-Fi. In-hotel: restaurant, room service, bar, pool, no elevator, laundry service, executive floor, public Internet, public Wi-Fi, parking, no-smoking rooms* ⊟*AE, DC, MC, V* ⊠*BP.*

$$ ⊞**The Guest House.** The aroma of fresh coffee greets you all day long, and little homemade chocolates wait on your pillow at this B&B, a

---

WORD OF MOUTH

"The Lake Crossing is a whole day event that entails crossing through the Andes both by bus and by boat. The scenery, particularly on our beautiful day, was breath taking: snow topped mountains reflected in perfectly blue lakes. The event is also well organized. Luggage and humans are escorted from place to place, nothing is lost, food is available, and tour descriptions are in both English and Spanish." –leelabell

7

restored 1926 mansion just a couple of blocks from downtown. Period furnishings and antiques fill the cheery rooms. Vicky Johnson, Guest House's exuberant American owner, a longtime resident of Chile and a font of information, will provide personalized attention. **Pros:** Good location. **Cons:** Not much privacy. ⊠*Av. Bernardo O'Higgins 608* ☎*65/231–521* 🖷*65/232–240* ⊕*www.vicki-johnson.com/guesthouse* ↘*9 rooms* ⚹*In-room: no a/c, no TV, Wi-Fi. In-hotel: room service, no elevator, laundry service, public Internet, public Wi-Fi, airport shuttle, parking, no-smoking rooms* ⊟*No credit cards* ⦿*BP.*

$$$ 🏨**Hotel Bellavista.** This hotel, an eclectic mix of traditional Bavarian and modern architectural styles, sits right on the lake. Most of the bright rooms have views of the nearby volcanoes, and some have their own balconies. Stylish contemporary furnishings are upholstered in tailored stripes. **Pros:** Great views. **Cons:** None of the frills you might expect. ⊠*Av. Vicente Pérez Rosales 60* ☎*65/232–011* 🖷*65/232–013* ↘*70 rooms, 3 suites* ⚹*In-room: no a/c, safe, refrigerator, ethernet, Wi-Fi. In-hotel: restaurant, bar, room service, laundry service, public Internet, public Wi-Fi, airport shuttle, parking* ⊟*AE, DC, MC, V* ⦿*BP.*

$$$ 🏨**Hotel Cabañas del Lago.** The pine-paneled cabins, hidden among carefully tended gardens, make this place special. Each A-frame unit, which can accommodate five people, is decorated with lace curtains and floral-pattern bedding, and has a woodstove and full kitchen. Most rooms in the main hotel are a little on the small side, but they're cozy and have lovely views of Volcán Osorno. **Pros:** Great views. **Cons:** Small rooms. ⊠*Klenner 195* ☎*65/232–291* 🖷*65/232–707* ⊕*www.cabanas dellago.cl* ↘*130 rooms, 11 cabins, 3 suites* ⚹*In-room: no a/c, safe, refrigerator (some), ethernet (some). In-hotel: restaurant, bar, room service, pool, spa, laundry service, public Internet, public Wi-Fi, parking, airport shuttle, no-smoking rooms* ⊟*AE, DC, MC, V.*

$$ 🏨**Hotel El Greco.** In a remodeled, German school house more than a century old, this hotel is a friendly, comfy place to stay. It's also literally a minute from the town center, and its hill setting affords it wonderful views. ⊠*Mirador 134* ☎*65/233–880* ⊕*www.hotelelgreco.cl* ↘*12 rooms* ⚹*In-room: no a/c. In-hotel: no elevator, laundry service, public Internet, airport shuttle, parking* ⊟*AE, DC, MC, V* ⦿*BP.*

$$ 🏨**Hotel Licarayén.** Balcony rooms overlook Lago Llanquihue at this rambling Bavarian-style chalet. Other rooms are bright, with wood paneling and pleasant views of the garden. The fireplace in the common sitting room keeps things warm. **Pros:** Great locations. **Cons:** Plain. ⊠*San José 114* ☎*65/232–305* 🖷*65/232–955* ⊕*www.hotelicarayen. cl* ↘*23 rooms, 1 suite* ⚹*In-room: no a/c, ethernet, Wi-Fi. In-hotel: room service, gym, public Internet, public Wi-Fi, laundry service, parking, no elevator* ⊟*AE, DC, MC, V* ⦿*CP.*

$$$ 🏨**Melia Patagonia.** One of the few legitimate five-star hotels to be found
★ in southern Chile, this relaxing, comfortable hotel is close to downtown. For the hotel's opening in 2007, the Chilean owners entirely renovated and modernized what was once Puerto Varas's most prestigious hotel and casino. Rooms are immaculate, the service personalized and attentive, and the views from the hotel terrace superb. A regular happy hour and live music make Bar Kutral a popular town hangout. **Pros:** Excellent

service, attention to detail, spacious rooms, bar. **Cons:** Gym and pool are small, not all rooms have lake views. ⊠*Klenner 349* ☎*65/201–000* ⊕*www.solmelia.com* ↪*91 rooms, 2 suites* ⚷*In-room: safe, refrigerator, ethernet, Wi-Fi. In-hotel: 2 restaurants, room service, bar, pool, gym, spa, laundry service, executive floor, public Internet, public Wi-Fi, parking* ▤*AE, DC, MC, V* ¶◎│*BP.*

NIGHTLIFE

Puerto Varas is a small town, so don't expect much, but the bars the town does have are friendly and fun. On Thursdays, virtually all of the restaurants and bars offer happy hour specials.

The flashy **Casino de Puerto Varas** (⊠*Del Salvador 21* ☎*65/346–600*) dominates the center of town these days. It has all the Vegas-style trappings, from slot machines to roulette, along with weekly Vegas-style entertainment.

The popular **Barómetro** (⊠*Walker Martinez 584* ☎*65/346–100*) is the town's most lively bar for both locals and the constant flow of tourists. Expect a DJ most nights, and often live music. On Friday nights, the live jazz at **The Garage** (⊠*Walker Martinez 220*) is an uplifting event and the beer flows fast at the long bar. Young people in their teens or twenties in search of a place to dance the night away go to **La Playa** (⊠*Av. Vicente Pérez Rosales 1400* ☎*8/839–8577*), located in Puerto Chico across the street from the town's main beach.

SPORTS & THE OUTDOORS

Puerto Varas has a plethora of outdoor options. Fly-fishing is king in the region, with many rivers and the huge Lake Llanquihue making attractive targets. But the region has much more to offer: mountain biking, canyoning, hiking in Vicente Pérez Rosales Park, or just enjoying the lake by kayak. You can also hike up the nearby volcanoes, which makes for an exciting and scenic excursion. With so much attractive nature in its backyard, it's no wonder Puerto Varas is becoming a prime destination for outdoor-adventure enthusiasts.

Al Sur Expediciones (⊠*Del Salvador 100* ☎*65/232–300* ⊕*www.alsur-expeditions.com*) is known for rafting and kayaking trips on the Class III Río Petrohué. It also runs horseback-riding and fly-fishing trips, and handles hotel reservations and guided tours for Pumalin Park. **Aqua Motion** (⊠*San Pedro 422* ☎*65/232–747* ⊕*www.aqua-motion.com*) is a longtime provider of rafting and kayaking excursions on the nearby Río Petrohué, as well as trekking, horseback riding, helicopter rides, bird-watching, and fly-fishing tours. **Margouya Tours** (⊠*Santa Rosa 318* ☎*65/237–640*) specializes in half- and full-day canyoning and rappelling trips near Volcán Calbuco, in addition to kayaking and hiking excursions. **Miralejos** (⊠*San Pedro 311* ☎*65/234–892* ⊕*www.miralejos.com*) offers trekking, kayaking, mountaineering, horseback-riding trips throughout the region.

For fly-fishing in Puerto Varas, try **Tres Piedras** (⊠*Ruta 225, Km 22, Los Riscos* ☎*65/330–157* ⊕*www.trespiedras.cl*).

ENSENADA

47 km (28 mi) east of Puerto Varas.

A drive along the southern shore of Lago Llanquihue to Ensenada takes you through the heart of Chile's *murta*-growing country. Queen Victoria is said to have developed a fondness for these tart, red berries, and today you'll find them used as ingredients in the region's syrups, jams, and küchen. Frutillar, Puerto Varas, and Puerto Octay might all boast about their views of Volcán Osorno, but you can really feel up close and personal with the volcano when you arrive in the town of Ensenada, which also neighbors the jagged Volcán Calbuca. The lake drive also illustrates how volcanoes play hide-and-seek on you: you'll see neither along a given stretch of road; then suddenly, you round a bend, or the clouds will part, and there they are.

WHERE TO STAY & EAT

$$ ☎ Hotel Puerto Pilar. Set on the shore of Lago Llanquihue, this hotel's many activities and perfect volcano views make it immensely popular among Chileans in summer. If you want a bit more of the get-away-from-it-all feel for which the place was originally known, opt for one of the fully furnished cabins. Eight of them are constructed in *palafito*-style, held up with stilts right on the lakeshore (a style most commonly seen on the island of Chiloé); you can even fish right from your deck. Carpeted rooms in the main lodge all come with king beds and enormous windows. ⊠*Ruta 225, Km 27* ☎*65/335–378, 2/650–8118 in Santiago* ☎*65/335–344, 2/650–8111 in Santiago* ⊕*www.hotelpuerto pilar.cl* ➪*18 rooms, 2 suites, 13 cabins* ⚒*In-room: no a/c, safe, refrigerator, Wi-Fi. In-hotel: restaurant, bar, room service, tennis court, pool, beachfront, laundry service, public Internet, public Wi-Fi, parking, no-smoking rooms* ⊟*AE, DC, MC, V* ⊙*BP.*

$$ ✕☎ Onces de Bellavista. If you're traveling by car in the afternoon near
★ Ensenada, be sure to stop here. They only serve "onces," which is a sort of Chilean tea time. For 6,500 pesos you get great küchen, cake, bread, cheese, salami, coffee, tea, chocolate, and more. You'll have a panoramic view of the volcanoes and lake while you dine. There is also a mini-zoo with animals such as llamas and guanaco, a tennis court, and a private lakeside beach. They have six well-equipped cabins if you want to stay overnight. In summer, onces are served every day from 4 PM to 9 PM. The rest of the year they only serve onces on weekends and holidays. ⊠*Ruta 225, Km 34* ☎*65/335–323* ⊕*www.oncesbellavista.cl* ➪*6 cabins* ⚒*In-room: no a/c, kitchen, refrigerator. In-hotel: restaurant, beachfront, tennis court, parking* ⊟*No credit cards.*

$$$$ ✕☎ Yan Kee Way. With a striking view of Volcán Osorno and Lago
Fodor'sChoice Lllanquihue as its backdrop, this fly-fishing lodge and hotel has first-
★ class rooms and cabins. Central heating and goose-down comforters are unheard-of amenities for this part of the world, and Yan Kee Way has them. Moreover, the restaurant, Latitude 42, is outstanding. The kitchen was actually designed and constructed in the United States, then shipped to Chile. Unique artwork from around the world adorns rooms and common spaces. And there is the "cave," a one-of-a-kind cigar smoker's haven carved out of ancient, volcanic boulders. **Pros:**

Great all-around amenities. **Cons:** Expensive. ☒*Ruta 225, Km 42* ☎*65/212–030* ⊕*www.southernchilexp.com* ⇱*19 rooms, 8 bungalows, 2 chalets* ☝*In-room: no a/c, safe, refrigerator, no TV, Wi-Fi. In-hotel: restaurant, room service, bar, gym, spa, beachfront, water sports, bicycles, laundry service, public Internet, public Wi-Fi, airport shuttle, parking, no-smoking rooms* ▤*AE, DC, MC, V* ⦿*BP.*

PARQUE NACIONAL VICENTE PÉREZ ROSALES

3 km (2 mi) east of Ensenada.

GETTING HERE & AROUND

Take a one-hour drive along Ruta 224, Camino a Ensenada, from Puerto Varas. Several agencies in Puerto Varas offer guided trips and transport to the park.

EXPLORING

Chile's oldest national park, Parque Nacional Vicente Pérez Rosales was established in 1926. South of Parque Nacional Puyehue, the 2,538-square-km (980-square-mi) preserve includes the Osorno and lesser-known Puntiagudo volcanoes, as well as the deep-blue Lago Todos los Santos. The visitor center opposite the Hotel Petrohué provides access to some fairly easy hikes. The Rincón del Osorno trail hugs the lake; the Saltos de Petrohué trail runs parallel to the river of the same name. Rudimentary campsites are available for 10,000 pesos per person. ☎*65/290–711* ☒*1,000 pesos* ⊘*Dec.–Feb., daily 9–8; Mar.–Nov., daily 9–6.*

The Volcán Osorno begins to appear in your car window soon after you drive south from Osorno and doesn't disappear until shortly before your arrival in Puerto Montt. (The almost-perfectly conical volcano has been featured in a Samsung television commercial shown in the United States.)

The mountain forms the foundation for Chile's newest ski area, **Ski & Outdoors Volcán Osorno** (☒*San Francisco 333, Puerto Varas* ☎*65/233–445 or 09/262–3323* ⊕*www.volcanosorno.com*), which offers ski and snowboard rentals and lessons. Adults pay 16,500 pesos for a full day of skiing; 12,000 pesos for a half day, with transportation offered from the office in the center of Puerto Varas.

One of the Lake District's signature excursions is a binational one. The **Cruce de Lagos** takes in a combination of bus and boat transport from Puerto Varas to San Carlos de Bariloche, Argentina, via the park's Lago Todos los Santos and Argentina's Lago Nahuel Huapi. **Andina del Sud** (☒*Del Salvador 72, Puerto Varas* ☎*65/232–811* ⊕*www.crucedelagos.cl*) offers the trip starting from Puerto Varas or Puerto Montt.

WHERE TO STAY

$$$$ ⊞**Hotel Petrohué.** The common areas in this stately, rustic orange chalet have vaulted ceilings and huge fireplaces. Guest rooms are a mix of dark woods and stone and have brightly colored drapes and spreads. Cabins echo the design of the main building and have their own fire-

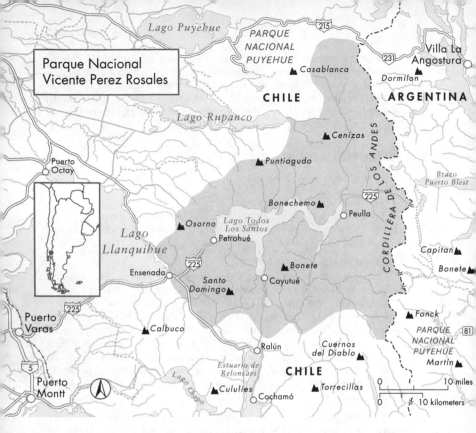

places. The hotel's tour office can set you up with cruises on nearby lakes, take you to scale Volcán Osorno if you're an experienced climber, or send you on guided hikes in the park. ⊠ *Ruta 225, Km 64, Petrohué s/n* ☎📠 *65/212–025* ⊕ *www.petrohue.com* ◄⊐ *20 rooms, 4 cabins* ⌂ *In-room: no a/c, no phone, safe, no TV. In-hotel: restaurant, bar, pool, bicycles, water sports, beachfront, no elevator, laundry service, parking, no-smoking rooms* ⊟ *AE, DC, MC, V* ⫯○⫯ *AI, BP, MAP.*

SPORTS & THE OUTDOORS
Make like Tarzan (or Jane) and swing through the treetops in the shadow of Volcán Osorno with **Canopy Chile** (☎ *65/330–922 or 09/638–2644* ⊕ *www.canopychile.cl*). A helmet, a very secure harness, 2 km (1 mi) of zip line strung out over 12 platforms, and experienced guides give you a bird's-eye view of the forest below.

PUERTO MONTT

20 km (12 mi) south of Puerto Varas via Ruta 5, Pan-American Hwy.

For most of its history, windy Puerto Montt was the end of the line for just about everyone traveling in the Lake District. Now the Carretera Austral carries on southward, but for all intents and purposes Puerto Montt remains the region's last significant outpost, a provincial city that is the hub of local fishing, textile, and tourist activity. Today the city center is quickly sprouting malls, condos, and office towers—it's the fastest-growing city in Chile—but away from downtown, Puerto Montt consists mainly of low clapboard houses perched above its bay, the Seno de Reloncaví. If it's a sunny day, head east to Playa Pelluco or one of the city's other beaches. If you're more interested in exploring the countryside, drive along the shore for a good view of the surrounding hills.

GETTING HERE & AROUND
Puerto Montt is a main transit hub in the region. Buses from Santiago and all points in southern Chile ramble through here at some point, while many cruise ships dock at the port. Puerto Montt's El Tepual Airport has daily air traffic from all the major airlines that serve Chile. The Pan-American Highway also stops here, while the mostly unpaved Carretera Austral, which winds it ways through Chilean Patagonia, begins south of the city. To cross over into Argentina by boat, buses leave from here and from Puerto Varas. Chiloé Island is less than two hours' drive from Puerto Montt. Take the last part of Ruta 5, or the Pan-American Highway to Pargua, where two ferries cross the Chacao Channel every hour.

ESSENTIALS
Bus Contacts Cruz del Sur (⊠*Av. Diego Portales* ☎*65/254–731*). **Puerto Montt Bus Depot** (⊠*Av. Diego Portales* ☎*65/349–010*). **Tas-Choapa** (⊠*Av. Diego Portales* ☎*65/259–320*). **Tur-Bus** (⊠*Av. Diego Portales* ☎*65/259–320*).

Currency Exchange Eureka Turismo (⊠*Guillermo Gallardo 65* ☎*65/250–412*). **Inter Money Exchange** (⊠*Talca 84* ☎*65/253–745*).

Internet Cybercafé Navegante (⊠*Illapel 10, Local 304A, Mall Paseo Costanera* ☎*65/435–858*). **Mundosur** (⊠*San Martin 232* ☎*65/295–415*).

Medical Asístanse Farmacias Ahumada (⊠*Antonio Varas 651, Puerto Montt* ☎*65/344–419*).**Hospital Base Puerto Montt** (⊠*Seminario s/n* ☎*65/261–100*).

Post Office Correos de Chile (⊠*Av. Rancagua 126*).

Rental Cars Avis (⊠*Benavente 570* ☎*65/253–307* ⊠*Urmeneta1037* ☎*65/255–065*). **Budget** (⊠*Antonio Varas 162* ☎*65/286–277* ⊠*Aeropuerto El Tepual* ☎*65/294–100*). **Hertz** (⊠*Calle de Servicio 1431, Parque Industrial Tyrol* ☎*65/313–445* ⊠*Aeropuerto El Tepual* ☎*65/268–944*).

Visitor & Tour Info Puerto Montt Tourist Office (⊠*Plaza de Armas* ☎*65/261–823*). **Sernatur** (⊠*Av. de la Décima Región 480* ☎*65/254–850*).

EXPLORING
Latin America's ornate church architecture is nowhere to be found in the Lake District. More typical of the region is Puerto Montt's stark 1856 **Catedral.** The alerce-wood structure, modeled on the Pantheon in Paris, is the city's oldest surviving building. ⊠*Plaza de Armas* ☎*No phone* ☉*Mass: Mon.–Sat. noon and 7 PM, Sun. 8:30, 10, and noon.*

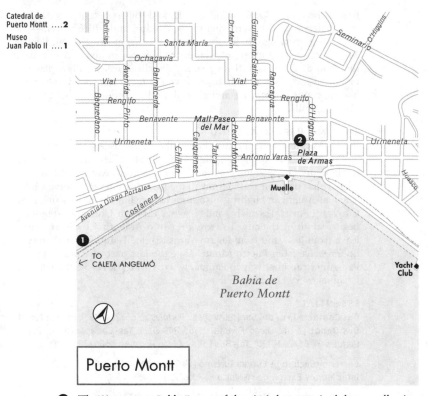

Puerto Montt

❶ The **Museo Juan Pablo II**, east of the city's bus terminal, has a collection of crafts and relics from the nearby archipelago of Chiloé. Historical photos of Puerto Montt itself give a sense of the area's slow and often difficult growth and the impact of the 1960 earthquake, which virtually destroyed the port. Pope John Paul II celebrated Mass on the grounds during his 1987 visit. One exhibit documents the event. ✉ *Av. Diego Portales 991* ☎ *65/261–822* 💲 *250 pesos* 🕑 *Jan. and Feb., daily 9–7; Mar.–Dec., daily 9–noon and 2–6.*

About 3 km (2 mi) west of downtown along the coastal road lies the **Caleta Angelmó,** Puerto Montt's fishing cove. This busy port serves small fishing boats, large ferries, and cruisers carrying travelers and cargo southward through the straits and fjords that form much of Chile's shoreline. On weekdays small launches from Isla Tenglo and other outlying islands arrive early in the morning and leave late in the afternoon. The fish market here has one of the most varied selections of seafood in all of Chile.

Beaches at Maullín. About 70 km (43 mi) southwest of Puerto Montt, at this small town near Pargua—the ferry crossing to Chiloé—the Maullín River merges with the Pacific Ocean. It's a spectacular setting. Be sure to visit Pangal Beach, an extensive beach with large sand dunes that is teeming with birds. If you choose to stay overnight, there are cabins and a campground. ⊠*Ruta 5 south from Puerto Montt, about a 1-hr drive.*

Barely a stone's throw from Cochamó, the mountainous 398-square-km (154-square-mi) **Parque Nacional Alerce Andino,** with more than 40 small lakes, was established to protect some 20,000 endangered alerce trees. Comparable to California's hardy sequoia, alerce grow to average heights of 40 meters (130 feet), and can reach 4 meters (13 feet) in diameter. Immensely popular as a building material for houses in southern Chile, they are quickly disappearing from the landscape. Many of these are 3,000–4,000 years old. ⊠*Carretera Austral, 35 km (21 mi) east of Puerto Montt* ☎*65/212–036* 🎫*1,700 pesos* ⊙*Daily 9–6.*

WHERE TO EAT

$ ✕**Café Central.** This old-style café in the heart of Puerto Montt retains the spirit of the 1920s and 1930s. It's a good place for a filling afternoon tea, with its menu of sandwiches, ice cream, and pastries. The raspberry küchen is a particular favorite here. ⊠*Rancagua 117* ☎*65/482–888* ⊟*AE, DC, MC, V.*

$$ ✕**Café Haussmann.** Its pale-wood-and-chrome decor might make this place seem trendy, but it's actually fun and friendly. The great sandwiches and light meals of crudos, cakes, and küchen make it a great destination for late-night noshing. ⊠*San Martín 185* ☎*65/293–380* ⊟*AE, DC, MC, V.*

$ ✕**Dino's.** Part of a chain of similar restaurants in southern Chile, for years this centrally located spot has been the place for locals to meet and be seen. Sandwiches can be served up extra big if you like. Standard Chilean beef and chicken plates are served, and diverse salads (such as the calamari salad) are excellent. The place also doubles as a coffee shop, so don't hesitate to inquire about the cakes and other desserts. ⊠*Antonio Varas 550* ☎*65/252–785* ⊟*AE, DC, MC, V.*

$$ ✕**Feria Artesanal Angelmó.** Several kitchens here prepare *mariscal* (shellfish soup) and *caldillo* (seafood chowder), as well as *almejas* (clams), *machas* (razor clams), and *ostiones* (scallops) with Parmesan cheese. Separate tables and counters are at each kitchen in this enclosed market, which is 3 km (2 mi) west of Puerto Montt along the coast road. Don't expect anything as formal as set hours, but most open around 11 AM for lunch and serve for about three hours, and then from about 6 to 9 PM for dinner every day in the January–March high season. The rest of the year, most close some days of the week. ⊠*Caleta Angelmó* ☎*No phone* ⊟*No credit cards.*

$$ ✕**El Fogon de Pepe.** If you need a change of pace from the ubiquitous seafood found in these parts, this is a great option. Exquisite roast beef plates in addition to roasted ribs, chicken, and steaks are all great. ⊠*Rengifo 845* ☎*65/271–527* ⊟*AE, DC, MC, V.*

$$ ✕**Pazos.** One of the best things to do in Puerto Montt is to eat curanto, a southern Chilean potpourri of shellfish served together with various meats and potatoes. Pazos, located in a large house across the street from the beach in Peulluco, is where you'll want to start. They also have an array of other seafood delicacies, and meat and chicken alternatives if you're not up for fish. ⊠*Juan Soler Manfredini, Pelluco,*

Fodor's Choice
★

7

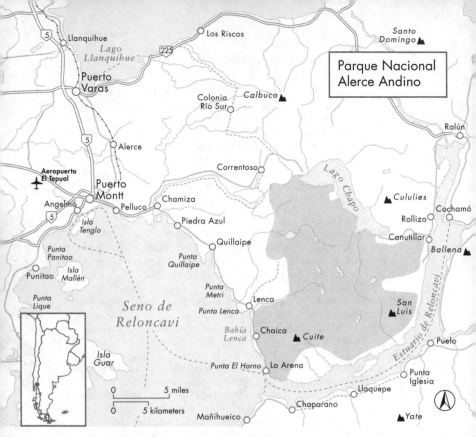

across the street from beach ☎65/252–552 ⚓Reservations essential ▭AE, DC, MC, V.

$$ ✗**Restaurant Kiel.** Hospitable German-born proprietor Helga Birkir stands guard at this Chilean-Teutonic seafood restaurant on the coast west of Puerto Montt. Helga offers a little bit of everything else, but it's her curanto that draws crowds. Fresh produce from her well-kept garden makes lunch here a delight. ✉*Camino Chinquihue, Km 8, Chinquihue* ☎65/255–010 ▭*AE, DC, MC, V.*

WHERE TO STAY

¢ ⛺**Los Alamos.** You can camp here at a site with fine views of the Seno de Reloncaví and Isla Tenglo. Sites have electricity and water, and hot showers are nearby. There's also a dock with boats you can rent. The campground is 11 km (7 mi) west of Caleta Angelmó. **Pros:** Cheap. **Cons:** Bring your own linens. ✉*Costanera, highway to Chinquihue* ☎65/264–666 ▭*No credit cards.*

$$–$$$ 🏨**Don Luis Gran Hotel.** This modern lodging down the street from the cathedral, a favorite among upscale business travelers, has panoramic vistas of the Seno de Reloncaví. (Rooms on the seventh and eighth floors have the best views.) The carpeted rooms have undergone a welcome renovation and have either queen-size beds or two full-size beds. A big American-style breakfast, served in a cozy salon, is included in

the rate. **Pros:** Good for business travelers. **Cons:** Not all rooms have good views. ✉ *Urmeneta at Quillota* ☎ *65/259–001* 🖶 *65/259–005* 🌐 *www.hoteldonluis.cl* 🛏 *60 rooms, 1 suite* ⬦ *In-room: no a/c, safe, refrigerator (some), Wi-Fi. In-hotel: restaurant, bar, room service, gym, laundry service, public Internet, public Wi-Fi, parking, no-smoking rooms* ☰ *AE, DC, MC, V.*

$$ 🏨 **Gran Hotel Vicente Costanera.** The grandest of Puerto Montt's hotels underwent a much-needed face-lift in 2002–2003 and, more than ever, it retains its Gstaad-by-the-sea glory. Its Bavarian-style facade resembles that of countless other Lake District lodgings, but the lobby's huge picture window overlooking the Seno de Reloncaví lets you know this place is something special. The modern guest rooms are comfy, with carpets and contemporary wood furniture—but do yourself a favor and spring for a standard room, rather than an economy one. The difference in price is tiny, but the difference in quality of the rooms is substantial. **Pros:** Clean and modern. **Cons:** Low on personality. ✉ *Diego Portales 450* ☎ *65/432–900* 🖶 *65/437–699* 🌐 *www.granhotelvicente costanera.cl* 🛏 *82 rooms, 4 suites* ⬦ *In-room: no a/c, safe, refrigerator. In-hotel: restaurant, bar, room service, concierge, laundry service, airport shuttle, public Internet, public Wi-Fi, parking, no-smoking rooms* ☰ *AE, DC, MC, V* 🍽 *BP.*

$$ ★ 🏨 **Holiday Inn Express.** Stunning views of Puerto Montt Bay and the city itself make this place an excellent choice. Combine the view, which almost all the rooms have (some rooms even have their own private terrace), with modern facilities, and this is easily one of the best hotels in the city. As an added bonus, the hotel sits above a large mall that includes a movie theater with six movie screens. **Pros:** Amazing views. **Cons:** Can be noisy. ✉ *Av. Costanera, above Mall Paseo Costanera* ☎ *65/566–000* 🌐 *www.holidayinnexpress.cl* 🛏 *105 rooms* ⬦ *In-room: safe, ethernet, Wi-Fi. In-hotel: restaurant, bar, gym, public Internet, public Wi-Fi, parking, no-smoking rooms* ☰ *AE, DC, MC, V.*

$ 🏨 **Hostal Pacífico.** European travelers favor this solid budget option up the hill from the bus station. The rooms are small, but they have comfy beds with lots of pillows. Look at a few before you pick one, as some of the interior rooms have skylights rather than windows. The staff is exceptionally friendly and helpful. **Pros:** Great staff. **Cons:** Small rooms. ✉ *Juan J. Mira 1088* ☎ *65/256–229* 🌐 *www.hostalpacifico. cl* 🛏 *30 rooms* ⬦ *In-room: no a/c, Wi-Fi. In-hotel: restaurant, laundry service, public Internet, public Wi-Fi, airport shuttle, parking, no-smoking rooms* ☰ *No credit cards* 🍽 *CP.*

NIGHTLIFE & THE ARTS

Puerto Montt is a growing city, and the nightlife seems to improve ever year. Most of the better bars and discos are in Pelluco. If you do venture out late at night, be careful where you walk as with the city's growth in size has come a growth in street crime.

Sherlock (✉ *Antonio Varas 452* ☎ *65/288–888*), a bar-restaurant in the city center, is a good place to drink wine or cocktails. In summer, pull up to a table outside. Downstairs on the bar's ground floor they often have live music or karaoke. **Boule Bar** (✉ *Benavente 435, 2nd* *floor* ☎65/348–973 ⊕*www.boulebar.cl*) is a good drinking hole in the city center. The upbeat disco **Kamikaze** (✉*Juan Soler Mafredini 1667* ☎8/499–1262 ⊕*www.kamikazeclub.cl*) fills up with people of all ages. Puerto Montt's biggest disco, **Apache** (✉*Pelluco* ☎65/345–867 or 9/703–5348 ⊕*www.apachepub.com*) also has a separate bar with live music. It's usually packed on weekends, mostly with a younger crowd.

The **Casa de Arte Diego Rivera** (✉*Quillota 116* ☎65/261–859), a gift of the government of Mexico, commemorates the famed muralist of the same name. It hosts art exhibitions in the gallery, as well as evening theater productions and occasional music and film festivals.

SHOPPING

An excellent selection of handicrafts is sold at the best prices in the country at the **Feria Artesanal Angelmó,** on the coastal road near Caleta Angelmó. Chileans know there's a better selection of crafts from Chiloé for sale here than in Chiloé itself. Baskets, ponchos, figures woven from different kinds of grasses and straw, and warm sweaters of raw, hand-spun, and hand-dyed wool are all offered. Much of the merchandise is geared toward tourists, so look carefully for more authentic offerings. Haggling is expected. It's open daily 9–dusk.

COCHAMÓ

94 km (59 mi) southwest of Puerto Varas via Ruta 225, Camino a Ensenada, following the signs south to Ralun, which is 15 km (9 mi) north of Cochamó.

The small fishing villages of Cochamó are blessed with friendly people but little infrastructure. Only a few farms dot the countryside. In short, nature with a capital "N" is the real reason to come here. Civilization has barely touched these great, vast nature areas, some of Chile's (and the world's) last. Think of Yosemite National Park in California without the crowds. Granite walls and domes reminiscent of Yosemite are prevalent throughout the valley. At Río Puelo, the emerald-blue water seems like a dream amid the rare, ancient alerce forests and Andean mountain scenery. An old frontier cattle trail in Cochamó Valley, once used as a hideout by Butch Cassidy and the Sundance Kid, reminds the visitor that the only way through this natural wonderland is by foot or horse. You won't find any cars or roads here.

GETTING HERE & AROUND

There are few cars in Cochamó, and even fewer gas stations (though you can get gas by the container). Walking is probably the most efficient way to get around. Nearby Puelo is even smaller than Cochamó. If you must, rent a car in Puerto Montt or Puerto Varas. Roads in the region are mostly gravel and dirt, so four-wheel drive would be good. Buses do service these towns, however. If you take the bus, arrange with a travel agency or outfitter beforehand to help with transport to the nature areas on your wish list.

ESSENTIALS

Medical Assistance Posta Salud Rural Río Puelo (⊠ *Puelo* ☎ *45/197–2507*).

Visitor & Tour Info Cochamó Municipalidad (⊠ *Calle Santiago Bueras, Puelo* ☎ *65/255–474* ⊕ *www.cochamo.cl*).

WHERE TO STAY & EAT

$$$ ⊞**Andes Lodge.** Billed as a fly-fishing and outdoors lodge, the Andes Lodge has earned a highly favorable reputation among locals and frequent visitors. The restaurant has a fixed menu that features many of the basics, including salmon and beef. The food is not the focus, though. Around Puelo, this is definitely a top lodging spot. **Pros:** Great for those focused on fly fishing. **Cons:** No frills. ⊠ *Puelo,* ☎ *65/234– 454 or 08/501–5478* ⊕ *www.andeslodge.com* ⟿ *8 rooms* ♿ *In-room: no a/c, no phone, no TV. In-hotel: restaurant, room service, bar, pool, water sports, bicycles, no elevator, laundry service, public Internet, airport shuttle, parking, no-smoking rooms* ☰ *AE, DC, MC, V* ⅊*BP.*

$ ⊞**Campo Aventura.** Although mosts guests of this hostal are also clients of the Campo Aventura tour company that owns it, you can still stay here without any touring commitments if you wish. Campo Aventura does offer horseback riding, trekking, rafting, kayaking, or canyoning excursions. In Cochamó this is certainly the best place to stay. They also have a vegetarian restaurant and camping area. **Pros:** Plenty to do. **Cons:** No frills. ⊠ *5 km (3 mi) south of Cochamó on Ruta 225 (Camino a Ensenada)* ☎ *65/232–910* ⊕ *www.campo-aventura.cl* ⟿ *3 rooms, 1 cabin* ♿ *In-room: no a/c, no phone, no TV. In-hotel: restaurant, beachfront, no elevator, laundry service, parking* ☰ *AE, DC, MC, V* ⅊*BP.*

$ ✕⊞**Domo Camp and Tique Restaurant.** You won't soon forget this innovative concept. Five extra-large, dome-like tents with wooden floors, a wood stove, and mattresses are connected by wooden walkways that twist through a lovely forest. A cedar-wood hot tub is available. Nearby there are hiking trails. The Tique Restaurant serves up good food, with an eclectic array of dishes such as roasted salmon, steak and fries, roast lamb, spicy pork, or zucchini pie. **Pros:** Unique concept. **Cons:** Rustic! ⊠ *Río Puelo Alto, Cochamó* ☎ *9/9549–1069* ⊕ *www.andespatagonia. cl* ⟿ *5 cabins* ♿ *In-room: no a/c, no phone, no TV. In-hotel: restaurant, bar, no elevator, parking* ☰ *No credit cards* ⅊*BP.*

SPORTS & THE OUTDOORS

Cochamó and Río Puelo's vast forests, fast-flowing rivers, and mountains are an outdoors-lover's mecca. Before you pursue any of the myriad activities available, though, be sure to get your bearings. Unlike national parks, these areas are not formally protected and maintained, and therefore often lack well-marked trails. Check with a local outfitter or travel agency to get more info on where to go and how.

Campo Aventura (⊠ *San Bernardo 318, Puerto Varas* ☎ *65/232–910* ⊕ *www.campo-aventura.cl*) offers treks, rafting, kayaking, and biking trips in Cochamó and Puelo, but they specialize in horseback-riding trips from one to 14 days.

Continued on page 298

FLY FISHING by Jack Trout

Chile and Argentina are the final frontier of fly fishing. With so many unexplored rivers, lakes, and spring creeks—most of which are un-dammed and free flowing to the ocean—every type of fishing is available for all levels of experience. You'll find many different species of fish, including rainbow trout, browns, sea-run browns, brooks, sea-trout, and steelhead.

The Southern Cone has endless—and endlessly evolving—rivers, streams, and lakes, which is why they're so good for fly fishing. These waterways formed millions of years ago, as volcanic eruptions and receding glaciers carved out the paths for riverbeds and lakes that feed into the Pacific or Atlantic Oceans. With more than 2,006 volcanoes in Chile alone (including South America's most active mountain, Volcano Llaima, outside of Temuco), the Lake Districts of both countries are still evolving, creating raw and pristine fishing grounds.

Why choose Chile or Argentina for your next fly fishing adventure? If you're only after huge fish, stick to California. What these two South American countries offer is a chance to combine fishing, culture, and food in a unique package during the northern hemisphere's off season. With the right guide, you just might find yourself two hours down a dirt road, fishing turquoise water in the shadow of a glacial peak, with not a soul in sight but the occasional *gaucho* or *huaso*. It's an experience you will find nowhere else.

Top: Trout angler casts fly to trout/salmon, Llanquihue, Chile.
Right: Tronador Mountain and Hess Lake, Bariloche, Argentina.

NOT NATIVE

Trout, salmon, and other common species aren't indigenous to South America. These fish were introduced during the late 19th century, mostly as a result of demand from European settlers. Germans, Scots, and others needed trout-filled rivers to survive, so they stocked the New World streams in the image of those in the Old World. For more information, consult *Fly Fishing in Chilean Patagonia* by Gonzalo Cortes and Nicolas Piwonka or *Fly Fishing the Best Rivers of Patagonia Argentina* by Francisco Bedeschi.

WHAT TO EXPECT ON THE GROUND

LOGISTICS

You'll probably fly into Bariloche, Argentina, or Chaiten, Chile. You won't need more than two weeks for a good trip, and hiring a guide can make a big difference in the quality of your experience. Since most rivers are un-dammed, you'll need the extra help managing your drift boat or locating foot access for wading that stream you've spotted around the bend. Having the help of someone who knows each section of river can save you a lot of time.

Good fishing near Chaitén, Chile

GUIDES VS. LODGES

You can purchase your trip package (usually they run between US $2900 and US $5500) through either an independent guide or a specific lodge property. In both cases, packages usually last one week to 10 days, and include breakfast, lunch, and dinner. If you opt to purchase through a lodge, you have the benefit of property-specific guides who know every nook and cranny of stream surrounding the lodge. On the other hand, hiring an independent guide will give you more power to customize your trip and go farther afield.

TIMING

You should make first contact with your guide or lodge in November, during the southern hemisphere's spring. They will be able to predict the upcoming season's peak fishing times, since the depth and speed of the streams depends on snow melt. You can safely plan your trip for sometime during February or March.

CHOOSING YOUR GUIDE

When talking to your guide, it is important to describe what type of fishing you enjoy most. Do you prefer to fish out of a boat, allowing you to travel greater distances, or do you prefer the personal zen of wading the river as it rushes by? Also, ask the right questions.

WHAT TO ASK A GUIDE:

- How early do you start in the morning?
- Do you mainly spin cast or fly fish?
- How long have you been in business?
- Do you always catch and release?
- Will I fish with you or another guide?
- Can I see pictures of your raft or drift boat?
- Do you supply the flies?
- Where do you get your flies?
- Can we fish a river twice if we like it?
- Which rivers and lakes do you float?
- Can we set an itinerary before I arrive?

WHAT TO BRING

5 to 7 Weight Rod: at least 9 foot (consider bringing 9½ foot for larger rivers, windy days, lakes, and sink-tip streamer fishing).

Floating Lines: for dry fly fishing and nymphing.

Streamers: for use while wading to or from the drift boat.

Lines: 15 to 20 foot sink-tip lines with a sink rate of 5.5 to 8 inches per second. It's good to carry two to four different sink rate lines.

Intermediate sink lines: for lakes and shallow depth fishing.

Line Cleaner: because low-ozone areas (the hole in the ozone is close to Antarctica) will eat up lines if you don't treat and clean the lines daily.

Hook sharpener: most guides don't have this very important item.

Small gifts: for the people you meet. Gift-giving can help you gain access to private rivers and lakes. Chocolates, such as Hershey Kisses, or some unique fly pattern, such as a dragon fly, always go over well.

Patagonian brown trout caught on surface fly

Good map: Turistel, in Chile, puts out the best maps and internal information for that country (⊕ www.turistel.cl). Check Argentina Tourism (⊕ www.turismo.gov.ar) for help with that country.

Coffee: Chile has Nescafé instant coffee just about everywhere you go. So if you like a good cup of joe, bring a filter and your favorite coffee. That way all you need is a cup and hot water, and you're all set for your morning fishing.

FLIES

■ Ask your guide where he or she gets flies. Those bought at a discount in countries outside of the United States are often sub-par, so get good guidance on this.

■ If you can, get a list of flies for the time of year you're scheduled to arrive and buy them in the United States before you go. Pay particular attention to the size as well type of insect.

■ The big fish and the quality catches are fooled by the flies that are tied by the guides themselves, because the guides know the hatches and the times they occur.

■ Flies are divided up into similar categories in Chile and Argentina since South America has many of the same insects as we do in North America. Check and see what time each insect is hatching. Note their sizes and colors. You'll need both dry and nymph versions of the following:

❶❷May
❸❹Caddis
❽Stone flies
❼Terrestrials
❺Midges
❻Streamers

in a variety of sizes, colors, and patterns

ARGENTINA FLY FISHING GUIDES AND RIVERS

Region, Trip Length, Season & Lake or Stream	Guides, Lodges, and Hostel Names	Phone	Web
SAN MARTIN DE LOS ANDES 5 to 7 days December–February	Alejandro Bucannan	2972/424–767	www.flyfishing-sma.com
	Jorge Trucco	2972/427–561 or 429–561	www.jorgetrucco.com
Río Filo Huaum/ Parque y Reserva Nacional Lanin	Pablo Zaleski / San Huberto Lodge	2972/422–921	www.chimehuinsp.com
Río Careufu Río Collon Cura	Estancia Tipiliuke	2972/429–466	www.tipiliuke.com
Río Quiquihue	La Chiminee	2972/427–617	n/a
	Lucas Rodriquez	2972/428–270	n/a
JUNIN DE LOS ANDES 5 to 7 days December–February	Alejandro Bucannan	2972/424–767 or 2944/1530–9469	www.flyfishing-sma.com
Río Malleo Río Chimehuin	Estancia Quemquemtreu	2972/424–410	www.quemquemtreu.com
Río Alumine	Redding Fly Shop Travel	800/669–3474 (in US)	www.flyfishingtravel.com
BARILOCHE 4 to 6 days December–February	Martin Rebora / Montan Cabins	2944/525–314	www.patagoniasinfronteras.com
	Río Manso Lodge	2944/490–546	www.Ríomansolodge.com
Río Limay Río Manso Río Traful	Estancia Peuma Hue	2944/501–030	www.peuma-hue.com
Lago Fonk Parque y Reserva Nacional Nahuel Huapi	Estancia Arroyo Verde	5411/4801–7448	www.estanciaarroyoverde.com.ar
	Hotel Piedras	2944/435–073	www.laspiedrashotel.com.ar
ESQUEL 5 to 7 days December–February	Esquel Outfitters	2944/462–776	www.esqueloutfitters.com
	Guided Connections	307/734–2716 (in US)	www.guidedconnections.com
Río Rivadavia Arroyo Pescado Río Carrileufu Río Pico -	Patagonia River Guides	2945/457–020 (in Argentina) or 406/835–3122 (in US)	www.patagoniariverguides.com
Lago Senquer Parque Argentino Los Alerces	Angelina Hostel	2945/452–763	n/a
	Hotel Tehuelche	2945/452–420	n/a

CHILE FLY FISHING GUIDES AND RIVERS

Region, Trip length, Season & Lake or Stream	Guides, Lodges, and Hostel Names	Phone	Web
PALENA AREA 5 to 7 days December–April Río Palena Río Rosselott Río Yelcho Río Futaleufu Lago Yelcho Parque y Reserva Nacional Palena Parque y Reserva Nacional Corcovado	Jack Trout	530/926–4540 (in US)	www.jacktrout.com
	Chucao Lodge	201–8571	www.chucaolodge.com
	Yelcho Lodge	65/731–337	www.yelcho.cl
	Tres Piedras / Francisco Constano	65/330–157	www.trespiedras.cl
	Martin Pescador Lodge	207/350–8178 (in US)	martinpescadorfishing.com
PUERTO VARAS AREA 4 to 6 days December–March Río Petrohue Río Puelo Río Maullin Parque y Reserva Saltos de Petrohue	Jack Trout	530/926–4540 (in US)	www.jacktrout.com
	Tres Piedras / Francisco Constano	65/330–157	www.trespiedras.cl
	Gray Fly Fishing	65/232–496	www.grayfly.com
	Hotel Licarayen Puerto Varas	65/232–305	www.hotellicarayen.cl
	Hotel Puerto Pilar	65/335–378	www.hotelpuertopilar.cl
	Cabins Río Puelo	90/940–643	www.southernchilexp.com
COYHAIQUE AREA 4 to 7 days December–April Río Simpson Río Nirehuoa Río Paloma Río Azul Río Manihuales Lago Pollux Parque y Reserva Nacional Simpson Parque y Reserva Nacional Cerro Castillo	La Pasarela Lodge & Cabins	67/525–101	www.lapasarela.cl
	Heart of Patagonia Lodge		www.patagoniachileflyfishing.com
	Nicolas Gonzales	98/406–3371	n/a
	Eduardo Otarola	99/946–1943	n/a
	David Federick	98/138–3530	n/a
	Alex PRíor	98/920–9132	www.flyfishingcoyhaique.com
	El Saltamontes Lodge	67/232–779	www.elsaltamonteslodge.com
	Troy Cowles	99/992–3199	n/a
RÍO BAKER & COCHRANE AREAS 4 to 6 days Janurary–April Río Baker Río Cochrane Parque Reserva Nacional Cerro Castillo	David Frederick	406/842–7158 (in US) 98/138–3530 (in Chile)	n/a
	Alex PRíor	98/920–9132	www.flyfishingcoyhaique.com
	Green Baker Lodge - Río Baker	72/491-418	www.flyfishing-baker.com
LAKES DISTRICT: PUCON & VILLARRICA 2 to 4 days Nov.–Dec., then Mar.–May Río Trancura, Parque Villarrica Lago Quillen, Parque Nacional Lanin Río Quillen, Parque Nacional Lanin	MaRío's Fishing Zone	99/760–7280	www.flyfishingpucon.com
	Hostal Aileen Colo	45/441–944	n/a
	Del Volcan Apart Hotel	45/442–055	n/a

Miralejos (✉*San Pedro 311, Puerto Varas* ☎*65/234–892* ⊕*www. miralejos.com*) offers trekking, kayaking, mountaineering, and horse-back-riding trips in both Cochamó and Puelo.

For horseback-riding, boating, hiking, and kayaking trips throughout the Río Puelo area, including ascents of Volcán Yates and hikes to ancient alerce forests and glaciers, check with **Andes Patagonia** (✉*Río Puelo Alto, Cochamó* ☎*9/9549–1069* ⊕*www.andespatagonia.cl*).

Chiloé

Queilén, Chiloé Island

WORD OF MOUTH

"Although you'll have many opportunities to view penguins on your planned trip further south, if you have the time and inclination to visit Chiloé Island, we enjoyed tremendously our excursion to the penguin colonies at Bahía Puñihuil (ca. 28 km from Ancud), a beautiful & serene bay on the Pacific. Three local families of farmers and fishermen built the "Restaurant Bahía Puñihuil", where we enjoyed a hearty lunch. They provide gum boots and Wellington pants for the ride on their boats to the penguin islands.

—waggis

WELCOME TO CHILOÉ

Fishing ship, Chonchi

TOP REASONS TO GO

★ **Fantastic Folklore:** Spirits of all stripes haunt Chiloé—or at least populate its colorful folklore, which is full of trolls, witches, mermaids, and ghost ships. Don't let curmudgeonly disbelief spoil your fun on this misty, foggy island.

★ **Traditional Crafts:** Chiloé's sweaters, ponchos, blankets, and rugs are a defining feature of the island. You won't find anything warmer, woollier, or more wonderful anywhere else in Chile.

★ **Charming Churches:** Within Chile, Chiloé is known for the simply elegant churches that dot Isla Grande. A few are open to the public, and a visit to one is essential.

★ **Nature:** Chiloé's close proximity to breeding grounds for blue whales, a globally endangered species, makes it one of the planet's top destinations for whale-watching. Many other animals call Chiloé home, too: there's spectacular bird-watching, including massive penguin colonies and rare birds like the little Chucao Tapaculo.

1 Ancud and Environs. Your ferry will arrive on Chiloé at Pargua, but Ancud is the main transportation hub of this area and also the island's largest city. Using it as your base, explore the nearby towns of Quemchi and Quicaví, two places steeped in folklore and fog. A few of Chiloé's famous churches dot the landscape here in northeastern Chiloé. If you venture over to Isla Quinchao (via the ferry from Dalcahue) be sure to stop in Achao, a busy fishing town.

2 Castro and Environs. Though smaller, Castro is the more cosmopolitan answer to Ancud. You can see a lot from here, including the brightly painted houses of Chonci and the Parque Nacional Chiloé. Other small towns dot the east coast all the way down to Quellón, where you can catch a ferry to Chaiten and the mainland.

PACIFIC OCEAN

Gaubún
Quetalmahue
Chepu

Sector Chepu

Parque Nacional Chiloé

Sector Anay

Cucao
Lago Cucao

Lago Tepuhuico

Isla Grande de Chiloé

Río Medina

Punta Roble

Isla Quilán

GETTING ORIENTED

If you're like most people, you'll explore Chiloé by car. Because of the island's relatively small size, driving is a pleasure. Major towns and landmarks are usually no more than an hour or two away. The Pan-American Highway (Ruta 5) that meanders through northern Chile ends at the Golfo de Ancud and continues again on Isla Grande. It connects the major cities of Ancud, Castro, and Chonchi before coming to its end in Quellón. Paved roads also connect the Pan-American to Quemchi and Dalcahue, and Achao on Isla Quinchao. There are plans to pave the coastal route that connects the village of San Antonio de Chacao with Dalcahue. Another, more scenic, route than the Pan-American leads from Chacao to Caulín and Ancud, via Huicha. The road west from Ancud has been paved as far as the crossroads to the lighthouse at Corona Point and the colonial fort at Ahui.

8

CHILOÉ PLANNER

When to Go

When best to visit Chiloé? In one word, summer. The islands usually get only 60 days of sunshine a year, mostly during the summer months of December to March. Some parts of Chiloé, much like the the Pacific Northwest or Ireland, receive more than 150 inches of rain annually, and most of that falls between April and November. You should be prepared for rain any time of year, though. The high-season crowds are not overwhelming, and they make the island look festive. Off-season Chiloé is beguilingly forlorn. Though admittedly not for everyone, the mist and fog that prevail here deepen the mystery of the island, while the crisp, breezy air is refreshing.

Festivals & Seasonal Events

As elsewhere in southern Chile, most of Chiloé's festivals take place in summer, when there's the best chance of good weather. Fiestas Costumbritsas, which celebrate Chilote customs and folklore, take place over several weekends between December and February in Ancud, Castro, and other towns. Ancud hosts a small open-air film festival the first few days in February.

Eat Well & Rest Easy

As befits an island culture, seafood reigns in Chiloé. The signature Chilote dish is the *curanto,* a hearty stew of shellfish, chicken, sausages, and smoked pork ribs. It's served with plenty of potato bread, known as *milcao* and *chapaleles.* Most restaurants here serve curanto, though not every day of the week and usually only at lunchtime. *Salmón ahumado* (smoked salmon) is another favorite, though salmon are not native to this area.

The archipelago is also known for its tasty fruit liqueurs, usually from the central Chiloé town of Chonchi. Islanders take varieties of berries and apples and turn them into the *licor de oro* that often awaits you at your hotel check in.

There are several good hotels on Chiloé, but none would pass for luxury lodgings on the mainland. That said, the islands have perfectly acceptable, reasonably priced hotels. Castro and Ancud have the most varied choices; Chonchi, Achao, and Quellón less so. Much-appreciated central heating and a light breakfast are standard in better hostelries. Not all places, especially hotels in rural towns, are equipped to handle credit cards, but ATMs are more readily available than you might expect.

Outside the major cities, lodgings are slim. *Hospedaje* ("lodging") signs seem to sprout in front of every other house in Castro and Ancud in summer as homeowners rent rooms to visitors.

WHAT IT COSTS IN CHILEAN PESOS (IN THOUSANDS)				
¢	$	$$	$$$	$$$$
RESTAURANTS				
under 3 pesos	3 pesos– 5 pesos	5 pesos– 8 pesos	8 pesos– 11 pesos	over 11 pesos
HOTELS				
under 15 pesos	15 pesos– 45 pesos	45 pesos– 75 pesos	75 pesos– 105 pesos	over 105 pesos

Restaurant prices are based on the median main course price at dinner. Hotel prices are for a double room in high season, excluding tax.

Chiloé's Chapels

More than 150 wooden churches are scattered across the eastern half of Chiloé's main island and the smaller islands nearby. Jesuit missionaries came to the archipelago after the 1598 Mapuche rebellion on the mainland, and the chapels they built were an integral part of the effort to convert the indigenous peoples. Pairs of missionaries traveled the region by boat, making sure to celebrate Mass in each community at least once a year. Franciscan missionaries continued the tradition after Spain expelled the Jesuits from its New World colonies in 1767.

The architectural style of the churches calls to mind those in rural Germany, the home of many of the missionaries. The complete lack of ornamentation is offset only by a steep roof covered with wooden shingles called *tejuelas* and a three-tier hexagonal bell tower. An arched portico fronts most of the churches. Getting to see more than the outside of many of the churches can be a challenge. Many stand seemingly alone on the coast, forlorn in their solitude and locked most of the year; others are open only for Sunday services. There are two main exceptions: Castro's orange-and-lavender Iglesia de San Francisco, dating from 1906—it's technically not one of the Jesuit churches but was built in the same style—opens its doors to visitors; and Achao's Iglesia de Santa María de Loreto gives daily guided Spanish-language tours.

Sample Itinerary

After crossing the Golfo de Ancud on the morning ferry on your first day, drive south to **Ancud.** Soak up the port town's atmosphere that afternoon. Head to **Dalcahue** the next day; if it's Sunday you can wander among the stalls of the morning market. Take the short ferry ride to **Isla Quinchao** and visit the colorful church of Santa María de Loreto. Back on Isla Grande, head to **Castro.** Spend the next day visiting the capital's historical and modern-art museums and the lovely church. The following day, head south to **Chonchi,** known to locals as the "City of Three Stories." From there it's a rough but doable drive to the sparsely populated Pacific coast to visit the **Parque Nacional Chiloé,** where you can enjoy one of the short hikes through the forest. On your last day head to Chiloé's southernmost town, **Quellón.**

Getting Here & Around

Air Travel. Chiloé has several small airports for regional flights and private planes but no airport for national or international flights. There are plans under way, however, to upgrade the airport at Castro. Most people flying to the region head to Aeropuerto El Tepual, 90 km (54 mi) northeast of Ancud near Puerto Montt. LAN maintains an office in Castro.

Boat & Ferry Travel. Since Chiloé is an archipelago, the only way to drive here is by taking one of the frequent ferries across the eastern end of the Chacao strait. Both Cruz del Sur and Transmarchilay operate the frequent ferry service connecting mainland Pargua with Chacao.

Bus Travel. Cruz del Sur and its subsidiary Transchiloé operate some 30 buses per day between Ancud and the mainland, usually terminating in Puerto Montt. Many of the routes continue north to Temuco, and a few travel all the way to Santiago. Buses arriving from the mainland provide *very* local service once they reach the island, making frequent stops.

Car Travel. Rather than terminating in Puerto Montt, the Pan-American Highway skips over the Golfo de Ancud and continues through Ancud, Castro, and Chonchi before stopping in Quellón. Paved roads also lead to Quemchi, Dalcahue, and Achao on Isla Quinchao.

8

Updated
by Jimmy
Langman

STEEPED IN MAGIC, SHROUDED IN MIST, the 41-island archipelago of Chiloé is that proverbial world apart, isolated not so much by distance from the mainland—it's barely more than 2 km (1 mi) at its nearest point—but by the quirks of history. Some 130,000 people populate 35 of these rainy islands, with most of them living on the 8,394-square-km (3,241-square-mi) Isla Grande de Chiloé. Almost all are descendants of a seamless blending of colonial and indigenous cultures, a tradition that entwines farming and fishing, devout Catholicism and spirits of good and evil, woolen sweaters and wooden churches.

Originally inhabited by the indigenous Chono people, Chiloé was gradually taken over by the Huilliche. Though Chiloé was claimed as part of Spain's empire in the 1550s, colonists dismissed the archipelago as a backwater despite its strategic importance. The 1598 rebellion by the Mapuche people on the mainland drove a contingent of Spanish settlers to the isolated safety of Chiloé. Left to their own devices, Spaniards and Huilliche lived and worked side by side. Their society was built on the concept of *minga,* a help-thy-neighbor spirit in the best tradition of the barn raisings and quilting bees in pioneer America. The outcome was a culture neither Spanish nor indigenous, but Chilote, a quintessential mestizo society.

Isolated from the rest of the continent, islanders had little interest in or awareness of the revolutionary fervor sweeping Latin America in the early 19th century. In fact, the mainland Spaniards recruited the Chilote to help put down rebellions in the region. When things got too hot in Santiago, the Spanish governor took refuge on the island, just as his predecessors had done two centuries earlier. Finally defeated, the Spaniards abandoned Chiloé in 1826, surrendering their last outpost in South America, and the island soon joined the new nation of Chile.

These days, the isolation is more psychological than physical. Some 40 buses per day and frequent ferries make the half-hour crossing between Chiloé and Pargua, near Puerto Montt in the Lake District on the mainland. Meanwhile, a $10 million grant from the Inter-American Development Bank will be used for improvement of sustainable tourism here, with a portion slated to restore Chiloé's historic Jesuit churches.

ANCUD AND ENVIRONS

Although it's the largest city in Chiloé, Ancud feels like a smaller town than perpetual rival Castro. Both have their fans. Castro has more activities, but Ancud, with its hills, irregular streets, and commanding ocean views, gets raves for its quiet charm.

Nearby Quemchi and Quicaví are the tranquil, mystical heart of Chiloé. You can catch the ferry to Isla Quinchao in Dalcahue, but linger there if you have time.

ANCUD

90 km (54 mi) southwest of Puerto Montt.

Interestingly, the village of Chacao (where your ferry arrives) was actually the site of one of the first Spanish shipyards in the Americas, but it was moved to Ancud in 1769 when Ancud was deemed a more defensible location. Ancud was repeatedly attacked during Chile's war for independence and remained the last stronghold of the Spaniards in the Americas, as well as the seat of their government-in-exile after fleeing from Santiago, until 1826, when the island was finally annexed by Chile.

GETTING HERE & AROUND

Boats leave Pargua, on the mainland, every 15 minutes from 7 AM until late in the evening. Trips take about 30 minutes. An additional 30 minutes down the road from Chacao, Ancud will be the first real stop on Chiloé Island for most visitors. Roads from Chacao to Ancud are paved, but if you venture north or west of town to visit attractions such as the beaches at Faro Corona or the penguin colony at Punihuil, the pavement turns into gravel road. There are several bus lines that serve Chiloé cities, particularly Ancud and Castro. Most visitors board buses in Puerto Montt, which is about 2½ hours from Ancud. Add one hour more to get to Castro. The main bus line serving Chiloé, Cruz del Sur, has frequent service throughout the island, including Chonchi and Quellon.

ESSENTIALS

Bus Contacts Cruz del Sur (☎ *65/622–249*). **Terminal Interurbano Ancud** (☎ *65/620–370*).

Currency Exchange Banco del Estado (✉ *Eleutorio Ramirez 229*). **BCI** (✉ *Eleutorio Ramirez 257*).

Ferry Service Cruz del Sur (✉ *Chacabuco 672, Ancud* ☎ *65/622–265*).

Internet Ciber Ares (✉ *Pudeto 364* ☎ *65/629–804*).

Medical Assistance Farmacia Ahumada (✉ *Pudeto 289* ☎ *65/620–345*). **Farmacia Cruz Verde** (✉ *Pudeto 298* ☎ *65/626–116*). **Hospital de Ancud** (✉ *Almirante Latorre 301* ☎ *65/326–352*).

Post Office Correos de Chile (✉ *Pudeto at Blanco Encalada, Ancud*).

Rental Cars Edgardo Ojeda (✉ *Anibal Pinto 1701* ☎ *65/623–793*).

Visitor & Tour Info Sernatur (✉ *Libertad 665, Ancud* ☎ *65/622–800*).

EXPLORING

Statues of mythical Chilote figures, such as the Pincoya and Trauco, greet you on the terrace of the fortresslike **Museo Regional de Ancud,** just uphill from the Plaza de Armas. The replica of the schooner *La Goleta Ancud* is the museum's centerpiece; the ship carried Chilean settlers to the Strait of Magellan in 1843. Inside is a collection of island handicrafts. ✉ *Libertad 370* ☎ *65/622–413* ⌫ *600 pesos* ☉ *Jan. and Feb., daily 10–7:30; Mar.–Dec., weekdays 10–5:30, weekends 10–2.*

8

Northwest of downtown Ancud, the 16 cannon emplacements of the **Fuerte de San Antonio** are nearly all that remain of Spain's last outpost in the New World. The fort, constructed in 1786, was a key component in the defense of the Canal de Chacao, especially after the Spanish colonial government fled to Chiloé during Chile's war for independence. ⊠*Lord Cohrane at San Antonio* ☎*No phone* 🍽*Free*.

WHERE TO EAT

\$\$ ✕ Kuranton. Around the corner from La Pincoya, this intimate establishment specializes in curanto, available at both dinner and lunch (most restaurants only offer curanto for lunch). They also have the standard Chilote seafood offerings along with pizza, beef, chicken, and sandwiches. The walls of the restaurant are lined with tasteful photos, statues, and other Chiloé memorabilia. The wood-burning stove in the center of the dining room is also much appreciated on the often cold and rainy nights. ⊠*94 Arturo Prat* ☎*65/623–090* 🗀*AE, DC, MC, V*.

\$\$ ✕ Restaurant La Pincoya. According to Chilote legend, the presence of the spirit La Pincoya signals an abundant catch. La Pincoya does serve up abundant fresh fish and shellfish and usually whips up curanto on the weekends. This friendly waterfront restaurant is nicely decorated and its views are stupendous. ⊠*Arturo Prat 61* ☎*65/622–613* 🗀*No credit cards* ⊙*Closed Sun. June–Aug*.

WHERE TO STAY

¢ 🏠 Hospedaje O'Higgins 6. The nicest of the many hospedajes in Ancud, this 60-year-old home sits on a hillside overlooking the bay. You have your pick of eight bright rooms. The furniture in the common areas is a bit worn, but the whole place has a cozy, lived-in feel. The friendly service will make you overlook any inadequacies. **Pros:** Amazing views of the bay from the breakfast room, location is good, hotel has character. **Cons:** Bathrooms are somewhat run-down, no Internet. ⊠*Av. Bernardo O'Higgins 6* ☎*65/622–266* 🛏*8 rooms, 2 with bath* 🛎*In-room: no a/c, no phone, no TV. In-hotel: laundry service, no elevator* 🗀*No credit cards* 🍴*CP*.

\$ 🏠 Hostal Lluhay. Don't let this hostal's drab exterior fool you: inside is a charming lobby filled with knickknacks, and a dining room dominated by a 200-year-old rosewood piano. Rooms are plain, but pleasant considering the reasonable rates. The amiable owners include a buffet breakfast in the price. **Pros:** Friendly, good location, reasonable price. **Cons:** Rooms are ordinary. ⊠*Lord Cochrane 458* ☎*65/622–656* ⊕*www.hostal-lluhay.cl* 🛏*18 rooms* 🛎*In-room: Wi-Fi, no a/c, no phone. In-hotel: bar, public Internet* 🗀*No credit cards* 🍴*BP*.

\$\$ ✕🏠 Hostería Ancud. Ancud's finest hotel—and one of the best in Chiloé—sits atop a bluff overlooking the Fuerte de San Antonio. It's part of Chile's Panamericana Hoteles chain, but that doesn't mean it lacks individuality. The rooms in the rustic main building, for example, have log-cabin walls. The wood-paneled lobby, with a huge fireplace inviting you to linger, opens into the town's loveliest restaurant, which feels spacious thanks to its vaulted ceilings and picture windows. Try the *salmón del caicavilú* (salmon stuffed with chicken, ham, cheese, and mushrooms).

Pros: Privileged views of Ancud Bay, good restaurant. **Cons:** Rooms are on the small side. ✉ *San Antonio 30* ☎ *65/622–340* 📠 *65/622–350* ⊕ *www.panamericanahoteles.cl* ⮐ *24 rooms* ⚿ *In-room: no a/c. In-hotel: public Wi-Fi, restaurant, room service, bar, laundry service, public Internet, parking, no-smoking rooms, no elevator* ▭ *AE, DC, MC, V* ⊠ *CP.*

$ 🏨 **Hotel Balai.** Facing the town plaza, this hotel has an ideal location in the center of town. The rooms are spacious, comfortable, and well-kept. The lobby, hallways, and dining area are decorated throughout with paintings and sculptures by local artists. Best of all, however, is the cheerful, attentive service they provide to guests. **Pros:** Location, ambience, friendly service. **Cons:** Paper-thin walls make for difficult sleeping if someone is snoring in a neighboring room, parking is two blocks away. ✉ *Pudeto 169* ☎ *65/622–541* ⊕ *www.hotelbalai.cl* ⮐ *12 rooms* ⚿ *In-room: no a/c, Wi-Fi. In-hotel: no elevator, laundry service, public Internet, parking* ▭ *AE, DC, MC, V* ⊗ *Closed on some holidays.*

$$ 🏨 **Hotel Galeón Azul.** Formerly a Catholic seminary, the Blue Galleon is, confusingly, painted bright yellow. The building is actually shaped like a ship run aground. Located on a bluff overlooking Ancud's waterfront, this modern hotel has pleasantly furnished rooms with big windows and great views of the sea. **Pros:** Waterfront views, proximity to downtown, parking. **Cons:** Walls in the rooms are thin, street noise. ✉ *Libertad 751* ☎ *65/622–567* 📠 *65/622–543* ✉ *galeonazul@surnet.cl* ⮐ *15 rooms* ⚿ *In-room: no a/c, no phone, Wi-Fi. In-hotel: restaurant, room service, laundry service, public Internet, no-smoking rooms, no elevator* ▭ *No credit cards* ⊠ *CP.*

AGROTURISMO

Following a trend seen elsewhere in Chile, Chiloé has developed a system of agro-tourism lodgings called the Red Agroturismo Chiloé (☎ 65/622–604), headquartered in the northern community of Ancud. The network of 19 farms, most of them on Isla Grande, gives the adventurous Spanish-speaking traveler a chance to partake of rural life, helping to milk the cows, churn the butter, or just relax. Rates run 10,000–12,000 pesos per person, including breakfast. Accommodations are in no-frills farmhouses, but plenty of smog- and traffic-weary Santiago residents are lapping up the experience.

NIGHTLIFE

Ancud has some good bars. The locals are friendly, upbeat sorts. Chilotes are known to enjoy a good night of drinking. Most of the bars are situated in the downtown shopping district, but a few nightspots can also be found closer to the waterfront.

Lumiere Bar (✉ *Eldiberto Ramirez 28* ⊗ *Mon.–Sat. noon–5 AM*), with its large square-shaped bar in the center, is an inviting place that's popular with the locals. They serve good bar food late into the evening.

Bar tunes blare loudly at the smoky, crowded **Retro's Pub** (✉ *Maipu 615* ☎ *65/ 626–410*). Their Mexican food offerings—burritos, fajitas, and nachos—are a nice change of pace from Chiloé's ubiquitous seafood.

8

SHOPPING

Shopping in Ancud is nothing extraordinary, though there's a fine artisans' market just below the town plaza and a few blocks up from the waterfront. There you will find woolen blankets, sweaters, dolls, wooden figurines, and other items hand made by Chiloé artisans.

SPORTS & THE OUTDOORS

Water sports such as sailing or sea kayaking are popular in Ancud. There are several fishing and trekking possibilities as well. Along the coastline you can see dolphins, penguins, and often whales from the safety of the area's picturesque beaches. Perhaps the best outdoor excursion in the Ancud area is a visit to Punihul (⊕ *www.pinguineraschiloe. cl*). Located 29 km (18 mi) southwest of Ancud, the three small islets here are home to a colony of Humboldt and Magellanic penguins along with a variety of other birds and wildlife.

Austral Adventures (⊠ *Lord Cochrane 43* ☎ *65/625–977* ⊕ *www.australadventures.com*) has a 50-foot vessel, the *Cahuella,* that takes visitors on extended trips throughout Chiloé.

Chepu Adventures (⊠ *Chepu* ☎ *9/379–2481* ✉ *chepuadventures@gmail. com*) offers kayaking, bird-watching, fishing, nature walks, and more.

Chiloe Indomito (⊠ *Chacao* ☎ *9/509–3741* ⊕ *www.chiloeindomito. com*) offers guided hiking and naturalist trips in northern Chiloé along the western coast.

Richard Dodge (☎ *9/097–6480* ✉ *Richard.dodge@gmail.com*) is a travel consultant, guide, and translator.

Rios Magicos (☎ *7/621–1859* ⊕ *www.riosmagicos.com*) runs fly-fishing, bird-watching, trekking, and canoeing trips.

QUEMCHI

62 km (37 mi) southeast of Ancud.

On the protected interior of the Golfo de Ancud, Quemchi is a small, tranquil fishing village that makes for a good stopover when visiting churches and other tourist sites in northeastern Chiloé. There are several historic churches and scenic islands nearby.

GETTING HERE & AROUND

You can reach Quemchi via paved roads from Ancud in less than an hour by car. To get to nearby tourist sites, be prepared for gravelly, dusty country roads that require careful driving, preferably in a four-wheel-drive vehicle. Additionally, there are a few small islands nearby worth seeing. You will need to hire a boat at the town port, where there are usually a handful of captains on hand ready to negotiate a fee for that service.

EXPLORING

Some 6 km (2½ mi) south of Quemchi is the tiny **Isla de Aucar,** a forested islet reached by walking across a stunning wooden bridge some 510 meters (1,673 feet) long. Black-necked swans and other birds frequent the area, and the Isla Aucar is host to a botanical garden and a Jesuit chapel and cemetery that date from 1761.

Reached by taking a 45-minute boat ride from the port of Quemchi, the immense rock outcropping called **Morrolobos** juts out of the sea off the coast of Caucahue Island. Hundreds of sea lions and marine birds call it home.

WHERE TO STAY & EAT

$
★ ✕**El Chejo.** The official El Chejo guestbook is jammed with raves and compliments about this small, waterfront restaurant. El Chejo offers the gamut of Chiloé seafood dishes, but it's the dozen types of empanadas—pastries filled with various ingredients, such as beef, cheese, clams, salmon, or crab meat, to name a few—that continually impress. ⊠*Diego Bahmonde 251* ☎*65/691–490* ⊟*No credit cards.*

¢ ⊞**Lafken.** This clean, comfortable lodging option is on the waterfront next to the town plaza. Its owners, Manuel Ojeda and his wife Maria Valdebenito, who are usually found working at the cash register in the mini-supermarket on the ground floor, can arrange guides and transport to nearby attractions for a modest price. If that's not enough to lure you in, their supermarket has three first-class pinball machines. **Pros:** Pleasant location. **Cons:** Plain. ⊠*Diego Bahamonde 360* ☎*65/691–373* ⇥*23 rooms, 19 with bath* ⚬*In-room: no a/c, no phone. In-hotel: restaurant, bar, no elevator* ⊟*No credit cards.*

QUICAVÍ

25 km (15 mi) southeast of Quemchi.

The center of all that is magical and mystical about Chiloé, Quicaví sits forlornly on the eastern coast of Isla Grande. Superstitious locals will strongly advise you against going anywhere near the coast to the south of town, where miles of caves extend to the village of Tenaún. They believe that witches, and evil ones at that, inhabit them. On the beaches are mermaids that lure fishermen to their deaths. (These are not the beautiful and benevolent Pincoya, also a legendary kelp-covered mermaid. A glimpse of her is thought to portend good fishing for the day.) And many a Quicaví denizen claims to have glimpsed Chiloé's notorious ghost ship, the *Caleuche,* roaming the waters on foggy nights, searching for its doomed passengers. Of course, a brief glimpse of the ship is all anyone dares admit, as legend holds that a longer gaze could spell death.

GETTING HERE & AROUND

From Ancud, Quicaví is reached by going first to Quemchi, then driving south along a two-lane dirt road for about 40 minutes through the Chiloé countryside.

EXPLORING

In an effort to win converts, the Jesuits constructed the enormous **Iglesia de San Pedro** on the Plaza de Armas. The original structure survives from colonial times, though it underwent extensive remodeling in the early 20th century. It's open for services the first Sunday of every month at 11 AM, which is the only time you can get a look inside.

EN ROUTE

A small fishing village, Tenaún is notable for its 1861 neoclassical **Iglesia de Tenaún,** on the Plaza de Armas, which replaced the original 1734 structure built by the Jesuits. The style differs markedly from that of other Chilote churches, as the two towers flanking the usual hexagonal central bell tower are painted a striking deep blue. You can see the interior during services on Sunday at 9:30 AM and the rest of the week at 5 PM.

DALCAHUE

40 km (24 mi) west of Tenaún, 74 km (44 mi) southeast of Ancud.

Most days travelers in Dalcahue stop only long enough to board the ferry that deposits them 15 minutes later on Isla Quinchao. But everyone lingers in Dalcahue if it's a Sunday morning, when they can visit the weekly artisan market. Dalcahue is a pleasant coastal town—one that deserves a longer visit.

GETTING HERE & AROUND

Like most destinations in Chiloé, this laid-back port town is not very far from Ancud—about one hour along paved roads. There is also frequent bus service, particularly from Castro, which is about a 15-minute drive from Dalcahue.

EXPLORING

The 1850 **Iglesia de Nuestra Señora de los Dolores,** modeled on the churches constructed during the Jesuit era, sits on the main square. A portico with nine arches, an unusually high number for a Chilote church, fronts the structure. The church, which is on Plaza de Armas, holds a small museum and is open daily 9–6.

A *fogón*—a traditional indigenous cooking pit—sits in the center of the small *palafito* (a shingled house built on stilts and hanging over the water) housing the **Museo Histórico de Dalcahue,** which displays historical exhibits from this part of the island. ⊠ *Av. Pedro Montt 105* 🕾 *65/641–214* 🎫 *Free* ⊗ *Weekdays 9–5.*

WHERE TO STAY

$ 🏨 **Hotel La Isla.** One of Chiloé's nicest lodgings, the wood-shingled Hotel La Isla greets you with a cozy sitting room and big fireplace off the lobby. Huge windows and vaulted ceilings make the wood-paneled rooms bright and airy. Comfortable mattresses with plush pillows and warm comforters invite you to sleep tight. **Pros:** Comfortable, friendly service. **Cons:** Pricey for what you get, no credit cards. ⊠ *Mocopulli 113* 🕾 *65/641–241* ✎ *hotellaisla@hotmail.com* 🛏 *14 rooms* ♨ *In-room: no a/c, no phone, Wi-Fi. In-hotel: restaurant, bar, laundry* *service, no elevator, parking* ▭*No credit cards* |◎|*CP.*

SHOPPING

Dalcahue's Sunday-morning art market, **Feria Artesanal,** on Avenida Pedro Montt near the waterfront municipal building, draws crowds who come to shop for Chilote woolens, baskets, and woven mythical figures. Things get under way about 8 AM and begin to wind down about noon. Bargaining is expected, though the prices are already quite reasonable. There's

UNDER RESTORATION
A nonprofit support organization, the Fundación de Amigos de las Iglesias de Chiloé, raises funds for restoration of the archipelago's churches, many of which are in urgent need of repair. Sixteen churches are undergoing major restoration at the time of this edition in a project expected to be completed by 2009.

fun to be had and bargains to be found, but the market is more touristy than the ramshackle daily market in nearby Castro.

ISLA QUINCHAO

1 km (½ mi) southeast of Dalcahue.

For many visitors, the elongated Isla Quinchao, the easiest to reach of the islands in the eastern archipelago, defines Chiloé. Populated by hardworking farmers and fisherfolk, Isla Quinchao provides a glimpse into the region's past. Head to Achao, Quinchao's largest community, to see the alerce-shingle houses, busy fishing pier, and colonial church.

GETTING HERE & AROUND

The roads from Dalcahue, and the main road through Isla Quinchao, are paved. About two hours from Ancud, Achao is a 30-minute journey from Dalcahue, the town from which you catch the ferry to cross Ayacara Bay. The ferry ride lasts a mere five minutes, and there are frequent departures from 7 AM to midnight. It's free for pedestrians and 2,000 pesos each way for cars. Once on the island, the road to Achao winds its way through verdant countryside, often with tremendous views of the surrounding sea.

EXPLORING

Fodor's Choice On Achao's Plaza de Armas, the town's centerpiece is its 1706 **Iglesia**
★ **de Santa María de Loreto,** the oldest remaining house of worship on the archipelago. In addition to the alerce so commonly used to construct buildings in the region, the church also uses wood from cypress and *mañío* trees. Its typically unadorned exterior contrasts with the deep-blue ceiling embellished with gold stars inside. Rich baroque carvings grace the altar. Mass is celebrated Sunday at 11 AM and Tuesday at 7 PM, but docents give guided tours in Spanish while the church is open. An informative Spanish-language museum behind the altar is dedicated to the period of Chiloé's Jesuit missions. All proceeds go to much-needed church restoration—termites have taken their toll. ✉*Delicias at Amunategui* ☎*65/661–881* 💲*500 pesos* ☉*Daily 10:30–1 and 2:30–7.*

8

About 10 km (6 mi) south of Achao is the archipelago's largest church, the 1869 **Iglesia de Nuestra Señora de Gracia.** As with many other Chilote churches, the 200-foot structure sits in solitude near the coast. The church has no tours, but may be visited during Sunday Mass at 11 AM.

WHERE TO STAY & EAT

$$ ✕**Hosteria La Nave.** The beachfront Hosteria La Nave serves seafood, beef, and other dishes in a rambling building that arches over the street. Try the oysters or a *merluza margarita,* hake fish in a shellfish seafood sauce. Above the restaurant is a hosteria with 30 rooms. The rooms are nothing special, but this is a clean, fine option in a pinch. ⊠*Arturo Prat at Sargento Aldea, Achao* ☎*65/661–219* ⊟*No credit cards.*

$$ ✕**Mar y Velas.** Scrumptious oysters and a panoply of other gifts from the sea are served on the top floor, accessible via a side stairway, of this big wooden house at the foot of Achao's dock. Many in town say the food here is the best around. That said, service can be slow at times. ⊠*Serrano 2, Achao* ☎*65/661–375* ⊟*AE, DC, MC, V.*

¢ ⊞**Hospedaje Sol y Lluvia.** If you plan to stay in Isla Quinchao overnight, come here first. It's the best option in town. Located across the street from the police station, the rooms are impeccable and the breakfast included is ample. **Pros:** Clean, pleasant, secure parking. **Cons:** Not close to the beach. ⊠*Ricardo Jara 9* ☎*65/661–383* ↩*9 rooms, 4 with bath* ₺*In room: no a/c, no phone. In hotel: parking, no-smoking rooms* ⊟*No credit cards.*

CASTRO & ENVIRONS

With a population of 20,000, Castro is Chiloé's second-largest city. Though hardly an urban jungle, this is big-city life Chiloé-style. Residents of more rural parts of the island who visit the capital—no more often than necessary, of course—return home with tales of traffic so heavy that it has to be regulated with stoplights.

South of Castro, Chanchi's colorful wooden houses climb the hillside. Parque Nacional Chiloé, one of the islands main attractions, is a great place to spend the night before the ferry ride back to the mainland from Quellón.

CASTRO

45 km (27 mi) southeast of Achao, 88 km (53 mi) south of Ancud.

Founded in 1567, Castro is Chile's third-oldest city. Its history has been one of destruction, with three fires and three earthquakes laying waste to the city over four centuries. The most recent disaster was in 1960, when a tidal wave caused by an earthquake on the mainland engulfed the city.

Castro's future as Isla Grande's governmental and commercial center looked promising after the 1598 Mapuche rebellion on the mainland drove the Spaniards to Chiloé, but then Dutch pirates sacked the city in 1600. Many of Castro's residents fled to the safety of more isolated parts of the island. It wasn't until 1982 that the city finally became Chiloé's administrative capital.

Next to its wooden churches, palafitos are the best-known architectural symbol of Chiloé. These shingled houses are all along the island's coast. Avenida Pedro Montt, which becomes a coastal highway as it leads out of town, is the best place to see palafitos in Castro. Many of these ramshackle structures have been turned into restaurants and artisan markets.

GETTING HERE & AROUND

Situated in the central part of the island, Castro is only about one hour's drive from Ancud along Ruta 5, the Pan-American Highway. For a more interesting route, take the coastal, unpaved road to Castro via Quemchi. That will take twice as long, but you pass by numerous tourist sites. There is regular and frequent bus service from the bus terminal in Puerto Montt to Castro. It's about 4 hours. Catamaranes del Sur provides twice-weekly catamaran service between Castro and mainland Chaitén, with continuing service to Puerto Montt.

ESSENTIALS

Bus Contacts Buses Arroyo (⊠ *San Martin s/n* ☎ *65/635–604*). **Buses Gallardo** (⊠ *San Martin 667* ☎ *65/634–521*). **Cruz del Sur** (⊠ *San Martin 486* ☎ *65/632–389*). **Dalcahue Expreso** (⊠ *Ramirez 233* ☎ *65/635–164*). **Queilen Bus** (⊠ *San Martin 667* ☎ *65/632–173*).

Currency Exchange Banco de Chile (⊠ *Blanco Encalada 201*). **BCI** (⊠ *Gamboa 397*).

Internet Café la Brujula del Cuerpo (⊠ *Av. Bernardo O'Higgins 308, Castro* ☎ *65/633–229*). **Chiloé Virtual** (⊠ *Esmeralda232, Castro* ☎ *65/633–427*). **Entel** (⊠ *Av. Bernardo O'Higgins 480, Castro*).

Medical Assistance Hospital de Castro (⊠ *Ramon Freire 852* ☎ *65/632–486*).

Post Office Correos de Chile (⊠ *Av. Bernardo O'Higgins 388, Castro*).

Rental Cars ADS Rent-a-Car (⊠ *Esmeralda 260, Castro* ☎ *65/637–777*). **Salfa Sur Rent-a-Car** (⊠ *Gabriela Mistral 499, Castro* ☎ *65/630–422*).

Visitor & Tour Info Tourism Office of the Castro Municipality (⊠ *Blanco 273, Castro* ☎ *65/635–039*).

EXPLORING

Any tour of Castro begins with the much-photographed 1906 **Iglesia de San Francisco,** constructed in the style of the archipelago's wooden churches, only bigger and grander. Depending on your perspective, terms like "pretty" or "pretty garish" describe the orange-and-lavender exterior, colors chosen when the structure was spruced up before Pope John Paul II's 1987 visit. It's infinitely more reserved on the inside. The dark-wood interior's centerpiece is the monumental carved crucifix hanging from the ceiling. In the evening, a soft, energy-efficient external illumination system makes the church one of Chiloé's most impressive sights. ⊠*Plaza de Armas* ☎*No phone* ⊙*Dec.–Feb., daily 9–12:30 and 3–11:30; Mar.–Nov., daily 9–12:30 and 3–9:30.*

The **Museo Regional de Castro**, just off the Plaza de Armas, gives the best Spanish-language introduction to the region's history and culture. Packed into a fairly small space are artifacts from the Huilliche era (primarily rudimentary farming and fishing implements) through the 19th century (looms, spinning wheels, and plows). One exhibit displays the history of the archipelago's wooden churches; another shows black-and-white photographs of the damage caused by the 1960 earthquake that rocked southern Chile. The museum has a collection of quotations about Chiloé culture by outsiders: "The Chilote talks little, but thinks a lot. He is rarely spontaneous with outsiders, and even with his own countrymen he isn't too communicative," wrote one ethnographer. The portrait is dated, of course, but even today, residents have been compared with the stereotypical taciturn New Englander. ⊠*Esmeralda 205* ☎*65/635–967* ⊠*Free* ⊙*Jan. and Feb., daily 9:30–8; Mar.–Dec., daily 9:30–1 and 3–6:30.*

All that remains of Chiloé's once-thriving Castro–Ancud rail service is the locomotive and a few old photographs displayed on the outdoor **Plazuela del Tren** down on the waterfront road. Nobel laureate Pablo Neruda called the narrow-gauge rail service "a slow, rainy train, a slim, damp mushroom." Service ended with the 1960 earthquake. ⊠*Av. Pedro Montt s/n.*

Northwest of downtown, the **Museo de Arte Moderno de Chiloé** is housed in five refurbished barns. Referred to locally as the MAM, this modern-art complex in a city park exhibits works by Chilean artists. The museum opens to the public only in summer, but holds occasional temporary exhibitions the rest of the year. ⊠*Pasaje Díaz 181* ☎*65/635–454* ⊠*Free* ⊙*Jan.–Mar., daily 10–6.*

WHERE TO EAT

$$ ✗**Anos Luz.** If you're looking for a nice place for drinks and appetizers, try Anos Luz. It has become a popular spot for tourists. They serve a trendy version of typical Chilean food. Try the *Pollo a la diabla,* or chicken with ginger, chilies, shallots, and onions. ⊠*San Martin 309* ☎*65/532–700* ⊟*No credit cards* ⊙*Closed Sun.*

$$ ✗**Café la Brújula del Cuerpo.** Next to the fire station on the Plaza de Armas, this little place, whose name translates oddly as "the body's compass," bustles with all the commotion of a big-city diner. Sandwiches are standard fare—burgers and clubs are favorites. ⊠*Av. Bernardo O'Higgins 308* ☎*65/633–229* ⊟*AE, DC, MC, V.*

$ ✗**Donde Eladio.** Well-situated in the Castro port in front of the artisans' market, Donde Eladio is a big, lively restaurant with good Chilote food. There are more than 60 plates on offer, from curanto to varied fish plates to Hawaiian-style roast beef. The owner, Eladio La Playa, has been a restaurateur in the neighborhood since 1973. ⊠*Av. Lillo 97* ☎*65/631–470* ⊟*No credit cards.*

$$ ✗**Octavio.** A longtime tourist hot spot, the waterside Octavio is well-known for its Chilote-style seafood and friendly service. You can also

chow down on steak and pork chops here. Their alerce-shingled building has nice views over the water. ⊠*Av. Pedro Montt 261* ☏*65/632–
855* ▤*No credit cards.*

WHERE TO STAY

$ ⊡**Hostal Don Camilo.** The rooms are spacious at Hostal Don Camilo,
an upbeat hotel with a nice, friendly staff. This hotel also has ample
parking, and a restaurant popular with the locals. **Pros:** Parking,
friendly staff, large rooms. **Cons:** Location is not the best. ⊠*Ramirez
566* ☏*65/632–180* ☜*23 rooms, 19 with bath* ♿*In-room: no a/c, no
phone, Wi-Fi. In-hotel: restaurant, room service, no elevator, laundry
service, parking, some pets allowed* ▤*No credit cards.*

$ ⊡**Hostal Kolping.** Great inexpensive lodging is yours at this alerce-shin-
gled building with a big porch in the center of town. Paneled rooms are
bright, sunny, spacious, and sparkling clean, with comfortable beds and
lots of pillows. **Pros:** Good budget option. **Cons:** No frills. ⊠*Chacabuco 217* ☏▤*65/633–273* ☜*11 rooms* ♿*In-room: no a/c, no phone.
In-hotel: public Wi-Fi* ▤*No credit cards* ❡*CP.*

$$ ⊡**Hostería de Castro Hotel & Spa.** Looming over downtown near the estu-
Fodor'sChoice   ary, this *hostería* has a sloped chalet-style roof with a long skylight, which
★   makes the interior seem bright and airy even on a cloudy day. Designed
by one of Chile's most important architects, and built more than 40 years
ago, the structure underwent significant remodeling in 2007 and a new
wing, with 20 suites and a spa, was added. The downstairs seafood res-
taurant has huge windows with great views of the Golfo de Corcovado.
They also have a dance club that opens on weekends. ⊠*Chacabuco 202*
☏*65/632–301* ▤*65/635–688* ⊕*www.hosteriadecastro.cl* ☜*49 rooms,
20 junior suites* ♿*In-room: no a/c, refrigerator (some), Wi-Fi. In-hotel:
restaurant, bar, pool, spa, laundry service, public Internet, no elevator,
parking* ▤*AE, DC, MC, V* ❡*BP.*

¢–$ ⊡**Hotel Chilhue.** This is a good budget option. On Castro's liveliest street,
and just a half block from the plaza, the rooms are clean and comfort-
able. **Pros:** Affordable price, good location. **Cons:** Rooms are plain.
⊠*Calle Blanco 278* ☏*65/632–596* ☜*34 rooms, 29 with bath* ♿*In-
room: no a/c, no phone, Wi-Fi. In-hotel: laundry service, parking.*

$ ⊡**Hotel Esmeralda.** This hot-pink storefront hotel sits just off the bus-
tling Plaza de Armas. The compact four-story building has lots of
windows and all the amenities that you would expect from such a
modern place. It's popular among corporate travelers due to the meet-
ing rooms and business services. **Pros:** Good location. **Cons:** Low on
personality. ⊠*Esmeralda 266* ☏*65/637–900* ▤*65/637–910* ⊕*www.
hotelesmeralda.cl* ☜*32 rooms, 2 suites* ♿*In-room: no a/c. In-hotel:
restaurant, bar, pool, laundry service* ▤*AE, DC, MC, V* ❡*BP.*

SHOPPING

The city's **Feria Artesanal,** a lively, often chaotic artisan market on Euse-
bio Lillo, is regarded by most as the best place on the island to pick up
the woolen sweaters, woven baskets, and the straw figures for which
Chiloé is known. Prices are already quite reasonable, but vendors
expect a bit of bargaining. The stalls share a ramshackle collection of
palafitos with several seafood restaurants. It's open daily 9–dusk.

SPORTS & THE OUTDOORS

Sea kayaking around the outlying islands near Castro has become one of Chiloé's main draws. There are also interesting options for fishing, horseback riding, and hiking in the surrounding countryside, particularly in and around Chiloé National Park.

Probably the best tourism agency in Chiloé is **Turismo Pehuen** (⊠ *Blanco 208* ☎ *65/635–254* ⊕ *www.turismopehuen.cl*). They have a variety of excursions, including horseback riding and hiking.

Altue Sea Kayaking (⊠ *Encomenderos 83, Santiago* ☎ *2/232–1103* ⊕ *www.seakayakchile.com*) specializes in sea-kayaking trips, which range in length from two to nine days.

CHONCHI

23 km (14 mi) south of Castro.

The colorful wooden houses of Chonchi are on a hillside so steep that it's known in Spanish as the *Ciudad de los Tres Pisos* (City of Three Stories). The town's name means "slippery earth" in the Huilliche language, and if you tromp up the town's steep streets on a rainy day you'll understand why. Arranged around a scenic harbor, Chonchi wins raves as one of Chiloé's most picturesque towns.

GETTING HERE & AROUND

Chonchi is just 15 minutes south of Castro via the Pan-Amercan Highway, Ruta 5.

EXPLORING

The town's centerpiece is the **Iglesia de San Carlos,** on the Plaza de Armas. Started by the Jesuits in 1754, it was left unfinished until 1859. Rebuilt in the neoclassical style, the church is now a national monument. An unusually ornate arcade with five arches fronts the church, and inside are an intricately carved altar and wooden columns. The church contains Chonchi's most prized relic, a statue of the Virgen de la Candelaria. According to tradition, this image of the Virgin Mary protected the town from the Dutch pirates who destroyed neighboring Castro in 1600. Townspeople celebrate the event every February 2 with fireworks and gunpowder symbolizing the pirate attack. A March 2002 storm felled the church's tower; fund-raising for reconstruction has been painfully slow, but an infusion of funds from the Inter-American Development Bank means restoration is expected to be completed by 2008. Tower or no tower, the building is open for Mass Sunday at 11 AM.

The small **Museo de las Tradiciones Chonchinas** documents life in Chonchi through furnishings and photos in a 19th-century house. ⊠ *Centenario 116* ☎ *No phone* ☜ *Free* ♡ *Sept.–May, weekdays 9–7; June–Aug., weekdays 9–1.*

WHERE TO STAY & EAT

$ ✕ **Mercado Chonchi.** In a tidy new building that opened in late 2007, this is a great spot for lunch. Four restaurants, in a food court over looking the water, mainly serve the standard Chiloé fare such as curanto and assorted seafoods. A favorite is the restaurant Ballena Azul, which offers great pizza. ⊠ *Located at the end of the waterfront* ⊟ *No credit cards.*

¢–$ 🏨 **Hotel & Cabanas Huildin.** Housed in a historic building more than a century old, this hotel offers comfortable rooms. Behind the main building are 10 fully equipped cabins overlooking the harbor. Given Chonchi's relatively short distance to both Castro and Chiloé Park, this is a good option for those travelers moving through Chiloé by car. **Pros:** Hstoric building, views of the bay, comfortable. **Cons:** Some rooms are small, no restaurant. ⊠ *Centenario 102,* ☎ *65/671–388* ⊕ *www. hotelhuildin.cl* 🛏 *12 rooms, 10 cabins* ⅃ *In-room: no a/c, no phone, kitchen (some), Wi-Fi. In-hotel: no elevator, laundry service, public Wi-Fi, public Internet, parking* ⊟ *No credit cards.*

PARQUE NACIONAL CHILOÉ

35 km (21 mi) west of Chonchi.

The 430-square-km (166-square-mi) Parque Nacional Chiloé hugs Isla Grande's sparsely populated Pacific coast. The park's two sectors differ dramatically in terms of landscape and access. Heavily forested with evergreens, Sector Anay, to the south, is most easily entered from the coastal village of Cucao. A road heads west to the park from the Pan-American Highway at Notuco, just south of Chonchi. Sector Anay is popular among backpackers, who hike the short El Tepual trail, which begins at the Chanquín Visitor Center 1 km (½ mi) north of the park entrance. The El Tepual trail is a wooden path that winds through a rare, intact forest of tepu trees, whose large, twisted trunks are visible above and below your walking path. Along the path as well are signs explaining the significance of the forest and what it holds.

The longer Dunas trail also begins there and leads through the forest to the beach dunes near Cacao. Hiking through the park will give you the best chance of seeing the Chiloé fox, native to Isla Grande; more reclusive is the *pudú*, a miniature deer found throughout southern Chile. Some 3 km (2 mi) north of the Cucao entrance is a Huilliche community on the shore of Lago Huelde. Unobtrusive visitors are welcome.

Cucao beach at the southern end of the park extends 1½ km (1 mi). Dunes extend all along this unusually wide beach. This is one of the best beaches in Chile. Camping is permitted.

Accessible only during the drier months of January through March, the northern Sector Chepu of Chiloé National Park is primarily wetlands created by the tidal wave that rocked the island in 1960. The sector now shelters a large bird population (most notably penguins) as well as a sea-lion colony. Reaching this portion of the park is difficult—take a gravel road turnoff at Coipomó, about 20 km (12 mi) south of Ancud on the Pan-American Highway, to Chepu on the Pacific coast. From there, it's about a 90-minute hike to the park's northern border. ⊠*North of Cucao and south of Chepu* ☎*65/532–501 in Castro* ⬛*Each sector, 1,000 pesos* ⊙*Daily 7–5.*

GETTING HERE & AROUND
To get to Chiloé National Park, take the Pan-American Highway, or Ruta 5, south from Ancud or Castro. A paved side road from the highway leading to the park is found at Notuco, near the town of Chonchi, which is only 22½ km (14 mi) south of Castro.

WHERE TO STAY & EAT
¢   ✕▥ **Parador Darwin.** This bed-and-breakfast has many fans. Owned by a Chilean artist and his German wife, the menu at their popular restaurant includes vegetarian fare, goulash, and authentic küchen (pie). The rooms are comfortable. **Pros:** Restaurant, friendly service, cheap. **Cons:** Small place. ⊠*Located near the Cucao entrance to Chiloé National Park* ☎*9/884–0702 or 9/799–9923* ⌐*4 rooms* ⟁*In-room: no a/c, no phone, no TV. In-hotel: restaurant, parking* ⬛*No credit cards.*

¢–$ ▥ **El Fogon de Cucao.** Founded in 1997 by Miguel Angel, a longtime
Fodor'sChoice   reporter for some of Chile's most important newspapers, the Fogon
★   de Cucao is a cozy architectural gem of a hotel. Some rooms have their own terraces, where guests can sit and gaze out at a tremendous view of the park and Cucao Lake. Facilities are spotless. The restaurant occasionally hosts live music, and there's also a campground and a general store. The hotel will happily arrange horseback excursions through the park's hills, forests, and beaches. **Pros:** Excellent service, comfortable rooms, lakeside. **Cons:** Few rooms, no Internet. ⊠*Located near the Cucao entrance in the southern end of Chiloé National Park* ☎*9/946–5685* ⌐*9 rooms, 1 cabin* ⟁*In-room: no a/c, no phone, no TV. In-hotel: restaurant, bar, beachfront, water sports, no elevator, laundry service, parking* ⬛*No credit cards.*

QUEILÉN

47 km (29 mi) southeast of Chonchi.

This town named for the red cypress trees that dot the area sits on an elongated peninsula and, as such, is the only town on Isla Grande with two seafronts. Two of Isla Grande's best bathing beaches are the town's central **Playa de Queilén,** and the **Playa Lelbun,** 15 km (9 mi) northwest of the city.

GETTING HERE & AROUND
From Castro, go south on Ruta 5 until you get to the Chonchi exit; from Chonchi there is a gravel road that leads to Queilen.

EXPLORING
The **Refugio de Navegantes** serves as the town's cultural center and contains a small museum with artifacts and old black-and-white photographs. Nothing is very colorful here—the muted tones of the pottery, the fabrics, and the farm implements reflect the stark life of colonial

Chiloé. ⊠*Pedro Aguirre Cerda s/n* 🕾*No phone* 🖃*Free* ⊙*Weekdays 9–12:30 and 2:30–6.*

Uphill on Calle Presidente Kennedy is a **mirador.** The observation point has stupendous views of the Golfo de Ancud, the smaller islands in the archipelago, and, on a clear day, the Volcán Corcovado on the mainland.

QUELLÓN

99 km (60 mi) south of Castro.

The Pan-American Highway, which begins in Alaska and stretches for most of the length of North and South America, ends without fanfare here in Quellón, Chiloé's southernmost city. Quellón was the famed "end of Christendom" described by Charles Darwin during his 19th-century visit. Just a few years earlier it had been the southernmost outpost of Spain's empire in the New World. For most visitors today, Quellón is also the end of the line. But if you're truly adventurous, it's the starting point for ferries that head to the Southern Coast.

GETTING HERE & AROUND

Quellón is about a one-hour drive south of Castro, on the paved Ruta 5. From Quellón, you can also catch a bi-weekly ferry with Naviera Austral (Wednesdays and Sundays in summer) to get to Chaiten on the mainland, the jumping off point for the Carretera Austral.

EXPLORING

Taking its name from a Huilliche phrase meaning "from our past," the **Museo Inchin Cuivi Ant** stands apart from other museums in Chiloé because of its "living" exhibitions: Chilote women spin woolens on their looms, make empanadas in a traditional fogón, and cultivate a botanical garden with herbs, plants, and trees native to Chiloé. ⊠*Ladrilleros 225* 🕾*No phone* 🖃*500 pesos* ⊙*Daily 9–1 and 2:30–8.*

WHERE TO STAY & EAT

$$ ✕**Hostería Romeo Alfa.** This imposing seafood restaurant, which resembles a Bavarian chalet, sits right on Quellón's pier. Choose one of the tables along the window and watch all the comings and goings while you enjoy fish or other Chiloé-style seafood plates. The atmosphere is informal and friendly. ⊠*Capitán Luis Alcazar 554* 🕾*65/680–177* ▭*No credit cards.*

¢–$ ✕🖬**Hotel El Chico Leo.** A nice waterfront hotel and restaurant. The especially popular restaurant serves up curanto and other seafoods. Ask for a room with a view (room numbers 6, 7, or 8 are the best). **Pros:** Good location. **Cons:** Small. ⊠*Pedro Montt 325* 🕾*65/681–567* 🛏*17 rooms* ⚏*In-room: no a/c, no phone, Wi-Fi. In-hotel: restaurant, bar, no elevator, laundry service* ▭*AE, DC, MC, V.*

$$ 🖬**Hotel Patagonia Insular.** Opened in September 2007, the hotel right-
★ fully bills itself as the most modern hotel on Chiloé. Its location, perched on a hill overlooking Quellón Bay, provides spectacular views. The rooms have all the amenities you'd expect from a top hotel. **Pros:** Modern, panoramic views of Quellón Bay. **Cons:** No gym or spa.

8

⊠*Av. Juan Ladrilleros 1737* ☎*65/681–610* ⊕*www.hotelpatagonia insular.cl* ⟳*30 rooms* ⚘*In-room: safe, DVD, Wi-Fi. In-hotel: restaurant, room service, bar, no elevator, laundry service, public Internet, parking* ⊟*AE, DC, MC, V.*

¢–$ ✕▣ **Hotel Tierra del Fuego.** This rambling alerce-shingle house, dating from the 1920s, is on Quellón's waterfront. You'll notice a significant change of light when you've crossed the threshold between the original rooms, with their small windows, and those added in the past decade. Opt for one of the wood-paneled rooms in the newer wing or on the third floor; they maintain the style of the original house, but sunlight streams in through big windows. Everyone in town seems to stop by for lunch at the bustling restaurant downstairs. **Pros:** Great location, good restaurant, friendly service. **Cons:** Rooms vary in quality. ⊠*Av. Pedro Montt 445* ☎☎*65/682–079* ⟳*30 rooms, 21 with bath* ⚘*In-room: no a/c, no phone, Wi-Fi. In-hotel: restaurant, bar, no elevator* ⊟*No credit cards.*

SHOPPING

Quellón's **Feria Artesanal Llauquil,** on Avenida Gómez García, doesn't have the hustle and bustle of similar artisan markets in Castro and Dalcahue, but there are some good buys on woolens and straw folkloric figures. Don't bother to bargain; you'll find the prices are already extremely reasonable. The market is open daily until 7 December–February, and Monday–Saturday until 6 the rest of the year.

The Southern Coast

Bertrand Lake Laguna San Rafael National Park

WORD OF MOUTH

Patagonia would probably be one of the safest places to drive. From El Calafate to Torres del Paine, we only saw a hand full of cars and everyone was really courteous of one another and even waved hello!

—oceania

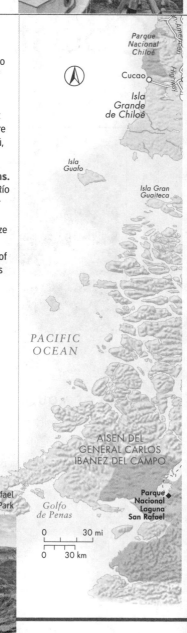

WELCOME TO THE SOUTHERN COAST

TOP REASONS TO GO

★ **Scenery:** The Carretera Austral, a dusty dirt road blazed through southern Chile by Augusto Pinochet, has opened up one of the most beautiful places in the world to tourists. Rent a four-wheel-drive truck or jeep, or bring a mountain bike, and soak it all in.

★ **Glaciers:** To watch a chunk of ice break off the glaciers near Mount San Valentín, and fall with a thundering splash into the lake below, is reason enough for a trip to Laguna San Rafael National Park (which has 19 different glaciers).

★ **Fishing:** Fly-fishing fanatics were among the first to explore this area thoroughly. You'll be able to step right outside your door for great fishing at any number of lodges. A short boat trip will bring you to isolated spots where you won't run into another soul for the entire day.

★ **Rafting and Kayaking:** The Futalefeu River is Class V-plus. That's raft speak for very fast-moving water. In fact, this river is considered one of the fastest in the world.

1 Chaitén & Puerto Puyuhuapi. Although Chaitén itself isn't much to see, you will find yourself passing through it on the way from Chiloé or the Lake District. It's a perfect spot from which to explore Parque Pumalín, Futaleufú, and Puerto Puyuhuapi.

2 Coyhaique & Environs. Where Río Simpson and Río Coyhaique come together you'll find Coyhaique, the only community of any size on the Carretera Austral. Calling itself "the capital of Patagonia," Coyhaique has some 50,000 residents—more than half of the region's population.

Baker River, Laguna San Rafael National Park

Cohaique Region

LOS LAGOS

Pichanco
Fiordo
Largo
Cta
Gonzalo ◆ **Parque
Pumalín** 1
Chaitén
Termas de
Amarillo
Volcán
Corcovado
Villa
Santa
Lucia
Palena
Parque
Nacional
Patena
La Junta
Volcán
Melimoyu
Parque Nacional
Queulat ◆
Puerto
Puyuhuapi
Lago
Verde
Puyuhuapi
Lodge & Spa
Villa
Amegual
Isla
Magdalena
Puerto
Cisnes
Volcán
Co Maca
Mañihuales
Puerto
Aisén
Puerto
Chacabuco
Coyhaique
2
Balmaceda
Volcán
Hudson
Villa Cerro
Castillo
Puerto
Murta
Lago
General
Carrera
Chile
Chico
Lago
Buenos
Aires
Puerto
Tranquilo
Campos de
Hielo Sur
Cochrane

Castro
Chonchi
5
Quellón
Golfo de Corcovado
Nevado
Canal Moraleda

ARGENTINA

Futaleufú
Puerto
Ramirez

9

GETTING
ORIENTED

The Southern Coast is a
tranquil, expansive region
covered with pristine na-
ture, much of it protected
in national parks and
reserves. By and large,
this is territory for people
who love the outdoors.
Here you will find unpar-
alleled fishing, kayaking,
white-water rafting, and
a road through natural
beauty that is ideal for a
long mountain-bike trip.
Intrepid explorers will be
rewarded with relatively
untrammeled trails and
rarely viewed vistas.

Baker River, Laguna San Rafael
National Park

THE SOUTHERN COAST PLANNER

When to Go

Late spring through summer—late November to mid-March—is considered high season in this part of southern Chile. It's highly recommended that you make advance reservations if your intention is to stay at high-end hotels or resorts during this time. Although the weather is likely to be cooler and rainier in the spring (September into November) and fall (March to May), it's also a fine time for travel here.

Money Matters

Converting cash can be a bureaucratic headache, particularly in smaller towns like Chaitén. A better option is using your ATM card at numerous local banks connected to Cirrus or Plus networks.

When you're anticipating smaller purchases, try to have coins and small bills on hand at all times. Small vendors do not always have change for large bills.

Eat Well & Rest Easy

All manner of fish, lamb, beef, and chicken dishes are available in the Southern Coast. By and large, entrées are simple and hearty. Given the area's great distance from Chile's Central Valley, where most of Chile's fruits and vegetables are grown, most things that appear on your plate probably grew somewhere nearby. Many dishes are prepared from scratch when you order.

Traveling by road throughout the region, you may see crudely printed signs with an arrow pointing to a nearby farmhouse advertising _küchen_ (rich, fruit-filled pastries)—clear evidence of the many pockets of German influence.

This region offers a surprisingly wide choice of accommodations. What you won't find is the blandness of chain hotels. Most of the region's establishments reflect the distinct personalities and idiosyncrasies of their owners.

Some of the most humble homes in villages along the Carretera Austral are supplementing their family income by becoming bed-and-breakfasts. A stay in one of these _hospedajes_ is an ideal way to meet the people and experience the culture. These accommodations are not regulated, so inquire about the availability of hot water and confirm that breakfast is included. Don't hesitate to ask to see the room—you may even get a choice.

WHAT IT COSTS IN CHILEAN PESOS (IN THOUSANDS)

¢	$	$$	$$$	$$$$
RESTAURANTS				
under 3 pesos	3 pesos–5 pesos	5 pesos–8 pesos	8 pesos–11 pesos	over 11 pesos
HOTELS				
under 15 pesos	15 pesos–45 pesos	45 pesos–75 pesos	75 pesos–105 pesos	over 105 pesos

Restaurant prices are based on the median main course price at dinner. Hotel prices are for a double room in high season, excluding tax.

The Carretera Austral

As you drive south along the Carretera Austral, Chile's southernmost reaches seem to simply disintegrate into a tangle of sounds and straits, channels and fjords. Here you'll find lands laden with lush vegetation or layered in fields of ice. The road struggles valiantly along this route, connecting tiny fishing towns and farming villages all the way from Puerto Montt to Villa O'Higgins. There, the huge Campo de Hielo Sur (Southern Ice Field) forces it to a halt.

Navigating the Carretera Austral requires some planning, as communities along the way are few and far between. Some parts of the highway, especially in the southernmost reaches, are deserted. Check out your car thoroughly, especially the air in the spare tire. Make sure you have a jack and jumper cables. Bring along enough food in case you find yourself stuck far from the nearest restaurant.

Sample Itinerary

On your first day head to the port town of **Chaitén** by ferry from Puerto Montt. Devote a day or two to visiting **Parque Pumalín,** which has some of the most pristine landscape in the region. Then, spend a day going down the Carretera Austral, or Southern Highway, to **Puerto Puyuhuapi,** preferably doing so in your own rented, four-wheel-drive truck or jeep to give you more flexibility. A stay at Puyuhuapi Lodge & Spa, a resort accessible only by boat, is a great way to relax and recharge for the next phase of your journey. While in Puyuhuapi, consider spending an extra day there to visit the "hanging glacier" at **Parque Nacional Queulat.** Afterward, go to **Coyhaique,** located about five hours south. The largest city in the region, Coyhaique will be a good place for shopping and eating a nice meal before heading to nearby **Puerto Chacabuco,** where you can board a boat bound for the unforgettable glaciers at **Parque Nacional Laguna San Rafael.** If you lack the time to continue farther south to see still more of Patagonia's incredible landscape, return to Puerto Montt by a ferry boat that departs from Puerto Chacabuco.

Getting Here & Around

Air Travel. LAN has flights to the region from Santiago, Puerto Montt, and Punta Arenas. They arrive at the Southern Coast's only major airport, 55 km (34 mi) south of Coyhaique, in the town of Balmaceda. Other carriers serving southern Chile include Aerolineas del Sur, Empresa CieloMarAustral, and Empresa Aero Taxi.

Boat & Ferry Travel. Be warned that ferries in southern Chile are slow and not always scenic, particularly if skies are the least bit clouded, but they are reliable. If you're touring the region by car, the ferry is a good choice. The main companies serving this area are Navimag and Transmarchilay.

Bus Travel. Service between Puerto Montt and Cochrane is by private operators such as Tur-Bus. Travel along the Carretera Austral is often agonizingly and inexplicably slow, so don't plan on getting anywhere on schedule.

Car Travel. You can drive the northern part of the Southern Coast without the aid of a ferry, but you'll need to spend some time in Argentina along the way, eventually crossing back into Chile near Futaleufú. The best route takes you to Bariloche, crossing the Argentina border near Osorno and Puyehue, just north of Puerto Montt.

9

Updated
by Jimmy
Langman

THE SLIVER OF LAND KNOWN as the Southern Coast stretches for more than 1,000 km (620 mi), from the southernmost part of the administrative district of Los Lagos through the northern part of Aisén (locally spelled Aysén). Sandwiched between the tranquil valleys of the Lake District and the wondrous ice fields of Patagonia, it largely consists of heavily forested mountains, some of which rise dramatically from the shores of shimmering lakes, others directly out of the Pacific Ocean. Slender waterfalls and nearly vertical streams, often seeming to emerge from the rock itself, tumble and slide from neck-craning heights. Some dissipate into misty nothingness before touching the ground, others flow into the innumerable rivers—large and small, wild and gentle— heading westward to the sea. Chile has designated vast tracts of this truly magnificent landscape as national parks and reserves, but most are accessible only on foot. The few roads available to vehicles are slightly widened trails or the occasional logging route navigable only by the most rugged of four-wheel-drive vehicles.

The Southern Coast is one of the least-populated areas remaining in South America: the population density here is said to be lower than that of the Sahara Desert. The infrequent hamlets scattered along the low-lying areas of this rugged region subsist as fishing villages or small farming centers. The gradual increase of boat and ferry service to some of these towns and the expansion of the major highway called the Carretera Austral have begun to encourage migration to the region. Coyhaique, the only town here of any size, with a population of 50,000, has lots of dining, lodging, and shopping. Meanwhile, a few intrepid entrepreneurs have established world-class accommodations in remote locations near spectacular mountain peaks, ancient volcanoes, and glaciers, with their concomitant fjords and lakes.

Planning a visit to the region's widely separated points of interest can be challenging, as getting from place to place is often difficult. Creating a logical itinerary in southern Chile is as much about choosing how to get here as it is about choosing where you want to go. The most rewarding mode of transport through this area is a combination of travel by boat and by plane, with an occasional car rental if you want to journey a little deeper into the hinterlands.

CHAITÉN & PUERTO PUYUHUAPI

CHAITÉN

201 km (125 mi) south of Puerto Montt.

A century ago, Chaitén wasn't even on the map. Today it's a small port town, with a population of barely more than 3,000. Although it's not really a destination itself, Chaitén serves as a convenient base for exploring the area, including Parque Pumalín.

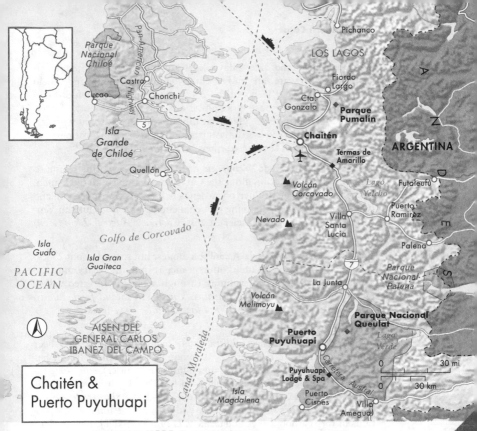

Chaitén &
Puerto Puyuhuapi

GETTING HERE & AROUND

Getting here is fairly easy: both Navimag (⊕ *www.navimag.com*) and Transmarchilay (⊕ *www.transmarchilay.com*) operate regular ferry service between Chaitén and Puerto Montt in the Lake District and Quellón on Chiloé. Flying is also an option; a few small airlines offer flights between Chaitén and Puerto Montt.

It's also possible to drive to Chaitén from Puerto Montt via the Carretera Austral, but you have to make use of two car ferries. The first is fine, as Transmarchilay ferries make nine daily trips between La Arena and Puelche all year. The second leg is tougher because Transmarchilay's ferries between Hornopirén and Caleta Gonzalo operate only in January and February.

ESSENTIALS

Currency Exchange Banco del Estado (⊠ *Calle Libertad 298* ☎ *65/565–540*).

Medical Asístanse Hospital de Chaitén (⊠ *Ignacio Carrera Pinto 153* ☎ *65/731–244*).

Visitor & Tour Info Chaitur (⊠ *Terminal de Buses, O'Higgins 67* ☎ *65/731–429* ⊕ *www.chaitur.com*). **Sernatur** (⊠ *Edificio del Gobernacion, 1st Floor, Av. Bernardo O'Higgins 254* ☎ *65/731–280*).

EXPLORING

Michimahuida Volcano. Take a day hike through dense temperate rainforest dotted with waterfalls and rare native trees like coihue and canelo to enjoy spectacular views of the 2,438-meter-high (8,000-foot-high) Michimahuida. For those more ambitious and physically fit, an overnight camping trip to the glacier at the summit rewards you with tremendous, bird's-eye views of the surrounding area. One local outfitter for trips like this is **Chaitur Excursions** (⊕www.chaitur.com).

The emerald-green **Lago Yelcho,** one of the best places in the region to fish for brown trout, runs along the Carretera Austral south of Chaitén. Just past the village of Puerto Cárdenas is Puente Ventisquero Yelcho (Glacier Bridge), the beginning of a challenging two-hour hike to Ventisquero Cavi (Hanging Glacier). ⊠*Off Carretera Austral, 2 km (1 mi) past Puerto Cardenas.*

The much-lauded **Termas del Amarillo,** a modest hot springs about 25 km (16 mi) southeast of Chaitén, offers a nice respite for weary muscles. The setting, along a river running through a heavily forested valley, is lovely. ⊠*Off Carretera Austral, 6 km (4 mi) inland from Puerto Cardenas* ☎*No phone* 🎫*2,000 pesos* ☉*Daily 8* AM*–9* PM.

WHERE TO EAT

$$ ✕**Brisas del Mar.** This cheerful little eatery overlooks the sea. The sheer number of items on the menu is astounding. Try excellent fish dishes such as *salmón en mantequilla* (salmon braised in butter), *congrio* (conger eel), and *loco* (abalone). They also have six cabins available for weary tourists. ⊠*Corcovado 278* ☎*65/731–284* 🚫*No credit cards.*

$ ✕**Corcovado.** Here's one place where you won't leave hungry: the portions of the seafood dishes and *asado a la brasa* (mixed grilled meats), served with a baked potato and salad, are huge, but the prices are small. This wooden building sits near the water, so you are treated to great views. The restaurant also adjoins a small hotel under the same ownership. ⊠*Corcovado 408* ☎*65/731–221* 🚫*No credit cards.*

WHERE TO STAY

$ 🏨**Hosteria Puma Verde.** This adorable, wood-shingled B&B is run by
★ Parque Pumalín, which explains why it's in a class of its own. Locally crafted furniture sits atop polished wood floors. Woolen blankets and piles of pillows add to the coziness. Puma Verde has three rooms (one double, two triples), and one apartment that sleeps five. The large apartment, filled with hand-carved wood furniture, rents for a bargain 60,000 pesos without breakfast. **Pros:** Tastefully decorated, cozy. **Cons:** Not a lot of rooms, no TV. ⊠*Av. Bernardo O'Higgins 54* ☎*65/731–184* ⊕*www.parquepumalin.cl* 🛏*3 rooms, 1 apartment* ⚷*In-room: no a/c, no phone, no TV. In-hotel: no elevator* 🚫*AE, DC, MC, V* 🍴*BP.*

$ 🏨**Hotel Mi Casa.** This friendly hotel has spectacular views of the bay and town from its large, wooden terrace. The restaurant has good regional and international dishes. And the staff goes out of its way to cater to your specific needs. **Pros:** Terrace views, friendly service, good restaurant. **Cons:** Somewhat outside of town, no phone, no TV in some rooms.

Chile's Road to Riches

The Pan-American Highway, which snakes its way through the northern half of Chile, never quite makes it to the Southern Coast. To connect this remote region with the rest of the country, former President Augusto Pinochet proposed a massive public works project to construct a highway called the Carretera Austral. But the $300 million venture had another purpose as well. Pinochet was afraid that without a strong military presence in the region, neighboring Argentina could begin chipping away at Chile's territory. The highway would allow the army easier access to an area that until then was accessible only by boat.

Ground was broken on the Carretera Austral in 1976, and in 1982 the first section, running from Chaitén to Coyhaique, opened to great fanfare. The only trouble was that you still couldn't get there from the mainland. It took another five years for the extension from Chaitén north to Puerto Montt to be completed. An extension from Coyhaique south to Cochrane was finished the following year.

The word *finished* is misleading, as construction continues to this day. Although the Carretera Austral is nicely paved near Puerto Montt, it soon reveals its true nature as a two-lane gravel surface that crawls inexorably southward for 1,156 km (718 mi) toward the outpost of Villa O'Higgins. And the highway isn't even contiguous. In places the road actually ends abruptly at water's edge—ferries link these broken stretches of highway. The segment from Chaitén to Coyhaique is mostly gravel road, but every year the paved sections grow longer.

The Carretera Austral is lauded in tourism brochures as "a beautiful road studded with rivers, waterfalls, forests, lakes, glaciers, and the occasional hamlet." This description is accurate—you may live the rest of your life and never see anything half as beautiful as the scenery. However, the highway itself is far from perfection. The mostly unpaved road has dozens of single-lane, wide-board bridges over streams and rivers. Shoulders are nonexistent or made of soft, wheel-grabbing gravel. Periodically, traffic must wend its way through construction, amid heavy equipment and workers.

What the Carretera Austral offers adventurous travelers is a chance to see a part of the world where few have ventured. The views from the highway are truly amazing, from the conical top of Volcán Corcovado near Chaitén to the sprawling valleys around Coyhaique. Here you'll find national parks where the trails are virtually deserted, such as Parque Nacional Queulat and Reserva Nacional Río Simpson. The region's crowning glory, of course, is the vast glacier at Laguna San Rafael. It may be a tough journey today, but when it is eventually finished, the Carretera Austral could rival the most spectacular scenic roadways in the world.

—Pete Nelson

9

✉*Av. Norte 206* ☎*65/731–285* ⊕*www.hotelmicasa.cl* ⟿*20 rooms* ♿*In-room: no phone, no TV (some). In-hotel: restaurant, room service, bar, gym, laundry service, public Internet, public W-Fi, no elevator, airport shuttle, parking, no-smoking rooms* ☰*No credit cards* ⍩*BP.*

$ ▦**Hotel Schilling.** Of the town's numerous family-run hospedajes, Hotel Schilling is the most professional and hospitable. Rooms are enlivened by bedspreads in a rainbow of colors. Its location, just across from the ocean, is a major draw. **Pros:** Location, good service. **Cons:** Simple rooms. ✉*Corcovado 230* ☎*65/731–295* ⊕*www.hotelschilling.patagoniatour. cl* ⟿*12 rooms* ♿*In-room: no a/c, no phone, ethernet, Wi-Fi. In hotel: restaurant, parking, no elevator* ☰*No credit cards* ⍩*CP.*

PARQUE PUMALÍN

Fodor'sChoice
★ *56 km (35 mi) north of Chaitén.*

Parque Pumalín is an extraordinary venture that began when conservationist Douglas Tompkins bought a 42,000-acre *araucaria* (an indigenous evergreen tree) forest south of Puerto Montt. Since 1988, he has spent more than $25 million to purchase the nearly 800,000 acres that make up Parque Pumalín. In addition to araucaria trees, the park shelters one of the largest—and one of the few remaining—intact alerce forests in the world. Alerces, the world's second-longest-lived tree species, which can live up to 4,000 years, are often compared to the equally giant California redwood. The Chilean government declared the park a nature sanctuary in August 2005.

Tompkins, an American who made his fortune founding the clothing companies Esprit and North Face, owns two strips of land that stretch from one side of the country to the other. He tried to buy the parcel between the two halves that would have connected them, but the sale was fiercely opposed by some government officials who questioned whether a foreigner should own so much of Chile. The Pan-American Highway, which trundles all the way north to Alaska, is interrupted here. No public roads, with their accompanying pollution, pass through the preserve, except for a well-maintained road stretching from Chaitén to park headquarters at Caleta Gonzalo.

Parque Pumalín encompasses some of the most pristine landscape in the region, if not the world. There are a dozen or so trails that wind past lakes and waterfalls. Stay in log cabins, at traditional or covered campsites, or put up your tent on one of the local farms scattered across the area that welcome travelers. The entrance to the park is at Caleta Gonzalo, where the ferries from Hornopirén arrive. Buses run from Chaitén in January and February. ✉*Information centers: Calle Klenner 299, Puerto Varas* ☎*65/250–079* 🖷*65/255–145* ✉*Av. Bernardo O'Higgins 62, Chaitén* ☎*65/731–341* ⊕*www.parquepumalin.cl* 🎫*Free* ⊙*Daily.*

GETTING HERE & AROUND

Caleta Gonzalo, headquarters of Pumalín Park, is about 60 km (37 mi) north of Chaitén. The road from Chaitén to Caleta Gonzalo is well-maintained but not paved. One can also reach Caleta Gonzalo by ferry. To venture to the northernmost areas of the park, such as Cahuelmo hot springs, you will need to rent a boat in Hornopiren, a small town about 110 km (68 mi) southeast of Puerto Montt.

WHERE TO STAY

$$ ★ ⊞ **Cabañas Caleta Gonzalo.** Nine gray-shingled cabanas, each designed to be distinct from its neighbor, sit high on stilts against the backdrop of the misty mountains. Broad front porches and tall windows let in lots of light. The interiors are rustic yet luxurious, with handcrafted furniture and hand-woven woolen blankets. There are also two cabanas, with kitchen and wood stoves for heating, at the Rio Gonzalo Farm. To access these cabanas, you must cross a wooden hanging bridge. The complex includes an attractive visitor center and handicraft shop stocking books, guides, and maps, as well as organic honey and jams. A copper-hooded corner fireplace welcomes you at the adjacent café for meals from early morning until midnight year-round. **Pros:** Unique, close to nature. **Cons:** Remote. ⊠ *Caleta Gonzalo* ☎*65/232–300* ☞*9 cabins* ⚐ *In-room: no a/c, no TV. In-hotel: restaurant, bar, parking, no elevator* ▤*AE, DC, MC, V* ⦿ *BP.*

¢ ⊞ **Camping in Pumalín.** There are more than a dozen camping sites near Cabañas Caleta Gonzalo. You must cross the hanging bridge over the Gonzalo River and walk to Rio Gonzalo Farm. The campground there includes cold-water showers, bathrooms, and three covered shelters for cooking and eating. There is also a covered shelter for sleeping. Throughout the park, there are several other camping sites at lakes and along trails. Inquire at Caleta Gonzalo.

FUTALEUFÚ

159 km (99 mi) east of Chaitén.

Near the town of Villa Lucia, Ruta 231 branches east from the Carretera Austral and winds around Lago Yelcho. About 159 km (99 mi) later, not far from the Argentine border, it reaches the tiny town of Futaleufú. Despite being barely five square blocks, Futaleufú is on many travelers' itineraries. World-class adventure sports await here, where the Río Espolón and the Río Futaleufú collide. It's the staging center for serious river and sea kayaking, white-water rafting, and mountain biking, as well as fly-fishing, canyon hiking, and horseback riding. Day trips for less-experienced travelers are available.

GETTING HERE & AROUND

The road from Chaitén to Futaleufú, which takes about four hours to drive, is almost entirely unpaved, and conditions are spotty at times. However, it's also possible to enter Futaleufú from Argentina, which is about 190 km (118 mi) southwest of Esquel. From Bariloche, Argentina, proceed south, about four hours' drive, passing through pleasant Argentine tourist towns such as El Bolson and Esquel. After Esquel you will come upon the road that leads to Futaleufú. The roads are paved throughout the Argentine portion of the trip, and a car rented in Puerto Montt costs less than 40,000 pesos, although better deals can be had in Santiago. Some bus companies offer service to Futaleufú from Puerto Montt and Osorno. Some minivans do make the trip from Chaitén to Futaleufú, but this service is irregular and you may have to wait a day or two.

ESSENTIALS

Currency Exchange Para Ti Store (✉ *Pedro Aguirre Cerda 505* ☎ *65/721–215*).

Medical Assistance Hospital de Futaleufú (✉ *Juan Manuel Balmaceda 382* ☎ *65/721–231*).

Visitor & Tour Info Tourist Office (✉ *Av. Bernardo O'Higgins 334* ☎ *65/721–241*).

WHERE TO STAY & EAT

$ ✕▢**Hostería Antigua Casona.** Built in the 1940s, this three-story house is
★ one of the better stays you will find in southern Chile. The Coronado family, who run the place, will quickly make you feel at home. The place has a rustic feel with tasteful decorations throughout, and the restaurant is wonderful. Fine handicrafts are sold on the first floor. The Coronados can help arrange tours and transportation as well. And ask them about staying at their country house, Posada Anchileufu, a good alternative if you want to get a taste of Patagonian country life. **Pros:** Intimate with few other guests, friendly hosts, good food. **Cons:** Not a lot of luxury, no TV, no phone. ✉ *Manuel Rodriguez 215* ☎ *65/721–311* ⊕ *www.futaleufupatagonia.cl* ➷ *4 rooms* ☖ *In-room: no a/c, no phone, no TV, Wi-Fi. In-hotel: restaurant, bar, no elevator, laundry service, public Wi-Fi, parking, no-smoking rooms* ▤ *AE, DC, MC, V.*

$$$ ▢**Hostería Río Grande.** This sleek wooden hotel is adventure-travel headquarters for the area. It hosts the Futaleufú Adventure Center, a branch of **Expediciones Chile** (⊕ www.exchile.com), operated by former U.S. Olympic paddler Chris Spelius. December–March it offers four- to seven-night packages that include kayaking, rafting, and hiking trips throughout the region. There is cable TV in the salon. **Pros:** Modern facilities, rafting and other excursions, restaurant. **Cons:** Gets crowded in dining room. ✉ *Manuel Rodriguez 315; office: Gabriel Mistral 296* ☎ *65/721–320, 888/488-9082 in U.S.* ⊕ *www.pachile.com* ➷ *12 rooms* ☖ *In-room: no a/c, no TV. In-hotel: restaurant, room service, bar, laundry service, public Internet, no elevator, parking* ▤ *AE, DC, MC, V* ⦿*BP.*

$$$ ▢**Hotel El Barranco.** Easily one of the Futa's best lodging options, it offers first-class rooms and facilities, including a pool. **Pros:** Rooms are comfortable, pool. **Cons:** No business center. ✉ *Av. Bernardo O'Higgins 172* ☎ *65/721–267* ⊕ *www.elbarrancochile.cl* ➷ *10 rooms* ☖ *In-room: no a/c, no TV, Wi-Fi. In-hotel: restaurant, bar, pool, bicycles, no elevator, laundry service, public Wi-Fi, parking* ▤ *AE, DC, MC, V* ⦿*BP.*

PUERTO PUYUHUAPI

196 km (123 mi) south of Chaitén.

This mossy fishing village of about 500 residents is one of the old est along the Carretera Austral. It was founded in 1935 by German immigrants fleeing the economic ravages of post–World War I Europe. As in much of Patagonia, Chile offered free land to settlers with the idea of making annexation by Argentina more difficult. Those early immigrants ventured into the wilderness to clear the forests and make way for farms.

Today this sleepy town near Quelat National Park is a convenient stopover for those headed farther south in the region. It has a few modest guesthouses, as well as some markets and a gas station.

GETTING HERE & AROUND

The mostly unpaved 210-km (130 mi) drive from Coyhaique along the Carretera Austral, or Southern Highway, can be undertaken by car or bus. Patagonia Connection (⊕ *www.patagonia-connection.com*), a Santiago tour company, also gets you here in five hours by boat if you plan to stay at their Puyuhuapi Lodge. A small landing strip nearby serves private planes only.

WHERE TO STAY & EAT

$ ☶**Cabanas Aonikenk.** Relatively new to the area, Veronica Gallardo immigrated to this quiet town some five years ago and built this little establishment on her own with few resources. Her hard work has resulted in a more than adequate place to sleep and a great café. **Pros:** Friendly service, good location, affordable price. **Cons:** Facilities are far from luxurious. ⊠ *Hamburgo 16* ☎ *67/325-208* ⇆ *2 rooms, 3 cabins* △ *In-room: no a/c, no phone. In-hotel: restaurant, no elevator, parking* ⊟ *No credit cards* ⏛*BP.*

$ ☶**Hosteria Alemana.** The home of Ursula Flack, the last of the town's original German settlers, is a great choice for budget-minded travelers who want to explore the beautiful countryside. Flack moved here in 1958, 10 years after her husband, who built this large Bavarian-style home with gardens in the middle of town. Rooms with functional baths are simple but charming. Fresh flowers fill the quaint dining room. Ursula also runs perhaps the best eatery in town, Café Ross bach, just a five-minute walk down the road, next to the carpet work shop run by her son, Helmut. **Pros:** Hotel has character, clean. **Cons:** Located outside of town. ⊠ *Puerto Puyuhuapi s/n* ☎ *67/325-118* ⇆ *9 rooms* △ *In-room: no a/c, no phone, no TV. In-hotel: laundry facilities, laundry service, no elevator, parking, no-smoking rooms* ⊟ *AE, MC, V* ⏛*BP.*

$$$–$$$$ ✕☶**Puyuhuapi Lodge & Spa.** If you arrive at night, your catamaran sails
Fodor'sChoice past a dark fjord to a spectacular welcome—drums, bonfires along
★ the shore, and fireworks illuminating the grounds. Accessible only by water (it's a five-hour boat ride from Puerto Chacabuco to the south), the property is remote and profoundly secluded. Luckily, your every need is taken care of here, whether you're in the mood for hiking and kayaking, excursions to glaciers, or just relaxing with a massage or

9

in one of the many indoor and outdoor hot-spring pools. Pathways wind among flower beds, where hummingbirds hover, and between the low-roofed but spacious accommodations, with decks extending over the lakefront. The dining room *($$$)* has terrific views of the fjord, and a wonderful selection of wines. **Pros:** Spa, pool, views. **Cons:** Hard to get here, no Wi-Fi. ⊠*Bahia Dorita s/n, Carretera Austral, 13 km (8 mi) south of Puerto Puyuhuapi* ☎*67/325–103, 2/225–6489 in Santiago* ⊞*2/274–8111 in Santiago* ⊕*www.patagonia-connection.com* ⌑*44 rooms* ⚿*In-room: no TV, safe. In-hotel: restaurant, bar, pools, gym, spa, laundry service, public Internet, no elevator* ⊟*AE, DC, MC, V* ⦿*BP.*

FISHING

More than 50 rivers are within easy driving distance of Puerto Puyuhuapi, making this a cherished destination among fishing enthusiasts. Here are rainbow and brown trout, silver and steelhead salmon, and local species such as the robalo. The average size is about 6 pounds, but it's not rare to catch monsters twice that size. Daily trips are organized by the staff at the resort hotel, Puyuhuapi Lodge & Spa.

SHOPPING

Carpets at **Alfombras de Puyuhuapi** (⊠*E. Ludwig s/n* ☎*67/325–131* ⊕*www.puyuhuapi.com*) are handwoven by three generations of women from Chiloé who use only natural wool thread and cotton fibers. The rustic vertical looms, designed and built specifically for this shop, allow the weavers to make carpets with a density of 20,000 knots per square meter. Trained by his father and grandfather, who opened the shop here in the 1940s, proprietor Helmut E. Hopperdietzel proudly displays the extensive stock of finished carpets of various sizes and designs. Carpets can be shipped. The shop is closed in June.

PARQUE NACIONAL QUEULAT

175 km (109 mi) south of Chaitén.

The rugged 350,000-acre Parque Nacional Queulat begins to rise and roll to either side of the Carretera Austral some 20 km (12 mi) south of the town of La Junta. Rivers and streams that crisscross dense virgin forests attract fishing aficionados from all over the world. At the higher altitudes, brilliant blue glaciers can be found in the valleys between snowcapped peaks. If you're lucky you'll spot a *pudú,* one of the diminutive deer that make their home in the forest.

Less than 1 km (½ mi) off the east side of the Carretera Austral you are treated to a close-up view of the hanging glacier, **Ventisquero Colgante.** This sheet of ice slides forward between a pair of gentle rock faces. Several waterfalls cascade down the cliffs to either side of the glacier's foot. There is an easy 15-minute walk leading to one side of the lake below the glacier, which is not visible from the overlook. Another, longer hike takes you deeper into the park's interior.

A short drive farther south, where the Carretera Austral makes one of its sharp switchback turns as it climbs higher, a small sign points into the undergrowth, indicating the trailhead for the **Salto Padre García.** There is no parking area, but you can leave your car on the shoulder. This short hike through dense forest is well worth attempting for a close-up view of this waterfall of striking proportions.

There are two CONAF stations (the national forestry service), one at the Ventisquero Colgante overlook, the other a few miles north of the southern park gateway. ✉ *Carretera Austral, 20 km (12 mi) south of La Junta* ☎ *67/231–065 or 67/232–599* ⊕ *www.conaf.cl* 🎫 *1,500 pesos* ⊙ *Daily 8:30–6:30.*

WHERE TO STAY

$$ 🖼 **Hotel El Pangue.** Follow the driveway to the sprawling complex of reddish buildings on the sheltered shores of Lake Risopatrón. Several shingle-roofed cabanas, all with central heating and ample hot water, were constructed by local craftspeople from native wood. The club-house has a fireplace and a panoramic view of the lake. The dining room serves barbecued lamb prepared on a traditional *quincho* (grill). Activities include trolling and fly-fishing on the lake and nearby rivers. Canoes, mountain bikes, and horses are available for exploring the lake and park trails. It's 5 km (3 mi) south of the entrance of Parque Nacional Queulat. **Pros:** Pool, near Queulat Park, helps arrange outdoor activities. **Cons:** Not near town, no TV. ✉ *Carretera Austral, Km 240* ☎ *67/325–128* ⊕ *www.elpangue.cl* 🛏 *8 rooms, 5 cabanas* 🛆 *In-room: no a/c, kitchen (some), no TV, Wi-Fi. In-hotel: restaurant, bar, pool, beachfront, water sports, bicycles, laundry service, public Internet, public Wi-Fi, parking, no elevator* 🖃 *AE, MC, V* 🍴*BP.*

COYHAIQUE & ENVIRONS

COYHAIQUE

224 km (140 mi) south of Puerto Puyuhuapi.

Ten streets radiate from the central plaza. Horn, one of the most colorful, holds the crafts stands of the Feria Artesanal. Balmaceda connects the central square with the smaller Plaza Prat. Navigating the area around the plaza is confusing at first, but the streets, bearing those traditional names used throughout the country, soon yield to a simple grid system.

GETTING HERE & AROUND

There are regular domestic flights every day to the Southern Coast's only major airport, 55 km (34 mi) south of Coyhaique in the town of Balmaceda. Ferry lines operating in southern Chile sail the interwoven fjords, rivers, and lakes of the region. Navimag (short for "Navigacion Magallanes") operates a cargo and passenger fleet throughout the region. Transmarchilay operates a cargo and passenger ferry fleet similar to that of Navimag, with ships that start in Puerto Montt and sail to nearby Puerto Chacabuco. Tour companies also often offer more luxurious transport that includes stops in Chacabuco.

9

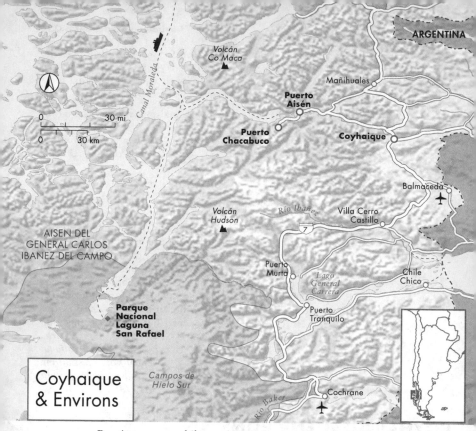

Coyhaique & Environs

Renting a car, while expensive, is a worthwhile option for getting around. At Balmaceda airport there are several rental agencies. Make sure you understand the extent of your liability for any damage to the vehicle, including routine events such as a chipped or cracked windshield. If you want to visit one of the more popular parks, check out tour prices. They may prove far cheaper than driving yourself. There are also a number of bus companies with offices in Coyhaique that serve most destinations in the area.

ESSENTIALS

Bus Contacts Don Carlos (✉ *Subteniente Cruz 63* ☎ *67/232–981*). **Suray** (✉ *Eleuterio Ramirez 501* ☎ *67/332–779*). **Transfer Valencia** (✉ *Balmaceda Airport* ☎ *67/233–030*). **Tur-Bus** (✉ *Magallanes 303* ☎ *67/237–571*).

Currency Exchange Emperador (✉ *Bilbao 222, Local 3*). **Turismo Prado** (✉ *21 de Mayo 417*).

Medical Assistance Hospital Regional Coyhaique (✉ *Dr. Jorge Ibar 068* ☎ *67/233–172*).

Post Office Correos (✉ *Lord Cochrane 202*).

Rental Cars AGS Rent A Car (✉ *Av. Ugana 1298* ☎ *67/235–354*). **Automotriz Los Carrera** (✉ *Carrera 330* ☎ *67/231–457*). **Budget** (✉ *Balmaceda Airport* ☎ *67/255–177*). **Int'l Rent A Car** (✉ *Balmaceda Airport* ☎ *67/272–220*).

Visitor & Tour Info Sernatur (✉ *Bulnes 35* ☎ *67/231–752*).

EXPLORING

The pentagonal **Plaza de Armas** is the center of town and the nexus for its attractions, including the town's **Catedral** and **Intendencia**, the government building.

The Carretera Austral leads into the northeastern corner of town and to the **Monumento al Ovejero.** On the broad median of the Avenida General Baquedano a solitary shepherd with his horse and his dog lean motionless into the wind behind a plodding flock of sheep. ✉ *Av. General Baquedano.*

The **Museo Regional de la Patagonia** is worth the small fee for the black-and-white photos of early 20th-century pioneering in this region, as well as for the collections of household, farming, and early industrial artifacts from the same era. To visit is to be reminded of how recently many parts of southern Chile began to develop. ✉ *Calle Eusebio Lillo 23, Casa de la Cultura* ☎ *No phone* 💲 *400 pesos* ⊗ *Weekdays 8:30–5:30.*

The 5,313-acre **Reserva Nacional Coyhaique,** about 4 km (2½ mi) north of Coyhaique, provides hikers with some stunning views when the weather cooperates. If it's raining you can drive a 9-km (5½-mi) circuit through the park. ✉ *54 km (34 mi) east of Coyhaique* ☎ *No phone* ⊕ *www.conaf.cl* 💲 *800 pesos* ⊗ *Jan. and Feb., daily 8 AM–9 PM; Mar.–Dec., daily 8:30–5.*

The evergreen forests of **Reserva Nacional Río Simpson,** just north of Reserva Nacional Coyhaique, are filled with waterfalls tumbling down steep canyon walls. A lovely waterfall called the Cascada de la Virgen is a 1-km (½-mi) hike from the information center, and another called the Velo de la Novia is 8 km (5 mi) farther. About 1 km from Coyhaique, along the banks of the Simpson River, you can also see the Piedra del Indio, a rock shaped in the profile of an Indian. ✉ *Carretera Austral, Km 32* ☎ *No phone* ⊕ *www.conaf.cl* 💲 *800 pesos* ⊗ *Jan. and Feb., daily 8 AM–9 PM; Mar.–Dec., daily 8:30–5.*

The only skiing in northern Patagonia can be had 32 km (20 mi) outside town at **El Fraile.** You can rent equipment for the three trails here. There are no accommodations and it's wise to bring food and water with you. The season runs May–September. ✉ *Camino Lago Pollux* ☎ *67/232–277.*

OFF THE BEATEN PATH

Lago General Carrera. It takes a 280-km (174-mi) drive from Coyhaique along the rutted, unpaved Carretera Austral to reach this beautiful, almost surreally blue lake, the biggest in Chile (and the second-largest in South America, after Lake Titicaca). But this spectacular place is more than worth the trip. Tourism has only just started developing here, but already, travelers have been making the pilgrimage in four-wheel-drive vehicles to fish, hike, and gasp at the mountains, glaciers, and waterfalls that dot the landscape. A great place to stay in the area

9

is **Terra Luna,** which occupies 15 peaceful acres at the southeastern edge of the lake. The property is serene, with charming (very basic) redwood cabins, grazing horses, and a beautiful main lodge where all meals are served. Excursion packages are offered; you can trek in nearby mountains, raft or kayak on the lake or more lively rivers, or take scenic flights over ice fields and glaciers. The remoteness and changeable weather of the region mean these excursions aren't always guaranteed to happen as planned—but if it's too windy for your plane ride, you can always borrow a mountain bike, or relax in the waterfront hot tub. ⊠ *Km 1.5, Carretera Austral, Puerto Guadal* ☎*67/431–263* ⌨*67/431–264* ⊕*www.terraluna.cl.*

Cerro Castillo National Reserve. Just 64 km (40 mi) south of Coyhaique, this national reserve is home to one of the most beautiful mountain chains in the region, crowned majestically by the rugged Cerro Castillo. Glacier runoff fills the lakes below the mountain, and the reserve is also home to several species of wildlife. Cerro Castillo could be called one of the best hikes in Patagonia, but it gets perhaps only one-tenth of a percent of visitors compared to its more popular counterpart to the south, Torres del Paine. One excellent hiking route begins at Las Horquetas Grandes, 8 km (5 mi) south of the park entrance. From there, go along La Lima River until Laguna Cerro Castillo, where you can begin your walk around the peak and then head toward the nearby village Villa Cerro Castillo. In addition to hikes, there are some good fishing spots in the area. There is bus service to the reserve from Coyhaique, but it's better to come here in your own rented vehicle. It's also preferable to hike here with a guide, as trails are not always clearly marked. ⊠*Km 59, Carretera Austral Villa Cerro Castillo* ⊙ *Daily* ⌨*Camping at Laguna Chiguay, 2,000 pesos.*

WHERE TO EAT

$ ✕ **Casona.** A fire crackles in the corner wood-burning stove in this tidy
★ little restaurant. Vases filled with fresh flowers adorn tables covered with white linen. The place is run by the González family—the mother cooks, her husband and son serve—who exude a genuine warmth to everyone who walks in the door. There's plenty of traditional fare on the menu, including the standout *centolla* (king crab) and *langostino* (lobster), not to mention the hearty *filete casona,* roast beef with bacon, mushrooms, and potatoes. ⊠*Obispo Vielmo 77* ☎*67/238–894* ⊟*AE, DC, MC, V.*

$ ✕ **La Olla.** Starched linen tablecloths lend an unmistakable aura of European gentility to this modest restaurant, operated by a courtly Spaniard and his son. Among the specialties are a fine paella and a hearty *estofado de cordero* (lamb stew). ⊠*Av. Arturo Prat 176* ☎*67/234–700* ⊟*AE, DC, MC, V.*

$ ✕ **Restaurant Histórico Ricer.** Operated by the same family for decades, this popular restaurant is a Coyhaique institution. The stairs in the back lead to a wooden dinner parlor; the walls are covered with fascinating sepia photos from the town's archives. An upper loft here makes a cozy place for tea. Among the most popular items on the extensive menu are salmon, rabbit, and grilled leg of lamb. Lighter fare includes excellent empanadas filled with *locate* (a local mollusk), and a host of sandwiches. The pottery and crocheted hangings that decorate the restaurant were created by the family's matriarch. ⊠*Horn 40 at 48* ☎*67/232–920 or 67/237–950* ▤*AE, DC, MC, V.*

WHERE TO STAY

$$ ✕▣**El Reloj.** Simple, very clean, wood-paneled rooms contain just the basic pieces of furniture. But the salon is warmly decorated with antiques and wood furnishings, and it has a large fireplace. Request a second-floor room for a view of the Coyhaique River. The restaurant offers award-winning regional dishes like lamb and salmon. **Pros:** On the river, great food. **Cons:** No frills. ⊠*Av. General Baquedano 828* ☎*67/231–108* ⊕*www.elrelojhotel.cl* ⊳*17 rooms* ⌂*In-room: no a/c. In-hotel: restaurant, room service, bar, laundry service, public Internet, no elevator, airport shuttle, no-smoking rooms* ▤*AE, DC, MC, V* ⵌ*CP.*

$$ ▣**Hostal Belisario Jara.** You realize how much attention has been paid to
★ the detail here when the proprietor points out that the weather vane on
· the peak of the single turret is a copy of one at Chilean poet Pablo Neruda's home in Isla Negra. In the quaint lodging's various nooks and crannies, you'll find plenty of wide windows and natural woods. In the small but tasteful rooms, terra-cotta floors complement the rustic carved-pine beds, spread with nubby cream linens. **Pros:** Nice atmosphere, central location. **Cons:** Rooms somewhat small, no credit cards. ⊠*Francisco Bilbao 662* ☎*67/234–150* ⊕*www.belisariojara.itgo.com* ⵌ*8 rooms* ⌂*In-rooms: Wi-Fi. In-hotel: bar, no elevator, laundry service, public Internet, airport shuttle, parking* ▤*No credit cards* ⵌ*BP.*

$ ▣**Hotel Coyhaique.** This nicely landscaped lodging is in a quiet corner of town, but it's within easy walking distance of the Plaza de Armas. Rooms are a bit motel-like, with pale-green comforters and drapes, a bed, a TV, and not much else. But they are clean and spacious. **Pros:** Clean, good location, pool. **Cons:** Rooms are underwhelming. ⊠*Magallanes 131* ☎*67/231–137 or 67/231–737* ⊕*www.hotelcoyhaique.cl* ⵌ*40 rooms* ⌂*In-room: Wi-Fi. In-hotel: restaurant, room service, bar, pool, laundry service, airport shuttle, public Internet, refrigerator, no elevator* ▤*AE, MC, V* ⵌ*CP.*

$ ▣**Minchos Lodge.** A homey place just 200 meters (656 feet) from the Simpson River, the lodge is popular among fishermen because of its fishing guides and boats. There are great views of the mountains and Simpson River Valley. Victoria Moya, the owner, is also a geologist who has detailed knowledge of the regional landscape. **Pros:** Fishing options, views, homey atmosphere. **Cons:** The place is not well-marked and can be hard to find. ⊠*Camino del Bosque 1170,* ☎*67/233–273* ⵌ*10 rooms* ⌂*In-room: no phone, no TV (some), Wi-Fi. In-hotel: restaurant, bar, water sports, no elevator, laundry service, public Internet, public Wi-Fi, airport shuttle, parking, no kids under 14, no-smoking rooms* ▤*AE, MC, V* ⵌ*BP.*

9

NIGHTLIFE & THE ARTS

Coyhaique's nightlife is about what you'd expect from a city of its size. There isn't a huge number of bars and discos, but the places they do have are hopping at times and worth checking out if you are in the mood to go out.

The outrageous stylishness of **Piel Roja** (✉*Moraleda 495* ☎*67/236–635*) is given a further boost by its remote location. The bar-disco, whose name translates into "Red Skin," opens relatively early, at 7 PM. Nosh on pizza and explore the four levels of sculptural decor, several bars, a large dance floor, and a private nook. The furnishings are over-size and slightly surreal, a mix of motifs from art nouveau to Chinese. The weekend cover price of 6,000 pesos for men and 3,000 pesos for women is credited toward drinks or food.

Just down the road from Piel Roja, another bar-disco, **El Cuervo** (✉*Moraleda 420* ☎*67/215–015* ⊕*www.elcuervopub.cl* ☾*Mon.–Sat. 7 PM–4 AM*), is the new favorite for Coyhaique's young and festive folk. The atmosphere is upbeat and there's plenty of dancing. The weekend cover price at the disco is 6,000 pesos for men, and 3,000 pesos for women.

SHOPPING

Coyhaique is no shopping mecca, but the Feria Artesenal does host some unique handicrafts. As Coyhaique is the largest settlement around, it's also the place to stock up on general supplies if you're heading off on a long exploring expedition.

The **Feria Artesenal** (✉*Plaza de Armas between Dussen and Horn* ☎*No phone*) has stalls selling woolen clothing, small leather items, and pottery.

PUERTO CHACABUCO & PUERTO AISÉN

68 km (43 mi) northwest of Coyhaique.

It's hard to imagine a drive more beautiful—anywhere in the world—than the one from Coyhaique to the town of Puerto Aisén and its port, Chacabuco. The mist hangs low over farmland, adding a dripping somnolence to the scenery. Dozens of waterfalls and rivers wend their way through mountain formations. Yellow poplars surround charming rustic lodges. And sheep and cattle graze on mossy, vibrant fields. The picture of serenity terminates at the sea, where the nondescript town of Puerto Aisén and its port Chacabuco, Coyhaique's link to the ocean, sits, a conduit to further beauty. This harbor ringed by snowcapped mountains is where you board the ferries that transport you north to Puerto Montt in the Lake District and Quellón on Chiloé, as well as boats headed south to the spectacular Laguna San Rafael.

GETTING HERE & AROUND

Puerto Chacabuco is less than an hour's drive from Coyhaique, and about 10 minutes from nearby Puerto Aisén. Several bus lines in Coyhaique serve Chacabuco. The town is also the jumping off point for

Continued on page 350

INTO THE WILD

by Tim Patterson

Patagonia will shatter your sense of scale. You will feel very small, surrounded by an epic expanse of mountains and plains, sea, and sky. Whether facing down an advancing wall of glacial ice, watching an ostrich-like rhea racing across the open steppe, or getting splashed by a breaching right whale off the Valdez Peninsula, prepare to gasp at the majesty of the Patagonian wild.

GLACIERS OF PATAGONIA

The Patagonia ice field covers much of the southern end of the Andean mountain range, straddling the Argentina-Chile border. The glaciers that spill off the high altitude ice field are basically rivers of slowly moving ice and snow that grind and push their way across the mountains, crushing soft rock and sculpting granite peaks.

Most of Patagonia's glaciers spill into lakes, rivers or fjords. Chunks of ice calve off the face of the glacier into the water, a dramatic display of nature's power that you can view at several locations. The larger pieces of ice become icebergs that scud across the water surface like white sailboats blown by the wind.

WEATHER

Weather is unpredictable around glaciers: it's not uncommon to experience sunshine, rain, and snow squalls in a single afternoon.

ICE COLORS

Although clear days are best for panoramas, cloudy days bring out the translucent blue of the glacial ice, creating great opportunities for magical photographs. You'll also see black or gray streaks in the ice caused by sediment picked up by the glacier as it grinds down the mountain valley. When that sediment is deposited into lakes, it hangs suspended in the water, turning the lake a pale milky blue.

ENVIRONMENTAL CONCERN

There's no question that human-induced climate change is taking its toll on Patagonia's glaciers. Although the famous Perito Moreno glacier is still advancing, nearly all the others have shrunk in recent years, some dramatically. The retreat of the Upsala glacier near El Calafate is featured in Al Gore's award-winning documentary, *An Inconvenient Truth*.

Below: Cruise on Lago Argentino, Santa Cruz province, Glaciers National Park, Argentina

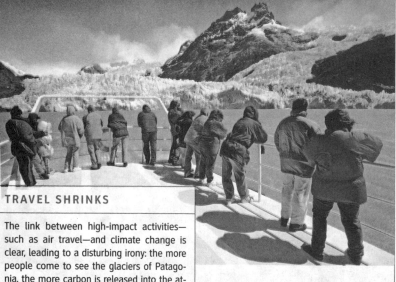

TRAVEL SHRINKS

The link between high-impact activities—such as air travel—and climate change is clear, leading to a disturbing irony: the more people come to see the glaciers of Patagonia, the more carbon is released into the atmosphere, and the more the glaciers shrink.

Right: Glacier Grey, Paine Circuit, Torres del Paine National Park, Chile

GLACIERS TO SEE

- Perito Moreno Glacier, Santa Cruz, Argentina
- Upsala Glacier, Santa Cruz, Argentina
- Martial Glacier, Tierra del Fuego, Argentina
- Serrano Glacier, Tierra del Fuego, Chile
- O'Higgins Glacier, Southern Coast, Chile

FIRE & ICE: MOUNTAINS OF PATAGONIA

Trekker, Cerro Torre and Fitz Roy in background, Los Glaciares National Park, Patagonia

In Patagonia, mountains mean the Andes, a relatively young range but a precocious one that stretches for more than 4,000 miles. The Patagonian Andes are of special interest to geologists, who study how fire, water, and ice have shaped the mountains into their present form.

CREATION

Plate tectonics are the most fundamental factor in the formation of the southern Andes, with the oceanic Nazca plate slipping beneath the continental South American plate and forcing the peaks skyward. Volcanic activity is a symptom of this dynamic process, and there are several active volcanoes on the Chilean side of the range.

GLACIAL IMPRINT

Glacial activity has also played an important role in chiseling the most iconic Patagonian peaks. The spires that form the distinctive skylines of Torres del Paine and the Fitzroy range are solid columns that were created when rising glaciers ripped away weaker rock, leaving only hard granite skeletons that stand rigid at the edge of the ice fields.

MOUNTAIN HIGH BORDERS

Because the border between Chile and Argentina cuts through the most impenetrable reaches of the ice field, the actual border line is unclear in areas of the far south. Even in the more temperate north, border crossings are often located at mountain passes, and the officials who stamp visas seem more like mountain guides than bureaucrats.

MOUNTAINS OF THE SEA

Tierra del Fuego and the countless islands off the coast of southern Chile were once connected to the mainland. Over the years the sea swept into the valleys, isolated the peaks, and created an archipelago that, viewed on a map, looks as abstract as a Jackson Pollack painting. From the water these island mountains appear especially dramatic, misty pinnacles of rock and ice rising from the crashing sea.

Right: Mt. Fitzroy

PROMINENT PEAKS AND RANGES

- ■ Mt. Fitzroy and Cerro Torre, Santa Cruz, Argentina
- ■ Cuernos of Torres del Paine, Chile
- ■ Beagle Channel Mountains, Tierra del Fuego, Chile/ Argentina
- ■ Cerro Piltriqitron, El Bolson, Argentina
- ■ Osorno Volcano, Lake District, Chile

YAY, PENGUINOS!

Magellanic Penguin walking to his nest in Peninsula Valdes

Everyone loves penguins. How could you not feel affection for such cute, curious, and loyal little creatures? On land, their awkward waddle is endearing, and you can get close enough to see the inquisitive gaze in their eyes as they turn their heads from side to side for a good look at you. In the water, penguins transform from goofballs into Olympic athletes, streaking through the waves and returning to the nest with mouthfuls of fish and squid for their chicks.

TYPES

Most of the penguins you'll see here are Magellanic penguins, black and white colored birds that gather in large breeding colonies on the beaches of Patagonia in the summer and retreat north to warmer climes during winter. Also keep an eye out for the red-beaked Gentoo penguins that nest among the Magellanics.

If your image of penguins is the large and colorful Emperor penguins of Antarctica that featured in the documentary *March of the Penguins*, you might be slightly underwhelmed by the little Magellanics. Adults stand about 30 inches tall and weigh between 15 and 20 pounds. What they lack in glamor, Patagonia's penguins make up in vanity—and numbers. Many breeding sites are home to tens of thousands of individuals, all preening and strutting as if they were about to walk the red carpet at the Academy Awards.

PENGUIN RELATIONS

Male and female penguins form monogamous pairs and share the task of raising the chicks, which hatch in small burrows that the parents return to year after year. If you sit and observe a pair of penguins for a little while you'll notice how affectionate they appear, grooming each other with their beaks and huddling together on the nest.

HUMAN CONTACT

Although penguins are not shy of humans who keep a respectful distance (about 8 feet is a good rule of thumb), the history of penguin-human relations is not entirely one of peaceful curiosity. Early pioneers and stranded sailors would raid penguin nests for food, and in modern times, oil spills have devastated penguin colonies in Patagonia.

Magellanic Penguins

The best time to see penguins is from November through February, which coincides with the best weather in coastal Patagonia. Some of the most convenient and impressive colonies to visit are:

■ Punta Tombo, Chubut, Argentina

■ Cabo Virgenes, Santa Cruz, Argentina

■ Isla Madalena, Chile

■ Martillo Island, Tierra del Fuego, Argentina

■ Puerto San Julian, Santa Cruz, Argentina

IN FOCUS INTO THE WILD

9

IN THE SEA

The Patagonian coast teems with marine life, including numerous "charismatic megafauna" such as whales, dolphins, sea lions, and seals.

DOLPHINS

Dolphins are easy to spot on tours, because they're curious and swim up to the boat, sometimes even surfing the bow wake. Commerson's dolphins are a common species in coastal Argentina and the Straights of Magellan. Among the world's tiniest dolphins, their white and black coloring has earned them the nickname "skunk dolphin" and prompted comparisons with their distant cousins, orcas.

WHALES

The Valdez Peninsula is also one of the best places to observe right whales, gentle giants of the ocean. Although the name right whale derives from whalers who designated it as the "right" whale to kill, the right whale is now protected by both national legislation and international agreements.

ORCAS

Orcas aren't as common as dolphins, but you can spot them off the Valdez Peninsula, Argentina, hunting seals and sea lions along the shore. Sometimes hungry orcas will chase their prey a few feet too far and beach themselves above the tide line, where they perish of dehydration.

SEALS & SEA LIONS

In the springtime massive elephant seals and southern sea lions drag themselves onto Patagonian beaches for mating season—hopefully out of range of hungry orcas. These giant pinnipeds form two groups in the breeding colonies. Big, tough alpha bulls have their own harems of breeding females and their young, while so-called bachelor males hang out nearby like freshman boys at a fraternity party, hoping to entice a stray female away from the alpha bull's harem.

Southern Sea Lions
(Otaria flavescens),
Valdes Peninsula, Patagonia

IN THE AIR

Patagonia is a twitcher's paradise. Even non-bird-lovers marvel at the colorful species that squawk, flutter, and soar through Patagonia's skies.

ANDEAN CONDOR
You probably won't see a condor up close. They nest on high-altitude rock ledges and spend their days soaring in circles on high thermals, scanning mountain slopes and plains for carrion. With a wing span of up to 10 feet, however, the king of the Andean skies is impressive even when viewed from a distance. Condors live longer than almost any other bird. Some could qualify for Social Security.

MAGELLANIC WOODPECKER
You can hear the distinctive rat-tat of this enormous woodpecker in nothofagus forests of Chilean Patagonia and parts of Argentina. Males have a bright red head and a black body, while females are almost entirely black.

ALBATROSS
You can spot several species of albatross off the Patagonian coast, gliding on fixed wings above the waves. The albatross lives almost entirely at sea, touching down on land to breed and raise its young. Unless you're visiting Antarctica or the Falklands, your best bet for seeing an albatross is to take a cruise from Punta Arenas or Ushuaia.

RHEA (NANDU)
No, it's not an ostrich. The rhea is an extremely large flightless bird that roams the Patagonian steppe. Although they're not normally aggressive, males have been known to charge humans who get too close to their partner's nests.

KELP GOOSE
As the name implies, kelp geese love kelp. In fact, kelp is the only thing they eat. The geese travel along the rocky shores of Tierra del Fuego in search of their favorite seaweed salad.

Laguna San Rafael, although the boats that go to the park are almost all luxury tour vessels that you will need to contract in Coyhaique or in Santiago. Consult a travel agent beforehand if you plan to use one of these.

A hanging bridge leads from Chacabuco to **Puerto Aisén,** founded in 1928 to serve the region's burgeoning cattle ranches. Devastating forest fires that swept through the interior in 1955 filled the once-deep harbor with silt, making it all but useless for transoceanic vessels. The busy main street is a good place to stock up on supplies for boat trips to the nearby national parks.

WHERE TO STAY & EAT

$ ▒ **Hotel Caicahues.** Owned by the municipality of Puerto Aisén, this is a quiet, homey place that is frequented by business travelers and tourists in transit to Laguna San Rafael. It's also conveniently in the town center. **Pros:** Quiet, centrally located. **Cons:** Restaurant serves food by a set menu only, no credit cards. ⊠*Michimalonco 660* ☎*67/336–326* ✈*20 rooms* ☾*In-room: no phone, Wi-Fi. In-hotel: restaurant, room service, bar, no elevator, laundry service, public Wi-Fi, parking, no-smoking rooms* ⊟*No credit cards* ۞|*BP.*

$$$$ ✕▒ **Hotel Loberías del Sur.** On a hill overlooking the port, Hotel Loberías del Sur is a luxurious hotel in an unlikely place. The owner, who runs a catamaran service to Parque Nacional Laguna San Rafael, needed a place to pamper foreign vacationers for the night, and so the hotel was born. It provides real comforts after a blustery day at sea, such as firm queen-size beds and separate showers and bathtubs. The restaurant ($$$), as you might expect, has the finest service in town. **Pros:** Luxury, spa, boat tour to the Laguna San Rafael Park. **Cons:** Expensive, nothing to do in port itself. ⊠*Carrera 50* ☎*67/351–112* 🖷*67/351–188* ⊕*www.catamaranesdelsur.cl* ✈*60 rooms* ☾*In-room: safe. In-hotel: restaurant, room service, bar, spa, pool, gym, water sports, laundry service, public Internet, public Wi-Fi, airport shuttle, parking, no-smoking rooms* ⊟*AE, DC, MC, V* ۞|*BP.*

$ ▒ **Patagonia Green.** The cabins at Patagonia Green are extremely comfortable, and the nice, attentive owner/manager can help arrange all kinds of excursions to nearby nature areas, including Laguna San Rafael Park. **Pros:** Independent, good location, tour programs. **Cons:** No restaurant. ⊠*Located 400 meters from Puerto Aisén bridge, on the Chacabuco side* ☎*67/336–796* ⊕*www.patagoniagreen.cl* ✈*4 cabins* ☾*In-room: no phone, safe, kitchen, refrigerator, Wi-Fi. In-hotel: water sports, laundry service, parking* ⊟*AE, DC, MC, V* ۞|*BP (optional).*

SPORTS & THE OUTDOORS

The principal reason for coming here for many travelers will be to board a boat bound for the spectacular glaciers and ice at Laguna San Rafael Park. To do so, you must arrange with one of four tour operators, or organize your own private boat. But given that it's a 10-hour round-trip deal, organizing your own transportation can be quite expensive. That said, the area around Puerto Aisén is nature-rich and worth checking out too if you have the time. Nearby, for example, is Parque Aiken del Sur, a small private park situated on the banks of

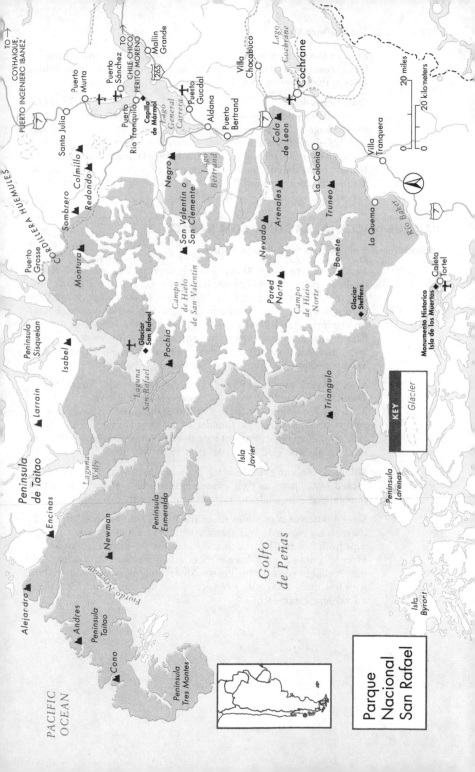

Riesco Lake with excellent walks through native flora and strong fly-fishing possibilities. For fishermen, the area is bountiful in prime fishing spots at the numerous rivers and lakes.

Catamaranes del Sur (⊠ *Carrera 50, Puerto Chacabuco* ☎ *67/351–112, 2/333–7127 in Santiago* ⊕ *www.catamaranesdelsur.cl*) arranges boat trips to Laguna San Rafael. **Patagonia Connection** (⊠ *Puerto Puyuhuapi* ☎ *2/225–6489* ⊕ *www.patagonia-connection.com*) arranges boat trips to Laguna San Rafael and Puyuhuapi. **Patagonia Green** (☎ *67/336–796* ⊕ *www.patagoniagreen.cl*) can arrange all kinds of excursions to nature attractions around Puerto Aisén, including an overflight of glaciers at nearby Laguna San Rafael Park.

PARQUE NACIONAL LAGUNA SAN RAFAEL

Fodor'sChoice   *5 hrs by boat from Puerto Chacabuco.*
★

Nearly all of the 101,000-acre Parque Nacional Laguna San Rafael is totally inaccessible fields of ice. But only a handful of the people who come here ever set foot on land. Most travel by boat from Puerto Chacabuco or Puerto Montt through the maze of fjords along the coast to the expansive San Rafael Lagoon. Floating on the surface of the brilliant blue water are scores of icebergs that rock from side to side as boats pass. Most surprising is the variety of forms and colors in each iceberg, including a shimmering, translucent cobalt blue.

Massive Ventisquero San Rafael extends 4 km (2½ mi) from end to end. The glacier is receding about 182 meters (600 feet) a year: paint on a bordering mountain marks the location of the glacier in past years. It's a noisy beast, roaring like thunder as the sheets of ice shift. If you're lucky you'll see huge pieces of ice calve off, causing violent waves that should make you glad your boat is at a safe distance.

Wildlife lovers can glimpse black-browed albatross and elegant black-necked swans here, as well as sea lions, dolphins, elephant seals, and *chungungos*—the Chilean version of the sea otter.

Several different companies make the trip to Laguna San Rafael. The cheapest are Navimag and Transmarchilay, which offer both two-night trips from Puerto Chacabuco and four-night trips from Puerto Montt. More luxurious are the three-night cruises from Puerto Chacabuco and the six-night cruises from Puerto Montt run by Skorpios. For those with less time, Patagonia Connection has day trips from Chacabuco on a deluxe catamaran.

Southern Chilean Patagonia & Tierra del Fuego

Penguins, Península Valdés

WORD OF MOUTH

"Have you thought of going to Patagonia? Kids enjoy it tremendously because almost every species in the area gives birth in November, and by January there are babies everywhere. Not to mention, most of the species are unique to Patagonia. Adults enjoy it because it is one of the most beautiful places to photograph on the face of the earth. And I've never been anywhere more relaxing."

—hills27

WELCOME TO SOUTHERN CHILEAN PATAGONIA & TIERRA DEL FUEGO

TOP REASONS TO GO

★ **Mad About Ornithology:** With plentiful fish food courtesy of the frosty Humboldt Current, southern Chile enjoys one of the richest populations of sea birds in the world. Perhaps most dazzling is the largest of all sea birds, the albatross, eight species of which migrate through Chilean waters.

★ **Glaciers Galore:** One of the prime justifications for traveling thousands of miles via sea, air, and land is to set yourself opposite an impossibly massive wall of ice, contemplating the blue-green-turquoise spectrum trapped within.

★ **Penguin Encounters:** Humboldt, Rockhopper, and Magellanic penguins congregate around the southern Patagonian coast—at the noisy, malodorous colony of Isla Magdalena you'll find a half-burnt lighthouse and over 120,000 of our waddling friends.

1 Puerto Natales & Torres del Paine. Puerto Natales serves as last stop before what many consider the finest national park in South America, Parque Nacional Torres del Paine 91 mi north. A worthy break in your journey is the city itself, commonly called Natales, which boasts an array of fine eateries and super-supportive local hosts.

2 Punta Arenas. Lord Byron's legendary mariner grandfather gave Chile's southernmost city its name, meaning Sandy Point. Situated at the foot of the Andes, monument-laden Punta Arenas faces the island of Tierra del Fuego, where the Atlantic and Pacific oceans convene—and there it thrived as a key 19th-century refueling port for maritime traffic.

3 El Calafate & the Parque Nacional los Glaciares. The wild, icy expanse of the Hielo Continental ice-cap and the exquisite turquoise surface of Lago Argentino exist in dramatic contrast to the tourist boomtown atmosphere of El Calafate, where international visitors flock to fancy restaurants and modern hotels.

4 Tierra del Fuego. The common name of Isla Grande, the largest island of southern Patagonia's archipelago, this is where the world's longest mountain chain peters out to become "el fin del mundo" (the end of the world). Part-Chilean, part-Argentinean, Tierra del Fuego is synonymous with seclusion and natural beauty, though you will find plenty of company in Ushuaia, the world's most southern *city*.

GETTING ORIENTED

Punta Arenas, more than 2,000 km (1,360 mi) south of Santiago, is the capital of this Chilean province. The only other settlement of any size in Magallanes is Puerto Natales, 240 km to the northwest, a well-positioned gateway to Parque Nacional Torres del Paine. Frequent bus service links the two cities. But the archipelagic breadth of Chilean Patagonia—consisting of countless remote, hardly visited islands—is impossible to see without a boat. At the bottom end of the continent, separated by the Magellan Strait and split between Chile and Argentina, lies Tierra del Fuego. Though comprising a number of islands, it's more or less equivalent to Isla Grande. The resort town of Ushuaia, Argentina, base camp for explorations of the Beagle Channel and the forested peaks of the Cordillera Darwin, is by a long stretch the leading tourist attraction of the region.

10

SOUTHERN CHILEAN PATAGONIA & TIERRA DEL FUEGO PLANNER

When to Go

Late November to early March—summer in the Southern Hemisphere—is considered high season in Patagonia. Demand for accommodations is highest in January and February, so advance reservations are vital. Summer weather in these latitudes is by no means warm, but rather pleasantly cool. Bring an extra layer or two, even when the sun is shining. Windbreakers are essential. On or near these Antarctic waters, stiff breezes can be biting. In spring (September to November) and fall (March to May) the weather is usually delightfully mild, but can also be downright cold, depending on clouds and the wind. The region goes into virtual hibernation in the winter months of June, July, and August.

Eat Well & Rest Easy

Menus tend to be extensive, although two items in particular might be considered specialties: *centolla* (king crab), and moist, tender *cordero magallánico* (Magellanic lamb). Many Chilean restaurants offer salmon *a la plancha* (grilled), a satisfying local delicacy. If you hop the border into Argentina, the dining options are cheaper and often tastier. You'll find the same fire-roasted centolla and cordero (in Argentina it's *cordero a la cruz* or *al asador*) but you'll also get a chance to try the famous Argentine *parrillas* (grilled-meat restaurants). Many restaurants close for several hours in the afternoon and early evening (3–8).

Punta Arenas has many historic hotels offering luxurious amenities and fine service. A night or two in one of them should be part of your trip. Several good resorts and lodges skirt Puerto Natales or are within Parque Nacional Torres del Paine. The terms *hospedaje* and *hostal* are used interchangeably in the region, so don't make assumptions based on the name. Many hostals are fine hotels—not youth hostels with multiple beds—just very small. By contrast, some *hospedajes* are little more than a spare room in someone's home.

Health & Safety

Emergency services and hospitals are widely available in the cities. At Torres del Paine, there is an emergency clinic during the summer at the National Park administration office. The closest hospital is in Puerto Natales. Additionally, every park guide is trained in first aid.

What It Costs

IN CHILEAN PESOS (IN THOUSANDS)				
¢	$	$$	$$$	$$$$
RESTAURANTS				
under 3 pesos	3 pesos– 5 pesos	5 pesos– 8 pesos	8 pesos– 11 pesos	over 11 pesos
HOTELS				
under 15 pesos	15 pesos– 45 pesos	45 pesos– 75 pesos	75 pesos– 105 pesos	over 105 pesos

Restaurant prices are based on the median main course price at dinner. Hotel prices are for a standard double room in high season, excluding taxes.

Getting Here & Around

If you want to begin your trip in Chile, fly into Punta Arenas, the region's principal city, or drive in from Argentina—if you've been visiting El Calafate—and head directly to Puerto Natales and Torres del Paine. If you'd rather begin touring the area in Argentina, head on down to Ushuaia. Many fly or cruise from Punta Arenas to Ushuaia or vice versa. Remote spots, such as Isla Magdalena or Puerto Williams, can be reached only by boat or airplane.

Air Travel. LAN (⊕ www.lan.com) operate flights daily between Punta Arenas and Santiago, Coihaique, and Puerto Montt. Sky (www.skyairline.com) and Air Comet (www.aircomet.com) also offer competitive fares.

Aerovías DAP (⊕ www.aeroviasdap.cl) has regularly scheduled flights exclusively in Patagonia, between Punta Arenas, Porvenir, and Puerto Williams. Aerolíneas Argentinas (⊕ www.aerolineas.com.ar) has service between Buenos Aires and Ushuaia, Argentina.

Boat Travel. Boat tours are a popular way to see otherwise inaccessible parts of Patagonia and Tierra del Fuego. *See the Tierra del Fuego by Sea box at the end of this chapter for further information.*

Bus Travel. The four-hour trip between Punta Arenas and Puerto Natales is serviced by small, private companies. One of the best is Buses Fernández. To travel the longer haul between Punta Arenas, Río Gallegos, and Ushuaia, Argentina, your best bet is Tecni-Austral, based in Argentina. Book your ticket in advance.

What It Costs

IN ARGENTINA PESOS

¢	$	$$	$$$	$$$$
RESTAURANTS				
under 8 pesos	8 pesos–15 pesos	15 pesos–25 pesos	25 pesos–35 pesos	over 35 pesos
HOTELS				
under 80 pesos	80 pesos–140 pesos	140 pesos–220 pesos	220 pesos–300 pesos	over 300 pesos

Restaurant prices are based on the median main course price at dinner. Hotel prices are for a standard double room in high season, excluding taxes.

Visitor Info

Sernatur, Chile's national tourism agency, has offices in Punta Arenas and in Puerto Natales. The Punta Arenas office is open daily 8–7 except Sundays, and the small Puerto Natales office is open Monday–Thursday 8:15–6 and Friday 8:15–5. You can also try the helpful folks at the Punta Arenas City Tourism Office, in an attractive kiosk in the main square. It's open December–March, Monday–Saturday 8–8 and Sunday 9–2; April–November, Monday–Thursday 8–6 and Friday 8–5. They offer a free Internet connection. Sometimes they offer last-minute specials to fill remaining seats on popular tours. Don't hesitate to ask for complete printouts of transportation timetables, since this information is subject to change on short notice.

Border Crossing

The border between Chile and Argentina is still strictly maintained, but crossing it doesn't present much difficulty beyond getting out your passport and waiting in a line to get the stamp. Most travelers end up crossing the border by bus, which means getting out of the vehicle for 30–45 minutes to go through the bureaucratic proceedings, then loading back in. Crossing by car is also quite manageable (check with your car-rental company for restrictions on international travel).

10

Updated by
Jonathan Yevin

CHILEAN PATAGONIA MAY TRADITIONALLY CLAIM the bottom half of Chile, but the spirit of the region resides in the southernmost province of Magallanes (in honor of 16th-century conquistador Hernando de Magallanes), the waterway of Seno Última Esperanza ("Last Hope Sound"), and the infamous misnomer Tierra del Fuego ("Land of Fire"). It's one of the least inhabited areas in South America, physically cut off from by the rest of the continent by two vast ice caps and the Strait of Magellan. The only links with the north are via air or water— or through Argentina. It's amidst this seclusion that you will find the daunting rocky spires of Torres del Paine, horseback sheep-wrangling gauchos, islands inhabited solely by elephant seals and penguin colonies, and the austere landscapes that captivated everyone from Charles Darwin to Butch Cassidy and the Sundance Kid.

Navigating the channel that today bears his name, conquistador Hernando de Magallanes arrived on these shores in 1520, claiming the region for Spain. Although early attempts at colonization failed, the forbidding landscape continued to fascinate explorers. Naturalist Charles Darwin, who sailed through the Estrecho de Magallanes (Strait of Magellan) in 1833 and 1834, called it a "mountainous land, partly submerged in the sea, so that deep inlets and bays occupy the place where valleys should exist."

The newly formed nation of Chile showed little interest in Patagonia until 1843, when other countries began to eye the region, and Chilean President Manuel Bulnes sent down a ragtag group of soldiers to claim some of it for Chile. Five years later the town of Punta Arenas was founded.

Shortly thereafter, Punta Arenas became a major stop on the trade route around the tip of South America. Steam navigation intensified the city's commercial importance, leading to its short-lived age of splendor from 1892 to 1914, when its population rose from approximately 2,000 to 20,000. The opening of the Panama Canal all but bumped Punta Arenas off the map, and you will still hear Chileans down here bemoaning the loss of shipping. By 1920 many of the founding families had decided to move on, leaving behind the lavish mansions and the impressive public buildings they'd built.

North from Punta Arenas the land is flat and vast; this terrain gave rise to the book of poems *Desolation* by Nobel prize–winning Chilean poet Gabriela Mistral. The road peters out to the north at Parque Nacional Torres del Paine, where snow-covered pillars of stone seem to rise vertically from the plains below. To the east, across the Argentine border, is the only glacier in the world that is still growing after 30,000 years—Glaciar Perito Moreno, one of Argentina's national landmarks. To the south is Tierra del Fuego, the storm-lashed island at the continent's southernmost tip. This bleak wilderness, which still calls out to explorers today, is literally the end of the Earth.

CLOSE UP

The Giants of Patagonia

Antonio Pigafetta was an Italian aristocrat who shelled out a great sum of money for the privilege of playing passenger on Ferdinand Magellan's famed circumnavigation, and his story is told in *Relazione del Primo Viaggio Intorno Al Mondo* (Reflections on the first voyage around the world). Among the most curious details of his book is its depiction of the native Patagonians as a race of giants. Patagonia itself, according to one etymological account, was named by Magellan as a remark upon the great size of the natives' feet ("Patagones" roughly translates as "bigfoots"). Pigafetta describes the initial encounter with the Patagones:

"One day we suddenly saw a naked man of giant stature on the shore of the port, dancing, singing, and throwing dust on his head. The captain-general sent one of our men to the giant so that he might perform the same actions as a sign of peace. Having done that, the man led the giant to an islet where the captain-general was waiting. When the giant was in the captain-general's and our presence he marveled greatly, and made signs with one finger raised upward, believing that we had come from the sky. He was so tall that we reached only to his waist..."

Half a century later, in 1578, Sir Francis Drake's chaplain Francis Fletcher also wrote a manuscript that described meeting very tall Patagonians. In the 1590s, Anthonie Knivet, who had sailed with Sir Thomas Cavendish, claimed that he had seen dead bodies in Patagonia measuring over 12 feet in length. Soon the region of Patagonia was noted on maps as "Regio Gigantum."

The rumors of Patagonian giants were only definitively proven fictitious when the official account of Commodore John Byron's voyage appeared in 1773. This account revealed that Byron, also known as "Foul-Weather Jack," had indeed encountered a tribe of Patagonians, but that the tallest among them measured 6 feet, 6 inches. They were tall, but not 12-foot giants. The tribe that Byron met was probably the Tehuelche, who were later wiped out by the Rocca expedition in 1880.

10

PUERTO NATALES

242 km (150 mi) northwest of Punta Arenas.

The land around Puerto Natales held very little interest for Spanish explorers in search of riches. A not-so-warm welcome from the indigenous peoples encouraged them to continue up the coast, leaving only a name for the channel running through it: Seno Última Esperanza (Last Hope Sound).

The town of Puerto Natales wasn't founded until 1911. A community of fading fishing and meat-packing enterprises, with some 20,000 friendly residents, it has recently seen a large increase in tourism and is repositioning itself as a vacation town; it's now rapidly emerging as the staging center for visits to Parque Nacional Torres del Paine, Parque Nacional Bernardo O'Higgins, and other attractions, including

Sendero de Chile: Chile's Ridiculously Long Trail

The Sendero de Chile ("Chilean path") trail system is one of the most ambitious trekking trail projects in the world, over 9,700 km (6,000 mi) of trails when completed in 2010. This is one of many initiatives the government kicked off to celebrate the 200th anniversary of Chile's 1810 independence from Spain. The aim is to create an ecological connection across the country—through deserts, mountains, valleys, forest, and glaciers—to demonstrate the natural and cultural diversity of Chile. One of the major stated goals underlying the government's initiative is to raise awareness for conservation and the protection of the environment. The path is designed to fill the need for safe public access to natural spaces inside the country for Chileans and tourists. All the infrastructure—signs, refuges, camping areas, bridges—is geared towards reducing human impact on the natural environment. Keep up with the progress at ⊕ *senderodechile.cl.*

the Perito Moreno Glacier across the border in Argentina. A lot of tourism is also generated by the scenic **Navimag cruise** that makes four-day journeys between here and Puerto Montt, to the north.

Hotels and restaurants are simpler than in Punta Arenas, and shops older and more basic. Serious hikers often come to this area and spend four or five days—or more—hiking and camping in **Torres del Paine,** either before or after stopping in Puerto Natales. Others choose to spend a couple of nights in one of the park's luxury hotels, and take in the sights during day hikes from that base.

If you have less time, however, it's quite possible to spend just one day touring the park, as many people do, with Puerto Natales as your base. In that case, rather than drive, you'll want to book a one-day Torres del Paine tour with one of the many tour operators in Natales. Most tours pick you up at your hotel between 8 and 9 AM, and most go along the same route, visiting several lakes and mountain vistas, seeing Lago Grey and its glacier, and stopping for lunch in Hostería Lago Grey or one of the other hotels inside the park. These tours return around sunset.

Argentina's magnificent **Perito Moreno Glacier,** near El Calafate, can be visited on a popular (long) one-day tour, leaving at the crack of dawn and returning late at night—don't forget your passport. It's a four-hour-plus trip in each direction. (Some tours instead include overnights in El Calafate.) *For some recommended tour agencies, see Chapter 2 Choosing Your Cruise & Tour, but there are many in town, most of them booking the same vans.*

GETTING HERE & AROUND

Puerto Natales centers on the Plaza de Armas, a lovely, well-landscaped sanctuary. A few blocks west of the plaza on Avenida Bulnes you'll find the small Museo Historico Municipal. On a clear day, an early morning walk along Avenida Pedro Montt, which follows the shoreline of the

Puerto Natales
& Environs

Seno Última Esperanza (or Canal Señoret, as it's called on some maps), can be a soul-cleansing experience. The rising sun gradually casts a glow on the mountain peaks to the west.

ESSENTIALS

Bus Contacts Buses Fernández (✉ *Eleuterio Ramirez 399* ☎ *61/411–111* ⊕ *www.busesfernandez.com).* **Internet Cafés El Rincón del Tata** (✉ *Arturo Prat 23* ☎ *61/413–845).*

Rental Cars Avis (✉ *Av. Bulnes 632* ☎ *61/410–775).*

Visitor & Tour Info Sernatur Puerto Natales (✉ *Av. Pedro Montt 19* ☎ *61/412–125).*

WHAT TO SEE

A few blocks east of the Seno Última Esperanza is the not-quite-central **Plaza de Armas**. An incongruous railway engine sits prominently in the middle of the square. ✉ *Arturo Prat at Eberhard.*

Across from the Plaza de Armas is the squat little **Iglesia Parroquial**. The ornate altarpiece in this church depicts the town's founders, indigenous peoples, and the Virgin Mary all in front of the Torres del Paine.

A highlight in the small but interesting **Museo Historico Municipal** is a room filled with antique prints of Aonikenk and Kaweshkar indigenous

10

peoples. Another room is devoted to the exploits of Hermann Eberhard, a German explorer considered the region's first settler. Check out his celebrated collapsible boat. In an adjacent room you will find some vestiges of the old Bories sheep plant, which processed over 300,000 sheep a year. ⊠ *Av. Bulnes 285* 🕿 *61/411–263* 🖃 *1,000 pesos* ☺ *Weekdays 8:30–12:30 and 2:30–8, weekends 2:30–6.*

> ## BORDER CROSSING
>
> There are three crossings to and from Argentina near Puerto Natales. Dorotea Pass is 27 km (17 mi) along Route CH-250 from Puerto Natales. There are 14 km (9 mi) to Río Turbio in Argentina. It's open 24 hours from November to March, 8–midnight April–October. Casas Viejas Pass is located 14 km (9 mi) from Puerto Natales. It's about 19 km (12 mi) to Río Turbio (open all year 8 AM–10 PM). From December to March, Cancha Carrera provides access from Puerto Natales through the Cerro Castillo area to El Calafate.

In 1896, Hermann Eberhard stumbled upon a gaping cave that extended 200 meters (650 feet) into the earth. Venturing inside, he discovered the bones and dried pieces of hide of an animal he could not identify. It was later determined that what Eberhard had discovered were the extraordinarily well-preserved remains of a prehistoric herbivorous mammal, *mylodon darwini,* about twice the height of a man, which they called a *milodón.* The discovery of a stone wall in the cave, and of neatly cut grass stalks in the animal's feces led researchers to conclude that 10,000 years ago a group of Tehuelche Indians captured this beast. The cave and a somewhat kitschy life-size fiberglass rendering of the creature are at the **Monumento Natural Cueva de Milodón.** ⊠ *5 km (3 mi) off Ruta 9 signpost, 28 km (17 mi) northwest of Puerto Natales* 🕿 *No phone* 🖃 *3,000 pesos* ☺ *Summer, daily 8* AM– *9* PM; *winter, daily 9–6.*

WHERE TO EAT

$$ ✕**Asador Patagónico.** This bright spot in the Puerto Natales dining scene
★　is zealous about meat. So zealous, in fact, that there's no seafood on the menu. Incredible care is taken with the excellent *lomo* and other grilled steaks, as well as the steak carpaccio starter. Though the wine list is serious, the atmosphere is less so—the place used to be a pharmacy, and much of the furniture is still labeled with the remedies (*catgut crin* anyone?) they once contained. There's good music, dim lighting, an open fire, and a friendly buzz. ⊠ *Prat 158* 🕿 *61/412–197* 🖃 *AE, DC, MC, V.*

¢–$ ✕**Café Melissa.** The best espresso in town is found at this café, which also serves pastries and cakes baked on the premises. In the heart of downtown, this is a popular meeting place for residents and visitors, and there's Internet access. It's open until 9 PM. ⊠ *Blanco Encalada 258* 🕿 *61/411–944* 🖃 *No credit cards.*

$–$$ ✕**Centro Español.** Tables swathed in bright red, and hardwood floors that would be perfect for flamenco dancing create this restaurant's subtly Spanish style. It's a bit formal, but never stuffy. There's a wide selection of simply prepared meat and fish entrées, including succulent squid, served in ample portions. ⊠ *Av. Magallanes 247* ☎ *61/411–181* ⊟ *AE, MC, V.*

¢–$$ ✕ **Pez Glaciar.** Eco friendly vibes waft from this bright newly renovated seafood spot. Marine fossils collected from the adjacent fjord, piles of *National Geographic*s, subtle cuisine, and an English-speaking staff make this restaurant a hit. The fresh lemon-marinated ceviche is amazing, as are the dinner-plate-size sandwiches served on homemade wheat bread. The corner location within the Indigo Hotel, overlooking the water and a backdrop of snowy peaks, makes for a pleasant visit, even if you come just for a cup of coffee. ⊠ *Ladrilleros 105* ☎ *61/413–609* ⊕ *www.indigopatagonia.com* ⊟ *AE, DC, MC, V* ⊙ *Closed in winter; months vary.*

$–$$ ✕ **Restaurant Última Esperanza.** Named for the strait on which Puerto Natales is located, the Last Hope Restaurant sounds as if it might be a bleak place. It's known, however, for its attentive service and top-quality dishes from chefs Miguel Risco and Manuel Marín. *Cordero* (lamb) and *salmón a la plancha* (grilled salmon) are specialties. The room is big and impersonal. ⊠ *Av. Eberhard 354* ☎ *61/413–626* ⊟ *No credit cards.*

¢–$$ ✕ **El Rincón del Tata.** It's all about the low-lighting groove at this funky little spot. Artifacts, mainly household items, from the town's early days fill the dining room, which has a working wood-burning stove to keep you warm, and Internet access. Pizza is a specialty, and it's not bad by Chilean standards; the *salmón à la mantequilla* (salmon baked in butter and black pepper) is also decent, and the grilled lamb with garlic sauce is a Patagonian highlight. The waiters' modish tango hats, however, are not. ⊠ *Arturo Prat 236* ☎ *61/614–291* ⊟ *AE, DC, MC, V.*

WHERE TO STAY

$–$$ 🏨 **Hostal Lady Florence Dixie.** Named after an aristocratic English immigrant and tireless traveler, this modern yet long-established hotel with an alpine-inspired facade is on the town's main street. Its bright, spacious lounge is a great people-watching perch. Guest rooms are spartan—not much more than a bed—although the "superior" rooms are bigger and have bathtubs. **Pros:** Very convenient location. **Cons:** Not quite the boutique hotel it purports to be. ⊠ *Av. Bulnes 655* ☎ *61/411–158* 🖷 *61/411–943* ⊕ *www.chileanpatagonia.com/florence* ⟿ *19 rooms* ⚷ *In-room: safe. In-hotel: laundry service, public Internet* ⊟ *AE, MC, V* ⧖ *CP.*

$ 🏨 **Hotel Alberto de Agostini.** The Agostini is one of the modern hotels that have cropped up in Puerto Natales in the past few years. Small rooms—some with hot tubs—are unremarkable in decor, but a comfortably furnished lounge on the second floor looks out over the Seno Última Esperanza. **Pros:** Perfectly functional. **Cons:** Rooms small, not distinctive. ⊠ *Av. Bernardo O'Higgins 632* ☎ *61/410–060* 🖷 *61/410–070* ⊕ *www.hotelalbertodeagostini.cl* ⟿ *25 rooms* ⚷ *In-hotel: restaurant, room service, bar, laundry service, public Internet, minibar* ⊟ *AE, DC, MC, V.*

$$$–$$$$ ⊞ **Hotel CostAustralis.** Designed by a local architect, this venerable three-story hotel is one of the most distinctive buildings in Puerto Natales; its peaked, turreted roof dominates the waterfront. Rooms have wood-paneled entryways, thermo-acoustic windows, and Venetian and Czech furnishings. Some have a majestic view of the Seno Última Esperanza and the snowcapped mountain peaks beyond, and others look out over the city. **Pros:** Great views from bay-facing rooms, good restaurant. **Cons:** Rooms are somewhat bland. ⊠ *Av. Pedro Montt 262, at Av. Bulnes* ☎ *61/412–000* 📠 *61/411–881* ⊕ *www. hoteles-australis.com* 🛏 *72 rooms, 2 suites* △ *In-room: safe. In-hotel: restaurant, room service, bar, laundry service, public Internet station* 🖃 *AE, DC, MC, V* ⦿*BP.*

$–$$$ ⊞ **Hotel Martín Gusinde.** Part of Chile's modern AustroHoteles chain, this intimate inn possesses an aura of sophistication that contrasts with the laid-back atmosphere of Puerto Natales. The hotel is named after an Austrian ethnologist who studied the native inhabitants of Tierra del Fuego. Rooms are decorated with wood furniture and colorfully patterned wallpaper. It's across from the casino, a block south of the Plaza de Armas. The hotel has the same owners as Hostería Lago Grey in Parque Nacional Torres del Paine, so joint bookings are a good idea. In low season, prices drop by almost two thirds. **Pros:** Atmosphere is urbane. **Cons:** Staff language barrier, seedy casino neighbor. ⊠ *Carlos Bories 278* ☎ *61/412–770* 📠 *61/412–820* ⊕ *www.hotelmartingusinde. com* 🛏 *20 rooms* △ *In-room: safe. In-hotel: restaurant, room service, bar, public Internet* 🖃 *AE, MC, V* ⦿*CP.*

$$$$ ⊞ **Indigo Patagonia Hotel & Spa.** Rooms in this completely renovated
★   hotel have amazing views down the Canal Señoret, stretching as far as the Mt. Balmaceda glacier and the Paine Grande. Very minimalist modern natural-wood design abounds. Blankets are made of hand-woven wool. With three open-air Jacuzzis and a dry sauna, the rooftop spa is a treat for the senses. Down below common spaces are filled with plush couches and there's a lounge bar where you can enjoy brownies and cappuccinos—or a late-night pisco sour. English is spoken well, as exhibited in the Friday-night shows about Torres del Paine park. Ask for one of the corner rooms, which have windows along two walls. **Pros:** Steeped in ultramodern luxury. **Cons:** Standard rooms do not have bathtubs (though the showers are excellent). ⊠ *Ladrilleros 105* ☎ *61/413–609* 📠 *61/410–169* ⊕ *www.conceptoindigo.com* 🛏 *23 rooms, 6 suites* △ *In-room: no TV. In-hotel: restaurant, bar, laundry service, spa, public Wi-Fi* 🖃 *AE, DC, MC, V* ⊙ *Closed in winter; months vary.*

WHERE TO STAY JUST OUTSIDE TOWN

Recently, several lodges have been constructed on a bluff overlooking the Seno Última Esperanza, about a mile outside of town. The views at these hotels are amazing—broad panoramas with unforgettable sunsets. It's too far to walk to town comfortably (about 20 minutes), but there is dependable taxi service for 1,000 pesos.

$$$ ☷**Altiplanico Sur.** This is the Patagonian representative of the Altiplanico line of thoughtfully designed eco-hotels. Nature takes center stage at Altiplanico Sur. The hotel blends seamlessly with its surroundings due to an interesting construction technique which involves the use of natural materials in its exterior. The roofs are covered with grass and flowers so it looks like the hotel is cascading down the hillside. If you are looking for TVs, Wi-Fi, and other modern day accoutrements, there are more appropriate choices. Clean, comfortable, and well-designed rooms are in a minimalist style, with great views of the Última Esperanza Sound. The dining area is bright and open. Staff do their best to help, but sometimes language proves a barrier. **Pros:** You couldn't be closer to nature. **Cons:** No mod-cons, staff speaks little English. ✉*Ruta 9 Norte, Km 1.5 Huerto 282* ☎*61/411–919* ⊕*www.altiplanico.cl* 🛏*22 rooms* ♿*In-room: no TV, safe. In-hotel: restaurant* ☐*AE, V, MC.*

$$$$
Fodor'sChoice
★
☷**Remota.** For most of its guests the Remota experience begins a long way off from the hotel, when they are scooped up from the Punta Arenas airport. Not your conventional boring old transfer, however, as the driver stops to point out animals and other items of interest. On arrival you meet what seems like the entire staff, check into your ultramodern room, have a drink from a top-shelf open bar, and run off to the open-air Jacuzzis and impossibly serene infinity pool—before you unpack. The hotel is the paragon of style, deliberately designed (by the same architect as Explora) in a way that blocks out everything but the exquisite vistas. The various buildings are connected by enclosed walkways in the style that shepherds built for local sheep ranches. The lenga walls are natural and unfinished. The staff feels like family, and all meals and excursions are included in the price. Every day a guide proposes a wide range of activities, demanding various levels of exertion, so you are sure to find something to suit your speed. Equipment is supplied and includes everything from Zodiacs to mountain-climbing gear to bikes. Horseback riding with local gauchos is a hard activity to pass up. The guides are helpful, patient, demonstrate an infectious love for the outdoors, and know how to crack a joke. **Pros:** After a few days the staff feels like family. **Cons:** All-inclusiveness discourages sampling local restaurants. ✉*Ruta 9 Norte, Km 1.5, Huerto 279* ☎*61/414–040* ⊕*www.remota.cl* 🛏*72 rooms* ♿*In-room: no phone, no TV, safe. In-hotel: spa, pool, bicycles, restaurant, bar* ☐*AE, V, MC* ⦿*AI.*

$ ☷**Weskar Patagonian Lodge.** Weskar stands for "hill" in the language of the indigenous Kaweskar, the forebears owner Juan José Pantoja, a marine biologist, pays homage to in creating this lodge. Looking over the Última Esperanza fjord, the wooden building is surrounded by parkland and has fabulous views from the terrace. It has a welcoming lounge with rustic fireplaces, ideal when coming back from the windy and cold outdoors. The hotel also boasts a bar and restaurant with a somewhat overpriced standard lunch and dinner menu. The rooms are simply decorated but warm and welcoming—ask for one with a lake view. The staff are unremittingly helpful, and keep the grounds spotless. **Pros:** Great views, helpful staff. **Cons:** Restaurant is so-so given the prices. ✉*Ruta 9 Norte, Km 1 / Puerto Natales* ☎*61/414–168* ⊕*www.weskar.cl* 🛏*16 rooms, 2 suites* ♿*In-room: no phone, no TV, safe. In-hotel: restaurant, bar, bicycles, public Internet.*

10

PARQUE NACIONAL TORRES DEL PAINE

Fodor'sChoice *80 km northwest of Puerto Natales.*

★ A raging inferno broke out in the Parque Nacional Torres del Paine on February 17, 2005, when a Czech trekker's gas camp stove was accidentally knocked over. At the time, he was camped in an unauthorized campsite in an area intended for grazing. The park's famous winds accelerated the blaze, which went on for over a month and required 800 firefighters from Chile and Argentina to rein in. According to reports by CONAF the fire consumed 13,880 hectares, equivalent to 7% of the park. The most ravaged zones were Lake Azul, Lake Cebolla, and the Paine Waterfall. The tourist later apologized in an interview with *El Mercurio* newspaper, was fined $200 by authorities, and donated another $1,000 to the restoration fund. "What happened changed my life...I'll never forget the flames. I would like to express my most profound regret to the Chilean people for the damage caused." The total cost of the damage is estimated to be over $5 million. CONAF's restoration program involved erosion prevention techniques, reforestation with indigenous species, and transplantation of young samples from neighboring forests. CONAF asks that visitors to the park respect the camping zones and the indications of park staff. The institution posts a series of recommendations for camping, and on how to prevent future disasters, on their Web page.

Some 12 million years ago, lava flows pushed up through the thick sedimentary crust that covered the southwestern coast of South America, cooling to form a granite mass. Glaciers then swept through the region, grinding away all but the twisted ash-gray spires—the "towers" of Paine (pronounced "pie-nay"), the old Tehuelche word for "blue"—that rise over the landscape of one of the world's most beautiful natural phenomena, now the Parque Nacional Torres del Paine (established in 1959). Snow formations dazzle at every turn of road, and the sunset views are spectacular. The 2,420-square-km (934-square-mi) park's most astonishing attractions are its lakes of turquoise, aquamarine, and emerald green waters; and the Cuernos del Paine ("Paine Horns"), the geological showpiece of the immense granite massif.

Another draw is the park's unusual wildlife. Creatures like the guanaco (a woollier version of the llama) and the *ñandú* (a rhea, like a small ostrich) abound. They are used to visitors, and don't seem to be bothered by the proximity of automobile traffic and the snapping of cameras. Predators like the gray fox make less-frequent appearances. You may also spot the dramatic aerobatics of falcons and the graceful soaring of endangered condors. The beautiful puma, celebrated in a National Geographic video filmed here, is especially elusive, but sightings have grown more common. Pumas follow the guanaco herds and eat an estimated 40% of their young, so don't dress as one.

The vast majority of visitors come during the summer months of January and February, which means the trails can get congested. Early spring, when wildflowers add flashes of color to the meadows, is an ideal time to visit because the crowds have not yet arrived. In summer,

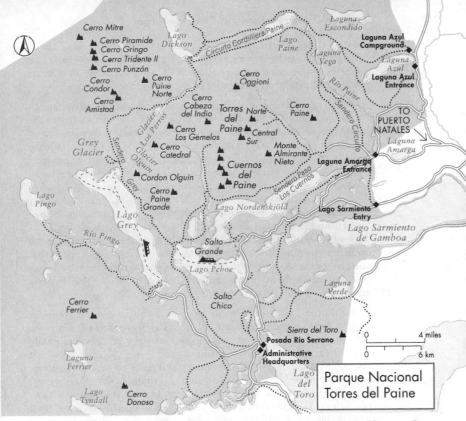

Parque Nacional
Torres del Paine

the winds are incredibly fierce. During the wintertime of June to September, the days are sunnier yet colder (averaging around freezing) and shorter, but the winds all but disappear. The park is open all year, and trails are almost always accessible. Storms can hit without warning, so be prepared for sudden rain or snow. The sight of the Paine peaks in clear weather is stunning; if you have any flexibility in your itinerary, visit the park on the first clear day.

VISITOR INFORMATION

CONAF, the national forestry service, has an office at the northern end of Lago del Toro with a scale model of the park, and numerous exhibits (some in English) about the flora and fauna. ✉ *CONAF station in southern section of the park past Hotel Explora* ☎ *61/247-845* ⊕ *www. conaf.cl* ✉ *Summer 15,000 pesos, winter 5,000 pesos* ☉ *Ranger station: Nov.–Feb., daily 8–8; Mar.–Oct., daily 8–12:30 and 2–6:30* ✉ *Punta Arenas Branch, Av. Bulnes 0309* ☎ *61/238-581* ✉ *Puerto Natales Branch, Av. Bernardo O'Higgins 584* ☎ *61/411-438.*

EXPLORING THE PARK

There are three entrances to the park: Laguna Amarga (all bus arrivals), Lago Sarmiento, and Laguna Azul. You are required to sign in when you arrive. *Guardaparques* (park rangers) staff six stations around the reserve, and can provide a map and up-to-the-day information about the state of various trails. A regular minivan service connects Laguna Amarga with the Hostería Las Torres, 7 km (4½ mi) to the west, for 1,000 pesos. Alternatively, you can walk approximately two hours before reaching the starting point of the hiking circuits.

Although considerable walking is necessary to take full advantage of Parque Nacional Torres del Paine, you need not be a hard-core trekker. Many people choose to hike the **"W" route,** which takes four days, but others prefer to stay in one of the comfortable lodges and hit the trails in the morning or afternoon. **Glaciar Grey,** with its fragmented icebergs, makes a rewarding and easy hike; equally rewarding is the spectacular boat or kayak ride across the lake, past icebergs, and up to the glacier, which leaves from Hostería Lago Grey (⇨below). Another great excursion is the 900-meter (3,000-foot) ascent to the sensational views from **Mirador Las Torres,** four hours one way from Hostería Las Torres (⇨below). Even if you're not staying at the Hostería, you can arrange a morning drop-off there, and a late-afternoon pickup, so that you can see the Mirador while still keeping your base in Puerto Natales or elsewhere in the park; alternatively, you can drive to the Hostería and park there for the day.

If you do the "W," you'll begin (or end, if you reverse the route) at Laguna Amarga and continue to Mirador Las Torres and Los Cuernos, then continue along a breathtaking path to Valle Frances and finally Lago Grey. An even more ambitious route is the "Circuito," which essentially leads around the entire park and takes up to a week. Along the way, some people sleep at the dozen or so humble *refugios* (shelters) found along the trails, and others in tents. Driving is an easier way to enjoy the park: a new road cuts the distance to Puerto Natales from a meandering 140 km (87 mi) to a more direct 80 km (50 mi). Inside the national park, more than 100 km (62 mi) of roads leading to the most popular sites are safe and well maintained, though unpaved.

You can also hire horses from the Hosteria Las Torres and trek to the Torres, the Cuernos, or along the shore of Lago Nordenskjold (which offers the finest views in the park, as the lake's waters reflect the chiseled massif). The hotel offers tours demanding various levels of expertise (prices start at 25,000 pesos). Alternatively, many Puerto Natales–based operators offer multi-day horseback tours. Water transport is also available, with numerous tour operators offering sailboat, kayak, and inflatable Zodiac speedboat options along the Río Serrano (prices start around 50,000 pesos for the Zodiac trips) towards the Paine massif and the southern ice field. Additionally, the Hostería Lago Grey operates the *Grey II,* a large catamaran making a three-hour return trip twice daily to Glaciar Grey, at 10 AM and 3 PM; as well as dinghy runs down the Pingo and Grey rivers. Another boat runs between Refugio Pudeto and Refugio Lago Pehoé.

WHERE TO STAY & EAT

$$$$ 🗙 **Hostería Lago Grey.** The panoramic view past the lake dappled with floating icebergs and to the glacier beyond is worth the journey here, which doesn't change the fact that this older hotel is overpriced and not

very attractive. Rooms seem cheaply built, but are comfortable and have small baths. There's a TV with a VCR in the lounge. The view—and it's one you're not likely to forget—can also be enjoyed through the picture windows in the dining room (breakfast is included; lunch costs about 10,000 pesos per person, and dinner about 20,000 pesos per person with wine). The food is mediocre, though—simple sandwiches are your best bet. The hotel operates its own sightseeing vessel, the *Grey II,* for close-up tours to Glaciar Grey. **Pros:** The views, the location, heated bathroom floors. **Cons:** Thin walls, the price, English-speaking staff is scarce. ⊠ *Lago Grey* ☎ *61/410–172* ⊕ *www.lagogrey.com* ⤶ *30 rooms* ♿ *In-room: no TV. In-hotel: restaurant, bar, laundry service* ⊟ *AE, DC, MC, V* ⦿*BP.*

$$$–$$$$ 🏨 **Hostería Pehoé.** Cross a 100-foot footbridge to get to this hotel on its own island with a volcanic black-sand beach in the middle of glistening Lake Pehoé, across from the beautiful Torres del Paine mountain peaks. Upon seeing the setting, nonguests are often tempted to cancel other reservations. Unfortunately, rooms at Pehoé—built in 1970 as the first hotel in the park—are dark, poorly furnished, windowless, and face an interior lawn. In the new wing, the higher the room number the better the quality. However, it's a delight to walk over the footbridge and have a drink at the ski lodge–like bar, where the views are jaw-dropping. **Pros:** Views are jaw-dropping. **Cons:** Far from attractive grounds, with miserably appointed rooms. ⊠ *Lago Pehoé* ☎ *61/411–390* 🖷 *61/248–052* ⊕ *www.pehoe.com* ⤶ *40 rooms* ♿ *In-room: no phone, no TV. In-hotel: restaurant, bar, laundry service* ⊟ *AE, DC, MC, V* ⦿*CP.*

$$$ 🏨 **Hostería Tyndall.** A boat ferries you from the end of the road the few minutes along the Serrano River to this wooden lodge. The simple rooms in the main building are small but cute, with attractive wood paneling. The hallways are poorly lit and the lodge itself can be noisy—a problem solved by renting a log cottage (at $220 a great value for groups of four). There's also a much more basic refugio with dorm-style rooms that are very cheap. Owner Christian Bore is a wildlife enthusiast and bird-watcher; ask him for a tour of the grassy plain looking out toward the central cluster of snowy peaks. Or go fishing—the kitchen staff will cook your catch for free. The prix-fixe lunch costs $14, dinner $25. **Pros:** Cheaper lodging and dining options than other places in the park. **Cons:** Hallways are poorly lit and the lodge itself can get noisy. ⊠ *Ladrilleros 256, Lago Tyndall* ☎ *61/614–682* ⊕ *www.hosteria tyndall.com* ⤶ *24 rooms, 6 cottages* ♿ *In-room: no phone, no TV. In-hotel: restaurant, bar, laundry service* ⊟ *AE, DC, MC, V* ⦿*CP.*

$$$$ 🏨 **Hotel Explora.** On the southeast corner of Lago Pehoé, this lodge
Fodor'sChoice is one of the most luxurious—and the most expensive—in Chile.
★ Although there may be some debate about the aesthetics of the hotel's low-slung minimalist exterior, the interior is impeccable: it's Scandinavian in style, with local woods used for ceilings, floors, and furniture. No expense has been spared—even the bed linens were imported from Spain. A dozen full-time guides tailor all-inclusive park outings to guests' interests. A four-night minimum stay is required, for which you'll pay a minimum of US$4,952 for two people, including airport transfers, three meals a day, drinks, and excursions. Rooms with better

10

views go up to almost double that. Yet, as a testament to the value, the place consistently sells out even during the winter. Nonguests may also enjoy a pricey prix-fixe dinner ($60) at the restaurant. **Pros:** The grande dame of Patagonian hospitality and perhaps the best hotel in all South America. **Cons:** A bank breaker. ⊠ *Lago Pehoé* ☎ *2/206–6060 in Santiago* ☎ *2/228–4655 in Santiago* ⊕ *www.explora.com* 📠 *44 rooms, 6 suites* ♿ *In-room: no TV. In-hotel: restaurant, bar, pool, gym, laundry service, airport shuttle, public Internet* ☐ *AE, DC, MC, V* ⦿⎮*AI.*

$$$–$$$$ ✕📷 **Posada Río Serrano.** A welcoming staff will show you a selection of small, clean rooms with colorful bedspreads. Insist on the ones with lake views. A warm and cheerful salon with a fireplace makes for a nice place to relax. The restaurant serves filling fish dishes, as well as lamb; in summer there might be an outdoor asado. They recently expanded and even added a golf course to the grounds. The inn also has a general store where you can find basic necessities such as batteries and cookies. **Pros:** Good service and location. **Cons:** Rooms a little small—ask for lake views. ⊠ *Lago Toro* ☎ *61/410–684 for reservations (Puerto Natales)* ⊕ *www.hotelrioserrano.cl* 📠 *56 rooms* ♿ *In-room: minibar. In-hotel: restaurant, bar, golf course* ☐ *No credit cards* ⦿⎮*CP.*

$$$$ 📷 **Las Torres Patagonia.** Owned by one of the earliest families to settle ★ in what became the park, Las Torres has a long history. Originally an estancia, then a popular hosteria, the facility recently upgraded to a three-night-minimum, all-food-and-excursion-inclusive resort, in the style of Remota and Explora. Stretched across several vast fields, the location is perfect if you want to day-hike to Mirador Torres, one of the park's highlights. Don't forget to check out the informative mini-museum with the stuffed ñandú. **Pros:** Friendly and efficient, with a homey atmosphere. **Cons:** Not cheap. ⊠ *Lago Amarga* ☎📷 *61/360–364* ⊕ *www.lastorres.com* 📠 *57 rooms* ♿ *In room: no TV. In-hotel: restaurant, bar, spa* ☐ *AE, MC, V.*

PARQUE NACIONAL BERNARDO O'HIGGINS

Southwest of Parque Nacional Torres del Paine.

Bordering the Parque Nacional Torres del Paine on the southwest, Parque Nacional Bernardo O'Higgins is composed primarily of the southern tip of the vast Campo de Hielo Sur (Southern Ice Field). As it is inaccessible by land, the only way to visit the park is to take a boat up the Seno Última Esperanza. The Navimag boat passes through, but only the Puerto Natales–based, family-run outfit Turismo 21 de Mayo (⇨ *By Boat in Patagonia & Tierra del Fuego Essentials*) operates boats here—the *21 de Mayo* and the *Alberto de Agostini*. These well-equipped boating day trips are a good option if for some reason you don't have the time to make it to Torres del Paine. On your way to the park you approach a cormorant colony with nests clinging to sheer cliff walls, venture to a glacier at the foot of Mt. Balmaceda, and finally dock at Puerto Toro for a 1-km (½-mi) hike to the foot of the Serrano Glacier. Congratulations, you made it to the least-visited national park in the whole of Chile. In recognition of the feat, on the trip back to Puerto Natales the crew treats you to a pisco sour served over a chunk of glacier ice. As with many full-day tours, you must bring your own lunch. Warm clothing, including gloves, is recommended year-round, particularly if there's even the slightest breeze.

EL CALAFATE & THE PARQUE NACIONAL LOS GLACIARES

320 km (225 mi) north of Río Gallegos via R5, 253 km (157 mi) east of Río Turbio on Chilean border via R40, 213 km (123 mi) south of El Chaltén via R40.

Founded in 1927 as a frontier town, El Calafate is the base for excursions to the Parque Nacional los Glaciares (Glaciers National Park), which was created in 1937 as a showcase for one of South America's most spectacular sights, the Perito Moreno glacier. Because it's on the southern shore of Lago Argentino, the town enjoys a microclimate much milder than the rest of southern Patagonia. During the long summer days between December and February (when the sun sets around 10 PM), and during Easter vacation, tens of thousands of visitors come from all corners of the world and fill the hotels and restaurants. This is the area's high season, so make reservations well in advance. October, November, March, and April are less crowded and less expensive periods to visit. March through May can be rainy and cool, but it's also less windy and often quite pleasant. The only bad time to visit is winter, particularly June, July, and August, when many of the hotels and tour agencies are closed.

> **MINES**
>
> On the drive between Punta Arenas and Puerto Natales, Argentina is just a stone's throw away. Chile lined this border with mines in the 1980s, right before the Falklands war, when Argentina was threatening to invade Chile over some uninhabitable islands. The mines are only now being removed. Obviously, this is not an area to take a stroll, but there's not much reason to, either—it's just flat, scrubby land with wind-bent trees, and the occasional bomb.

To call El Calafate a boomtown would be to put it mildly. Between 2001 and 2008, the town's population exploded from 4,000 to 22,000, and it shows no signs of slowing down; at every turn you'll see new construction. As a result, the downtown has a very new sheen to it, although most buildings are constructed of wood, with a rustic aesthetic that respects the majestic natural environment. One exception is the brand-new casino in the heart of downtown, the facade of which seems to mock the face of the Perito Moreno glacier. As the paving of the road between El Calafate and the glacier nears completion, the visitors continue to flock in—whether luxury package tourists bound for the legendary Hostería Los Notros, backpackers over from Chile's Parque Nacional Torres del Paine, or *porteños* (those from Buenes Aires) in town for a long weekend.

10

The booming economy means prices are substantially higher than in most parts of Patagonia—they seem to rise every other week—and many longtime locals bemoan the rampant commercialization of their hometown.

GETTING HERE & AROUND

Daily flights from Buenos Aires, Ushuaia, and Río Gallegos, and direct flights from Bariloche transport tourists to El Calafate's 21st-century glass-and-steel airport with the promise of adventure and discovery in distant mountains and glaciers. El Calafate is so popular that the flights are selling out weeks in advance, so don't plan on booking at the last minute.

Driving from Río Gallegos takes about four hours across desolate plains, enlivened by occasional sightings of a gaucho, his dogs, and a herd of sheep, and *ñandú* (rheas), shy llama-like guanacos, silver-gray foxes, and fleet-footed hares the size of small deer. **Esperanza** is the only gas, food, and bathroom stop halfway between the two towns.

Avenida del Libertador San Martín (known simply as Libertador, or San Martín) is El Calafate's main street, with tour offices, restaurants, and shops selling regional specialties, sportswear, camping and fishing equipment, and food.

A staircase in the middle of San Martín ascends to Avenida Julio Roca, where you'll find the bus terminal and a very busy **Oficina de Turismo** with a board listing available accommodations and campgrounds; you can also get brochures and maps, and there's a multilingual staff to help plan excursions. It's open daily 7 AM–10 PM.

The **Parques Nacionales Office** (⊠ *Av. Libertador 1302* ☎ *2902/491– 005*), open weekdays 7–2, has information on the entire park, the glaciers, area history, hiking trails, and flora and fauna.

ESSENTIALS

Bus Contacts Bus Sur (☎ *2966/442–765, 2902/491–631 in El Calafate*). **Cal Tur** (⊠ *Terminal Ómnibus, El Calafate* ☎ *2962/491–842*). **Interlagos** (⊠ *Bus terminal* ☎ *2902/491–179*). **TAQSA** (⊠ *Bus terminal* ☎ *2902/491–843* ⊕ *www.taqsa.com. ar*). **Turismo Zaahj** (☎ *5661/412–260*).

Currency Exchange Provincia de Santa Cruz (⊠ *Av. Libertador 1285* ☎ *2902/492–320*).

Medical Asístanse Hospital Distrital (⊠ *Av. Roca 1487* ☎ *2902/491–001*). **Farmacia El Calafate** (⊠ *Av. Libertador 1190* ☎ *9405/491–407*).

Post Office El Calafate (⊠ *Av. Libertador 1133*).

Remis El Calafate (⊠ *Av. Roca* ☎ *2902/492–005*).

Rental Cars Cristina (⊠ *Av. Libertador 1711,* ☎ *2902/491–674* ✎ *crisrent@arnet. com.ar*) **Dollar Rent a Car** (⊠ *Av. Libertador 1341,* ☎ *2902/492–634*).

Visitor & Tour Info Oficina de Turismo (⊠ *Av. Roca 1004* ☎ *2902/491–090* ⊕ *www.elcalafate.gov.ar*).

WHAT TO SEE

The Hielo Continental (Continental ice cap) spreads its icy mantle from the Pacific Ocean across Chile and the Andes into Argentina, covering an area of 21,700 square km (8,400 square mi). Approximately 1.5 million acres of it are contained within the **Parque Nacional los Glaciares**, a UNESCO World Heritage site. The park extends along the Chilean border for 350 km (217 mi), and 40% of it is covered by ice fields that branch off into 47 glaciers feeding two enormous lakes—the 15,000-year-old **Lago Argentino** (Argentine Lake, the largest body of water in Argentina and the third-largest in South America) in the park's southern end, and **Lago Viedma** (Lake Viedma) at the northern end near **Cerro Fitzroy**, which rises 11,138 feet. Plan on a minimum of two to three days to see the glaciers and enjoy the town—more if you plan to visit El Chaltén or any of the other lakes. Entrance to the southern section of the park costs 40 pesos.

The **Glaciar Perito Moreno** lies 80 km (50 mi) away on R11, which is almost entirely paved. From the park entrance, the road winds through hills and forests of lengas and ñires, until suddenly, the startling sight of the glacier comes into full view. Descending like a long white tongue through distant mountains, it ends abruptly in a translucent azure wall 3 km (2 mi) wide and 165 feet high at the edge of frosty green Lago Argentino.

Although it's possible to rent a car and go on your own, virtually everyone visits the park by day-trip tours booked through one of the many travel agents in El Calafate (unless you're staying in Los Notros, the only hotel inside the park—which arranges all excursions). The most basic tours take you to see the glacier from a viewing area composed of a series of platforms wrapped around the point of the Península de Magallanes. The platforms, which offer perhaps the most impressive view of the glacier, allow you to wander back and forth, looking across the Canal de los Tempanos (Iceberg Channel). Here you listen and wait for nature's number-one ice show—first, a cracking sound, followed by tons of ice breaking away and falling with a thunderous crash into the lake. As the glacier creeps across this narrow channel and meets the land on the other side, an ice dam sometimes builds up between the inlet of Brazo Rico on the left and the rest of the lake on the right. As the pressure on the dam increases, everyone waits for the day it will rupture again. The last time was in March 2004, when the whole thing collapsed in a series of explosions that lasted hours and could be heard in El Calafate.

In recent years, the sky-rocketing increase in the number of visitors to Glaciar Perito Moreno has created a scene that is not always conducive to reflective encounters with nature's majesty. Although the glacier remains spectacular, savvy travelers would do well to minimize time at the madhouse that the viewing area becomes at midday in high season, and instead encounter the glacier by boat, on a mini-trekking excursion, or by supplementing Perito Moreno with a visit to one of the less crowded glaciers in the region.

10

SHHH!! IT'S A SECRET!!

Lago Roca is a little-visited lake located inside the National Park just south of Brazo Rico, 46 km (29 mi) from El Calafate. This area receives about five times as much annual precipitation as El Calafate, creating a relatively lush climate of green meadows by the lakeshore, where locals come to picnic and cast for trophy rainbow and lake trout. Don't miss a hike into the hills behind Lago Roca—the view of dark-blue Lago Roca backed by a pale-green inlet of Lago Argentino with the Perito Moreno glacier and jagged snowcapped peaks beyond is truly outstanding. "Shhh," said the local who suggested a visit to Lago Roca. "It's the best place in El Calafate. Don't tell everyone." Never trust a guidebook writer.

There are gorgeous campsites, simple cabins, fishing-tackle rentals, hot showers, and a basic restaurant at **Camping Lago Roca** (☎ *2902/499–500 ⊕ www.losglaciares.com/camping lagoroca ☉ Closed May–Sept.*). Make reservations in advance if visiting over the Christmas holidays; at other times the campground is seldom crowded. For more comfortable accommodations, you can arrange to stay at the Nibepo Aike Estancia at the western end of Lago Roca, about 5 km (3 mi) past the campground. The National Park entrance fee is only collected on the road to Perito Moreno Glacier or at Puerto Banderas, where cruises depart, so admission to the Lago Roca corner of the park is free.

Glaciar Upsala, the largest glacier in South America, is 55 km (35 mi) long and 10 km (6 mi) wide, and accessible only by boat. Daily cruises depart from Puerto Banderas (40 km [25 mi] west of El Calafate via R11) for the 2½-hour trip. While dodging floating icebergs (*tempanos*), some as large as a small island, the boats maneuver as close as they dare to the wall of ice rising from the aqua-green water of Lago Argentino. The seven glaciers that feed the lake deposit their debris into the run-off, causing the water to cloud with minerals ground to fine powder by the glacier's moraine (the accumulation of earth and stones left by the glacier). Condors and black-chested buzzard eagles build their nests in the rocky cliffs above the lake. When the boat stops for lunch at Onelli Bay, don't miss the walk behind the restaurant into a wild landscape of small glaciers and milky rivers carrying chunks of ice from four glaciers into Lago Onelli. Glaciar Upsala has diminished in size in recent years, a trend many attribute to climate change.

The **Nimez Lagoon Ecological Reserve** is a marshy area on the shore of Lago Argentino just a short walk from downtown El Calafate. It's home to many species of waterfowl including black-necked swans, buff-necked ibises, southern lapwings, and the occasional flamingo. Strolling the footpaths among grazing horses and flocks of birds may not be as intense an experience as—say—trekking on a glacier, but a trip to the lagoon provides a good sense of the local landscape. For some reason, the gate is sometimes locked until 9 AM, frustrating early morning bird enthusiasts. If you get there early go ahead and hop the fence, no one will mind. ⊠ *1 km (½ mi) north of downtown, just off Av. Alem* ☎ *2 pesos.*

OUTDOOR ACTIVITIES

BOAT TOURS

The two most popular scenic boat rides in the Parque Nacional los Glaciares are the hour-long **Safari Náutico,** in which your boat cruises a few meters away from the face of the Glaciar Perito Moreno, and the full-day **Upsala Glacier Tour,** in which you navigate through a more extensive selection of glaciers, including Upsala and Onelli, and sections of Lago Argentino that are inaccessible by land. The Safari Náutico costs 35 pesos, not including transportation from El Calafate. **René Fernández Campbell** (⊠ *Av. Libertador 867, El Calafate* ☎*2902/491–155* ✆*fernandez_campbell@infovia.com.ar*) is currently the only local tour operator that runs boat tours to Upsala and Onelli glaciers. Any hotel can arrange reservations.

HIKING

Although it's possible to find trails along the shore of Lago Argentino and in the hills south and west of town, these hikes traverse a rather barren landscape and are not terribly interesting. The mountain peaks and forests are in the park, an hour by car from El Calafate. If you want to lace up your boots in your hotel, walk outside and hit the trail, go to El Chaltén—it's a much better base than El Calafate for hikes in the National Park. Good hiking trails are accessible from the camping areas and cabins by Lago Roca, 50 km (31 mi) from El Calafate.

HORSEBACK RIDING

Anything from a short day ride along Lago Argentino to a weeklong camping excursion in and around the glaciers can be arranged in El Calafate by **Gustavo Holzmann** (⊠ *Av. Libertador 4315* ☎*2902/493–278* ✆*cabalgataenpatagonia@cotecal.com.ar* ⊕*www.cabalgataenpatagonia.com*) or through the tourist office. *Estancias Turísticas* (tourist ranches) are ideal for a combination of horseback riding, ranch activities, and local excursions. Information on **Estancias de Santa Cruz** is in Buenos Aires at the **Provincial tourist office** (⊠ *Suipacha 1120* ☎*11/4325–3098* ⊕*www.estanciasdesantacruz.com*). **Estancia El Galpón del Glaciar** (⊠ *Ruta 11, Km 22* ☎☎*2902/492–509 or 11/4774–1069* ⊕*www.estanciaalice.com.ar*) welcomes guests overnight or for the day—for a horseback ride, bird-watching, or an afternoon program that includes a demonstration of sheep dogs working, a walk to the lake with a naturalist, sheep-shearing, and dinner in the former sheep-shearing barn, served right off the grill and the asador by knife-wielding gauchos. **Estancia Maria Elisa** (☎☎*2902/492–583 or 11/4774–1069* ✆*estanciamariaelisa@cotecal.com.ar*) is an upscale choice among estancias. Other estancias close to El Calafate are **Nibepo Aike** (⊠ *50 km [31 mi] from El Calafate near Lago Roca* ☎*2966/492–797* ⊕*www.nibepoaike.com.ar*), **Alta Vista** (⊠ *33 km [20 mi] from El Calafate* ☎*2966/491–247* ✆*altavista@cotecal.com.ar*), and **Huyliche** (⊠ *3 km [2 mi] from El Calafate* ☎*2902/491–025* ✆*teresanegro@cotecal.com.ar*).

10

ICE TREKKING

★ A two-hour mini-trek on the Perito Moreno Glacier involves a transfer from El Calafate to Brazo Rico by bus and a short lake crossing to a dock and refugio, where you set off with a guide, put crampons over your shoes, and literally walk across a stable portion of the glacier, scaling ridges of ice, and ducking through bright-blue ice tunnels. It is one of the most unique experiences in Argentina. The entire outing lasts about five hours. Hotels arrange mini-treks through **Hielo y Aventura** (⊠ *Av. Libertador 935* ☏ *2902/492–205* ⊕ *www.hieloyaventura.com*), which also organizes much longer, more difficult trips of eight hours to a week to other glaciers; you can arrange the trek directly through their office in downtown El Calafate. Mini-trekking runs about 300 pesos for the day. Hielo y Aventura also runs a longer "Big Ice" trek that traverses a much more extensive area of the glacier and costs 420 pesos. If you're between the ages of 18 and 40 and want a more extreme experience, Big Ice is highly recommended.

MOUNTAIN BIKING

Mountain biking is popular along the dirt roads and mountain paths that lead to the lakes, glaciers, and ranches. Rent bikes and get information at **Alquiler de Bicicletas** (⊠ *Av. Buenos Aires 173* ☏ *2902/493–806*).

LAND ROVER EXCURSIONS

If pedaling uphill sound like too much work, check out the Land Rover expeditions offered by **MIL Outdoor Adventure.** These trips follow dirt tracks into the hills above town for stunning views of Lago Argentino. On a clear day, you can even see the peaks of Cerro Torre and Cerro Fitzroy on the horizon. MIL's Land Rovers are converted to run on vegetable oil, so environmentalists can enjoy bouncing up the trail with a clean conscience. ⊠ *Av. Libertador 1029* ☏ *2902/495–446* ⊕ *www. miloutdoor.com*.

WHERE TO EAT

$$$ ╳ **Barricas de Enopio.** The emphasis at this restaurant-bar is on the extensive wine list and great cheeses that accompany each glass. A variety of brochettes and dinner entrées are big enough to share. The menu includes eclectic dishes such as pasta stuffed with venison or wild boar. The space is chic, casual, and cozy, with natural-cotton curtains and tablecloths, handmade lamps, and Tehuelche influences. ⊠ *Av. Libertador 1610* ☏ *2902/493–414* ⊟ *AE, MC, V.*

$$–$$$$ ╳ **Casimiro Biguá.** This restaurant and wine bar boasts a hipper-than-thou interior and an inventive menu serving such delights as Patagonian lamb with *Calafate* sauce (Calafate is a local wild berry). The **Casimiro Biguá Parrilla,** down the street from the main restaurant, has a similar trendy feel. You can recognize the *parrilla* by the *cordero al asador* (spit-roasted lamb) displayed in the window. ⊠ *Av. Libertador 963* ☏ *2902/492–590* ⊕ *http://casimirobigua.com* ⊟ *AE, DC, MC, V.*

$$–$$$ ╳ **La Cocina.** This casual café on the main shopping street serves homemade pasta, quiches, crepes, and hamburgers. Homemade ice cream and delicious cakes make for good treats. *Postre Chancho* (Pig's Dessert)

is ice cream with hot dulce de leche sauce. There is a long siesta daily from 2 to 7. ⊠*Av. Libertador 1245* ☎*2902/491–758* ▭*MC, V.*

$$ ✕**La Lechuza.** This cozy, bustling joint is known for having some of the best pizza in town. The brick oven and thin crust make for a more Italian-style taste and texture than at most spots. ⊠*Av. Libertador at 1 de Mayo* ☎*2902/491–610* ▭*No credit cards* ⊗*No lunch Sun.*

$$-$$$ ✕**Pura Vida.** Modernity merges with tradition at this hippie-ish, veggie-friendly restaurant a few blocks out of the center of El Calafate. It's a treat to find such creative fare, funky decor, cool candles, and modern art in such a frontier town. The beef stew served inside a *calabaza* (pumpkin) has an irresistible flair and is excellently seasoned, although the beef isn't particularly tender. Even if the cooking isn't quite top-flight, Pura Vida is more than the sum of its parts, drawing in backpackers and older folks alike with an almost mystical allure. ⊠*Av. Libertador 1876* ☎*2902/493–356* ▭*V.*

$$$ ✕**Rick's Parrillá.** It's *tenedor libre* (literally, "free fork," or all you can eat) for 35 pesos at this immensely popular *parrilla* in a big yellow building on El Calafate's main street. The place is packed full of tourists day and night. The room is big and bustling, if not particularly interesting, and the spread includes lamb and *vacío* (flank steak). ⊠*Av. Libertador 1091* ☎*2902/492–148* ▭*MC, V.*

$$-$$$ ✕**La Tablita.** It's a couple of extra blocks from downtown, across a
Fodor'sChoice little white bridge, but this parrilla is where the locals go for a special
★ night out. You can watch your food as it's prepared: Patagonian lamb and beef ribs cooking gaucho-style on an asador, or meat sizzling on the grill, including steaks, chorizos, and excellent *morcilla* (blood sausage). The enormous *parrillada* for two is a great way to sample it all, and the wine list is well priced and well chosen. ⊠*Coronel Rosales 28* ☎*2902/491–065* ⊕*www.interpatagonia.com/latablita* ▭*AE, DC, MC, V* ⊗*No lunch Mon.–Thurs. June and July.*

WHERE TO STAY

¢–$ ⊞**América del Sur.** The only downside to this established hostel, which caters to younger backpackers, is its location (a 10-minute uphill walk from downtown). But beautiful views of the lake and mountains and a free shuttle service compensate for the distance. Otherwise, the hostel is simple but spectacular—sparklingly clean and legendarily friendly. There are rooms with two and four beds. It's a particularly cheap deal for groups of four. **Pros:** Great view, friendly staff. **Cons:** A hike from downtown. ⊠*Punto Deseado* ☎*2902/493–525* ⊕*www.americahostel.com.ar* &*In-room: no TV. In-hotel: restaurant, bar, public Wi-Fi, no elevator* ▭*No credit cards.*

$$$$ ⊞**Helsingfors.** If we could recommend only one property in southern
Fodor'sChoice Patagonia, it would be Estancia Helsingfors, a luxurious, converted
★ ranch-house with an absolutely spectacular location in the middle of the National Park on the shore of Lago Viedma. The scenery is straight out of a *Lord of the Rings* movie and knowledgeable guides can point out dozens of species of birds; inside, a cozy fire warms the sitting room, friendly staff serve fine food and delicious house wine, and the beds are perhaps the most comfortable in Patagonia. Don't

10

leave without visiting the jewel of Helsingfors, a breathtaking blue lake at the foot of a glacier that's a three-hour hike or horseback ride from the inn. **Pros:** Unique location, wonderful staff. **Cons:** Three hours by dirt road from El Calafate. ✉*Reservations in Buenos Aires: Cordoba 827* ☎*11/4315–1222 in Buenos Aires* ⊕*www.helsingfors. ar* ⇨*8 rooms* &*In-room: no TV. In-hotel: restaurant* ☰*AE, MC, V* ⊗*Closed May–Sept.*

$$$$ ✗⊡ **Hostería los Notros.** Weathered wood buildings cling to the mountainside that overlooks the Perito Moreno Glacier as it descends into Lago Argentino. This inn, seemingly at the end of the world, is 73 km (45 mi) west of El Calafate. The glacier is framed in the windows of every room. A path through the garden and over a bridge spanning a canyon, connects rooms to the main lodge. Appetizers and wine are served in full view of sunset (or moonrise) over the glacier, followed by an absolutely spectacular menu that spotlights game, including delicious venison and creative preparations of Argentine classics. A two-night minimum stay is required. This property is extremely expensive; prices include all meals, cocktails, park entry, and a glacier excursion. If you don't feel like spending that much, come just for a meal. **Pros:** Unique location, totally luxurious. **Cons:** Very expensive, crowds bound for Perito Moreno can detract from the secluded atmosphere. ✉*Reservations in Buenos Aires: Arenales 1457* ☎*11/4814–3934 in Buenos Aires, 2902/499–510 in El Calafate* ⊕*www.losnotros.com* ⇨*32 rooms* &*In-room: no phone, no TV. In-hotel: restaurant, bar, airport shuttle, public Wi-Fi, no elevator* ☰*AE, DC, MC, V* ⊗*Closed June–mid-Sept.* ⍟*FAP.*

$$$$ ✗⊡ **Hotel Kau-Yatun.** From the homemade chocolates and flower bouquets that appear in the rooms each evening to the sweeping back ⟳ yard complete with swing sets for the kids, every detail of this con-
Fodor'sChoice verted ranch property is tailored to thoughtful hospitality. Guests
★ rave about the attentive staff, the excellent food with a focus on local and organic ingredients, and the building, which feels more well-loved than the newer hotels in town. **Pros:** Great food, loving attention to detail. **Cons:** Water pressure is only adequate. ✉*25 de Mayo* ☎*2902/491–059* ✐*kauyatun@cotecal.com.ar* ⇨*44 rooms* &*In-hotel: restaurant, bar, airport shuttle, bicycles, public Wi-Fi, no elevator* ☰*AE, MC, V* ⍟*CP.*

$$$$ ⊡ **Kosten Aike.** The wood balconies outside, and the slate floors, wood-beamed ceilings, and unfailing attention to detail inside, will please aficionados of Andean Patagonian architecture. Tehuelche symbols and designs are used on everything from the curtains to the room plaques. A lobby bar and living room with fireplace, card tables, magazines, and a large TV is dangerously conducive to lounging about. **Pros:** Large rooms, central location. **Cons:** Dining room decor is uninspired. ✉*25 de Mayo 1243, at G. Moyano* ☎*2902/492–424, 11/4811–1314 in Buenos Aires* ⊕*www.kostenaike.com.ar* ⇨*78 rooms, 2 suites* &*In-hotel: restaurant, bar, gym, public Wi-Fi* ☰*AE, DC, MC, V* ⊗*Closed May–Sept.*

¢–$$ ⊡ **Lago Argentino Hostel.** Just steps from the bus terminal, this chill new hostel is operated by the same family that runs the popular Pura Vida restaurant. Like Pura Vida, the atmosphere is cozy and eclectic. *Amor y paz* (love and peace) reads a sign in the entryway, and the friendly staff would not look out of place at a music festival. Private rooms in an annex across the street from the main building are much nicer, but more expensive, than the functional rooms in the main dorms. **Pros:** Convenient location, pleasant garden. **Cons:** Earplugs recommended, mattresses and pillows could be thicker. ⊠ *Campana del desierto 1050* ☎ *2902/491–423* ⊕ *www.interpatagonia.com/lagoargentino* ⚐ *In-hotel: laundry facilities, public Wi-Fi, no elevator* ⊟ *No credit cards.*

$$ 🏨 **Michelangelo.** Bright red and yellow native flowers line the front of the low log-and-stucco building with its distinctive A-frames over rooms, restaurant, and lobby. A fine collection of local photographs is displayed next to a sunken lobby, where easy chairs and a banquette surround the fireplace. The restaurant next door is excellent. **Pros:** Good value, convenient location. **Cons:** Limited views. ⊠ *Moyano 1020* ☎ *2902/491–045* ✉ *michelangelohotel@cotecal.com.ar* ⇱ *20 rooms* ⚐ *In-hotel: restaurant, no elevator* ⊟ *AE, MC, V* ⊙ *Closed June* ⊚ *CP.*

$$ 🏨 **Miyazato Inn.** Jorge Miyasato and his wife Elizabeth have brought the flawless hospitality of a traditional Japanese country inn to El Calafate. Comfortably removed from the tourist scene downtown, and only a short walk from the Ecological Preserve, each of the five rooms has hardwood floors and comfortable twin beds. The Miyasatos have two young children, and the family atmosphere makes this cozy inn a refuge of intimacy and calm. **Pros:** Clean, homey, good value. **Cons:** Neighborhood dogs are noisy. ⊠ *Egidio Feruglio 150* ☎ *2902/491–953* ✉ *miyazatoinn@cotecal.com.ar* ⊕ *www.interpatagonia.com/miyazatoinn* ⇱ *5 rooms* ⚐ *In-hotel: public Wi-Fi, no elevator* ⊟ *MC, V* ⊚ *CP.*

$$$$ 🏨 **Nibepo Aike.** This is a lovely estancia within a day-trip's distance
★ from El Calafate in a bucolic valley overlooking Lago Roca and backed by snowcapped mountain peaks. Sheep, horses, and cows graze among purple lupine flowers, and friendly gauchos give horse-racing and sheep-shearing demonstrations. The attached restaurant serves up a truly exceptional lamb and beef barbecue. It's possible to visit Nibepo Aike by booking a day-trip at the office in downtown El Calafate but the best way to experience this unique property is with an overnight stay in comfortable rooms decorated with original antiques and ranching memorabilia. The name Nibepo is a combination of the nicknames of the original owner's three daughters—Nini, Bebe, and Porota. All-inclusive packages are available, with mini-trekking and a cruise to the Upsala Glacier. **Pros:** Spectacular scenery, welcoming staff. **Cons:** An hour by dirt road from downtown. ⊠ *For reservations: Av. Libertador 1215* ☎ *For reservations: 2902/492–797* ⊕ *www.nibepoaike.com.ar* ⇱ *11 rooms* ⚐ *In-room: no TV. In-hotel: restaurant* ⊟ *AE, MC, V* ⊙ *Closed May–Sept.*

$$$$ 🏨 **Posada los Alamos.** Surrounded by tall, leafy alamo trees and con-
★ structed of brick and dark *quebracho* (ironwood), this attractive country manor house uses rich woods, leather, and handwoven fabrics to produce conversation-friendly furniture groupings in the large lobby. Plush comforters and fresh flowers in the rooms, and a deferential

10

staff make this a top-notch hotel. Lovingly tended gardens surround the building and line a walkway through the woods to the restaurant and the shore of Lago Argentino. **Pros:** Nice interiors, beautiful gardens. **Cons:** Staff can be overly formal. ✉ *Moyano 1355, at Bustillo* ☎ *2902/491–144* ⊕ *www.posadalosalamos.com* 📠 *140 rooms, 4 suites* 🖧 *In-hotel: restaurant, bar, golf course* ☰ *AE, MC, V* ⦿*CP.*

$$$$ 📺 **El Quijote.** Sun shines through picture windows onto polished slate floors and high beams in this modern hotel next to Sancho restaurant a few blocks from the main street. Rooms are carpeted and have plain white walls (which some readers have reported are paper-thin) and wood furniture. **Pros:** Central location, attentive staff. **Cons:** Lacks personality, uncreative room decor. ✉ *Gregores 1155* ☎ *2902/491–017* ✍ *elquijote@cotecal.com.ar* 📠 *80 rooms* 🖧 *In-hotel: bar, public Wi-Fi* ☰ *AE, DC, MC, V* ⊗ *Closed June and July* ⦿*CP.*

PUNTA ARENAS

Founded a little more than 150 years ago, Punta Arenas ("Sandy Point") was Chile's first permanent settlement in Patagonia. Great developments in cattle-keeping, mining, and wood production led to an economic and social boom at the end of the 19th century; today, though the port is no longer an important stop on trade routes, it exudes an aura of faded grandeur. Plaza Muñoz Gamero, the central square (also known as the Plaza de Armas), is surrounded by evidence of its early prosperity: buildings whose then-opulent brick exteriors recall a time when this was one of Chile's wealthiest cities.

The newer houses here have colorful tin roofs, best appreciated when seen from a high vantage point such as the Mirador Cerro la Cruz. Although the city as a whole is not particularly attractive, look for details: the pink-and-white house on a corner, the bay window full of potted plants, and schoolchildren in identical naval peacoats reminding you how the city's identity is tied to the sea.

Although Punta Arenas is 3,141 km (1,960 mi) from Santiago, daily flights from the capital make it an easy journey. As the transportation hub of southern Patagonia, Punta Arenas is within reach of Chile's Parque Nacional Torres del Paine (about a four- to five-hour drive, thanks to a new road) and Argentina's Parque Nacional los Glaciares. It's also a major base for penguin-watchers and a key point of embarkation for boat travel to Ushuaia and Antarctica.

The sights of Punta Arenas can basically be done in a day or two. The city is mainly a jumping off point for cruises, or for traveling up to Torres del Paine, which is most pleasantly done by staying in closeby Puerto Natales, a town that's gaining ground over Punta Arenas as a vacation destination. Something of a giant service station of a city catering to energy companies, its port, tax-free electronics, the military, and only some tourism, Punta Arenas seems unable to make up its mind what it wants to be, and it suffers from a lack of cultural activities (a few good museums notwithstanding) and an exodus of its young people.

GETTING HERE & AROUND

Most travelers will arrive at Aeropuerto Presidente Carlos Ibanez de Campo, a modern terminal approximately 12 mi from town. Public bus service from the airport into the central square of Punta Arenas is 2,000 pesos. Private transfers by small companies running minivans out of the airport (with no other pickup points or call-in service) run 3,000 pesos per person, while a taxi for two or more is your best deal at 5,000 pesos.

Set on a windy bank of the Magellan Strait, eastward-facing Punta Arenas has four main thoroughfares which were originally planned wide enough to accommodate flocks of sheep. Bustling with pedestrians, Avenida Bories is the main drag for shopping. Overall, the city is quite compact, and navigating its central grid of streets is fairly straightforward.

ESSENTIALS

Bus Contacts Buses Fernández (⊠*Armando Sanhueza 745, Punta Arenas* ☎*61/221–429* ⊕*www.busesfernandez.com*). **Tecni-Austral** (⊠*Lautaro Navarro 975* ☎*61/222–078 or 61/223–205*).

Internet Cafés Austro Internet (⊠*Croacica 690* ☎*61/222–297*). **El Calafate** (⊠*Av. Magallanes 922* ☎*61/241–281*). **Cyber Café** (⊠*Av. Colón 778, 2nd fl.* ☎*61/200–610*).

Medical Assistance Clinica Magallanes Medical Center (⊠*Av. Bulnes 1448* ☎*61/211–527*). **Hospital Cirujano Guzman** (⊠*Av. Bulnes at Capitan Guillermos* ☎*61/207--500*). **Hospital Mutual de Seguridad** (⊠*Av. España 1890* ☎*61/212–369*).

Postal Services DHL (⊠*Pedro Montt 840, Local 4* ☎*61/228–462* ⊕*www.dhl.com*). **Post Office** (⊠*Bories 911*).

Rental Cars Avis (⊠*Roca 1044* ☎*61/241–182* ⊠*Aeropuerto Presidente Ibañez*). **Budget** (⊠*Av. Bernardo O'Higgins 964* ☎*61/241–696* ⊠*Aeropuerto Presidente Ibañez*). **Hertz** (⊠*Av. Bernardo O'Higgins 987* ☎*61/248–742* ⊠*Aeropuerto Presidente Ibañez* ☎*61/210–096*). **International Rent A Car** (⊠*Aeropuerto Presidente Ibañez* ☎*61/212–401*). **Payne** (⊠*José Menéndez 631* ☎*61/240–852*). **RUS** (⊠*Av. Colón 614* ☎*61/221–529*).

Visitor & Tour Info Punta Arenas City Tourism (⊠*Plaza Muñoz Gamero* ☎*61/200–610* ⊕*www.puntaarenas.cl*). **Sernatur Punta Arenas** (⊠*Av. Magallanes 960* ☎*61/225–385* ⊕*www.sernatur.cl*).

WHAT TO SEE

❼ Cementerio Municipal. ★ The fascinating history of this region is chiseled into stone at the Municipal Cemetery. Bizarrely ornate mausoleums honoring the original families are crowded together along paths lined by sculpted cypress trees. In a strange effort to recognize Punta Arenas's indigenous past, there's a shrine in the northern part of the cemetery where the last member of the Selk'nam tribe was buried. Local legend says that rubbing the statue's left knee brings good luck. ⊠ *Av. Bulnes 949* 🕾 *No phone* 🖾 *Free* ⊙ *Daily dawn–dusk.*

FodorśChoice   **Isla Magdalena.** Punta Arenas is the launching point for a boat trip to see
★   the more than 120,000 Magellanic penguins at the **Monumento Natural Los Pingüinos** on this island. Visitors walk a single trail, marked off by rope, and penguins are everywhere—wandering across your path, sitting in burrows, skipping along just off the shore, strutting around in packs. The trip to the island, in the middle of the Estrecho de Magallanes, takes about two hours. To get here, you must take a tour boat. If you haven't booked in advance, you can stop at any of the local travel agencies and try to get on a trip at the last minute, which is often possible. You can go only from December to February; the penguin population peaks in January and February. However you get here, bring warm clothing, even in summer; the island can be chilly, and it's definitely windy, which helps with the odor. If you like penguins, you'll have a blast. If you don't like penguins, what are you doing in Patagonia?

❶   **Mirador Cerro la Cruz.** From a platform beside the white cross that gives this hill lookout its name, you have a panoramic view of the city's colorful corrugated rooftops leading to the Strait of Magellan. Stand with the amorous local couples gazing out toward the flat expanse of Tierra del Fuego in the distance. ⊠ *Fagnano at Señoret* 🖾 *Free* ⊙ *Daily.*

❺   **Museo Naval y Marítimo.** The Naval and Maritime Museum extols Chile's high-seas prowess, particularly concerning Antarctica. Its exhibits are worth a visit by anyone with an interest in ships and sailing, merchant and military alike. The second floor is designed in part like the interior of a ship, including a map and radio room. Aging exhibits include an account of the 1908 visit to Punta Arenas by an American naval fleet. Ask for a tour or an explanatory brochure in English. ⊠ *Av. Pedro Montt 981* 🕾 *61/205–558* 🖾 *700 pesos* ⊙ *Tues.–Sat. 9:30–5.*

❹   **Museo Regional de Magallanes.** Housed in what was once the mansion
★   of the powerful Braun-Menéndez family, the Regional Museum of Magallanes is an intriguing glimpse into the daily life of a wealthy provincial family at the beginning of the 20th century. Lavish Carrara marble hearths, English bath fixtures, and cordovan leather walls are among the original bling. The museum has an excellent group of displays depicting Punta Arenas's past, from European contact to its decline with the opening of the Panama Canal. The museum is half a block north of the main square. ⊠ *Av. Magallanes 949* 🕾 *61/244–216* 🖾 *1,000 pesos* ⊙ *Oct.–Mar., Mon.–Sat. 10:30–5, Sun. 10:30–2; Apr.–Sept., daily 10:30–2.*

❻   **Museo Salesiano de Maggiorino Borgatello.** Commonly referred to simply as "El Salesiano," this museum is operated by Italian missionaries whose order arrived in Punta Arenas in the 19th century. The Salesians, most of whom spoke no Spanish, proved to be daring explorers. Traveling throughout the region, they collected the artifacts made by indigenous tribes that are currently on display. They also relocated many

Punta Arenas

Angamos
Maipú
Sarmiento
Croacia
Jorge Montt
Quillota
Bulnes
Magallanes
Bories
Chiloé
Armando Sanhueza
Mejicana
Carrera Pinto
Navarro
O'Higgins
Av. Colón
José Menéndez
Post Office
Waldo Seguel
Cathedral
Fagnano
Av. España
Armando Sanhueza
Chiloé
José Nogueira
21 de Mayo
Navarro
Pedro Montt
Roca
Errázuriz
Balmaceda
Av. Independencia
Port
Estrecho de Magallanes

KEY

i Tourist information

Patagonia's Penguins

As the ferry slowly approaches Isla Magdalena, you begin to make out thousands of black dots along the shore. You catch your breath, knowing that this is your first look at the 120,000 seasonal residents of Monumento Natural Los Pingüinos, one of the continent's largest penguin sanctuaries, a population that is at its height during the breeding season, which peaks in January and February.

But the squat little birds are much closer than you think. You soon realize that on either side of the ferry are large groups of penguins catching their breakfast. They are amazingly agile swimmers, leaping almost entirely out of the water before diving down below the surface once again. A few swim alongside the boat, but most simply ignore the intrusion.

Several different types of penguins, including the Magellanic penguins found on the gentle hills of Isla Magdalena, make their homes along the Chilean coast. For the thrill of seeing tens of thousands in one place, nothing beats Monumento Natural Los Pingüinos, open only from December to February. At this reserve, a two-hour trip by boat from Punta Arenas, the birds can safely reproduce and raise their young.

Found only along the coast of Chile and Argentina, Magellanic penguins are named for Spanish explorer Hernando de Magallanes, who spotted them when he arrived on these shores in 1520. They are often called jackass penguins because of the braying sound they make when excited. Adults, with the characteristic black-and-white markings, are easy to distinguish from the adolescents, which are a mottled gray. Also gray are the

chicks, which hide inside their burrows when their parents are searching for food. A good time to get a look at the fluffy little fellows is when their parents return to feed them regurgitated fish.

A single trail runs across Isla Magdalena, starting at the dock and ending on a hilltop at a red-and-white lighthouse. Ropes on either side keep humans from wandering too far afield. The penguins, however, have the run of the place. They waddle across the path, alone or in small groups, to get to the rocky beach. Familiar with the boatloads of people arriving two or three times a week, the penguins usually don't pay much attention to the camera-clutching crowds. A few of the more curious ones will walk up to people and inspect a shoelace or pants leg. If someone gets too close to a nest, however, they cock their heads sharply from side to side as a warning.

An easier way to see penguins in their natural habitat is to drive to Pingüinera de Seno Otway, on the mainland about an hour northwest of Punta Arenas. It's open longer than Isla Magdalena—from October to March. Founded in 1990, the reserve occupies 2 km (1 mi) of coastline. There are far fewer penguins here— only about 4,000—but the number is still astounding. The sanctuary is run by a nonprofit group, which can provide English-language guides. Travel companies from Punta Arenas arrange frequent tours to the reserve.

–Pete Nelson

of the indigenous people to nearby Dawson Island, where they died by the hundreds (from diseases like influenza and pneumonia). The museum contains an extraordinary collection of everything from skulls and native crafts to stuffed animals. ⊠ *Av. Bulnes 336* ☎ *61/241–096* ⊠ *1,500 pesos* ☉ *Oct.–Mar., Tues.–Sun. 10–6; Apr.–Sept., Tues.–Sun. 10–1 and 3–6.*

❸ **Palacio Sara Braun.** This resplendent 1895 mansion, a national landmark
★ and architectural showpiece of southern Patagonia, was designed by French architect Numa Meyer at the behest of Sara Braun (the wealthy widow of wool baron José Nogueira). Materials and craftsmen were imported from Europe during the home's four years of construction. The city's central plaza and surrounding buildings soon followed, ushering in the region's golden era. The Club de la Unión, a social organization that now owns the building, opens its doors to nonmembers for tours of some of the rooms and salons, which have magnificent parquet floors, marble fireplaces, and hand-painted ceilings. After touring the rooms, head to the cellar tavern for a drink or snack. ⊠ *Plaza Muñoz Gamero 716* ☎ *61/241–489* ⊠ *1,000 pesos* ☉ *Tues.–Fri. 10:30–1 and 5–8:30, Sat. 10:30–1 and 8–10, Sun. 11–2.*

NEED A BREAK? Tea and coffee house, chocolate shop, and bakery, **Chocolatta** (⊠ *Bories 852* ☎ *61/268–606*) is a perfect refueling stop during a day of wandering Punta Arenas. The interior is cozy, the staff friendly, and you can hang out, perhaps over a creamy hot chocolate, for as long as you like.

❷ **Plaza Muñoz Gamero.** A canopy of pine trees shades this square, which is surrounded by splendid baroque-style mansions from the 19th century. A bronze sculpture commemorating the voyage of Hernando de Magallanes dominates the center of the plaza. Local lore has it that a kiss on the shiny toe of Calafate, one of the Fuegian statues at the base of the monument, will one day bring you back to Punta Arenas. ⊠ *José Nogueira at 21 de Mayo.*

WHERE TO EAT

10

$–$$ ✗**El Estribo.** Centered around a large fireplace used to grill the meats, this narrow restaurant is filled with intimate little white-clothed tables. The name means "The Stirrup," and the walls are adorned with bridles, bits, lariats, and all manner of stirrups. The longtime popularity of the place has more to do with its excellent regional food (which it ambitiously dubs *platos exóticos patagónicos*) than novelty of decor. More unusual preparations include rabbit Stroganoff and fillet of guanaco (a local animal that resembles a llama) in sherry sauce. There's also delicious spit-roasted lamb. For dessert try rhubarb pie—uncommon in these parts. ⊠ *Ignacio Carrera Pinto 762, at Av. Magallanes* ☎ *61/244–714* ⊟ *No credit cards.*

$–$$ ✗**La Leyenda del Remezón.** This cheerful little restaurant stands out because of its deliciously seasoned grilled fish and meats. The dining room is unpretentious and homey, with a welcoming fireplace, and the day's menu is scrawled onto a chalkboard; if you're lucky, it might include a delicious pisco-marinated goose. Although it's near the port, away from the main part of town, the terrific food and potent pisco sours (brandy mixed with lemon, egg whites, and sugar) make it a walk rewarded. ⌂ *21 de Mayo 1469* ☎ *61/241–029* ⊟ *AE.*

¢ ✕ **Lomit's.** A fast-moving but friendly staff serves Chilean-style blue-plate specials at this bustling deli. In addition to traditional hamburgers, you can try the ubiquitous *completos*—hot dogs buried under

> ### CORDERO AL ASADOR
>
> In Argentine and Chilean Patagonia, lamb is deliciously prepared in the traditional manner: spit-roasted whole over an open fire. Restaurants offering *cordero al asador* often have grills positioned in their front windows to tempt you; you can smell, as well as see, the meat roasting to a delectable crispness.

mounds of toppings, from spicy mayonnaise to guacamole. Or seat yourself at the counter and treat yourself to a heavenly gelato. Try not to get too distracted by the televisions. Locals gather here for coffee and drinks, morning to midnight. ⌂ *José Menéndez 722, between Bories and Av. Magallanes* ☎ *61/243–399* ⊟ *No credit cards.*

¢–$$$ ✕ **Parrilla Los Ganaderos.** You'll feel like you're on the range in this
★ enormous restaurant resembling a rural *estancia* (ranch). The waiters, dressed in gaucho costumes, serve up spectacular *cordero al ruedo* (spit-roasted lamb) cooked in the *salón de parilla* (grill room); a serving comes with three different cuts of meat. Complement your meal with a choice from the long list of Chilean wines. Black-and-white photographs of past and contemporary ranch life are displayed along the walls. The restaurant is several blocks north of the center of town, but it's worth the small detour. ⌂ *Av. Bulnes 0977, at Manantiales* ☎ *61/214–597* ⊕ *www.parrillalosganaderos.cl* ⊟ *AE, MC, V* ☉ *Closed Sun.*

$$–$$$ ✕ **La Pérgola.** In what was once the sunroom and winter garden of Sara Braun's turn-of-the-20th-century mansion, La Pérgola has one of the city's most refined settings. A 100-year-old vine festoons the glass windows and ceiling. The photo-illustrated menu lists mainly Chilean seafood and meat dishes; you might start with fried calamari and then have whitefish in garlic sauce. The service is formal and attentive as in the rest of the Hotel José Nogueira, to which the restaurant belongs. ⌂ *Bories 959* ☎ *61/248–840* ⊕ *www.hotelnogueira.com* ⊟ *AE, DC, MC, V.*

¢ ✕ **Pub Olijoe.** This tastefully designed two-floor bar is reminiscent of an upscale English pub, with paneled walls, ceiling, and bar, and reasonably priced drinks—especially during happy hour. Austral on tap is particularly tasty. Later in the evening, be warned, the music can get loud for conversation. It's a good joint for a pizza or *picoteos* (little snacks). Open until 2 AM. ⌂ *José Errázuriz 970* ☎ *61/223–728* ⊟ *No credit cards.*

¢–$$$ ✕ **Puerto Viejo.** The paragon of stylish modern design, Puerto Viejo is
Fodor's Choice down by the old port, appropriately enough. All-glass and untreated-
★ wood partitions cordon off the smoking section. Seafood is the specialty, but good lamb and steak are also available. Owned by a local farmers' association, its sister restaurant is Los Ganaderos. Reserva-

tions are recommended. ⊠*Av. Bernardo O'Higgins 1166* ☎*61/225–103* ⊕*www.puertoviejo.cl* ⊟*AE, MC, V* ☉*Closed Sun.*

$$ ✕**Restaurant Asturias.** Rough-hewn wood beams and white-stucco walls are meant to evoke the Asturias region of Spain. The warmly lighted dining room is an inviting place to linger over *salmón papillote* (salmon poached in white wine with cured ham, cream cheese, and tomatoes), paella, or *congrio a la vasca* (conger eel—Chile's ubiquitous whitefish—in cream sauce). ⊠*Lautaro Navarro 967* ☎*61/243–763* ⊟*AE, DC, MC, V.*

¢–$ ✕**Santino Bar-Resto.** This downtown bar has friendly service, good pizzas and crepes, and an excellent assortment of Chilean cocktails. It's most popular for its drinks; perhaps the most interesting libation is the beer that's frothed up with egg whites. It was nicknamed the "Shourtney" after a young couple from Texas and Uruguay, who declared their undying love for the egg beer—and for each other—at Santino. ⊠*Av. Colón 657, between Bories and Chiloé* ☎*61/220–511* ⊟*AE, DC, MC, V* ☉*Closed Sun.*

$–$$$ ✕**Sotito's Restaurant.** A virtual institution in Punta Arenas, Sotito's has dining rooms that are intimate and cozy, with subdued lighting, exposed-brick walls, and wood-beamed ceilings. Locals gather to enjoy some of the best *centolla* (king crab) in the area. It's prepared in several imaginative ways, including a dish called *chupé*, with bread, milk, cream, and cheese. The restaurant is near the water, a few blocks east of Plaza Muñoz Gamero. ⊠*Av. Bernardo O'Higgins 1138* ☎*61/243–565* ⊕*www.chileaustral.com/sotitos* ⊟*AE, DC, MC, V.*

$–$$ ✕**Taberna Club de la Unión.** A jovial, publike atmosphere prevails in
Fodor's Choice this wonderful, labyrinthine cellar redoubt down the side stairway of
★ Sara Braun's old mansion on the main plaza. A series of nearly hidden rooms in cozy stone and brick have black-and-white photos of historical Punta Arenas adorning the walls. You're likely to hear ragtime and jazz on the stereo while you enjoy beers served cold in frosted mugs, tapas-style meat and cheese appetizers, sandwiches, tacos, pizza, fajitas, and carpaccio (the menu has more bar snacks than dinner entrées). The bar is affiliated with the Club de la Unión headquartered upstairs, and many members relax down here. Unfortunately, due to a lack of proper ventilation, this smoker-tolerant venue reeks of cigarette smoke. ⊠*Plaza Muñoz Gamero 716* ☎*61/241–317* ⊟*AE, DC, MC, V* ☉*Closed Sun. No lunch.*

$–$$$ ✕**La Tasca.** Inside the Sociedad Española, on Punta Arenas's main square, is this rustically elegant Spanish restaurant, operated by the same owners as the legendary Taberna Club de la Unión. You can look out the windows of the gracious, wood-ceilinged dining room onto the plaza while enjoying a typical Chilean *vaina* (port, sherry, chocolate, cinnamon, and egg whites), followed by paella *con centolla* (with king crab). If you're ordering fish, keep it simple; some of the heavy cream sauces can be overwhelming. ⊠*Sociedad Española, Plaza Muñoz Gamero 771, 2nd fl.* ☎*61/242–807* ⊟*AE, DC, MC, V.*

10

WHERE TO STAY

$ **Hostal de la Avenida.** The rooms of this pea-green guesthouse all over-look a garden lovingly tended by the owner, a local of Yugoslav origin. Flowers spill out from a wheelbarrow and a bathtub, birdhouses hang from trees, and a statue of Mary rests in a shrine with a grotto. The rooms offer modest comforts for those on a budget. The ones across the garden, away from the street, are the newest. Beside them is a funky bar that Chilean poet Pablo Neruda would have approved of; it seems hunkered down for blustery winters. **Pros:** Quaint, simple, nice contrast to the big hotels. **Cons:** No Internet. ✉ *Av. Colón 534* ☎ *61/247–532* ➥ *10 rooms, 6 with bath* ♿ *In-room: minibar, safe. In-hotel: bar, laundry service, public Wi-Fi* ☰*AE, DC, MC, V* ⓘ*CP.*

$ **Hostal Oro Fueguino.** On a sloping cobblestone street near the obser-
★ vation deck at Cerro la Cruz, this charming little hostelry—tall, narrow, and rambling—welcomes you with lots of color. The first thing you notice is the facade, painted bright orange and blue. Inside are homey wall hangings and lamp shades made of eye-catching fabrics from as far off as India. The dining and living rooms are cheerful, and there's a wealth of tourist information. The warmth is enhanced by the personal zeal of the proprietor, Dinka Ocampo. **Pros:** Much of its charm comes from its quirkiness. **Cons:** Somewhat isolated. ✉ *Fagnano 365* ☎ *61/249–401* ⊕ *www.orofueguino.cl* ➥ *12 rooms* ♿ *In-room: no a/c. In-hotel: laundry service, public Internet* ☰*AE, DC, MC, V* ⓘ*BP.*

$$$ **Hotel Finis Terrae.** A Best Western affiliate, this contemporary hotel has a good location (a couple of blocks from the main square) and a very professional staff. Guest rooms are comfortable, with traditional floral-print bedcovers and overstuffed chairs, and the baths are spacious and modern. There's a pleasant lounge with a fireplace, and the sixth-floor restaurant and bar has panoramic views. Stick with the superior rooms or, better yet, the junior suites, and avoid the tiny standard rooms; if you need two beds in a room, look elsewhere. Discounts are considerable March–September. **Pros:** American franchise standards. **Cons:** Small rooms. ✉ *Av. Colón 766* ☎ *61/228–200* 🖷 *61/248–124* ⊕ *www.hotelfinisterrae.com* ➥ *60 rooms, 4 suites* ♿ *In-room: safe. In-hotel: restaurant, bars, airport shuttle, public Internet, minibar* ☰*AE, DC, MC, V* ⓘ*BP.*

$$ **Hotel Isla Rey Jorge.** Lofty wood-framed windows let lots of light into the intimate rooms, decorated in mint and deep rose, at this English-style hotel with impeccable service. The hotel's richly toned *lenga* and *coigüe* woodwork in the lobby continues down into the popular basement pub, El Galeón. The hotel is just one block from Plaza Muñoz Gamero. **Pros:** Staff is friendly and efficient, inviting interior. **Cons:** Some rooms are rather indifferently appointed. ✉ *21 de Mayo 1243* ☎ *61/248–220 or 61/222–681* ⊕ *www.islareyjorge.com* ➥ *21 rooms, 4 suites* ♿ *In-hotel: restaurant, bar, airport shuttle, public Wi-Fi* ☰*AE, DC, MC, V.*

$$$ **Hotel José Nogueira.** Originally the home of Sara Braun, this opulent
★ 19th-century mansion also contains a museum. The location—steps off the main plaza—couldn't be better. Carefully restored over many

years, the building retains the original crystal chandeliers, marble floors, and polished bronze details that were imported from France. Rooms are stunning—especially on the third floor—with high ceilings, thick carpets, and period furniture. Suites have hot tubs and in-room faxes. **Pros:** Central location, authentic. **Cons:** None really. ⊠*Bories 959* ☎*61/711–000* 🖷*61/711–011* ⊕*www.hotelnogueira.com* 🛏*17 rooms, 5 suites* ⛬*In-room: safe, dial-up. In-hotel: restaurant, bar, laundry service, minibar, public Wi-Fi* ▤*AE, DC, MC, V.*

$$ ✕☲ **Hotel Los Navegantes.** This unpretentious older hotel, just a block from the Plaza de Armas, has spacious burgundy-and-green rooms and a nautical theme (an enormous maritime map graces the lobby wall). There's a charming dark-wood bar and a garden-view restaurant that serves delicious roast lamb. **Pros:** Superb mattress and bedding quality. **Cons:** Don't get burned by the radiators; few electrical outlets. ⊠*José Menéndez 647* ☎*61/617–700* 🖷*61/617–717* ⊕*www.hotel-losnaveg-antes.com* 🛏*50 rooms, 2 suites* ⛬*In-room: safe. In-hotel: restaurant, bar, airport shuttle, minibar, public Wi-Fi* ▤*AE, DC, MC, V.*

$$ ✕☲ **Hotel Tierra del Fuego**. Just a couple of blocks from the main plaza, this hotel is aging with grace. The place is clean and simple, with an old-world pub that serves sandwiches and drinks into the wee hours. Rooms are brightened by pretty rugs and marble bathroom sinks; some even have kitchenettes. The prices are reasonable; it's a good value in this category, especially given the amount of space you get. **Pros:** Close to much of the town's action. **Cons:** Not the most romantic. ⊠*Av. Colón 716* ☎*61/226–200* ⊕*www.puntaarenas.com* 🛏*26 rooms* ⛬*In-room: kitchen (some), Wi-fi. In-hotel: bar, restaurant, public Wi-Fi* ▤*AE, DC, MC, V* ❍|*BP.*

NIGHTLIFE

During the Chilean summer, because Punta Arenas is so far south, the sun doesn't set until well into the evening. That means that locals don't think about hitting the bars until midnight. If you can't stay up late, try the hotel bars, such as Hotel Tierra del Fuego's **Pub 1900** (⊠*Av. Colón 716* ☎*61/242–759*), which attract an early crowd. The city's classic speakeasy, **La Taberna Club de la Unión,** hops into the wee hours with a healthy mix of younger and older patrons. Claustrophobes head to Pub Olijoe's for a roomier option. If you're in the mood for dancing, try **Kamikaze** (⊠*Bories 655* ☎*61/248–744*) or the gothier **El Templo** (⊠*Pedro Montt 927* ☎*61/257–384*) where the younger set goes to party until dawn.

10

SHOPPING

You don't have to go far to find local handicrafts, pricey souvenirs, wool clothing, hiking gear, postcards, custom chocolates, or semiprecious stones like lapis lazuli. You will see penguins of every variety, from keychain size to larger than life. Warm wool clothing is for sale in almost every shop, but it isn't cheap. Unfortunately, few things are actually made in Chile—often a design is sent to England to be knitted and then returned with a handsome markup.

Almacén de Antaño (✉ *Av. Colón 1000* ☎61/227–283) offers a fascinatingly eclectic selection of pewter, ceramics, mirrors, and graphics frames. **Dagorret** (✉*Bories 587* ☎61/228–692 ⊕*www.dagorret.cl*), a Chilean chain with other outlets in Puerto Montt and Puerto Natales, carries top-quality leather clothing, including *gamuza* (suede) and *gamulán* (buckskin), some with wool trim. **Quilpué** (✉*José Nogueira 1256* ☎61/220–960) is a shoe-repair shop that also sells *huaso* (cowboy) supplies such as bridles, bits, and spurs. Pick up some boots for folk dancing.

PUERTO HAMBRE

50 km (31 mi) south of Punta Arenas.

In an attempt to gain a foothold in the region, Spain founded Ciudad Rey Don Felipe in 1584. Pedro Sarmiento de Gamboa constructed a church and homes for more than 100 settlers. But just three years later, British navigator Thomas Cavendish came ashore to find that all but one person had died of hunger, which some might say is a natural result of founding a town where there isn't any fresh water. He renamed the town Port Famine. Today a tranquil fishing village, Puerto Hambre still has traces of the original settlement, a sobering reminder of bad government planning.

WHAT TO SEE

About 2 km (1 mi) west of Puerto Hambre is a small white **monolith** that marks the geographical center of Chile, the midway point between northernmost Arica and the South Pole.

In the middle of a Chilean winter in 1843, a frigate under the command of Captain Juan Williams Rebolledo sailed southward from the island of Chiloé carrying a ragtag contingent of 11 sailors and eight soldiers. In October, on a rocky promontory called Santa Ana overlooking the Estrecho de Magallanes, they built a wooden fort, which they named **Fuerte Bulnes,** thereby founding the first Chilean settlement in the southern reaches of Patagonia. Much of the fort has been restored. ✉*5 km (3 mi) south of Puerto Hambre* ☎*No phone* ✉*Free* ☉ *Weekdays 8:30–12:30 and 2:30–6:30.*

The 47,000-acre **Reserva Nacional Laguna Parrillar,** west of Puerto Hambre, stretches around a shimmering lake in a valley flanked by hills. It's a great place for a picnic, if the weather cooperates. A number of well-marked paths lead to sweeping vistas over the Estrecho de Magallanes. ✉*Off Ruta 9, 52 km (32 mi) south of Punta Arenas* ☎*No phone* ✉*650 pesos* ☉*Oct. 16–Mar. 15, weekdays 8:30–5:30, weekends 8:30–8:30.*

PINGÜINERA DE SENO OTWAY

65 km (40 mi) northwest of Punta Arenas.

Magellanic penguins, which live up to 20 years in the wild, return repeatedly to their birthplace to mate with the same partner. For about

2,000 penguin couples—no singles make the trip—home is this desolate and windswept land off the Otway Sound. In late September the penguins begin to arrive from the southern coast of Brazil and the Falkland Islands. They mate and lay their eggs in early October, and brood their eggs in November. Offspring are hatched mid-November through early December. If you're lucky, you'll see downy gray chicks stick their heads out of the burrows when their parents return to feed them. Otherwise you might see scores of the adult penguins waddling to the ocean from their nesting burrows. They swim for food every eight hours and dive up to 30 meters (100 feet) deep. The penguins depart from the sound in late March.

The road to the sanctuary begins 30 km (18 mi) north of Punta Arenas, where the main road, Ruta 9, diverges near a checkpoint booth. A gravel road then traverses another fierce and winding 30 km (18 mi), but the rough trip (mud will be a problem if there's been recent rain) should reward you with the sight of hundreds of sheep, cows, and birds, including, if you're lucky, rheas and flamingos. The sanctuary is a 1-km (½-mi) walk from the parking lot. It gets chilly, so bring a windbreaker.

The best time to appreciate the penguins is in the morning before 10 AM, or the evening after 5 PM, when they are not out fishing. If you don't have a car, Comapa, like many other tour companies based in Punta Arenas, offers tours to the Pingüinera (⇨ *By Boat in Patagonia & Tierra del Fuego Essentials*). The tours generally leave from Punta Arenas, return about 3½ hours later, and range in price from 7,000 to 10,000 pesos. ⊠*Off Ruta 9* ⌨*2,000 pesos* ☉*Oct.–Mar., daily 8–7.*

PORVENIR

30 km (18 mi) by boat from Punta Arenas.

A short trip eastward across the Estrecho de Magallanes, Porvenir ("Future"!) is the principal town on Chile's half of Tierra del Fuego. It's not much to speak of, with a landscape dominated by brightly painted corrugated-iron houses and neat topiary. Located at the eastern end of narrow Bahía Porvenir, it was born during the gold rush of the 1880s. After the boom went bust, it continued to be an important port for the burgeoning cattle and sheep industries. Today Porvenir is home to 6,000 inhabitants, many of whom are of Croatian descent. A signpost in the town even marks the distance to Croatia. There are a number of reasonable places to stay, but nothing noteworthy. We recommend Hotel Rosas (Philippi 196 ☎61/580–088), with cozy, simple accommodations and a knowledgeable staff.

Porvenir's small **Museo Provincial Fernando Cordero Rusque** includes collections of memorabilia about subjects as eclectic as early Chilean filmmaking and the culture of the indigenous peoples. There are interesting photos of the gold rush and the first sheep ranches. The museum also functions as a tourist office. ⊠*Plaza de Armas* ☎*61/580–098* ⌨*500 pesos* ☉*Weekdays 9–5, weekends 11–5.*

10

TIERRA DEL FUEGO

Tierra del Fuego, a more or less triangular island separated from the southernmost tip of South America by the twists and bends of the Estrecho de Magallanes, is indeed a world unto itself. The vast plains on its northern reaches are dotted with trees bent low by the savage winds that frequently lash the coast. The mountains that rise in the south are equally forbidding, traversed by huge glaciers slowly making their way to the sea.

The first European to set foot on this island was Spanish explorer Hernando de Magallanes, who sailed here in 1520. The smoke that he saw coming from the fires lighted by the native peoples prompted him to call it Tierra del Humo (Land of Smoke). King Charles V of Spain, disliking that name, rechristened it Tierra del Fuego, or Land of Fire.

Tierra del Fuego is split in half. The island's northernmost tip, well within Chilean territory, is its closest point to the continent. The only town of any size here is Porvenir. Its southern extremity, part of Argentina, points out into the Atlantic toward the Falkland Islands. Here is Ushuaia, the main destination, on the shores of the Canal Beagle. Farther south is Cape Horn, the southernmost point of land before Antarctica (still a good 500 mi accross the brutal Drake Passage).

USHUAIA

230 km (143 mi) south of Río Grande, 596 km (370 mi) south of Río Gallegos, 914 km (567 mi) south of El Calafate, 3,580 km (2,212 mi) south of Buenos Aires.

At 55 degrees latitude south, Ushuaia (pronounced oo-swy-ah; the Argentines don't pronounce the "h") is closer to the South Pole than to Argentina's northern border with Bolivia. It is the capital and tourism base for Tierra del Fuego, the island at the southernmost tip of Argentina.

Although its stark physical beauty is striking, Tierra del Fuego's historical allure is based more on its mythical past than on reality. The island was inhabited for 6,000 years by Yámana, Haush, Selk'nam, and Alakaluf Indians. But in 1902, Argentina, eager to populate Patagonia to bolster its territorial claims, moved to initiate an Ushuaian penal colony, establishing the permanent settlement of its most southern territories and, by implication, everything in between.

When the prison closed in 1947, Ushuaia had a population of about 3,000, made up mainly of former inmates and prison staff. Today, the Indians of Darwin's "missing link" theory are long gone—wiped out by diseases brought by settlers, and by indifference to their plight—and the 50,000 residents of Ushuaia are hitching their star to tourism. The city rightly (if perhaps too loudly) promotes itself as the southernmost city in the world (Puerto Williams, a few miles south on the Chilean side of the Beagle Channel, is a small town). Ushuaia feels like a frontier boomtown, at heart still a rugged, weather-beaten fishing village, but

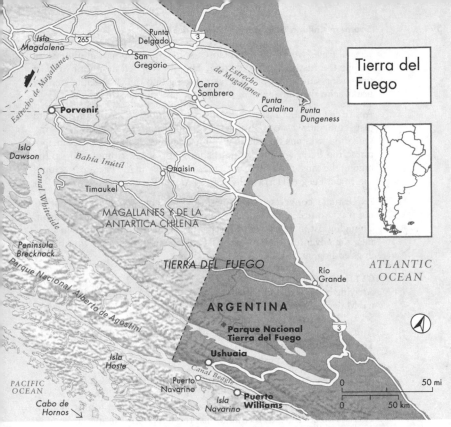

exhibiting the frayed edges of a city that quadrupled in size in the '70s and '80s. Unpaved portions of R3, the last stretch of the Pan-American Highway, which connects Alaska to Tierra del Fuego, are finally being paved. The summer months—December through March—draw 120,000 visitors, and the city is trying to extend those visits with events like March's Marathon at the End of the World.

A terrific trail winds through the town up to the Martial Glacier, where a ski-lift can help cut down a steep kilometer of your journey. The chaotic and contradictory urban landscape includes a handful of luxury hotels amid the concrete of public housing projects. Scores of "sled houses" (wooden shacks) sit precariously on upright piers, ready for speedy displacement to a different site. But there are also many small, picturesque homes with tiny, carefully tended gardens. Many of the newer homes are built in a Swiss-chalet style, reinforcing the idea that this is a town into which tourism has breathed new life. At the same time, the weather-worn pastel colors that dominate the town's landscape remind you that Ushuaia was once just a tiny fishing village, populated by criminals, snuggled at the end of the Earth.

As you stand on the banks of the Canal Beagle (Beagle Channel) near Ushuaia, the spirit of the farthest corner of the world takes hold. What stands out is the light: at sundown the landscape is cast in a subdued, sensual tone; everything feels closer, softer, more human in dimension despite the vastness of the setting. The snowcapped mountains reflect the setting sun back onto a stream rolling into the channel, as nearby peaks echo their image—on a windless day—in the still waters.

Above the city, the last mountains of the Andean Cordillera rise, and just south and west of Ushuaia they finally vanish into the often stormy sea. Snow whitens the peaks well into summer. Nature is the principal attraction here, with trekking, fishing, horseback riding, and sailing among the most rewarding activities, especially in the Parque Nacional Tierra del Fuego (Tierra del Fuego National Park).

As Ushuaia converts to a tourism-based economy, the city is seeking ways to utilize its 3,000 hotel rooms in the lonely winter season. Though most international tourists stay home to enjoy their own summer, the adventurous have the place to themselves for snowmobiling, dogsledding, and skiing at Cerro Castor.

GETTING HERE & AROUND

Arriving by air is the preferred option. Ushuaia's Aeropuerto Internacional Malvinas Argentinas (⊠ Peninsula de Ushuaia ☎ 2901/431–232) is 5 km (3 mi) from town, and is served daily by flights to/from Buenos Aires, Río Gallegos, El Calafate, Trelew, and Comodoro Rivadavía. There are also flights to Santiago via Punta Arenas in Chile. A taxi into town costs about 7 pesos.

Arriving by road on the RN3 involves Argentinean and Chilean immigrations/customs, a ferry crossing, and a lot of time. Buses to/from Punta Arenas make the trip five days a week in summer, four in winter. There is no central bus terminal, just three separate companies.

There is no regular passenger transport (besides cruises) by sea.

ESSENTIALS

Bus Services Tecni-Austral (⊠ *Roca 157* ☎ *2901/431–408*). **Trans los Carlos** (⊠ *Av. San Martín 880* ☎ *2901/22337*).

Postal Services Ushuaia Post Office (⊠ *Belgrano 96*).

Visitor Information Tierra del Fuego Tourism Institute (⊠ *Maipú 505,* ☎ *2901/421–423*). **Ushuaia Tourist Office** (⊠ *Av. San Martín 674* ☎ *2901/432–000* ⊕ *www.e-ushuaia.com*).

WHAT TO SEE

The **Antigua Casa Beben** (Old Beben House) is one of Ushuaia's original houses, and long served as the city's social center. Built between 1911 and 1913 by Fortunato Beben, it's said he ordered the house through a Swiss catalog. In the 1980s the Beben family donated the house to the city to avoid demolition. It was moved to its current location along the coast and restored, and is now a cultural center with art exhibits. ⊠ *Maipú at Pluschow* ☎ *No phone* ☎ *Free* ☉ *Tues.–Fri. 10–8, weekends 4–8.*

CLOSE UP

Next Stop: Antarctica

Antarctica. The White Continent. The last frontier of adventure travel. If you've come all the way to southern Patagonia, why not extend your journey, venture a bit farther south and catch a glimpse of the land of eternal winter at the bottom of the world?

Although tourism to Antarctica has increased dramatically in recent years, as the 2007 sinking of the cruise ship *Explorer* demonstrated, Antarctica is not a risk-free destination. Travel companies might offer gourmet meals and Pilates classes for passengers cruising off the Antarctic peninsula, but travelers should always keep in mind that luxury aside, the beauty of Antarctica is matched only by its isolation and utterly inhospitable environment. By all means, go to Antarctica, but choose your tour company with great care, searching out operators who prioritize safety, not price or amenities.

Most Antarctic cruises depart from Ushuaia, cross the Drake Passage, and spend about a week cruising the Antarctic peninsula. The cruising season runs from November through March. Early season is best for viewing icebergs, although whales and other marine wildlife are especially plentiful in February and March. Most ships incorporate landings via Zodiac at various points along the peninsula, but remember that as with everything in Antarctica, these excursions are totally weather dependent.

The size of the cruise ship you take to Antarctica is an important and oft-overlooked consideration. Although large ships may offer more in the way of lectures and amenities, they have major drawbacks. There is a limit on the number of passengers who can disembark at any given attraction, so passengers on a large ship will have to take turns, and may miss out on the best landing points. Likewise, the sinking of the small *Explorer* notwithstanding, smaller ships are generally safer than the larger alternatives, because many are former ice-breakers converted to cruise ships. One good one is the **Antarctic Dream** (⊕ *www.antarctic.cl*), a former Chilean navy vessel now operated by the Antarctic Shipping company.

Safety should always be your first priority, but if price is a sticking point, you can look into booking last-minute at a steep discount in Ushuaia. Doing so can save you thousands of dollars, but you will not be able to choose your ship with the proper care.

The **International Association of Antarctic Tour Operators** is an exemplary organization that promotes safe and environmentally friendly Antarctic tourism. Their Web site (⊕ *www.iaato.org*) is a good place to start your research.

—Tim Patterson

10

Rainy days are a reality in Ushuaia, but two museums give you an avenue for urban exploration and a glimpse into Tierra del Fuego's fascinating past. Part of the original penal colony, the Presidio building was built to hold political prisoners, street orphans, and a variety of other social undesirables from the north. In its day it held 600 inmates in 380 cells. Today it holds the **Museo Marítimo** (Maritime Museum), within Ushuaia's naval base, which has exhibits on the town's extinct indigenous population, Tierra del Fuego's navigational past, Antarctic explorations, and life and times in an Argentine penitentiary. You can enter cell blocks and read the stories of the prisoners who lived in them while gazing upon their eerie effigies. Well-presented tours (in Spanish only) are conducted at 3:30 daily. ⊠ *Gobernador Paz at Yaganes* ☎ *2901/437–481* 🎫 *15 pesos* ⊙ *Daily 10–8.*

At the **Museo del Fin del Mundo** (End of the World Museum), you can see a large stuffed condor and other native birds, indigenous artifacts, maritime instruments, and such seafaring-related objects as an impressive mermaid figurehead taken from the bowsprit of a galleon. There are also photographs and histories of El Presidio's original inmates, such as Simon Radowitzky, a Russian immigrant anarchist who received a life sentence for killing an Argentine police colonel. The museum is in the 1905 residence of a Fuegonian governor. The home was later converted into a bank, and some of the exhibits are showcased in the former vault. ⊠ *Maipú 173, at Rivadavía* ☎ *2901/421–863* 🎫 *10 pesos* ⊙ *Oct.–Mar., daily 9–8; Apr.–Sept., daily noon–7.*

Tierra del Fuego was the last land mass in the world to be inhabited—it was not until 9,000 BC that the ancestors of those native coastal inhabitants, the Yamana, arrived. The **Museo Yamana** chronicles their lifestyle and history. The group was decimated in the late 19th century, mostly by European diseases. Photographs and good English placards depict the unusual, hunched posture of the Yamana; their characteristic wobbly walk; and their way of hunting of cormorants, which were killed with a bite through the neck. ⊠ *Rivadavía 56* ☎ *2901/422–874* ⊕ *www. tierradelfuego.org.ar/mundoyamana* 🎫 *5 pesos* ⊙ *Daily 10–8.*

The **Tren del Fin del Mundo** (End of the World Train) takes you inside the Parque Nacional Tierra del Fuego, 12 km (7½ mi) away. The touristy 40-minute train ride's gimmick is a simulation of the trip on which El Presidio prisoners were taken into the forest to chop wood; but unlike them, you'll also get a good presentation of Ushuaia's history (in Spanish and English). The train departs daily at 9:30 AM, noon, and 3 PM in summer, and just once a day, at 10 AM, in winter, from a stop near the national park entrance. If you have a rental car, you'll want to do the round trip, but if not, one common way to do the trip is to hire a *remis* (car service) that will drop you at the station for a one-way train ride, pick you up at the other end, and then drive you around the Parque Nacional for two or three hours of sightseeing (which is more scenic than the train ride itself). ⊠ *Ruta 3, Km 3042* ☎ *2901/431–600* ⊕ *www.trendelfindelmundo.com.ar* 🎫 *95 pesos first-class ticket, 50 pesos tourist-class ticket, 20 pesos national park entrance fee (no park fee in winter).*

Tour operators run trips along the **Canal Beagle,** on which you can get a startling close-up view of sea mammals and birds on **Isla de los Lobos, Isla de los Pájaros,** and near **Les Eclaireurs Lighthouse.** There are catamarans that make three-hour trips, generally leaving from the Tourist Pier at 3 PM, and motorboats and sailboats that leave twice a day, once at 9:30 AM and once at 3 PM (trips depend on weather; few trips go in winter). Prices range 60 pesos–140 pesos; some include hikes on the islands. Check with the tourist office for the latest details; you can also book through any of the local travel agencies.

One good excursion in the area is to **Lago Escondido** (Hidden Lake) and **Lago Fagnano** (Fagnano Lake). The Pan-American Highway out of Ushuaia goes through deciduous beechwood forest and past beavers' dams, peat bogs, and glaciers. The lakes have campsites and fishing and are good spots for a picnic or a hike. This can be done on your own or as a seven-hour trip, including lunch, booked through the local travel agencies (75 pesos without lunch, 95 pesos with lunch).

One recommended operator, offering a comfortable bus, a bilingual guide, and lunch at Las Cotorras, is **All Patagonia** (⊠ *Juana Fadul 26* ☎ *2901/433–622 or 2901/430–725).*

A rougher, more unconventional tour of the lake area goes to **Monte Olivia** (Mt. Olivia), the tallest mountain along the Canal Beagle, rising 4,455 feet above sea level. You also pass the **Five Brothers Mountains** and go through the **Garibaldi Pass,** which begins at the Rancho Hambre, climbs into the mountain range, and ends with a spectacular view of Lago Escondido. From here you continue on to Lago Fagnano through the countryside past sawmills and lumber yards. To do this tour in a four-wheel-drive truck with an excellent bilingual guide, contact **Canal Fun** (⊠ *Rivadavía 82* ☎ *2901/437–395);* you'll drive *through* Lago Fagnano (about 3 feet of water at this point) to a secluded cabin on the shore and have a delicious *asado,* complete with wine and dessert.

Estancia Harberton (Harberton Ranch), consists of 50,000 acres of coastal marshland and wooded hillsides. The property was a late-19th-century gift from the Argentine government to Reverend Thomas Bridges, who authored a Yamana–English dictionary and is considered the patriarch of Tierra del Fuego. Today the ranch is managed by Bridges's great-grandson, Thomas Goodall, and his American wife, Natalie, a scientist and author who has cooperated with the National Geographic Society on conservation projects and operates the impressive marine mammal museum, Museo Acatushun (⊕ www.acatushun.com ☒ 5 pesos). Most people visit as part of organized tours, but you'll be welcome if you arrive alone. They serve up a tasty tea in their home, the oldest building on the island. For safety reasons, exploration of the ranch can only be done on guided tours (45–90 minutes). Lodging is available, either in the Old Shepherd's House (240 pesos per person with breakfast) or the Old Cook's House (210 pesos per person with breakfast). Additionally, you can arrange a three-course lunch at the ranch by calling two days ahead for a reservation. Most tours reach the estancia by boat, offering a rare opportunity to explore the **Isla Martillo** penguin colony, in addition to a sea-lion refuge on **Isla de los Lobos** (Island of the Wolves) along the way. ⊠ *85 km (53 mi) east of Ushuaia* ☎ *2901/422–742* ⊕ *www.estanciaharberton.com* 💲 *15 pesos* ⊙ *By tour only, daily 9–7, last tour 5:30.*

★   If you've never butted heads with a glacier, and especially if you won't be covering El Calafate on your trip, then you should check out **Glaciar Martial,** in the mountain range just above Ushuaia. Named after Frenchman Luís F. Martial, a 19th-century scientist who wandered this way aboard the warship *Romanche* to observe the passing of planet Venus, the glacier is reached via a panoramic *aerosilla* (ski lift). Take the Camino al Glaciar (Glacier Road) 7 km (4 mi) out of town until it ends (this route is also served by the local tour companies). Even if you don't plan to hike to see the glacier, it's a great pleasure to ride the 15-minute lift (and hiking this stretch is unrewarding), which is open daily 10–5, weather permitting (it's often closed from mid-May until August) and costs 25 pesos. If you're afraid of heights, you can instead enjoy a small nature trail here, and a teahouse. You can return on the lift, or continue on to the beginning of a 1-km (½-mi) trail that winds its way over lichen and shale straight up the mountain. After a steep, strenuous 90-minute hike, you can cool your heels in one of the many gurgling, icy rivulets that cascade down water-worn shale shoots or enjoy a picnic while you wait for sunset (you can walk all the way down if you want to linger until after the *aerosilla* closes). When the sun drops behind the glacier's jagged crown of peaks, brilliant rays beam over the mountain's crest, spilling a halo of gold-flecked light on the glacier, valley, and channel below. Moments like these are why this land is so magical. Note that temperatures drop dramatically after sunset, so come prepared with warm clothing.

WHERE TO EAT

Choosing a place to stay depends in part on whether you want to spend the night in town, out of town several miles west towards the national park, or above town several miles uphill. Las Hayas Resort, Hotel Glaciar, Cumbres de Martial, and Los Yámanas have stunning views, but require a taxi ride or the various complimentary shuttle services to reach Ushuaia.

$–$$$ ✕ **Arco Iris.** This restaurant in the center of town is one of the finest of the good-value *tenedor libre* (all-you-can-eat) parrillas on the main strip—nobody orders à la carte. Skip the Italian buffet and fill up instead on the spit-roasted Patagonian lamb, grilled meats, and delicious *morcilla* (blood sausage). It's all you can eat for 38 pesos. Sit by the glass wall to see the *parrillero* artfully coordinate the flames and spits. ⊠ *Av. San Martín 96* ☎ *2901/431–306* ⊟ *AE, DC, MC, V.*

$–$$$ ✕ **La Cabaña Casa de Té.** This cottage, in a verdant wood of lenga trees beside the surge of a powerful river, overlooks the Beagle Channel and provides a warm, cozy spot for tea or snacks before or after a hike to the Martial Glacier—it's at the end of the Martial road that leads up from Ushuaia. Fondues are a specialty at lunchtime; at 8 PM the menu shifts to pricier dinner fare with dishes like salmon in wine sauce.

☒*Camino Luís Martial 3560* ☎*2901/434–699* ▱*AE, DC, MC, V*
⊗*Closed Mon.*

$$–$$$$ ✗**Chez Manu.** *Herbes de provence* in the greeting room tip French quasi-
Fodor's Choice   celebrity chef Manu Herbin's hand: he gives local seafood a French
★   touch to diversify the Argentine gastronomy and create some of Ush-
uaia's most memorable meals. Perched a couple of miles above town,
across the street from the Hotel Glaciar, the restaurant has grand views
of the Beagle Canal. The first-rate wine list includes Patagonian selec-
tions. Don't miss the *trucha fueguina* (local trout) in white wine sauce,
served with buttery rice cooked in fish stock, or the *centolla* (king crab)
au gratin. ☒*Camino Luís Martial 2135* ☎*2901/432–253* ▱*AE, MC,
V* ⊗*Closed Mon., May, and June.*

$–$$$ ✗**Ramos Generales.** Entering this café on the waterfront is like entering
a time machine transporting you back a hundred years. As you travel
from room to room admiring the stories behind various antique relics
(such as the hand-cranked Victrola phonograph), imagine that warehouses like this were not only providers of all kinds of products for the
city's denizens, but also a point of social encounter. Try the submarino,
a glorified hot chocolate which may prove the best one you've ever
had. Goes well with a panini. ☒*Maípu 749* ☎*2901/424–317* ⊕*www.
ramosgeneralesushuaia.com* ▱*AE, MC, V* ⊗*Closed Mon.*

$$–$$$$ ✗**Tía Elvira.** On the street that runs right along the Beagle Channel,
this is an excellent place to sample the local catch. Garlicky shellfish
appetizers and centolla are delicious, and even more memorable is the
tender *merluza negra* (black sea bass). The room is decked out with
nautical knickknacks that may seem on the tacky side for such a pricey
place. The service is friendly and familial. ☒*Maipú 349* ☎*2901/424–
725* ▱*AE, DC, MC, V* ⊗*Closed Sun. and July.*

$$–$$$ ✗**Volver.** A giant king crab sign beckons you into this red tin restaurant,
★   which provides some major relief from Avenida San Martín's row of
all-you-can-eat parrillas. The name means "return" and it succeeds in
getting repeat visits. Newspapers from the 1930s line the walls in this
century-old home; informal table settings have placemats depicting old
London landmarks; and fishing nets hang from the ceiling, along with
hams, a disco ball, tricycles, and antique lamps. The culinary highlight
is king crab (*centolla*), which comes served with a choice of five differ-
ent sauces. ☒*Maipú 37* ☎*2901/423–977* ▱*AE, DC, MC, V* ⊗*No
lunch May–Aug.*

WHERE TO STAY

$$$ ⊡**Los Acebos.** The new offering from the owners of Las Hayas (just
down the winding mountain road), Los Acebos is a modern hotel sur-
rounded by forests and mountains with a commanding view out to the
Beagle Channel. Spacious and superclean rooms feature the same icon-
oclastic decor as Las Hayas, including the trademark fabric-padded
walls. The restaurant serves international dishes in beautiful surroundings and in a warm friendly atmosphere. The bar serves a variety of
drinks, regional and international. Guests can imbibe by the lounge fireplace or in the game room. **Pros:** A great value for spacious and superclean rooms. **Cons:** A tad out of the way for a spa-less facility. ☒*Luis
F. Martial 1911, Ushuaia* ☎*4393-0621* ⊕*www.losacebos.com.ar*

10

📶*56 rooms, 4 suites* ⟜*In-room: safe minibar. In hotel: restaurant, room service, public Internet, spa, gym, laundry, parking* ▤*AE, MC, V.*

$$$$ ▦**Los Cauquenes Resort and Spa.** This resort hotel is more of a gated campus, with a series of buildings and cabanas along the Beagle Channel shore about 8 km (5 mi) west of town. Privileged beach access and sparse development in the Barrio Bahía Cauquén (for now) means a nature hike starts right outside your room. Request one on a higher floor, as many of the ground-floor rooms are partially underground. Rooms can get uncomfortably hot, and noise goes through the walls. Yet the water pressure is excellent, and the heated pool which flows from inside to out is spectacular. The gym, sauna, and massage/relaxation studios are top-notch. On the relatively cheap menu of the restaurant Reinamora you will find the standard Patagonian lamb, rainbow trout, and a delicious king crab served with berries. **Pros:** Great amenities to soothe body and mind. **Cons:** No air-conditioning in rooms, thin walls can make for noisy nights. ✉*Reinamora s/n, Barrio Bahía Cauquén, Ushuaia* ☎*2901/441–300* ⊕*www.loscauquenesushuaia.com.ar* 📶*49 rooms, 5 suites, 13 cabanas* ⟜*In room: safe, minibar. In-hotel: gym, pool, sauna, restaurant, bar, public Wi-Fi, parking* ▤*AE, MC, V.*

$$$$ ▦**Cumbres de Martial.** This charming wood complex, painted fire-engine red, is high above Ushuaia at the foot of the ski lift that leads to the Martial glacier. Each spacious room has an extremely comfortable bed and a small wooden deck with terrific views down to the Beagle Channel. The *cabañas* are beautiful self-contained log cabins. There are also a teahouse and a small nature trail beside the Martial River. There is, however, no complimentary shuttle service to town, so you'll need to take a 10- to 15-peso taxi to access Ushuaia. **Pros:** Easy access to the glacier, views. **Cons:** You need to cab it to and from town. ✉*Camino Luís Martial 3560,* ☎*2901/424–779* ⊕*www.cumbresdelmartial. com.ar* 📶*6 rooms, 4 cabins* ⟜*In-room: safe. In-hotel: restaurant, bar, laundry service, airport shuttle* ▤*AE, DC, MC, V* ☽*Closed Apr. and May* ⏻❘*BP.*

$$ ▦**Hostería Patagonia Jarké.** Jarké means "spark" in a local native lan-
★ guage, and indeed this B&B is a vibrant addition to Ushuaia. This three-story lodge, cantilevered down a hillside on a dead-end street in the heart of town, is an amalgam of alpine and Victorian styles on the outside; inside, a spacious contemporary design incorporates a glass-roofed lobby, several living rooms, and breakfast room. Rooms have polished wood floors, peaked-roof ceilings, artisanal soaps, woven floor mats, bidets, Jacuzzi tubs, and lovely views. **Pros:** Feels like home. **Cons:** Steep walk home. ✉*Sarmiento 310,* ☎*2901/437–245* ⊕*www.hosteriapatagoniaj.com* 📶*15 rooms* ⟜*In-room: safe. In-hotel: bar, laundry service, public Wi-Fi* ▤*AE, DC, MC, V* ⏻❘*BP.*

$$ ▦**Hotel Cabo de Hornos.** Cabo de Hornos is a cut above other downtown hotels in the same price category. The rooms are clean and simple, and all have cable TV and telephones. The lobby-lounge is tacky and taste-ful at the same time, decorated with currency and postcards from all over the world. Its old ski-lodge feel makes it a nice place to relax and watch *fútbol* with a cup of coffee or a beer. They also run a quaint local history museum. **Pros:** Good value. **Cons:** Nothing spectacular. ✉*San*

Martín at Rosas, ☎2901/430–677 ⊕*www.hotelcabodehornos.com.ar* ⟿*30 rooms* ⚲ *In-hotel: restaurant, bar* ▭*AE, MC, V* ⦿*CP.*

$$$$ 🖥 **Hotel Fueguino.** A gleaming ultramodern addition to Ushuaia's down-
★ town offerings, the Fueguino boasts all the amenities: conference center
with four Internet stations, extensive gym and spa, shuttle service, multilingual staff, and some of the most thorough Wi-Fi coverage we've
seen. Rooms feature custom Italian wood furnishings with stainless
steel, leather accents, frosted glass, and blackout blinds. The Fueguino
name is branded on every trinket you can think of, from bathrobes
to shoe mitts. And whatever it's not stamped on is still top of the line
(even the bidets are Ferrum Marina). Beds with padded headboards
and California king-size mattresses are as firm as it gets. Downstairs
the Komenk restaurant serves Mediterranean cuisine with Patagonian
influences. A junior suite is worth the upgrade. **Pros:** Ultramodern syb-
aritic excess. **Cons:** Immediate vicinity a shambles, making this place
a stark contrast with its environment. ✉*Gobernador Deloqui 1282,*
☎*2901/424–894* ⊕*www.fueguinohotel.com* ⟿*50 rooms, 3 suites*
⚲*In-room: safe, minibar. In-hotel: spa, gym, room service, public
Internet, Wi-Fi, restaurant, bar* ▭*AE, MC, V.*

$$$$ 🖥 **Hotel del Glaciar.** Just above the Las Hayas hotel in the Martial
Mountains, this hotel has the best views of Ushuaia and the Beagle
Channel. The rooms are bright, clean, and very comfortable. After a
long day in the woods, you can curl up on the large sofa next to the
fire pit or make your way over to the cozy wood-paneled bar for a
drink. Hourly shuttle buses take you to the town center. **Pros:** Old-
style colonial atmosphere sets it apart from the modern behemoths on
the mountain. **Cons:** Still very big. ✉*Camino Glaciar Martial 2355,
Km 3.5,* ☎*2901/430–640* ⊕*www.hoteldelglaciar.com* ⟿*119 rooms,
1 suites* ⚲*In-hotel: restaurant, bar, laundry service, airport shuttle,
public Internet, minibar* ▭*AE, DC, MC, V* ⦿*CP.*

$$$$ 🖥 **Hotel y Resort Las Hayas.** Las Hayas is in the wooded foothills of the
Fodor's Choice Andes, overlooking the town and channel below. Ask for a *canal* view
★ and, since the rooms are all decorated differently and idiosyncratically,
sample a variety before settling in. All feature Portuguese linen, solid
oak furnishings, and the Las Hayas trademark: fabric-padded walls. A
suspended glass bridge connects the hotel to a spectacular health spa,
which includes a heated pool, Jacuzzi, and even a squash court. The
wonderful five-star restaurant Le Martial prepares an excellent version
of *mollejas de cordero* (lamb sweetbreads) with scallops, and boasts the
best wine list in town. Frequent shuttle buses take you into town. **Pros:**
Four Internet stations, good restaurant. **Cons:** Decor doesn't suit everyone. ✉*Camino Luís Martial 1650, Km 3,* ☎*2901/430–710, 11/4393–
4750 in Buenos Aires* ⊕*www.lashayashotel.com* ⟿*85 rooms, 7 suites*
⚲*In-room: safe. In-hotel: restaurant, bar, pool, gym, spa, laundry service, airport shuttle* ▭*AE, DC, MC, V* ⦿*CP.*

$$$$ 🖥 **Hotel Los Yámanas.** This cozy hotel 4 km (2½ mi) from the center
of town is named after the local tribe and offers a rustic mountain
aesthetic. Some rooms have stunning views over the Beagle Channel,
and all have wrought-iron bed frames, and are furnished with simple
good taste. The expansive lobby, second-floor restaurant, games room

10

with billiards, and sauna are just as welcoming. Never overlook the virtues of a 100-peso per hour massage. **Pros:** Top notch gym. **Cons:** Questionable taste in lobby decoration. ✉*Los Ñires 1850, Km 3,* ☎*2901/445–960* ⊕*hotelyamanas.com.ar* ⤳*39 rooms, 2 suites* ⬧*In-room: safe. In-hotel: restaurant, bar, gym, pool, laundry service, public Wi-Fi, minibar* ☰*AE, DC, MC, V* ⍟*CP.*

$$$ ⛺ **La Tierra de Leyendas.** The Land of Legends is Sebas and Maia's honeymooners' delight. The couple put this adorable B&B together on the heels of careers in hospitality working for Marriott. The hotel is in the Estancia Río Pipo, on a wind-battered hill 4 km (2½ mi) west of town, in an area once inhabited by canoeist nomads. The five bedrooms—with names such as La Coqueta and La Mision—boast large windows facing the Beagle Channel or the snow-capped Andes; a cozy living room offers a book exchange, board games, video library, and glass display tables with antique arrows, bones, and currency. The restaurant has a top-notch gourmet menu—offering such exotic fare as *conejo a la cazadora* (stuffed Fuegian rabbit)—prepared by the owner. **Pros:** An extraordinarily quaint find for western Ushuaia. **Cons:** Insanely windy—hold on to your hat. ✉*Tierra de Vientos 2448,* ☎*2901/443–565* ⊕*www.tierradeleyendas.com.ar* ⤳*5 rooms* ⬧*In-room: DVD, safe. In-hotel: laundry service, public Wi-Fi* ☰*AE, MC, V.*

NIGHTLIFE

Ushuaia has a lively nightlife in summer, with its casino, discos, and intimate cafés all close to each other. The biggest and most popular pub is **El Náutico** (✉*Maipú 1210* ☎*2901/430–415*). **Bar Ideal** (✉*San Martín 393*) is a cozy and historic bar and café. **Kaitek Lounge Bar** (✉*Antartida Argentina 239* ☎*2901/431–723*) is a place to eat until 2 AM, and to dance to pop music until 6 AM. **Tante Sara** (✉*San Martín 701* ☎*2901/433–710* ⊕*cafebartantesara.com.ar*) is a popular café-bar with a casual, old-world feel, in the heart of town, where locals kick back with a book or a beer (they pour Beagle, the local artisanal brew). During the day it's one of the few eateries to defy the 3–6 PM siesta.

PARQUE NACIONAL TIERRA DEL FUEGO

★ The pristine park, 21 km (13 mi) west of Ushuaia, offers a chance to wander through peat bogs, stumble upon hidden lakes, trek through native *canelo, lenga,* and wild cherry forests, and experience the wonders of wind-whipped Tierra del Fuego's rich flora and fauna. Everywhere, lichens line the trunks of the ubiquitous lenga trees, and "chinese lantern" parasites hang from the branches.

Everywhere, too, you'll see *castoreros* (beaver dams) and lodges. Fifty beaver couples were first brought in from Canada in 1948 so that they would breed and create a fur industry. In the years since, however, the beaver population has grown to more than 50,000 and now represents a major threat to the forests, as the dams flood the roots of the trees; you can see their effects on the gnawed-down trees everywhere. Believe it or not, the government now pays hunters a bounty of 30 pesos for each beaver they kill (they need to show a tail and head as proof). (To make matters worse, the government, after creating the beaver problem, then introduced weasels to kill the beavers, but the weasels killed birds instead; they then introduced foxes to kill the beavers and weasels, but they also killed the birds.)

Visits to the park, which is tucked up against the Chilean border, are commonly arranged through tour companies. Trips range from bus tours to horseback riding to more adventurous excursions, such as canoe trips across Lapataia Bay. Another way to get to the park is to take the Tren del Fin del Mundo *(⇨above)*. **Transportes Kaupen** (☎*2901/434–015*), one of several private bus companies, has buses that travel through the park, making several stops within it; you can get off the bus, explore the park, and then wait for the next bus to come by or trek to the next stop (the service only operates in summer). Yet one more option is to drive to the park on R3 (take it until it ends and you see the famous sign indicating the end of the Pan-American Highway, which starts 17,848 km [11,065 mi] away in Alaska, and ends here). If you don't have a car, you can also hire a private *remis* to spend a few hours driving through the park, including the Pan-American terminus, and perhaps also combining the excursion with the Tren del Fin del Mundo. Trail and camping information is available at the park-entrance ranger station or at the Ushuaia tourist office. At the park entrance is a gleaming new restaurant and teahouse set amidst the hills, **Patagonia Mia** (✉*Ruta 3, Entrada Parque Nacional* ☎*2901/1560–2757* ⊕*www.patagoniamia.com*); it's a great place to stop for tea or coffee, or a full meal of roast lamb or Fuegian seafood. A nice excursion in the park is by boat from lovely **Bahía Ensenada** to **Isla Redonda,** a wildlife refuge where you can follow a footpath to the western side and see a wonderful view of the Canal Beagle. This is included on some of the day tours; it's harder to arrange on your own, but you can contact the tourist office to try. While on Isla Redonda you can send a postcard and get your passport stamped at the world's southernmost post office. You can also see the Ensenada bay and island (from afar) from a point on the shore that is reachable by car.

Other highlights of the park include the spectacular mountain-ringed lake, **Lago Roca,** as well as **Laguna Verde,** a lagoon whose green color comes from algae at its bottom. Much of the park is closed from roughly June through September, when the descent to Bahía Ensenada is blocked by up to 6 feet of snow. Even in May and October, chains for your car are a good idea. No hotels are within the park—the only one burned down in the 1980s, and you can see its carcass as you drive by—but there are three simple camping areas around Lago Roca. Tours to the park are run by **All Patagonia** (✉*Juana Fadul 26* ☎*2901/433– 622 or 2901/430–725*).

OUTDOOR ACTIVITIES

FISHING The rivers of Tierra del Fuego are home to trophy-size freshwater trout—including browns, rainbows, and brooks. Both fly- and spin-casting are available. The fishing season runs November–March; fees range from 10 pesos a day to 40 pesos for a month. Fishing expeditions are organized by the following companies. Founded in

1959, the **Asociación de Caza y Pesca** (✉*Av. Maipú 822* ☎*2901/423–168*) is the principal hunting and fishing organization in the city. **Rumbo Sur** (✉*Av. San Martín 350* ☎*2901/421–139* ⊕*www.rumbosur.com.ar*) is the city's oldest travel agency and can assist in setting up fishing trips. **Wind Fly** (✉*Av. 25 de Mayo 143* ☎*2901/431–713 or 2901/1544–9116* ⊕*www.windflyushuaia.com.ar*) is dedicated exclusively to fishing, and offers classes, arranges trips, and rents equipment.

MOUNTAIN
BIKING

A mountain bike is an excellent mode of transport in Ushuaia, giving you the freedom to roam without the rental-car price tag. Good mountain bikes normally cost about 5 pesos an hour or 15 pesos–20 pesos for a full day. Bikes can be rented at the base of the glacier, at the **Refugio de Montaña** (✉*Base Glaciar Martial* ☎*2901/1556–8587*), or at **D.T.T. Cycles** (✉*Av. San Martín 903* ☎*2901/434–939*). Guided bicycle tours (including rides through the national park), for about 50 pesos a day, are organized by **All Patagonia** (✉*Fadul 26* ☎*2901/430–725*). **Rumbo Sur** (✉*San Martín 350* ☎*2901/421–139* ⊕*www.rumbosur.com.ar*) is the city's biggest travel agency and can arrange trips. **Tolkeyén Patagonia** (✉*San Martín 1267* ☎*2901/437–073*) rents bikes and arranges trips.

SCENIC
FLIGHTS

The gorgeous scenery and island topography of the area is readily appreciated on a Cessna tour. A half-hour flight (US$35, or 102 pesos per passenger; US$50, or 145 pesos for one passenger alone) with a local pilot takes you over Ushuaia and the Beagle Channel with views of area glaciers and snowcapped islands south to Cape Horn. A 60-minute flight (US$70, or 203 pesos per passenger; US$100, or 290 pesos for one passenger alone) crosses the Andes to the Escondida and Fagnano lakes. **Aero Club Ushuaia** (✉*Antiguo Aeropuerto* ☎*2901/421–717* ⊕*www.aeroclubushuaia.org.ar*) offers half-hour and hour-long trips.

SKIING

Ushuaia is the cross-country skiing (*esqui de fondo* in Spanish) center of South America, thanks to enthusiastic **Club Andino** (☎*2901/422–335*) members who took to the sport in the 1980s and made the forested hills of a high valley about 20 minutes from town a favorite destination for skiers. **Hostería Tierra Mayor** (☎*2901/423–240*), **Hostería Los Cotorras** (☎*2901/499–300*), and **Haruwen** (☎*2901/424–058*) are three places where you can ride in dog-pulled sleds, rent skis, go cross-country skiing, get lessons, and eat; contact the Ushuaia tourist office for more information.

Glaciar Martial Ski Lodge (☎*2901/243–3712*), open year-round, Tuesday–Sunday 10–7, functions as a cross-country ski center from June to October. Skis can also be rented in town, as can snowmobiles.

For downhill (or *alpino*) skiers, Club Andino has bulldozed a couple of short, flat runs directly above Ushuaia. The newest downhill ski area, **Cerro Castor** (☎*2901/422–244* ⊕*www.cerrocastor.com*), is 26 km (17 mi) northeast of Ushuaia on R3, and has 19 trails and four high-speed ski lifts. More than half the trails are at the beginner level, six are intermediate, and three are expert trails, but none of this terrain is very challenging for an experienced skier. You can rent skis and snowboards and take ski lessons. **Transportes Kaupen** (*⇨above*) and other local bus companies run service back and forth from town.

WHERE TO STAY

Dotting the perimeter of the park are five free campgrounds, none of which has much more than a spot to pitch a tent and a fire pit. Call the **park office** (☎2901/421–315) or consult the ranger station at the park entrance for more information. **Camping Lago Roca** (✉*South on R3 for 20 km [12 mi]* ☎*No phone*), within the park, charges 8 pesos per person per day and has bathrooms, hot showers, and a small market. Of all the campgrounds, **La Pista del Andino** (✉*Av. Alem 2873* ☎*2901/435–890*) is the only one within the city limits. Outside of town, **Camping Río Pipo** (☎2901/435–796) is the closest to Ushuaia (it's 18 km [11 mi] away).

PUERTO WILLIAMS

75-min flight southeast from Punta Arenas; 82 km (50 mi) southeast of Ushuaia, Argentina.

On an island southeast of Ushuaia, the town of Puerto Williams is the southernmost permanent settlement in the world. Originally called Puerto Luisa, it was renamed in 1956 in honor of the military officer who took possession of the Estrecho de Magallanes for the newly founded nation of Chile in 1843. Most of the 2,500 residents are troops at the naval base, but there are several hundred civilians in the adjacent village. A tiny community of indigenous Yaghan peoples makes its home in the nearby Ukika village.

Stop in at the Oficina de Turismo at Ibanez 130 (Dec.–Mar., weekdays 10–1 and 3–6 ☎61/621–011), but don't expect much beyond maps. Accommodation offerings are simple and huddled around the center of town.

For a quick history lesson on how Puerto Williams evolved, and some insight into the indigenous peoples, visit the **Museo Martín Gusinde,** named for the renowned anthropologist who traveled and studied in the region between 1918 and 1924. ✉*Aragay 1* ☎*No phone* 💲*500 pesos* 🕐 *Weekdays 10–1 and 3–6, weekends 3–6.*

Weather permitting, **Aerovis DAP** (✉*Av. Bernardo O'Higgins 891, Punta Arenas* ☎*61/223–340* 🌐*www.aeroviasdap.cl*) offers charter flights over Cabo de Hornos, the southernmost tip of South America. Although the water looks placid from the air, strong westerly winds make navigating around Cape Horn treacherous. Over the last few centuries, hundreds of ships have met their doom here trying to sail to the Pacific.

HIKING

A hike to the top of nearby **Cerro Bandera** is well worth the effort if you have the stamina. The trail is well marked, but very steep. The view from the top toward the south to the Cordón Dientes del Perro (Dog's Teeth Range) is impressive, but looking northward over the Beagle Channel to Argentina—with Puerto Williams nestled below and Ushuaia just visible to the west—is truly breathtaking. Near the start of the trail, 3 km (2 mi) west of Puerto Williams, is the Parque Etnobotanico

10

Omora visitor center (open daylight hours ⊕www.cabodehornos. org), which got its name from the Yahgan word for hummingbird. In the Yahgan cosmology Omora was more than a bird; he was also a revered mythological hero. The Omora Foundation is a Chilean NGO dedicated to biocultural conservation in the extreme southern tip of South America. Their work led UNESCO to designate the Cape Horn Biosphere Reserve in June 2005. Within the park interpretive trails explore the various habitats of the Isla Navarino region: coastal coigue forests, lenga parks, nirre forests, Sphagnum bogs, beaver wetlands, and alpine heath. Additionally, the Robalo River runs through the park and provides potable water to the town.

THE SOUTHERN DEBATE
The southernmost town on the globe, Puerto Williams, is just above the 55th parallel. It's closer to the South Pole than to the northern border of Chile. Bigger, and just to the northeast of Puerto Williams, is Ushuaia, Argentina, the world's southernmost *city*. At least, that's how the Argentineans describe it. The Chileans like to say that Puerto Williams is a city, too, resenting how Ushuaia has claimed that moniker in its tourist literature. Visit both, and decide for yourself.

WHERE TO STAY & EAT

When you arrive in Puerto Williams, your airline or ferry company will recommend a few of the hospedajes available, then take you around to see them. With the exception of Lakutaia Hotel, all are rustic inns that also serve meals.

$$$$ ▦ **Lakutaia Hotel.** From the people behind Punta Arenas's splendid José
★   Nogueira comes this endearing venue, the most southern luxury hotel in the world. Hotel Lakutaia takes advantage of Navarino's beautiful surroundings to offer a range of unique outdoors activities including kayaking and trekking in Lauta, mountain biking, golf, horseback riding, sailing, walks to Castors Lagoon, and matches of Rayuela, a typical Chilean sport. Lukutaia also organizes ecological excursions to nearby fjords, mountains, indigenous settlements, the waterfalls in Robalo River, a Zodiac boat ride to the Cormorans Island, and a trip to Cape Horn. One of the most interesting trips visits millenary glaciers, following the same path covered by Darwin over 150 years ago. The hotel's 24 double rooms are built with natural wood materials that fit perfectly with the forested world outside. Even the horse stables are impressive. The Lakutaia has a complete library–map room where you can find books and magazines with obscure details on the history and natural resources of the region. **Pro:** Offers a surprisingly impressive range of activities. **Con:** Comes with a high price. ⊠*Seno Lauta s/n* ☎*61/621–020* ⊕*www.lakutaia.cl* ⊐*24 rooms* ♨*In-room: no TV. In-hotel: laundry, restaurant* ☰*AE, MC, V* ¶◎¶*CP.*

CLOSE UP

Tierra del Fuego by Sea

The four-day Navimag trips from Puerto Montt to Puerto Natales, which pass the Amalia Glacier, are immensely popular with backpackers and other visitors. The ship isn't luxurious, but it has a restaurant, pub, and lectures on local culture. Depending on which sort of cabin you choose, cabins are priced US$720–$845 (380,000 pesos–446,000 pesos) per person for double occupancy in high season, and US$340–$410 (180,000 pesos–216,500 pesos) per person in low season. Prices include all meals. The boat calls at Puerto Edén, where you can get off and visit the town for a few hours. Navimag tickets can be bought online or at local travel agencies.

If you prefer to travel through the region's natural wonders in comfort, Comapa's affiliate Cruceros Australis runs two ships, the elegant 55-cabin *Mare Australis*, built in 2002, and the even newer 63-cabin *Vía Australis*, constructed in 2005. Both ships have the classic, wood-and-polished-brass design of old-world luxury liners, and both sail round-trip between Punta Arenas and Ushuaia (there are 4-day and 3-day options). On the way, the ships stop at a number of sights, including the Garibaldi Glacier, a breathtaking mass of blue ice. You also ride smaller motorboats ashore to visit Isla Magdalena's colony of 120,000 penguins, and Ainsworth Bay's family of elephant seals. The cruises include lectures in English, German, and Spanish on the region's geography and history, flora and fauna; all multi-course meals and cocktails (including some formidable pisco sours) are included.

Comapa also runs a ferry three times a week between Punta Arenas and Porvenir, and the *Barcaza Melinka*, which makes thrice-weekly trips to Isla Magdalena (during penguin season).

Turismo 21 de Mayo operates two ships, the *Cutter 21 de Mayo* and the *Alberto de Agostini*, to the Balmaceda and Serrano glaciers in Parque Nacional Bernardo O'Higgins. Passengers on these luxurious boats are treated to lectures about the region as the boat moves up the Seno Última Esperanza.

Lago Grey Tours offers boat trips to Glaciar Grey inside the Parque Nacional Torres del Paine.

In El Calafate, Upsala Explorer combines a day at an estancia and a boat trip to Upsala Glacier.

Comapa (✉ *Av. Magallanes 990, Punta Arenas* ☎ *61/200–200* ⊕ *www.comapa.cl* ✉ *Av. Bulnes 533Puerto Natales* ☎ *61/414–300*).

Cruceros Australis (✉ *Av. El Bosque Norte 0440, Piso 11, Santiago* ☎ *2/442–3110* 🖷 *2/203–5173* ⊕ *www.australis.com*).

Lago Grey Tours (✉ *Lago Grey* ☎🖷 *61/225–986* ⊕ *www.lagogrey.com*).

Navimag (✉ *Av. El Bosque Norte 0440, Santiago* ☎ *2/442–3120* 🖷 *2/203–5025* ⊕ *www.navimag.com*).

Turismo 21 de Mayo (✉ *Ladrilleros 171, Puerto Natales* ☎ *61/411–176* ⊕ *www.turismo21demayo.cl*).

10

CLOSE UP

Tierra Del Fuego by Land & Air

AIR TOURS

Air tours are often a little more expensive than cruises, but they provide an entirely different perspective, and may take you farther than you could otherwise go. Aerovías DAP operates charter flights over Cape Horn for about US$75 (39,500 pesos) per person. In the austral summer (December–February) they fly small groups to comfortable refuges in the Chilean Antarctic, where you can stay in a lodge for up to three nights. DAP staffs a resident guide in Antarctica, and visits include trips to the air force bases of Russia, China, and Chile. Single-day visits begin at US$2,500 (1,320,000 pesos). The flight is 3½ hours. DAP also has helicopter service across Patagonia. **Aerovís DAP** (⊠ Av. Bernardo O'Higgins 891, Punta Arenas ☎ 61/223–340 ⊕ www.aeroviasdap.cl).

LAND-BASED TOURS & EXCURSIONS

SportsTour, based in Santiago, offers half- and full-day city tours and multiday excursions throughout the region; the company also arranges individual tour itineraries. Most staff members speak excellent English. In Puerto Natales, TourExpress operates a fleet of small vans for comfortable tours into Parque Nacional Torres del Paine. The bilingual guides are well versed not only on the area's culture and history but on its geology, fauna, and flora.

The U.S.-based Lost World Adventures specializes in tailoring Patagonia and Tierra del Fuego itineraries around your specific interests.

In Ushuaia and the Tierra del Fuego, Tolkar offers a wide variety of adventurous treks through the Parque Nacional Tierra del Fuego and around the Canal Beagle. Tolkeyén Patagonia organizes tours of the Canal Beagle and bus trips that give an overview of the national park. All Patagonia organizes bus trips to Lago Escondido and other spots in the area.

TOUR OPERATORS

Lost World Adventures (⊠ 337 Shadowmoor Dr. South, Decatur, ☎ 404/373–5820 or 800/999–0558 ⊕ www.lostworldadventures.com). **SportsTour** (⊠ Moneda 970, 18th fl., Santiago ☎ 2/549–5200 ⊕ www. sportstour.cl). **Tolkar** (⊠ Roca 157, Ushuaia ☎ 2901/431–408 or 2901/437–421). **Tolkeyén Patagonia** (⊠ Maipú 237, Ushuaia ☎ 2901/437–073 or 2901/424–504). **TourExpress** (⊠ Av. Bulnes 769, Puerto Natales ☎ 61/410–734).

Adventure & Learning Vacations

Kayaking near floating icebergs, Lago Gray (Lake Gray), Torres del Paine National Park, Chile

WORD OF MOUTH

"Yes, you can go up for the day to ski [from Santiago]. Every morning on the way to work I pass a place with twenty minivans parked out front with people going for the day."

—Huentetu

Updated by
Nicholas Gill

WITH TERRAIN RANGING FROM TOWERING Andean peaks to vast grasslands, deserts, wetlands, glaciers, and the huge Amazonian rain forest, South America's natural attractions are virtually unsurpassed. This topographical diversity guarantees ideal settings for almost any type of active or ecotourism adventure. Additionally, the continent claims some of the world's most renowned archaeological sites, a number of indigenous cultures, and an impressive array of wildlife, creating the perfect destination for off-the-beaten-path cultural experiences. You can explore the Amazon by riverboat, trek, ski, or climb the Andes, kayak along a fjord-studded coast, or view the Galápagos Islands' astonishing wildlife up close.

As in the past, today's travelers yearn to see the world's great cities, historical sites, and natural wonders. The difference is that today, far fewer travelers are content to experience all this from the air-conditioned comfort of a huge coach. Even tour operators known for their trips' five-star comfort are including soft-adventure components, such as hiking, canoeing, biking, or horseback riding, in most itineraries and have added "best available" lodgings to satisfy the increased demand for visits to more traditional locales.

Choosing a tour package carefully is always important, but it becomes even more critical when the focus is adventure or sports. You can rough it or opt for comfortable, sometimes even luxurious accommodations. You can select easy hiking or canoeing adventures or trekking, rafting, or climbing expeditions that require high degrees of physical endurance and technical skill. Study multiple itineraries to find the trip that's right for you.

This chapter describes selected trips from some of today's best adventure-tour operators in the travel world. Wisely chosen, special-interest vacations lead to distinctive, memorable experiences—just pack flexibility and curiosity along with the bug spray.

For additional information about a specific destination, contact the country's tourist office (often attached to the embassy) or the **South American Explorers Club** (⊠*126 Indian Creek Rd., Ithaca, NY 14850* ☎*607/277–0488 or 800/274–0568* ⊕*www.saexplorers.org*). This nonprofit organization is a good source for current information regarding travel throughout the continent. The Explorers Club also has clubhouses in Buenos Aires, Quito, Lima, and Cusco.

CHOOSING A TRIP

With hundreds of choices for special-interest trips to South America, there are a number of factors to keep in mind when deciding which company and package will be right for you.

How strenuous a trip do you want? Adventure vacations commonly are split into "soft" and "hard" adventures. Hard adventures, such as strenuous treks (often at high altitudes), Class IV or V rafting, or ascents of some of the world's most challenging mountains, generally require excellent physical conditioning and previous experience. Most hiking, biking, canoeing/kayaking, and similar soft adventures can be enjoyed by persons of all ages who are in good health and are accustomed to a reasonable amount of exercise. A little honesty goes a long way—recognize your own level of physical fitness and discuss it with the tour operator before signing on.

How far off the beaten path do you want to go? Depending on the tour operator and itinerary selected for a particular trip, you'll often have a choice of relatively easy travel and comfortable accommodations or more strenuous going with overnights spent camping or in basic lodgings. Ask yourself if it's the *reality* or the *image* of roughing it that appeals to you. Stick with the reality.

Is sensitivity to the environment important to you? If so, then determine whether it is equally important to the tour operator. Does the company protect the fragile environments you'll be visiting? Are some of the company's profits designated for conservation efforts or put back into the communities visited? Does it encourage indigenous people to dress up (or dress down) so that your group can get great photos, or does it respect their cultures as they are? Many of the companies included in this chapter are actively involved in environmental organizations and projects with indigenous communities visited on their trips.

What sort of group is best for you? At its best, group travel offers curious, like-minded people with whom to share the day's experiences. Do you enjoy a mix of companions or would you prefer similar demographics—for example, age-specific, singles, same sex? Inquire about the group size; many companies have a maximum of 10 to 16 members, but 30 or more is not unknown. The larger the group, the more time spent (or wasted) at rest stops, meals, and hotel arrivals and departures.

If groups aren't your thing, most companies will customize a trip just for you. In fact, this has become a major part of many tour operators' business. The itinerary can be as loose or as complete as you choose. Such travel offers all the conveniences of a package tour, but the "group" is composed of only you and those you've chosen as travel companions. Responding to a renewed interest in multigenerational travel, many tour operators also offer designated family departures, with itineraries carefully crafted to appeal both to children and adults.

The client consideration factor—strong or absent? Gorgeous photos and well-written tour descriptions go a long way in selling a company's trips. But what's called the client consideration factor is important, too. Does the operator provide useful information about health (suggested or required inoculations, tips for dealing with high altitudes)? A list of frequently asked questions (FAQ) and their answers? Recommended readings? Equipment needed for sports trips? Packing tips when baggage is restricted? Climate info? Visa requirements? A list of client referrals? The option of using your credit card? What is the refund policy if you must cancel? If you're traveling alone, will the company match you up with a like-minded traveler so you can avoid the sometimes exorbitant single supplement?

Are there hidden costs? Make sure you know what is and is not included in basic trip costs when comparing companies. International airfare is usually extra. Sometimes domestic flights are additional. Is trip insurance required, and if so, is it included? Are airport transfers included? Visa fees? Departure taxes? Gratuities? Equipment? Meals? Bottled water? All excursions? Although some travelers prefer the option of an excursion or free time, many, especially those visiting a destination for the first time, want to see as much as possible. Paying extra for a number of excursions can significantly increase the total cost of the trip. Many factors affect the price, and the trip that looks cheapest in the brochure could well turn out to be the most expensive. Don't assume that roughing it will save you money, as prices rise when limited access and a lack of essential supplies on-site require costly special arrangements.

TOUR OPERATORS

Below you'll find contact information for all tour operators mentioned in this chapter. For international tour operators, we list both the tour operator and its North American representative. For example, Exodus is represented in North America by Adventure Center. Although those listed hardly exhaust the number of reputable companies, these tour operators were chosen because they are established firms that offer a good selection of itineraries. Such operators are usually the first to introduce great new destinations, forging ahead before luxury hotels and air-conditioned coaches tempt less hardy visitors.

CRUISES

ANTARCTICA CRUISES

Founded to promote environmentally responsible travel to Antarctica, the **International Association of Antarctica Tour Operators** (☎ *970/704–1047* ⊕ *www.iaato.org*) is a good source of information, including suggested readings. Most companies operating Antarctica trips are members of this organization and display its logo in their brochures.

Season: November–March.
Location: Most cruises depart from Ushuaia, Argentina.
Cost: From $2,995 (triple-occupancy cabin) for 12 days from Ushuaia.
Tour Operators: Abercrombie & Kent; Adventure Center; Adventure Life; Big Five Tours & Expeditions; ElderTreks; G.A.P. Adventures; Lindblad Expeditions; Mountain Travel Sobek; Quark Expeditions; Travcoa; Wilderness Travel; Zegrahm Expeditions.

Ever since Lars-Eric Lindblad operated the first cruise to the "White Continent" in 1966, Antarctica has exerted an almost magnetic pull for serious travelers. From Ushuaia, the world's southernmost city, you'll sail for two (sometimes rough) days through the Drake Passage and then on to the spectacular landscapes of Antarctica. Most visits are to the Antarctic Peninsula, the continent's most accessible region. Accompanied by naturalists, you'll travel ashore in motorized rubber craft called Zodiacs to view penguins and nesting seabirds. Some cruises visit research stations, and many call at the Falkland, South Orkney, South Shetland, or South Georgia Islands. Adventure Center, Adventure Life, and Big Five Tours & Expeditions offer sea kayaking and, at an extra cost, the chance to camp for a night on the ice.

Expedition vessels have been fitted with ice-strengthened hulls; many originally were built as polar-research vessels. On certain Quark Expeditions itineraries you can travel aboard an icebreaker, the *Kapitan Khlebnikov,* which rides up onto the ice, crushing it with its weight. This vessel carries helicopters for aerial viewing.

When choosing an expedition cruise, it's wise to inquire about the qualifications of the on-board naturalists and historians, the maximum number of passengers carried, the ice readiness of the vessel, onboard medical facilities, whether there is an open bridge policy, and the number of landings attempted per day.

PATAGONIA COASTAL & LAKE CRUISES

Cruising the southern tip of South America presents you some of the earth's most spectacular scenery: fjords, glaciers, lagoons, lakes, narrow channels, waterfalls, forested shorelines, fishing villages, penguins, and other wildlife. Although many tour operators include a one- or two-day boating excursion as part of their Patagonia itineraries, the companies listed below offer from 4 to 12 nights aboard ship.

ARGENTINA & CHILE
Season: October–April.
Locations: Chilean fjords; Puerto Montt and Punta Arenas, Chile; Tierra del Fuego and Ushuaia, Argentina.
Cost: From $1,395 for 12 days from Buenos Aires.
Tour Operators: Abercrombie & Kent; Adventure Life; Big Five Tours & Expeditions; Explore! Worldwide; International Expeditions; Mountain Travel Sobek; Off the Beaten Path; Wilderness Travel; Wildland Adventures.

Boarding the comfortable M/V *Mare Australis* or M/V *Via Australis* in Punta Arenas, Chile, or Ushuaia, Argentina, you'll cruise the Strait of Magellan and the Beagle Channel, visiting glaciers, penguin rookeries, and seal colonies before heading north along the fjords of Chile's western coast. With Adventure Life and Abercrombie & Kent you'll savor the mountain scenery of Torres del Paine National Park before or following the cruise, while Mountain Travel Sobek and International Expeditions visit Tierra del Fuego National Park. Several of the companies also include Cape Horn National Park. Wilderness Travel allows time for hiking at Volcano Osorno and in Alerce Andino National Park; the latter protects the second-largest temperate rainforest ecosystem in the world. Following a five-day cruise, Off the Beaten Path travelers fly to Puerto Montt for a three-night stay at nearby Lake

Llanquihue, with opportunities for hiking in the mountains. In addition to the typical Torres del Paine trip, Wildland Adventures also has a cruise in a 50-foot yacht along the Chiloé Archipelago, a region rich in folklore about ghost ships, witch-like brujas, and magical sea creatures. Stops at the virgin forests of Parque Pumalín and the Carretera Austral are included in this Chiloé trip.

LEARNING VACATIONS

CULTURAL TOURS

Among the many types of travel, some find the most rewarding to be an in-depth focus on one aspect of a country's culture. This could mean exploring the archaeological remains of great civilizations, learning about the lives and customs of indigenous peoples, or trying to master a foreign language or culinary skills.

CHILE
Season: Year-round.
Locations: Atacama Desert; Easter Island; Santa Cruz.
Cost: From $1,795 for seven days from Santiago.
Tour Operators: Abercrombie & Kent; Big Five Tours & Expeditions; Far Horizons; G.A.P. Adventures; Ladatco Tours; Myths and Mountains; Nature Expeditions International; PanAmerican Travel; South American Journeys; Tours International; World Expeditions.

In the Pacific Ocean 3,680 km (2,300 mi) west of the Chilean mainland, remote Easter Island is famed for its *moais,* nearly 1,000 stone statues whose brooding eyes gaze over the windswept landscape. Abercrombie & Kent, Far Horizons, Myths and Mountains, and Nature Expeditions are among the tour operators that will take you there. Far Horizons' departure is timed for the annual Tapati festival. Vying with Easter Island as a cultural experience, the Atacama, generally considered the world's driest desert, is a region of bizarre landscapes, ancient petroglyphs (designs scratched or cut into rock), geoglyphs (designs formed by arranging stones or earth), and mummies. Many of the above companies have Atacama programs. For a cultural experience of another sort, join PanAmerican Travel's nine-day round of Chilean vineyards, where you'll enjoy tours, tastings, and even the occasional vineyard lunch. World Expeditions offers a similar trip by bicycle: the eight-day Chile Wine Route By Bike, where you'll cycle from vineyard to vineyard in the Rosario, Casablanca, and Aconcagua valleys. G.A.P. Adventures takes you from Santiago to Buenos Aires, stopping for tastings at wineries and cooking classes along the way in Mendoza and Córdoba in their 10-day Gourmet Adventure.

SCIENTIFIC RESEARCH TRIPS

Joining a research expedition team gives you more than great photos. By assisting scientists, you can make significant contributions to better understanding the continent's unique ecosystems and cultural heritages. Flexibility and a sense of humor are important assets for these trips, which often require roughing it.

THE OUTDOORS

BIRD-WATCHING TOURS

When selecting a bird-watching tour, ask questions. What species might be seen? What are the guide's qualifications? Does the operator work to protect natural habitats? What equipment is used? (In addition to binoculars, this should include a high-powered telescope, an audio recorder to record and play back bird calls as a way of attracting birds, and a spotlight for night viewing.)

ANTARCTICA

Season: January; November–December.
Locations: Antarctic Peninsula; Falkland Islands; South Georgia.
Cost: From $14,595 for 19 days from Ushuaia.
Tour Operator: Victor Emanuel Nature Tours, Wild Wings.

Arguably the ultimate travel adventure, Antarctica exerts a strong pull on nature lovers. Now a trip has been designed to focus on the special interests of serious birders. Victor Emanuel brings you aboard the *Clipper Adventurer,* from which you'll view wandering, light-mantled, and royal albatrosses; snow petrels along with several other petrel species; and large colonies of king and macaroni penguins. Wild Wings cruises to Antarctica, as well as South Georgia and the Falkland Islands. Zodiac boats make coming ashore in remote locations easy.

CHILE

Seasons: October–November.
Locations: Atacama Desert; Lake District; Patagonia.
Cost: From $3,999 for 16 days from Santiago.
Tour Operators: Focus Tours; Victor Emanuel Nature Tours; WINGS.

Chile spans a number of distinctive vegetational and altitudinal zones, ensuring a varied and abundant avian population. On a 16-day journey to the northern and central regions, Focus Tours participants visit the ski areas of Farellones and Valle Nevado to spot the rare Crag Chilia, an earth-creeper-like bird; Los Cipreses Reserve, stronghold of the burrowing parrot; La Campana National Park, which holds five of Chile's eight endemic species; the Andes for the rare and threatened white-tailed shrike-tyrant; plus the arid Atacama and Lauca National Park. WINGS's itinerary covers the country from Tierra del Fuego in the south to the Atacama Desert in the north, also spending time in Patagonia and the Lake District. Victor Emanuel has created a unique tour that explores bird life while cruising for 23 days from Cape Horn in Southern Patagonia to the Cape of Good Hope in South Africa.

NATURAL HISTORY

Many operators have created nature-focused programs that provide insight into the importance and fragility of South America's ecological treasures. The itineraries mentioned below take in the deserts, glaciers, rain forests, mountains, and rivers of this continent, as well as the impressive variety of its wildlife.

ARGENTINA & CHILE
Season: October–April.
Locations: Atacama Desert; Buenos Aires; Lake District; Patagonia; Santiago.
Cost: From $790 for four days from Bariloche.
Tour Operators: Abercrombie & Kent; Adventure Life; Big Five Tours & Expeditions; ElderTreks; G.A.P. Adventures; Geographic Expeditions; Inca; Journeys International; Myths and Mountains; Nature Expeditions International; Off the Beaten Path; PanAmerican Travel; South American Journeys; Southwind Adventures; Wilderness Travel; Wildland Adventures; World Expeditions, Zeghram Expeditions.

The southern tip of Argentina and Chile, commonly referred to as Patagonia, has long been a prime ecotourism destination, and nature lovers will find no lack of tour offerings for this region. You'll view the glaciers of Los Glaciares National Park, where the Moreno Glacier towers 20 stories high; the soaring peaks of Torres del Paine; the fjords of the Chilean coast; and a Magellanic penguin colony. Most itineraries spend some days in the Lake District, possibly traversing the fantastic Cruce del Lagos ferry route between the countries. Many programs include day walks and, often, a one- to three-day cruise. Several operators feature a stay at a historic ranch, Estancia Helsingfors. The Atacama Desert of northern Chile is nature of another sort. Abercrombie & Kent has a "Fire and Ice" itinerary, combining the deep south with this arid zone. Zeghram Expeditions' 15-day program explores the natural highlights of Patagonia with stops in Torres del Paine, the Perito Moreno glacier, and the Península Valdéz.

PHOTO SAFARIS

An advantage of photo tours is the amount of time spent at each place visited. Whether the subject is a rarely spotted animal, a breathtaking waterfall, or villagers in traditional dress, you get a chance to focus both your camera and your mind on the scene before you. The tours listed below are led by professional photographers who offer instruction and hands-on tips. If you're not serious about improving your photographic skills, these trips might not be the best choice, as you could become impatient with the pace.

ANTARCTICA
Season: October; January–February.
Locations: Antarctic Peninsula; Falkland, South Georgia, and South Orkney Islands.
Cost: From 11,795 for 28 days from Ushuaia.
Tour Operator: Joseph Van Os Photo Safaris.

Photograph seabirds, Adélie and gentoo penguin colonies, albatross nesting areas, and elephant and fur seals, plus the spectacular landscapes of the Antarctic. With Joseph Van Os, you'll travel for 28 days aboard their research expedition ship *Ushuaia,* which carries its own fleet of Jacques Cousteau–designed Zodiac landing craft. Highlights include Paulet Island, home of Adélie Penguin colonies, and cruising the Neumayer and Lemaire Channels.

ARGENTINA & CHILE
Season: March–April.
Locations: Central Patagonia; Easter Island; Los Glaciares and Torres del Paine national parks.
Cost: From $5,395 for 15 days from Buenos Aires.
Tour Operators: Joseph Van Os Photo Safaris.

Timed for vibrant fall colors among ice fields, snowcapped mountains, glaciers, and rushing streams, Joseph Van Os has a 15-day departure during the Patagonian fall (during the months of the northern hemisphere's spring). The trip visits the famed Torres del Paine and Los Glaciares national parks and lesser-known regions in central Patagonia.

SPORTS

A sports-focused trip offers a great way to get a feel for the part of the country you're visiting and to interact with local people. A dozen bicyclists entering a village, for instance, would arouse more interest and be more approachable than a group of 30 stepping off a tour bus. Although many itineraries do not require a high level of skill, it is expected that your interest in the sport focused on in a particular tour be more than casual. On the other hand, some programs are designed for those who are highly experienced. In either case, good physical conditioning, experience with high altitudes (on certain itineraries), and a flexible attitude are important. Weather can be changeable, dictating the choices of hiking and climbing routes. If you're not a particularly strong hiker or cyclist, determine if support vehicles accompany the group or if alternate activities or turnaround points are available on more challenging days.

BICYCLING

ARGENTINA & CHILE
Season: October–March.
Locations: Atacama Desert; Bariloche; Lake District; Mendoza; Patagonia; Salta.

Cost: From $2,545 for eight days from San Carlos de Bariloche.
Tour Operators: Australian & Amazonian Adventures; Butterfield & Robinson; Experience Plus!; Global Adventure Guide.

Global Adventure's 15-day journey, graded moderate with some uphill challenges and occasional single-track riding, twice crosses the lower Andes as you ride along paved and dirt roads through forests and past volcanoes. The itinerary encompasses both the Lake District and Patagonia, with occasional opportunities for rafting, canyoning, or volcano climbing. Nicknamed a "two-wheeled tango," Butterfield & Robinson's nine-day trip begins in Santiago and ends in Buenos Aires (traveled mostly, but not all, by bike), stopping in Chile's Atacama Desert and Argentina's wine country along the way. Starting in Bariloche, Experience Plus! cycles up to 93 km (58 mi) a day around Lake Llanquihue for views of volcanoes; there's also the chance for Class III rafting on Río Petrohué. Choose from four biking journeys with Australian & Amazonian Adventures, one to Chile's Lake District, another biking from Salta to San Miguel de Tucumán, and others traversing the Andes between the countries. Most nights are spent camping.

CANOEING, KAYAKING & WHITE-WATER RAFTING

White-water rafting and kayaking can be exhilarating experiences. You don't have to be an expert paddler to enjoy many of these adventures, but you should be a strong swimmer. Rivers are rated from Class I to Class V according to difficulty of navigation. Generally speaking, Class I–III rapids are suitable for beginners, while Class IV–V rapids are strictly for the experienced. Canoeing is a gentler river experience.

CHILE
Season: November–March.
Locations: Chiloé Archipelago; Northern Patagonia; Río Futaleufú.
Cost: From $680 for four days from Castro, in Chiloé.
Tour Operators: Adventure Life; Australian & Amazonian Expeditions; Earth River Expeditions; Hidden Trails; PanAmerican Travel.

Chile has both scenic fjords for sea kayaking and challenging rivers for white-water rafting. With PanAmerican Travel, sea kayakers can spend nine days exploring the fjords, waterfalls, and hot springs of the country's rugged coast, camping at night. Australian & Amazonian Adventures offers three- to six-day kayaking experiences. On the four-day itinerary, you'll discover the islands of the Chiloé Archipelago, a region rich in folklore, while the six-day program explores the fjords of northern Patagonia. For the experienced rafter, the Class IV and V rapids of Río Futaleufú, often considered the best rafting river in the world, offer many challenges. Its sheer-walled canyons boast such well-named rapids as Infierno and Purgatorio. Earth River's 10-day program here includes a rock climb up 98-meter (320-foot) Torre de los Vientos and a Tyrolean traverse where, wearing a climbing harness attached to a pulley, you pull yourself across a rope strung above the rapids. With tree houses and riverside hot tubs formed from natural potholes, overnight camping becomes an exotic experience. Earth River also offers a kayaking journey over a chain of three lakes, surrounded by snowcapped mountains. Access is by floatplane. Hidden Trails and Adventure Life have Futaleufú rafting trips; the latter's program offers, in addition to shooting the rapids, horseback riding in the mountains, kayaking, and fishing.

FISHING

ARGENTINA & CHILE
Season: Year-round.
Locations: Chiloé; Lake District; Patagonia.
Cost: From $3,250 for seven days from Balmaceda, Chile.
Tour Operators: Fishing International; FishQuest; Fly Fishing And; Pan-American Travel; Rod & Reel Adventures.

For anglers, Argentina and Chile are the southern hemisphere's Alaska, offering world-class trout fishing in clear streams. An added bonus is the availability of landlocked salmon and golden dorado, known as the river tiger. Bilingual fishing guides accompany groups, and accommodations are in comfortable lodges with private baths. Although November is the usual opening date for freshwater fishing, the season begins two months earlier at Lago Llanquihue because of the large resident fish population. Rod & Reel takes advantage of this, basing participants at a lodge near Osorno volcano. With Fly Fishing And, your 10 days will be divided between El Encuentro and La Patagonia lodges, meaning you can fish several rivers and creeks, while PanAmerican's seven-day program breaks up lodge stays with a night of riverside camping. Fishing International offers an Argentina program fishing the Ibera marshes for dorado and a Chile trip based at an estancia (ranch) where you can fish two rivers for brown trout weighing up to 15 pounds, as well as trips to lodges throughout both countries including Tierra del Fuego. FishQuest has four itineraries, offering fishing at a variety of rivers for brown and rainbow trout, dorado, giant catfish, and salmon.

HIKING, RUNNING & TREKKING

South America's magnificent scenery and varied terrain make it a terrific place for trekkers and hikers. The southern part of Argentina and Chile, known as Patagonia, and Peru's Inca Trail are especially popular. Numerous tour operators offer hiking and trekking trips to these regions, so study several offerings to determine the program that's best suited to your ability and interests. The trips outlined below are organized tours led by qualified guides. Camping is often part of the experience, although on some trips you stay at inns and small hotels. Itineraries range from relatively easy hikes to serious trekking and even running.

ARGENTINA & CHILE
Season: October–April.
Locations: Atacama Desert; Lake District; Patagonia; Salta.
Cost: From $1,619 for 15 days from El Calafate, Argentina.

Tour Operators: Adventure Life; American Alpine Institute; Andes Adventures; Australian & Amazonian Adventures; BikeHike Adventures; Butterfield & Robinson; Country Walkers; Geographic Expeditions; KE Adventure Travel; Mountain Travel Sobek; Southwind Adventures; The World Outdoors; Wilderness Travel; Wildland Adventures; World Expeditions.

Patagonia may be the most trekked region in South America. All the above companies have programs here, ranging from relatively easy hikes (Butterfield & Robinson, Country Walkers) to serious treks that gain up to 800 meters (2,625 feet) in elevation daily and ice and snow traverses using crampons (American Alpine Institute). Almost every operator runs tours to Torres del Paine in Chile and places just across the border around El Calafate, often combining the two, while just a few operate in more remote places such as Tierra del Fuego or the Southern Ice Fields. Adventure Life's program lets you overnight in igloo-shaped tents at EcoCamp in Torres del Paine. In addition to its hiking trip, Andes Adventures offers an 18-day running itinerary with runs of as much as 31 km (19 mi) per day. Other options include an Atacama Desert trek with KE Adventure Travel that includes an ascent of Licancabur Volcano or a Futaleufú Canyon trek with Wilderness Travel.

HORSEBACK RIDING

CHILE
Season: October–April; year-round, Atacama.
Locations: Atacama Desert; Patagonia; Easter Island; Río Hurtado Valley.
Cost: From $1,100 for six days from Rapa Nui.
Tour Operators: Equitours; Hidden Trails.

On Equitours's 12-day "Patagonia Glacier Ride," you cross the pampas to Torres del Paine National Park, a region of mountains, lakes, and glaciers. Nights are spent camping or in lodges. Hidden Trails has 15 different itineraries. You can opt for a ride in southern Chile, along historic mule trails created by gold diggers, and into the Andes; join an Atacama Desert adventure riding over the crusted salt of the Salar de Atacama and visiting ancient ruins and petroglyphs; explore moais, caves, craters, and beaches on Easter Island; or choose from four Patagonia programs. If getting off the beaten path appeals to you, consider the company's "Glacier Camping Ride," which ventures into remote areas accessible only on foot or horseback.

MOUNTAINEERING

Only the most towering peaks of Asia vie with the Andes in the challenges and rewards awaiting mountaineers. This is no casual sport, so ask questions, and be honest about your level of fitness and experience. Safety should be the company's—and your—first priority. Are the guides certified by professional organizations such as the American Mountain Guides Association? Are they certified as wilderness first responders and trained in technical mountain rescue? What is the climber-to-guide ratio? Are extra days built into the schedule to allow for adverse weather? Is there serious adherence to "leave no trace" environmental ethics? Several of the tour operators mentioned below have their own schools in the United States and/or other countries that offer multilevel courses in mountaineering, ice climbing, rock climbing, and avalanche education.

ANTARCTICA

Season: November–January.
Location: Mt. Vinson.
Cost: $29,500 for 22 days from Punta Arenas.
Tour Operator: Alpine Ascents International; Mountain Madness.

If you have a solid mountaineering background and are accustomed to cold-weather camping, this could be the ultimate mountaineering adventure. A short flight from Patriot Hills brings you to the base camp of Antarctica's highest peak. With loaded sleds, you move up the mountain, establishing two or three camps before attempting the 4,897-meter (16,067-foot) summit of Mt. Vinson. Although the climb itself is considered technically moderate, strong winds and extreme temperatures, as low as -40°F, make this a serious challenge. Additionally, Alpine Ascents offers the chance to ski from the 89th to the 90th parallel. Aircraft will bring you within 70 mi of the South Pole; then ski the rest of the way. This unique adventure can be made independently or as an extension of the Vinson climb.

ARGENTINA & CHILE

Season: November–February.
Locations: Mt. Aconcagua.
Cost: From $2,980 for 11 days from Calafate, Argentina.
Tour Operators: Alpine Ascents International; American Alpine Institute; Colorado Mountain School; KE Adventure Travel; Mountain Madness; World Expeditions.

At 6,960 meters (22,835 feet), Argentina's Mt. Aconcagua is the highest peak in the world outside of a few in the Himalayas. Though some routes are not technically difficult, Aconcagua is quite demanding physically and requires the use of ice axes, crampons, and ropes. All the above operators offer climbs of Aconcagua, some via the more difficult Polish glacier route. Frequent high winds and ice make this route very challenging and only for those with extensive mountaineering experience at high altitudes. American Alpine Institute has a second expedition with ascents of Cerro Marconi Sur and Fitzroy Massifs, in southern Patagonia, where you can traverse part of the Patagonian ice cap.

Tour Operators

Abercrombie & Kent ✉ *1520 Kensington Rd., Oak Brook, IL 60523* ☎ *630/954–2944 or 800/554–7016* ⊕ *www.abercrombiekent.com.*

Adventure Center ✉ *1311 63rd St., Suite 200, Emeryville, CA 94608* ☎ *510/654–1879 or 800/227–8747* ⊕ *www.adventurecenter.com.*

Adventure Life ✉ *1655 S. 3rd St. W, Suite 1, Missoula, MT 59801* ☎ *406/541–2677 or 800/344–6118* ⊕ *www.adventure-life.com.*

Alpine Ascents International ✉ *121 Mercer St., Seattle, WA 98109* ☎ *206/378–1927* ⊕ *www.Alpine Ascents.com.*

American Alpine Institute ✉ *1515 12th St., Bellingham, WA 98225* ☎ *360/671–1505* ⊕ *www. mtnguide.com.*

Andes Adventures ✉ *1323 12th St., Suite F, Santa Monica, CA 90401* ☎ *310/395–5265 or 800/289–9470* ⊕ *www.andesadventures.com.*

Australian & Amazonian Adventures ✉ *2711 Market Garden, Austin, TX 78745* ☎ *512/443–5393 or 800/232–5658* ⊕ *www.amazon adventures.com.*

Big Five Tours & Expeditions ✉ *1551 S.E. Palm Ct., Stuart, FL 34994* ☎ *772/287–7995 or 800/244–3483* ⊕ *www.bigfive.com.*

BikeHike Adventures ✉ *200-1807 Maritime Mews, Vancouver, British Columbia V6H 3W7 Canada* ☎ *604/731–2442 or 888/805–0061* ⊕ *www.bikehike.com.*

Butterfield & Robinson ✉ *70 Bond St., Suite 300, Toronto, Ontario M5B 1X3 Canada* ☎ *416/864–1354 or 866/551–9090* ⊕ *www.butterfield.com.*

Colorado Mountain School ✉ *341 Moraine Ave., Estes Park, CO 80517* ☎ *800/836–4008* ⊕ *www.total climbing.com.*

Country Walkers ✉ *Box 180, Waterbury, VT 05676* ☎ *802/244–1387 or 800/464–9255* ⊕ *www.country walkers.com.*

Earth River Expeditions ✉ *180 Towpath Rd., Accord, NY 12404* ☎ *845/626–2665 or 800/643–2784* ⊕ *www.earthriver.com.*

ElderTreks ✉ *597 Markham St., Toronto, Ontario M6G 2L7 Canada* ☎ *416/588–5000 or 800/741–7956* ⊕ *www.eldertreks.com.*

Equitours ⊕ *Box 807, Dubois, WY 82513* ☎ *307/455–3363 or 800/545–0019* ⊕ *www.equitours.com.*

Experience Plus! ✉ *415 Mason Ct., #1, Fort Collins, CO 80524* ☎ *970/484–8489 or 800/685–4565* ⊕ *www.ExperiencePlus.com.*

Explore! Worldwide This company is represented in North America by Adventure Center (contact information under A, above). ✉ *Hampshire GU14 7PA U.K.* ⊕ *www.explore.co.uk.*

Far Horizons ⊕ *Box 2546, San Anselmo, CA 94979* ☎ *415/482–8400 or 800/552–4575* ⊕ *www. farhorizons.com.*

Fishing International ✉ *5510 Skylane Blvd., Suite 200, Santa Rosa, CA 95405* ☎ *707/542–4242 or 800/950–4242* ⊕ *www.fishinginternational.com.*

FishQuest ✉ *152 North Main St., Hiawassee, GA 30546* ☎ *706/896–1403 or 888/891–3474* ⊕ *www. fishquest.com.*

Fly Fishing And ✆ *Box 1719, Red Lodge, MT 59068* ☎ *406/425–9452* ⊕ *www.flyfishingand.com.*

Focus Tours ✉ *Box 22276, Santa Fe, NM 87502* ☎ *505/989–7193* ⊕ *www.focustours.com.*

G.A.P. Adventures ✉ *19 Charlotte St., Toronto, Ontario M5V 2H5 Canada* ☎ *416/260–0999 or 800/708–7761* ⊕ *www.gapadventures.com.*

Geographic Expeditions ✉ *1008 General Kennedy Ave., San Francisco, CA 94129* ☎ *415/922–0448 or 800/777–8183* ⊕ *www.geoex.com.*

Global Adventure Guide ✉ *14 Kennaway Rd., Unit 3, Christchurch, 8002 New Zealand* ☎ *800/732–0861 in North America* ⊕ *www.global adventureguide.com.*

Hidden Trails ✉ *659A Moberly Rd., Vancouver, British Columbia V5Z 4B3 Canada* ☎ *604/323–1141 or 888/987–2457* ⊕ *www.hiddentrails.com*

Inca ✉ *1311 63rd St., Emeryville, CA 94608* ☎ *510/420–1550* ⊕ *www.inca1.com.*

Joseph Van Os Photo Safaris ✆ *Box 655, Vashon Island, WA 98070* ☎ *206/463–5383* ⊕ *www.photo safaris.com.*

Journeys International ✉ *107 Aprill Dr., Suite 3, Ann Arbor, MI 48103* ☎ *734/665–4407 or 800/255–8735* ⊕ *www.journeys-intl.com.*

KE Adventure Travel ✉ *3300 E. 1st Ave., Suite 250, Denver, CO 81601* ☎ *303/321–0085 or 800/497–9675* ⊕ *www.keadventure.com.*

Ladatco Tours ✉ *2200 S. Dixie Hwy., Suite 704, Coconut Grove, FL 33133* ☎ *800/327–6162* ⊕ *www.ladatco.com.*

Lindblad Expeditions ✉ *96 Morton St., New York, NY 10014* ☎ *212/765–7740 or 800/397–3348* ⊕ *www.expeditions.com.*

Mountain Madness ✉ *3018 S.W. Charlestown St., Seattle, WA 98126* ☎ *206/937–8389 or 800/328–5925* ⊕ *www.mountainmadness.com.*

Mountain Travel Sobek ✉ *1266 66th St., Suite 4, Emeryville, CA 94608* ☎ *510/594–6000 or 888/687–6235* ⊕ *www.mtsobek.com.*

Myths and Mountains ✉ *976 Tee Ct., Incline Village, NV 89451* ☎ *775/832–5454 or 800/670–6984* ⊕ *www.mythsandmountains.com.*

Nature Expeditions International ✉ *7860 Peters Rd., Suite F-103, Plantation, FL 33324* ☎ *954/693–8852 or 800/869–0639* ⊕ *www.naturexp.com.*

Off the Beaten Path ✉ *7 E. Beall, Bozeman, MT 59715* ☎ *800/445–2995* ⊕ *www.offthebeatenpath.com.*

PanAmerican Travel Services ✉ *320 E. 900 S, Salt Lake City, UT 84111* ☎ *800/364–4359* ⊕ *www.panamtours.com.*

PowderQuest Tours ✉ *7108 Pinetree Rd., Richmond, VA 23229* ☎ *206/203–6065 or 888/565–7158* ⊕ *www.powderquest.com.*

Quark Expeditions ✉ *1019 Post Rd., Darien, CT 06820* ☎ *203/656–0499 or 800/356–5699* ⊕ *www.quarkexpeditions.com.*

Rod & Reel Adventures ✉ *32617 Skyhawk Way, Eugene, OR 97405* ☎ *541/349–0777 or 800/356–6982* ⊕ *www.rodreeladventures.com.*

Tour Operators (continued)

Snoventures ✉ Cedar Ave., Huddersfield HD1 5QH U.K. ☎ 775/586–9133 in North America ⊕ www.snoventures.com.

South American Journeys ✉ 9921 Cabanas Ave., Tujunga, CA 91042 ☎ 818/951–8986 or 800/884–7474 ⊕ www.southamericanjourneys.com.

Southwind Adventures ⊿ Box 621057, Littleton, CO 80162 ☎ 303/972–0701 or 800/377–9463 ⊕ www.southwindadventures.com.

The World Outdoors ✉ 2840 Wilderness Pl., Suite D, Boulder, CO 80301 ☎ 303/413–0938 or 800/488–8483 ⊕ www.theworldoutdoors.com.

Tours International ✉ 12750 Briar Forest Dr., Suite 603, Houston, TX 77077 ☎ 800/247–7965 ⊕ www.toursinternational.com.

Travcoa ✉ 4340 Von Karman Ave., Suite 400, Newport Beach, CA 92660 ☎ 949/476–2800 or 800/992–2003 ⊕ www.travcoa.com.

Victor Emanuel Nature Tours ✉ 2525 Wallingwood Dr., Suite 1003, Austin, TX 78746 ☎ 512/328–5221 or 800/328–8368 ⊕ www.ventbird.com.

Wilderness Travel ✉ 1102 9th St., Berkeley, CA 94710 ☎ 510/558–2488 or 800/368–2794 ⊕ www.wildernesstravel.com.

Wildland Adventures ✉ 3516 N.E. 155th St., Seattle, WA 98155 ☎ 206/365–0686 or 800/345–4453 ⊕ www.wildland.com.

Wild Wings ✉ 577–579 Fishponds Rd., Fishponds, Bristol, BS163AF U.K. ☎ 0117/965–333 ⊕ www.wildwings.co.uk.

WINGS ✉ 1643 N. Alvernon, Suite 109, Tucson, AZ 85712 ☎ 520/320–9868 or 888/293–6443 ⊕ www.wingsbirds.com.

World Expeditions ✉ 580 Market St., Suite 225, San Francisco, CA 94104 ☎ 415/989–2212 or 888/464–8735 ⊕ www.worldexpeditions.com.

Zegrahm & Eco Expeditions ✉ 192 Nickerson St., #200, Seattle, WA 98109 ☎ 206/285–4000 or 800/628–8747 ⊕ www.zeco.com.

MULTISPORT

Only a few years ago, multisport offerings were so sparse that the topic didn't merit inclusion in this chapter. Since then, such trips have grown in popularity every year and now form an important part of the programs of many adventure-tour operators. Innovative itineraries combine two or more sports, such as biking, fishing, canoeing, hiking, horseback riding, kayaking, rafting, and trekking.

ARGENTINA & CHILE
Season: November–April.
Locations: Lake District; northern Chile; Patagonia; Río Futaleufú, Chile.
Cost: From $1862 for 10 days from Buenos Aires, Argentina.
Tour Operators: American Alpine Institute; Australian & Amazonian Adventures; BikeHike Adventures; Earth River Expeditions; Hidden Trails; Mountain Madness; Mountain Travel Sobek; Nature Expedi-

tions International; The World Outdoors; Wilderness Travel; World Expeditions.

Mountain Travel Sobek and Hidden Trails combine horseback riding with sea kayaking in Southern Patagonia, while Mountain Madness offers hut-to-hut trekking and glacier walking in the Torres del Paine area along with kayaking on the Río Serrano. Nature Expeditions offers soft adventure options such as hiking, rafting (Class II and III rapids), and horseback riding. BikeHike has two multisport trips in Argentina and Chile; you can hike, raft, sea-kayak, bike, and ride horses in the Lake District or hike, ride horses, and sandboard in northern Chile. If you want to try serious rafting, consider one of the Río Futaleufú trips, such as those run by Earth River Expeditions and The World Outdoors; these programs also include hiking and horseback riding.

SKIING

When ski season's over in the Northern Hemisphere, it's time to pack the gear and head for resorts in Argentina or Chile. Advanced and expert skiers will find seemingly endless terrain, and powder hounds will discover the ultimate ski. If your present level leans more toward beginner or intermediate, not to worry. Adventures aplenty await you, too. Snowboarders, also, will find the southern mountains much to their liking. In addition to marked trails, there's off-piste terrain, often with steep chutes and deep powder bowls, plus backcountry areas to try. Those with strong skills could opt for heli-skiing on peaks reaching 4,200 meters (13,600 feet) as condors soar above. As hard as it might be to break away from the slopes, a day of hiking or snowshoeing would be well-spent. Many of the resorts exude a European ambience with a lively nightlife scene. Everywhere, you'll be surrounded by some of Earth's grandest natural beauty. The tour operators mentioned below have created all-inclusive ski packages covering airport/hotel and hotel/ski mountain transfers, accommodations, two meals daily, and lift tickets for a number of mountains and resorts in both Argentina and Chile; many packages combine the two countries. Costs vary with the accommodations selected. Prices quoted are per person double; costs are even lower if four people share a room. Be aware that less expensive packages, while providing the services mentioned, generally are not guided tours. Eight-day guided packages start around $1,795.

CHILE

Season: June–October.
Locations: El Colorado; La Parva; Portillo; Pucón; Termas de Chillán; Valle Nevado.
Cost: From $730 for a seven-day non-guided inclusive package from Santiago.
Tour Operators: Ladatco Tours; PowderQuest; Snoventures.

A short drive from Santiago, Valle Nevado has more than 300 acres of groomed runs and an 800-meter (2,600-foot) vertical drop. Famous for powder, it's also home to the Andes Express, a chair lift so super-fast you can get in extra runs each day. From Valle Nevado you can interconnect with the slopes of nearby El Colorado and La Parva, making for a vast amount of skiable terrain. First-rate heli-skiing, heli-board-ing, and even hang gliding can be taken out of Valle Nevado; the off-piste is excellent, as well. A snowboard camp is based here coached by North American AASI level-three certified instructors. Participation in the seven-day program, divided into first-time and advanced groups, can be arranged by PowderQuest. Near the base of Mt. Aconcagua, the highest mountain in the western hemisphere, Portillo is ranked on numerous lists as one of the top 10 ski resorts in the world. Several national ski teams have their off-season training here. The heli-ski-ing is enviable, and Portillo's lively après-ski life comes as an added bonus. Yet another world-class resort, Termas de Chillán, has what one tour operator terms "killer slopes," plus a network of forest tracks for cross-country skiers. Its 28 runs along 35 km (22 mi) of groomed trails include one that at 13 km (6 mi) is South America's longest. Boasting one of Chile's deepest snow packs, the resort offers varied terrain on two volcanoes for skiing or snowboarding, plus a thermal area com-prised of nine pools for end-of-the-day relaxation. At the small resort of Pucón, on the edge of Lago Villarrica, ski on the side of Chile's most active volcano. You can hike to the crater to gaze at molten magma, then ski or snowboard back down. Bordering two national parks plus a national reserve, Pucón boasts great snowshoeing. PowderQuest and Snoventures offer inclusive packages to all the resorts mentioned. Ski weeks without guides run in the $730–$800 range. PowderQuest's main focus is guided tours of 8–16 days, with time spent at as many as seven resorts in both Argentina and Chile. Ladatco offers packages to Valle Nevado, Portillo, and Chillán.

UNDERSTANDING
CHILE

Traveling in a Thin
Country

Spanish Vocabulary

TRAVELING IN A THIN COUNTRY

WHEN CHILEANS JOKE that their nation was crafted from the universe's leftovers, they are only partly jesting. Chile's thin ribbon of territory comprises some of nature's most spectacular anomalies: the looming Andes impose the country's eastern boundaries, stretching from the desolate Atacama Desert to the archipelagos and fjords of forbidding Patagonia, where the concept of the final frontier is still fresh in the hearts of its inhabitants. Just above Puerto Montt lies a land of alpine lakes, with its distinctively German and Swiss cultural enclaves. The central Maipo Valley, fertile home of Chile's famous vineyards and fruit fields, also houses the frenzy of cosmopolitan Santiago.

All of this fits into one sliver of land squeezed between the Andes and the Pacific Ocean. In some places the 320-km (200-mi) territorial limit is actually wider than the country itself, making Chile as much water as earth.

As might be expected in a country with a coastline stretching for more than 4,000 km (2,500 mi), many parts of Chile are inaccessible by land. Because of the unusual topography, highways simply end when they reach fjords or ice fields. You'll need to take a ship to see the mammoth glacier in the heart of Parque Nacional Laguna San Rafael. A ferry ride is necessary to visit Chiloé, an archipelago where you'll find charming wooden churches built by missionaries. Distant Easter Island, in the middle of the Pacific Ocean, is reachable only by a five-hour flight from the mainland.

The region known today as Chile has been inhabited for millennia. One of the oldest known people were the Chinchorros, who lived along the coast of El Norte Grande beginning about 6000 bc. This nomadic people learned the process of mummifying their dead 5,000 years ago—thousands of years before the Egyptians. Nearby in the antiplano lived the Aymara, who herded llamas and alpacas and cultivated barley and potatoes. In El Norte Chico were the Diaguitas, whose finely detailed bowls and pitchers are among the most beautiful of pre-Columbian ceramics, and the Molles, who carved the intricate petroglyphs in the Valle del Encanto.

The first invaders did not come from Europe, but from elsewhere in South America. The Mapuches crossed the Andes from what is today Argentina and established a stronghold in the Lake District. In the process they gradually absorbed the peoples already living in the region. The Incas, who arrived in the 15th century, were much more brutal. Pushing southward from their empire in Peru, the Incas dismantled existing cultures, forcing indigenous peoples to give up their language and their rituals. Only the fierce resistance of the Mapuches halted the expansion of the Inca empire.

The first European to reach Chile barely gave it a glance: Spanish conquistador Hernando de Magallanes left his name and little else behind when he journeyed up the Southern Coast in 1520. Diego de Almagro was the first Spaniard actually to explore the region. Setting out from Peru in 1535, Almagro and a ragged crew of 500 adventurers marched south in search of fame and fortune. When the band reached the Aconcagua Valley, they fled after an extended battle with the Mapuches. Pedro de Valdivia, who led another gang of adventurers south along the roads constructed by the Incas, broke ground for Santiago in 1541. He founded several other towns, including Concepción and Villarrica, before he died during a skirmish with the Mapuches.

Spain had its hands full with the rest of its empire in South America, so Chile was pretty much ignored. The residents, even those who had profited under colonial rule, eventually grew tired of having others govern their land. After Chile won its independence from Spain in a war that lasted from 1810 to 1818, the new nation sought to establish firm control of its entire territory. In 1843, it sent a frigate carrying a ragtag contingent of 19 men to the Strait of Magellan. There the men built a wooden fort called Fuerte Bulnes, thus establishing the country's first permanent settlement in the southernmost reaches of Patagonia. Chile also began to dream about expansion northward. The 1879 War of the Pacific pitted Chile against its two neighbors to the north, Bolivia and Peru. Chile gained much of the nitrate-rich land of the Atacama Desert, and Bolivia lost its only outlet to the sea.

For more than 300 years, the Mapuches successfully defended much of the Lake District against the encroachment of the Spanish. But the proud people could not hold out against the Chileans. The last great rebellion of the Mapuche people failed in 1881, and soon afterward the Chilean government started shipping in German, Swiss, and other European colonists to fill the "empty" lands.

Chile's government was hampered for almost a century by an 1830 constitution that granted enormous powers to the president, thus encouraging autocratic rule. After a civil war in 1891, Congress seized control, diminishing the president to a mere figurehead. This unstable system, which caused constant clashes between the presidential and legislative branches, was replaced in 1925 with a new constitution that sought to find a delicate balance.

By the 1950s, left-wing political parties representing working-class people began to gain considerable strength. In 1970, the push for governmental reform led to the election of Salvador Allende, Chile's first socialist president. Although widely popular at first, Allende lost favor when he failed to find a way to shore up the country's sagging economy. Strikes by

labor unions and protests by farmworkers made it clear that his administration was ailing.

From 1973 to 1990, Chile was virtually synonymous with the name of General Augusto Pinochet. With support from the United States, the military leader led a bloody coup in September 1973. He dissolved the legislature, banned political organizations, and exiled opponents. Tens of thousands are said to have been murdered during his years in power.

Pinochet's regime discouraged many visitors, but in the decades since his fall from power tourism has steadily increased. Chile's beaches draw sun worshippers from all over South America, and its towering volcanoes and roaring rivers attract adventure travelers from around the world. Fishing aficionados, skiers, hikers, and other outdoors enthusiasts head south to the Lake District, and armchair archaeologists are attracted to the 5,000-year-old mummies of the Atacama. Today Chile is one of the most popular destinations in South America. It doesn't hurt that the country also has one of the continent's most stable economies.

SPANISH VOCABULARY

	ENGLISH	SPANISH	PRONUNCIATION
BASICS			
	Yes/no	Sí/no	see/no
	Please	Por favor	pore fah-**vore**
	May I?	¿Me permite?	may pair-**mee**-tay
	Thank you (very much)	(Muchas) gracias	(**moo**-chas) **grah**-see-as
	You're welcome	De nada	day **nah**-dah
	Excuse me	Con permiso	con pair-**mee**-so
	Pardon me	¿Perdón?	pair-**dohn**
	Could you tell me?	¿Podría decirme?	po-dree-ah deh-**seer**-meh
	I'm sorry	Lo siento	lo see-**en**-toh
	Good morning!	¡Buenos días!	**bway**-nohs **dee**-ahs
	Good afternoon!	¡Buenas tardes!	**bway**-nahs **tar**-dess
	Good evening!	¡Buenas noches!	**bway**-nahs **no**-chess
	Goodbye!	¡Adiós!/¡Hasta luego!	ah-dee-**ohss**/ **ah**-stah **lwe**-go
	Mr./Mrs.	Señor/Señora	sen-**yor**/sen-**yohr**-ah
	Miss	Señorita	sen-yo-**ree**-tah
	Pleased to meet you	Mucho gusto	**moo**-cho **goose**-toh
	How are you?	¿Cómo está usted?	**ko**-mo es-**tah** oo-**sted**
	Very well, thank you.	Muy bien, gracias.	**moo**-ee bee-**en**, **grah**-see-as
	And you?	¿Y usted?	ee oos-**ted**
	Hello (on the telephone)	Diga	**dee**-gah
NUMBERS			
	1	un, uno	oon, **oo**-no
	2	dos	dos
	3	tres	tress
	4	cuatro	**kwah**-tro
	5	cinco	**sink**-oh

6	seis	saice
7	siete	see-**et**-eh
8	ocho	**o**-cho
9	nueve	new-**eh**-vey
10	diez	dee-**es**
11	once	**ohn**-seh
12	doce	**doh**-seh
13	trece	**treh**-seh
14	catorce	ka-**tohr**-seh
15	quince	**keen**-seh
16	dieciséis	dee-es-ee-**saice**
17	diecisiete	dee-es-ee-see-**et**-eh
18	dieciocho	dee-es-ee-**o**-cho
19	diecinueve	**dee**-es-ee-new-**ev**-eh
20	veinte	**vain**-teh
21	veinte y uno/veintiuno	**vain**-te-**oo**-noh
30	treinta	**train**-tah
32	treinta y dos	train-tay-**dohs**
40	cuarenta	kwah-**ren**-tah
43	cuarenta y tres	kwah-**ren**-tay-**tress**
50	cincuenta	seen-**kwen**-tah
54	cincuenta y cuatro	seen-**kwen**-tay **kwah**-tro
60	sesenta	sess-**en**-tah
65	sesenta y cinco	sess-**en**-tay **seen**-ko
70	setenta	set-**en**-tah
76	setenta y seis	set-**en**-tay **saice**
80	ochenta	oh-**chen**-tah
87	ochenta y siete	oh-**chen**-tay see-**yet**-eh
90	noventa	no-**ven**-tah
98	noventa y ocho	no-**ven**-tah-**o**-choh
100	cien	see-**en**

101	ciento uno	see-**en**-toh **oo**-noh
200	doscientos	doh-see-**en**-tohss
500	quinientos	keen-**yen**-tohss
700	setecientos	set-eh-see-**en**-tohss
900	novecientos	no-veh-see-**en**-tohss
1,000	mil	meel
2,000	dos mil	dohs meel
1,000,000	un millón	oon meel-**yohn**

COLORS

black	negro	**neh**-groh
blue	azul	ah-**sool**
brown	café	kah-**feh**
green	verde	**ver**-deh
pink	rosa	**ro**-sah
purple	morado	mo-**rah**-doh
orange	naranja	na-**rahn**-hah
red	rojo	**roh**-hoh
white	blanco	**blahn**-koh
yellow	amarillo	ah-mah-**ree**-yoh

DAYS OF THE WEEK

Sunday	domingo	doe-**meen**-goh
Monday	lunes	**loo**-ness
Tuesday	martes	**mahr**-tess
Wednesday	miércoles	me-**air**-koh-less
Thursday	jueves	hoo-**ev**-ess
Friday	viernes	vee-**air**-ness
Saturday	sábado	**sah**-bah-doh

MONTHS

January	enero	eh-**neh**-roh
February	febrero	feh-**breh**-roh
March	marzo	**mahr**-soh
April	abril	ah-**breel**

May	mayo	**my**-oh
June	junio	**hoo**-nee-oh
July	julio	**hoo**-lee-yoh
August	agosto	ah-**ghost**-toh
September	septiembre	sep-tee-**em**-breh
October	octubre	oak-**too**-breh
November	noviembre	no-vee-**em**-breh
December	diciembre	dee-see-**em**-breh

USEFUL PHRASES

Do you speak English?	¿Habla usted inglés?	**ah**-blah oos-**ted** in-**glehs**
I don't speak Spanish	No hablo español	no **ah**-bloh es-pahn-**yol**
I don't understand (you)	No entiendo	no en-tee-**en**-doh
I understand (you)	Entiendo	en-tee-**en**-doh
I don't know	No sé	no seh
I am American/ British	Soy americano (americana)/ inglés(a)	soy ah-meh-ree-**kah**-no (ah-meh-ree-**kah**-nah)/in-**glehs(ah)**
What's your name?	¿Cómo se llama usted?	koh-mo seh **yah**-mah oos-**ted**
My name is . . .	Me llamo . . .	may **yah**-moh
What time is it?	¿Qué hora es?	keh **o**-rah es
It is one, two, three . . . o'clock.	Es la una./Son las dos, tres . . .	es la **oo**-nah/sohn lahs dohs, tress
Yes, please/No, thank you	Sí, por favor/No, gracias	**see** pohr fah-**vor**/no **grah**-see-us
How?	¿Cómo?	**koh**-mo
When?	¿Cuándo?	**kwahn**-doh
This/Next week	Esta semana/ la semana que entra	**es**-teh seh-**mah**-nah/lah seh-**mah**-nah keh **en**-trah
This/Next month	Este mes/el próximo mes	**es**-teh mehs/el **proke**-see-mo mehs
This/Next year	Este año/el año que viene	**es**-teh **ahn**-yo/el **ahn**-yo keh vee-**yen**-ay

Yesterday/today/ tomorrow	Ayer/hoy/mañana	ah-**yehr**/oy/mahn-**yah**-nah
This morning/ afternoon	Esta mañana/ tarde	es-tah mahn-**yah**-nah/**tar**-deh
Tonight	Esta noche	es-tah **no**-cheh
What?	¿Qué?	keh
What is it?	¿Qué es esto?	keh es **es**-toh
Why?	¿Por qué?	pore **keh**
Who?	¿Quién?	kee-**yen**
Where is . . . ?	¿Dónde está . . . ?	**dohn**-deh es-**tah**
the train station?	la estación del tren?	la es-tah-see-on del trehn
the subway station?	la estación del tren subterráneo?	la es-ta-see-**on** del trehn la es-ta-see-**on** soob-teh-**rrahn**-eh-oh
the bus stop?	la parada del autobus?	la pah-**rah**-dah del ow-toh-**boos**
the post office?	la oficina de correos?	la oh-fee-**see**-nah deh koh-**rreh**-os
the bank?	el banco?	el **bahn**-koh
the hotel?	el hotel?	el oh-**tel**
the store?	la tienda?	la tee-**en**-dah
the cashier?	la caja?	la **kah**-hah
the museum?	el museo?	el moo-**seh**-oh
the hospital?	el hospital?	el ohss-pee-**tal**
the elevator?	el ascensor?	el ah-**sen**-sohr
the bathroom?	el baño?	el **bahn**-yoh
Here/there	Aquí/allá	ah-**key**/ah-**yah**
Open/closed	Abierto/cerrado	ah-bee-**er**-toh/ ser-**ah**-doh
Left/right	Izquierda/derecha	iss-key-**er**-dah/ dare-**eh**-chah
Straight ahead	Derecho	dare-**eh**-choh
Is it near/far?	¿Está cerca/lejos?	es-**tah sehr**-kah/ **leh**-hoss
I'd like . . .	Quisiera . . .	kee-see-ehr-ah
a room	un cuarto/una habitación	oon **kwahr**-toh/ **oo**-nah ah-bee-tah-see-**on**
the key	la llave	lah **yah**-veh
a newspaper	un periódico	oon pehr-ee-**oh**-dee-koh
a stamp	un sello de correo	oon **seh**-yo deh koh-**reh**-oh

I'd like to buy . . .	Quisiera comprar . . .	kee-see-**ehr**-ah kohm-**prahr**
cigarettes	cigarrillos	ce-ga-**ree**-yohs
matches	cerillos	ser-**ee**-ohs
a dictionary	un diccionario	oon deek-see-oh-**nah**-ree-oh
soap	jabón	hah-**bohn**
sunglasses	gafas de sol	**ga**-fahs deh sohl
suntan lotion	loción bronceadora	loh-see-**ohn** brohn-seh-ah-**do**-rah
a map	un mapa	oon **mah**-pah
a magazine	una revista	**oon**-ah reh-**veess**-tah
paper	papel	pah-**pel**
envelopes	sobres	**so**-brehs
a postcard	una tarjeta postal	**oon**-ah tar-**het**-ah post-**ahl**

How much is it?	¿Cuánto cuesta?	**kwahn**-toh **kwes**-tah
It's expensive/cheap	Está caro/barato	es-**tah kah**-roh/bah-**rah**-toh
A little/a lot	Un poquito/mucho	oon poh-**kee**-toh/**moo**-choh
More/less	Más/menos	mahss/**men**-ohss
Enough/too much/too little	Suficiente/demasiado/muy poco	soo-fee-see-**en**-teh/deh-mah-see-**ah**-doh/**moo**-ee poh-koh
Telephone	Teléfono	tel-**ef**-oh-no
Telegram	Telegrama	teh-leh-**grah**-mah
I am ill	Estoy enfermo(a)	es-**toy** en-**fehr**-moh(mah)
Please call a doctor	Por favor llame a un medico	pohr fah-**vor ya**-meh ah oon **med**-ee-koh
Help!	¡Auxilio! ¡Socorro!	owk-see-lee-oh/soh-kohr-roh
Fire!	¡Incendio!	en-sen-dee-oo
Caution!/Look out!	¡Cuidado!	kwee-dah-doh

ON THE ROAD

Avenue	Avenida	ah-ven-**ee**-dah
Broad, tree-lined boulevard	Bulevar	boo-leh-**var**
Fertile plain	Vega	**veh**-gah
Highway	Carretera	car-reh-**ter**-ah

Mountain pass	Puerto	poo-**ehr**-toh
Street	Calle	**cah**-yeh
Waterfront promenade	Rambla	**rahm**-blah
Wharf	Embarcadero	em-bar-cah-**deh**-ro

IN TOWN

Cathedral	Catedral	cah-teh-**dral**
Church	Templo/Iglesia	**tem**-plo/ee-**glehs**-see-ah
City hall	Casa de gobierno	kah-sah deh go-bee-**ehr**-no
Door, gate	Puerta portón	poo-**ehr**-tah por-**ton**
Entrance/exit	Entrada/salida	en-**trah**-dah/sah-lee-dah
Inn, rustic bar, or restaurant	Taverna	tah-**vehr**-nah
Main square	Plaza principal	plah-thah prin-see-**pahl**
Market	Mercado	mer-**kah**-doh
Neighborhood	Barrio	**bahr**-ree-o
Traffic circle	Glorieta	glor-ee-**eh**-tah
Wine cellar, wine bar, or wine shop	Bodega	boh-**deh**-gah

DINING OUT

A bottle of . . .	Una botella de . . .	**oo**-nah bo-**teh**-yah deh
A cup of . . .	Una taza de . . .	**oo**-nah **tah**-thah deh
A glass of . . .	Un vaso de . . .	oon **vah**-so deh
Ashtray	Un cenicero	oon sen-ee-**seh**-roh
Bill/check	La cuenta	lah **kwen**-tah
Bread	El pan	el pahn
Breakfast	El desayuno	el deh-sah-**yoon**-oh
Butter	La mantequilla	lah man-teh-**key**-yah
Cheers!	¡Salud!	sah-**lood**
Cocktail	Un aperitivo	oon ah-pehr-ee-**tee**-voh

Dinner	La cena	lah **seh**-nah
Dish	Un plato	oon **plah**-toh
Menu of the day	Menú del día	meh-**noo** del **dee**-ah
Enjoy!	¡Buen provecho!	bwehn pro-**veh**-cho
Fixed-price menu	Menú fijo o turistico	meh-**noo fee**-hoh oh too-**ree**-stee-coh
Fork	El tenedor	el ten-eh-**dor**
Is the tip included?	¿Está incluida la propina?	es-**tah** in-cloo-**ee**-dah lah pro-**pee**-nah
Knife	El cuchillo	el koo-**chee**-yo
Large portion of savory snacks	Raciónes	rah-see-**oh**-nehs
Lunch	La comida	lah koh-**mee**-dah
Menu	La carta, el menú	lah **cart**-ah, el meh-**noo**
Napkin	La servilleta	lah sehr-vee-**yet**-ah
Pepper	La pimienta	lah pee-me-**en**-tah
Please give me	Por favor déme	pore fah-**vor deh**-meh
Salt	La sal	lah sahl
Savory snacks	Tapas	**tah**-pahs
Spoon	Una cuchara	**oo**-nah koo-**chah** rah
Sugar	El azúcar	el ah-**thu**-kar
Waiter!/Waitress!	¡Por favor Señor/Señorita!	pohr fah-**vor** sen-**yor**/sen-yor-**ee**-tah

Travel Smart
Chile

WORD OF MOUTH

"We rented a car and drove from Santiago to Concepción and then back to Santiago to Valparaíso and Viña del Mar. Obviously traffic in Santiago was hectic much like other large cities...but the roads were good. We always felt safe driving in Chile."

—CollegeMom

GETTING HERE & AROUND

■ BY AIR

Traveling between the Americas is usually less tiring than traveling to Europe or Asia because you cross fewer time zones. New York is 1 hour behind Santiago, and Los Angeles is 4 hours behind Santiago. London is 3 to 5 hours ahead of Santiago, depending on the time of year. New Zealand and Australia are 11 hours ahead.

Miami (9 hour flight), New York (11½ hours), and Atlanta (9 hours) are the primary departure points for flights to Chile from the United States, though there are also frequent flights from Dallas and other cities. Other international flights often connect through other major South American cities like Buenos Aires and Lima.

Here's the bad news: arriving from abroad, American citizens must pay a "reciprocity" fee (to balance out fees Chileans pay upon entering the United States) of $130. The good news is that in addition to cash, credit cards are now also accepted. A departure tax of $18 is included in the cost of your ticket.

Always confirm international flights at least 72 hours ahead of the scheduled departure time. This is particularly true for travel within South America, where flights tend to operate at full capacity—often with passengers who have a great deal of baggage to process before departure.

LAN offers the LAN pass, where customers can earn miles (actually, kilometers) by flying with LAN, renting cars, or staying at associated LAN hotels. Like any such program, if you travel regularly this is worth looking into. Sky Airlines offers Sky Plus, which allows passengers a range of discounts on area hotels, restaurants, and other services within seven days of their flight.

AIRPORTS

Most international flights head to Santiago's Comodoro Arturo Merino Benítez International Airport (SCL), also known as Pudahuel, about 30 minutes west of the city. Domestic flights leave from the same terminal.

Airport Information Comodoro Arturo Merino Benítez International Airport (☎ 2/690–1900 ⊕ www.aeropuertosantiago.cl).

FLIGHTS

The largest North American carrier is American Airlines, which has direct service from Dallas and Miami; Delta flies from Atlanta. LAN flies nonstop to Santiago from both Miami and Los Angeles and with a layover in Lima from New York. Air Canada flies nonstop from Toronto.

LAN has daily flights from Santiago to most cities throughout Chile. Aerolineas del Sur (aka Air Comet Chile) and Sky also fly to most large cities within Chile.

Airline Contacts American Airlines (☎ 800/433–7300 in North America, 2/679–0000 in Chile). **Delta Airlines** (☎ 800/221–1212 for U.S. reservations, 800/241–4141 for international reservations, 2/690–1555 in Chile ⊕ www.delta.com). **LAN** (☎ 800/735–5526 in North America, 2/565–2000 in Chile). **United Airlines** (☎ 800/864–8331 for U.S. reservations, 800/538–2929 for international reservations ⊕ www.united.com).

Within Chile Aerolineas del Sur/Air Comet (☎ 600/625–0000 in Chile ⊕ www.aircomet chile.cl). **LAN** (☎ 2/565–2000 in Chile). **Sky** (☎ 600/600–2828 in Chile).

■ BY BOAT

Boats and ferries are the best way to reach many places in Chile, such as Chiloé and the Southern Coast. They are also a great alternative to flying when your destination is a southern port like Puerto Natales or Punta Arenas. Navimag and Transmarchilay are the two main companies operating routes in the south. Further details on boat travel are discussed in the various Getting Here & Around sections throughout each chapter of this guide.

Navimag and Transmarchilay both maintain excellent Web sites with complete schedule and pricing information. You can also buy tickets online, or book through a travel agent.

Information Navimag (⊠ Av. El Bosque Norte 0440, Piso 11, Las Condes, Santiago ☎ 2/442–3120 ⊕ www.navimag.com ⊠ Angelmó 2187, Puerto Montt ☎ 65/432–300). **Transmarchilay** (⊠ Av. Providencia 2653, Local 24, Providencia, Santiago ☎ 2/234–1464 ⊕ www.transmarchilay.cl ⊠ Angelmó 2187, Puerto Montt ☎ 65/270–430).

▌BY BUS

Long-distance buses are safe and affordable. Luxury bus travel between cities costs about one-third that of plane travel and is more comfortable, with wide reclining seats, movies, drinks, and snacks. The most expensive service offered by most bus companies is called *cama* or *semicama,* which indicate that the seats fold down into a bed. Service billed as *ejectivo* is nearly as luxurious.

Without doubt, the low cost of bus travel is its greatest advantage; its greatest drawback is the time you need to cover the distances involved. A trip from Santiago to San Pedro de Atacama, for example, takes between 23 and 24 hours.

When traveling by bus, pack light and dress comfortably. Be sure to get a receipt for any luggage you check beneath the bus and keep a close watch on belongings you take on the bus.

For more information on local bus service, see the Getting Here & Around sections within each town in this guide.

Bus fares are substantially cheaper than in North America or Europe. In Chile you'll usually pay between $1 and $3 per hour of travel. Competing bus companies serve all major and many minor routes, so it can pay to shop around. Always speak to the counter clerk, as cutthroat competition may mean you can ride for less than the posted fare.

Tickets are sold at bus-company offices and at city bus terminals. Note that in larger cities there may be different terminals for buses to different destinations, and some small towns may not have a terminal at all. You'll be picked up and dropped off at the bus line's office, invariably in a central location. Expect to pay with cash, as only the large bus companies such as Pullman Bus and Tur-Bus accept credit cards.

Note that reservations for advance ticket purchases aren't necessary except for trips to resort areas in high season or during major holidays. You should arrive at bus stations extra early for travel during peak seasons. Companies are notoriously difficult to reach by phone, so it's often better to stop by the terminal to check on prices and schedules.

Pullman Bus and Tur-Bus are two of the best-known companies in Chile. They travel to much of the country.

Bus Information Pullman Bus (☎ 600/320–3200 ⊕ www.pullman.cl). **Tur-Bus** (☎ 600/660–6600 ⊕ www.turbus.com).

▌BY CAR

Certain areas of Chile are most enjoyable when explored on your own in a car, such as the beaches of the Central Coast, the wineries of the Central Valley, the ski areas east of Santiago, and the Lake District in the south. Some regions, such as parts of the Atacama Desert, are impossible to explore without your own wheels.

Drivers in Chile are not particularly aggressive, but neither are they particularly polite. Some commonsense rules of the road: before you set out, establish an itinerary. Be sure to plan your daily driving distance conservatively, as distances are always longer than they appear on maps. Obey posted speed limits and traffic regulations. And above all, if you get a traffic ticket, don't argue—and plan to spend longer than you want settling it.

AUTO CLUBS

El Automóvil Club de Chile offers low-cost road service and towing in and around the main cities to members of the Automobile Association of America (AAA).

Auto Club Information El Automóvil Club de Chile (⊠ Av. Andrés Bello 1863, Providencia, Santiago ☎ 2/431–1000 ⊕ www. automovilclub.cl).

GASOLINE

Most service stations are operated by an attendant and accept credit cards. They are open 24 hours a day along the Pan-American Highway and in most major cities, but not in small towns and villages. Attendants will often ask you to glance at the zero reading on the gas pump to show that you are not being cheated.

At this writing, a liter of gas cost about 700 pesos ($1.50). To make sure you don't run out of gas, always ask about gas stations en route.

PARKING

Depending on the area, you can park on the street, in parking lots, or in parking garages in Santiago and large cities in Chile. Expect to pay anywhere from 600 to 800 pesos. There are parking meters for street parking, but more often a parking attendant will be there to direct and charge you.

RENTAL CARS

On average it costs 25,000 pesos (about $50) a day to rent the cheapest type of car with unlimited mileage. Hertz, Avis, and Budget have locations at Santiago's airport and elsewhere around the coun-

try. A locally owned Santiago company, United, lists slightly lower rates than the big chains on its Web site ⊕ www. united-chile.com. Nearly all companies list higher rates (about 20%) for the high season (November to February).

To access some of Chile's more remote regions, it may be necessary to rent a four-wheel-drive vehicle, which can cost up to 48,000 pesos (about $100) a day. You can often get a discounted weekly rate. The rate you are quoted usually includes insurance, but make sure to ask whether there is a deductible you will have to pay in case of an accident. You can usually pay slightly more and have no deductible.

It is by far easier to rent a car in Santiago, where all the international agencies have branches at the airport and in town. You'll find mostly local rental agencies in the rest of the country.

An annoying fact about Chilean rental companies is that they often deliver the car to you with an empty tank. Make sure to ask about the nearest gas station, or your trip may be extremely short.

If you don't want to drive yourself, consider hiring a car and driver through your hotel concierge, or make a deal with a taxi driver for some extended sightseeing at a longer-term rate. Drivers charge an hourly rate regardless of the distance traveled. You'll often spend less than you would for a rental car.

Local companies are sometimes a cheaper option. Rosselot and United are two reputable local companies with offices in Santiago and many other cities.

You need your own driver's license, but not the International Driver's Permit (IDP), to drive legally in Chile. The minimum age for driving is 18. To rent a car you usually have to be 25, but a few companies let you rent at 22.

ROAD CONDITIONS

Between May and August, roads, underpasses, and parks can flood when it rains. It's very dangerous, especially for drivers who don't know their way around. Avoid driving if it has been raining for several hours.

The Pan-American Highway runs from Arica in the far north down to Puerto Montt, in the Lake District. Much of it is now two-lane, or in the process of being widened, and bypasses most large cities. The Carretera Austral, an unpaved road that runs for more than 1,000 km (620 mi) as far as Villa O'Higgins in Patagonia, starts just south of Puerto Montt. A few stretches of the road are broken by water and are linked only by car ferries. Some parts of the Carretera can be washed away in heavy rain; it is wise to consult local police for details.

Many cyclists ride without lights in rural areas, so be careful when driving at night, particularly on roads without street lighting. This also applies to horse- and bull-drawn carts.

RULES OF THE ROAD

Keep in mind that the speed limit is 60 kph (37 mph) in cities and 120 kph (75 mph) on highways unless otherwise posted. The police regularly enforce the speed limit, handing out *partes* (tickets) to speeders.

Seat belts are mandatory in the front and back of the car, and police give on-the-spot fines for not wearing them. If the police find you with more than 0.5 milligrams of alcohol in your blood, you will be considered to be driving under the influence and arrested.

Plan to rent snow chains for driving on the road up to the ski resorts outside Santiago. Police will stop you and ask if you have them—if you don't, you will be forced to turn back.

▋ BY CRUISE SHIP

Several international cruise lines, including Celebrity Cruises, Holland America, Norwegian Cruise Lines, Princess Cruises, Royal Olympic, and Silversea Cruises, call at ports in Chile or offer cruises that start in Chile. Itineraries typically start in Valparaíso, following the coastline to the southern archipelago and its fjords. Some companies, such as Holland America and Orient Lines, have itineraries that include Antarctica. Victory Yacht Cruises and Adventure Associates operate in southern Chile and also have cruises to Antarctica.

You can spend a week aboard the luxury *Skorpios,* run by Cruceros Maritimos Skorpios, which leaves from Puerto Montt and sails through the archipelago to the San Rafael glacier. In the far south, you can board Navimag's *Terra Australis* and motor through the fjords to the Beagle Channel, stopping in Puerto Williams, Chile's most southerly settlement.

ESSENTIALS

■ ACCOMMODATIONS

The lodgings (all indicated with a 🏠 symbol) that we list are the cream of the crop in each price category. We always list the facilities that are available—but we don't specify whether they cost extra: when pricing accommodations, always ask what's included and what costs extra. All hotels listed have private bath unless otherwise noted. Properties indicated by ✗🏠 are lodging establishments whose restaurant warrants a special trip.

It's always good to look at any room before accepting it. Expense is no guarantee of charm or cleanliness, and accommodations can vary dramatically within one hotel. If you ask for a double room, you'll get a room for two people, but you're not guaranteed a double mattress. If you'd like to avoid twin beds, ask for a *cama de matrimonio*. Many older hotels in Chile have rooms with wrought-iron balconies or spacious terraces; ask if there's a room *con balcón* or *con terraza* when checking in.

Hotels in Chile do not charge taxes to foreign tourists. Knowing this in advance can save you some cash. When checking the price, make sure to ask for the *precio extranjero, sin impuestos* (foreign rate, without taxes). If you are traveling to Chile from neighboring Peru or Bolivia, expect a bump-up in price. Everything in Chile is a bit pricier than in those two countries.

Also, note that you can always ask for a *descuento* (discount) out of season or sometimes midweek during high season.

HOSTELS

Youth hostels in Chile are not very popular, perhaps due to the prevalence of *residenciales* and other low-cost lodging.

Information Hostelling Chile (☎301/495–1240 ⊕www.hostelchile.com).

HOTELS

All hotels listed have private bath unless otherwise noted.

Chile's urban areas and resort areas have hotels that come with all of the amenities that are taken for granted in North America and Europe, such as room service, a restaurant, or a swimming pool. Elsewhere you may not have television or a phone in your room, although you will find them somewhere in the hotel. Rooms that have a private bath may have only a shower, and in some cases, there will be a shared bath in the hall. In all but the most upscale hotels, you may be asked to leave your key at the reception desk whenever you leave.

RESIDENCIALES

Private homes that rent rooms, *residenciales,* are a unique way to get to know Chile, especially if you're on a budget. Sometimes residenciales are small, very basic accommodations and not necessarily private homes. *Hospedajes* are similar. Many rent rooms for less than $10. Some will be shabby, but others can be substantially better than hotel rooms. They also offer the added benefit of allowing you to interact with locals, though they are unlikely to speak English. Contact the local tourist office for details on residenciales and hospedajes.

LANGUAGE

Try to learn a little of the local language. You need not strive for fluency; even just mastering a few basic words and terms is bound to make chatting with the locals more rewarding.

Chile's official language is Spanish, so it's best to learn at least a few words and carry a good phrase book. Chilean Spanish is fast, clipped, and chock-full of colloquialisms. For example, the word for police officer isn't *policía,* but *carabinero.* Even foreigners with a good deal of experience in Spanish-speaking countries may feel like they are encountering a completely new language. However, receptionists at most upscale hotels speak English.

When giving directions, Chileans seldom use left and right, indicating the way instead with a mixture of sign language and *para acá, para allá* (toward here, toward there) instructions. At their clipped, rapid-fire rate, these often come off as two-syllable exchanges ("pa'ca," "pa'ya").

A phrase book and language-tape set can help get you started.

Fodor's Spanish for Travelers (available at bookstores everywhere) is excellent.

▌ COMMUNICATIONS

INTERNET

Chileans are generally savvy about the Internet, which is reflected by the number of Internet cafés around the country. Connection fees are generally no more than $1 for an hour. Very few hotels have wireless connections, but almost all have ethernet ports or a computer where you can get online.

If you're planning to bring a laptop computer into the country, check the manual first to see if it requires a converter. Newer laptops will require only an adapter plug. Remember to ask about electrical surges before plugging in your computer. Note that South America's luxury hotels typically offer business centers with computers.

Carrying a laptop computer could make you a target for thieves; conceal your laptop in a generic bag and keep it close to you at all times.

PHONES

The good news is that you can now make a direct-dial telephone call from virtually any point on earth. The bad news? You can't always do so cheaply. Calling from a hotel is almost always the most expensive option; hotels usually add huge surcharges to all calls, particularly international ones. In some countries you can phone from call centers or even the post office. Calling cards usually keep costs to a minimum, but only if you purchase them locally. And then there are mobile phones (⇨ *below*), which are sometimes more prevalent—particularly in the developing world—than land lines; as expensive as mobile phone calls can be, they are still usually a much cheaper option than calling from your hotel.

The country code for Chile is 56. When dialing a Chilean number from abroad, drop the initial 0 from the local area code. The area code is 2 for Santiago, 58 for Arica, 55 for Antofagasta and San Pedro de Atacama, 42 for Chillán, 57 for Iquique, 56 for La Serena, 65 for Puerto Montt, 61 for Puerto Natales and Punta Arenas, 45 for Temuco, 63 for Valdivia, 32 for Valparaíso and Viña del Mar.

Mobile phone numbers are preceded by a number 9 (sometimes you'll see it written out as 09) or a number 8 (sometimes 08). Dial the "0" first if you're calling from a land line; otherwise drop it.

From Chile the country code is 01 for the United States and Canada, 61 for Australia, 64 for New Zealand, and 44 for the United Kingdom.

CALLING WITHIN CHILE

A 100-peso piece is required to make a local call in a public phone booth, allowing 110 seconds of conversation between the hours of 9 AM and 8 PM, and 160 seconds of talk from 8 PM to 9 AM. Prefix codes are not needed for local dialing.

To call a cell phone within Chile you will need to insert 200 pesos in a phone box.

Having numerous telephone companies means that Chilean public phones all look different. Public phones use either coins (and require a 100-peso deposit) or phone cards. Telefónica and other companies sell telephone cards, but many locals continue to use coins. If you will be making only a few local calls, it's not necessary to purchase a phone card.

Most city areas have standing phone booths, but phones are also found at restaurants, calling centers, and even newsstands. You may have to wait several seconds after picking up the receiver before a steady humming sound signals that you may dial. After dialing, you'll hear a characteristic beep-beep as your call goes through; then there's a pause, followed by a long tone signaling that the other phone is ringing. A busy signal is similar but repeats itself with no pause in between. Some phones also include English-language instructions, accessed by pressing a button marked with a flag icon.

Instead of using a public phone, you can pay a little more and use a *centro de llamadas,* small phone shops divided into booths. Simply step into any available booth and dial the number. The charge will be displayed on a monitor near the phone.

You can reach directory assistance in Chile by calling 103. English-speaking operators are not available.

CALLING OUTSIDE CHILE

An international call at a public phone requires anywhere from a 400- or 500-peso deposit (depending on the phone box), which will give you anywhere between 47 and 66 seconds of talking time. You can call the United States for between 39 and 76 seconds (depending on the carrier you use) for 200 pesos.

The country code for the United States is 1.

CALLING CARDS

If you plan to call abroad while in Chile, it's in your best interest to buy a local phone card (sold in varying amounts at kiosks and calling centers) or use a calling center (*centro de llamadas*). For calls to the United States, EntelTicket phone cards, available in denominations rang-

ing from 1,000 to 15,000 pesos, are a good deal.

MOBILE PHONES

If you have a multiband phone (some countries use frequencies other than those used in the United States) and your service provider uses the world-standard GSM network (as do T-Mobile, AT&T, and Verizon), you can probably use your phone abroad. Roaming fees can be steep, however: 99¢ a minute is considered reasonable. And overseas you normally pay the toll charges for incoming calls. It's almost always cheaper to send a text message than to make a call, since text messages have a very low set fee (often less than 5¢).

If you just want to make local calls, consider buying a new SIM card (note that your provider may have to unlock your phone for you to use a different SIM card) and a prepaid service plan in the destination. You'll then have a local number and can make local calls at local rates. If your trip is extensive, you could also simply buy a new cell phone in your destination, as the initial cost will be offset over time.

Contacts Cellular Abroad (☎800/287–5072 ⊕www.cellularabroad.com) rents and sells GMS phones and sells SIM cards that work in many countries. **Mobal** (☎888/888–9162 ⊕www.mobalrental.com) rents mobiles and sells GSM phones (starting at $49) that will operate in 140 countries. Per-call rates vary throughout the world. **Planet Fone** (☎888/988–4777 ⊕www.planetfone.com) rents cell phones, but the per-minute rates are expensive.

▮ CUSTOMS & DUTIES

You may bring into Chile up to 400 cigarettes, 500 grams of tobacco, 50 cigars, two open bottles of perfume, 2.5 liters of alcoholic beverages, and gifts. Prohibited items include plants, fruit, seeds, meat, and honey. Spot checks take place at airports and border crossings.

Visitors, although seldom questioned, are prohibited from leaving with handicrafts and souvenirs worth more than $500. You are generally prohibited from taking antiques out of the country without special permission (⇨ *Shopping*).

Information **Chilean Embassy** (✉1732 Massachusetts Ave. NW, Washington, USA ☎202/785–1746 ⊕www.chile-usa.org).

U.S. Information **U.S. Customs and Border Protection** (⊕www.cbp.gov).

▪ EATING OUT

The restaurants (all of which are indicated by a ✗symbol) that we list are the cream of the crop in each price category. Properties indicated by a ✗⊡ are lodging establishments whose restaurant warrants a special trip. It is customary to tip 10% in Chile; tipping above this amount is uncommon among locals.

For more information on Chile's cuisine, see the Chile Planner in Experience Chile. For information on food-related health issues, see Health below.

▪ ELECTRICITY

Unlike the United States and Canada— which have a 110- to 120-volt standard— the current in Chile is 220 volts, 50 cycles alternating current (AC). The wall sockets accept plugs with two round prongs.

Consider making a small investment in a universal adapter, which has several types of plugs in one lightweight, compact unit. Most laptops and mobile phone chargers are dual voltage (i.e., they operate equally well on 110 and 220 volts), so require only an adapter. These days the same is true of small appliances such as hair dryers. Always check labels and manufacturer instructions to be sure. Don't use 110-volt outlets marked FOR SHAVERS ONLY for high-wattage appliances such as hair-dryers.

Contacts **Steve Kropla's Help for World Travelers** (⊕www.kropla.com) has information on electrical and telephone plugs around the world. **Walkabout Travel Gear** (⊕www. walkabouttravelgear.com) has a good coverage of electricity under "adapters."

▪ EMERGENCIES

The numbers to call in case of emergency are the same all over Chile.

Foreign Embassies Chile (✉1732 Massachusetts Ave. NW, Washington, USA ☎202/785–1746).

Chile United States (✉Av. Andrés Bello 2800, Las Condes, Santiago ☎2/232–2600).

General Emergency Contacts Ambulance (☎131). **Fire** (☎132). **Police** (☎133).

▪ HEALTH

SHOTS & MEDICATIONS

All travelers to Chile should get up-to-date tetanus, diphtheria, and measles boosters, and a hepatitis A inoculation is recommended. Children traveling to Chile should have current inoculations against mumps, rubella, and polio. Always check with your doctor before leaving.

According to the Centers for Disease Control and Prevention, there's some risk of food-borne diseases such as hepatitis A and typhoid. There's no risk of contracting malaria, but a limited risk of several other insect-borne diseases, including dengue fever. They are usually restricted to forest areas. The best way to avoid insect-borne diseases is to prevent insect bites by wearing long pants and long-sleeve shirts and by using insect repellents with DEET. If you plan to visit remote regions or stay for more than six weeks, check with the CDC's International Travelers Hot Line.

In 2005 there was an outbreak of Vibrio parahemolyticus in Puerto Montt. The infection causes severe diharrea and is caused by eating bad shellfish. You can consult ⊕ *www.mdtravelhealth.com* for a country-by-country listing of health precautions that should be taken prior to travel.

Health Warnings Centers for Disease Control & Prevention (CDC ☎877/394–8747 (FYI-TRIP) international travelers' health line ⊕www.cdc.gov/travel). **World Health Organization** (WHO ⊕www.who.int).

SPECIFIC ISSUES IN CHILE

From a health standpoint, Chile is one of the safer countries in which to travel. To be on the safe side, take the normal precautions you would traveling anywhere in South America.

In Santiago there are several large private *clinicas* (clinics; ⇨ *Santiago Essentials in Chapter 1*), and many doctors can speak at least a bit of English. In most other large cities there are one or two private clinics where you can be seen quickly. Generally, *hospitales* (hospitals) are for those receiving free or heavily subsidized treatment, and they are often crowded with long lines of patients waiting to be seen.

Altitude sickness—which causes shortness of breath, nausea, and splitting headaches—may be a problem when you visit Andean countries. The best way to prevent *soroche* is to ascend slowly. Spend a few nights at 6,000–9,000 feet before you head higher. If you must fly straight in, plan on doing next to nothing for your first few days. The traditional remedy is herbal tea made from coca leaves. Over-the-counter analgesics and napping also help. If symptoms persist, return to lower elevations. Note that if you have high blood pressure and/or a history of heart trouble, you should check with your doctor before traveling to the mountains.

When it comes to air quality, Santiago ranks as one of the most polluted cities in the world. The reason is that the city is surrounded by two mountain ranges that keep the pollutants from cars and other sources from dissipating. The pollution is worse in winter, when wind and rainfall levels are at their lowest.

What to do? First and foremost, avoid the traffic-clogged streets when air-pollution levels are high. Santiago has a wonderful subway that will whisk you to almost anywhere you want to go. Spend your days in museums and other indoor attractions. And take advantage of the city's many parks.

Visitors seldom encounter problems with drinking the water in Chile. Almost all drinking water receives proper treatment and is unlikely to produce health problems. If you have any doubts, stick to bottled water. Mineral water is good and comes carbonated (*con gas*) and noncarbonated (*sin gas*).

Food preparation is strictly regulated by the government, so outbreaks of foodborne diseases are very rare. But it's still a good idea to use the same commonsense rules you would in any other part of South America. Don't risk restaurants where the hygiene is suspect or street vendors where the food is allowed to sit around at room temperature. To be on the safe side, avoid raw shellfish, such as seviche. Remember to steer clear of raw fruits and vegetables unless you know they've been thoroughly washed and disinfected.

OVER-THE-COUNTER REMEDIES

Mild cases of diarrhea may respond to Imodium (known generically as loperamide), Pepto-Bismol (not as strong), and

Lomotil. Drink plenty of purified water or tea—chamomile (*manzanilla* in Spanish) is a good folk remedy.

You will need to visit a *farmacia* (pharmacy) to purchase medications such as Tylenol and *aspirina* (aspirin), which are readily available. Pharmacists can often recommend a medicine for your condition, but they are not always certain of the dosage. Quite often the packaging comes with no instructions unless the drug is imported, in which case it will cost two or three times the price of a local product.

■ HOURS OF OPERATION

Most retail businesses are open weekdays 10–7 and Saturday until 2; most are closed Sunday. Many businesses close for lunch between about 1 and 3 or 4, though this is becoming less common, especially in larger cities. Supermarkets often stay open until 10 or 11 PM.

Most banks are open weekdays 9–2, although some are open until 4. *Casas de cambio* are open weekdays 9–7 and weekends 9–3 for currency exchange.

Gas stations in major cities and along the Pan-American Highway tend to stay open 24 hours. Others follow regular business hours.

Most tourist attractions are open during normal business hours during the week and for at least the morning on Saturday and Sunday. Most museums are closed Monday.

Shops generally are open weekdays 9–8 and Saturday 9–2. Large malls often stay open daily 10–10. In small towns, shops often close for lunch between 1 and 3 or 4.

HOLIDAYS
New Year's Day (January 1), Good Friday (March or April depending on year), Labor Day (May 1), Day of Naval Glories (May 21), Corpus Christi (in June), Feast of the Virgen de Carmen (July 16), Feast of the Ascension of the Virgin (August 15), Feast of St. Peter and St. Paul (June 29), Independence Celebrations (September 18), Army Day (September 19), Discovery of the Americas (October 12), All Saints Day (November 1), Immaculate Conception (December 8), Christmas (December 25).

Many shops and services are open on most of these days, but transportation is always heavily booked up on and around the holidays. The two most important dates in the Chilean calendar are September 18 and New Year's Day. On these days shops close and public transportation is reduced to the bare minimum or is nonexistent. Trying to book a ticket around these dates will be impossible unless you do it well in advance.

■ MAIL

The postal system is efficient, and, on average, letters take five to seven days to reach the United States, Europe, Australia, and New Zealand. They will arrive sooner if you send them *prioritaria* (priority) post, but the price will almost double. You can send them *certificado* (registered), in which case the recipient will need to sign for them. Vendors often sell stamps at the entrances to larger post offices, which can save you a potentially long wait in line—the stamps are valid, and selling them this way is legal.

Postage on regular letters and postcards to Canada and the United States costs 250 pesos and 230 pesos, respectively. The postage to Australia, the United Kingdom, and New Zealand is 290 pesos for letters and postcards.

If you wish to receive a parcel in Chile and don't have a specific address to which it can be sent, you can have it labeled *poste restante* and sent to the nearest post office.

SHIPPING PACKAGES

A cheap, reliable method for sending parcels is to use the Chilean postal system, which although slow—up to 15 business days—is still reliable for sending packages weighing up to 33 kilograms (73 pounds). Shipping a small parcel of 2 kilograms (4 pounds) will cost 10,000 pesos to North America, 15,000 pesos to Europe, and 20,640 pesos to Australia and New Zealand. Express service is also available.

Federal Express has offices in Santiago and operates an international overnight service. DHL, with offices in Santiago and most cities throughout Chile, provides overnight service. If you want to send a package to North America, Europe, Australia, or New Zealand, it will take one–four days, depending on where you're sending it from in Chile.

Chile's post office can ship overnight parcels of up to 33 kilograms (73 pounds) within Chile and internationally. ChileExpress and LanCourier also offer overnight services between most cities within Chile.

Express Services ChileExpress (☏800/200–102). **DHL** (☏800/800–345). **Federal Express** (☏800/363–030). **LanCourier** (☏800/800–400).

▌ MONEY

Credit cards and traveler's checks are accepted in most resorts and in many shops and restaurants in major cities, though you should always carry some local currency for minor expenses like taxis and tipping. Once you stray from the beaten path, you can often pay only with pesos.

Typically you will pay 500 pesos for a cup of coffee, 1,200 pesos for a glass of beer in a bar, 1,200 pesos for a ham sandwich, and 800 pesos for an average museum admission.

Prices throughout this guide are given for adults. Substantially reduced fees are almost always available for children, students, and senior citizens.

■**TIP**→Banks never have every foreign currency on hand, and it may take as long as a week to order. If you're planning to exchange funds before leaving home, don't wait until the last minute.

ATMS & BANKS

Your own bank will probably charge a fee for using ATMs abroad; the foreign bank you use may also charge a fee. Nevertheless, you'll usually get a better rate of exchange at an ATM than you will at a currency-exchange office or even when changing money in a bank. And extracting funds as you need them is a safer option than carrying around a large amount of cash.

■**TIP**→PIN numbers with more than four digits are not recognized at ATMs in many countries. If yours has five or more, remember to change it before you leave.

ATMs, or "cajeros automaticos," are widely available, and you can get cash with a Cirrus- or Plus-linked debit card or with a major credit card. Most ATMs in Chile have a special screen—accessed after entering your PIN code—for foreign-account withdrawals. In this case, you need to access your account first via the "foreign client" option. ATMs offer excellent exchange rates because they are based on wholesale rates offered only by major banks.

Banco de Chile is probably the largest national bank; its Web site ⊕*www.bancochile.cl* lists branches and ATMs by location if you click on the "surcursales" (locations) link, then the "cajeros automaticos" link. Itua (⊕*www.itau.cl*), a Brazilian bank, recently bought all of the BostonBank locations in Chile and is also widely available. Citibank (⊕*www.citibank.com*) is another fairly common option.

CREDIT CARDS

Throughout this guide, the following abbreviations are used: **AE**, American Express; **DC**, Diners Club; **MC**, Master-Card; and **V**, Visa.

It's a good idea to inform your credit-card company before you travel, especially if you're going abroad and don't travel internationally very often. Otherwise, the credit-card company might put a hold on your card owing to unusual activity—not a good thing halfway through your trip. Record all your credit-card numbers—as well as the phone numbers to call if your cards are lost or stolen—in a safe place, so you're prepared should something go wrong. Both MasterCard and Visa have general numbers you can call (collect if you're abroad) if your card is lost, but you're better off calling the number of your issuing bank, since MasterCard and Visa usually just transfer you to your bank; your bank's number is usually printed on your card.

If you plan to use your credit card for cash advances, you'll need to apply for a PIN at least two weeks before your trip. Although it's usually cheaper (and safer) to use a credit card abroad for large purchases (so you can cancel payments or be reimbursed if there's a problem), note that some credit-card companies *and* the banks that issue them add substantial percentages to all foreign transactions, whether they're in a foreign currency or not. Check on these fees before leaving home, so there won't be any surprises when you get the bill.

Dynamic currency conversion programs are becoming increasingly widespread. Merchants who participate in them are supposed to ask whether you want to be charged in dollars or the local currency, but they don't always do so. And even if they do offer you a choice, they may well avoid mentioning the additional surcharges. The good news is that you *do* have a choice. And if this practice really gets your goat, you can avoid it entirely

thanks to American Express; with its cards, DCC simply isn't an option.

Credit cards are widely accepted in hotels, restaurants, and shops in most cities and tourist destinations. Fewer establishments accept credit cards in rural areas. It may be easier to use your credit card whenever possible. The exchange rate varies by only a fraction of a cent, so you won't need to worry about whether your purchase is charged on the day of purchase or at some point in the future. Note, however, that you may get a slightly better deal if you pay with cash, and that some businesses charge an extra fee for paying with a non-Chilean (International) credit card.

Reporting Lost Cards American Express (☎800/528–4800 in the U.S., 336/393–1111 collect from abroad ⊕www.american express.com). **Diners Club** (☎800/234–6377 in the U.S., 303/799–1504 collect from abroad ⊕www.dinersclub.com). **MasterCard** (☎800/627–8372 in the U.S., 636/722–7111 collect from abroad ⊕www.mastercard.com). **Visa** (☎800/847–2911 in the U.S., 410/581–9994 collect from abroad ⊕www.visa.com).

CURRENCY & EXCHANGE

The peso ($) is the unit of currency in Chile. Chilean bills are issued in 1,000, 2,000, 5,000, 10,000, and 20,000 pesos, and coins come in units of 1, 5, 10, 50, 100, and 500 pesos. Note that getting change for larger bills, especially from small shopkeepers, can be difficult. Make sure to get smaller bills when you exchange currency. Always check exchange rates in your local newspaper for the most current information; at press time, the exchange rate was approximately 475 pesos to the U.S. dollar.

Common to Santiago and other mid- to large-size cities are *casas de cambio,* or money-changing stores. Naturally, those at the airport will charge premium rates for convenience's sake. It may be more economical to change a small amount for your transfer to the city, where options are wider and rates more reasonable.

The U.S. State Department notes that travelers "should be aware that they might have difficulty using U.S. $100 bills due to concerns about falsification. The United States Secret Service has provided Chilean banks and local police with the tools and training needed to identify counterfeit U.S. currency. Although the training was very successful, many Chilean banks, exchange houses and business still refuse to accept the $100 notes. Whenever possible visitors to Chile should use traveler's checks or bring notes smaller than $50."

Currently, it's quite easy to figure out how much you're paying for something in Chile, as long as the U.S. dollar is equal to approximately 500 pesos: simply multiply what you're being charged by two (e.g., a 10,000-peso dinner is worth about 20 U.S. dollars).

Currency Conversion Google (⊕www. google.com). **Oanda.com** (⊕www.oanda.com). **XE.com** (⊕www.xe.com).

∎ PACKING

You'll need to pack for all seasons when visiting Chile, no matter what time of year you're traveling. Outside the cities, especially in the Lake District and Southern Chile, long-sleeve shirts, long pants, socks, sneakers, a hat, a light waterproof jacket, a bathing suit, and insect repellent are all essential. Light colors are best, since mosquitoes avoid them. If you're visiting Patagonia or the Andes, bring a jacket and sweater or a fleece pullover. A high-factor sunscreen is essential at all times, especially in the far south where the ozone layer is much depleted.

Other useful items include a screw-top water bottle that you can fill with purified water, a money pouch, a travel flashlight and extra batteries, a Swiss Army knife with a bottle opener, a medical kit, binoculars, and a pocket calculator to help with currency conversions. A sarong or light cotton blanket can have many uses: beach towel, picnic blanket, and cushion for hard seats, among other things. You can never have too many large resealable plastic bags, which are ideal for storing film, protecting things from rain and damp, and quarantining stinky socks.

Since it's sometimes hard to get a bottle of shampoo through customs these days, an easy workaround (and load-lightener) is to buy a handful of shampoo packets (about the size of a ketchup packet) in any Chilean drug store or street market. Of course many better hotels will already provide shampoo and soap. Note that in other South American countries, it's always handy to carry a small packet of tissues for bathroom use. Though Chile's bathrooms are generally well-stocked with toilet paper, it's still not a bad idea to have a packet in your pocket.

PASSPORTS & VISAS

While traveling in Chile you might want to carry a copy of your passport and leave the original in your hotel safe. If you plan on paying by credit card you will often be asked to show identification or at least write down your passport number.

American citizens must pay a "reciprocity" fee (to balance out fees Chileans pay upon entering the United States) of $100. Canadian and Australian citizens pay $132 and $56, respectively. The good news is that in addition to cash, credit cards are now also accepted. A departure tax of $18 is included in the cost of your ticket.

Citizens of the United States, Canada, Australia, New Zealand, and the United Kingdom need only a passport to enter Chile for up to three months.

Upon arrival in Chile, you will be given a flimsy piece of paper that is your three-month tourist visa. This has to be handed in when you leave. Because getting a new one involves waiting in many lines and a lot of bureaucracy, put it somewhere safe.

You can extend your visa an additional 90 days for a small fee, but do this before it expires to avoid paying a *multa* (fine).

▌SAFETY

The vast majority of visitors to Chile never experience a problem with crime. Violent crime is a rarity; far more common is pickpocketing or thefts from purses, backpacks, or rental cars. Be on your guard in crowded places, especially markets and festivals.

Wherever you go, don't wear expensive clothing or flashy jewelry, and don't handle money in public. Keep cameras in a secure camera bag, preferably one with a chain or wire embedded in the strap. Always remain alert for pickpockets, and don't walk alone at night, especially in the larger cities.

Volcano climbing is a popular pastime in Chile, with Volcán Villarrica, near Pucón, and Volcán Osorno the most popular. But some of these mountains are also among South America's most active volcanoes. CONAF, the agency in charge of national parks, cuts off access to any volcano at the slightest hint of abnormal activity. Check with CONAF before heading out on any hike in this region.

Many women travel alone or in groups in Chile with no problems. Chilean men are less aggressive in their machismo than men in other South American countries (they will seldom, for example, approach a woman they don't know), but it's still an aspect of the culture (they will make comments when a women walks by). It's a good idea for single women not to walk alone at night, especially in the larger cities.

▌TIP➔ Distribute your cash, credit cards, IDs, and other valuables between a deep front pocket, an inside jacket or vest pocket, and a hidden money pouch. Don't reach for the money pouch once you're in public.

Contact **CONAF** (☎45/298–221 in Temuco, 2/390–0125 in Santiago ⊕www.conaf.cl). **Transportation Security Administration** (TSA; ⊕www.tsa.gov).

▌TAXES

An 18% value-added tax (VAT, called IVA here) is added to the cost of most goods and services in Chile; often you won't notice because it's included in the price. When it's not, the seller gives you the price plus IVA. At many hotels you may receive an exemption from the IVA if you pay in American dollars or with a credit card.

▌TIME

Chile is one hour ahead of Eastern Standard Time and four hours ahead of Pacific Standard Time. Daylight saving time in Chile begins in October and ends in March.

Time Zones Timeanddate.com (⊕www.timeanddate.com/worldclock).

▌VISITOR INFORMATION

The national tourist office Sernatur (Servicio Nacional de Turismo) has branches in Santiago and major tourist destinations around the country. Sernatur offices, often the best source for general information about a region, are generally open daily from 9 to 6, but break for lunch (usually from 2 to 3).

Municipal tourist offices, often located near a central square, usually have better information about their town's sights, restaurants, and lodging. Many have shorter hours or close altogether during low season, however.

INDEX